Industrial organisation

Also available from Routledge

An Introduction to Industrial Economics (fourth edition)
P. Devine, N. Lee, R. Jones and W. Tyson

The Structure of British Industry (second edition)
Peter Johnson

The Economics of Industries and Firms (second edition)
Malcolm Sawyer

Industrial organisation

Competition, Growth and Structural Change

Fourth edition

Kenneth D. George,
Caroline Joll and
E.L. Lynk

London and New York

First published 1971
by the Academic Division of Unwin Hyman Ltd

This fourth edition first published 1992
by Routledge
11 New Fetter Lane, London EC4P 4EE

Simultaneously published in the USA and Canada
by Routledge
a division of Routledge, Chapman and Hall, Inc.
29 West 35th Street, New York, NY 10001

Typeset in September Roman by
Leaper & Gard Ltd, Bristol
Printed and bound in Great Britain by
Mackays of Chatham PLC, Chatham, Kent

British Library Cataloguing in Publication Data
A catalogue record for this book is available from the British Library.

Library of Congress Cataloging-in-Publication Data
George, Kenneth Desmond.
    Industrial organisation : competition, growth, and structural
change / Kenneth D. George, Caroline Joll, and E.L. Lynk. — 4th ed.
        p.   cm.
    Includes bibliographical references and index.
    ISBN 0–415–07850–4
    1. Industrial organization (Economic theory) 2. Great Britain–
Industries. 3. European Economic Community countries–Industries.
4. United States–Industries. I. Joll, Caroline. II. Lynk, E. L.
III. Title.
HD2326.G47 1992
338.7'0941–dc20   91-40389
                                                          CIP

ISBN 0–415–07850–4

Contents

Tables and figures

TABLES

FIGURES

Preface

This book is intended for a one-year undergraduate course in industrial economics. The only prior knowledge that is assumed is a first-year course in economic principles.

The structure of the fourth edition is broadly similar to that of the earlier editions of this book. However, each chapter has been substantially revised and updated to take account of developments in the subject since the publication of the third edition. In addition, four new chapters (on dominant firms, potential competition and entry deterrence, natural monopoly, and introducing competition) have been added, which reflect the major new areas of interest in industrial economics which have emerged during the last decade.

Industrial economics has seen substantial growth and development during the last ten or fifteen years, which has had the effect of raising the technical level at which industrial economics courses are generally taught. However, a high proportion of the undergraduate students who do industrial economics as an independent course are not economics specialists. Therefore, this book has been designed to keep to a minimum the technical demands, in terms of mathematical and econometric knowledge, made on the reader. In those places where a relatively technical treatment is unavoidable (such as the mathematical expressions for welfare loss in Chapter 12 or the survey of empirical work on the relationship between profitability and concentration in Chapter 11), this is accompanied by a full verbal explanation of the relevant points.

Lastly, we should like to record our sincere thanks to Sian Davies and Carolyn Phillips, of the Department of Economics at the University College of Swansea, who typed the manuscript with great goodwill and efficiency.

Introduction

Industrial economics has been an area of rapid growth over the last 20 years on both the theoretical and the empirical sides. In this book we are concerned with both, and in particular with the extent to which theoretical and empirical work can aid in the formulation of policies towards industry. The theory of the firm has given us some useful insights into the working of the market economy, and empirical work has also made an important contribution to our understanding of industry. However, theory and empirical work have not yet put us in the position of being able to draw simple and generally applicable prescriptions in the field of industrial economics, and it is hard to imagine that they will ever succeed in doing so. It has to be admitted that we do not know the answers to many of the most important questions. Common sense in using theory and econometric analysis is essential. An important role also exists for case studies. Throughout the book we make considerable use of case studies, particularly of the reports of the Monopolies and Mergers Commission and its predecessors in the UK. In the text the cases are referred to under abbreviated titles, and a complete list of all cases cited is given in the list of references.

Many of the issues discussed in this book apply to any advanced industrial country. This is obviously the case with such issues as the relationship between the size, growth and profitability of firms, the measurement of concentration, the relationship between market structure and performance, and the pricing policies of firms. Other issues are of importance to some but not all industrial economies. Thus, the UK has suffered a serious decline in the competitiveness of its manufacturing industry. Similar problems have been experienced in the USA but not in Japan and West Germany, which have an impressive postwar record of growth in manufacturing. The contents of this book therefore do not relate solely to the UK, and the experience of other countries is discussed. For instance, in our analysis of competition policy we adopt a comparative approach and examine the development and application of policy in the UK, the USA and the European Communities (EC).

Since this book is concerned with the economic problems and policy issues that arise from the activities of firms, the majority of the subject matter is the microeconomic analysis of the factors that determine how firms behave and their resulting performance. This is of vital importance to the level of economic welfare, which depends critically on the performance of firms in such respects as the rate of growth and structure of output, responsiveness to technical advance and linkage of prices to costs.

However, the manufacturing sector is also crucially dependent on macroeconomic variables. Indeed, the most effective ways of making industry competitive arise not from policies directed at particular industries (e.g. competition policy) but from macroeconomic policies designed to give industry a stably growing home market, which can be used as a base from which to export. For instance, in such a country as the UK, which is very open to international competition, it makes little sense to discuss industrial performance in isolation from international factors, and in particular without considering the effect of the exchange rate. Such macroeconomic variables as the level of domestic demand and the exchange rate clearly have a major impact on the general state of health of the industrial sector. To ignore these macroeconomic variables and to concentrate attention entirely on micro-policies is distinctly unrealistic. For this reason, in Chapter 1 we devote some space to a consideration of the effects of macroeconomic variables on industrial performance.

In Chapter 1 we start by reviewing the process of structural change in industrial economies by which resources are transferred between sectors in response to the changing pattern of consumer demand and to differential rates of productivity growth. All advanced economies have been characterised by the movement of resources out of agriculture into manufacturing and subsequently from manufacturing into services. However, these long-run tendencies do not appear to give a complete explanation of the decline of the manufacturing sector in the UK. The performance of UK manufacturing industry is examined in some detail. The analysis is based on hypotheses concerning the relationship between changes in output and productivity. The interrelationships here mean that fast-growing economies can get into a 'virtuous' and slow-growing economies into a 'vicious' circle. Such forces of cumulative causation make for increasingly serious structural imbalance between countries, and the role of investment and the exchange rate in maintaining or reducing such imbalances is examined. This chapter concludes with some thoughts on important macroeconomic policy issues.

The next three chapters are focused on the firm as a whole rather than on the activities of firms in individual markets. This is justified by the fact that a relatively small number of firms now account for a high proportion of industrial and commercial activity, and it is important to understand the process by which these firms have grown and also to examine how well they perform. Chapter 2 starts by looking at a question that is essential to understanding the behaviour and performance of firms, namely, business motivation and goals. Traditionally, the theory of the firm has assumed that firms aim to maximise profits, but this assumption has been subject to criticism. For instance, under conditions of uncertainty profit maximisation has no precise meaning; and the organisational complexity of large firms may make profit maximisation difficult to achieve.

These difficulties do not necessarily mean that the profit-maximising goal becomes less important, but they do suggest that profit-maximising behaviour may have to be viewed rather differently, as suggested, for instance, by the Behavioural School. Much recent work has also analysed the incentive mechanisms that may be employed within firms in order to get close to profit-maximising behaviour. Another criticism aimed at the profit-maximising assumption is that modern large firms are run by managers, not owners, and managers may well be concerned to maximise something other than profits. The importance of this criticism depends on a number of questions: to what extent is it true that modern firms are controlled by managers, not owners, and if managers do control firms what are their aims; that is, what do they try to maximise? Three alternative managerial theories of the firm are considered. Do these different aims mean that management-controlled firms will actually behave differently from profit-maximising ones? And how much discretion do managers have to maximise their own utility, unconstrained by profit considerations? Chapter 2 suggests that growth is likely to be a major aim of management-controlled firms and, more generally, that in a dynamic economy firms feel compelled to grow in order to succeed.

In Chapter 3 we examine the process of the growth of firms. Among the important dimensions of growth are vertical integration, diversification and take-overs and mergers. Each of these dimensions is examined in turn. There are several questions that need to be addressed. To what extent can vertical integration be explained by considerations of efficiency, and what part is played by the monopoly motive? Why do firms move into new lines of activity, and are there any systematic relationships between diversification and such factors as demand growth and market structure? What are the motives for mergers, and what factors influence the direction of growth by merger? After examining these and other questions relating to the process of growth, we turn to consider what factors limit the rate of growth that a firm can achieve.

Having looked at the reasons why firms are concerned with growth and at the various dimensions of growth, the next question that arises concerns the results of such growth. What can we say about the performance of large firms, and what are the consequences of the growth process for the allocation of resources? Chapter 4 reviews the arguments and some of the empirical evidence on these questions. We examine the relationships between size, growth and profitability, particularly the evidence concerning the effects of mergers and whether they yield efficiency gains not readily available through internal growth. We also look at the consequences of firms' growth for the level of aggregate concentration in the economy and at the extent to which production has become increasingly concentrated in the very largest firms. Lastly, we look at the implications of diversification for resource allocation and whether growth by diversification should be expected to improve or worsen the performance of the sectors in which the diversified firm operates.

The remainder of the book is concerned mainly with another level of aggre-

gation, namely the market. The activities of diversified firms are made up of
their operations in several individual markets, so the two levels of analysis are
interrelated. However, there is a central belief in industrial economics that the
behaviour of firms, and their resultant performance in a particular market,
will be importantly influenced by the structure of that market. This view, which
is known as the structure-conduct-performance paradigm, is oversimplified. As
Chapter 3 makes clear, firms' conduct decisions will feed back and affect market
structure. In addition, firms' behaviour is not dictated by structural factors alone
in any deterministic way. However, market structure is one factor that affects
business behaviour and industrial performance, and therefore in Chapter 5 we
review the main elements of structure.

The dimension of market structure that has received the most attention is the
level of concentration, which is one aspect of the size distribution of firms in the
market. We look at the problems of measuring concentration and at the determinants of both the level and the rate of change of concentration. The most interesting question about levels of concentration in individual markets is whether
these can be explained and justified by economies of large-scale production.
After examining some of the problems of measuring economies of scale we look
at the evidence from several countries. A major feature of industrial development
in many countries over the past 50 years has been the substantial increase in the
level of concentration. In Chapter 5 we turn to an examination of changes in
concentration in individual markets. There are several reasons why market
concentration changes over time. These include the effects of market growth,
advertising, changes in technology and government involvement in industry.
However, the single most important factor explaining why concentration has
increased is merger activity, and we review the evidence on the contribution of
mergers to increased concentration. After a detailed analysis of concentration, we
turn more briefly to other important aspects of structure that have been relatively
neglected, in empirical work at least, owing to data and measurement problems;
these are barriers to entry, vertical integration and diversification, product differentiation, growth, buyer concentration, and foreign competition.

The extreme case of market power is that of simple monopoly, where one firm
has complete control over the production of a product for which there are no
close substitutes. Although the textbook case of simple monopoly may be rare, it
is approximated in those cases where the leading firm is very much larger than its
competitors and thus dominates a market. Cases of dominance are of particular
interest to the economist from both the theoretical and policy viewpoints because
of the potential that exists for the abuse of market power. Chapter 6 examines
some of the main concerns, including the way in which dominant firms may
behave strategically, in both price and non-price policies, so as to maintain or
enhance positions of market power.

The distinction between dominance and oligopoly is one of degree. However,
where there are two or more fairly well-matched firms the issue of interdependence, which is the defining characteristic of oligopoly, comes sharply into focus.

Oligopolistic pricing behaviour is the subject matter of Chapter 7. Because the central feature of an oligopolistic market is the interdependence between firms, many important features of oligopolies can be illustrated using the techniques of game theory. This approach shows how interdependence creates simultaneous incentives for firms to compete and to cooperate. We consider non-cooperative models of oligopoly and then go on to analyse price-fixing cartels and joint profit maximisation, paying particular attention to those factors that facilitate collusive behaviour. A factor that is singled out for detailed analysis is the idea that, under conditions of uncertainty, firms may attempt to coordinate their prices by following behavioural rules. One such rule is average cost, or full cost, pricing. Average cost pricing, however, does not constitute a theory of pricing behaviour unless we know what determines the mark-up over costs, and various explanations are examined.

Pricing policy is not the only important aspect of inter-firm rivalry. Non-price competition can be just as important or indeed even more so. Chapters 8 and 9 consider two important aspects of non-price competition, namely, product differentiation and invention and innovation.

Product differentiation is both a dimension of market structure, which itself affects firms' pricing behaviour, and an important aspect of the behaviour of firms in oligopolistic markets. Interdependence between producers of heterogeneous products is difficult to analyse using the traditional theory of the firm in which 'markets' contain all sellers of the same good. In Chapter 8 we use Lancaster's theory of demand, which views goods as bundles of characteristics, to elucidate equilibrium between producers of differentiated products. We also consider the costs and benefits of product differentiation, and its associated advertising, as a form of competition and an inescapable part of life in modern capitalist economies. Product differentiation increases consumers' choice, but often only at the expense of economies of scale obtainable from producing fewer varieties in greater quantities. This implies that there may be a trade-off, which would identify an optimal level of product differentiation from society's point of view – a level that will vary from industry to industry. What type of market structure is most likely to lead to the optimal amount of product differentiation? We consider the argument that under certain circumstances the process of product differentiation will be carried too far (i.e. beyond the stage at which new varieties yield a net increase in consumer surplus).

Invention and innovation are an aspect of business that is of vital importance for the long-run growth of the economy. We first examine the relationship between R&D and firm size. Because the process of technological change is complex, and consists of several stages which differ greatly in costliness and the degree of risk involved, the general conclusion is that a wide range of firm sizes seems to be needed for optimal performance. Second, we ask whether innovative performance can be systematically related to market structure and find that, since innovative activity requires elements of both monopoly power and competition, neither an extremely concentrated nor an extremely unconcentrated structure is conducive to technical advance. The empirical work in this area supports this idea and also shows that concentration is not the most important determinant of R&D effort. More generally, we consider the question of whether a market economy will underinvest in R&D, which is a risky activity and has the characteristics of a public good. Information can be used by one person without becoming unavailable to others, and it is also difficult, if not impossible, to restrict the benefits of information to those who financed the research that produced it. Government activity can therefore take the form of state provision of funds for R&D to correct for private underallocation of resources, or of encouraging private investment in R&D by providing the right mix of monopoly and competition. The patent system is the main example of the latter type of policy, and we review the workings of such systems.

The aspect of competition that remains to be discussed is that from new firms entering a market. The basic presumption is that new entry is usually welfare-enhancing. Therefore, business behaviour designed to deter entry is to be condemned. A considerable literature has developed which seeks to explain the various price and non-price strategies which incumbents may pursue in order to prevent entry, and these strategies are reviewed in Chapter 10. This chapter also examines the special case of a contestable market, where entry is perfectly free and exit is completely costless. A market of this kind has many desirable welfare properties. Unfortunately, however, it can be shown that contestable market theory is not robust, i.e. small changes in the underlying assumptions completely upset the results. Even so, the theory has served to re-emphasise the importance of potential competition and of the importance of reducing entry barriers wherever possible.

Chapters 11 and 12 attempt to bring together some of the factors that have been considered in preceding chapters, first, by examining the empirical work that has been done on structure-performance relationships, and then by asking what welfare losses are likely to result from the existence of market power. The structure-conduct-performance paradigm suggests a positive correlation between concentration and profitability, with high concentration causing high profits. It has also been suggested that advertising expenditure increases profitability by raising entry barriers and increasing market power. Both these hypotheses, however, have been challenged. For instance, it has been argued that the positive association between concentration and profitability is the result of the superior efficiency of large firms.

A vast amount of empirical econometric work has been done to test hypotheses concerning structure-performance relationships, but very few strong systematic relationships have been found to exist. This means that, instead of having general policy rules about what structure will lead to desirable results, individual markets must be examined to look for the causes of their good or bad aspects of performance.

There are also substantial problems in measuring the welfare loss of monopoly power, which is the subject matter of Chapter 12. There are both theoretical and practical problems in measuring allocative losses, even when it is assumed that the costs of the industry are the same under monopoly as under perfect competition. In fact there is no reason why this should be so, and plausible arguments can be put forward to suggest either that costs will be higher under monopoly or that they will be lower. Either way, the estimated welfare loss of monopoly power will be affected. One of the most controversial issues in this area is the suggestion that the resources used up in competing for monopoly positions should be counted as part of the welfare loss of monopoly, a suggestion which is critically reviewed in the last section of Chapter 12.

Although there may be considerable doubt about the overall magnitude of the losses associated with monopoly there is still widespread agreement that some sort of policy aimed at protecting society against monopoly abuse and at fostering effective competition is needed. Chapters 13–16 deal with various aspects of policy.

One of the most problematic questions is to decide how to deal with 'natural monopolies'. These are cases where, because of large economies of scale and of scope, industry output can be produced more cheaply by one firm than by two or more firms. In the UK one approach to the problem has been to take industries into public ownership. However, the UK experience with public ownership has not been an entirely happy one; in particular there have been problems in maintaining internal efficiency, and successive governments have failed to lay down a consistent set of objectives for the nationalised industries to pursue. Chapter 13 examines these problems and also looks at the performance of the nationalised industries. The other main approach to the natural monopoly problem is to allow firms to be privately owned but to put in place regulatory agencies to control prices and other aspects of business conduct. Privatisation and regulation were major features of UK industrial policy in the 1980s. Chapter 13 examines the case for privatisation and the difficulties of finding an effective regulatory regime for large private sector monopolies.

The regulatory problems that have been experienced in the USA and UK suggest that, wherever possible, the burden of regulation should be eased by exposing incumbents to competition. This means that it is important to know which of the activities of a company such as British Gas or British Telecom have natural monopoly characteristics and which do not, and what measures can be taken to make industry structure more competitive without sacrificing much by way of efficiency. Chapter 14 considers the possibilities of restructuring industries with particular reference to telecommunications. We also consider the policy of introducing competition into an entirely different industry – stage-fare bus services – and find that competition can in fact be taken too far.

In some cases it is not possible to have competition in the market. An alternative policy is to have competition for the market in which firms bid for the right to be the monopoly supplier of a good or service. Franchising seems to offer a neat solution to the problem of avoiding monopoly abuse without sacrificing internal efficiency. However, the economics of franchising is far from straightforward and Chapter 14 shows that several subtle trade-offs are involved.

Elsewhere in the economy the problem is that of maintaining competition, and this is the problem which we examine in detail in Chapters 15 and 16.

Private firms can get together to restrict competition in a large number of ways; Chapter 15 reviews the main types of restrictive agreement and their effects. The policy attitudes of the UK, the EC and the USA are compared by looking at the legislation and how it is enforced, and it is found that restrictive agreements are generally condemned, with policy being most hostile in the USA except against the practice of resale price maintenance. Restrictive practices legislation may outlaw and strike down a large number of different agreements, but it is another and a more difficult matter to get firms behaving in a positively competitive manner. We discuss various doubts concerning the extent to which restrictive practices policy has actually led to more competitive behaviour.

Chapter 16 discusses policies for controlling the market power of large firms acting on their own (monopolies) or as a group without any restrictive agreements (oligopolies). The problem of market power is essentially a structural one and arises from the breakdown of atomistic market structures. However, the monopoly policies pursued by the UK, the USA and the EC place different emphases on structure, conduct and performance in their definition of a monopoly, in their criteria for intervention in the market and in the remedies applied. These approaches are assessed in the attempt to identify the most effective way of controlling large firms, and it is discovered that there is no simple, practicable and effective policy that doesn't use a great deal of resources. The conclusion that it is difficult to find effective ways of making firms with market power behave as if they were competitive brings out the importance for competition policy of preventing the emergence of market power. An essential policy for maintaining competitive market structures is control over mergers, and in the last section of Chapter 16 we examine the way in which merger policy has developed in the UK, the USA and the EC and how effective it has been.

This book has been designed so that each chapter can be read on its own. However, it is inevitable in a book of industrial economics that each topic is not self-contained. Instead the same themes recur in many different areas, and therefore cross-references between chapters are given in order to avoid unnecessary repetition. Lastly, all the references used throughout the book are listed in a single alphabetical list at the end.

Chapter 1

Structural change

1.1 INTRODUCTION

The development of an economy is characterised by changes in the structure of economic activity. Some sectors of the economy grow faster than others so that over time there are marked changes in their relative importance. The causes of such change are complex but include: changes in the pattern of demand; the invention of new products and processes; the different opportunities across sectors for technical progress and factor substitution; the changing importance of the role of government in economic activity, and the changing patterns of international competitiveness.

This chapter first considers, in section 1.2, certain systematic changes that tend to occur in the sectoral distribution of activity as economies develop, and draws attention in particular to the long-run growth in services. It then goes on in section 1.3 to consider some important implications of the tendency for productivity growth in many areas of service activity, especially the caring and nurturing services such as health and education, to lag behind that in the rest of the economy. This is followed in section 1.4 by an examination of trends in manufacturing activity, and addresses such questions as why manufacturing activity has declined in importance so much more in the UK than in the other major industrial countries, what the importance is of this relative decline, and why it has happened.

1.2 LONG-TERM CHANGES IN SECTOR SHARES

In the following discussion there will be frequent references to 'industry', 'goods' and 'services'. These categories of activity are defined as follows. Industry is made up of mining and quarrying; manufacturing; gas, electricity and water; and building and construction. These plus agriculture, forestry and fishing make up the goods sector of the economy. The service sector includes all other activities – transport and communications; distribution; insurance, banking and finance; professional and scientific services; hotels and catering; central and local government; and miscellaneous services.

One general feature which seems to fit the historical experience of all developed economies is a movement of resources out of agriculture into non-agricultural activities, followed by a shift from industry into services. In somewhat more detail the following main stages may be identified. In the first stage of development a high proportion of employed labour is attached to the land. As development proceeds there is a movement out of agriculture into industry and services but especially into the former. Service activity also expands because of the linkages between industry and services – most obviously transport, distribution and finance. Both industry and services will therefore tend to increase in relative importance. Eventually industry's share of total employment stabilises but services continue to expand in relative importance at the expense of agriculture. The final stage is when an economy reaches maturity. During this phase of development the service sector's share of activity continues to expand but now at the expense of industry, which declines in relative importance. If services are to continue to expand in relative importance then, in the absence of growth in the total employed labour force and with agricultural employment reduced to a very low level, this expansion can occur only at the expense of industry.

There is an abundance of empirical evidence to support these general structural changes that accompany development. Take for instance agriculture's share of total employment. In the UK of the 1850s this stood at around 20 per cent; by the 1920s it had fallen to less than 10 per cent and today it stands at around 2.5 per cent. For the USA the approximate figures for the same periods were 60 per cent, 20 per cent and 3.5 per cent respectively. Turning to the division between goods and services we find that the share of employment in the service sector has displayed a long-term upward trend, as is shown by the figures for the UK and USA given in Table 1.1.

Even though all developing economies may in the fullness of time experience similar long-term changes in employment patterns, at a particular point in time they are likely to be at a different stage in the development process. This may be due to the fact that industrialisation started earlier in some countries than in others or because countries spend different periods of time in a particular stage of development. Take, for instance, the position in the mid 1960s. At this time the UK had less than 4 per cent of its employed labour force in agriculture and the USA less than 6 per cent. This compares with about 10 per cent for West Germany, 17 per cent for France and over 20 per cent for Japan and Italy. There

Table 1.1 Service sector share of total employment, UK and USA (%)

	Mid 1920s	Early 1950s	Mid 1960s	Mid 1970s	Late 1980s
UK	48	48	50	56	67
USA	47	51	58	67	69

Sources: Kuznets (1977); OECD, Labour Force Statistics, Paris, 1988

was much less scope in the UK and USA therefore for industry to benefit from a transfer of labour out of agriculture than was the case for the other countries. This would be a matter for concern if the performance of the economy depended to a significant extent on an increase in the supply of labour to the industrial sector; we return to this argument later. Another interesting feature of the UK economy in the mid 1960s is that the service sector's share of employment had changed little since the 1920s, while in the USA services had grown steadily in relative importance. In the UK the goods sector's share of employment remained at a relatively high level for a longer period of time than was the case in the USA. The slower movement of manpower into services in the UK over the 40-year period up to the mid 1960s may in part be explained by the greater effect on the UK of industrial reconstruction following the two world wars. It is also likely to be due in part to the slower rise in living standards in the UK and also in part to the poor productivity performance of UK industry.

To the underlying secular forces affecting sector shares must be added shorter-term influences which may reinforce or weaken the underlying trend. These influences often come in the form of severe shocks to the economy. For instance, during the interwar years the high level of unemployment was a factor accounting for an increase in the proportion of UK labour employed in services. Some of the surplus labour of this period was taken up as underemployed labour in low-paid services industries – not only as low-wage employees but also as low-paid self-employed workers. During the war and immediate postwar years however these manpower movements were reversed. Again, the shock to the manufacturing sector resulting from the macroeconomic policies of the incoming Thatcher administration in 1979 served to strengthen the underlying movement of manpower away from industry into services.

Whatever the nature of the short-run movements in sector shares, the underlying long-term trends are inescapable. Two of the clearest of these trends are the decline in manufacturing and the growth of services. A summary of these trends for six major industrial countries over the period 1966–86 is given in Table 1.2.

What economic explanation can be offered for these long-term movements? Both supply- and demand-side factors are at work. Consider first the decline in the relative importance of agriculture. On the supply side, big gains in productivity have been made as a result of increased mechanisation, improved transportation, the greater use of chemical fertilisers and pesticides, and a general improvement in scientific knowledge and farm-management techniques. The productivity performance of the agricultural sector compares favourably with that of industry. For instance, over the period 1959–74 the volume of agricultural output in the UK increased by about 56 per cent, the same increase as in manufacturing. Over the same period employment declined slightly in manufacturing but by a substantial amount in agriculture, indicating that labour productivity increased faster in agriculture over this period than in manufacturing. No problem of labour reallocation would arise if these supply-side

Table 1.2 Civilian employment, UK and USA, 1966 and 1986

	UK				USA			
	1966		1986		1966		1986	
	'000	%	'000	%	'000	%	'000	%
Total civilian employment	24,934		24,221		72,895		109,597	
Agriculture	916	3.7	603	2.5	4,101	5.6	3,350	3.1
Industrial	11,560	46.4	7,478	30.9	26,278	36.0	30,339	27.7
Services	12,462	50.0	16,141	66.6	42,516	58.3	75,909	69.3
Manufacturing	8,691	34.9	5,455	22.5	20,243	27.8	20,962	19.1

	West Germany				France			
	1966		1986		1966		1986	
	'000	%	'000	%	'000	%	'000	%
Total civilian employment	26,320		25,267		19,688		20,965	
Agriculture	2,790	10.6	1,344	5.3	3,344	17.0	1,536	7.3
Industrial	12,879	48.9	10,345	40.9	7,705	39.1	6,567	31.3
Services	10,651	40.5	13,578	53.7	8,639	43.9	12,862	61.3
Manufacturing	10,051	38.2	8,126	32.2	5,401	27.4	4,748	22.6

	Japan				Italy			
	1966		1986		1966		1986	
	'000	%	'000	%	'000	%	'000	%
Total civilian employment	48,270		58,530		19,095		20,614	
Agriculture	10,720	22.2	4,950	8.5	4,810	25.2	2,242	10.9
Industrial	15,800	32.7	20,180	34.5	7,063	37.0	6,821	33.1
Services	21,750	45.1	33,410	57.1	7,222	37.8	11,551	56.0
Manufacturing	11,780	24.4	14,440	24.7				

Source: OECD, Labour Force Statistics, Paris, 1988

changes were counter-balanced by an increase in the demand for agricultural produce. However, as income per head rises so the income elasticity of demand for food declines. A combination of good productivity performance and falling income elasticity of demand tends over time to generate surpluses. As a result, farm prices and profitability and the wages of farm labourers fall relative to those elsewhere in the economy thus inducing a shift in resources. Alternatively, or in addition, the labour market adjustment mechanism may take the form of labour being forced to move away from agriculture because of few job opportunities at the going wage rates.

The growing importance of services can also be explained by a combination of supply- and demand-side factors. Early explanations placed the main emphasis on demand: the high income elasticity of demand for services as compared with goods at high levels of real income per head means that as an economy becomes more prosperous an increasing proportion of additional income tends to be spent on services. However, subsequent research on US data suggested that only a small part of the growth of service sector employment could be attributed to these demand-side forces, estimates of income elasticities of demand being rather similar for many kinds of goods and services. On reflection this is hardly surprising since many goods and services are closely linked. The growth in importance of travel, leisure and entertainment, for instance, involves expenditure on goods as well as services.

The main explanation for the growing importance of the service sector must therefore be found on the supply side. Here the main force accounting for changes in the pattern of employment is the difference between sectors in long-run productivity performance. On average, the rate of increase in labour productivity tends to be lower in services, both because of fewer opportunities for replacing labour with capital and because of a lower rate of technical change. As a result the service sector's share of employment must increase. It is worth noting that a lower rate of productivity growth for services implies that the prices of services will tend to increase more quickly than those for goods. This will offset part of any tendency for the demand for services to rise more quickly because of a higher income elasticity of demand. Overall, therefore, there may be even less of a difference in the growth rates of demand in the two sectors than might be suggested by a comparison of income elasticities of demand alone. All this suggests that changes in sector shares should be more noticeable in terms of employment than in terms of the volume of output.

Another supply-side explanation for the growth of services relates to shifting comparative advantage in international trade. The reasoning here is that, as industrial wages increase with the level of prosperity, comparative advantage in production switches to low-wage underdeveloped countries. In the richer countries, comparative advantage moves in the direction of professional services which, though intensive in labour are intensive in labour of high skill and expertise, which is lacking in the less developed countries. One problem with this explanation is that it may underestimate the extent to which any such tendency for comparative advantage to shift can be offset by the continual introduction of new products and processes which are also intensive in the skilled labour which is lacking in less-developed economies. The emergence of new industrialising countries may, that is, result in an overall expansion of world trade with little or no adverse effects on industrial employment in advanced countries. However, if the new industries which replace the old are less labour intensive, a net loss of labour will occur. Empirical work in this area suggests that the net displacement effect on labour in the advanced countries is small.

1.3 SERVICE SECTOR PRODUCTIVITY

The previous section pointed to the relatively low average productivity growth rate for service activities as a major factor explaining this sector's growing share of employment. It is important to note, however, that this is an average result and that within the service sector there are wide variations in productivity performance, and that productivity gains in some service activities may exceed those in manufacturing. This is most likely in areas such as communications, banking, insurance and finance, where there is substantial scope for technical progress and factor substitution.

In other areas, such as hotels, catering, health, education and public administration, productivity gains are more difficult to achieve. One problem to be noted at the outset is that of obtaining reliable productivity indices for many of these service activities and in particular of finding reliable indicators of output. As will be suggested later, some of the available productivity indices are at best incomplete and may be quite misleading for judging performance. It is with these service activities of low measured productivity growth that this section is mainly concerned.

One possible reason for poor productivity performance is of course that labour is used inefficiently. This is a serious possibility because many services, especially those in the public sector, do not face the competitive discipline of the market place. Some exposure to competitive forces or, where this is not feasible, the discipline of periodic efficiency audits may have beneficial effects. But the main point to emphasise is that, even if there is no noticeable inefficiency, labour productivity will still lag behind that of the rest of the economy because of fewer opportunities for labour-saving investment and technical change. Take for instance the caring and nurturing services – health and education. Over the period 1974–85 the average rate of growth in output per person employed for the UK as a whole was 2.5 per cent per annum. In education and health, on the other hand, various crude measures of labour productivity showed a decline. The pupil–teacher ratio fell slightly and health productivity indicators such as the number of new outpatients per medical staff member also declined.

Although productivity growth in these services lags behind the rest of the economy, the same is not true, or at least not true to the same extent, of wage and salary movements. Over the long run, wages and salaries must keep broadly in line with those on offer elsewhere if labour is to be kept and additional labour attracted as the services expand. This has important cost and financial implications.

Low productivity growth, and wages which tend to keep in line with those offered elsewhere in the economy, mean that unit costs will tend to increase faster in services. A widespread response to rising relative costs has been to reduce direct contact between suppliers of services and their customers. The clearest examples of this are self-service and self-selection in retailing and driver-only bus services, but similar pressures exist in health and education. These developments draw attention to the inadequacy of commonly used productivity indices. Because of the difficulty referred to earlier of measuring output, they fail to take account of an important dimension of output – the quality of service. Crude productivity indices may show an increase at the same time as the quality of service is deteriorating. In hospitals, for instance, the number of patients discharged per consultant may increase but at the cost of discharging patients too quickly because of a shortage of beds. Some of these patients may have to be readmitted for further hospital treatment, which would further improve the crude productivity indicator. Another factor to mention is that the cost savings may reflect not greater efficiency, in the sense of reduced inputs of labour or capital, but merely lower wages for the workers concerned or harder work for the same pay.

In the public sector, low productivity growth and escalating costs explain why the provision of services has placed an increasing financial burden on central and local government. One response has been an attempt to increase efficiency by measures such as competitive tendering. This may lead to improvements in efficiency without any material loss to the quality of service, but there is also the danger that the search for increased efficiency may be pursued on the basis of inappropriate or incomplete performance indicators, resulting in a serious decline in quality of service.

Another consequence of the escalating financial burden of public sector services has been a failure to maintain expenditure on some of these services at a level high enough to maintain standards. Hence, for instance, longer hospital waiting lists and the deteriorating condition of school buildings.

To summarise: a problem besetting many service industries is one of low productivity growth, and there is a danger that attempts to improve performance may be at the expense of a decline in the quality of service. The relative cost of these services increases over the long run not because nurses, doctors or teachers become less efficient but because productivity and wages in other sectors increase faster and, in a competitive labour market, service sector pay must keep broadly in line with wages in the rest of the economy. Lastly, it should be emphasised that a decline in standards in the service sector is not inevitable. As long as productivity in the economy as a whole is increasing, all sectors can benefit. The real issue is how the overall productivity gains are distributed, and this depends on the resource allocation choices made by individuals and by government.

1.4 MANUFACTURING INDUSTRY

A feature of economies in the mature stage of development is what has become known as de-industrialisation. Although common to almost all of the most industrialised economies, this process of de-industrialisation has over the past 20 years or so proceeded faster in the UK than in almost any other country. From Table 1.2 for instance it can be seen that the fall in industrial employment between 1966 and 1986 was far greater than anything experienced by the other major industrial countries. Indeed, in the USA and Japan industrial employment actually increased over this period. Here the focus of attention is on manufacturing. Much of the evidence on this topic is presented in terms of relative shares but it is also important to look at absolute numbers. A summary of the evidence in terms of employment and output is given in Tables 1.3 and 1.4 respectively.

Looking first at the employment figures, it can be seen that the share of manufacturing in total civilian employment decreased in every country except Japan, where there was little change. The UK therefore is not alone in experiencing a decline in the relative importance of the manufacturing sector, although the decline is certainly larger than that for the other countries shown in the table. Even this might not be regarded with too much concern when it is observed that in the 1950s and 1960s manufacturing in the UK was relatively more important than in the majority of other OECD countries. Indeed in 1955, when manufacturing activity reached a peak as a percentage of GDP, the UK had the highest share of employment in manufacturing of all the OECD countries. A decline in relative terms was thus to be expected, and starting from such a high level in the 1950s it is perhaps not surprising that the decline was greater than that experienced by other countries. Even so it has to be concluded that the extent of de-industrialisation has been greater in the UK than in the other major industrialised economies.

Table 1.3 Manufacturing employment, selected countries, 1966 and 1986

	Number ('000s)		Share of total civilian employment (%)	
	1966	1986	1966	1986
UK	8,691	5,455	34.9	22.5
USA	20,243	20,962	27.8	19.1
West Germany	10,051	8,126	38.2	32.2
France	5,401	4,748	27.4	22.6
Italy[a]	7,063	6,821	37.0	33.1
Japan	11,780	14,440	24.4	24.7

[a]Figures are for industrial production.
Source: OECD, Labour Force Statistics, Paris, 1988

However, the true magnitude of de-industrialisation in the UK can only be seen by looking at absolute figures. After all, when employment is growing the relative share of manufacturing may fall while the number employed increases. This is what has happened for instance in the USA. What is so striking about the UK experience is the massive decline in the numbers employed in manufacturing – a 35 per cent decline from 1966 to 1986. Numbers employed in manufacturing also fell substantially in Germany over this period, but the percentage fall was only half that suffered by the UK.

A similar picture emerges from the output figures (Table 1.4). Manufacturing output has declined as a proportion of GDP in all major industrial countries though, as one would expect, to different degrees. Once again the decline in the UK has been greater than that in the other countries, and once again it is when one looks at the level of output that the UK stands out. In this respect the UK's performance is clearly a lot worse than that of its main competitors. From 1960 to 1979 manufacturing output grew more slowly than in the other major industrial economies. Then in 1979/80 manufacturing was dealt a hammer blow by macroeconomic policy, which reduced output by 14 per cent in two years. It was not until 1987 that manufacturing output regained its 1979 level. Over this period France too performed relatively badly.

The changes that have been recorded could be the result of the forces that were outlined earlier – the long-term shift into services that is common to developing economies including, as part of this process, shifts in comparative advantage in international trade, which again are naturally occurring tendencies in a dynamic economy. However, these factors may not offer anything like a complete explanation of the UK experience. There is indeed sufficient evidence to suggest that there are additional factors at work – major underlying weaknesses in UK manufacturing that have overlain, and added impetus to, the tendencies discussed earlier.

Table 1.4 Manufacturing output, selected countries, 1960–86

	Index (1977 = 100)			Net output in manufacturing as % of GDP		
	1960	1979	1986	1960	1979	1985
UK	71.2	100.5	96.2	32.1	25.8	22.6
USA	52.5	108.1	125.9	28.3	23.0	20.4
West Germany	50.0	106.6	112.8	40.3	33.8	32.3
France	35.4	105.3	103.0	29.1	27.0	25.4
Italy	36.4	108.6	121.9	28.6	30.6	26.2
Japan	19.2	113.9	182.1	33.9	29.3	29.8

Source: US Department of Labor, Bureau of Labor Statistics, December 1987

To make progress it is necessary to define what is meant by an efficient manufacturing sector. For an open economy such as the UK, Singh (1977: 128) has suggested the following definition: 'Given the normal levels of the other components of the balance of payments, an efficient manufacturing sector is one which not only satisfies the demand of consumers at home at least cost, but is also able to sell enough of its products abroad to pay for the nation's import requirements', and this must be achieved 'at socially acceptable levels of output, employment and the exchange rate' – the last being used as a proxy for an acceptable rate of inflation.

The qualification is important because any manufacturing sector can be efficient in the terms described at some low enough level of output or at some low enough exchange rate. The reference to normal levels of the non-manufacturing components of the balance of payments is needed because the long-term consequences of an inefficient manufacturing sector may for a time be masked by abnormally high levels of some other item in the balance of payments. In the UK this item has taken the form of North Sea Oil. The latter may for a time keep the current account of the balance of payments in surplus at acceptable levels of output, employment and inflation, but, when the contribution of oil diminishes and greater reliance has once more to be placed on manufacturing activity, the desirable objectives of macroeconomic policy may not be so easily achievable.

Let us turn then to the UK's trade performance and see what light this throws on the efficiency of the manufacturing sector. One indicator frequently cited is the UK's share of world exports in manufactured goods. In 1950 this stood at 25 per cent, by 1979 it had fallen to 9.1 per cent and by 1988 to 7 per cent. The USA too experienced a big decline from 27 per cent in 1950 to 16 per cent in 1979, while the two countries that have gained most have been Japan and West Germany. Another commonly cited performance indicator is the trade balance in manufactured goods. A summary of what has happened since the early 1960s is given in Table 1.5, which shows a marked deterioration in the UK position. In the early 1960s the UK exported twice as much in value terms as it exported. At the end of the 1980s the country's trade balance was in deficit. A surplus of £3.6 billion in 1980 had changed to a deficit of £10.0 billion in 1987.

Although possibly suggestive of some deep-seated malaise, these indicators in themselves do not prove that the manufacturing sector is inefficient. It was inevitable that the countries which dominated world trade in the early postwar years should decline in relative importance as Germany and Japan reconstructed their industries and as new industrialised countries emerged. A decline in the UK's surplus on manufacturing trade was also inevitable given the changes that have occurred in the structure of UK trade. In the early 1960s only two of the main components of visible and invisible trade (i.e. the current account of the balance of payments) were in surplus – manufactured goods and 'interest, profits and dividends', the former being by far the most important. Everything else, including food, fuel, services and other invisibles, was in deficit. Over the next 20

Table 1.5 UK exports and imports of manufactured goods, 1962–88

	Value of exports (fob) £m	Value of imports (cif) £m	Exports/ imports
1962	3,336	1,556	2.14
1963	3,568	1,702	2.10
1970	6,806	4,572	1.49
1971	7,718	4,921	1.57
1980	34,811	31,177	1.12
1981	34,898	31,993	1.09
1987	61,037	70,995	0.86
1988	66,218	83,521	0.79

Sources: Central Statistical Office, *Monthly Digest of Statistics*, London: HMSO, various issues; Central Statistical Office, *Annual Abstract of Statistics*, London: HMSO, various issues

years the balance of trade in many non-manufacturing sectors improved: there was a growing surplus in services, a diminishing deficit in food, and of course a dramatic turn-around from deficit to surplus on the oil balance. As a result, by the 1980s the UK no longer had to generate large surpluses on manufacturing trade in order to pay for deficits on other visible and invisible trade.

However this cannot be the whole story. That there is something more to the explanation of the decline in manufacturing than the structural changes that have occurred in UK trade is suggested by the trend deterioration that has occurred in the current account (see Table 1.6). In 1965/66 the current account was roughly in balance, with the economy operating at full employment. In 1978/79 a near-balance on the current account was accompanied by an unemployment rate of 5 per cent. The next six years, 1980–85, were, thanks to North Sea Oil and a depressed economy (with unemployment climbing to over 11 per cent), years of substantial surplus. But, as the level of activity increased and the contribution of North Sea Oil diminished, the current account moved swiftly and spectacularly into deficit. In 1988 the current account deficit stood at £14 billion or 4.4 per cent of GDP – an unprecedentedly high level – with unemployment still standing at 8.2 per cent of the labour force. Over the 25-year period since the mid 1960s the decline in the UK trade balance had gone so far that by the end of the period the country could not support anything like full employment without an unsustainable deficit on the current account. It can hardly be doubted that this trend deterioration is a reflection of a fundamental problem in the manufacturing sector.

Importance of the decline in manufacturing

The conclusion to be drawn from the preceding discussion is that the decline in UK manufacturing is more than just the inevitable consequence of the long-term forces of structural change in a dynamically vibrant economy. This decline is a

Table 1.6 The UK current account balance and unemployment rate, 1965–88

	Current account balance £bn	Unemployment rate %
1965/66	–	1.5
1978/79	–	5.0
1980–85	Large surpluses £2bn–£8bn	6–11.4
1987	–2.7	10.2
1988	–14.3	8.2

Source: *National Institute Economic Review*, London: National Institute of Economic and Social Research, various issues.

cause for concern because of the contribution made by manufacturing to the growth of the economy, to the balance of payments, and to employment prospects. The effects of manufacturing on all these are, of course, interrelated, but for convenience and to emphasise the point they are dealt with separately.

The importance of manufacturing in the growth of the economy has been emphasised in particular by Kaldor (1966). He emphasised three things: first, the positive correlation across countries between growth of manufacturing output and growth of GDP; second, the dependence of other sectors on manufacturing; and, third, that the benefits deriving from increasing returns to scale in the broadest sense (i.e. external as well as internal economies) are generally more important in manufacturing than elsewhere in the economy.

In the context of the UK, Kaldor argued that the poor performance of the economy as a whole relative to that of other industrialised countries was due in the main to relatively slow output and productivity growth in manufacturing. UK economic performance has indeed been relatively poor in these respects (Rowthorn 1986). In the early 1950s the UK was one of the wealthiest countries in the world in terms of GDP per head and ahead of all the other countries that are presently members of the European Communities. Today the UK is one of the poorest of the industrial nations of the world. Within the EC its GDP per head exceeds that of only Greece, Portugal and Eire. In manufacturing, performance has lagged behind over long periods of time. The first two columns of Table 1.4 show, for instance, that whereas UK output increased by about 40 per cent over the period 1960–79, in the USA and West Germany output more than doubled, in France and Italy it increased nearly three-fold, and in Japan nearly six-fold. The long-run growth of productivity has also been relatively low. From 1960 to 1985, for instance, the annual percentage increase in manufacturing output per person employed was 2.9 for the UK compared with 3.7 for West Germany, 4.8 for Italy, 5.0 for France and 7.7 for Japan. The USA's productivity growth was also low at 2.8 per cent.

There can be no doubt that this poor performance in manufacturing is the dominant cause of the slow growth in the economy as a whole. It is easy enough to imagine what a stronger manufacturing sector would have meant – not only a higher level of output in manufacturing itself but higher output in complementary activities such as transport, distribution and construction, and, since the country would be better able to afford it, higher expenditure on public sector services such as health and education.

Turning to the balance of payments, it has already been noted that manufacturing now plays a smaller role in paying for the UK's imports. However, it still accounts for a third of the country's current account credits, which is still more than twice as much as service exports. It might be argued that in the short to medium term no disadvantage will result from the decline in manufacturing because other sectors, especially services and oil, will fill the gap. Furthermore, if in the longer run increased reliance has once again to be placed on manufacturing to pay for the country's imports, the market will ensure that the necessary adjustments will take place. However, it is not at all clear that other sectors can be relied upon to fill the gap left by a declining manufacturing sector. Oil is already diminishing in importance, and for services it has been estimated that a 1 per cent fall in manufacturing exports requires a 3 per cent rise in the export of services to compensate because value added in manufacturing exports is some three times higher than in services. It seems most unlikely that exports of services can rise quickly enough to compensate for a decline in manufacturing, especially in view of the growing international competition in services and the fact that a declining manufacturing sector, which purchases about one-fifth of service sector output, would itself have a damaging effect on the service sector. The trend deterioration in the current account balance is indeed strong evidence which suggests that the gap left by manufacturing has not been successfully filled. The evidence is quite clear: whenever growth in the economy has accelerated, the country has run up against a balance of payments and/or inflation constraint and governments have been forced to dampen down demand. If the manufacturing sector had been stronger these constraints would have been weaker and successive governments could have pursued more expansionary policies.

As to the view that market adjustments would, if needed, reverse the decline in manufacturing, this might be so, but it would certainly be a painful and lengthy process if only because there are important asymmetries in structural change. Physical capital can be scrapped more quickly than it is built; a trained labour force is easier to lose than to acquire; R&D effort is dissipated more easily than it can be put together. All are illustrations of the proposition that markets once lost are not easily recaptured.

The decline in manufacturing is also important because of what might happen to employment. The crucial question to ask is: are the jobs lost in manufacturing being made good elsewhere? And it is a matter not only of the number of new jobs generated but also of the quality of those jobs. Up to the mid 1970s much of the employment decline in industry did appear to be taken up by expansion in services. After 1979, however, there was a large movement of labour into unemployment, the level of unemployment reaching a peak in 1986. Over the following years unemployment fell as the economy recovered. However, a high proportion of the new jobs that have been created are part time and lower paid than the jobs lost in industry. So far the evidence suggests that not only has the service sector failed to generate a sufficient number of new jobs to make good those lost in industry but the quality of the new jobs has on average been lower than that of those that have been lost.

Reasons for the decline in manufacturing

There is no consensus on what has caused Britain's industrial decline. One thing that is clear is that the causes are complex. Various hypotheses have been presented and some of these are considered here as a means of gaining some insight into the problem.

One view that has been advanced is that the problem is somehow linked to employment. In 1966 Kaldor argued that it was a deficiency in the supply of labour to manufacturing industry that was the key. As a result the Selective Employment Tax was introduced in 1966 and remained in being until 1973. This was a discriminatory fiscal measure to make labour more expensive in sectors such as distribution, construction, hotels and restaurants. This, it was argued, would induce employers in these sectors to shed labour, which would then be available for employment in manufacturing. If manufacturing did indeed require more labour, a slowing down of employment growth in services was the only major source of additional supplies since there was very little growth in the labour force and the agricultural sector was very small.

Later, Bacon and Eltis (1976: 20) also laid emphasis on employment. Examining the period 1965–74 they argued that 'the fall in industrial employment in relation to non-industrial employment is what has caused Britain's difficulties'. In developing the argument they divided the economy into two broad sectors – one consisting of all marketable goods and services, the other of non-marketable goods and services. The latter, they argued, had increased, particularly because of government expenditure which absorbed manpower which would otherwise have gone into industry. At the same time the public resisted a decline in the consumption of marketable goods, and attempts by government to force a decline – by taxation and monetary expansion – led to inflation, a decline in private investment and a weakening of the balance of payments. The general argument can be illustrated with the aid of the familiar national income identity:

$$Y \equiv (C_m + C_{nm}) + (I_m + I_{nm}) + (X - M)_m$$

where consumption (C) and investment (I) are simply broken down into their marketable (m) and non-marketable (nm) components. All exports and imports are, of course, marketable. If C_{nm} and I_{nm} increase and C_m resists downward adjustment, then for a given Y there must be a decline in I_m and/or $(X - M)_m$.

However, this is an identity and does not prove anything about causality. The evidence is indeed consistent with both of the following hypotheses: (i) that there was an autonomous (e.g. government-induced) expansion of the non-marketable sector which caused the marketable sector, and particularly industry, to decline and to shed labour; (ii) that the expansion of the non-marketable sector was just a symptom of a more deep-seated problem.

Hypothesis (i) is difficult to sustain because there is no evidence of a labour shortage in the 1965–74 period. Furthermore, three-quarters of the increase in employment outside industry was female employment – much of it part time; whereas over 70 per cent of the fall in industrial employment affected males. After 1979 the fall in industrial employment continued at the same time as the government was attempting to reduce employment in the non-marketable public sector.

The earlier Kaldor emphasis on a deficiency of industrial employment is also difficult to justify. As pointed out earlier in this chapter, the proportion of the UK labour force employed in industry in the mid 1960s was still high compared with that of many other industrialised countries. There was little evidence that manufacturing was failing to expand because of an inadequate supply of labour, but a great deal of evidence that industry was suffering from overmanning.

Hypothesis (ii) seems much more plausible – industrial decline and the expansion of the non-marketable sector reflect basic structural weaknesses in the economy. These weaknesses manifest themselves in the form of low world income elasticity of demand for UK exports and high UK income elasticity of demand for imports. Thirlwall (1982) has estimated that the world income elasticity of demand for UK exports over the period 1953–70 was 0.9, which compares with 2.1 for West Germany, 2.2 for Italy and 3.6 for Japan. As a result, the growth of the economy has been constrained by the balance of payments with the exception of a short period in the 1980s when the constraint was relaxed by North Sea Oil. Far, therefore, from being the *cause* of industry's decline, the expansion of the non-marketable sector may simply have maintained aggregate demand at a higher level than would otherwise have been possible.

Another theme in the debate is that the problem is one of a failure to take advantage of productivity gains. Examining the period 1965–74 Bacon and Eltis (1976: 11) commented: 'the fast increase in productivity growth could have led to the economic miracle we've all been looking for', and 'it is not the rate of growth of productivity that has let Britain down; what has let Britain down is that this has been allowed to produce growing numbers of redundancies instead of an increase in employment'. In fact the 1960s and 1970s, unlike the 1980s, were not periods of high productivity growth in the UK, as is shown in Table 1.7. What needs to be emphasised, however, is the following. First, output growth cannot match productivity growth for long if income elasticities result in a balance of payments constraint. Second, short periods of exceptional growth in productivity can be achieved as a result of the closure of the most inefficient firms

Table 1.7 Manufacturing industry productivity growth, selected countries, 1960–88

	1960–70	1970–80	1980–88
UK	3.0	1.6	5.2
USA	3.5	3.0	4.0
Japan	8.8	5.3	3.1
West Germany	4.1	2.9	2.2
France	5.4	3.2	3.1
Italy	5.4	3.0	3.5

Source: HM Treasury, Autumn Statement, London: HMSO, November 1988

and a general shake-out of labour, but this is not sufficient for long-term success. It is important therefore to examine *how* productivity gains are achieved. Further insights can be gained by examining the interactions between output growth and productivity growth.

Changes in output and productivity – cumulative causation

Research into changes in industrial structure has commonly found a general tendency for industries with above-average increases in output to show above-average increases in output per head. The pioneering work on this association was undertaken by Verdoorn (1949). Major works by Kendrick (1961) in the USA and Salter (1966) in the UK confirmed the existence of a positive correlation between changes in output and changes in output per head.

The relationship between changes in output and productivity tend to be stronger over long time periods such as a decade or so than over short periods covering only a few years. The shorter the time period covered, the more likely it is that the forces which lie behind the relationship will be masked by special short-term factors. For instance, firms in industries which are facing conditions of adversity are forced to adopt measures to increase efficiency, and over short time periods such measures may result in larger productivity gains than are observed for industries experiencing faster growth. In addition there are often special factors which help to explain the good productivity of declining industries, particularly government-sponsored rationalisation schemes. However, high productivity growth is more difficult to sustain in declining industries over long periods, and the longer the period of time covered the more likely it is that growing industries will show greater productivity gains than the stagnating and declining ones because of the greater opportunities for profitable investment and for achieving the benefits of economies of scale and technical progress. The positive correlation between output and output per head is also observed in international comparisons of the performance of the manufacturing sector.

A positive correlation between changes in output and changes in output per head does not, of course, say anything about causation. The direction of causality could in fact run either way. On the one hand, above-average increases in output ($\hat{o}$) may be the cause of above-average increases in productivity ($\hat{o}/E$). In this case the gain in output is the autonomous variable and causes gains in productivity by inducing a high level of investment (I) which enables an industry to benefit from economies of scale and technical progress. Thus:

$$\hat{o} \rightarrow I \rightarrow \left\{ \begin{array}{l} \text{economies of scale} \\ \text{technical progress} \end{array} \right\} \rightarrow \hat{o}/E$$

On the other hand, the alternative explanation takes productivity change as the autonomous factor and argues that industries which are experiencing rapid improvements in technology experience falling costs and/or high profit margins relative to other industries. This increases their competitiveness in terms of price and/or non-price factors, which in turn results in an above-average rate of increase in output. Thus:

$$\hat{o}/E \rightarrow \left\{ \begin{array}{l} \downarrow \text{costs} \\ \uparrow \text{profit margins} \end{array} \right\} \rightarrow \left\{ \begin{array}{l} \downarrow \text{prices} \\ \uparrow \text{non-price} \\ \quad \text{competitiveness} \end{array} \right\} \rightarrow \hat{o}.$$

Some economists have placed emphasis on the first of these causal mechanisms; others have stressed the second. It should also be pointed out that there is a third possibility, which is that some other factor(s) is at work which causes the above-average increase in both output and productivity.

In his study of 12 industrially advanced countries over the period 1953–64, Kaldor (1966) laid emphasis firmly on increases in output leading to gains in productivity; the reverse direction of causation is explicitly rejected. Thus, according to Kaldor, if productivity growth rather than output growth were the autonomous factor inducing increases in demand by lowering costs and prices, this would not account for the large differences in performance in the *same* industry over the same period in different countries, since each had access to the same improvements in technology. Moreover, doubt is cast on the extent to which variations in productivity growth are likely to be reflected in movements in relative prices and, even if they are, whether the price elasticity of demand is always greater than unity for the relevant products. These arguments, however, are not altogether convincing. First, although it is not implausible to suggest that advanced countries have more or less equal access to technological improvements, the critical factor is whether each country has the same ability and willingness to apply such improvements. It is not unlikely of course that a reluctance to innovate might be overcome by a sufficiently high rate of growth, but, while a rapid growth rate will undoubtedly help, other considerations may also be of some importance. Relative factor prices, for instance, will affect the speed at which new techniques are introduced, but more important will be factors such as the quality of management and the state of industrial relations. Second, a number of studies have in fact found an inverse relationship both between changes in output and price and between changes in labour productivity and price, though admittedly these have been inter-industry rather than inter-country comparisons. Kaldor's other requirement that price elasticities be greater than unity has not been adequately tested. The importance of the point is obvious where growth is sought by price reductions for, unless the demand for a commodity is elastic, a lowering of price will not succeed in increasing the value of sales. The point is of less relevance, however, when the fruits of productivity improvements are used to increase growth in other ways such as more intensive advertising, product improvements and innovation.

In his cross-section study of UK industries, Salter took a different view about the direction of causation. He argued that a rapid rate of productivity growth produced a relative decline in cost and price and so stimulated an increase in the demand for the industry's output. Improvements in technical knowledge were seen to play the key role in determining productivity growth, although the realisation of economies of scale and factor substitution were also regarded as potentially important. The factors affecting productivity are highly interrelated. Salter's conclusion was that the 'realisation of economies of scale depends upon increases in output which are in part induced by technical advances; while factor substitution is prompted by changes in relative factor prices which to some extent originate in technical change itself' (1966: 143). These factors reduce the costs of the best-practice methods of production, which leads to an expansion of output and a fall in prices which forces the abandonment of high-cost obsolete methods of production. Labour productivity therefore increases both through the addition of new capacity and through the abandonment of old capacity, with industry output becoming concentrated in the most up-to-date plants. An increase in output would itself tend to produce this latter effect, and in this sense the relationship between the growth in productivity and output is simultaneous. However, there is little doubt that Salter regarded technical change as the main autonomous factor and capital investment as the instrument by which such change is implemented.

Caves (1968) also regarded productivity growth rather than output growth as the main explanatory variable, and he placed great emphasis on the evidence, which emerges from many studies, of a negative correlation between output growth and price changes. He argued that 'if output growth predominantly causes productivity growth, then the selling prices of fast-growing industries should generally be rising, if only to reflect short-run full utilisation of capacity' (1968: 298). However, this interpretation is open to debate, since it seems not only to disregard the possibility of increasing returns but also to ignore what is happening to prices in slow-growing industries.

In contrast, Kendrick, from his analysis of productivity trends in the USA, came to the conclusion that:

the significant association between relative changes in productivity and in output is not due just to the influence of productivity on prices and therefore on sales ... increases in output make possible economies of scale that augment autonomous innovation in producing productivity advance. In fact, our analysis suggests that the influence of relative changes in scale on relative productivity changes may be more important than the reverse influence working through relative price changes. (1961:209)

To sum up, while there is no disputing the widespread tendency for labour productivity growth to be closely associated with the expansion of output, there is still room for debate over the causal processes underlying the correlation. Perhaps the most sensible conclusion is that the direction of causation can run either way and that there is likely to be some interaction between the two processes in the sense that, whatever initiates the process, changes in one variable will facilitate changes in the other, i.e. a high rate of increase in output will induce a high rate of growth of productivity, which in turn will facilitate a further expansion of output, and so on. In other words, a process of 'cumulative causation' may get under way which benefits fast-growing sectors. Furthermore, one should add that conditions will be especially favourable to exceptional gains in both output and productivity for those products where, owing to rising incomes, there is a big increase in demand and where there are also many opportunities for technological advances. Thus to summarise and using the same format as previously:

$$\hat{o} \rightarrow I \rightarrow \left\{ \begin{array}{l} \text{economies of scale} \\ \text{technical progress} \end{array} \right\} \rightarrow$$

$$\hat{o}/E \rightarrow \left\{ \begin{array}{l} \downarrow \text{costs} \\ \uparrow \text{profit margins} \end{array} \right\} \rightarrow \left\{ \begin{array}{l} \downarrow \text{prices} \\ \uparrow \text{non-price} \\ \text{competitiveness} \end{array} \right\} \rightarrow \hat{o}.$$

The role of investment

It is clear from the foregoing discussion that, whatever the precise causal mechanism at work, investment plays a crucial role. If it is expansion of output that causes gains in productivity, it will do so in part as a result of investment in new plant. If on the other hand it is technological progress that starts the whole process moving, then again much of the advance will be embodied in new plant and equipment. Countries such as the UK and USA that have had a low rate of increase of output and productivity compared with their more successful competitors have also experienced poorer investment performance as measured by the ratio of gross investment to output in the manufacturing sector.

As well as having an indirect effect on efficiency through economies of scale and technical progress, gross investment is also an important component of final demand for a number of industries. It is particularly important for such sectors as mechanical and electrical engineering and vehicles. A period of low investment can clearly have a very damaging effect on the efficiency of sectors of this kind since it means a low level of demand, declining profitability and a weakening of the process of structural change whereby old plant is replaced by new. There is nothing to impede the closure of old plants and indeed this may be accelerated as industry runs into increasing difficulties. But low profits will mean that there is little inducement to invest in new capacity, so that the long-term competitiveness of the industry will be weakened. If cumulative causation is important, the closure of inefficient plants is not enough since this will simply reduce the size of the manufacturing base and do little to strengthen long-term competitiveness.

Further insight into the problem is obtained by considering the balance between safety and competition which is so crucial in determining investment. Neither extreme of all-out competition or entrenched monopoly power is likely to be conducive to a high rate of investment. The best results are likely to be associated with an intermediate position where firms are certainly threatened by their competitors but where they also have some element of market power in the short run. The problem of identifying the optimum balance between safety and competition is one that will be grappled with in later chapters. In the present context it is sufficient to note that, when cumulative factors are working in an industry's favour, the resulting fast rate of growth is an important element of safety which gives firms an expectation of an adequate return on capital. For investment and sales are each the precondition of the other. To have the capacity to satisfy customers, the producer must invest and hope that an adequate level of sales will be forthcoming, but he may not dare to invest without first knowing that the sales will be there. Uncertainty about buyers' reactions might prevent investment and thus cause production to remain at a low level.

There can of course be no complete certainty about the future, but an expanding market is the best insurance against being caught for a long period with excess capacity. This is particularly important where, because of economies of scale, the minimum optimal size of a new plant is large in relation to the annual growth in industry sales. If the rate of expansion of sales is low, firms may not be prepared to invest in new plants of optimal size but instead choose less risky sub-optimal capacity extensions. These may be in the form of new plant of sub-optimal size, or additions to existing plant so that new equipment operates alongside the old. If the production process is such that the new machines have to be used alongside old equipment then it may be impossible to operate the former to full advantage.

A slow rate of growth may also manifest itself in a failure to take full advantage of the economies of standardisation and long production runs within plants. Here again part of the explanation is found in the higher risks associated with specialisation when markets are growing only slowly.

It has already been noted that over the postwar period the level of manufacturing investment in the UK has not matched that achieved in more successful economies. From the preceding analysis it would not be surprising to find that, in view of the poor performance of manufacturing output since the mid 1970s, investment performance has also been disappointing, and this is precisely what the figures show (see Table 1.8). The slump in manufacturing output between 1978 and 1981 was accompanied by a fall of more than a quarter in gross fixed investment for the years 1980–83 compared with 1977–79. In 1985 both output and investment were still below their levels in the late 1970s, and regained that level only in 1987. Over the same period, direct investment by UK industrial and commercial companies overseas more than doubled while inward investment to the UK showed little change.

It is also possible by using the results of CBI questionnaires to get some idea of the growth of productive capacity of British manufacturing industry. The relevant data are given in Table 1.9. Even assuming no problems with the questionnaire itself, the figures in the first column give only a very rough measure of capacity working and must therefore be used with caution. What they suggest is that there was very little, if any, growth in manufacturing capacity over the period. For instance, comparing 1978 with 1987, manufacturing output was at

Table 1.8 UK manufacturing output and investment expenditure, 1977–88

	Manufacturing output index (1980 = 100)	Gross fixed investment Annual averages 1985 prices £m		Direct overseas investment £m	Inward direct investment £m
1978	109.6	1977–9	9,686	3,310	2,265
1981	94.0	1980–3	7,031	4,685	2,937
1985	103.8	1984–6	8,347	7,521	2,284
1987	110.7	1987–8	9,610	–	–

Sources: Central Statistical Office, *Economic Trends*, London: HMSO, various issues; Central Statistical Office, *Balance of Payments 'Pink Book'*, London: HMSO, various issues

Table 1.9 Estimated growth of productive capacity, British manufacturing industry, 1973–88

	CBI questionnaire % of respondents working below capacity	Manufacturing output Index (1980 = 100)
1973 (average of May, July, October)	43	114.2
1978 (Oct)	60	109.7
1987 (average of 4 surveys)	46	109.5
1988 (April, July)	32	116.5

Sources: Confederation of British Industry, Industrial Trends Survey in *National Institute Economic Review*. London National Institute of Economic and Social Research, various issues

about the same level, but a much smaller proportion of firms declared output below capacity. This suggests that capacity use in 1987 was higher and that capacity was lower.

The exchange rate

In an open economy the interactions between growth, investment and productivity involve the growth of exports. The expansion of output that can trigger off or reinforce the process of cumulative causation can occur in overseas markets as well as in the domestic one. In this respect the performance of an economy may be hampered by a failure to maintain international competitiveness, a failure that may in part be due to an overvalued exchange rate.

In order to appreciate fully the significance of the part played by exchange rates, consider what would happen in a world of freely floating exchange rates, starting from a position in which all countries are in balance of payments equilibrium. Assume further that the structure of manufacturing industries in all countries is highly competitive and that firms are profit maximisers. If one country suffers a decline in its competitiveness, its balance of trade will deteriorate and this will be reflected in a fall in the value of that country's currency on the foreign exchanges. This will serve to restore competitiveness in world markets by reducing prices and/or increasing the profit margins of exporters. For instance, suppose the £ falls in value. This will open up a number of strategies for UK exporters. They could decide to leave export prices unchanged in terms of domestic currency. The prices of exports would then fall by the full amount of the devaluation (strategy (a) in Table 1.10). Alternatively they could decide to keep export prices the same in terms of foreign currency. The effect of this would be to increase the price which an exporter gets in terms of his own currency, thus increasing his profit margin on exports (strategy (b) in the table). A third possibility is that some intermediate strategy will be pursued, giving the exporter some advantage in terms of keener prices and also some advantage in terms of a higher margin (strategy (c) in the table).

Table 1.10 Possible responses of UK exporters to a sterling devaluation

Strategy	Exchange rate	Price of product in UK market £	Price of product in W. German market DM
	£1 = 3.25 DM	1000	3250
a	£1 = 2.75 DM	1000	2750
b	"	1182	3250
c	"	1091	3000

Each firm will decide on the appropriate response to a devaluation in the light of its particular circumstances. Some will decide that their greatest need is to increase their price competitiveness and so will choose strategy (a). Others who might be on the verge of withdrawing entirely from the export market because it is unprofitable are more likely to choose strategy (b), and so on. In addition to these responses in export markets, devaluation also increases the competitiveness of firms in their domestic markets by making imports more expensive and/or less profitable to foreign producers.

A point which needs emphasising is that the sooner these adjustments are allowed to take place the easier the process of adjustment is likely to be. The market mechanism operates most effectively where departures from equilibrium are small. If exchange rate adjustments in response to a decline in competitiveness are prompt then the required devaluation will be small and so also will be its effect on the price of imports, the cost of living and the real wage. The longer the adjustment is delayed, however, the greater the structural imbalances that will develop and the more difficult it becomes for the exchange rate mechanism to correct them without causing serious damage to counter-inflation policy. In addition, the longer adjustment is delayed the more serious the effect on non-price competitiveness: product design and quality, marketing and after-sales service, the range of products and the number of producers will all suffer, and these dimensions of competitiveness are far more easily lost than regained.

Under the fixed exchange rate regime that existed for much of the 1950s and 1960s, an important element in the adjustment process was missing and this reinforced the cumulative process of advantage that benefited some countries and disadvantage that was suffered by others. In Japan and West Germany for instance, successful export performance was aided by a growing undervaluation of their currencies. This resulted in a rapid growth of manufacturing output, which stimulated a high level of investment and fast growth of productivity, which further strengthened their competitive position in world markets. In Britain and the USA the reverse process was at work. As competitiveness declined, the currencies became increasingly overvalued, and this reduced exports, which slowed the growth of manufacturing output, which adversely affected investment and the growth of productivity.

The most spectacular loss of international competitiveness suffered by British industry occurred in 1978–80. A commonly used indicator of competitiveness is the movement of relative unit labour costs, which equals:

$$\frac{\text{Relative labour costs}}{\text{Relative productivity}} \times \text{exchange rate.}$$

In 1978–80, all three components of this index moved to the UK's disadvantage. The value of sterling increased as a result of high interest rates (in November 1979 the minimum lending rate reached an all-time high of 17 per cent), the growth of North Sea oil production, and a restoration of confidence overseas following the government's announcement of firm fiscal and monetary policies.

At the beginning of 1980, sterling's effective exchange rate was 15 per cent above its average 1978 level. At the same time, relative labour costs were increasing rapidly and relative productivity was falling. The combined impact was to reduce Britain's international competitiveness by no less than 60 per cent between 1978 and the first quarter of 1981. Part of the loss in competitiveness was regained between 1981 and 1986 as a result of an improvement in relative productivity performance and a depreciation of sterling. However, in 1986 the index of competitiveness was still approximately 30 per cent below the 1978 level, and from 1986 to 1990 there was a further deterioration in industrial competitiveness.

Labour costs and productivity

The purpose of the preceding discussion has been to stress that, in an open economy, one of the important adjustment mechanisms is the exchange rate. A depreciation of the currency restores competitiveness. Unfortunately it also has an adverse impact on the rate of inflation, and this problem is particularly acute when a big loss of competitiveness has occurred and a substantial depreciation of the currency is needed to correct it. The analysis also points to the importance of relative movements in labour costs and productivity. If unit labour costs kept in line with those in other economies, a currency depreciation would not be required to maintain competitiveness. It is clearly better for managing the economy if depreciation doesn't have to be relied upon. There is also a further consideration. By eschewing depreciation, and making it known that this is a central plank of policy, a government may force firms and unions to exercise more discipline in pay bargaining and to seek more earnestly for ways of improving productivity. This is an issue of key importance, especially in view of the government's decision in 1990 to join the Exchange Rate Mechanism (ERM) of the European Communities. Can a firm exchange rate policy succeed in increasing efficiency at the level of the firm and industry without an unacceptable drop in output and employment, or are there fundamental weaknesses in the economy which cannot be remedied, at least in the short to medium term, so that depreciation is from time to time inevitable? The UK experience suggests that the latter is nearest the truth.

This brings us to one final point. The process of cumulative causation was summarised above as follows:

$$\hat{o} \rightarrow I \rightarrow \left\{\begin{array}{l} \text{economies of scale} \\ \text{technical progress} \end{array}\right\} \rightarrow$$

$$\hat{o}/E \rightarrow \left\{\begin{array}{l} \downarrow \text{costs} \\ \uparrow \text{profit margins} \end{array}\right\} \rightarrow \left\{\begin{array}{l} \downarrow \text{prices} \\ \uparrow \text{non-price} \\ \text{competitiveness} \end{array}\right\} \rightarrow \hat{o}.$$

The analysis is important in emphasising the relationships between variables such as output and investment, etc. But what it doesn't reveal directly is just as important as what it does – and that is the *strength* of these relationships. There is no reason to doubt that any manufacturing sector can, in principle, benefit from the process of cumulative causation. They are likely to differ however in the extent to which they can sustain the process, because this depends on such fundamentals as the quality of management, labour relations, the level of skill in the workforce, expenditure on research and development, and the relationship between manufacturing industry and the financial institutions. These factors will determine the strength of the relationships that have been discussed, and in Britain they are almost all a cause for concern. For instance, Prais (1989) has shown that Britain lags well behind West Germany in technical and industrial training and, as we shall see in Chapter 9, Britain's performance in civilian R&D expenditure is also relatively weak. Concern has also been expressed at the failure of financial institutions to take a sufficiently active interest in and long-term view of the companies in which they invest.

It is these weaknesses which, in the absence of a depreciating currency, make it difficult if not impossible for the UK to match the long-term output and productivity performance of its major competitors.

1.5 SOME POLICY ISSUES

There can be no doubt that the long-run performance of the British economy, and of manufacturing in particular, has been relatively weak. In 1979, the Conservative government announced the introduction of policies that would, it claimed, create the conditions needed for a sustainable growth in output and employment. These policies comprised the control of inflation by means of monetary policy, and various measures to strengthen the supply side of the economy, including tax reform, trade union reform, privatisation and deregulation. There is considerable disagreement on how effective these policies have been, though it must be said that evidence of improved performance is less than convincing. After the deep recession of 1979–82, national output recovered, at first gradually and then, after 1986, more quickly. The fast growth rate from 1986 to 1990 was a consumer-led boom fuelled by tax-cutting budgets and a boom in credit. It proved to be anything but sustainable. By the end of 1990 the economy was faced with an inflation rate touching double figures, very high interest rates, a massive balance of trade deficit and rising unemployment. In manufacturing it was not until 1987 that output regained its 1979 level. Then, after three years of growth, the sector was again, at the end of 1990, facing a major slump.

The causes of Britain's poor performance are complex. There are also no easy policy solutions. No attempt will be made here to discuss policy issues in detail, but the analysis of this chapter suggests one or two pointers.

First, there is widespread agreement that Britain has performed badly in some fundamental areas which are crucial to the underlying competitive strength of the economy. These areas include industrial training and R&D. Though there is general agreement that a skilled workforce and R&D expenditure are vitally important to long-run competitiveness, coherent policies still have to be worked out. One thing that does seem certain is that in both areas a substantial improvement in performance will depend on the government adopting a more positive approach to industrial matters than was typical in the 1980s. And in the area of R&D in particular a more positive approach might well mean some industrial planning.

Second, there is the matter of the right mix of macroeconomic policies. The analysis of this chapter has shown the importance of maintaining a high level of expenditure on investment, training and R&D, and also of maintaining profitable export markets. Given these objectives, a macroeconomic policy that relies exclusively on high interest rates and a high exchange rate to contain the level of domestic demand seems singularly inappropriate. If enough encouragement is to be given to investment, more direct ways must be used to control personal consumption, e.g. fiscal policy supplemented perhaps by some form of credit control.

Third, mention should be made of the means by which relative unit labour costs are to be contained. By entering the ERM in 1990 the government signalled that this would have to be achieved by bringing downward pressure to bear on wage settlements. With present institutional arrangements, however, this has to be done on a company-by-company basis. One problem with this is that companies with high productivity growth will be able to justify big wage awards, which in turn set the standard for companies with lower productivity growth. Many of the latter, especially when skilled labour is in short supply, will be forced to concede higher wage settlements than they would have liked. The alternative is a more centralised approach along German lines in which employers collectively set a norm for wage settlements which the country can afford. With this system, unit labour costs, and prices, fall where productivity growth is high, and comparable wage settlements can be achieved where productivity growth inevitably lags behind the norm, as in many of the non-traded sectors of the economy (see section 1.3).

A more centralised pay system will undoubtedly work best where there are no severe skill shortages which force companies to compete for the skilled labour available. However, one thing is clear. With a fixed exchange rate, failure to bring wage settlements into line with productivity growth will mean growing business bankruptcies and unemployment. Devaluation within the ERM is possible and, given the circumstances of the UK economy, likely to be inevitable if an unbearably high level of unemployment is to be avoided.

Acknowledgement

We are grateful to Professor R.E. Rowthorn for his constructive comments on this chapter.

Chapter 2

Business goals and behaviour

2.1 INTRODUCTION

In this chapter we look at a question that underlies much of the discussion in other chapters of the book, namely, the question of a firm's aims or objectives. The traditional theory of the firm assumes that firms aim simply to maximise profits, and on the basis of this assumption a large number of testable predictions about how profit-maximising firms will behave, and the resultant performance of the industry, can be derived.

However, the assumption of profit maximisation has been attacked from two directions. The first objection is that, while profit maximisation may appear to be a simple and unambiguous objective in theory, it will not be so in practice. The model of a profit-maximising firm is an owner-managed firm producing only one good, which knows all future cost and revenue streams with certainty. Such a firm could indeed choose the levels of output and price that would maximise its profits. But in fact firms are faced with much more complex decisions, to be taken in a dynamic and uncertain environment, and in this case it is far less clear how a profit-maximising firm will behave.

The second objection to profit maximisation is not that it will in fact be difficult, if not impossible, to maximise profits but that the whole idea of profit maximisation is misconceived, because firms may be motivated by other considerations. Consider, following Scitovsky (1943), what profit maximisation implies about the preferences of the profit maximiser. This we can do with the aid of Figure 2.1. Take the simple case of a firm with a single owner-manager and where output is proportional to managerial input or effort so that the latter can be measured in terms of output. The total revenue (TR), cost (TC) and profit (TP) curves can then be drawn from A – the point on the horizontal axis where managerial effort and output are zero. Profit is maximised at P where managerial effort is equal to AM. The diagram also shows an indifference curve, I, taken from the preference map of a manager for whom both money income and leisure are normal goods. In this case indifference curves will be negatively sloped and the optimum position for the manager will be at point L, representing that combination of income and leisure which maximises the manager's utility. But L

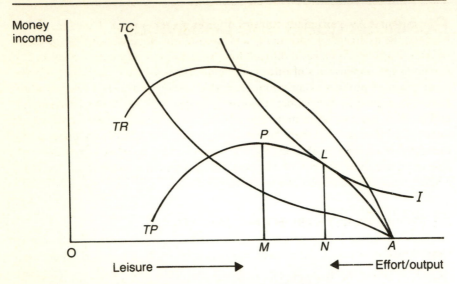

Figure 2.1 Profit maximisation and managers' preferences

is clearly not the profit-maximising position. Only if the indifference curves were horizontal would *P* be the optimum position; and horizontal indifference curves would imply that while money income has a positive marginal utility no extra utility is derived from consuming more leisure. In other words, the amount of leisure which the manager enjoys is of no concern to him; higher utility can be achieved only by more income. The profit-maximising businessman, therefore, is so keen on making money that he will not wish to increase his leisure at the cost of unexploited profit opportunities.

The profit-maximising assumption can therefore be questioned on the grounds that it is based on somewhat questionable assumptions about the psychology of decision-makers. The argument that decision-makers may well be interested in objectives other than profits is a general one, but it has received most emphasis in the case of companies that are not managed by their owners. In these cases profits accrue to the owner while the decisions about how the firm should behave are taken by managers, who may be interested in non-profit objectives.

These two objections to the assumption of profit maximisation raise a large number of issues which we examine in this chapter. Some of these issues are methodological: how should we assess whether profit maximisation is a 'good' assumption or not? Any theory must involve abstraction from the complexity of the real world, and the assumption of profit maximisation may be justified if it leads to correct predictions about firms' behaviour (i.e. if firms behave *as if* they aim to maximise profits, even if this is not an accurate description of firms' more complex motivations). On the other hand, correct predictions based on obviously false assumptions may be untrustworthy.

In section 2.2 we examine problems of profit maximisation. These are raised by, first, the existence of uncertainty and, second, the organisational complexity of large firms, which makes it difficult for a single aim to be pursued. Section 2.3 examines the implications of uncertainty and organisational complexity for the assumption of profit maximisation. Does this assumption merely need modification, as argued by behavioural theorists, or must it be replaced by alternative and possibly more complex motivations? The main alternatives are found in the 'managerial theories' and these are reviewed in section 2.4. Even if managers are interested in objectives other than profit maximisation, to what extent are they able to pursue these objectives? The possible constraints on managerial decision-making make up the subject matter of section 2.5.

2.2 PROBLEMS WITH PROFIT MAXIMISATION

Uncertainty

As already stated, the basic model of a profit-maximising firm is a static model in which the firm knows its revenue and cost curves with certainty and maximises profits by equating marginal cost and marginal revenue. In practice, however, firms are involved in making decisions in a dynamic, not a static, context, and maximising profits therefore involves maximising the difference between the revenues and costs associated with different courses of action, where both costs and revenues appear as streams of funds extending over future periods.

In order to choose between these courses of action they must be compared on a basis that abstracts from the problem that they bring in different returns at different times in the future. To deal with this problem the future streams of costs and revenues must be discounted to yield a net present value (NPV) associated with each course of action.

If in future year i revenue is R_i and costs are C_i, profits in future year i are given by

$$\pi_i = R_i - C_i$$

and the present value of the stream of profits (π_i) is given by

$$NPV = \sum_{i=1}^{n} \frac{\pi_i}{(1 + r)^i}$$

where n is the time horizon and r is the discount rate.

Profit maximisation means choosing the course of action that yields the highest NPV. However, this apparently simple reformulation of profit maximisation in dynamic terms raises a number of problems, which we deal with below. First, the firm does not know the value of its future profits stream, because this is uncertain. Second, treating profit maximisation as a dynamic problem shows that the firm has to specify both a discount rate (r) and a time horizon (n) for its decisions.

The values of both cost and revenue streams in the future are uncertain because they are affected by factors that the firm cannot predict: for example, the reactions of existing and potential competitors, the rate of growth of real incomes, changes in tastes and technology, changes in the cost and availability of raw materials or factor inputs, and government policy changes. The profit-maximising firm's choice between alternative courses of action therefore becomes much more complicated. Instead of yielding a single NPV of profits, each course of action is associated with a large number of possible outcomes, each with a probability attached.

How does the firm react in these circumstances? In effect the firm has to choose between a series of probability distributions of profits, and under these conditions of uncertainty profit maximisation ceases to have a unique meaning, as we shall see. Imagine a profit-maximising firm trying to decide between two policies whose profits in year i appear as the following distributions. Policy A promises a 25 per cent chance of zero profits, a 50 per cent chance of £40 and a 25 per cent chance of £100. Policy B promises an equal (50 per cent) chance of zero profits or of making £100.

Initially, the firm will look at the expected value of profits, $E(\pi_i)$, associated with each policy:

$$E(\pi_i) = \Sigma\, \pi_i\, p\,(\pi_i)$$

where $p(\pi_i)$ is the probability attached to each value that profits may take in year i. Policy B has an expected value of profits in year i of £50, and policy A of £45. This kind of calculation can be carried out for each year within the time horizon, and so it may be thought that the profit-maximising firm's choice between alternative courses of action can be reduced to choosing that which promises the highest present value of expected profits:

$$NPV = \sum_{i=1}^{n} \frac{E(\pi_i)}{(1+r)^i}$$

However, this ignores the fact that there are other characteristics of a probability distribution, as well as its expected value, that influence a firm's behaviour; the variance of the distribution measures its dispersion around the expected value and provides some measure of the risk attached to that particular course of action. The firm's choice between alternative courses of action will be influenced by its attitude to risk. The policy with the highest present value of expected profits will be the obvious one to choose only if it also has a low variance; otherwise a risk-averse profit-maximising firm may choose a policy with a lower value of expected profits but with less risk attached to this value. In the example given above, policy B has the highest present value of expected profits in year i, but it also has a higher variance than policy A; that is, the chance of making no money at all is higher with policy B.

This is what is meant when we say that profit maximisation has no unique meaning under uncertainty; which course of action a profit-maximising firm will choose depends on its degree of risk aversion as shown in the firm's utility function, which will show some kind of trade-off between expected return and variance of return. Since little information is available on individual decision-makers' degree of risk aversion it is difficult to derive any clear-cut predictions based on the assumption of profit maximisation.

The recognition that profit maximisation must be interpreted in a dynamic rather than a static sense raises problems connected with the choice of time period and discount rate; both these factors can influence the behaviour adopted by a profit-maximising firm, and here again the relevance of uncertainty is apparent. One response to uncertainty is to maximise short-run profits. A firm may, for instance, be convinced that, whatever strategy it pursues, new entrants are likely to enter the market; it therefore decides to charge high prices while it can. Another firm may respond by increasing sales as fast as it possibly can, so as to establish a market dominance which may deter entry or give it a strong market position should entry occur. In this case the emphasis is on long-run competitiveness and long-run profits.

A factor which will have a widespread effect on the choice of time period over which profits are maximised is the general business environment. This can vary substantially in the pressure it exerts on firms to cut costs and concentrate on the short term. This was true in UK manufacturing in the early 1980s. Faced with a massive decline in competitiveness many firms survived only by cutting investment, reducing research and development expenditure and spending less on training, including apprenticeships – a classic case of conflict between what may be necessary for short-term survival and what is sensible in terms of long-run competitiveness.

The choice of time horizon over which profits are to be maximised is linked to the choice of discount rate. A higher discount rate will reduce the present value of any course of action whose profits appear further into the future more than that of a course whose profits are reaped relatively soon, and thus the higher the discount rate used, the more likely is the latter course of action to be chosen.

What is the relevant discount rate for firms to use to discount future streams of profits? In terms of the expression on page 30, what value of r should the firm use in computing the present value of expected profits attached to different courses of action? The appropriate rate to use will usually be the rate at which the firm can borrow or lend money, since this rate measures the cost of borrowing money, if necessary, or the opportunity cost of using the firm's own funds in a particular course of action rather than lending the money out.

As previously implied, the firm's choice of discount rate can determine which of the alternative policies open to it appears as profit maximising. This is because the NPV method of comparing alternative courses of action makes them comparable by implicitly assuming that, where policies cover different time periods, the revenue from the action that has returns earliest can be reinvested at the rate of discount. But this is not the only problem raised by the firm's choice of discount rate. Should a firm use the same rate to discount all future streams, although streams further into the future may inherently be more uncertain? The choice of a discount rate higher than the current cost of funds may be defended on the grounds that, since this discounts further-away yields more strongly, some sort of allowance for risk is included.

Organisational complexity

The paradigm of a profit-maximising firm in the static model is an owner-managed firm, where the owner-manager both takes the decisions and carries them out. The reality of a large modern firm is far more complicated than this. The 'owners' of the firm are a large number of shareholders, who have nothing to do with the running of the firm, while the main decisions are made by the board of directors of the firm and implemented by managers and workers all through the different levels and departments of the firm.

This more realistic model of a firm has two main implications for the assumption of profit maximising. First, the managers who take the decisions may be interested not in the maximisation of profits but in some other goal. This problem is dealt with later in this chapter. Second, the problem to which we now turn is that, even if managers do wish to maximise profits, this objective will be difficult to achieve in a complex structure like a large firm. Problems may arise for a number of reasons, and the implications of these problems for the profit-maximising firm have been analysed by organisation theory.

One problem that has received a great deal of attention, and which has been blamed for many of the industrial relations problems of large firms, is that of communication difficulties within companies. These difficulties operate in both directions. Decisions made at the top, at board level, may be inadequately explained to those lower down in the firm who have to implement the decisions, which may consequently be misunderstood; also, the problems and grievances of lower management and non-managerial employees may have difficulty in filtering up through the firm to the decision-making level. One argument put forward for the extension of 'industrial democracy' – the increased involvement of employees at all levels in decision-making, by such mechanisms as workers elected to sit on the board of directors – is that such arrangements ease the communication problems of large firms and can benefit everyone concerned by improving the performance of the firm.

For a firm to be actively engaged in profit maximisation it is not enough for the directors to take profit-maximising decisions; it is necessary also that everyone concerned in implementing these decisions should accede to them. This implies that they must not only understand and accept the decisions but also see how they themselves are involved in the goal of profit maximisation. In fact, in a large complex organisation it may be difficult for an individual employee, at either lower management or shopfloor level, to make any connection between his own behaviour and the firm's aims, because each employee is only a small part of the organisation. However, if enough employees feel like this, it is not surprising that the goal of maximum profits may not be reached. Individual employees are likely to feel not only that their own behaviour makes little difference to the overall performance of the firm, but also that they themselves derive little benefit from profits being maximised. For managers, the level of their salary may be thought to depend on variables other than profits, while trade union negotiators may sometimes argue that high profits justify large wage increases but will rarely accept low profits or even losses as a reason for low or negative wage increases. If lower-level managers are interested in goals other than the maximisation of profits, they will be able to exert a significant influence on the firm's behaviour through their control over the information channels in the firm. Decisions made at board level must be based on information collected from lower down the firm, and it is therefore possible for low-level managers to feed the board distorted information in order to influence these decisions.

The model of a profit-maximising firm assumes that the firm behaves as a monolithic entity concentrating on a single goal. We have already seen that this may not be so for reasons involving control loss and lack of involvement by employees. The behavioural theory of the firm, however, argues that the firm is not at all monolithic but represents a coalition of different interest groups, whose goals may well conflict. This problem is likely to be more acute in large firms organised into separate divisions: for example, research and development (R&D), sales, marketing, industrial relations, and so on. These divisions will compete for the allocation of funds within the firm, and, to the extent that members of each division see themselves primarily as engineers, say, or accountants rather than as members of the firm itself, there is room for different goals to develop, which can hinder the overall aim of profit maximisation. For instance, the professional interests of engineers may incline them to push the introduction of complex and sophisticated products without much thought for the cost implications and market requirements. Other examples of cases in which the interests of one group of employees conflict with the central aim of profit maximisation are not hard to think of.

It is of course the function of top management to resolve these difficulties. In endeavouring to do this the style of management will clearly be important. More specifically the difficulties may be resolved by employment contracts that offer incentives to compliant behaviour on the part of the employee, and by organisational changes that make it easier to monitor performance.

Employment relations

Many of the problems considered in the previous section stem from *information deficiency*. In an uncertain world, information may be costly to acquire and it can never be complete. In making decisions businessmen cannot possibly take into account every piece of information that might conceivably be relevant to a particular problem. They are therefore subject to what is known as *bounded rationality*, i.e. rational decision-making based on a sub-set of all the information that is potentially available. Information may also be *asymmetric*, i.e. one of the parties to a contract is better informed than the others and this may give rise to transactional problems such as *opportunistic behaviour*. Applicants for jobs may, for instance, deliberately misrepresent their skills in order to get employment. Employees may shirk on the job when they are not being supervised or behave opportunistically in other ways. A large theoretical literature has developed around these various problems. Our task here is the modest one of illustrating their relevance to the business world and to suggest that solutions cannot be fully understood in terms of maximising behaviour because important elements of bilateral bargaining and satisficing are involved.

One possible approach to the transactional problems embedded in the employment relation would be a package along the following lines: an explicit contract with a carefully defined list of tasks for each worker; close monitoring of the employee; and the dismissal of workers who are found shirking. This is the stick rather than the carrot approach to the problem and it is clear that some elements of this approach are commonly found in employment relations. How appropriate the approach is will vary from one firm to another depending on the nature of the tasks to be done, the characteristics of the employees, and the labour market and product market conditions facing the firm. With easily defined tasks, an unskilled labour force, a ready supply of labour, and demand fluctuations in product markets so that the firm attaches little importance to continuity of employment, explicit employment contracts which rely on monitoring may be appropriate.

However, in many circumstances this approach will prove inadequate and will have to be amended or replaced. The major difficulties are the following. First, tasks may be difficult to define with sufficient precision to be embodied in an explicit contract, especially when conditions facing the firm are continually changing. It will simply be impossible to anticipate every possible state of the world and to work out the implications for the contracts. In other words, the problem of bounded rationality exists. The conditions that may change include those over which the employee has no control. In addition, through learning by doing, the dexterity with which the employee performs his task will improve over time. As a result the employer may wish to vary the wage contract. Continual renegotiation of contracts is a way of dealing with changing circumstances, but this involves heavy transactions costs. Second, monitoring may be costly and difficult to implement, especially where production is the result of team effort. It can also lead to friction and have a damaging effect on workforce morale. Third, there is a cost involved in hiring and firing, which becomes important once it is recognised that labour is heterogeneous so that the firm has an interest in the quality of its labour force.

The upshot is that the problems may be met not by a confrontational approach but by building up a relationship of trust between the firm and its employees. This relationship is built on the investment which the firm has made in the worker and the investment which the worker has made in the firm. Because both employer and worker have made such an investment, each side stands to lose if the employment relationship breaks down. It therefore follows that each side can impose a cost on the other party by violating the relationship. This is an example of a type of problem associated with asymmetry of information known as *moral hazard*. Moral hazard arises when one party to an agreement is unable to control the behaviour of the other party. One way in which the problem can be reduced is by the development of structured internal labour markets.

For its part the firm shows its interest in the worker by screening at the point of entry, offering training in specific skills and holding out the prospect of continuity of employment and promotion. A problem facing the firm is that it will fail to recover its investment if workers leave as soon as they have been trained. It will therefore require from the worker some sign of commitment to the firm. One way of showing such commitment is for the worker to accept a two-tier wage offer – a low wage to start with and a higher wage when training is completed. The firm is thus able to recover its investment in the worker and the worker has an incentive to stay with the firm so as to enjoy the benefit of the higher wage. But why should the worker trust the firm? The worker too is faced with a problem of moral hazard, because the firm may renege on the deal by finding some excuse to dismiss the worker before the higher wage comes into effect. The answer to this dilemma is the interest which the firm has in maintaining its reputation as a good employer. That reputation would quickly be destroyed if it failed to keep its side of the bargain.

The mutual trust between firm and employee is further strengthened by other features of internal labour markets. In structured internal labour markets there is a considerable degree of closure from the wider labour market, which is attributable to a number of factors. To minimise internal disruption, a single unified basic pay structure is developed across all job slots in the work unit, with wages being related to jobs rather than to individual workers. This rules out individual bargaining and weakens the incentive for workers to behave opportunistically. Wages will not be highly sensitive to demand and supply forces operating in the wider market but will reflect the skill requirements of jobs. Because the quality of labour is important to the firm, careful screening takes place both at entry and when selecting workers for promotion. Entry is largely confined to the lowest grade, higher positions being filled by internal promotions. By confining higher positions to internal candidates the firm is offering an inducement to reduce shirking. The importance of specific skills necessitates the continuous involvement of the firm in the finance and provision of training. The investment that the firm has in the worker gives it an incentive to promote stability within the workforce. It will thus offer wages and conditions of work conducive to low voluntary turnover. In addition, hiring and firing as a means of adjusting labour to fluctuations in output will be used only as a last resort. Instead the emphasis is on overtime, shift variations, short-time working and temporary lay-offs.

The implicit contract of the internal labour market is an institutional device to reduce transactions costs, a device that is based on developing a mutual trust between firm and employee. Clearly this approach to solving employer–labour relationships contains important elements of satisficing and bilateral bargaining. Certainly neither employee nor firm takes advantage of every opportunity to gain at the expense of the other. The emphasis is on continuity and long-term commitments. There is a cost in terms of a loss of short-run allocative efficiency but also a benefit in terms of lower transactions costs.

How well the internal labour market solves the problems of moral hazard and how successful it is in offering incentives is another matter (see for instance George and Shorey 1985). Promotion prospects may for instance be very limited in terms of job slots and benefit only a tiny percentage of the workforce. Furthermore the degree of closure of the internal labour market is partial not complete. The accepted procedures of the internal market are likely to work well so long as conditions of relative stability exist in product markets. But if there is a severe and prolonged slump, accepted procedures will have to give way to more fundamental market forces, though some firms will succumb to these forces more readily than others.

It is clearly difficult to solve the incentive problems that exist within firms. The general picture that emerges is that considerable discretion may be exercised by those involved in the chain of command in terms of both the choice of employment contract and the precise way in which a particular contract is enforced.

Organisational form

Is it possible to restructure the firm in a way that will get all the employees working towards profit maximisation? It has been observed that, as firm size increases and organisational problems begin to intrude, the structure of firms tends to adapt to deal with these problems. Specifically, the organisation of firms changes from what Williamson (1971) called unitary-form (U-form) to multidivisional-form (M-form). The implications for efficiency and resource allocation are discussed in Chapter 4. Here, we are concerned only with the implications of a change from U-form to M-form for profit maximisation and with the idea that resources will be allocated more efficiently within a large diversified firm if it adopts the multidivisional form of organisation. We draw heavily on Williamson's analysis of the relative merits of the two forms of organisation. The examples shown in Figure 2.2 are highly simplified versions of reality, but they serve to bring out the salient points. The purpose of the exercise is to see what sort of problems are likely to emerge as a firm grows in size and why these difficulties may be less acute in the decentralised form of organisation.

In the U-form of organisation, the chief executive coordinates the activities of the functional divisions (e.g. manufacturing) and also plans the overall strategy of the firm. Between the chief executive's office and the workers in the functional divisions are the middle management layers, the number of layers depending on the employment size of the firm. As a firm expands, the number of management

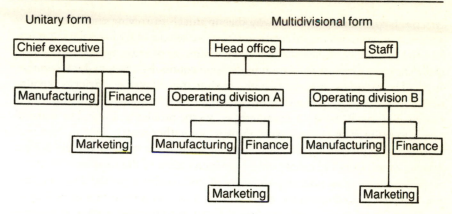

Figure 2.2 Unitary and multidivisional forms of organisation

layers increases, because there is a limit to the number of subordinates who can effectively be supervised. As the number of management layers increases, there is a loss of internal efficiency brought about by increasing communication problems. As information is transmitted across successive management levels, mistakes are made and, furthermore, these mistakes may be cumulative. The communication problems and consequent loss of control by the chief executive will tend to occur merely as a result of increasing the number of management layers. Further problems are caused in the processing and interpretation of the commands and information that flow between head office and the shopfloor, because individuals may have an interest in deliberately distorting messages in order to protect their own position.

As a result of growing communication problems and increasing difficulties of coordination, continued expansion will render the task of the chief executive impossible. The capacity of the head office will have to be expanded, and this is done by drawing the heads of the functional divisions into the office in order to help coordinate the firm's activities.

The heads of the functional divisions thus play a dual role. They have exclusive responsibility for the performance of their own divisions and also partial responsibility for company-wide issues. Since each head will to a greater or lesser extent have a vested interest in safeguarding the interests of his own division, the result is a weakening of company-wide decision-making.

Now let us look at the M-form of organisation. Here, responsibility for operating decisions is left to the divisions. Divisions A and B in Figure 2.2 may refer to different products or to the same product sold in separate geographical markets. This immediately reduces the flow of information to and from head office. The general executives at head office have no direct operating responsibilities and are thus free to concentrate on overall planning. In this role they are assisted by specialist staff. The divisional managers can, of course, be expected to work for the expansion of their own divisions, but head office can exercise more effective control than is typically the case in the U-form of organisation. This is partly because the divisional managers play no role in company-wide decisions, and so the conflict of interests that arises when people play dual roles does not occur. Because of this separation it is also easier for head office to fire lower-level executives. Another important factor is that the divisions can form separate profit centres, whose performances can be meaningfully compared. This is not the case in the U-form of organisation, where it clearly makes no sense to compare the profit performances of the operating divisions.

For all these reasons it is argued that the M-form of organisation will achieve greater internal efficiency than a U-form organisation of similar size.

Intermediate cases involving elements of both the U-form and M-form types may also be found, i.e. some aspects of a firm's activities may be organised on functional lines (e.g. personnel and research and development) while other activities may be divisionalised, as illustrated in Figure 2.3.

Underlying the choice of organisational form is the managerial need to collect information, interpret that information and respond to it, the need to monitor behaviour and to provide incentives. Depending on the informational requirements, etc., one organisation form will be preferred to another; for instance the M-form is better adapted to conglomerate firms. Differences in managerial ability and style will also ensure that, in the short run at least, different organisational firms will exist side by side, but over the longer term it can be expected that superior forms will be imitated and will tend to prevail.

2.3 MANAGERIAL OBJECTIVES

It was noted above that, once the existence of uncertainty is admitted, analysis of the behaviour of the profit-maximising firm becomes much more complex; behaviour in fact becomes impossible to predict without knowledge of the firm's attitude to risk. Does this mean that the assumption of profit maximisation loses its usefulness? Certainly one might question whether the firm actually takes its

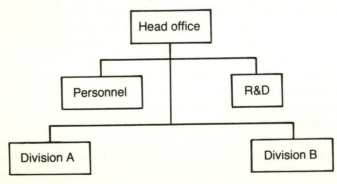

Figure 2.3 Intermediate organisational form

decisions in the formal way outlined above, by calculating the expected values and variances of probability distributions and taking into account the effect of different time horizons and rates of discount. However, unless one wants to argue that firms lose their interest in profits under conditions of uncertainty, which seems unlikely, then the assumption of profit maximisation needs to be modified rather than discarded.

The Behavioural School approach

The Behavioural School approach is to argue that firms will continue to choose a course of action which offers more profits rather than one promising less, but in conditions of uncertainty profit-maximising behaviour will have to take place in a more gradual step-by-step manner: it is no longer possible to choose the policy that will definitely lead to maximum profits over the period under consideration. Instead, aims and policies will have to be subject to constant revision, and a policy which goes wrong will have to be abandoned or modified in the light of experience.

In this approach profit maximisation is an iterative process which of necessity is limited to a consideration of a small number of the vast array of alternative strategies that are in principle open to the firm. The firm does not have perfect information on such matters as demand and cost functions, the competitive position of its suppliers, customers and competitors, and the strategies being considered by them. It is impossible to imagine all possible states of the world, and to contemplate the optimum response to each state. This is the problem of bounded rationality which we have already encountered. In a world characterised by uncertainty and complexity, firms cannot take everything into account. They can be viewed as behaving rationally only within bounds which are determined by the ability of the organisation to absorb and process information. The firm must therefore make decisions on the basis of the best estimates it can get from its information systems.

Management establishes a number of different goals that it wishes to achieve in any decision period. These goals represent the best judgement of each member of the management team as to the achievement necessary in sales, profit, etc. for the firm to survive and grow. They also represent the desires of individuals for the survival and growth of the sub-units they represent within the firm.

The goals are acceptable-level goals and the decisions made on price, investment, etc. must be expected to achieve them. They also depend on the level of achievement of the firm. Easy achievement of goals in one period will lead to more challenging goals being set in the next. Failure leads to a search process aimed at changing internal or external conditions to enable a set of decisions to be found that will achieve the goals.

This approach clearly does not deny that profit maximisation is a goal, because more profit is preferred to less. What it serves to emphasise is that the decision-making process of a profit-maximising firm is likely to be much more costly in terms of resources than is suggested by the static model. New information must constantly be collected, the results of past decisions assessed and plans revised.

Alternatives to profit maximisation

Another approach to analysing the possible consequences of uncertainty and organisational complexity has been to emphasise other objectives. It was pointed out earlier that incentive schemes and organisational reforms can do something to overcome the problems posed by uncertainty and organisational complexity. But they do not address another serious objection to the assumption of profit maximisation – that top managers may not be motivated by this aim. The M-form of organisation for instance may represent the best way for top managers to keep control over those below them and impose their own objectives on the company, but it is not necessarily true that this objective will be profit maximisation. Who, in other words, monitors the monitor?

The central observation on which this objection to profit maximisation rests is that in modern advanced capitalist economies the ownership of companies is divorced from their control. Typically, a large company is owned by many shareholders and controlled by a relatively small number of paid managers. The managers are nominally employed by the shareholders and are responsible to them at the annual general meeting of the company, but in fact the diffusion of ownership among so many people means that the owners can exercise little control over the managers, who are therefore free within wide limits to run the company as they wish.

This phenomenon of the divorce between the ownership and the control of firms raises a number of questions, which we look at in this section. First, is it true that shareholders have no effective control over how their company is run? And second, to the extent that this is true and decisions on firm behaviour are made by managers, not owners, what are the implications of this finding? Do managers wish to pursue objectives other than profit maximisation? If so, what are these objectives, and how will the pursuit of these objectives affect the behaviour of management-controlled firms? And if managers do wish to pursue other objectives, will they be free to do so, or are there pressures of various kinds on the firm that compel them to pursue profits?

The divorce between ownership and control

The seminal work on the ownership of corporations in the USA is that of Berle and Means (1932). They suggested that nearly half (88) of the largest 200 US firms were under management control in 1929, in the sense that in these 88 firms no individual or clearly defined group of individuals owned as much as the 25–50 per cent of total votes needed to exercise effective ownership control. Following on from this work it has been widely accepted that a managerial revolution has taken place – that most modern firms are management controlled and that the importance of management control is inexorably increasing. Before looking at the implications of management control for the behaviour of the firm, it is obviously important to ask whether this widely held view is in fact true.

The first study of this subject in the UK was by Sargant Florence (1961). He used a number of alternative criteria for establishing ownership control and found that, of the 98 largest UK companies in 1951, only 30 were owner controlled and that the trend towards the divorce of ownership from control between 1938 and 1951 was marked. Of all the UK companies with nominal share capital over £3 million, only 7 per cent had a single majority shareholder, and in only another 5.5 per cent did as few as the largest 20 shareholders have a majority position between them. Florence's work was thus taken as confirming the US picture of such a wide dispersion of ownership that managers were able to run their firms free from control by the owners.

More recently, this view has been criticised as presenting an oversimplified and misleading account of the separation of ownership control. In part this criticism depends on the definition of 'control' used: where shareholdings are widely dispersed, the percentage of votes needed to exercise control may be very much lower than the percentages (always in excess of 10 per cent) used to identify 'owner-controlled' firms in the studies mentioned above. An individual or group owning as little as 2 per cent of the shares of a company may be able to maintain control over its managers.

Second, figures on the concentration or dispersion of share ownership reveal only a part of the truth about who controls the company. Such figures show only the crude quantitative dimension of control and miss out altogether on the more subtle aspects of ownership and control, which can be elucidated only by a case-by-case approach to the study of firms. The amount of control exercised by a given block of shares can vary according to whom the shares belong to. Members of a family may unite to form a group not identifiable from share ownership records unless they all share the same name. Through their involvement in a large number of companies, banks and other financial institutions wield power out of all proportion to their holdings in any one company, and the same applies to significant individuals in the business community, through interlocking direc-torates. Also, a given number of shares will count for more when held by a member of the board of directors of the company or by a close relation of a director.

This last point shows that the separation between ownership and control is to some extent an artificial one, since managers do have some equity stake in the companies that they manage. It is true that modern managers do not own their firms in the traditional sense. Prais (1976) found that in 1972 directors owned less than 2 per cent of the company's shares in 73 of the largest 100 UK manufac-turing firms, and that in only 11 of these firms did the directors own more than 10 per cent. The size of large manufacturing companies is such that paid managers are extremely unlikely to hold a high proportion of the company's shares, but the above data suggest that managers do have significant holdings in their own companies, large enough, where shareholdings are dispersed, to give them some control over the company. To the extent that managers are involved in ownership they will have an interest in the firm's continuing ability to earn high profits.

A major and increasingly important potential source of control over managers comes from institutional share-owners. In 1970 over 40 per cent of all shares were held by insurance companies, banks, pension funds, investment and unit trusts, and this percentage has increased in recent years. In the UK such financial institutions have adopted a passive attitude towards the companies that they invest in and have usually spread their shareholdings thinly across a large number of firms. However, Nyman and Silberston (1978) suggested that there was evidence of an increase in the amount of control exercised by financial institutions and they cited two examples of large UK firms where financial institutions stepped in when the company's performance began to deteriorate.

In their article, Nyman and Silberston severely criticised the quantitative method of assessing control by looking at the distribution of share ownership, and they emphasised that control is a subtle and complex concept, which can be assessed only on a case-by-case approach. They also suggested that the dichotomy between owner-controlled and management-controlled firms is too sharp, since different types of ownership control (e.g. ownership by a family, a financial institution or another company) may lead to different behaviour. Of 224 of the largest UK companies in 1975, Nyman and Silberston estimated that at least 126 (50 per cent) were owner controlled. Of these firms, 77 were controlled through the shareholdings of their boards of directors or family chairmen, 23 were controlled by other industrial firms and 7 by charitable trusts or government organisations.

Nyman and Silberston also suggested, contrary to Berle and Means and other earlier work, that the extent of ownership control may actually be increasing in the UK, partly owing to the growing importance of institutional shareholders. Their work on the top 250 firms shows that manufacturing firms are more likely to be management-controlled than service firms, because, for one thing, the former are more capital intensive.

The conclusion to be drawn from this section is that for the majority of UK industry there is by no means a total separation of ownership from control. Many small shareholders are not in a position to exercise any control over the behaviour of the firms in which they have shares, but in most large UK companies the managers are subject to control from one or another kind of ownership interest. The implications of this conclusion for the behaviour of firms are that profits must still be regarded as important, although institutional shareholders have tended to intervene only in extreme cases when the firm is threatened with bankruptcy.

What about those firms, though, which are controlled by managers? What reasons are there to suppose that these firms will behave differently from owner-controlled firms?

Managerial motivation

Management-controlled firms will certainly not be indifferent to profits. For one thing, managers have a direct financial stake in the firm's profits through their shareholdings. More generally, the firm's profit record is one aspect of performance on which the firm will be judged, and the managers will have to maintain a satisfactory record in this respect to keep their jobs. This fact is recognised in the managerial theories of the firm by the inclusion of a minimum profit constraint, subject to which managerial utility is to be maximised. Firms may be under more direct pressure to maximise profits in order to survive in competitive product markets or in order to be able to raise money in a competitive capital market. If this pressure is strong enough, managers will have little chance to adopt any objective other than profit maximisation. This question of how much discretion managers actually have is dealt with later on.

The relationship between a salaried manager and the profits of his company is not as simple as that between an owner-manager and his profits, since the owner-manager gets all the profits of the firm and may therefore realistically be assumed to be interested in maximising them. One implication is that management-controlled firms may be more risk averse than owner-controlled firms and thus will tend to avoid more risky projects and courses of action. An owner-manager will bear any losses associated with a risky policy but will stand to get all the benefits if the project pays off. For a manager the balance of gain and loss appears different. If the risky project is successful, the rewards go to the shareholders, and only a small part comes to the manager himself, but if the project makes a loss, the manager is quite likely to lose his job. This implies that, even if managers are interested in profit maximisation, their greater risk aversion may lead them to choose different policies from a profit-maximising owner-controlled firm. (See earlier section on the indeterminacy of profit-maximising behaviour in conditions of uncertainty.)

If a salaried manager is not motivated by profit maximisation, what are his objectives likely to be? Managerial theories of the firm have suggested that managers are interested in their own levels of income, status and power and that they are also concerned with security and the avoidance of uncertainty. If this is a correct characterisation of managerial motivation, how will the behaviour of management-controlled firms differ from that of owner-controlled ones? The main theory here is that managers' own utility levels will depend more closely on the size of the company that they run than on its profitability, so that management-controlled firms will be concerned to maximise the size of the firm, and not profits.

It seems plausible to suggest that a manager's status is more closely related to size of firm than to profits. Large firms confer prestige, which is to a considerable extent independent of the firm's profitability record. The larger the firm, the more power its managers have in the form of controlling the resources of the firm, and also the more likely they are to have market power, to be involved in bodies like the Confederation of British Industry (CBI) and to receive a knight-hood. Large size makes for security in that it reduces the probability of the firm being taken over or going out of business in any other way. Evidence discussed elsewhere in this book suggests that in most mergers it is large companies that absorb smaller ones, and not more efficient firms that take over less efficient ones as a competitive model would suggest.

Is it also true that managers' incomes are more dependent on size than on profitability? A number of studies have reached apparently conflicting answers to this question. Before 1970 the accepted view, based on the work of Roberts (1956) and of McGuire, Chiu and Elbing (1962), was that executive pay was significantly correlated with sales, but not with profits. This view was first challenged by the work of Llewellyn and Huntsman (1970). They argued, first, that salaries account for only a minority (about one-sixth) of executives' total remun-eration and that the majority comes from dividends, bonuses and capital gains, all of which depend on profitability. Second, they argued that earlier work was mis-specified and that a revised formulation of the relationship between direc-tors' pay, size and profits shows that salaries are positively and significantly correlated with profits, but not with sales.

This is in fact a complex question, which needs to be viewed dynamically rather than statically, and this brings out the possible importance of growth, rather than absolute size of firm, in contributing to managers' objectives. If the level of managers' status, power and pay depends on the size of the firm, and if there is only limited mobility of managers between firms, the only way for managers to increase their utility is by achieving a rapid rate of growth. Thus, managerial emphasis on growth as an objective is increased by the operation of internal markets for managerial employees. If firms operate internal labour markets, managers will be recruited to the firm from outside only at a limited number of job levels (ports of entry), probably at the lower management levels, and promotion from this level will take place purely within the firm. Much mana-gerial skill may be specific to the firm, and this makes for the development of internal labour markets and reduces mobility between firms; managers can move to another firm only by moving down the ladder to the level of job that is recruited externally.

Meeks and Whittington (1975) argued that growth, not sales, is the most important determinant of directors' pay in an article that goes some way towards reconciling the conflicting evidence already cited. In their work, the size variable is used in logarithmic form, on the argument that directors will be paid according to the proportionate growth of their firms; for example, £100,000 of extra size will add more to the pay of the directors of a £1 million firm than to that of the directors of a £10 million firm. Using this formulation, Meeks and Whittington found that the coefficient on size is larger and more significant than that on profitability. However, although this supports the argument that levels of pay are correlated more closely with size than with profitability, Meeks and Whittington also argued that changes in profitability have more effect than changes in size, because a firm cannot move as rapidly along the size distribution of firms as it can along the profitability distribution. However, the importance of 'going for growth' is increased relative to that of profitability, because growth increases size and thus leads to a permanent increase in salary.

The conclusion of this debate is an eclectic one. There are a number of reasons for supposing that profits are a source of motivation for management-controlled firms, since a large part of managers' remuneration comes from stocks and shares. However, size, and therefore the growth rate of the firm, are also important to managers, since there is a correlation between size and managers' pay, and size also contributes to the other objectives of managers, namely status, power and security.

2.4 MANAGERIAL THEORIES OF THE FIRM

Given that there are no wholly convincing reasons for believing that firms are bound by profit-maximising considerations, it is necessary to look at models of firms that aim to maximise sales, or growth, and to see in what respects their behaviour will differ from that of profit-maximising firms. Three such managerial non-profit-maximising models are discussed below, and subsequently we make some assessment of these models.

Discretionary expenditures

The first model to be discussed is that of Williamson (1963), who analysed the effects on firm behaviour of discretionary behaviour by managers. He argued that managers aim to maximise a utility function that contains discretionary expenditures on staff and on all forms of management perquisites (e.g. lavish expense and entertainment allowances), subject to a profit constraint imposed by the need to keep reported profits at an acceptable level.

Such a utility function can be represented by the normal sort of indifference map, with curves drawn between staff expenditure (S) and discretionary profit (π_D); i.e. net profit in excess of the minimum required to meet the constraint.

Managers' utility is constrained by the relationship between profits and staff expenditure. Up to the level of maximum profits, staff expenditures and discretionary profits expand together, but if output continues to increase, profits decline as staff expenditures increase. This relationship is shown in Figure 2.4 by the profit–staff curve, which is drawn net of the profit constraint. The firm reaches equilibrium at point P, where this curve is tangential to the highest possible managerial indifference curve.

This shows that a firm with this kind of managerial utility function will always spend more on staff than a profit-maximising firm and will also have higher output, lower price and lower profits. It will also exhibit more management 'slack'; no slack is allowed in a profit-maximising model.

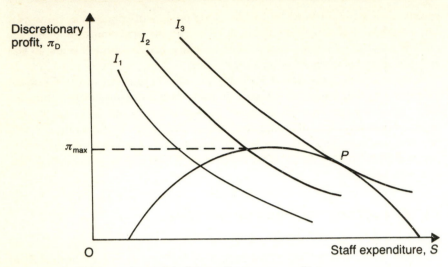

Figure 2.4 Williamson's model of discretionary expenditure

Sales maximisation

The idea that managers are concerned to maximise sales revenue rather than profits was first put forward by Baumol (1967) and justified on several grounds, including the closer dependence of managers' pay on size than on profits. Sales-maximising firms, however, are not able to ignore profits altogether; sales are constrained by the need to keep profits at some minimum adequate level to finance investment. Provided that this constraint is met, the firm is prepared to sacrifice further increases in profit for the sake of more revenue.

In Figure 2.5 *TR* and *TC* are the total revenue and total cost curves of the firm respectively; the difference between them gives the level of profits (π). The profit-maximising firm would produce output *OM*. The sales-maximising firm, if it were unconstrained, would produce output *ON*, and this will be the level of output chosen as long as the profit constraint is at or below the level of π_1. If the profit constraint is above this level, however, say at π_2, then sales will be effectively constrained to the level *OS*. The sales-maximising firm will always choose a larger output than the profit-maximising firm as long as the profit constraint is below the level of maximum profits.

The predictions derived from Baumol's model depend on whether the profit constraint is operative or not. A change in costs that affects profits but not total revenue will lead to a change in price and output only if the profit constraint is effective, because then the cost increase will reduce profits below the minimum acceptable level and output will have to be reduced to restore profits. However, Baumol argued that, if the firm is concerned to maximise long-run sales, the profits constraint will always tend to be effective, because the firm will use any

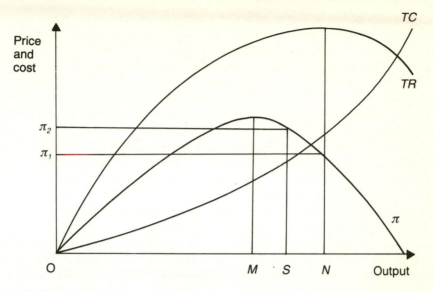

Figure 2.5 Baumol's model of sales revenue maximisation

profits earned above the minimum level to advertise and increase sales revenue. Thus, profits will always be at the level given by the constraint, but the constrained sales-maximising level of output is still greater than the profit-maximising level.

   In the model outlined above it is clear that sales revenue maximisation may take place at the expense of current profits. The conflict between sales and profits is less obvious in the dynamic sales-maximisation model also put forward by Baumol. In this model the firm aims to maximise the present value of future sales revenue, and, since sales expansion is financed mainly or completely from retained profits, profits become an endogenously determined choice variable rather than an exogenously imposed constraint.

   If profits provide the finance for sales growth, will the multiperiod sales-maximising firm behave any differently from the profit-maximising firm? The answer is that the sales maximiser will again choose a higher level of output. Suppose that the current value of sales revenue is S and the annual growth rate of sales g. Then the future revenue stream of the firm is

$$S, S(I + g), S(I + g)^2 \ldots S(I + g)^n$$

and the present value of this stream is given by

$$PV(S) = \sum_{i=0}^{n} S \left[\frac{I + g}{I + r} \right]^i$$

where r is the rate of discount.

The firm wishes to choose values of g and S to maximise the present value. The nature of this choice is illuminated by considering the growth function of the firm, Figure 2.6, which is derived from the profits function of Figure 2.5, and shows the attainable growth rate for any value of current revenue. Up to the level of maximum profits both g and S increase. Beyond this level of output, S continues to increase, but g (the rate of growth) falls, because it depends on profits. Therefore, there is a trade-off between high current sales (S) and a high rate of growth of sales (g).

Thus, a number of different negatively related combinations of S and g will yield the same present value of sales revenue, as shown in the iso-present-value lines of $V_0, V_1, \ldots$ in Figure 2.7. In order to maximise present value, the firm will be in equilibrium where the growth function is tangential to an iso-present-value line (i.e. at point P in Figure 2.7). This point determines the present-value-maximising levels of current revenue (S^*) and the growth rate of revenue (g^*).

Lastly, in Figure 2.8 the level of revenue S^* is related to current output (Q^*), and the profit constraint is shown to be endogeneously determined. The multi-period sales-maximising firm, then, will maximise the present value of future sales by choosing current output Q^* (and revenue S^*) and a rate of growth of revenue g^* that requires a level of profits π^*_{min} to finance it.

Figure 2.8 shows that a multiperiod sales-maximising firm, like that in the static model, will produce a higher output than a profit-maximising firm. The point of tangency between the growth function and the negatively sloped iso-present-value curve must come on the downward-sloping section of the growth function.

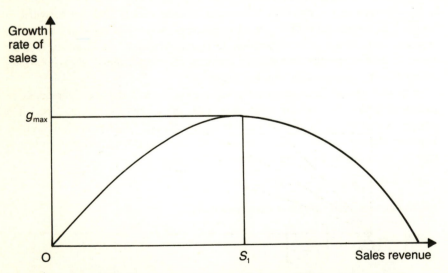

Figure 2.6 The relationship between the level and growth of sales revenue

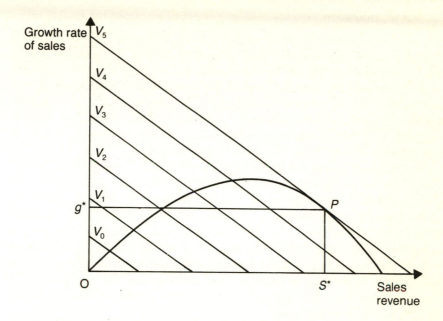

Figure 2.7 Derivation of present value of sales revenue

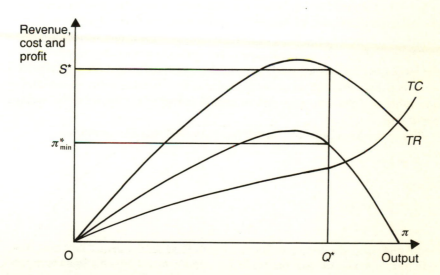

Figure 2.8 Equilibrium of the multiperiod sales-revenue-maximising firm

Growth maximisation

The third non-profit-maximising model that we look at is a model in which managers aim to maximise the rate of growth of the firm. The possible reasons for such an aim have already been discussed, and we have seen that a concern with size becomes in a dynamic context a concern with growth, although growth and current size may conflict as objectives. A coherent model of a growth-maximising firm has been presented by Marris (1963), whose firm aims to maximise its balanced rate of growth; that is, the rate of growth of product demand must match the rate of growth of capital inputs.

The balanced growth rate of the firm is constrained by two separate factors. First, there is a managerial constraint set by the ability of the management team to expand both demand and supply. Second, on the supply side only, the ability of the firm to grow is subject to a financial constraint imposed by the management's desire for security, which, we have previously argued, is an important component of managers' utility. This means that managers must pursue financial policies with regard to borrowing, liquidity and profits retention that give a low risk of either bankruptcy or takeover, since in either case the managers would lose their jobs. The value assigned to the security constraint depends on the attitude to risk of the managers.

If this security constraint is assumed to remain constant, the maximum balanced rate of growth of the firm depends on two variables, which affect both the growth of demand (g_d) and that of capital (g_c). The first is the rate of diversification (d) and the second is the average rate of profit (m). It is only through diversification that product demand grows in this model; Marris viewed the control of diversification as the most important task of management. The rate of growth of demand (g_d) increases with d at a decreasing rate and for any rate of diversification is lower the higher the profit rate, because a higher profit rate implies less demand-expanding expenditure on advertising and R&D.

The rate of growth of capital supply rises with the rate of diversification up to the level at which existing R&D personnel are optimally used. Beyond this level too much diversification means a fall in profits and the availability of capital. For any value of d the rate of growth of capital is higher the higher is the average profit rate.

The above description of Marris's model implies that for equilibrium

$$g_c = g_d = g^*$$

where

$$g_c = \bar{a} f_1 (m, d)$$
$$g_d = f_2 (m, d)$$

and $\bar{a}$ represents the given security constraint. In other words, we have one equation in two unknown variables (m and d), and it is not possible to solve for the equilibrium balanced growth rate without predetermining the value of one of these variables. In Figure 2.9, g_c and g_d curves are drawn against d for each of four values of m (where $m_3 > m_2 > m_1 > m_0$). The balanced growth curve *BGC* is formed by joining up the points where $g_c = g_d$ for a given value of m.

The highest point on this curve determines the maximum value of balanced growth ($g^* = g_c = g_d$) and simultaneously determines the values of m^* and d^*. The level of profits required to finance this rate of growth will also be endogenously determined.

So far we have assumed that the security constraint remains constant. If we relax this assumption, how is the analysis affected? Suppose that managers become less risk averse (i.e. less concerned about security). This implies that the firm should be willing either to borrow more, or to hold less liquid assets, or that it retains more profits. Any of these changes will shift the g_c curves in Figure 2.9 upwards; it becomes easier to accumulate capital. Thus, for a given value of m, the g_c and g_d curves intersect at a higher value of g, and the balanced growth curve moves upwards. Allowing the security constraint to vary implies that profits and growth may conflict. This is not the case with a fixed security constraint, under which maximising the growth rate implies maximising profits.

This is an important difference from the point of view of distinguishing between the behaviour of owner- and management-controlled firms. As long as the security constraint is fixed, utility maximisation for managers coincides with that of owners concerned to maximise profits. However, the interests of managers and owner-shareholders can conflict when the financial policy of firms is allowed to vary; managers concerned to maximise growth will retain profits for reinvestment at the expense of dividend payments to shareholders.

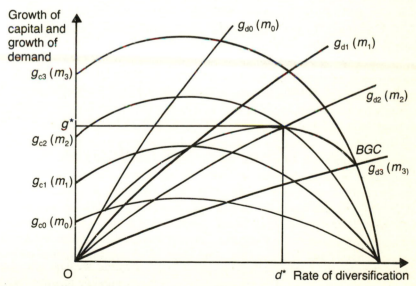

Figure 2.9 Marris's model of growth maximisation

An assessment of non-profit-maximising theories of the firm

We have now looked at three different 'new' theories of the firm, which argue that in our advanced industrial society corporations are controlled not by their owners but by their managers. This being the case, firms do not aim to maximise profits but behave in the way that will maximise the utility of the managers who take the decisions. The content of the managerial utility function varies between these three models: Baumol's firm maximises sales, Marris's firm maximises growth, and Williamson's maximises discretionary expenditures. How can we assess the success of these theories in superseding the traditional profit-maximising theory of the firm?

A first relevant point to make is that the need for such theories is not proven. We have already reviewed the evidence on the separation of ownership from control, which shows it to be by no means complete. We have also seen that managers will be interested in profits for a number of reasons.

If we accept, however, that there are some firms whose goal cannot accurately be described as profit maximisation, how much of an advance do the managerial theories represent? This is in part a methodological question, which takes us back to the points raised in the introduction to this chapter. Do the managerial theories of the firm help us to understand features of firms' behaviour that traditional theory cannot? How do their predictions differ from those based on the assumption of profit maximisation? And does the empirical evidence support the predictions of the managerial theories or not?

Baumol certainly claimed that his sales-maximisation hypothesis helps to explain certain features of business behaviour not readily explicable on the assumption of profit maximisation. The first such feature is that businessmen do pass on an increase in fixed costs to the consumer by raising prices, while for a profit-maximising firm such an increase in costs has no effect on marginal cost and therefore no effect on equilibrium price and output. For a sales-maximising firm, however, an increase in fixed costs implies a reduction in profits. Provided that the profits constraint was effective before the increase in fixed costs, it will no longer be met, and output will have to be reduced before the profit constraint can again be satisfied; the reduced output will be sold at a higher price.

If firms do react to a change in fixed costs by changing price and output, does this provide conclusive proof that they are sales maximisers rather than profit maximisers? Unfortunately not, and here we encounter a problem that makes assessment of the managerial theories of the firm extremely difficult. This is that it is very hard to distinguish between the different managerial theories on the one hand, and to decide between them and profit maximisation on the other hand, because their predictions are so similar. Take the above example of reacting to an increase in fixed costs. It is true that a short-run profit-maximising firm will not react in this way, but a firm that sets its price at an entry-preventing level so as to maximise long-run profits *will* raise its price in response to an increase in fixed costs, because all the firms in the industry will be affected in the same way, and therefore market shares won't change. The other managerial theories of the firm, apart from Baumol's sales-maximisation theory, also predict that a firm will react to an increase in fixed costs by reducing output, and therefore the observation that firms do behave like this is certainly not conclusive proof that they are sales maximisers.

In fact, the behavioural differences between long-run profit maximisation and the alternative managerial theories are so subtle that no conclusive econometric tests can be carried out with the available data. All attempts to do such econometric tests have been subject to a great many problems. For instance, Hall's attempt to test Baumol's theory empirically ran into difficulties in specifying the minimum profits constraint (Hall 1967). Empirical work on Marris's model has found it difficult to distinguish between management- and owner-controlled firms clearly enough to look for differences in behaviour between them; this is not surprising in view of Nyman and Silberston's work, referred to earlier, on the variety of forms that 'control' can take. It is therefore not possible to make a satisfactory assessment of non-profit-maximising theories of the firm by strict econometric testing of the predictions, as Friedman's positive methodology of economics would have us do, and we shall have to make our assessment on other grounds.

Compared with the profit-maximising theory of the firm, managerial theories pay less attention to price competition and more to non-price competition. In fact, these theories have no satisfactory explanation of the determination of prices; we return to this point below. In Baumol's model, firms maximise sales revenue by spending any profits in excess of the minimum constraint level on advertising to expand sales, and in Marris's model demand for the firm's product is assumed to grow by means of diversification. Thus, these two theories both assume that via sufficient marketing and promotional campaigns the firm can always increase sales. It may be true that managerial theories are applicable to large firms with market power in oligopolistic industries where competition is indeed likely to take the form of non-price rather than price competition, but the managerial theories go a long way away from the idea of consumer sovereignty towards the Galbraithian theory that firms can create new consumer demand for their products endlessly by manipulative advertising. There is no conclusive evidence to support this view. Indeed, within an oligopolistic industry where all the firms go in for a lot of advertising, the effects may cancel out, so that it becomes extremely difficult for one firm to expand its market share at the expense of the others by this means.

We have now come to a central criticism of the managerial non-profit-maximising theories of the firm. Compared with the profit-maximising assumption, the managerial theories introduce a number of considerations (e.g. management preference for sales, discretionary expenditure on staff or management perquisites) that may be important and helpful in analysing the behaviour of single large firms. However, these theories are no help at all in explaining the interdependence between firms that lies at the heart of any satisfactory theory of the firm in oligopolistic industries. Neither the equilibrium price structure of competing firms nor any other aspect of competition between them is analysed satisfactorily.

Thus, the claim of managerial theories of the firm to have supplanted the traditional profit-maximising approach *as a general theory* cannot be accepted. Yet, undoubtedly the managerial approach is in some sense a more realistic one than profit maximisation and is more descriptively accurate. Do we lose anything, apart from such realism, by retaining the assumption of profit maximisation? Solow (1971) concluded that we don't, if what we wish to be able to do is predict or control firms' behaviour, because growth-oriented and profit-oriented firms will respond in qualitatively similar ways to such stimuli as changes in factor prices, discount rate and excise and profits taxes. It must also be remembered that managerial maximisation of the arguments of their utility function, whether these be sales, growth or discretionary expenditure, is in each version of managerial theory constrained by the need to earn a satisfactory minimum level of profits. The higher this level, the more quantitatively, as well as qualitatively, similar will be the behaviour of a profit-maximising and a management-controlled firm.

2.5 CONSTRAINTS ON MANAGERIAL DECISION-MAKING

How much discretion do managers actually have to determine firms' behaviour? If managers are concerned with objectives other than profit maximisation, to what extent will they be able to pursue these objectives?

Shareholder control

It has been observed earlier in this chapter that even in large firms the separation of ownership from control is by no means total. Effective constraints may be imposed by shareholders, although the effectiveness of shareholder monitoring will depend on the type of shareholder and the dispersion of holdings. It is likely to be least effective when shares are highly dispersed among individuals. The small individual shareholder will find it difficult and costly to obtain information on company performance and to judge that performance against what could have been achieved by a more profit-conscious management. The more widely dispersed the holdings, the more difficult it will be to organise a revolt. Moreover, the incentive for a small number of shareholders to upstage management is weakened by the fact that any ensuing gains will have to be shared with all the other owners, who thus benefit by free-riding on the backs of the activists. Free-riding thus acts as a disincentive to effective monitoring. This is not to say that a minority of activists may not have some impact, but their ability to exercise effective monitoring may be further blunted if management can use the weapon of the proxy vote to enlist the support of the majority of sleeping shareholders.

When institutional shareholders are important, the prospect for effective monitoring would appear to be brighter, as indeed it should be in those cases where a large block of shares in one industrial company is owned by another. But whether the potential for successful monitoring is grasped is another matter. Without detailed knowledge of the opportunities facing the firm it will be difficult for outsiders to judge the size of the gap between actual and potential performance. They may therefore settle for a satisfactory performance using readily available indicators such as the growth of earnings per share. Monitoring may be further attenuated if institutional shareholders are themselves motivated by considerations other than profit maximisation. In addition, where an institution owns a relatively small percentage of the total stock, the free-rider disincentive to intervention remains. The alternative to getting involved, which is to sell the shares, then becomes particularly attractive. In some countries effective monitoring systems do exist, as in the case for instance of the German supervisory boards. In the UK on the other hand the emphasis is on passive portfolio adjustment rather than active intervention. In these circumstances the amount of discretion that managers have to pursue non-profit goals depends on how much they are exposed to, or protected from, the forces of competition in product or capital markets.

Product markets

It is clear that, in the textbook model of a competitive industry, firms have no choice about whether or not to aim for profit maximisation. Freedom of entry into, and exit from, the industry will ensure that, except in the short run, firms will be able to earn no more than normal profits. Any firm that expands output beyond the profit-maximising level because it is concerned with sales or growth, or that lets costs rise above their minimum level by spending too much money on managers' perks, will find that it is earning less than the minimum necessary level of profit and will be eliminated from the market.

How realistic is this model? We argue throughout this book that the effect of different types of market imperfection is to shield some firms from competition to a considerable extent. In Chapter 5, which discusses market structure, we see that in an advanced industrial economy many markets are not even approximately perfectly competitive but have an imperfectly competitive oligopolistic structure, owing to the importance of such factors as economies of scale, product differentiation, patent protection and the level of capital requirements. In such industries the number of existing firms of any size is typically small, and the threat of potential competition from new entrants is reduced by barriers to entry. Under these circumstances the existing firms in the industry have market power, and this gives them a choice about how to behave that firms in competitive industries do not have. One facet of this choice is the ability to pursue aims other than short-run profit maximisation, since this is no longer necessary to ensure survival.

The implication seems to be that the constraints imposed on managers become more binding as the business environment becomes more hostile. Leibenstein (1979) suggests a two-way relationship between the firm's average costs and the effort expended to maintain efficiency as shown in Figure 2.10. As effort increases through, for instance, closer supervision and monitoring, average costs fall. This relationship is depicted by curve C in the diagram. The intensity of monitoring and supervisory control is in turn a function of the firm's average costs. As average costs increase, the firm feels increasingly threatened and the pressure to intensify monitoring goes up, a relationship summarised in curve B. However, there is a family of B curves, each related to a different market environment. The more protected the firm, the less pressure there is to maintain efficiency and the less supervisory control, etc. there will be for any given level of average cost. If for a given environment the relevant curve is B_1, the optimal amount of effort for the firm to expend is E_1 with average costs at C_1. However, if the market becomes more hostile, the B curve shifts to B_2, the new optimum position having lower average costs and a higher level of supervisory effort.

This analysis leaves unexplained however the mechanism which induces management to greater effort. A sudden change in the general business climate such as occurred in the UK in the early 1980s (see Chapter 1) will certainly force managers to pay much closer attention to costs, but all that this suggests is that the degree of discretion which managers have will tend to vary with general economic conditions – increasing during an upturn in business activity and

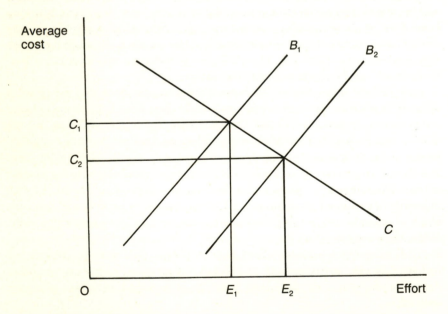

Figure 2.10 An X-efficiency theory of costs

falling during the downturn. A more interesting question is whether the incentive to supply greater effort is a function of the number of competitors in an industry. Is an industry with a large number of firms likely to pay more attention to cost minimisation than one with a smaller number? The answer is not necessarily, because if *all* firms are similarly motivated by non profit-maximising goals the 'extra' competition will not pose a threat to any one firm. For such a threat to exist there must be firms which *are* cost minimisers. They will be able to expand their market share by cutting prices and thereby force the managerial firms to reduce managerial slack so that they can meet their minimum profit constraints. But, to repeat, this will happen only if the industry is not populated entirely by managerial firms.

It is not the case therefore that only profit-maximising/cost-minimising firms will survive. The outcome will certainly depend in part on the ownership structure of firms in an industry and how these firms are motivated. It can also be added that if profit maximisation is interpreted as a short-run objective there may be circumstances when it is the profit maximiser who is most at risk. For instance, in an industry where economies of scale and learning by doing are important, the firms most likely to survive are those with a competitive advantage derived from expanding output, moving down the long-run average cost curve and producing at lower cost. Growth-maximising firms may, in other words, eliminate the profit maximisers by being quicker to seize the benefits of large scale.

Where firms have market power, then, we cannot rely on competitive forces in the product market to constrain firms to act as profit maximisers. The discretion that firms with market power have may be manifested in a number of different ways. First, there is the active pursuit of goals other than profits, which has already been discussed, and which is more likely to occur in large diversified management-controlled firms, which do typically have market power. Second, rather than actively pursuing other goals, profits may simply be maintained at a satisfactory level rather than maximised. Thus, the rewards of market power may be taken in the form of 'a quiet life' rather than profits. This implies that costs will be permitted to rise above the minimum attainable level by the existence of either management slack or X-inefficiency. Management slack represents the difference between maximum performance and acceptable performance and is one of the arguments of Williamson's managerial utility function (see next section). X-inefficiency, discussed in the context of the welfare costs of monopoly in Chapter 12, represents a related concept of inefficient resource use, which is possible where firms have market power and are relieved from the pressure to minimise costs.

The behavioural approach to the theory of the firm suggests however that any tendency towards inefficiency may be attenuated by the firm's efforts to attain ever-increasing goals, and, in particular, that internal growth may act as a control mechanism.

Internal growth as a control mechanism

The basic idea here is that, in striving to attain ever-increasing goals, the firm will tend to move to the point where costs are minimised. Consider, following Cyert and George (1969), a firm with an output goal and a profit goal. In Figure 2.11 the average cost function is initially at C^1 and it is assumed for simplifying purposes that actual and estimated costs are the same. The output goal in period t is set at Q_t so that estimated average costs are C_t. Assume that output Q_t, average cost of C_t and the given price of the product allow the profit goal π_t to be achieved. As a result the output and profit goals for the next period will be raised to Q_{t+1} and π_{t+1}. Estimated average costs are now C_{t+1} and when these are used along with the output goal and the given price it is found that the profit goal cannot be met. This is the signal for the firm to invoke a search routine which it is assumed results in economies which produce a new estimated average cost curve C^2. If the lower cost estimates C^2_{t+1} are consistent with the attainment of the profit goal, the search for greater efficiency ends. The same process of search would result from goal failure, i.e. when actual costs (or revenue) are not equal to estimated levels. But, whether the search process is invoked when firms fail to attain their goals or when it is anticipated that goals will not be attained, in the absence of shocks the firm would approach closely the cost curve assumed in economic theory.

The problem is that, although firms may indeed behave in this way, the behavioural theory does not provide a convincing explanation as to why there

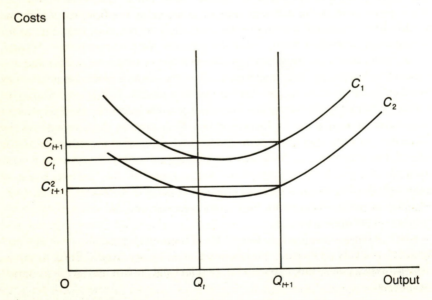

Figure 2.11 A behavioural theory of costs

will never be a relaxation of the motive to be as efficient as possible. Furthermore, it is management that chooses the profit and output goals and may, for instance, sacrifice the former in favour of the latter. Once more it appears that it is only competition in product and capital markets that can impose the necessary discipline. The former has already been considered; we now turn to consider capital market discipline.

Capital markets

If the capital market functions competitively, it will allocate limited investment funds to those firms which promise the highest ratio of earnings to capital. These firms will be able to attract capital on the basis of their share prices; in other words, shares will be valued on the basis of the future earnings prospects of the firms concerned. In this case, as long as firms have to go to the capital market to raise money for new investment they will be under pressure to pursue profit-maximising policies, since these will produce the highest earnings ratio and therefore the highest share price and this will make it easier for the firm to raise capital. This requirement also means that firms will be forced to use their existing assets efficiently for the same reason (i.e. to increase share prices and make it possible to raise new capital).

Competition for investment funds in the capital market thus provides a form of direct control over firms' behaviour that forces them to be efficient and aim for maximum profits. However, the strength of this direct control is weakened by imperfections in the capital market and by uncertainty about the future earnings prospects of companies. Shareholders have only limited information about the likely profit outcome of different courses of action by the firm, so they are not easily able to assess whether a more profit-oriented management team would produce better results from the shareholders' point of view.

To the extent that managers are interested in profits, perhaps because they have significant shareholdings themselves, this lack of information is less important. Also, institutional shareholders may be in a better position than individuals to assess the profit performance of firms and relate it to their behaviour. It is true that institutional shareholders have become increasingly important, and the work of Nyman and Silberston, referred to earlier, has shown that institutions have recently been exercising greater control than formerly when firms have a bad profit record. However, the cases that Nyman and Silberston cited relate to intervention when profits had reached the disaster stage rather than to continuing pressure for profit-maximising strategies.

Lack of information and uncertainty mean that share prices are only tenuously related to future earnings prospects, so that the mechanism by which funds should be allocated to the most profitable firms is weakened. Large firms are further able to avoid direct control over their performance by financing investment out of retained earnings, so that they don't need to raise funds from the capital market at all.

In addition to the direct control over firms' behaviour already discussed, which, we have seen, may not be as powerful as the model of a competitive capital market would suggest, the capital market exercises indirect control over firms through the takeover mechanism. The argument that the takeover mechanism exercises pressure on firms to act as profit maximisers (which suggests that takeovers increase efficiency and should not be controlled by government policy) once again depends on the capital market functioning competitively and valuing firms according to their expected stream of future profits. In this case relatively inefficient firms will have low share prices and will be liable to be taken over by more efficient firms with higher share prices.

Unfortunately, the empirical evidence does not support the view that takeover bids exert strong pressure on firms to behave as profit maximisers. For one thing, shares are not closely related to earnings prospects, as already mentioned. Second, as discussed in Chapter 5, the tendency for more profitable firms to acquire less profitable ones is weak. The relationship between profitability and acquisition is weaker than that between size and acquisition. In other words, it is small rather than unprofitable firms that are most likely to be taken over, and therefore stock market discipline may be said to encourage the maximisation of growth rather than of profits. In addition, the transactions costs of making a takeover may be large, thus allowing scope for a considerable degree of managerial slack before a takeover bid is attracted.

Chapter 3

The growth of firms

3.1 INTRODUCTION

This chapter is concerned with a more detailed examination of the process of change, and attention is therefore focused on the firm which is the decision-making unit. Structural change has been associated with the varying fortunes of individual firms. In declining industries, firms which have failed to adapt themselves and move into new growth areas have declined and often passed out of existence. In expanding industries, existing firms have been able to increase in size, and capacity in the industry has also been expanded by the birth of entirely new firms and by the extension of the activities of firms whose main interests lie in other fields. Little needs to be said about the unsuccessful firm which finds itself in a declining market and, because of its failure to adapt to changing circumstances, ultimately ceases to exist. Our concern is rather with those firms that make a more positive contribution to structural change, that is, with the way in which the successful firm adapts itself to changing circumstances.

Apart from simply expanding within its existing industry, a firm can achieve growth by vertical integration or by diversification, and in each case it can do so either through internal expansion or through acquiring other firms. These dimensions of growth are not, of course, of equal importance to all firms, and for the same firm they are likely to change in relative importance over time. Thus, for instance, diversification is more likely to be an important feature of the growth of established firms in mature oligopolistic industries than for young firms in new industries. Some large firms have grown mainly by internal growth whereas others have relied heavily on acquisitions. Further elaboration is unnecessary in order to emphasise the diversity of experience which is likely to characterise the processes of growth of any randomly selected group of firms.

The ability to grow and the desire for growth

In a pioneering work on the growth of firms, Penrose (1966) argued that the ability to grow is found in the existence of unused resources within the firm. Resources may be unused because of indivisibilities in factors of production. In addition, as experience is accumulated in existing lines of activity and previously complex work becomes routine, managerial services are released for other uses. The firm's management is a team with experience of working together, and many of the skills that are accumulated by the team are firm specific not product specific. This facilitates movement into new lines of activity as new opportunities present themselves. These opportunities are themselves perceived on the basis of information generated within the firm through the activities of the purchasing, marketing and R&D departments. The unused resources that exist within the firm have nothing to do of course with static inefficiency. They are generated as a result of change and the accumulation of experience and new knowledge. In a sense, the existence of unused managerial resources is a necessary condition for expansion. For if management is completely absorbed in the day-to-day problems of current production there can be no planning for future developments. There must be some freedom therefore from short-term production, marketing and financial problems if management is to give any thought at all to longer-term strategy. In this context market structure is clearly important. It is unlikely, for instance, that the textbook model of perfect competition would be conducive to growth. Under such conditions it is hardly feasible for the firm to devote resources to activities, such as research and development, which are not relevant to current production and marketing problems.

But the ability to grow is not enough. There must also be a desire for growth. Up to a point of course success will breed success. The firm which has built up a good name for itself will attract additional business. But, in general, continuing success requires constant marketing efforts on the part of the firm. Why then, it may be asked, are firms so interested in growth?

One reason which has been advanced is that growth, and the consequent attainment of large size, is of particular importance to managements. Managerial status, prestige and salaries are positively related to the size of the firm and more closely related to size in fact than to profitability. The managing directors of ICI or General Motors get paid more than the managing directors of much smaller companies even if the latter are a lot more profitable, and they also enjoy far greater prestige in the business community. Furthermore, a growing firm offers the prospect of more rapid promotion up the managerial ladder, especially, as is frequently the case, when appointments to more senior positions are made from amongst existing staff. In other words, for the incentives offered by internal labour markets to be effective the firm has to adapt to changing market conditions and to grow. These considerations have been given particular emphasis in explaining the interest in growth shown by those companies where there is a divorce between the shareholders who own the company, and the managers who control it.

A more general explanation, which applies to firms under all forms of control, is that, in a market which is generally expanding, growth is part of the competitive process. Under such conditions to stand still is to fall behind. The faster-growing firms will be in a position to benefit from a number of advantages as compared with their slower growing competitors. Faster growth will mean a higher level of gross investment. This in turn will allow the quicker realisation of economies of scale and the speedier adoption of technological improvements so that a larger proportion of the firm's capital stock will embody up-to-date techniques. Furthermore, expanding firms are likely to attract better-quality managers. A comparison of fast- with slow-growing firms in the same industry, therefore, would be expected to show that the former would have a higher growth rate of productivity which would be reflected in higher profitability, or lower prices, or better quality products, or some combination of the three.

Determinants – a brief review

Firms may find opportunities for expansion in existing product lines, in vertical integration or in diversification. They can achieve this expansion either by internal growth or by acquisition. Before turning to a detailed consideration of these issues it is useful to summarise some of the main factors that help shape the outcome.

Perhaps the main point to emphasise is that whichever direction of growth is considered there are many factors at work. As a result the boundaries between firms and markets are constantly shifting.

With horizontal growth it is clear that basic technological conditions play an important role via their influence on economies of scale. In many industries, however, it appears that firms are larger than can be explained by economies of scale, suggesting the role of other factors in determining size. There may be *learning* effects in which lower costs are achieved as a result of an increase in the *cumulative* volume of production. Firms may wish to extend their size beyond the point where scale economies and learning economies are exhausted in order to increase market power. There may also be random forces at work affecting relative firm sizes. Technology, learning effects, managerial motivation and random forces thus all interact to influence horizontal expansion.

Technology also plays a part in vertical integration, which involves the addition of an earlier or later activity in the production and distribution process so that the new activities are 'vertically' related to the old. Much of the emphasis in explaining vertical integration however has been on the argument that firms seek to economise not on production costs alone but on production plus *transactions costs*. Three important dimensions of a transaction are the frequency with which it occurs, the degree of uncertainty to which it is subject, and the degree of *asset specificity* involved, i.e. the extent to which a transaction requires the use of assets which would have a much lower value if employed elsewhere. These dimensions or attributes of transactions influence the extent to which activities will be integrated within the firm rather than transacted in the market. Vertical integration is not however motivated solely by prospects of efficiency gains. It may also be a response to market imperfections or indeed be a source of such imperfections. Thus a firm may integrate forwards in order to escape the power of large buyers. And integration may increase barriers to entry and so protect the market power of incumbent firms.

One of the factors determining the extent of diversification is *economies of scope*, which exist when total cost can be reduced by producing a number of products within the firm. Products which have common components may be produced more cheaply together than separately. Alternatively, the economies may be in distribution, as when the same vehicles can be used to transport a range of products to the same wholesale or retail outlets. As in the case of horizontal and vertical integration, efficiency considerations do not explain everything. Diversification may also be a response to uncertainty or to the growth motives of managers or to the empire-building ambitions of owners.

In considering the extent to which growth is achieved by acquisition rather than internal growth a variety of motives can again be found. Efficiency, security, market power and financial and promotional factors all play a part.

Relevant to all aspects of growth is the organisation of the firm and the capacity of management to absorb change. The importance of these factors is most clearly seen in takeover activity and the fact that many takeovers fail as a result of management deficiency. But the internal organisation of the firm, the ability of members of the management team, and the entrepreneurial skills of the chief executive are just as important in dealing with internal expansion.

The remaining sections of this chapter now go on to consider some of the main dimensions of growth in some detail. Section 3.2 examines the complex considerations underlying vertical relationships; this is followed in section 3.3 by an analysis of the factors influencing diversification, and in section 3.4 by the determinants of takeover activity. Lastly, in section 3.5 some consideration is given to the factors limiting the growth of firms. The factors influencing horizontal growth are not considered here, but they are discussed fully in Chapter 5 which deals with market structure and its determinants.

3.2 VERTICAL INTEGRATION

Vertical integration may be considered either as a static dimension of market structure or as a dynamic process which alters market structure and possibly business behaviour and performance.

As a static measure of the extent to which vertically related activities take place within a firm there is no difficulty in identifying individual industries where vertical integration is extremely important and those where it is not. The petroleum industry clearly falls into the first category since the largest firms carry out all the activities from exploration, through refining to the final marketing of the products. On the other hand retailing is largely unintegrated, with most retailing giants doing very little manufacturing.

Although clear-cut cases are not difficult to identify there are problems in devising quantitative measures that allow systematic comparisons across industries. A measure of integration that would appear suitable and which can be computed from available data is the ratio of value added to sales. However this will give misleading comparisons when firms are located at different stages in the vertical chain. Take the simple case of an economy consisting of three unintegrated firms A, B and C; the first a raw material producer, the second a fabricator and the third a distributor. Assume that firm A buys nothing in and that each firm contributes one-third of total value added in the economy. A's value added/sales ratio is 1, which gives the totally misleading impression that it is totally integrated vertically. B buys inputs from A equal to one-third of total value added and adds its own labour, etc. valued at one-third. B's value added/sales ratio is thus 0.5. Firm C's value added/sales ratio is 0.33. Although each firm is equally integrated, the measure of integration used shows them to be quite different. This is because the nearer the raw material end of the production/distribution stream a specialist firm's operations are located, the higher *ceteris paribus* its value added/sales ratio tends to be. To avoid this problem we have to rely on more detailed empirical studies.

Vertical integration as a process

Our main concern, however, is with vertical integration as a dynamic process. We are therefore interested in the motives that lie behind the integration of activities and ultimately in the way in which integration may affect efficiency and economic welfare.

One important motive for vertical integration is cost minimisation; another is the desire for greater security, i.e. more control over the market environment. The two are not unrelated. If a firm is better able to control its environment this may result in lower costs. On the other hand, it may also result in market power and monopoly abuse. Another factor which may have an effect is the tax structure. The main purpose of this section however is to unravel the complex interactions that exist between efficiency, security and market power.

Cost minimisation

An important determinant of the boundaries between firms and markets is the transactions costs of using the market. These costs include the cost of obtaining information on prices and product specification, and the cost of negotiating and concluding separate contracts. Costs may also be incurred from delay in delivery or from the delivery of inferior intermediate products or from marketing through inferior outlets. Given these costs, 'a firm will tend to expand until the cost of organising an extra transaction within the firm becomes equal to the cost of carrying out the same transaction by means of an exchange in the open market or the cost of organising in another firm.' This quotation from Coase's celebrated 1937 article (Coase 1937: 395) draws attention to the fact that the coordination of economic activity may take place either through the market or within the firm and the high transactions costs which are often incurred in using the market are one of the reasons why firms exist.

The classic example is that of steel production, where integration of the various processes from blast furnace to rolling mill reduces handling and the need for reheating. In principle the different stages of steel production could be in the hands of separate firms, but the transactions costs would be very high in comparison with the costs of organisation within a single firm. The relationship between the various stages of steel production integrated on a single site is one that displays a very high degree of asset specificity. If, for instance, the furnaces and rolling mills were owned by separate companies, the value of both the companies would decline sharply if the contract between them broke down. High degrees of asset specificity are therefore predicted to lead to either long-term contracts or complete integration within a single firm. In the case of steel production, the technological factors dictate the choice of complete integration as the optimum solution.

Whether transactions costs are higher or lower than the cost of organising activities within a firm will depend on several factors. Since transactions costs include the cost of obtaining information on price, product quality and the cost of negotiating and concluding separate contracts, it can be expected that they are likely to be especially high when goods have to be contracted for frequently. Upstream integration may also give the firm better information about supply conditions and therefore the future price of an input, which can lead to more efficient production planning.

The benefits from integration are also likely to increase the more complex are product-component interrelationships, especially when combined with frequent changes in design and technical specification. Where specification of inputs is important, careful monitoring will be needed to ensure that the supplier is meeting the specifications. Apart from this moral hazard problem of determining *ex post* whether the terms of a contract have been fulfilled, there is also the danger of opportunistic behaviour on the part of the supplier. Where product specification is important, an existing supplier may have developed advantages over its competitors which it may use to renegotiate a contract in its favour. Faced with heavy monitoring costs and the danger of opportunistic behaviour, the buying firm may respond by upstream integration. This may also occur as a means of maintaining design secrets and, in the absence of a vigorous independent sector, of ensuring that it is well placed to adapt quickly to competitive developments.

Forward integration, too, may occur because of the transactions costs of using the market. Take, for instance, the well-known case of a monopoly supplier of an input who integrates with a competitive firm downstream, thereby reducing the cost of producing the downstream product. In Figure 3.1, isoquant Q depicts the input substitution possibilities available to the competitive firm in the production of a given quantity of the downstream product. Input x is supplied by the upstream monopolist and input y is supplied competitively. The monopoly price

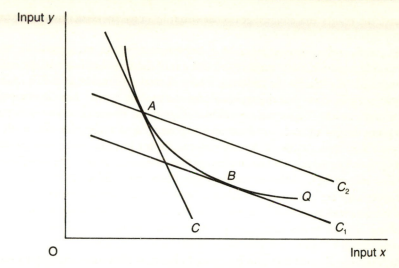

Figure 3.1 Vertical integration and choice of inputs

charged for x is reflected in the slope of isocost line C, and the optimum combination of inputs is at A. If the monopoly supplier integrates forward it will not use the monopoly price of x as the basis for choosing the optimum combination of inputs, but rather the marginal cost of supplying x. This lower price of x is reflected in isocost line C_1 and the combination of inputs used will be at point B with more of input x used and less of y. With this price ratio, B is clearly on a lower isocost line than A, the distance between C_1 and C_2 indicating the cost savings that the integrated firm has been able to achieve.

These cost savings could in principle have been secured without resort to vertical integration. For instance, discriminatory pricing on the part of the monopoly input supplier could induce the downstream firm to operate with the combination of inputs at B. However, the transactions costs of discriminatory pricing may be prohibitive, leaving integration as the only practical means of ensuring an optimal combination of inputs.

There are other aspects of a firm's competitive situation which may also be best safeguarded by forward integration. For instance, where product differentiation and brand image are important, a firm may decide that its reputation is best protected by by-passing wholesalers and selling direct to retailers. It may go further and, as is common in the clothing industry, set up a chain of 'shops within shops' or decide in favour of full integration and purchase its own retail outlets.

In summary, it would appear that, with static conditions and product homogeneity, contracts can be kept simple, and this favours the use of markets and short-term relationships. On the other hand, the greater the degree of change, the more uncertainty there is, and, the more complex contractual relationships become, the bigger the advantages of developing long-term links including full integration.

The balance of advantage between coordinating transactions within the firm and using the market may be perceived differently by different firms in the same industry. This may be due, for instance, to different experiences which firms have had with suppliers and customers, which determines the cost to them of using the market mechanism. Firms may reach different conclusions therefore over the merits, say, of buying in a particular component as opposed to manufacturing it in-house. Differences in the degree of vertical integration will also be due to the fact that some firms react more quickly than others to changing circumstances, and may indeed have different expectations about the speed and direction of market developments. Our observations of changes in the extent of vertical integration take place against the background of a set of industry boundaries which have been shaped by yesterday's technology and organisational know-how and yesterday's market sizes. As technology, organisational techniques and the size of markets change, so traditional industry boundaries may become less appropriate to the most efficient organisation of production, and the boundaries between firms and markets also change.

Technological change may work either way. Technological advances may result in the hiving off of a section of an industry into the hands of specialist firms. However, the complicated nature of much modern production means that many highly specialised processes and skills need close coordination, and this tends towards more integration. Integration may also be needed for the speedy introduction of new methods of production or distribution where independent suppliers or distributors are reluctant to depart from traditional methods. Organisational changes have, on balance, worked in the direction of increasing the level of integration. The development of new forms of organisation such as the multidivisional firm, discussed in Chapter 2, has greatly widened the range of activity that can be coordinated efficiently within the firm. So too have developments in computing and telecommunications and the associated advances in data retrieval and analysis.

The effect of changes in market size depends very much on the stage of development that the market has reached. In the early stages of development of a new product or process, a high level of integration within firms may be necessary because specialist firms with the necessary knowledge to manufacture components or market final products may not exist. Or it may be the case that, though the know-how exists, firms may be unwilling to sink capital into highly specific investments when the future of the market is still highly uncertain. As the market expands however, and the specialist knowledge needed for producing components and marketing the end product spreads, opportunities for vertical disintegration will arise. An often-quoted example where the benefits of disintegration may be especially great is where, in a sequence of operations, economies of scale are much more important at some stages than at others. The full advantage of technical economies of scale might then only be realisable within an integrated firm so large that there are offsetting costs arising out of substantial managerial diseconomies.

To illustrate the point, assume that there are three separate operations consisting of the manufacture of two components A and B, with one unit of each entering into the assembly of product C. The lowest output at which costs are minimised is 600,000 units for A, 400,000 units for B and 300,000 units for C. If an integrated firm is to benefit fully from the technical economies of scale it would have to produce a total of 1,200,000 units. At this output the firm might suffer from managerial diseconomies and thus incur a cost penalty. In this case it might be advantageous to have specialist components manufacturers supplying the downstream assemblers. Technical economies of scale could thereby be realised without the danger of running into the organisational problems associated with large size. These considerations are important in a number of industries. In the motor vehicle industry, for example, economies of scale in body pressings and the manufacture of engine blocks and other components are far more important than economies of scale in final assembly. The same is true of other consumer durables such as refrigerators and washing machines. In these cases there would appear to be rewards from having specialist component producers and a high degree of vertical disintegration.

Security and control of the market environment

At this point, however, the security aspect of vertical integration becomes relevant. 'Vertical integration is sometimes the consequence of a reuniting of separated processes of production. It is more often the consequence of a search for security' (Robinson: 1958: 110). From this point of view the incentive to integrate will be influenced by the structure of markets, the efficiency and reliability of suppliers, and the state of trade. Take, for instance, the scenario outlined above of the incentive which firms may have to integrate upstream. This was due to the fact that economies of scale in the manufacture of components may be so large that there is room for only a small number of suppliers each with market power. Buyers of components then have to live with the fear of actual or potential exploitation. In order to avoid total dependence on monopoly suppliers, some downstream firms may integrate backwards. If they do so and produce components in sub-optimal plants, or if integration results in problems of managing a firm with a wider range of activities, they will suffer some cost disadvantage. However, they gain the advantage of not being at the mercy of dominant suppliers.

If one or more firms decide to integrate backwards, the remaining non-integrated firms will be further disadvantaged. With integrated firms now accounting for part of the upstream activity, the number of specialist independent supplying firms is likely to fall, thus heightening still further the dependence of non-integrated buyers. The latter in some cases may find that they have to buy at least part of their input requirements from integrated firms who are their main competitors at the downstream stage. Once one firm integrates backwards, therefore, the incentive for others to do so is increased.

The key to the scenario just outlined was fewness of producers at the upstream stage as a result of scale economies and the opportunities that these firms had for exploiting their positions of market power. If the component-producing industry had been structured differently, with effective competition between many suppliers, this particular incentive to integrate would not exist. The incentive to search for greater security through vertical integration is thus likely to depend on the number and size distribution of firms at different stages in the chain of production and distribution, and that incentive is stronger the more liable markets are to competitive breakdown.

The incentive to integrate is also influenced by the state of trade. The incentive to integrate backwards is greatest when demand is buoyant. This is when suppliers have greatest leverage over buyers which they can use to charge higher prices. Backward integration may thus be induced in order to eliminate the excess profit element in supply price and also to ensure greater reliability of supply. In times of low demand, however, the integrated firm may be at a disadvantage in so far as it will not be entirely free to purchase from the cheapest source. Similar considerations apply to forward integration but, whereas the incentive to integrate backwards is greatest at times of high demand, the incentive to integrate forward will be greatest when demand is falling, as suppliers become more conscious of the need to secure their markets.

In summary, there are several forces at work which change the pattern of vertical integration, some pulling in one direction and some in the other. Integration may result in higher costs if it means a loss of some of the advantages of scale, or if there are problems in managing a more diversified business, or if the level of trade declines. On the other hand, integration may result in savings in transactions costs, greater reliability of supply and more efficient planning of production schedules.

Bilateral monopoly

The transactions costs of using the market are comprised largely of the cost of bargaining and the consequences of bargaining failure in terms of interruptions in supply. These problems are illustrated in the following model, depicted in Figure 3.2, of bilateral monopoly in which a single seller S of good j confronts a single buyer, B.

S produces j at a total cost of $C(j)$ which gives rise to S's average and marginal cost curves AC_S and MC_S respectively. B uses j to produce output x according to the production function $x = f(j)$, and B's total revenue function $R = R(f(j))$ gives rise to the average revenue product and marginal revenue product curves ARP_B and MRP_B. Under competitive conditions, input purchases would be at j_c where the demand and supply curves intersect, and there would be a single determinate price for input j. Under bargaining conditions, the price is indeterminate

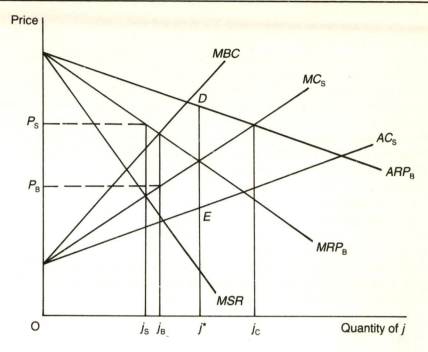

Figure 3.2 Bilateral monopoly

and, to see the limits to the range of indeterminacy, consider first the case where B has the power to set the price, and second the case where all the bargaining power lies with S.

If the price is set by B and S simply responds to it, S will produce where $P = MC_S$. MC_S is thus S's supply curve and also the supply curve facing B. But what price will B set? This depends upon the amount of the input that B wishes to buy. As a monopsonist, B must recognise that the more of the input it buys the higher the price will be. Since it faces supply curve MC_S, the marginal cost of its purchases is given by the marginal buyer cost curve *MBC*. If B also has monopoly power in the market for x, it will recognise that the more it buys of the input j and the more it sells of the final product x the lower the price of x will be. Given that the derived demand curve for j is ARP_B, the benefit from purchasing additional amounts of j is given by the marginal revenue product curve MRP_B. To maximise profits B will want to produce where $MRP_B = MBC$. It will thus quote a price of P_B and the seller S will supply j_B.

Consider now the case where all the bargaining power rests with the seller. Whatever price is set, B will wish to purchase an amount of j such that $P = MRP_B$. In other words, MRP_B is B's demand curve for the input and thus the demand curve facing S. What amount of j will S wish to sell? Given that the demand curve facing S is MRP_B, S's marginal revenue curve is *MSR*, reflecting the fact that P must fall as more j is sold. S's marginal cost curve for supplying j is MC_S, so to maximise profits S must sell the amount where $MC = MSR$. In other words, S will wish to supply j_s and will set a price of P_S which will induce B to purchase just this amount.

Assuming, then, that all the bargaining power rests with one or other of the two parties, the amount of the input produced will be either j_S or j_B and the price charged either P_S or P_B, depending on which party is in the driving seat. Either outcome entails a lower output than would be forthcoming under joint profit-maximisation. The latter is found at j^* where $MC_S = MRP_B$. However, although the joint profit-maximising output can be determined, the price is indeterminate between points D and E in Figure 3.2. At D the buyer gets no benefit; at E the seller gets none. The outcome depends upon the bargaining strength of the two. If a joint profit-maximising deal could be struck, the consumer would probably benefit because the larger production of j implies a larger output of the end product x and therefore a lower price.

However, costs involved in the bargaining process may be high and there is always a danger that a breakdown in bargaining could disrupt supply. A more stable and secure solution might be found through vertical integration.

Monopoly power

As a motive for vertical integration, monopoly power may not easily be disentangled from other considerations such as the search for greater efficiency and increased security. For instance, we have stressed that both backward and forward integration may be a response to the transactions costs of using markets. However, this may give rise to firms which have substantial market power. The earlier example (Figure 3.1) in which forward integration resulted in lower-cost production of the downstream product could, by giving the integrated firm control over all substitute inputs at the downstream stage, allow the firm to charge monopoly prices. The pursuit of greater efficiency may then lead to positions of market power. Similarly the search for greater security and control over an uncertain business environment is not always easily distinguishable from monopoly power considerations. But this is not to deny that monopoly is an important motive in its own right. The market power which vertically integrated firms may have over their more specialist rivals could be an important driving force behind integration and not just the 'incidental' outcome of the drive to achieve other more desirable objectives.

Price squeezes and refusal to supply are just two of the available weapons at the disposal of the integrated firm, and the mere threat to use these weapons may be sufficient to have the desired effect. If these market power opportunities exist and one firm starts taking advantage of them, others are likely to follow.

One possible reason for this behaviour is that it raises entry barriers. An integrated firm will of course be able to prevent entry altogether if it controls the entire supply of an essential input or all the distributive outlets. Short of this extreme, barriers may be heightened by refusal to supply, or by price squeezes, i.e. supply on unfavourable terms, and new entrants may then feel compelled to enter as integrated firms. This raises the capital requirements for entry and if the capital market is less than perfect entry barriers will be raised. How important this effect is depends on the additional capital sums required and the type of new entrant. If the potential entrant is an existing large company, the additional capital sum required for entry may not pose much difficulty.

Another explanation for the price squeeze or refusal to supply is that this may be an effective way of promoting industry discipline by discouraging price-cutting by non-integrated firms downstream. If necessary the strategy can be pursued until the offending downstream firms are driven from the market. This strategy may also be used to increase the level of industrial concentration at an upstream stage. Suppose stage A in a production chain is loosely oligopolistic with an oligopolistic core and a competitive fringe and that there is partial integration downstream to stage B. Furthermore, suppose the non-integrated firms at stage B have a preference for purchasing from the non-integrated suppliers but also have, of necessity, to source some of their supplies from the integrated firms. The latter, by means of discriminatory pricing, can impose a price squeeze on the non-integrated firms at B. The non-integrated firms at B will thus lose market share, and in some cases perhaps be acquired by the integrated firms, who will divert purchases to their own upstream production facilities at A. As a result the non-integrated firms at stage A will lose market share and the industry becomes more tightly oligopolistic. For this strategy to be successful, however, there must be some sort of entry barrier at stage A. Otherwise the high prices charged to non-integrated firms would attract new firms and so expand the competitive fringe.

Discriminatory pricing behaviour of the type just outlined may be facilitated by a tax system which gives special tax incentives to upstream activities such as those commonly found in oil and mineral extraction. Integrated firms will then have an incentive to adopt a structure of internal transfer prices which shifts the bulk of reported profits to the extraction stage. High prices are charged at that stage and low margins are accepted downstream. If internal transfer prices are reflected in 'arm's length' market prices, this will result in a price squeeze being imposed on non-integrated firms downstream.

Forces limiting the incentive to integrate

If there are so many advantages to integration, why is it that integration isn't more widespread? Why is it, for instance, that retailing firms do relatively little manufacturing?

Bargaining power of large buyers

Part of the reason is that where buyers have substantial power they may be able to secure satisfactory vertical relationships which obviate the need for full integration. The bargaining power of big buyers may take several forms. Buyers may, for instance, face highly competitive suppliers who are unable to exercise effective price discipline. Buyers will then be able to secure supplies at little more than cost plus normal profit. Buyers may be able to exercise effective bargaining power by pursuing a policy of dual sourcing and keep each supplier on its toes by threatening to switch more orders to the other. Alternatively a buyer may, if it suspects monopoly pricing on the part of a supplier or is dissatisfied with the quality of bought-in components, threaten backward integration. To be effective, a threat may eventually have to be carried out, so that the buyer integrates backwards in order to supply a fraction of its component requirements. This partial or tapered integration has a number of advantages. It affords the buyer a check on the production costs of the independent suppliers. This removes information asymmetries and so strengthens the buyer's bargaining position. In addition, by producing only part of total input requirements, the buyer is able to operate its own production facilities more or less continuously at full capacity while forcing the independent suppliers to bear the brunt of demand fluctuations.

Although buyers may have considerable monopsony power, they may at the same time operate in highly competitive final markets. Take the case of a buyer with monopsony power in the market for its inputs but no power at all in the market in which it sells its final product. In this case, and referring back to Figure 3.2, the buyer will expand purchases of input j until perceived marginal cost $(MBC) = ARP$.

More interestingly, consider the application of the theory when input suppliers operate under conditions of constant costs (Figure 3.3) – which fits more closely the empirical evidence. Assume that the buyer who sets the price of

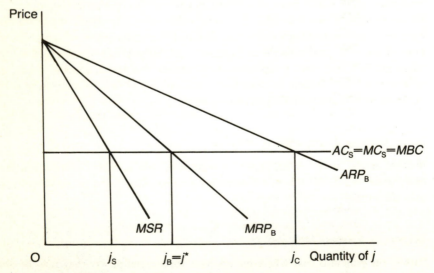

Figure 3.3 Bilateral monopoly with constant costs

input j has monopsony power and monopoly power. The result as before is exchange of the intermediate input at j_B where $MRP_B = MBC$. But because of constant costs this point now coincides with the joint profit-maximising solution. When the buyer has monopsony power but operates in competitive end markets, the input is exchanged at a level where $ARP = MBC$, which in the case of constant costs is the same as the competitive outcome.

Customer attachments and goodwill

So far the emphasis has been on the point that vertical integration may be limited by virtue of the fact that alternative vertical relationships may be sufficient to control the opportunistic behaviour of suppliers. There is another explanation. This is that firms do not typically attempt to milk the market for what it is worth even when the opportunity is there for them to do so. Rather they emphasise the importance of long-term relationships. In other words, opportunistic behaviour and moral hazard problems may be less important than commonly supposed and customer attachments and goodwill more important. The more this is so, the more will markets be seen as a satisfactory way of dealing with vertical relationships. The emphasis on customer attachments owes much to the work of Okun (1981).

Briefly, Okun's analysis is as follows. In searching for the best source of supply the buyer incurs search, or shopping costs. Buyers have an idea of the *distribution* of offers but not of who is making a particular offer. Suppose the distribution of prices forms a normal distribution with a mean of £38; that search has found a supplier A who charges £36; that one-quarter of the distribution lies below £36; and that the average of these better offers is £34.23 (see Figure 3.4). If the buyer continues the search and approaches even more suppliers, there is a probability of one-quarter that a better offer would result and the expected gain from this extra search would be $(0.25)(£1.77) = £0.44$. If the cost of search is less than £0.44, the buyer will continue searching. If the cost of extra search is equal to or greater than this amount, the buyer will find it just worthwhile to accept the offer of £36.

A decision to purchase from firm A means that the buyer has declared satisfaction with A's offer, and if satisfied is likely to stick with the supplier for repeat purchases so long as the supplier can pledge continuity of the offer. If continuity is offered there is a benefit to the buyer in terms of reduced search costs, and there is benefit to the supplier in terms of increased predictability of sales and more efficient production scheduling.

Reputation is clearly an important consideration in this analysis. The supplier who places much emphasis on customer attachments and goodwill is seeking to establish or maintain a reputation. He cannot afford therefore to take advantage of every market opportunity, increasing prices for instance when there is a temporary shortage, or failing to maintain uniform product specification because of indifferent quality control.

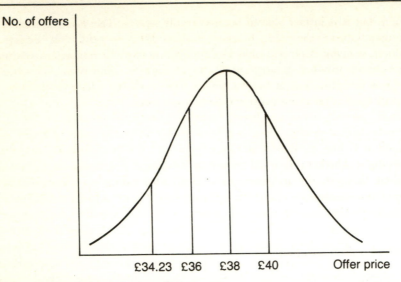

Figure 3.4 Distribution of price offers

The pricing policy implications of the customer attachments model will be considered in Chapter 7. Here we note that the more important are customer attachments and the emphasis on continuity, the lower will be the costs of using the market. In Okun's own development of the customer attachments model the illustrations are taken in the main from the retailing and hotel trades. However it may well be that his ideas are more relevant in analysing inter-firm relationships in the market for intermediate goods.

The forces shaping the extent and pattern of vertical relationships are complex and it should not be a surprise to find differences in the degree of integration even between firms in the same general field of activity. This may be due for instance to differences in managerial ability to coordinate the different stages of production and distribution. Or it may be due to the different experiences which firms have had with suppliers and thus different perceptions about the transactions costs of using the market. The fact that one firm is more highly integrated than another may also reflect differences in profitability and in the finance available for integration, or it may reflect a different view about future supply and demand conditions. In determining future strategy, some firms will see vertical integration as the most profitable use of funds, others will choose to extend their production horizontally in existing markets or to diversify into new areas of activity.

3.3 DIVERSIFICATION

Diversification involves the addition to the firm's activities of other products or services that are not vertically related to existing ones. The distinction between diversification and horizontal expansion in existing lines may appear to be self-evident, but it is in fact blurred because of the widespread practice of product differentiation (i.e. the production by a firm of different varieties of the 'same' product). In many instances it may be difficult in practice to draw a sharp distinction between product differentiation and product diversification. Quite apart from this problem, the degree of diversification itself can vary substantially. In terms of the Census of Production classification (see Chapter 5), a firm may, for instance, diversify from one broad industry group into another, or from one narrowly defined product class to another within the same industry group. The distinction is important because the explanation for diversification may vary according to whether it is broad or narrow in scope.

What, then, are the main motives for diversification? What factors influence the direction of diversification? What factors will determine its extent? These are the questions that we now want to examine.

Motives for diversification

Uncertainty

An important motive for diversification is associated with the fact that firms operate under conditions of uncertainty. A highly specialised firm will, in the event of a sharp downturn in the demand for its products, be faced with a drastic and perhaps fatal decline in profits. It is often to guard against this outcome that firms move into new product lines. Even in a world characterised by change and uncertainty there will be some businessmen who are sufficiently confident about the future course of demand to concentrate all their resources on the production of one commodity. But the general effect of an uncertain future is to cause firms to modify their choice of products towards producing a wider range.

Fluctuations in demand which are seasonal can of course be foreseen and the firm can accordingly plan its production to allow for them. Such circumstances exist in the case of summer and winter clothing, icecream, and the hotel industry. Other fluctuations, however, are more erratic and thus difficult to foresee. They pose a particular difficulty to firms whose products are made to individual order and specification. Under these conditions the firm's main line of production will commonly be supplemented at times of low demand by the production of secondary products, whose function is to make some contribution to overhead costs and to help keep together a skilled workforce. For this purpose a firm may be prepared to sell its secondary products at very little above their prime costs of production.

The secondary activities of one firm will of course be the main activity of another. If each firm in an industrial sector reacts to periodic downturns in demand by diversifying into products which are the main line activities of the other firms, it may happen that all of them end up being worse off. Competition will intensify in all lines and prices everywhere may fall below the full costs of production.

A related suggestion is that diversification can be explained in part by the existence of product cycles. Products go through stages of rapid expansion, maturity and decline and the onset of maturity or decline in existing products combined with the desire for growth gives a powerful inducement to diversify.

A rather different aspect of the risk and uncertainty motive is the financial one. Those who lend money to a firm are interested in both the level and the variation of the expected return. Comparing a diversified firm with an alternative situation where the individual products are produced by specialised firms, the variation in the combined earnings of the diversified firm will be lower than the variation in the earnings of each of the specialised firms. This will be true as long as the earnings streams of the separate activities are not perfectly correlated but rather tend to offset one another so that high earnings in one area compensate for low earnings in another. This lower variance in the earnings stream might, other things being equal, be an attraction to lenders, and put the diversified firm in a stronger position to attract funds.

However, as far as lenders are concerned they can achieve the same benefits of a lower variation in the return on their investment by investing in a range of specialised firms, a strategy which has been facilitated by the growth of unit and investment trusts. But there is still an advantage in investing in diversified firms for holders of fixed-interest debt. If a specialised firm is unable to pay its fixed-interest debts, the lender suffers a loss. In a diversified firm, however, the failure of one activity to make enough money to cover its fixed-interest debt may be made good by profits elsewhere, so that the fixed-interest lender suffers no loss of income. The importance of this factor may be particularly great where much of the fixed-interest lending is done by a relatively small number of institutions.

This benefit to fixed-interest lenders is, however, at the expense of equity-holders, and if the above argument is correct, diversified firms will tend to have a higher proportion of fixed-interest debt to total capital than specialised firms. This will in turn lead to further benefits as a result of the tax system, because interest payments are a deductible expense for tax purposes. A higher proportion of debt to equity finance therefore means a lower overall tax burden on the firm.

Another way in which the tax system may benefit the diversified firm is by allowing the firm to offset losses in one area of activity against profits in another. The knowledge that losses can be offset in this way weakens one of the obstacles to diversification, namely, the fear that a move into a new line of activity may prove to be a mistake or may take longer to put on a profitable footing than was originally anticipated.

Lastly, it should be noted that, in so far as diversification is seen as a response to uncertainty and unexpected declines in product demand, it cannot afford to be too narrowly based. If diversification is confined to products which are closely related, the pattern of earnings across products may be highly correlated, with the result that the variance of earnings will be much the same as that for specialist firms. The uncertainty motive for diversification is thus likely to be most powerful in the case of broadly based diversification of the sort found in truly conglomerate firms.

Growth

The growth objective of firms is another motive for diversification. Diversification will often occur because it is difficult for a firm to grow faster than the industry in which it operates, even if it has the resources to do so. In other words, for a firm that has growth as an important goal, diversification is not necessarily a response to the decline of existing markets but rather a response to the fact that existing markets are not expanding quickly enough. Similarly, even if a firm's existing fields of operation are profitable, diversification may still be the most profitable way of using new investment funds.

For the growth-motivated firm, integration into closely related products or processes comes entirely naturally because the information generated within the firm concerning markets or production methods is not entirely product specific but may have wide-ranging applications. This, together with the unused resources generated within the firm as a result of a changing external environment and the accumulation of experience and new knowledge, is a powerful force tending towards diversification.

Another powerful force is provided where, as outlined in the previous section, the firm sees continuity and long-term commitments as central to the incentives which it offers its employees. The incentives offered by internal labour markets will be effective only if employees perceive the firm as having an indefinite life. This means a commitment to growth and the necessity of adapting to changing external conditions and of generating new opportunities from within.

It has become clear that although in principle we can distinguish between the uncertainty motive for diversification and the growth motive, which would exist even in the absence of uncertainty, in practice it is often difficult to do this. Diversification to guard against adverse changes in demand for existing products will often be hard to distinguish from diversification based on the growth motive, for the latter is also a question of the relative growth rates of demand for different products. There is another way in which the two motives are interrelated. Growth and the attainment of larger size in themselves add to the security of the firm. One important aspect of this is that, over a certain size range, larger size means a greater ability to undertake R&D work and thus to generate new opportunities for expansion from within the firm. This may come about from the development of new products and processes as well as from the improvement of existing ones. A detailed examination of the relationship between R&D and firm size is left to Chapter 9. Here we simply note that the evidence shows that, whereas almost all large firms engage in some R&D, only a small fraction of small firms do so, and that the great bulk of recorded R&D expenditure is undertaken by large firms.

Market power

Lastly, under the motives for diversification we should mention the role of market power. A firm may see in diversification an opportunity both to extend its market power into new product lines and also to increase its market power in existing lines. These considerations are dealt with in more detail in the next chapter, in the section dealing with the large diversified firm and resource allocation (section 4.5).

A quite different aspect of the market power issue is the role played by monopoly and merger legislation in promoting diversification. Fear of the consequences of monopoly legislation may, for instance, induce a firm to diversify, even though it would be more profitable to increase its market share in existing lines. More directly, tight controls on horizontal and vertical mergers, as operated in the USA, may induce more diversification or conglomerate mergers.

The direction of diversification

Given the above motives for diversification, what factors are liable to influence its direction?

In the majority of cases the direction of diversification seems to be dictated by the advantages that established firms have in the form of experience in either technology or marketing. Diversification based primarily on a high level of technological competence is characteristic of many of the largest firms in the economy, particularly those in areas such as chemicals and electrical engineering. In these industries the possession of technical know-how is clearly seen as a spur to diversification. Firms with competent R&D teams have a built-in tendency to diversify. These teams are needed to develop new products or processes, but, once they are established and the initial problems are ironed out, the staff are free to pursue new ideas. In addition, of course, the possession of qualified technical personnel places a firm in a favourable position to take advantage of new opportunities arising from the R&D work of other organisations. It can be expected that these effects would be strongest where diversification is into related products and processes, and weakest for very broad diversification into a new industry group. There is some support for this expectation in empirical work on the relationship between diversification and R&D, but the data available for testing the hypothesis are far from ideal and the results have to be treated with considerable caution.

In other industries, diversification seems to be based mainly on the special advantages that big firms have in the large-scale marketing of consumer goods. A good example of this kind of diversification is the cigarettes and tobacco industry. Firms that have developed expertise in selling tobacco products by heavy promotional expenditures will find this a useful asset in selling many other types of consumer goods. Tobacco firms have diversified into a considerable range of other industries but most commonly into food and drink products, which can be marketed by the same methods as cigarettes. By 1969 the largest five US 'tobacco' companies were already deriving between 12 and 40 per cent of total sales revenue from non- tobacco products.

An important aspect of marketing is the goodwill that a firm generates for itself when it has produced a 'good value for money' product. Success in marketing one product enhances the reputation of the firm, and this in turn gives it an advantage when diversifying into new lines. Thus, a firm that has succeeded in establishing a high reputation for quality and reliability in, say, the manufacture of one item of hi-fi equipment will be able to trade on this reputation when it moves into new lines. Each new appliance will be backed in advertising campaigns by the 'good name' of the firm. In this way a firm may quickly establish itself in a wide range of products in a particular area. The diversification of camera manufacturers such as Canon, Minolta and Ricoh into photocopying is a case in point. And once one firm has developed in this way, other firms in that sector of industry may feel obliged to follow suit to maintain their competitive position.

Another question worth asking is whether the direction of diversification is related in any systematic way to industrial structure. It has been argued that one of the main factors inducing diversification is the fact that a firm is unable to realise its full growth potential in existing markets. This is most likely to be the case in highly concentrated industries that have advanced beyond the stage of rapid growth and where competition is between a relatively small number of large firms. In these circumstances it may be difficult for one firm to increase its share of the market at the expense of the others, particularly where the differences in efficiency between firms are small and where competition has been blunted by restrictive practices. This hypothesis suggests therefore that diversification will tend to be out of industries with high concentration and a small dispersion of efficiency into industries with low concentration and a large dispersion of efficiency. A new entrant into one of the latter industries will be able to expand rapidly at the expense of the least efficient existing firms.

There is in fact some evidence to suggest that diversification is positively associated with the level of concentration in the diversifying firm's main industry. It does not appear, however, that the industries into which large firms diversify are distinguished by having low levels of concentration. One reason for this is that high concentration need not prove a major obstacle to the entry of a diversifying firm, particularly when entry can take place by acquisition or merger. More important, however, is the fact that concentration is only one element of market structure that affects the pattern of diversification. Other important elements include the rate of growth of demand and the opportunities for technological change. Firms seeking new outlets for their investment funds will be attracted to industries with rapid growth and technological change, even if they are highly concentrated. For one thing, diversification into such industries is most likely to satisfy the growth and profitability objectives of firms, provided that the new field is within the range of the firm's marketing and technological competence.

For another, a high growth rate means that a firm can set up a new unit of production in the industry with a smaller risk of a response from established firms that would be the case where the growth of demand was low. Furthermore, in areas of rapid technological change, some innovations are likely to be made by firms outside the industry, which will be able to enter with a product or cost advantage over established firms.

The extent of diversification

The question of what factors determine the extent to which a firm will diversify into new areas can perhaps be adequately answered only by detailed historical studies of individual businesses. The complexities of business life, the range of managerial talent, the importance of chance factors, and so on make it difficult to capture all the relevant factors. Nevertheless, a few general influences may be mentioned.

First, the more closely products are related in either production or distribution, the more important will be economies of scope which make it cheaper for several products to be manufactured and/or distributed by the same firm rather than separately in different firms. Products which have common components may, for instance, be produced more cheaply together than separately, and economies in distribution may be achieved when the same vehicles are used to transport a range of products to the same outlets.

Second, the motivation of management, and in particular the weight attached to growth in the preference function of management, is important. This is most clearly seen in the case of the 'empire-builders' who wish to build a giant enterprise in a short space of time and who see growth by diversification as the easiest way of doing this.

Third, the success with which the firm tackles the problems of controlling separate internal interests has an important bearing on the extent to which it can handle the production and marketing of several products. There is no doubt that problems of coordination do exist in large firms. Problems of communication between different levels of management become more severe as the organisation gets larger; vested interests within the firm may be powerful enough to succeed in delaying necessary changes; the capacity of the top executive to coordinate effectively is limited, especially for firms operating in constantly changing environments. The decentralisation of management and the more effective monitoring systems associated with the multidivisional form of organisation, the development of more sophisticated accounting and budgeting techniques, and the use of computers have helped to reduce these problems, but they have not eliminated them. Clearly, it is dangerous to generalise. Some large diversified firms seem to be very well managed, but others could hardly be put forward as models of efficiency.

Fourth, and following directly from the previous points, the quality of management, and particularly of top management, is of crucial importance.

Although much emphasis is placed, and rightly so, on management being a team effort, the important contribution made by individuals with outstanding entrepreneurial and managerial ability should not be underestimated. Where that ability exists, conglomerate firms spanning a very wide range of activity can develop. Frequently it results from the identification of profitable takeover opportunities. The entrepreneurial function is to spot these opportunities. When the assets have been acquired, their longer-term management may be a relatively routine affair with performance continually monitored by head office. Hanson Trust, a good example of a conglomerate successful in the 1980s, includes cigarettes, bricks, batteries and health products amongst its activities.

Fifth, competition exercises a pervasive influence. We have already noted that competition may induce or force a firm to diversify into new products, but it will also set limits to diversification. The diversifying firm must expect to meet competition in each of its areas of production, and it must therefore have sufficient resources both to maintain its competitive position in existing fields and to establish and strengthen its position in new ones. Thus, the importance of economies of scale and entry barriers, and the intensity of competition among existing producers in new and existing lines of activity, will play an important role in determining the extent of diversification. Inevitably, mistakes will be made. A firm may underestimate the problems of producing or marketing in a new area of activity. For instance, in 1986 British Telecom (BT) took a majority stake in the Canadian manufacturer of computerised telephone switchboards Mitel, a deal which, subject to some safeguards, was approved by the Monopolies and Mergers Commission. This move of a telecommunications services company into manufacturing proved less than successful and in January 1990 BT announced that it was putting its stake in Mitel up for sale. Or it may be that a fundamental change in market conditions occurs which forces a firm to reconsider its strategy. An intensification of competition either generally or in particular industries may convince a firm that it should become less diversified in order to strengthen its position in a narrower range of activities. Certainly, as we shall see in the next section, the sale of subsidiaries between companies is a common phenomenon.

Lastly, it has been suggested that diversification is affected by wider considerations of social and political power. To the extent that this motivation exists, it will give rise to firms that are even larger than those which would otherwise have emerged.

3.4 ACQUISITIONS AND MERGERS

Mergers are an important feature of the growth of firms. In an early UK study, Evely and Little (1960) drew attention to the major importance of external expansion in the growth of leading firms in trades that were dominated by a small number of sellers, and they concluded that there were few firms among the leaders that had not been created by amalgamation or had not resorted to acquisition or merger at some stage in their growth. More recently, Hannah and Kay

(1977) emphasised the important role played by mergers in increasing the concentration of industry in the UK. Again, in a study of large companies in the USA, Weston (1961) concluded that mergers make a significant contribution to growth in all firms.

One of the most noticeable features of merger activity is that it occurs in waves, with periods of boom followed by periods of relative calm. As Table 3.1 shows, the late 1960s and early 1970s was a period of intense merger activity in the UK in terms of both the number of acquisitions and expenditure on them. Over the seven years 1967–73, annual expenditure on mergers as a percentage of gross domestic fixed capital formation in the industrial and commercial sector averaged over 40 per cent. Merger activity was at a low level during the mid 1970s. There were signs of a resurgence in activity in 1978–79 and again in 1982

Table 3.1 Merger activity within the United Kingdom, industrial and commercial companies, 1968–89

	Number acquired	Expenditure Current prices £m	1987 prices[a] £m	Expenditure as % of gross domestic fixed capital formation
1967	763	822	8,107	35
1968	946	1,946	13,580	73
1969	846	1,069	7,549	37
1970	793	1,123	8,951	34
1971	884	911	6,144	27
1972	1,210	2,532	13,409	67
1973	1,205	1,304	7,982	27
1974	504	508	5,296	9
1975	315	291	2,423	4
1976	353	448	3,118	6
1977	481	824	4,472	8
1978	567	1,140	5,489	9
1979	534	1,656	7,025	12
1980	469	1,475	5,855	10
1981	452	1,144	4,024	8
1982	463	2,206	6,712	14
1983	447	2,343	5,636	15
1984	568	5,474	11,069	28
1985	474	7,090	11,614	29
1986	696	14,935	19,718	56
1987	1,125	15,363	15,363	48
1988	1,224	22,123	24,592	55
1989	1,039	26,104	24,220	57

Sources: Business Statistics Office, Business Monitor MQ7, *Acquisitions and mergers of industrial and commercial companies*, London: HMSO, various issues; Central Statistical Office, *Economic Trends*, Annual Supplement, 1990 edition, London: HMSO, various issues.
Notes: [a]Figures derived by using the FT Actuaries, Industrial (500 share) Index.

but the whole period from 1974 to 1983 was, by and large, one of relative calm. Over this ten-year period annual expenditure on acquisitions was, on average, less than 10 per cent of gross domestic fixed capital formation.

Over ther six-year period 1984–89, the UK experienced the largest merger wave in its postwar history. During this period several very large companies, many of them household names, were acquired, including Imperial Tobacco, Distillers, Coats Patons, British Home Stores and Debenhams. Expenditure, in real terms, peaked in 1988 at a level well exceeding the previous peaks of 1968 and 1972. As in the late 1960s and early 1970s, expenditure on mergers was high as a proportion of fixed capital formation, averaging 54 per cent over the four years 1986–89.

The information in Table 3.2 suggests that the intensity of merger activity is related to the state of both financial markets and product markets. The peak year of 1968 was followed by a fall in the stock market and less buoyant product markets; the 1972 merger boom coincided with big gains in share prices and with a recovery in output from the 1970–71 recession; the low level of merger activity in 1974–76 followed the fall in share prices in 1973–74 and the slump in output in 1974–75; the resurgence in merger activity in 1977–79 was accompanied by steady gains in both share prices and output, a resurgence which was brought to an end by the recession of 1980–81. Lastly, the 1980s merger boom coincided with several years of boom on the stock exchange and recovery from the 1980–81 recession.

The figures on mergers in Tables 3.1 and 3.2 include sales of subsidiaries between company groups. Over the period since 1969 the number of these transactions as a percentage of all acquisitions has varied from a low of 12.1 per cent to a high of 36.5 per cent (Table 3.3). As a proportion of all takeovers, the sale of subsidiaries tends to be highest during or immediately following periods of depression in financial and/or product markets such as 1970–71, 1975–76, 1982–83, and 1989.

An important feature of the 1980s was the size of subsidiary sales. In real terms the average value of these sales was substantially greater in the 1980s than in the previous decade, with very large sales occurring in 1982 and 1984, and in the four-year period 1986–89.

The sale of subsidiaries is an inevitable product of merger booms as companies undo past mistakes and hive off acquisitions that have been unsuccessful. And the more diversified companies become, particularly in the medium and large size classes, the more likely it is that some asset disposals will prove necessary during the rationalisation period following a merger; and the more likely also perhaps that takeover bids will be aimed initially at certain parts of a company rather than the company as a whole. Indeed in some recent cases (e.g. the Guinness takeover of Distillers) a bidder has been required by the Office of Fair Trading (OFT) to agree to the disposal of parts of the company it was seeking to acquire, in order to avoid a reference to the Monopolies and Mergers Commission (MMC).

Table 3.2 Expenditure on mergers and changes in financial and product markets, UK, 1967–89

	Expenditure 1987 prices £m	Industrial share prices (500 share index)	Index of output of production & construction industries
		% change on previous year	% change on previous year
1967	8,107	+ 6.8	+1.2
1968	13,580	+41.3	+6.3
1969	7,549	− 1.1	+2.8
1970	8,951	−11.4	+0.1
1971	6,144	+18.2	−0.3
1972	13,409	+27.3	+2.0
1973	7,982	−13.4	+8.0
1974	5,296	−41.2	−3.7
1975	2,423	+24.9	−5.4
1976	3,118	+19.8	+2.5
1977	4,472	+28.2	+4.2
1978	5,489	+12.7	+3.6
1979	7,025	+13.6	+3.4
1980	5,855	+ 6.9	−6.4
1981	4,024	+12.8	−4.6
1982	6,712	+15.6	+1.9
1983	5,636	+26.5	+3.7
1984	11,069	+19.0	+1.6
1985	11,614	+23.5	+4.1
1986	19,718	+24.1	+2.0
1987	15,363	+32.0	+3.3
1988	24,592	−11.0	+3.8
1989	24,220	+19.8	+0.5

Sources: Business Statistics Office, Business Monitor MQ7, *Acquisitions and mergers of industrial and commercial companies*, London: HMSO, various issues; Central Statistical Office, *Economic Trends*, Annual Supplement, 1990 edition, London: HMSO, various issues

Another feature of the merger boom in the second half of the 1980s was the increased vulnerability of very large companies. Over the period 1972–82 the pattern of death by merger amongst companies included in *The Times* 1000 list for 1972 was such that companies ranked in the top 200 in 1972 had approximately half the death rate of those with a lower ranking. For the period March 1982 to March 1986, however, the death rate for companies ranked 101–200 in 1982 turned out to be one of the highest and over three times higher than for the earlier period. In every case except one the predator was an even larger company. In recent years, therefore, only the true giants have enjoyed relative immunity from takeover.

Table 3.3 Sales of subsidiaries between companies, UK, 1969–89

	Number acquired	Number as % of all acquisitions	Expenditure 1987 prices £m	Average expenditure 1987 prices £m
1969	102	12.1	704	6.9
1970	179	22.6	1,004	5.6
1971	264	29.9	1,116	4.2
1972	272	22.5	982	3.6
1973	254	21.1	1,510	5.9
1974	137	27.2	514	3.8
1975	115	36.5	582	5.1
1976	111	31.4	694	6.3
1977	109	22.7	508	4.7
1978	126	22.2	785	6.2
1979	117	21.9	789	6.7
1980	101	21.5	835	8.3
1981	125	27.7	921	7.4
1982	164	35.4	2,446	14.9
1983	142	31.8	1,048	7.4
1984	170	29.9	2,267	13.3
1985	134	28.3	1,298	9.7
1986	159	22.8	3,710	23.3
1987	220	19.6	4,086	18.6
1988	287	23.4	5,839	20.3
1989	321	30.9	4,779	14.9

Sources: Business Statistics Office, Business Monitor MQ7, Acquisitions and mergers of industrial and commercial companies, London: HMSO, various issues; Central Statistical Office, Economic Trends, Annual Supplement, 1990 edition, London: HMSO, various issues

Mergers are conventionally classified into three categories; horizontal, vertical and conglomerate. What is the balance between these three categories? The Office of Fair Trading classification of merger proposals that fall within the scope of merger legislation shows that with the exception of 1985, when conglomerate or diversification mergers accounted for 54 per cent by value of all qualifying mergers, horizontal mergers were the dominant type in each year over the period 1969–87. However, the division into categories cannot be done with precision. For instance, whether a merger is counted as horizontal or conglomerate depends on how products are classified into industries. The narrower the classification, the greater the apparent incidence of conglomerate mergers, and vice versa. In practice many mergers contain elements of more than one category of expansion.

The remainder of this section examines the varied and complex motives for mergers. In trying to identify these motives both the direct method of questioning business executives and the indirect one of deducing motives from effects may fail to get at the truth. Executives may, for instance, rationalise past decisions and in so doing obscure the factors that were uppermost in the minds of the decision-takers at the time of the merger. The fact that many mergers fail to achieve their objectives makes the indirect method a hazardous way of identifying the underlying motives for the mergers.

If the truth could be ascertained, it would surely show that no one motive is of equal importance in all cases. It might also show the existence of strong underlying currents that contribute to the explanation of many mergers in particular periods but that would not be revealed by the replies of individual executives or by data on industry structure and business performance.

Motives of the acquired firm

For many mergers, particularly those involving the acquisition of small firms, an important part of the explanation of the mergers is to be found in the motives of the owners of acquired firms. In fact, an interest, on the part of the victim, in being acquired is probably a relevant factor in a substantial majority of mergers. The following examples illustrate some of the possibilities.

First, there is the firm that has hit upon hard times and become bankrupt or is on the verge of bankruptcy. In this case acquisition by an existing firm may be the only way of keeping at least part of the capital and workforce intact.

Second, there are cases where the owner of a firm is forced to sell in order to meet tax liabilities.

Third, firms will at some stage in their growth enter a critical stage 'which combines the technical disadvantage of smallness with the managerial disadvantage of being too large for individual control'. Robinson (1958) referred to such a firm as one of 'pessimum' size. Such a stage may in fact be experienced more than once in the growth of a firm, and a major reorganisation of management and finance has to take place in order to form a sounder basis for sustained growth. In some cases the owners may decide not to attempt to construct the managerial and financial launching pad for further growth but may instead decide either to continue at the same size or to accept the offer of a takeover by another company. In other cases owners will recognise and accept the need for change and will attempt to grow out of the critical stage. Substantial difficulties, however, may be faced, particularly in recruiting new management personnel and in raising capital. Acquisition by another firm may be the only effective way of overcoming these difficulties.

In any of the cases outlined above, an acquiring firm will have the chance of a bargain, for in such situations the owners of the firm that is in difficulty may be only too happy to sell at a price that is below the value placed on it by an acquirer. If in each case there were several interested purchasers, all with access to finance on the same terms and all with access to full information on the current position of the firm that is for sale, the price of the firm for sale would be bid up to its market value (i.e. to the present discounted value of the expected future stream of profits as seen by the successful bidder). However, the market for firms is typically very imperfect. The number of interested buyers who are aware that a firm is likely to be for sale is often small; they may have unequal access to funds; and some may be better informed than others about the current position of the firm that is to be sold. In addition, firms will hold different expectations about the future. In such circumstances the acquiring firm may well be able to make a purchase at a price that it considers attractive compared with the alternative of internal expansion by building a comparable plant.

One further point that should be made is that a firm may be in difficulties and ripe for takeover because of the predatory behaviour of a larger competitor. In this case the explanation of the merger should be sought in the motives of the acquiring and not the acquired firm.

Motives of the acquiring firm

Where bargain buys of the kind mentioned above are available, mergers will obviously be a profitable way to expand. However, to complete the picture we need to look at the possible motives of buyers.

Economies of scale

A frequently heard argument is that mergers result in the realisation of scale economies. This may come about in a number of ways. First, there may be the possibility of benefiting from product- specific economies as a result of increased specialisation and longer production runs within plants. It may be argued that if there are big gains to be realised it should pay some firms to operate plants with these advantages, and these firms would gain market share at the expense of their less efficient competitors. However, if competitors produce overlapping product ranges the competitive process could well be prolonged and may indeed result in widespread price-cutting behaviour, with all firms suffering lower profits and gaining little from increased specialisation. By combining plants into a smaller number of firms, mergers can result in the speedy rearrangement of production schedules and bring about benefits that could only be achieved, if at all, over a much longer period as a result of all-out competition between existing firms.

Second, mergers may lead to plant-specific economies. For instance, an industry may be operating with chronic excess capacity and, if fixed costs are large, prices, although above short-run average variable costs, may be well below unit total costs. Mergers would allow the speedy scrapping of the most inefficient plants and the concentration of production into a smaller number of the most efficient ones. Again, existing industry capacity may be more than adequate to meet demand but individual plants may be of sub-optimal size; and even in an expanding market the incentive to build optimal-sized units may be blunted because the optimal-sized plant may be large in relation to annual increments in demand. Here too, the risks can be reduced and the willingness to build optimal-sized units increased by the merger of competing companies. In principle, plant scale economies, where they are significant, should also be realisable as a result of sufficiently strong competition between independent firms. Once again, however, all-out competition may be prolonged, and managers may simply be unwilling to take the risks involved in building new plants in such a hostile environment.

Third, mergers may result in marketing economies as a result of such actions as the pooling of advertising campaigns, the sharing and rationalisation of distribution channels, or the offer of a wider range of products to distributors, thus benefiting from economies of scope.

That mergers may lead to scale-economy advantages is more easily argued than demonstrated. The evidence is far from impressive. Very frequently the realisation of scale economies is limited by customer demand for product differentiation; just as often economies may fail to be exploited because of poor management.

Complementarities

If one firm is strong in production but weak in marketing and financial control and another has the opposite characteristics a merger of the two should lead to substantial benefits. Or the amalgamation may be between firms in the same broad line of business but which have established reputations, with valuable brand names, in different product lines (e.g. the merger in 1989 between Nestlé and Rowntree). Similar motives may explain a vertical merger: a firm may acquire another because one supplies an important input for the other's production process, or controls outlets for the other's products.

Again it must be asked why these benefits cannot be realised by internal expansion, and once more the answer may be found in part at least in market 'imperfections'. If a firm wants access to research and development knowledge or brand names there may in practice be no alternative to acquiring a competitor, and in some industries (brewing is a good example) the limitation on the number of sales outlets may make merger the only feasible means of forward integration.

Speed and safety factors

Even when internal growth is feasible, merger is a quicker and often a safer way of growing. In some cases the emphasis on speed is simply a reflection of the importance of time in the estimates that a firm makes of the profitability of alternative courses of action. To take an extreme case, the time needed for internal expansion may be too long to save a firm from collapse. The rapid acquisition of outlets or of new knowledge may be necessary for survival. In the case of diversification there may be difficulties in moving into a new industry because of patent protection, the attachment of consumers to established brands, or the need to acquire new production and marketing skills. If a firm chooses to expand internally it has somehow to overcome these difficulties. The problems will often be solved more quickly by acquiring an existing firm with its own patents, brand names and appropriate management skills.

Merger may be a safer as well as a faster way to expand. This is most evident in those industries where there is excess capacity or where there is a danger that excess capacity will emerge because of sluggish demand growth. In these circumstances, competitive investment plans carry the danger that output from additional capacity will drive down prices and profitability. Acquisitions, on the other hand, leave industry capacity unchanged. The desire to stave off competitive investment plans is undoubtedly an important factor in explaining some horizontal mergers. For instance, in explaining a merger between two large firms in the milling and baking business, the deputy chairman of one of the companies said: 'Both of us were considering further capital investment, and quickly realised it might lead to duplication. Once that investment was on the ground in terms of new plant and equipment, each of us would have been committed to making it pay. So in a very real sense the merger was now or never.' The safety motive can clearly be translated into the relative profitability of different methods of expansion. In the example just given, the effect of internal expansion on industry capacity and the likely effects on subsequent profits were clearly factors telling against internal growth and in favour of acquisition.

Monopoly and market power

'Whenever merger is considered to be the most profitable way to expand there will surely be a tendency for merger to occur. Economic analysis that treats it only as a means of reducing competition, or establishing monopolistic dominance, is placing the wrong emphasis on one of the most significant characteristics of the firm in the modern economy' (Penrose 1966: 155).

There is no need to quarrel with the statement that firms will resort to external expansion when this is the most profitable course open to them. This, however, does not get us away from the monopoly issue. Indeed, mergers will be especially profitable when they result in increases in market power or when they eliminate a threatened increase in the intensity of competition. Such an increase in the intensity of competition could be due to competitive investment plans, as in the example above, and this shows that the speed, safety and market power motives for mergers are not necessarily independent.

Once a dominant position has been established, mergers may be used to protect it. For instance, the position of a large established firm may be threatened by a new product or process developed by a small competitor. There are a number of alternatives open to the threatened firm: it can do nothing and suffer a decline in its market share; it can attempt to develop a similar product or process; or it can make a takeover bid for the smaller firm. The last response is particularly likely when the threatened firm is much larger than the innovator. The profits that the small firm makes at its existing scale of operations will be a lot lower than the potential losses of the large firm if it fails to counter with its own improved product or process. Under these circumstances the large firm may be prepared to pay more for the innovating firm than it is worth to its current owners (i.e. more than the present value of the future stream of profits that they expect).

There is also a wider aspect to the market power motive. For the market system to work at all there must be *some* element of market power. The textbook model of perfect competition is not one that could survive for long in reality. Firms must have some protection from the day-to-day ravages of competition. At the same time, the threat of competition is often important in ensuring that markets function efficiently. Businessmen have a view of what is an acceptable balance between safety and competition, although this is hard to define. It is not a precise combination of factors but rather a range within which executives find the problems of conducting a business to be tolerable. From time to time major changes take place that drastically alter the environment within which firms have to operate and that upset the acceptable balance between safety and competition. These changes may be brought about by such factors as the widening of markets resulting from improvements in transport and communications or a reduction in trade barriers; prolonged recession; changes in competition policy or regulatory policy; and changes in technology and techniques of management. Factors such as these help explain upsurges in merger activity which may last several years and which may also be experienced more or less simultaneously in several countries. Over the postwar period, for instance, all the industrialised countries of the Western world have had to contend with more intensive competition from imports. During the 1950s and 1960s several countries experienced a strengthening of antitrust legislation. Technical and managerial changes have created a revolution in the distributive trades, and deregulation has created a more competitive environment in the UK financial sector. The much-publicised single European market which comes into effect in 1992 signals both a wider and a more competitive market for many products. A widening of markets, the entry of new competitors, the introduction of more efficient forms of organisation and so on, upset 'traditional' balances. When this happens, firms will look to merger as one means of protecting their positions and restoring balance. And once some firms resort to this course of action it is likely to trigger off defensive acquisitions by others.

The fact that an increase in the intensity of competition can be an important cause of mergers does not mean that we should necessarily find that mergers occur most often during a recession. For one thing, competition may intensify without there being a recession and over a much longer period than the business cycle. For another, the timing of mergers is affected by the availability and cost of finance. The underlying motive for a merger may be to increase market power, but the timing of the merger will be dictated in the main by financial considerations.

A market for corporate control

The most influential argument advanced in recent years to explain, and to justify, merger activity is that mergers are a sign of an active market for corporate control which ensures that assets are managed efficiently. Competition between rival management teams for the right to manage assets ensures the survival of the fittest, i.e. those with the best profit performance. The inefficient use of assets, or inflated discretionary expenditures by management teams at the expense of shareholders, result in poor profit performance, weak share prices and the exposure of the firm to a takeover bid. The threat of takeover may itself be sufficient to force management to improve its performance. If not, the firm is likely to be acquired by another whose management sees the opportunity for more efficient use of the assets, improved performance and increased benefits to shareholders. A free market in corporate control thus provides the best guarantee of efficiency in the use of existing assets. Without takeovers there would be no effective constraint on the tendency of management teams to inflate discretionary expenditures such as head office costs, staff costs and wasteful research and development expenditure at the expense of shareholders.

For the market to work in this way the stock market must be efficient, in the sense that companies are valued according to their expected future profit streams. Of two companies, therefore, the one with the higher earnings prospects will have the higher share price. In addition, there have to be a sufficient number of predators whose motivation is to maximise shareholder returns.

The proponents of the view that the stock market does work efficiently base their case on evidence of share price movements before and after takeover bids. Their interpretation of the evidence is that takeovers result in substantial gains to the shareholders of acquired firms and also in gains, albeit on a much more modest scale, to the shareholders of acquiring firms. (These results are examined in the next chapter.)

There can be little doubt that takeovers do frequently occur because a predator sees an opportunity for making more profitable use of the assets of another firm. However, considerable doubt exists over whether the market works in quite the beneficial way claimed for it by the free marketeers. Consideration of these doubts helps cast some further light on the causes of merger activity.

As mentioned earlier, for the stock market to operate efficiently share prices must reflect the expected future earnings potential of firms. There is little evidence, however, that they do so systematically or continuously. At the very least there is a considerable element of short-run disequilibrium embodied in share values, which has an important impact on both the pattern and extent of merger activity. Some companies will at a particular moment in time be undervalued relative to their long-run earnings potential, and thus be vulnerable to a takeover bid from companies whose shares are properly valued or overvalued. In the Guest Keen and Nettlefolds/Associated Engineering reference to the MMC, for instance, AE argued that its low share price was due to low dividend payments resulting from the priority it had given to investment in rationalisation, modernisation and research and development. Hepworth's bid for Steetley came at a time of reorganisation and rationalisation when Steetley's profits and share prices were depressed. In the event both bids were blocked by the MMC, although AE was subsequently acquired by Turner & Newall.

Measures to improve long-term competitiveness may make a firm vulnerable to takeover. Against this it may be argued that if shareholders are fully informed of the measures being taken, and are convinced of their effectiveness, a firm would not be exposed to a takeover bid on this account alone. Mistakes would, it is true, be made because of uncertainty surrounding future prospects, but if this were all that was involved there would be little reason for believing that interference with the market would improve matters.

However, there are a number of reasons for believing that this may be too sanguine an interpretation of reality. Even if shareholders are typically well informed about the measures that are being taken to improve long-run competitiveness, they may still attach greater weight to dividends in the short run than to the prospect of higher dividends in the future. For this reason alone, short-run disequilibrium in share values will result in a bias against the survival of firms whose shares are temporarily undervalued.

Financial and promotional factors

The different expectations that are held about the future performance of companies, as reflected in financial indicators, may give their own added impetus. By the very nature of things considerable uncertainty surrounds stock market valuations especially during stock market booms. But although a period of stock market boom is a good time to buy, because funds will be readily available, prices will also be higher. The boom however will not affect all firms equally. For various reasons investors will view the prospects of some firms more favourably than those of others. In addition, and this may itself partly explain the last point, some executives will be more optimistic about the future and more aggressive in their intentions than others. If their optimism is supported by the market, their companies will be accorded high price/earnings ratios, which will place them in a strong position to acquire companies whose shares are rated less highly, and at the same time improve their apparent performance.

Take, for instance, the example in Table 3.4. Suppose that firm A acquires firm B by offering one of its shares for one of B's. Assume also that A finances the deal by issuing 1 million new shares. The financial position of the firm will then be as follows: profits = £3 million; issued shares = 5 million; earnings per share = 60p; and, assuming that a price/earnings (P/E) ratio of 30 is maintained, price per share = £18. The merger will have resulted in an increase in the market value of A's shares from £15 to £18.

The crucial factor in explaining this bit of financial wizardry is the high P/E

Table 3.4 Mergers and financial performance

	Firm A	Firm B	Firm A + B
Profits after tax and interest	£2m	£1m	£3m
Number of issued shares	4m	1m	5m
∴ Earnings per share	50p	£1	60p
Ratio of price per share to earnings per share	30	12	30
∴ Price per share	£15	£12	£18

ratio of firm A, whose share price is 30 times earnings per share, reflecting the fact that the market views the future prospects of the firm very favourably. As long as it is able to maintain a high P/E ratio – or, in other words, as long as it keeps the confidence of investors – it will be in a good position to acquire other firms and at the same time to improve its apparent financial performance.

The reasons why the P/E ratios of some firms reach a higher level than others during a stock market boom are not clear. The reasons may be soundly based on long-term commercial considerations, but this need not be so in all cases or indeed in the majority of cases. During the euphoria of a stock market boom many mergers will occur simply because of the opportunities for short-run profit-making rather than because of any industrial logic.

Other factors may give further impetus to the short-run pursuit of profit. For instance, high P/E ratios may be supported by accounting procedures designed to inflate reported post-merger profitability. One device is to record acquired assets at values less than the purchase price, thus raising the reported return on assets. When undervalued assets are subsequently sold, a profit gain can be reported. A company may, for instance, make large provisions for writing off stocks, or to cover extraordinary reorganisation costs. The release of these reserves into the profit and loss account at a later date results in a boost to profits. Fully informed investors should see through what is happening, but the fact that the average investor is less than fully knowledgeable gives opportunities for large profits to be made by knowledgeable insiders.

The fees and commissions (sometimes huge by any standards) paid to company promoters are also a factor to be considered. In 1986 and 1987 these fees and commissions added up to several hundreds of millions of pounds. There have been cases where massive payments have been made to individuals for specialist advice; there have been allegations of insider dealing and of the manipulation of share prices. A small number of knowledgeable insiders do clearly have more information than the average investor, and this coupled with the enormous rewards that accompany success means that there is at least a tendency for those who have most to gain (or lose) to be unscrupulous in their share dealings. In this sort of world it is not necessarily the case that mergers are based on any industrial logic or that the best managers win.

One point that is particularly important in the context of financial and promotional motives, but also has wider significance, is the fact that mergers often take place on the basis of inadequate information for at least one of the parties involved. Of course, there cannot be complete information on the out-turn of events with or without a merger. Yet it may be that all the facts are not available to all the interested parties and also that there is insufficient consideration of the alternatives open to the acquired company. In order to ensure that merger decisions are based on a full knowledge of the relevant facts and to have at least two views of the future, it may be in the public interest that merger bids be fought tooth and nail. Contested bids will usually bring more information to light and also force the firm that is the subject of a bid to consider alternative courses of action.

3.5 LIMITS TO GROWTH

For many firms there will be an absolute limit to size under existing management. There is no evidence, however, that the idea of an absolute size limit is one that is applicable to all firms. Successful firms seem to be able to grow without limit, but there are factors that limit the rate of growth of all firms, including the successful ones.

Security

First, and quite apart from any managerial constraints, there are considerations of security to take into account – both security against bankruptcy and security against a takeover bid. The faster a firm attempts to expand, the more it will be driven to accept high-risk investments and the more it may have to rely on fixed-interest debt. Both endanger the future of the firm. The failure of a major investment or the high level of fixed charges that the firm is obliged to meet when trade is depressed may bring it to its knees. Too rapid a rate of growth may also expose a firm to the danger of a takeover bid. This may occur if rapid expansion depresses the firm's profitability or if it results in high retention of profits and low dividend payments to shareholders. Too low a rate of growth, on the other hand, may also attract a takeover bid. A profitable firm with a highly conservative management may have a high level of liquidity. A prospective acquirer may feel confident that the funds can be put to more profitable use.

Management

Within the constraints that are dictated by considerations of security there will be managerial limits to growth. The nature of this limit as seen by Penrose is as follows. First, management is a team with experience of working together. Second, it takes time for an outsider to become an effective part of the team. A new member has to undergo a training period before being able to contribute effectively to the overall management effort. Third, the training period is related to the number of new recruits. The greater the number of new people taken on, the longer the training period tends to be. From this it follows that there is a twofold managerial limit to expansion. The size of the existing management team limits the amount of expansion that can be planned, and this in turn limits the number of new people who can be absorbed into the management team.

Finance and uncertainty

Two other factors that have been considered as possible constraints on the growth of firms are the availability of finance and the existence of uncertainty. The difficulty here is in determining whether they are truly independent constraints, because both are related to the management function.

Where financial constraints are concerned, there is a relationship between the amount of finance that a firm can obtain and entrepreneurial and managerial ability, simply because success in attracting funds is an important part of the entrepreneurial function. Yet it would be unwise, given the existence of capital market imperfections, to assume that finance is never a real problem.

Because of this close relationship with the management function it is difficult to prove conclusively that financial constraints do exist. Take, for instance, the firm that answers 'yes' to the question 'Has finance been a major constraint to growth?' The answer may truly reflect the facts, but on the other hand it may be an attempt to hide managerial weaknesses. If the answer is 'no', here again we may not be able to accept it at face value. It may be true, or it may be that the firm adopts a conservative attitude and is content with the amount of expansion that available finance allows. It is also common to hear a member of a financial institution say that there is no shortage of finance for profitable investment projects. This statement, however, is based on the financial institution's own, possibly highly conservative, assessment of the likely outcome of different projects.

This brings us finally to the role of uncertainty in limiting the growth of firms. It is clear that the seriousness of this problem can be reduced, but only at the cost of additional management effort, which may affect the pattern as well as the rate of growth. This can be illustrated by considering some of the ways in which a firm may respond to uncertainty. One possible response is to increase the variety of goods produced. This would clearly affect the pattern of growth and might increase the managerial resources needed to coordinate the firm's activities. Indeed, management problems in a diversified firm might be so acute that they lead either to voluntary divestments (in the form of management buy-out or the sale of subsidiaries to other companies), or to the exposure of the firm to a take-over bid. Part of the attraction of a takeover for the predator might also be the profitable sale of subsidiaries of the acquired company to more specialist producers. Another response may be to emphasise short-term projects to the neglect of longer-term ones, which again would affect the pattern of growth as well as the long-term growth rate. Yet another possibility is to take longer in arriving at investment decisions: for instance, by carrying out more market research before deciding to launch a new product. In this respect different attitudes to uncertainty would have a crucial impact on business performance, for the firm that is particularly risk averse may find that it delays for so long before making a decision that it loses a potential position of market leadership to a competitor.

Given the managerial resources available, therefore, uncertainty will place a limit on the rate of expansion by affecting the volume of managerial services required for a given amount of expansion.

Chapter 4

Business performance

4.1 INTRODUCTION

In the previous chapter we have examined various aspects of the process of firm growth. We now turn to examine some of the results of this process. In section 4.2 we look at the empirical results of studies that have examined the inter-relationship between profitability, size and growth. Section 4.3 focuses attention on one aspect of growth, namely, growth by merger, to see if there is any evidence to suggest that growth by merger is less beneficial to society than internal growth. Section 4.4 examines trends in aggregate concentration, i.e. the extent to which a relatively small number of large firms dominate the manufacturing sector. Lastly, in section 4.5 we look at some of the consequences of the growth in importance of the large diversified firm for the efficient allocation of resources.

4.2 SIZE, GROWTH AND PROFITABILITY

Before proceeding to an examination of the evidence, it should be stressed that empirical results may differ for a variety of reasons. For instance, two studies on the relationship between size and profitability may reach different conclusions because the time periods are not the same, the samples of firms are not the same or different measures of size and profitability are used. One reason why the time period covered can affect the results is that large firms, because of their greater market power, do relatively better in terms of profits when business is slack than when it is booming.

The choice of variable to measure size can affect empirical results for the following reasons. There are several alternative measures available: for example, total assets, net assets, sales, employment and value added. If these measures were perfectly correlated – so that, say, firm X, which is twice as big as firm Y in terms of sales, was also twice as big in terms of all other variables – there would be no problem, and the choice of size measure would not affect results. This, however, will not be the case. The best that we can hope for is that measures of size are highly correlated. In this case, studies using different size variables are likely to arrive at qualitatively similar conclusions, but the quantitative effect on the dependent variable of changing size may differ considerably according to the size measure used.

For instance, suppose that the relationship between initial size and average growth rate over a certain period for four firms is as given in Table 4.1. The two measures of size are positively correlated but not perfectly so; there is a greater difference between the sizes of these firms measured in assets than in sales. A regression of growth on size will indicate a positive relationship whichever size measure is used, but the goodness of fit of the relationship (i.e. the correlation coefficient) and the effect on growth rate of changing size (i.e. the regression coefficient) will be different for the two variables. In fact, the independent variable with the lower variance (i.e. sales) gives a higher correlation and a greater estimated impact of size on growth.

Furthermore, it is possible that the same firm will be assigned to different size groups according to which size measure is used. In this case a small positive association between two variables using one measure of size can disappear or even become negative when an alternative measure of size is used. The same warning applies to profits. There are several alternative measures of profit performance, including the post-tax return on net assets, return on sales, and the price–cost margin. Since these measures are not perfectly correlated, the choice of variable to measure profitability may affect empirical results. Bearing these points in mind, we can now turn to look at the empirical evidence.

Size and profitability

Studies of the relationship between size and profitability have in general found little systematic association between the two. An early study by Downie (1958), which looked in fact at size and productivity, found that no association between the two variables could be distinguished when size was measured by employment, and the results were not much stronger when size was measured by net output. For the period 1948–60 Singh and Whittington (1968: 144) found that:

> average profitability (rate of return on net assets) was on the whole (with some exceptions) lower the larger the size of the firm (measured by net assets) but the differences in average profitability of firms between size-classes were not found to be statistically significant at the 5 per cent level, by the usual tests, for most of the populations of firms considered.

Table 4.1 Measures of the size and growth of firms

	Firm 1	Firm 2	Firm 3	Firm 4
Growth of net assets and sales (%)	5	6	7	7
Initial size, by net assets (index)	100	150	200	300
Initial size, by sales (index)	250	300	350	400

This conclusion was based on a study of four broad industries in UK manufacturing. An extension of the analysis to cover a much larger number of industries also found very little association between size and the average level of profitability. Other studies, however, have found a positive relationship between size and profitability. For instance, a study by Hall and Weiss (1967) of US manufacturing corporations over the period 1956–62 found that post-tax profits as a percentage of total assets increased with size.

More conclusive evidence exists of significant differences between size classes in the dispersion of profit rates, the tendency being for the degree of dispersion to vary inversely with the size of the firm. A number of reasons may be advanced to explain this finding. First, large firms are more diversified than small ones, and their reported profit is an average of the profits of the various branches and subsidiaries. Provided that the profits attributable to individual products do not show perfect positive correlation, the variation in profits will be less for a diversified firm producing, say, five products than it will be for individual specialised firms producing one of those products. This is because in the diversified firm the variations in the profits on individual products will tend to be offsetting. A second possible explanation is that the management of large firms may be more skilful at avoiding projects that result in losses, but also less adventurous and thus less likely to take advantage of opportunities of making exceptional gains. Third, large firms have greater market power and during good times may have relatively more organisational slack. During a downturn in demand they may be more successful in maintaining profits, both because they can use their power in the market and also because they have greater scope for increasing internal efficiency.

Growth and profitability

We would expect to find a positive relationship between growth and profitability for two reasons: because of a firm's *ability* to grow, and also because of its *desire* to grow.

The link between profitability and the ability to grow is clear. A growing firm requires finance for expansion, and the supply of this finance, whether originating internally from ploughed-back profits or externally from loans or new share issues, is related to the firm's profit record. In so far as the firm's growth is financed from retained profits, the greater the profit, the more growth it will be able to finance. In so far as growth is financed externally, the profitability of the firm is again important, because the ease of raising outside funds depends upon the prospects of dividends.

The firm's desire to grow is also related to profitability. As we have argued in an earlier chapter, in an expanding economy growth is an essential ingredient of the forces of competition. The growing firm has an advantage over stable or contracting ones in attracting and holding skilled workers, including good management, because of the increased opportunities and resources available to members of the organisation. In other words, internal labour markets are likely to work most successfully in companies that are growing. The rate of productivity growth in the firm is also likely to vary positively with the rate at which its output is expanding. The faster the increase in output, the faster the accumulation of new machines and the scrapping of old ones. We would expect the age distribution of the capital stock of the growth firm to have a lower mean and a lower variance than that of firms of stable or declining size: firms that are on the downgrade as indicated by an aged capital stock typically do not reverse the trend, whilst the more dynamic firms continue to 'rejuvenate' their capital stock by investing at higher rates. The faster-growing firms in an industry are therefore likely to have a higher productivity growth than their rivals and will tend to be more competitive in terms of price and quality of product and/or more profitable, which will give them an advantage in striving to increase market share or in diversifying into new lines of activity.

The empirical work that has been done in this area falls into two main groups. The first examines the relationship between changes in output and output per head, differential changes in output being a measure of relative growth and in output per head a measure of relative efficiency gains. On an industry basis the positive correlation between these variables has, as we have seen in Chapter 1, been well established. On an individual firm basis there is less evidence. However, Downie (1958) found a very definite association in most industries between changes in productivity and growth. Statistical results such as these do not tell us whether it is high output increases that cause high productivity gains or vice versa. However, either direction of causation is consistent with the behaviour of a firm for which growth is an important goal.

The second group of empirical studies has examined the relationship between profitability and the rate of growth of firms in terms of assets. These studies have in general found a strong positive association between growth and profitability. For instance, Singh and Whittington (1968: 189) found 'a fairly strong association between growth and profitability with profitability "explaining" on average about 50 per cent of the variation in growth rates.' A few points are worth making about such findings.

First, in these cross-section studies, profits rather than growth are likely to be the causal factor, so that above-average profitability brings about above-average growth rates rather than vice versa. The economic reasons for this are as follows. The profits that a firm has for expansion come either from retentions or from external sources. A firm's retentions (i.e. its dividend policy) and the amount of external finance that it can raise for a given profit performance and dividend policy are both influenced by the capital market, and the influence or constraints imposed by the capital market apply to all quoted companies. These constraints will not in practice impinge equally on all companies, but nevertheless we would expect them to be fairly systematic. On the other hand, no such external factor affects the growth-to-profits relationship. Attainable growth rates will vary substantially from one firm to another, reflecting such things as the organisational abilities of management, the product line of the firm, the skills of the marketing managers, and so on. The growth-to-profits relationship is therefore likely to vary much more between firms, so that it is the more stable profits-to-growth relationship that is captured in the cross-section study mentioned earlier. This is not to say, of course, that, for the individual firm, growth is not an important factor in determining profitability. Some growth rather than no growth or decline may well be important in maintaining efficiency and profitability, and too rapid a rate of growth can have an adverse effect on profits.

Second, only part of the variation in one of the variables is 'explained' by variations in the other. A substantial part remains to be explained by other factors. This is not surprising, because there are other important variables at work, notably differences in the quality and goals of management and in the intensity of competition.

Third, the observed positive relationship between profitability and growth does not say anything about the *direction* of expansion of the most profitable firms. The evidence is consistent with a range of growth patterns. Thus, in some cases high profitability will be associated with rapid expansion in existing lines, in others with expansion that has been achieved largely by diversification.

Size and growth

Traditional neoclassical theory, with its notion of an optimum size of firm, has very little to say about the relationship between size and growth. The emphasis is on describing equilibrium and comparing different equilibrium positions rather than on the process of change. In long-run equilibrium there will, of course, be no relationship between size and growth, because all firms will be of optimum size and none will have any inducement to get larger or smaller. Under conditions of disequilibrium, some sort of relationship will exist, and the most plausible hypothesis to put forward is that the relationship between size and growth will be negative. Assume that all firms have the same U-shaped long-run average-cost curve (*LRAC* in Figure 4.1). Assume also that there is initially a wide range of firm sizes, some operating at or near the optimum size *OM*, others operating well above or well below this size. During the time period between the initial position shown in Figure 4.1 and the attainment of long-run equilibrium, when all firms are of size *OM*, we would find that firms well below optimum size (e.g. firm A) will grow the most; firms at or near the optimum size (e.g. firm B) will show zero or near-zero growth; whereas firms that are initially well above optimum size (e.g. firm C) will experience negative growth.

As we have seen in Chapter 2, more recent theories of the firm emphasise the importance of growth, particularly the importance of the growth motive in management-controlled firms. Here there is no absolute limit to size, only a limit to the rate of growth per unit of time. Up to a certain size at least we might expect that the larger the size of firm, the more management-dominated it is and the stronger therefore is the growth motive. This would lead us to expect a

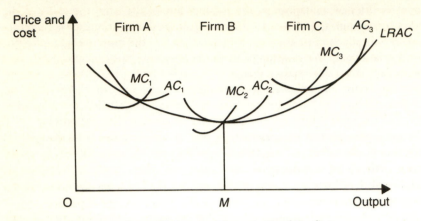

Figure 4.1 Short-run disequilibrium and the growth of the firm

positive association between size and growth. Even if it were true, however, that the growth motive is stronger in larger management-controlled firms than in smaller owner-controlled ones, this in itself would not necessarily lead us to anticipate a significant positive relationship between size and growth, because the desire for growth is only one factor affecting growth performance.

The evidence on this question is mixed. Some studies have found no significant difference between the growth rates of large and small firms. This was one of Hart's findings for a sample of UK companies over the period 1950–55 (Hart 1962). Later work by Samuels (1965), however, revealed a strong positive association between size and growth for a sample of 400 companies over the period 1951–60. A positive but weak association was also found by Singh and Whittington (1975) for the period 1948–60.

The finding of a positive association between size and growth may be explained by the stronger growth motive in large firms. Alternatively, the explanation may be that whatever diseconomies a firm faces as it gets larger are outweighed by economies of scale and market power advantages in production, finance and marketing.

Another finding of interest is that large firms have a lower dispersion of growth rates than small ones. As in the case of the dispersion of profit rates, this can be explained by the fact that the greater diversification of large firms allows them to offset poor performance in some markets against good performance in others.

4.3 THE EFFECTS OF MERGERS

In view of the importance of mergers in the growth of many firms, it is necessary to examine the role of mergers in influencing the interrelationships between growth, size and profitability. We are concerned with three main issues. First, does the stock market impose a strict discipline on firms as evidenced by a strong tendency for unprofitable firms to be acquired by profitable ones? Second, do mergers typically lead to improvements in efficiency and profitability? Third, is there any systematic relationship between the intensity of merger activity, overall growth, and investment in new assets?

Stock market discipline

On *a priori* grounds it is possible to argue that mergers play an important part in maintaining allocative and productive efficiency, because of their role in the process of stock market discipline. In essence, the efficient enforcement of this discipline is dependent on a strong tendency for the stock market to value the shares of companies according to their expected future stream of profits. Of two companies, therefore, the one with the higher earnings prospects will have the higher share prices. Part of the difference in expected profitability between firms will, of course, reflect differences in the earning power of assets. In other words, if there are two firms with equally good management but with different asset bases and, therefore, different expected future profits, the market will value the two firms accordingly.

There is no reason to expect, however, that the lower-valued firm will be the target of a takeover bid, because the low value in this case reflects the low earning power of assets. On the other hand, differences in market valuation may in part be due to the variable quality of management. Two firms with the same asset structure may be valued differently because the quality of management in one is much inferior, and therefore its expected future profits are lower. When differences in the quality of management are reflected in market valuations, there will be a tendency for those firms which are least efficiently managed to be acquired by those which are well managed. The latter will be able to acquire the former on attractive terms and, by better use of the assets, improve performance and future profit prospects. On this argument, therefore, mergers are an important part of the process whereby resources are transferred from less efficient to more efficient firms.

In practice, however, things may turn out rather differently. For instance, the above view of the world assumes that there are, at least, a sufficient number of predators who are concerned with maximising returns to shareholders. In so far as this is not their main or only important goal, the view that there is a strong tendency for mergers to eliminate the inefficient may need serious qualification. Even if maximisation of shareholder interests is the only concern of management, the stock market selection mechanism will still operate only imperfectly. This is partly because of imperfect information about the past performance and present position of companies and partly because decisions have to be made under conditions of uncertainty about the future prospects of companies.

UK research undertaken in this area has involved comparisons of groups of firms in terms of pre-merger characteristics such as size, growth, profitability and market value. For instance, acquired companies may be compared with non-acquired companies, or with a rather narrower group such as non-acquired and non-acquiring companies, or with a wider group such as all firms including the acquired. The choice of control group may clearly have some effect on the empirical results. The selection of firms for inclusion in the sample is also important because business performance varies over time, across industries, and across different size classes of firm. Ideally comparisons should be made between firms which are closely matched by industry, year and size. Many studies however fall far short of this ideal. The various studies that have been made differ in terms of both the control groups used and the sample design. The results are too numerous and complex to report in full but we hope that the following summary does no great violence to the truth.

Comparisons of acquired companies with other groups, such as non-acquired or non-acquired plus non-acquiring, show a tendency for acquired companies to be smaller and to have a lower growth rate. The valuation ratio (i.e. stock market value of assets ÷ reported book value) of acquired companies also tends to be lower. Any tendency for acquired firms to have poorer profitability performance seems very often to be concentrated in the year or two immediately preceding a takeover, suggesting perhaps opportunistic behaviour on the part of the acquirer (see the examples given in Chapter 3, section 3.4). There is little evidence of poorer profit performance in the medium to long term. A point to emphasise is that all studies show a *big overlap* between the groups of firms. For instance, a tendency may be found for non-acquired firms to have superior growth performance compared with acquired companies, but this tendency may be very weak, with just over 50 per cent of non-acquired firms coming out on top and just under 50 per cent doing relatively badly. Weak rather than strong tendencies are typical of results in this area.

Compared with companies in general, acquiring companies tend to be larger and faster growing. Profitability comparisons are again less clear. Generally, acquiring companies are shown not to be especially profitable compared with companies in general. An interesting finding of some studies is that, in so far as acquiring companies do have superior pre-merger profitability performance, this is found mainly amongst non-horizontal acquirers. A possible explanation of this finding is that horizontal mergers tend to be more defensive and that non-horizontal mergers reflect a more positive management approach. Again emphasis must be placed on the big overlap between groups of firms.

Lastly, comparisons of acquired and acquiring companies show that acquirers are usually faster growing but not invariably so. For profitability the findings are mixed and, even when on average the acquirers have superior profitability, there is a big overlap between the groups. What comes out most clearly from these comparisons is that size is the best discriminator. Thus, whereas the probability of being acquired within a particular time period is noticeably higher than average only for firms with *very* poor profit performance, there is a more systematic, inverse, relationship between the probability of being acquired and size. For a relatively small and unprofitable firm wishing to avoid acquisition it would appear that management should concentrate on growth rather than on profitability. It would, of course, be even better to improve performance in both respects, and indeed it might not be possible to achieve one goal without the other.

Mergers, profitability and efficiency

The effects of mergers on prices, costs and output, and their implications for welfare, may be examined in terms of Williamson's trade-off model (Williamson 1968).

Consider the case of a merger that transforms a competitive industry into a monopoly (Figure 4.2). The industry demand curve both before and after the merger is DD'. The unit cost curve before the merger is $C_1 C_1'$, constant cost conditions are assumed for simplicity of exposition, price is equal to unit cost OC_1, and output is OQ_1. As a result of the merger it is assumed that costs are reduced to $C_2 C_2'$, price is elevated to OP_m and output reduced to OQ_2. To establish the net effect on welfare we have to balance gains against losses. The gains in this case are equal to area c; that is, they are the lower costs of producing the output of the monopolist. The loss is the reduction in consumer surplus which is associated with the fall in output brought about by the increase in price. The total loss of consumer surplus is area $(a + b)$, but area b is matched by an equivalent increase in producer surplus, so that the net loss is equal to area a. The net gain in welfare is therefore equal to area $(c - a)$. It is clear from the figure that the more the merger raises price and the more elastic demand is, *ceteris paribus* the larger area a will be, and therefore the more cost savings are needed to offset this loss. In addition, if there is pre-merger market power that maintains price above unit cost, the cost saving must be greater if the merger is to

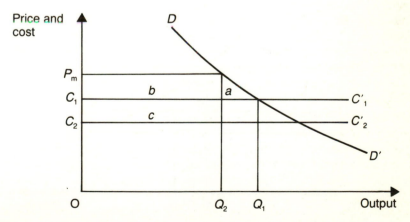

Figure 4.2 The welfare effect of a merger which achieves cost saving

result in a net increase in economic welfare. In this case (Figure 4.3), pre-merger price, P_1 is already above the competitive level C_1, and the merger strengthens market power allowing price to be elevated further to P_m. If the merger leads to increased efficiency so that costs are reduced to C_2, there is, as before, an efficiency gain equal to area c, but this must now be large enough to outweigh the loss of $(a + d)$ if there is to be a net gain. Area a represents, as before, net loss in consumer surplus and area d measures the loss in producer surplus caused by the fall in output from Q_1 to Q_2.

The examples given in Figures 4.2 and 4.3, in which the merger results in lower unit costs and higher prices, describe only one possible outcome. It is possible that in some cases a merger between firms will increase competitiveness and lower prices compared with the pre-merger position. This is most likely where the merger is between small or medium-sized firms, which are then able to compete more effectively with the giants. On the other hand, a merger may result in less efficiency and higher unit costs compared with a no-merger position. This possibility is discussed in Chapter 11, where the above framework of analysis is applied more generally to the welfare costs of monopoly.

There are, however, major data problems in making this analysis operational. They relate to the difficulties in obtaining reliable measures of market power and efficiency. It is common for some measure of industry concentration to be used as a proxy measure of market power, but there are well-known problems in such usage which are discussed in Chapter 5. As to measuring changes in efficiency, where these changes cannot be estimated directly, changes in profitability have been used as a proxy measure so that an increase in profitability is taken as a sign of increased efficiency and vice versa. An obvious difficulty here is that profitability may increase as a result of higher prices as well as of lower costs. These difficulties may be overcome, in part at least, if it can safely be assumed that any price increase resulting from a merger benefits all firms in an industry equally. If

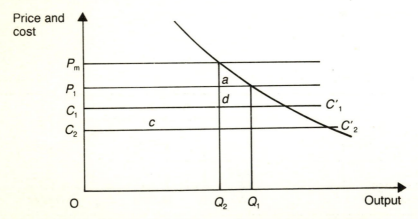

Figure 4.3 The welfare effect of a merger with pre-merger market power

the relative profitability performance of the merged company improves, this can then be taken as a sign of efficiency gains because all firms will have benefited from higher prices. It is important to note that it is the profit performance of the merged firm relative to that of an appropriate control group which has to be estimated – i.e. profitability performance has to be *normalised*. For instance, post-merger profitability may have fallen but by less than the industry average so that normalised profitability has increased.

Assuming, then, that it is possible to obtain some independent measure of the monopoly power effects of a merger, and that changes in normalised profitability can be used as a reasonable proxy for changes in efficiency, a summary can be compiled of the static welfare effects of mergers (see Table 4.2) (Hughes 1989).

The problems with this approach are not just those of data availability. There are major conceptual weaknesses as well. It is a partial equilibrium analysis that abstracts from all interactions between the various sectors of the economy, including for instance the knock-on effects which one merger may have in inducing further mergers amongst competing firms. It does not take account of the distributive effects of a merger. If the merger redistributes income from consumers to producers, this will normally mean a redistribution in favour of the better off. If such a change is regarded as undesirable it will count against the merger and allowance has to be made for this. Another complication is that there may be 'external effects' associated with a merger. For instance, a merger may increase market power, but it may also result in the internalising of an externality. In this case there are two effects of the merger with opposing impacts on the efficiency of resource allocation. Yet another difficulty is posed by the theory of second best. Given the existence of monopoly power elsewhere in the economy, it is not clear that a merger which increases monopoly power in a particular industry will have adverse resource allocation effects. Quite apart from any efficiency benefits that may be associated with a merger, the latter may result in an improvement in resource allocation. Lastly, and perhaps most important, the model presented on page 108 is a static one, which does not take account of the effects of a merger on investment in new assets and on technical progress.

Table 4.2 Static welfare effects of mergers

| Monopoly power | Normalised profits | | |
	Raised	No change	Reduced
Raised	W?	W–	W–
No change	W+	Wo	W–
Reduced	W+	W+	W?

W = social welfare (ignoring distributional considerations)

Data, even for the simple static analysis of the effects of mergers, are not readily available, and attempts at estimating these effects have had to rely on relatively crude methods. We now summarise briefly some of the main findings.

Empirical studies in this area differ with respect to the time period covered, the sample of firms chosen, the dimensions of performance chosen for investigation and also the methodology used. One approach that has been used is the case study of a relatively small number of companies, in which published information and evidence obtained from questionnaires are used to analyse the causes of mergers and to estimate their effects on efficiency and profitability. For instance, a US study by Kitching (1967) found that about a third of a sample of 19 acquisitions were judged as failures by the executives involved. Where the acquiring firms reported benefits from the merger, gains from improving the availability and cost of finance were found to be more important than economies in production. For the UK, Newbould (1970) found that post-merger performance was similarly unimpressive and that efficiency considerations were less important than market power in explaining merger activity. Another case-study treatment by Hart et al. (1973) revealed evidence of managerial diseconomies following merger. Several of the investigations of the Monopolies and Mergers Commission have also concluded that the evidence that mergers result in benefits of scale is very slim indeed.

One of the most ambitious case studies is that of Cowling et al. (1980), who examined the performance of 11 large mergers which occurred in the period 1966–69. They estimated post-merger efficiency gains using, as their measure of efficiency gain, changes in factor requirements per unit of output, i.e. average costs deflated by input prices, changes in this measure being inversely proportional to changes in efficiency. The methodology adopted was to measure the post-merger efficiency gains against an assumed counterfactual growth rate in efficiency of 1.5 per cent per annum. Post-merger comparisons were also made with industry averages and comparator firms. The authors encountered many data problems in this study and a great deal of judgement had to be used in interpreting the evidence. However, the overall result was that 5 out of the 11 mergers were judged to be successful in that their annual efficiency gains over the post-merger period exceeded 1.5 per cent.

A second approach is to compare the performance of firms that have grown exclusively or predominantly by internal growth with the performance of firms in the same industry or sector that have had an important merger component in their expansion. In the USA, a study by Reid (1968) relating to 478 of the 500 largest industrial corporations over the period 1951–61 showed that the profit performance (as measured by the growth in earnings for original stockholders) of pure internal-growth firms was very much superior to that of the active acquirers. The latter, however, had superior sales growth, which perhaps is not surprising. We would expect firms that have engaged in extensive merger activity to have a high growth rate, especially over relatively short periods. This rapid growth, however, need not result in any benefit to the economy as a whole, unless the growth of the consolidated firms is greater than that which would have been achieved had the acquired firms remained independent. However, it is not always the case that merger-prone firms achieve faster growth. For instance, a study by Scherer (1965) of the growth of 448 large manufacturing firms over the period 1955–59 found that the average sales growth of the 365 firms that had grown almost entirely through internal expansion was slightly higher than that of the 83 firms that had engaged in substantial merger activity. In the UK, a study by Utton (1974) compared the profit performance (pre-tax profits as a percentage of net assets) of merger-intensive firms with both industry performance and the performance of a randomly selected group of internal-growth firms. Both comparisons came out unfavourably to the merger-intensive growers.

A third approach to evaluating the effects of mergers is the 'before and after' comparison of profitability, in which the profit performance of the firm in the years following a merger is compared with the weighted average of the profitability of the separate firms before the merger took place. A simple comparison of profit performance will not do, because profitability is affected by so many other factors. For instance, post-merger profitability may show a decline, but this may be due to a general adverse change in the state of trade that has nothing to do with the merger itself. Some normalisation procedure therefore has to be used to make allowance for these factors. One possibility is to relate the profitability of the merging companies, both before and after the merger takes place, to the average profit performance of the industries in which the firms operate. Such a procedure was followed by Singh (1971), who, for a sample of 35 mergers in the period 1955–60, found that in just over half of the cases there was a decline in the pre-tax profitability of the acquiring firms relative to the industry average both in the year of takeover and also one and two years after the takeover took place. A similar but much larger study by Meeks (1977), covering the period 1964–71, came to much the same conclusion. He restricted his analysis to estimating the effects of one acquisition on the profit performance of his sample of firms, and he proceeded by comparing the weighted-average normalised pre-tax profitability of the sample of firms for three years before a merger with the normalised profitability of the merged firm in post-merger years. In all years up to the seventh year after merger, the firms in his sample showed a decline in profitability relative to the industry average. In all years the results also showed that a majority of mergers experienced a decline in profitability. The proportion was greatest in the fourth year following merger, when profitability was lower than in the pre-merger position in 66 per cent of the cases, and lowest in the second year after merger, when 52 per cent of the cases showed an adverse movement in profitability. In all years, therefore, there was a large minority of cases where post-merger profitability showed an improvement.

An alternative method of normalising pre- and post-merger performance is to compare the profit performance of active acquirers with a matched sample of non-acquirers. One such study by Kelly (1967), using US data for the period 1948–60, gave similar results to those already quoted. He took 20 pairs of firms with roughly comparable product lines and compared the average profit performance (profits as a percentage of sales) five years before and five years after merger activity on the part of the merging firm. The result was that, in 12 out of the 20 comparisons, the non-merging firm showed the bigger improvement in profit performance.

A UK study by Cosh *et al*. (1980) on mergers in the period 1967–69 reached rather different conclusions. In this study of quoted companies, the control group consisted of companies that were paired with the merging firms in terms of year, size and industry group and that were free from merger activity involving quoted companies. Three measures of profitability were used: trading profits on sales, net income on net assets, and net dividends and retentions on equity assets. A comparison of the post-merger profitability of the merging and non-merging firms showed no general tendency for the former to have worse performance. Indeed, statistically, the most striking result was that the merging firms had, on average, better performance in terms of post-tax profitability on equity assets. Furthermore, an analysis of post-merger changes in profitability showed merging firms to have the better performance on all three profit measures. Another interesting finding of this study is that non-horizontal acquisitions seem to come out best. Why is this? One possible reason is that integration costs might be less for non-horizontal acquisitions, and for diversification acquisitions in particular; a tendency that may be reinforced by the fact that in the sample of firms included in the study the size of the victim was usually smaller in non-horizontal acquisitions. Another possible explanation is that the management structure in diversified firms, in particular the M-form of organisation, might be better able to deal with the managerial problems of acquisitions.

There are clearly substantial problems in attempting to evaluate the effects of mergers on efficiency. Case studies may fail to be representative of mergers in general, and there are obvious dangers in relying on the replies to questionnaires. For those studies that rely on the published accounts of quoted companies, there are accounting problems that may not be fully resolved. Different definitions of profitability may yield different results. There are difficulties of finding a control group of companies with which to compare the performance of merging firms, particularly with regard to product range and relative opportunities for internal and external growth. There are problems in determining how long an adjustment period should be allowed before one can expect to see the real effects of a merger. Those who tend to support merger activity are critical of some studies, because insufficient allowance has been made for post-merger reorganisation and not enough time allowed, therefore, for the benefits of a merger to be realised. But this argument may work the other way as well. Since individual studies relate to a relatively short time period, they fail to pick up possible longer-term adverse effects on efficiency. A number of studies of the effects of mergers in a sector of industry covering only a few years may each find only a small adverse effect on efficiency, yet the total effect over the whole period may be substantial. Indeed, in many studies where the effect of mergers on profitability has been found to be adverse, the size of this adverse effect has been small. This, however, is hardly a strong defence of mergers, especially if these small adverse effects are repeated in subsequent merger activity. There are also problems in using profitability as a guide to efficiency. Where post-merger profitability improves relative to the industry average or to a matched sample of firms, this may be due to increased efficiency, to increased market power, or to some combination of the two. It is reasonable to assume that, in the majority of cases, mergers do not reduce market power, in which case a decline in post-merger profitability signifies a loss in efficiency. However, market power may decrease as a result of other factors; for example, increased competition in overseas markets. Ideally, this should be allowed for in the normalisation procedures, but full allowance may not be made if, for instance, merging firms are more heavily engaged in international competition than non-merging ones. Lastly, none of these studies tells us what the alternative position would actually have been in the absence of mergers. Even where profitability declines owing to a loss of efficiency in the merging firm, there may have been no better alternative.

Because of the difficulties in evaluating the effects of mergers using accounting data, a number of investigators have adopted a different approach, which is to examine movements in the return on securities. The methodology adopted in most of these studies has been the 'event' study, where the procedure is to compare actual returns to shareholders, in a sample of acquiring and acquired companies, with what the returns would have been in the absence of merger (the counterfactual return). The counterfactual return is estimated from an equation based on a data set which excludes data for a period before and after merger. The difference between the actual and counterfactual return is the abnormal return attributable to the merger 'event'. By choosing a reference point at some date prior to the merger, the cumulative abnormal return can be calculated, and this can be positive, negative or zero.

One example of a counterfactual model is the following:

$$R^*_{jt} = \alpha_j + \beta_j rm_t$$

$$AR_{jt} = r_{jt} - (\alpha_j + \beta_j rm_t)$$

where R^*_{jt} is the counterfactual return on security j in month t,

rm is the return on a market index,

α and β are the coefficients of the regression equation used to estimate R^*_{jt},

r is the actual return on the security,

AR is the abnormal return.

The results of studies using this type of methodology can be summarised as follows. For acquiring firms there are usually positive abnormal returns in the period close to the bid announcement. However, these positive short-run effects are outweighed in the longer term by negative effects. For acquired companies the most striking finding is that typically there are slightly negative abnormal returns in the year or so before an acquisition but large positive abnormal returns near to the bid date, with estimated cumulative abnormal returns ranging between 20 and 30 per cent. Taking acquiring and acquired firms together there seem, at best, to be positive abnormal effects typically lasting for just a few months after a merger. However, over the longer term, cumulative abnormal returns tend to be negative – i.e. short-term gains are typically not sustained and the share prices of merging companies decline relative to the values that would have been attained had the shares performed as well as those of non-merging firms.

By and large, therefore, the analysis of shareholder returns support the analysis of the effects of mergers based on company accounts. Positive abnormal returns tend, on average, to be very short-lived. Furthermore there is considerable doubt as to whether share movements resulting from merger reflect systematically changes in the efficiency with which assets are managed. They may also reflect other factors such as enhanced prospects of exploiting market power.

In view of the formidable array of problems involved in conducting research in this field and in interpreting the evidence, it is as well to be cautious in one's conclusions. The balance of evidence to date, however, does suggest that considerable scepticism should be displayed towards the alleged benefits of mergers.

Mergers, investment and growth

We mentioned in the previous section that an important weakness of the simple approach to the effects of merger based on a trade-off between monopoly pricing and cost reduction is its static nature and its failure to take account of the possible wider repercussions that mergers may have on investment, structural change and growth.

It should be emphasised that, although expansion by merger may have several advantages from the point of view of the firm, there need be no corresponding benefits to the economy as a whole. The economy benefits only if a merger results in advantages (e.g. economies of scale, rationalisation of production) that would not otherwise be realised or, more generally, results in a more competitive industry than would otherwise be the case.

What relationship may be expected between mergers and the rate of capital accumulation? There are arguments that suggest that mergers may lead to less rapid capital accumulation than internal growth. Other arguments point in the opposite direction.

In the short run, a merger may have an adverse effect on investment because of the greater proportion of managerial resources required to coordinate activities within the enlarged firm. In time the managerial problems associated with a merger may be sorted out, but these problems often cause acute short-to medium-term difficulties.

In the long run, the possible adverse effect that mergers may have on investment is associated with the monopolisation of an industry. Take the extreme case where a highly competitive industry is transformed by a series of mergers into a monopoly. In the initial position, firms plan to compete by expanding capacity, although each firm's expansion may involve the others in losses. If the industry is transformed into a monopoly, these losses are internalised, with the result that investment will be reduced. Similar effects may occur if mergers so reduce the number of competitors that competition between the remaining firms is seriously blunted.

However, there are other considerations which suggest that the impact of mergers on investment may be a positive one. Of particular importance is the balance between safety and competition, to which attention has been drawn in the previous chapter. The distinction made above between a highly competitive and a monopolised industry can give the wrong impression of the typical effect of a merger. Closer attention needs to be paid to both the initial market structure and that which will come into being as the result of a merger. It may be that in the initial situation the intensity of competition is so great, and the risks associated with rationalisation schemes or new capacity so high, that businessmen in general are simply not prepared to undertake the necessary investment. In such cases mergers may be a precondition for investment and structural change. Nor does it follow that mergers necessarily result in a lessening of competition, higher prices and lower output. They may in fact intensify competition, particularly when they result in a market structure of more evenly balanced rivals in which there is more oligopolistic rivalry – including rivalry in the creation of new capacity.

Empirical work in this area by Meeks (1977) and Kumar (1984) suggests that on balance the impact of merger on investment is favourable, the evidence being that active acquirers on average also invest more heavily than average in new fixed assets. Although suggestive, the evidence is not of course conclusive because we do not know what the investment performance of the active acquirers would have been had they been prevented from making so many acquisitions and put more emphasis on internal expansion. Again it is important to emphasise the big overlap between groups of firms. A majority of firms may be found to have better post-merger investment performance than the control group, but a large minority (typically 40–49 per cent) do not.

It is also interesting to note some of the other findings of research in this area, particularly those reported by Kumar. First, for acquisitions where investment expenditure of the acquired firm was a large proportion of the combined investment of the acquired and acquiring firms, the majority of cases showed a worsening of performance for several years after the date of acquisition. Second, for horizontal mergers very little difference was found between pre- and post-merger performance. Third, the difference between pre- and post-merger performance, and the beneficial effects of mergers, were found to be greatest for non-horizontal acquisitions. If investment performance is better for non-horizontal mergers why is this? One possibility is that these mergers often involve diversification into sectors that offer better investment opportunities to the acquiring firm. Another is that, whereas the motive for horizontal mergers may often be defensive and market power seeking, diversification mergers are more closely associated with growth and a more positive management approach in seeking out new opportunities. It may also be the case, as noted earlier, that fewer managerial resources are needed to integrate activities in a diversification merger, so that a higher proportion of managerial resources is available for planning new investment.

4.4 AGGREGATE CONCENTRATION

Predictions

What concrete predictions does the economic analysis of the growth of firms offer about the likely course of aggregate concentration? Over the years many economists have predicted a growing concentration of industry, this prediction being based on such factors as technological and organisational imperatives or the outcome of the competitive process. Writing in 1887, Karl Marx saw technological change and the growing importance of large-scale production as a major factor in the centralisation of capital. An essential instrument in this process was the emergence of the joint stock company and of a reliable market in securities, which allowed large amounts of capital to be concentrated in one firm. As centralisation proceeds Marx argued that price competition between surviving firms would become increasingly intense and that this would encourage the formation of cartels and mergers. The process of centralisation would be aided by the role of the banks and other financial institutions in promoting acquisitions and mergers.

Technological and organisational factors also feature in Galbraith's writing in the 1960s (Galbraith 1972). He argued that the development of modern technology has resulted in longer gestation periods for investment, increased capital requirements, more inflexible methods of production and more internal organisation. Where these developments occur – mainly, according to Galbraith, in the industrial and financial sectors – it becomes increasingly necessary for the firm to control its environment. This means a measure of control over such factors as product prices, demand and the supply of inputs. In seeking to achieve this control the firm may expand well beyond the technically optimum size.

In Penrose's analysis, the focus of attention is on whether there are any managerial limits to the growth of firms (Penrose 1966). It is argued that a firm with appropriate managerial services will be able to expand without limit. There is no limit on absolute size, only on the growth rate per unit of time. Does this mean that large firms will tend to absorb ever-larger proportions of the economy's resources?

A firm's attainable growth rate will be determined by the ratio between the managerial services available for expansion and the managerial services required per unit of expansion. With increased size there may be a tendency for the proportion of managerial services required for current operations to increase, thus leaving a smaller proportion available for planning expansion. However, the administrative task need not grow proportionately with the size of the firm. New management methods (including new organisational forms such as the multi-divisional form of organisation), the use of labour-saving devices in management and the use of more capital-intensive methods in production may contribute to making the management task relatively easier. The factor most likely to increase the proportion of managerial services required for current operations is competition with other large firms. The managerial services required per unit of expansion depend on the character of the expansion, and particularly on such factors as the variety of products that are produced, the number of separate plants and, again, the intensity of competition.

The implications of this analysis for concentration are rather weak. Penrose herself expected overall concentration to stabilise and even fall as it becomes more difficult for large firms as a group to take advantage of the same percentage of total opportunities. There is nothing in the analysis, however, that tells us at what level of concentration this is likely to happen. It should also be added that the outcome will depend rather heavily on the rate of expansion of the economy as a whole, which in turn will determine the number of opportunities for productive investment.

Further insights into the likely course of industrial concentration are obtained from Downie's analysis of the competitive process (Downie 1958). His theorising is constructed around two fundamental competitive mechanisms: the transfer mechanism and the innovation mechanism. The former is the process whereby efficient firms gain market share at the expense of the inefficient, and the latter summarises the forces that bear upon the incentive to innovate.

At any moment in time an industry will be composed of firms of varying degrees of efficiency, because innovations come about as a result of the efforts of individual firms and because any new knowledge embodied in these innovations is diffused only slowly. Thus, currently, the most efficient firms are the ones that have been the most successful innovators in preceding periods. The inefficient firms are the ones that have consistently failed to undertake research or to seek access to improved technology. Given the pattern of relative efficiencies, the more efficient firms will steadily expand at the expense of the less efficient, so that output becomes concentrated in fewer hands. The transfer mechanism will be particularly powerful where there are many firms and where differences in efficiency are initially very large. As the most inefficient firms are successively eliminated from the market, however, efficiency differences will diminish, and the transfer mechanism is weakened. This tendency will be reinforced if the move towards more concentrated oligopolistic structures is accompanied by more entrenched collusive behaviour.

The transfer mechanism, it seems, will push an industry, at first quickly and then more slowly, towards higher levels of concentration. However, the threat to the existence of the inefficient firm embodied in this mechanism is itself the stimulant to the innovation mechanism. The incentive to innovate is strongly related to external trading conditions, so the greater the competitive pressure upon firms, the more they are forced to look to a technological breakthrough for economic salvation. At the same time, the most efficient firms, whose current market leadership is based upon their past technological superiority, will feel little pressure to continue their search for advances. If the innovation mechanism is governed mainly by these forces acting upon the incentive to innovate, it will tend to undo the work of the transfer mechanism and arrest the move towards higher concentration. Leadership in innovation will change hands, and this will mean continual changes in the efficiency ranking of firms.

However, the conditions necessary for the innovation mechanism to be powerful enough to offset the transfer mechanism are clearly very stringent indeed and are unlikely in practice to be fully satisfied. For instance, even if there is a strong tendency for innovative leadership to change hands, the interval between innovations may mean that long time lags are involved. In this case the transfer mechanism may result in the emergence of a small group of large firms with market power, which a much smaller innovative firm will have difficulty in dislodging. Furthermore, large firms may well adopt the strategy of acquiring any small competitor likely to pose a threat because of its technological expertise. Failing this, they may adopt predatory tactics to drive such firms into bankruptcy. For the innovative mechanism to operate effectively it has to be responsive to competitive pressures and highly unresponsive to such factors as luck and the availability of finance.

Another important element in Downie's analysis is the role of new entry, which is seen to be dominated by the diversifying activities of large firms moving in the main from high-concentration to low-concentration industries. In highly concentrated industries the transfer mechanism will be weak, because only very small differences in efficiency between firms persist and because collusive behaviour is highly probable. The innovation mechanism will also be weak, since there will be little threat to the existence of individual firms. Consequently, there will be a tendency for market shares to stabilise. The growth aspirations of firms will therefore have to be satisfied by diversification into industries with lower concentration and considerable dispersion of efficiency. It follows that there will be a certain irreversibility about the process of concentration. Industries that have become highly concentrated will tend to remain so, and the diversification of large firms from high-concentration to low-concentration industries will tend to push the latter in the same direction by speeding up the transfer mechanism.

Overall, therefore, Downie's analysis seems to predict that there will be a general tendency in a free enterprise economy for the level of aggregate concentration to increase and for large firms to come to hold positions of market power in more than one industry.

Downie's theory predicts an increase in concentration due to mechanisms inherent in the market economy. Stochastic models take an entirely different approach to the explanation of concentration. One such model is the 'law of proportionate effect', which in its strong form states that, irrespective of initial size, all firms have the same probability of growing at a given proportionate rate during any period of time: that is,

$$S_{it}/S_{it-1} = E$$

where S_{it} and S_{it-1} are the size of firm i at the end and beginning respectively of a period of time, and E is a random variable that is distributed independently of initial firm size. In other words, the size distribution of firms will be the result of a large number of random influences affecting all firms. The implication is that, with a given population of firms, there will be an increase in concentration. The reason for this is that, although each firm faces the same distribution of growth possibilities regardless of past history and initial size, actual growth rates will nevertheless differ over any particular period simply because some firms will have more luck than others. Consequently, starting from a situation where there are many firms of equal size, at the end of, say, a five-year period some firms will have jumped ahead of the pack. In the next period each firm, from the largest to the smallest, will again have the same chance of growing by a given proportionate amount. As a result, some of the leading firms at the end of the first five-year period will jump even further ahead, again because of chance factors. In this way a small number of firms will attain positions of dominance. How quickly concentration increases will depend on the variation in growth rates. If the variation in growth rates is large, concentration will increase rapidly.

It should be noted that some of the results noted earlier in this chapter are not consistent with the strict version of the law of proportionate effect. According to this version there should be no relationship between size and growth, and also there should be no relationship between size and the dispersion of growth rates. Yet some empirical studies have found these relationships to exist. This, of course, does not mean that chance factors are unimportant in explaining increases in concentration. There are in fact weaker forms of the law of proportionate effect, which, while maintaining the importance of chance factors, also allow for other influences. Many of these stochastic models do produce firm size distributions that are similar to those observed in the real world.

What are the non-stochastic, systematic influences on concentration? For one thing, if the growth rates of firms in one year and the next are not independent of each other, the forces that favour some firms and penalise others may be even more powerful. Thus, for instance, if a firm is fortunate in the appointment of a chief executive, it will reap the benefit over a run of years, while others may suffer over several years the misfortune of incompetent management. Where such periods of good or bad management occur, cumulative forces may come into play, with success breeding success in one group of firms and failure breeding failure in another. Again, the initial boost to one firm's fortunes as a consequence of pure luck may be reinforced if there are scale advantages to be reaped, by means of which the firm gains a competitive advantage over its rivals and the trend towards high concentration accelerates.

One other factor that must be mentioned is the role of mergers. An important weakness of stochastic models is their treatment of births and deaths. The disappearance of medium- and large-sized firms is due overwhelmingly to acquisitions and mergers, whose role in explaining increases in concentration needs careful assessment. This assessment is left to the next chapter.

We should note two other factors that work against the forces making for greater concentration. One is changing comparative advantage in international trade. Many of our largest companies have declined in importance or indeed have suffered extinction because comparative advantage in the industries in which they were based has moved to newly developing economies. Such has been the fate of many businesses in textiles, iron and steel, and shipbuilding. The other factor is innovation. There is little doubt that any tendency towards higher levels of concentration would be much stronger but for the effects of product and process innovation. Product innovation in particular has created entirely new industries. This has opened up completely new opportunities for all firms and represents an important offsetting factor to the forces tending towards more monopolistic structures.

Evidence

Precise comparisons of the levels of aggregate concentration over a very long period are not possible because of data problems. There can be little doubt, however, that the share of the 100 or 200 largest companies in manufacturing activity is substantially higher today than it was in the first quarter of this century. For the UK it has been estimated that the share of the 100 largest manufacturing companies in total manufacturing net output was about 16 per cent in 1909 and 41 per cent in 1970. In the USA it has been estimated that the share of the 100 largest firms in manufacturing net output was about 22 per cent in 1909 and about 33 per cent in 1970 (see Prais 1976).

These long-term upward movements have not, however, been uninterrupted. In both countries aggregate concentration seems to have declined during the Second World War and immediate postwar years after increasing over the previous two or three decades. This may be due to the fact that the small-firm sector was able to gain relative to large firms during the boom of the war and early postwar years. Furthermore, after showing an upward trend from the late 1940s to the late 1960s–early 1970s, aggregate concentration seems once again to have stabilised.

In the UK the share of the largest 100 firms in manufacturing net output stood at around 20 per cent in 1948, 37 per cent in 1963 and just over 40 per cent in 1970. Over the period 1948–70, therefore, the 100 largest manufacturing firms just about doubled their share. This finding of a substantial increase in the share of the largest firms, which is based on Census of Production data, is confirmed by data on the balance sheet value of net assets of the 100 largest industrial companies whose ordinary or preference shares were quoted on the UK stock exchange. Companies in manufacturing, construction, transport and communication, distributive trades and miscellaneous services are included. The figures show that in 1948 the 100 largest firms controlled 47 per cent of company assets, while in 1968 they controlled 69 per cent. For the 50 largest firms the figures were 35 per cent and 51 per cent respectively. The rate of increase in the share of these large firms was particularly strong after the mid 1950s. The share of the 100 largest firms in total net assets showed a relatively small increase between 1948 and 1957, from 46.5 per cent to 50.7 per cent, but a much more marked increase between 1957 and 1968, from 50.7 per cent to over 60 per cent. The latter period coincided with one of intense merger activity in the UK. The contribution of mergers to increased levels of concentration is examined in Chapter 5. At this point suffice it to say that mergers may well have played an important part in the changes that took place during the period 1948–68.

In the USA there has also been an upward trend in aggregate concentration in the postwar years, although not so marked as that in the UK. The 100 largest firms accounted for 23 per cent of manufacturing value added in 1947, 30 per cent in 1958, 33 per cent in 1963 and 33 per cent in 1970. In terms of company assets, the 100 largest firms controlled about 40 per cent of the manufacturing sector in 1947 and about 50 per cent in 1968. Figures for the six original European Communities (EC) countries over the 1960s also suggest a substantial increase in aggregate concentration (see Jacquemin and de Jong 1977).

In contrast to the period before 1970, aggregate concentration seems to have remained stable or even declined slightly in many countries during the 1970s. For the UK, Clarke and Davies (1983) using Census of Production data found a very slight reduction in the level of aggregate concentration (measured by the Herfindahl index) for the manufacturing sector.

All the work on aggregate concentration discussed so far has concentrated on manufacturing industry. It could be argued that this is no longer appropriate in a world in which large manufacturing firms are diversified into sectors of the economy such as mining, transportation, distribution, and finance. To get a true picture of levels and trends in aggregate concentration some measure of aggregate concentration which goes beyond manufacturing is needed. The main problem here is that the data are not readily available. However, Hughes and Kumar (1984) have provided a range of measures for the period 1968–80. Their conclusions are, broadly, that aggregate concentration in more widely defined sectors (e.g. the non-financial private sector and the whole private sector of the economy) continued to increase until the mid 1970s (later than indicated for manufacturing above) and then fell slightly. Their estimates of the share of the top 100 companies in the non-financial private sector for the years 1968, 1975 and 1980 are 24.0 per cent, 26.5 per cent and 26.4 per cent respectively.

The figures that have been given so far relate to the largest companies in any particular year, but the membership of the top 100 club is not stable. The rate of turnover among the largest firms is also a matter of some importance. For instance, a study by Whittington (1972) of UK companies in manufacturing, construction, transport and communications, distribution, and miscellaneous services found that, of the top 100 companies in 1948, 52 were still in the top 100 in 1968 and 48 had 'died'. This implies an average death rate of 2.4 firms per annum, which is similar to US experience over the same period.

What conclusions can be drawn from figures on turnover among large firms? First, the changing identity of the top companies reflects in part the shifting pattern of demand for goods and services. Firms whose main interests lie in declining sectors of the economy (e.g. shipbuilding, traditional textiles) will give way to those in the expanding sectors (e.g. chemicals, electronics).

Second, in so far as there has been a tendency for the position of the giants to become more entrenched, this may be associated with the emergence of a management class that has a vested interest in preserving the firm as an organis-ation. In general it has been in the interests of this class to seek greater security and status by emphasising the growth of the organisation, including growth by diversification.

Third, we may ask what implications, if any, the rate of turnover among the top firms has for assessing the degree of competitiveness of the economy. Here in particular it is difficult to draw any firm conclusions. Whereas some obervers may be impressed by the fact that in the UK, for example, as many as 52 firms managed to keep in the top 100 over a 20-year period, others will want to emphasise the fact that 48 firms failed to maintain their position at the top.

However, even if we could agree what constituted a high rate of turnover, before we could take it as a sign of competitiveness we would need to examine the reasons why the companies disappeared. The suggestion that a high rate of turnover indicates a high degree of competitiveness would be most convincing if it were found that the majority of firms disappearing from the top 100 were displaced by faster-growing firms moving up from further down the list. This, however, may not be the case. In the UK, 36 of the 48 companies that left the top 100 between 1948 and 1968 disappeared because of acquisition or merger or nationalisation. In only 12 cases was a company relegated from the top 100 without losing its independent identity, and, as one would expect, the majority of these firms were at the lower end of the top 100 ranking in 1948. In the 1980s also, many large companies (e.g. Distillers, Imperial Tobacco and Rowntree/ Macintosh) disappeared as a result of acquisition. It is not at all clear that a high rate of turnover should be regarded as evidence of a high degree of competition, if the turnover is mainly due to intensive merger activity. In fact, this process may weaken competition by increasing the dominance of the largest companies.

4.5 THE LARGE DIVERSIFIED FIRM AND RESOURCE ALLOCATION

In the previous section we have noted the extent to which industrial activity in many countries has become dominated by a relatively small number of large companies. The existence of large, highly diversified firms is a major feature of modern-day economies, and it is important to have some idea of the quantitative importance of this development and of its significance for resource allocation.

Quantitative importance of diversification

A major problem in measuring the extent of diversification is that of defining the product and of classifying products to industries. Should we use the two-digit level of classification, which divides activity into broad classes (e.g. electrical and electronic engineering, vehicles, rubber and plastic products), or the four-digit grouping into more narrowly specified activities? Use of the broad two-digit classification will grossly underestimate the extent of diversification. A firm in the electrical engineering field, for instance, has a large number of quite distinct products to choose from without venturing outside the two-digit class. A finer breakdown is clearly desirable, but not so fine as to count as separate products different varieties of what is essentially a single product. Such a distinction cannot always be easily drawn. In any event it is obvious that the measured degree of diversification will depend on how fine an industrial classification is used (see Chapter 5).

It will also depend on the measure of diversification used. One possibility is simply to count the number of products. The weakness of this method is that some of the products may account for only a tiny proportion of the total sales of the firm. In addition, two firms may be producing the same number of products, but the products of one may be in very different trades (e.g. vehicles and aircraft engines) whereas the products of the other are confined to one sector (e.g. vehicles). Another method is to take the ratio of the output of non-primary product lines to total output. In this case, however, the measured diversification of two firms may be the same, even though diversification in one could quite reasonably be argued to be greater than that in the other. For instance, firm A may have 70 per cent of its output in one product and the remaining 30 per cent in another, while firm B has the same percentage of output accounted for by its primary product but the remaining 30 per cent spread evenly over another three products. These difficulties can be overcome to some extent by a measure that combines information on the number of products and on their share in total output. One such method is to multiply the ratio of non-primary to total output by the number of industries in which the firm has at least, say, 5 per cent of sales. Another suggestion is that the Herfindahl index of concentration should be applied to the distribution of a firm's output over different products. Thus, the index is

$$D_H = 1 - \sum_{i=1}^{n} P_i^2$$

where P_i is the proportion of the firm's sales in industry i.

No one summary measure, however, can capture the full complicated picture of diversification, and the problems of product classification and also of data availability will themselves pose formidable obstacles to accurate measurement.

Nevertheless, in spite of the measurement problems there can be little doubt that diversification is an extremely important aspect of modern-day industrial society. As one might expect, the largest companies tend to be the most diversified. Highly diversified giants that spring to mind include General Electric and International Telephone and Telegraph (ITT) in the USA; ICI and GEC in the UK; and Philips in the Netherlands. Utton (1979) attempted to measure systematically the extent of diversification in UK manufacturing industry. He used Census of Production data for 1972 to measure the distribution of the activities of the 200 largest firms across 120 industries. On average, these firms were found to have 43 per cent of their employment outside their primary industry, equivalent, on average, to a firm operating equally in 4.4 industries. Utton also found evidence of a marked increase in the extent of diversification in the postwar period, and that the decade 1958–68 could be viewed as one of intensive diversification. The increase in diversification within manufacturing in this period is confirmed by Clarke and Davies (1983), but their findings suggest that it was due entirely to an increase in narrow-spectrum diversification and that diversification across broad classes actually declined.

However, as mentioned earlier it may be misleading to restrict the study of diversification to the manufacturing sector when it is known that large manufacturing companies have substantial interests in non-manufacturing activities. Using sales data obtained from company accounts, Cosh et al. (1985) found a substantial increase in the diversification of large UK quoted companies during the 1970s.

Consequences for resource allocation

Diversification is not, of course, a new element in the growth of firms. The outstanding reason for the growing importance of diversification over the past 30 years is that it has become a strategy of development rather than simply a response to adverse market conditions. This has been associated with the growing professionalisation of management and with the growth of a managerial class whose main interest is to preserve the firm as a successful organisation. In pursuing this goal, managers have sought to reduce their insecurity and enhance their status by expansion, including expansion by diversification. Diversification has been facilitated by developments in management techniques, especially the greater use of computers and the adoption of decentralised forms of organisation.

What are the consequences of increased diversification for the performance of the competitive system? The integration of economic activity in a capitalist economy takes place in three main ways: by means of transactions in the market between completely independent buyers and sellers, by cooperation between decision-making units, and by the administration of resources within firms. The growing importance of the large diversified firm means that the integration of economic activity has come to depend more on the planning of activities within firms and less on competition in the market. Managerial decision-making and the allocation of resources within the firm have thus become much more important matters for investigation. The key issue is that of the relative efficiency of resource allocation within the firm and by means of the market mechanism. To what extent is competition for investment funds in the market adequately replaced by competition for funds between the various branches within a firm, and to what extent is the large firm forced, or indeed able, to maintain a high level of efficiency in the use of existing assets in each of its main activities? A great deal obviously depends on the form of organisation, the extent to which the internal transactions of the firm are based on 'arm's length' prices, and the extent to which individual branches or divisions are tightly controlled on a profit and loss basis. From this point of view it has been argued that the multidivisional form of organisation has the advantage over more centralised or unitary forms.

Before turning to this issue, however, it should be mentioned that there are those who see little need to be concerned about the large diversified company. Thus, for instance, it is pointed out that high levels of aggregate concentration are compatible with no firms having significant power in individual markets. Market shares may be relatively low, and competition between firms may be intense. This view would not deny that positions of market power exist; it simply holds that it would be a mistake to draw conclusions about competitiveness from information on aggregate concentration alone.

It has already been seen (Chapter 2) that an argument in favour of the multi-divisional form of organisation is that it is likely to achieve greater internal efficiency than other forms of organisation of similar size. It is also claimed that there are important resource allocation advantages associated with the M-form of organisation. Where retained profits are an important source of finance for investment, the argument in essence is that the firm can act as a mini capital market, channelling funds from low- to high-profit areas more quickly than would occur in a system characterised by several specialised U-form organis-ations. In this case, therefore, the diversified company may facilitate more rapid resource reallocation and thus contribute towards a more adaptable economic system.

Another possible advantage of the large diversified company is that it increases competition by facilitating entry into industries where the barriers to entry are too high for smaller, more specialised firms. Entry into a new industry may take place either by building entirely new facilities or by acquiring an existing firm. In the former case there is an increase in the productive capacity and in the number of decision-making units in the industry. This does not necessarily mean that competitive pressures in the industry will be intensified. For instance, the new entrant may join existing tacit arrangements relating to prices and output rather than act independently. However, the addition of new capacity, particularly if it embodies more advanced technology, is very likely to give competitive pressures a boost. Diversification by acquisition leaves the number of decision-making units unchanged and, initially at least, has no effect on capacity. Even so, it may result in the replacement of an inefficient management, or simply in the loosening of long-standing collusive behaviour in an industry, and thus increase competitiveness.

The existence of large diversified firms also poses problems for the efficient allocation of resources, however.

First, the efficiency of resource allocation within the firm still depends on the control exercised by top management. Even though the decentralised form of organisation may have eased the problems of managing large companies, it has not eliminated the problems of coordination and of adaptation to change. The basic strategic decisions (e.g. the hiring of key management personnel, the allocation of investment funds) remain in the hands of top management. When the large firm has monopoly power in individual markets, management is not *compelled* to be as efficient as possible. Furthermore, any organisational form will eventually run into problems of communication and control if it continues to grow. Also, in the field of invention and innovation, it has been pointed out by several investigators that the contribution of large corporations has often fallen far short of what might be expected of them, given their resources. Outside a small number of areas, large firms have been accused of concentrating the bulk of their research and development (R&D) on projects that result in modest advances rather than on the introduction of radically new products and processes. Indeed, it has been suggested that, if inventiveness and innovation are to be accelerated, the need is for less emphasis on the large corporation. In relation to these questions of efficiency, one can safely say that, while the form of organisation will undoubtedly affect the performance of large firms, a great deal will also depend on the excellence of a few top managers. For large firms as a group this implies reliance on the widespread and continuing availability of high-quality management, but experience shows that the quality of top management in large firms varies greatly.

Second, the large firm by virtue of its sheer size will have financial power, which may be used to distort competition. The most familiar possibility is that of cross-subsidisation. The large diversified firm may use its financial power to discipline specialist rivals who engage in price-cutting. Smaller producers, recognising the much greater financial strength of the large firm, may well be forced to modify their competitive policies for fear of retaliation. The mere expectation of a reaction may itself be sufficient to restrain the behaviour of specialised firms. Price-cutting, subsidised by profits from other markets where the firm has monopoly power, may also be carried further in an attempt to eliminate rivals from the market or to forestall the entry of new firms. The firm pursuing such a strategy must, of course, have monopoly profits in at least one protected market. Even where such profits exist, there is a limit to the extent to which it is worth using them to subsidise price-cutting behaviour. Whether such a strategy is worthwhile depends on whether entry barriers can be raised sufficiently to ensure higher long-term profits and also on the feasibility and cost of alternative strategies (e.g. acquisition, collusion) to achieve the same result. It must not be forgotten, however, that the mere presence of diversified firms in an industry may increase the barriers to entry for specialised firms. This will be the case if potential entrants *expect* diversified firms to react to new entry by various forms of predatory behaviour not available to specialised firms.

The large firm may also use excess profits in one market to finance heavy advertising in another, so as to extend its sphere of monopoly influence. This possibility is present in particular where marketing rather than technology is the main basis of diversification. It is in the field of marketing that large firms have perhaps their greatest advantage over small ones, especially where such factors as brand names, national advertising and style changes are important. In such circumstances a small number of diversified firms may build up a position in one industry to finance heavy sales promotion in another. Furthermore, once a dominant position has been established, the heavy marketing expenditures themselves constitute an entry barrier to new competition.

Other adverse forms of behaviour available to diversified firms are tie-in sales and full-line forcing. In the former the sale of product A (the tying product) is made conditional on the sale of another product B (the tied product), as when the price of colour film is set at a level that covers the cost of developing and printing, so that the buyer is not free to choose where to have his film processed. Full-line forcing is a similar practice by which a purchaser is forced to buy the full range of goods offered by a supplier and not just those which the purchaser wishes to buy. An example of full-line forcing in the UK involved oil companies, which required petrol stations to stock named brands of lubricants, antifreeze, paraffin, tyres and batteries. Exclusive dealing is another restrictive practice by which a firm producing two goods A and B will supply customers with A only on condition that any B that the customer wants is bought from the same source and not from rival firms.

These practices must obviously benefit the firm that engages in them, otherwise they would not be pursued. How successful they are will depend on whether retailers and other customers can secure supplies in adequate quantities from other manufacturers who do not enforce tying arrangements or exclusive dealing. Where these practices are firmly entrenched, however, are they likely to have an adverse effect on competition? The answer is that they may have. The more successful large manufacturers are in negotiating tying or exclusive-dealing arrangements with their customers, the more difficult life becomes for the smaller specialist producer. In addition, by restricting the available marketing outlets, the entry barriers facing new firms are raised. A freely competitive distributive sector is important for maintaining competition among manufacturers, and it is for this reason that tying arrangements and exclusive dealings are generally condemned by those responsible for framing monopoly and restrictive practices legislation.

A further possible distortion to competition associated with large diversified firms arises from their interdependence as buyers and sellers. The greater the proportion of activity accounted for by a relatively small number of large firms, the more frequently will we find that firm A is not only an important supplier of firm B but also an important customer of firm B. There is then a danger that a growing proportion of inter-firm transactions will be determined more by considerations of bargaining power than by strict comparisons of price and quality. In other words, inputs may be purchased from a good customer rather than from a smaller lower-cost firm that has little to offer by way of a reciprocal order. Here again there are clearly limits, in this case one suspects rather sharp ones, to the extent to which firms are prepared to accept higher-priced or lower-quality inputs even from important customers. However, even where no sacrifice is made on price, quality, reliability of supply, and so on, any tendency towards reciprocal dealing may still have anti-competitive effects, both by enabling large firms to increase their market shares and also by increasing obstacles to new entry.

It has to be recognised that, even if the economy is dominated by large firms, there can still be substantial competition between large firms themselves. Exploitation of a monopoly position by one large firm carries with it the danger of attracting competition from another. It is most unlikely, however, that the actual and potential competition will be sufficient to ensure a competitive outcome in all cases. Rather, it is probable that in some cases the main activity of one firm will be a secondary activity of another and that, recognising the dangers of spoiling each other's markets, firms will develop 'spheres of influence'. Alternatively, when firms have the same product range, spheres of influence may develop on a geographical basis. If mutual interpenetration of markets does occur and profits are eroded to unacceptably low levels, this may be followed by restrictive agreements or mergers or schemes designed to 'rationalise production'. There is certainly a danger that an increase in aggregate concentration resulting from the diversification activities of large firms will subsequently result in increased market dominance in the interests of what businessmen frequently describe as 'more orderly marketing'.

Examples of cross-subsidisation, tie-in sales, reciprocal dealing and other anti-competitive practices are not difficult to find. Although one suspects that in some cases the number of publicly known examples may be only the tip of the iceberg, one must also guard against the danger of exaggerating the anti-competitive consequences of the emergence of large diversified firms. The foregoing analysis shows clearly that the arguments do not all lie on the same side. As far as policy is concerned, the important point is to be aware not only of the advantages of large diversified firms but also of the dangers that they carry for the maintenance of competitive market structures.

Chapter 5

Market structure

5.1 INTRODUCTION

The previous two chapters have focused attention on the firm, and particularly on large diversified companies. This emphasis on the behaviour and performance of the firm as a whole is justified by the high proportion of manufacturing activity which is now accounted for in all industrialised countries by a relatively small number of companies. However, firms do of course operate in markets and their behaviour can be expected to be influenced by the structure of these markets. Therefore, we turn in this chapter to examining the main structural features of individual markets. One problem which immediately arises is that of defining the market; in principle a market consists of all the firms which produce a particular product, but the need to find a definition of the market which both makes economic sense and can be used in empirical work is a recurrent problem.

The next section deals with seller concentration, the dimension of market structure which has received most attention in the literature and particularly in empirical studies. The emphasis throughout this chapter is on concentration in individual markets rather than aggregate concentration, which measures the extent to which total manufacturing output is dominated by the largest 100, say, firms, and which has already been discussed in section 4.4 of Chapter 4.

The final section of this chapter will discuss other dimensions of structure, some of which have recently become the subject of more theoretical interest. These are: barriers to entry; vertical integration; diversification; product differentiation; growth and elasticity of demand; buyer concentration; and foreign competition. Barriers to entry, which are a very significant element of market structure in that they are the main determinant of potential competition, i.e. of the extent to which the existing firms in a market are subject to the threat of new entry, are dealt with in greater detail in Chapter 10.

Before moving on to discuss seller concentration, we briefly consider what is meant by 'market structure' and its significance. The importance attached to market structure stems from the hypothesis, founded on neoclassical economic theory, that the prices, outputs, costs and profits which result in a specific market ('market performance') depend on the decisions taken by the firms in that market

('market conduct') and that, in turn, these decisions reflect the amount of autonomy firms have in terms of the competitive environment in which they make decisions. This environment is what is called 'market structure' and this hypothesis is called the 'structure–conduct–performance paradigm'. At its simplest, this paradigm identifies structure as those elements over which the firm has little control, i.e. which provide constraints on its decisions, and suggests that structural factors are the most important determinants of industrial performance because the causal links run from structure to conduct to performance. Hence any attempt to understand the performance of industries should start by analysing their structure.

Undoubtedly the structure–conduct–performance paradigm has provided much insight into industrial economics, but it is unwise to take the simplest version too literally. Industrial economists have always recognised, for instance, that two oligopolistic markets might share a number of structural features but end up with very different price–cost margins because the firms in those industries chose to behave differently in terms of colluding or competing. More generally, the structure of individual industries is not fixed and exogenous but changing, and some of the factors which influence structure are aspects of the conduct and performance of the firms in the industry. For instance, firms may seek to create barriers to entry by engaging in advertising, or drive other firms out of the market by predatory pricing. Hence the direction of the causal links between market structure, conduct and performance is more complex than the simplest version of the paradigm would suggest. However, recognising that it is more fruitful to treat market structure as endogenous does not mean that structural features are unimportant in explaining industrial performance, and we now turn to examining the most widely studied dimension of market structure.

5.2 SELLER CONCENTRATION

Seller concentration refers to the size distribution of the firms that sell a specific product, i.e. how many firms are there in a market, and how big are they? The smaller the number of firms in a market, the more highly concentrated that market is. Also, if two markets contain the same number of firms, the one in which the firms are most equal in size is less concentrated. As already stated, seller concentration is the dimension of market structure which has received far and away most attention in the empirical analysis of market structure; partly because concentration is thought to play a significant role in determining business behaviour and performance, but also because data on concentration are relatively plentiful. As we shall see, however, the empirical measurement of concentration is not a simple matter.

The theoretical link between seller concentration and business behaviour argues that in an oligopolistic market the firms are interdependent, i.e. each firm's decision about how much to produce and how much to charge depends on how it expects its rivals to react. In turn, these expectations are influenced by the size distribution of those firms. For instance, in a market which is not growing and which contains a small number of firms each with a sizeable market share, a substantial increase in the sales of one firm will mean a noticeable loss to the others. These firms will quickly learn why they have lost sales and are likely to respond in an attempt to regain their share of the market. This train of thought may deter the firm from taking aggressive competitive action in the first place. Furthermore, the size distribution of firms influences the likelihood of collusion, whereby the firms recognise their interdependence and agree to act together to maximise joint profits. Successful collusive behaviour is more likely, other things being equal, the smaller the number of firms involved.

The argument, then, is that the higher the level of concentration in a market, the less competitively the firms are likely to behave, with consequent effects on performance. As we shall see in Chapter 11, this hypothesis has been subject to numerous empirical tests. It also plays an important role in monopoly and merger policy. Thus, for instance, in the UK a 'monopoly situation' is defined in law with reference simply to a market share criterion; a monopoly exists if one firm accounts for 25 per cent or more of the sales of a product. In the USA, also, restrictions have been placed on both horizontal and vertical mergers by reference to concentration levels. We return to these issues in Chapter 16. Before moving on to the measurement of concentration it is advisable to make an important caveat. Despite what has been said above, there is no deterministic link between the level of concentration and the intensity of competition. In some markets a small number of firms compete fiercely while in others a large number live in harmony. The relationship between the size distribution of firms and business behaviour is affected by many other important factors which are ignored if we look only at concentration.

The measurement of concentration

In order to test the hypothesis that concentration has a significant effect on firms' behaviour and hence on market performance, it is necessary to be able to measure the level of concentration and rank different markets in order of concentration. This involves summarising data on firms' size distribution into a concentration index. Many different statistical measures of concentration are available; these emphasise different aspects of the size distribution, and may well give different rankings. Hence the choice of concentration measure may affect the findings of empirical work and becomes an important question.

All measures of concentration offer some sort of combination or weighting of the market shares of the firms in the industry. Before looking at the measures most commonly used, we need to consider two prior problems. The first problem is that of defining the market, with respect to both product and geographical boundaries. In principle, a market contains firms producing goods or services that are regarded as close substitutes by buyers and sellers, i.e. products for which the cross-elasticities are significant. This concept is difficult to put into practice : cross-elasticities are not easily calculated, nor would it be simple to decide where to put the cut-off point between 'significant' and 'insignificant' cross-elasticities. Moreover, Census of Production data are classified by industry, and usually the establishments in an industry have common supply-side rather than demand-side characteristics. That is, they use similar raw materials or technology, but don't necessarily produce competing products, so a census industry may not even approximate an economic market.

Census data are collected on a national basis, i.e. the market is defined as being national. For many products this is quite inappropriate. Where regional markets are important, as for cement, the real market is much smaller, but for a product like cars where there is extensive international trade, the use of domestic sales will seriously underestimate the true size of the market.

The second problem is the choice of size variable: should the market shares, which any measure of concentration combines into an index, be shares of sales, employment, assets or value added? This is a serious problem in practice if the different measures give different rankings of industries by concentration. For instance, if large firms are more capital intensive than smaller firms in the same market, then asset concentration will exceed sales or employment concentration. Value-added offers the most theoretically appropriate measure of a firm's activities, but concentration measures using value added will be affected by the degree of vertical integration. If large firms are more integrated than smaller ones, then value added concentration will exceed sales concentration. In practice, sales and employment are the variables most likely to be available for use in the measurement of concentration: the above points show that care must be exercised in interpreting the results of such measurement. Diversification provides a final problem; where firms are engaged in more than one industry it may not be possible to divide assets or employment between the different markets except arbitrarily.

Next we consider the concentration measures most widely used and show how they are calculated using the following simple example. Suppose we have two industries, A and B, with the market shares given in Table 5.1. This

Table 5.1 Market shares of firms in two industries

	Industry A		Industry B	
Firm number	Market share %	Cumulative market share %	Market share %	Cumulative market share %
1	30	30	40	40
2	25	55	20	60
3	20	75	15	75
4	15	90	12	87
5	10	100	8	95
6	–	–	5	100

information can also be presented graphically, by drawing the concentration curves shown. Industry A contains fewer firms, but the biggest firm in B has a larger market share than the biggest firm in A. Which market is more concentrated?

The concentration ratio

The concentration ratio is the most widely used measure of concentration. It simply gives the sum of the shares of the largest r firms, i.e.

$$C = \sum_{i=1}^{n} P_i$$

where P_i is the market share of the ith largest firm.

Clearly, the concentration ratio provides extremely limited information on the size distribution of firms; its popularity results from the fact that it is available from official sources such as the UK Census of Production. This carries the disadvantage that the data source dictates the choice of r, the number of firms included in the group whose market share is cumulated. In the case of the industries shown above, for $r > 3$ the concentration ratio shows industry B to be more concentrated than industry A; for $r = 3$ they are equally concentrated; and for $r < 3$ A is more concentrated than B. This example shows that where concentration curves intersect then the ranking of industries by concentration ratio will depend on r; information for a range of values of r will be needed in order to find out whether this is a problem.

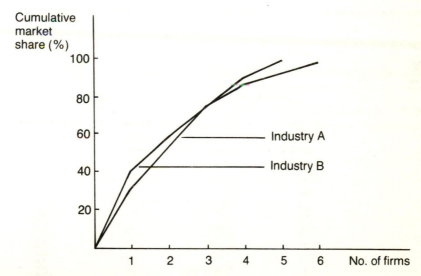

Figure 5.1 Cumulative market shares

The concentration ratio gives no information on the number or sizes of the firms outside the r group, and no information on the relative size of the firms in the r group (all of which are given a weight of 1 in calculating the index). Hence the main criticism of this widely used measure of concentration is that it fails to take account of a lot of information about the size distribution of firms.

The Herfindahl index

The Herfindahl index, on the other hand, does take account of all the firms in an industry. It is defined as:

$$H = \sum_{i=1}^{n} P_i^2$$

where P_i is the share of the ith firm, as above, and n is the total number of firms in the industry. Calculation of this index for the industries above would give the figures shown in Table 5.2. This calculation shows industry B to be more concentrated; although the two markets have the same three-firm concentration ratio (75 per cent), the fact that the largest firm in B has a higher market share than the largest firm in A causes B's Herfindahl index to be higher. In general, it is obvious that the squaring of market shares means that the smaller firms contribute less than proportionately to the index; in industry A, for instance, the smallest firm is one-third as big as the largest firm, but contributes only one-ninth as much to the index.

The maximum value of the Herfindahl index is 1, where the industry is a monopoly. Its minimum value, attained when all the firms in the industry are the same size, depends on n, the number of firms in the industry, and is equal to $1/n$.

Table 5.2 Calculation of Herfindahl index for two industries

	Industry A		Industry B	
Firm number	Market share % P_i	Squared Squared shares P_i^2	Market share % P_i	Squared shares P_i^2
1	30	.09	40	.16
2	25	.0625	20	.04
3	20	.04	15	.0225
4	15	.0225	12	.0144
5	10	.01	8	.0064
6	–	–	5	.0025
Total	100	.225	100	.2458

The entropy coefficient

This is another concentration index which includes all the firms in the industry: each firm's market share is weighted by the (natural) log of its reciprocal, i.e.

$$E = \sum_{i=1}^{n} P_i \log(1/P_i).$$

The entropy coefficient is an inverse measure of concentration: a lower value of E indicates a more concentrated industry. It may be interpreted as relating to uncertainty: the higher the coefficient, the less certain a firm is to retain a customer.

The calculation for industries A and B is given in Table 5.3. Industry A has a lower entropy coefficient than B; however, the absolute value of the coefficient is affected by the number of firms in the industry. Concentration can be compared between industries containing different numbers of firms using a *relative* measure of entropy, calculated as follows. For a given number of firms, n, entropy is maximised when all the firms have equal market shares, and E is then equal to $\log n$. If the entropy coefficient, calculated as above, is divided by maximum entropy for the appropriate number of firms, a coefficient of relative entropy is obtained which must lie between 0 and 1. For industry A, the relative entropy index $= (1.55/\log 5) = 0.96$, while for industry B it is given by $(1.58/\log 6) = 0.88$. This concentration measure therefore shows industry B to be more concentrated than industry A.

The variance of logs

The concentration ratio, Herfindahl index and entropy coefficient are the most commonly encountered measures of concentration, but by no means the only

Table 5.3 Calculation of entropy coefficient for two industries

Firm number	Industry A			Industry B		
	P_i %	$\log(1/P_i)$	$P_i.\log(1/P_i)$	P_i %	$\log(1/P_i)$	$P_i.\log(1/P_i)$
1	30	1.20	0.36	40	0.92	0.37
2	25	1.39	0.35	20	1.61	0.32
3	20	1.61	0.32	15	1.90	0.29
4	15	1.90	0.29	12	2.12	0.25
5	10	2.30	0.23	8	2.53	0.20
6	–	–	–	5	3.00	0.15
Total	100		1.55	100		1.58

ones available. It is also common to find concentration measured by an index of *inequality* of firm size, e.g. the variance of their logs. This is defined as the variance of the logarithms of market shares. Concentration and inequality are however distinct concepts, and inequality indices do not always work well as measures of market concentration. For instance, there is complete equality, and thus a variance of zero, both when there are two firms of equal size and when there are 100 firms of equal size. We show in Table 5.4 the calculation of the variance of logs for industries A and B. This calculation gives $\sigma^2 = 0.16$ for industry A and $\sigma^2 = 0.49$ for industry B, i.e. B is shown to be more concentrated than A.

Assessment of different concentration measures

We have now described four common indices of concentration, and shown how these are calculated. The Herfindahl index, entropy coefficient and variance of logs agree in ranking industry B as more concentrated than A, while the result of using the concentration ratio depends on the number of firms included in the ratio. How can we compare these indices to decide which is the best way of measuring concentration? One way of proceeding is to list desirable properties for a concentration index to possess, and use the list as criteria by which to assess different measures. One such list has been suggested by Hannah and Kay (1977), their five essential properties being:

1   A concentration curve (see Figure 5.1) that lies entirely above another represents a higher level of concentration.
2   If a large firm wins a customer from a small firm, concentration has increased; that is, the principle of transfers must hold.
3   The entry of a new firm below some significant size reduces concentration.
4   Mergers increase concentration.

Table 5.4 Calculation of variance of logs for two industries

Firm number	Industry A			Industry B		
	P_i %	$\log P_i$	$(\log P_i)^2$	P_i %	$\log P_i$	$(\log P_i)^2$
1	30	−1.20	1.44	40	−0.92	0.85
2	25	−1.39	1.93	20	−1.61	2.59
3	20	−1.61	2.59	15	−1.90	3.61
4	15	−1.90	3.61	12	−2.12	4.49
5	10	−2.30	5.29	8	−2.53	6.40
6	–	–	–	5	−3.00	9.00
Total	100		14.86	100		26.94

5   The contribution of a firm to the concentration measure tends to zero with its market share.

To use just one example from Hannah and Kay's list, the merger of two firms should increase measured concentration. The Herfindahl and entropy coefficients do meet this condition, but the concentration index will do so only if the merger involves a firm included in the r group (otherwise it will be unaffected). If the merger involves two smallish firms which hence attain a size nearer that of the larger firms in the industry, the variance of logs will actually fall, since inequality has declined. This shows that inequality is indeed different from concentration: for one thing inequality ignores the number of firms in the industry, which is relevant to the measurement of concentration.

An alternative way of assessing concentration indices is in terms of their theoretical properties. The aim of measuring concentration is to relate market structure to conduct and performance; it may be that different types of oligopolistic behaviour are best captured by different measures. For instance, price–cost margins in Cournot and related models (see Chapter 7) may be shown to depend positively on the Herfindahl index, while in the case of an industry containing a cartel of the k largest firms and a competitive fringe of smaller firms, the price–cost margin in the whole market depends directly on the k-firm concentration ratio.

Lastly, there is the empirical issue of how closely different concentration measures agree in comparing concentration across markets. There is no general answer here. Where the number of firms in the industry is small, using inequality indices such as the variance of logs may give results which seriously conflict with true concentration measures. In an industry with two firms of equal size, for instance, the two-firm concentration ratio reaches its highest value of 100 per cent but the variance of logs reaches the lower limit of zero. Also under these circumstances the relationship between the concentration ratio and the Herfindahl index becomes weaker.

Where does this discussion on the measurement of concentration leave us? No single index is ideal for all situations, and it is important always to exercise caution in empirical work on the relationship between concentration and market performance. Data availability acts as a severe constraint in practice on the indices used to measure concentration, as we shall find out in the next section where we consider the evidence on industrial concentration.

Empirical evidence on seller concentration

In this section we examine data on the level of seller concentration. Although the level of aggregate concentration is related to the level of concentration in individual markets (to an extent which depends on the degree of diversification) we consider only the latter aspect here. There are two separate questions to bear in mind when looking at these data. The first is a cross-sectional question concerning variations across industries in their levels of concentration: how much do markets differ in the extent to which they are dominated by a few large firms, and why? The second question concerns changes in concentration over time: have industries become more or less concentrated over the past 40 years, and why? The factors explaining cross-sectional and time-series variations in concentration levels are likely to overlap; these are the subject of the next section.

It will become clear in this section that the ability to assess patterns and trends in concentration is seriously constrained by the availability of suitable data. For one thing, most published data, including the primary source for the UK which is the annual Census of Production, use the (five- or three-firm) concentration ratio, which as we saw in the last section is a far from perfect measure of concentration. For another, data often are not available for industries defined narrowly enough to constitute economic markets, and lastly the classification of industries changes, which makes time-series comparisons difficult if not impossible.

Let us start by looking at recent evidence on concentration levels across industries. Published tables of the Census of Production give the five-firm concentration ratio (C_5) for 104 three-digit manufacturing industries (non-manufacturing activity, which accounts for some 75 per cent of UK GDP, is excluded from the Census of Production) using a variety of measures of firm size: employment, sales, net output and gross output. These data give an indication of the range of variation in concentration levels across industries, but in many cases these three-digit industries are too broad to correspond to economic markets. Census of Production data, which provide the raw material for much of the empirical work done in Britain on industrial economics, are now tabulated and analysed using the 1980 Standard Industrial Classification. This uses a decimal structure: economic activity is initially classified into ten divisions, numbered 0–9. Division 4, for instance, is 'other manufacturing industry'. Each division is split into ten two-digit classes; class 45 contains footwear and clothing industries. Each class is further sub-divided into three-digit groups, and each group into four-digit activities. For instance, group 453 consists of clothing, hats and gloves, which in turn contains nine activities numbered from 4531 (weatherproof outerwear) to 4539 (other dress industries).

When studying concentration levels, the practical issue of data availability will often overpower the theoretical problems of how to define a market, and studies have to be made using a broader definition than is desirable. The issue of narrow or broad definition of industries affects many types of empirical work; we have already seen in both Chapters 3 and 4 that the measured degree of diversification depends on the level of industry classification; another example from Chapter 3 is that the classification of mergers as horizontal or conglomerate will also depend on whether firms are classified to broadly defined (two-digit) classes or narrower (four-digit) activities.

The figures in Table 5.5 show that there is indeed substantial variation in the level of concentration. The reasons for this are taken up in more detail in the next section, but we note here that the highest- and lowest-concentration industries

Table 5.5 Most and least concentrated industries, UK, 1983

(a) *Most concentrated industries* ($C_5 \geqslant 90\%$)		C_5
420	sugar	100
429	tobacco	90
426	wines, cider, perry	95
260	man-made fibres	93
242	cement, lime & plaster	92
362	rail and tram vehicles	90

(b) *Least concentrated industries* ($C_5 \leqslant 15\%$)		
467	wooden & upholstered furniture & shop & office fittings	9
464	wooden containers	10
483	processing of plastics	10
328	miscellaneous machinery	13
313	bolts, nuts, washers, rivets, springs, chains	13
316	hand tools	14
322	metal-working machine tools	15
442	leather goods	15
453	clothing, hats, gloves	15

Source: Business Statistics Office, *Report on the Census of Production 1983* – Summary Volume, Business Monitor PA 1002, London: HMSO

are not scattered evenly through the classification; instead certain types of industry (e.g. the capital-intensive ones) tend to have high concentration, while more traditional, small-scale and labour-intensive industries usually have lower concentration. International evidence shows that the same kinds of industries are characterised by high and low concentration levels in different countries.

At the bottom end of the concentration ranking, a concentration ratio of less than 15 per cent indicates that certain parts of the timber, metal goods, leather, and clothing and footwear industries are competitive. However, in general there is no simple relationship between the numerical value of the five-firm concentration ratio and the theoretical classification of market structures into monopolies, oligopolies and so on. The use of five-firm concentration ratios means that the market share of the biggest firm in an industry cannot be identified; it is impossible to distinguish from census data an industry with a five-firm concentration ratio of, say, 90 per cent in which five firms have 18 per cent each of the market, from one in which one firm has 86 per cent while the other four have 1 per cent each.

Table 5.6 shows the distribution of the 104 three-digit industries included in the Census of Production according to their five-firm concentration ratio: half the industries have five-firm concentration ratios less than 40 per cent.

We now turn to the second, time-series, issue distinguished above, i.e. to a

Table 5.6 Distribution of industries by concentration ratio, UK, 1983

Five-firm concentration ratio	Number of industries
≥ 90%	6
80% and < 90%	5
70% and < 80%	5
60% and < 70%	7
50% and < 60%	12
40% and < 50%	16
30% and < 40%	20
20% and < 30%	16
< 20%	17
	104

discussion of how industry concentration levels have evolved over time. Changes in the level of concentration can be assessed by seeing how many industries experience increases and how many decreases in their r-firm concentration ratios, and by calculating average concentration ratios for the same sample of industries at different dates. The 'average' here may be the simple arithmetic average, or industries' concentration ratios may be weighted by employment, say, or sales so that bigger markets get more weight in the calculation of the overall level of concentration. This question is made more difficult to answer by changes over time in the classification of industries and in the ways in which data are collected.

The available evidence suggests that concentration in British industries increased between 1935 and 1968; the average level of concentration rose and more industries recorded increased than decreased concentration. Since the late 1960s, however, there has been little increase in average concentration. Table 5.7, which uses gross output-weighted five-firm concentration ratios, shows that the average concentration ratio across 93 three-digit industries rose slightly between 1970 and 1975, then fell again to record only a 0.5 per cent increase for 1970–79. The table also shows that over this period seven industries experienced falling concentration and two industries showed no change. The remaining eight industries had rising concentration ratios, but only shipbuilding experienced a major increase in concentration.

It is impossible to extend Table 5.7 into the 1980s because of the introduction of the 1980 Standard Industrial Classification, which uses a different industry breakdown. However, analysis for 1979–84 using the new classification suggests that the average concentration ratio has continued to fall. Also, if gross output-weighted five-firm concentration ratios for 199 two-digit industries are averaged within the 15 sectors of the new classification (approximating to the three-digit level used in Table 5.7), then the average concentration ratio fell in 12 of the 15 groups, and rose slightly in only three.

Table 5.7 Industry concentration by UK manufacturing sector, 1970, 1975 and 1979: constant (1970) weighted mean C_5 (gross output), %

SIC Order	Description	No. of industries	1970	1975	1979	Change 1970–79
III	Food, drink & tobacco	11	51.9	53.4	51.5	−0.4
IV	Coal, petroleum products	1	45.1	47.4	35.2	−9.9
V	Chemicals, allied indus.	14	54.7	54.9	54.7	0.0
VI	Metal manufactures	4	57.7	59.4	52.0	−5.7
VII	Mechanical engineering	9	38.3	42.4	40.1	1.8
VIII	Instrument engineering	2	30.8	30.6	29.8	−1.0
IX	Electrical engineering	6	61.7	59.0	55.8	−6.0
X	Shipbuilding	1	48.5	48.1	72.3	23.8
XI	Vehicles	3	81.3	78.0	80.3	−1.0
XII	Metal goods nes	6	37.8	38.0	37.8	0.0
XIII	Textiles	10	33.5	38.3	37.8	4.3
XIV	Leather, leather goods, fur	2	18.9	22.1	24.9	6.0
XV	Clothing and footwear	5	24.5	27.4	25.7	1.1
XVI	Bricks, pottery, glass, etc.	4	36.7	41.5	41.5	4.8
XVII	Timber, furniture, etc.	4	12.1	13.3	13.7	1.5
XVIII	Paper, publishing, etc.	4	43.1	40.8	40.8	−2.3
XIX	Other manufacturing goods	7	35.4	35.0	36.3	0.9
Average over 93 industries:						
equal weights			46.2	47.9	46.8	+0.6
output weights			46.6	48.1	47.1	+0.5

Source: Business Statistics Office, Business Monitor PA 1002, London: HMSO

Therefore, the postwar record is of a long period of rising concentration in the UK, followed by a period of little change. Since 1975 industry concentration has been declining, and there is now some indication that this decline accelerated during the 1980s. In the next section we look for explanations for both the inter-industry variation in the level of concentration, and changes in concentration over time.

Determinants of concentration

In this section we recognise that, while seller concentration is an important influence on the behaviour of the firms in an industry, it cannot be regarded as exogenous. Instead, we need to be able to explain the previous observations that concentration both varies between industries and changes over time. Different approaches stress respectively the importance of random, stochastic forces and the predictable effects of technology. No single factor is able to explain all the observed variations in concentration levels, and a realistic attempt to explain concentration must take into account the effects of mergers, new entry, market growth, advertising and government policy. In this section we concentrate first on determinants of inter-industry variations in concentration, and then turn to examine changes over time.

Economies of scale

The influence on cross-sectional concentration levels which has received most attention is the basically technological issue of the economies of large-scale production. Economies of scale are a big subject in their own right; here we focus on their relationship with concentration. Therefore, we first explain briefly the relevance of economies of scale to explaining concentration, then examine the sources of economies of scale and techniques of measuring such economies, before considering the empirical evidence on the significance of economies of scale and their importance in explaining inter-industry variations in concentration.

The technological possibilities facing a firm will determine the shape of its long-run cost curves, and the long-run average cost curve will show how much of an advantage, if any, big firms have over their smaller rivals by being able to produce the goods at a lower average cost per unit. A typical long-run average cost curve is shown in Figure 5.2. Over the range of output q_1q_2 the firm experiences economies of scale, i.e. average cost falls as output increases. At output q_2 the *LRAC* curve becomes horizontal and no further cost advantages are gained by increasing output. q_2 therefore represents *minimum efficient size* (MES).

Cost information alone, as summarised in the cost curve in Figure 5.2, cannot explain the size at which firms operate and hence the level of concentration. It is necessary also to know the size of the market, i.e. the level of demand for the product. If the MES is half of the market size, the market can support only two firms of optimal size, while if MES is only 2 per cent of market size then the market could contain 50 firms of optimal size. In the extreme case, where MES represents 100 per cent or more of market size, the industry is called a natural

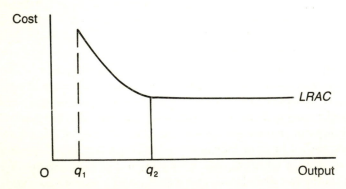

Figure 5.2 The minimum efficient size of firm

monopoly. The problems of regulating natural monopolies are dealt with in Chapter 13. The higher is MES in relation to market size, the higher would we expect concentration to be, *ceteris paribus*. However, if the *LRAC* curve is L-shaped as in Figure 5.2 (a shape which has some empirical support), then firms at or above output level q_2 are equally efficient and, rather than predict that concentration will be at the level consistent with n firms of optimal size where n = market size/MES, we can predict only that concentration will be at least this high. Another relevant issue is the slope of the average cost curve to the left of q_2; a steeper curve indicates greater cost disadvantage from being of sub-optimal size, and makes it less likely that small firms could survive.

Sources of economies of scale

Figure 5.2, showing how long-run average cost falls as output increases, does not adequately reveal the multi-dimensional nature of economies of scale. Increased scale may come from a bigger firm, or a bigger plant, or from longer production runs of a given product with a given plant, and in each case the precise source of the economies is likely to differ. Let us start by considering the sources of economies of scale at the plant level. The fundamental source of economies is the existence of indivisibilities in factors of production. The first example of such economies is that some elements of production costs are fixed or quasi-fixed with respect to output, so that increased output permits these costs to be spread over more units. Examples of such indivisible costs are costs of research and development and 'first copy costs' incurred in printing books and newspapers.

Sources of economies of scale which are related to indivisibility of factors but which are important enough to be discussed separately are specialisation and increased dimensions. It has been recognised since at least Adam Smith's time that costs can be reduced as output increases through the division of labour; if a worker can concentrate on one task she will become skilled at it and no time will be wasted moving from task to task. The same principle applies with other factors of production; bigger scale permits the introduction of more specialised machinery. Economies of scale may be gained from increased dimensions if the costs of constructing and operating a large plant rise less than proportionately to the increased output of the plant. For instance, the cost of building tankers or containers in general is proportionate to the surface area of the vessel, while their capacity and hence output depends on cubic capacity. Building costs will therefore rise less than proportionately with output. Operating costs will also give rise to economies of increased dimension if, for instance, doubling the capacity of an oil tanker does not double the necessary size of the crew.

In reality the production process is likely to consist of many separate processes, each subject to indivisibilities and each needing a different level of output to operate efficiently, i.e. at minimum cost. These indivisibilities will interact via the so-called 'law of multiples' in such a way that the most efficient way of integrating production will depend on the level of output. If the expansion of output permits the introduction of more efficient techniques, then this represents another source of economies of scale. Let us consider a simple example in which production involves using two machines A and B. Machine A operates most efficiently at an output level of 300,000 units per year; machine B has an optimal output of 400,000 units. The smallest output level needed to minimise unit costs in this case will be 1,200,000 units a year, in which case four machines of type A and three of type B will be able to work at full capacity. At any lower level of output at least one machine will be working at less than full capacity and unit costs will be higher. If one process demands a much higher level of output than the others, then at low levels of output the firm will find it more profitable to hire a separate specialist firm to do this part of the production process. Suppose we add a third process to the firm above, involving machine C with a full-capacity output of 800,000 units per year. The lowest common multiple is now 2,400,000 units a year, twice as high as before. If the cost disadvantage of operating a machine of type C below full capacity is high, and the firm can get this process performed by a specialist firm, then it will not be worth the firm owning its own C machines until its output reaches 2,400,000 units. Thus the expansion of output will actually change the efficient way of organising production, making it worthwhile buying specialised machinery (as in this example) or perhaps to substitute flow for batch production.

A final example of plant-specific economies of scale, also related to indivisibilities, is those which arise from massed resources. A small firm which has only one of a certain kind of machine will have to carry spare parts, or even a whole spare machine, in case of breakdown. A larger firm with several machines would not need proportionately more parts in reserve. The same argument applies to inventories, i.e. holdings of stocks of the finished product.

All the above types of economies of scale are real or technical economies, i.e. they involve resource savings. However, they are not all related to the same dimension of scale. For instance, the spreading of fixed costs depends on the total output of the product over its lifetime and hence can be increased by reducing the number of different products made and/or by extending the interval between changes in the design of the product. Economies of increased dimension or massed resources, on the other hand, are related to the size of the plant irrespective of the degree of specialisation within it.

We turn now to economies of scale which are related to the size of the firm rather than the plant. Some of these economies of multiplant operation are also real, but others are pecuniary economies which benefit the large firm at the expense of someone else. Firm-specific economies may be found in all the major functions undertaken by the firm. The following are some examples.

First, the kinds of economies from division of labour already discussed may be seen to apply at the level of the firm with respect to management economies. The managers of large firms can specialise in certain functions, and big firms can benefit from being able to use fully the services of specialised managers. Secondly, large firms can obtain economies from bulk buying of inputs. To the extent that these arise because suppliers actually face lower unit costs in supplying large quantities, these are real economies, but large firms also have a bargaining advantage when negotiating terms with their suppliers which can give rise to pecuniary economies. Third, there are economies of scale in advertising; developing and running an advertising campaign is another kind of fixed cost which can be spread over more units of output the larger the firm's scale of production. Fourth, by a similar argument, come economies in research and development. Lastly, big firms find it easier than small ones to raise capital, and are also able to secure finance on more favourable terms. This is partly because the fixed transactions costs of raising new money will be spread over a larger sum, and partly because the profit performance of large firms is subject to less risk, and therefore lenders require less return as an incentive for making finance available.

Before we go on to discuss ways of estimating economies of scale we should consider the possible reasons why economies of scale may be limited, so that beyond a certain level of output average costs begin to rise, and the long-run average cost curve is in fact U-shaped rather than L-shaped as in Figure 5.2. Again, different factors limit plant- and firm-specific economies of scale, and we consider them in this order.

Above a certain size, the economies of increased dimensions outlined above may be reversed if the building of an enormous plant requires different and more costly materials and techniques. A second source of diseconomies of scale is transport and distribution costs; as the plant expands it may be necessary to sell the extra output in a more geographically dispersed market, or to put more resources into finding new customers. This problem is likely to be most acute for bulky products of low unit value such as sand and cement; even if the actual production process favoured very large plants for these products, the heavy transport costs would make it impossible for the biggest firms to compete with smaller firms located nearer to the customer. Thirdly, although this argument does not apply only at the plant level, there is some evidence that large plants may suffer diseconomies from deteriorating labour relations (see Shorey 1975).

These sources of plant-specific diseconomies of scale need not limit the growth of firms, because firms can expand by operating a larger number of plants, all of optimal size. Therefore, we need to consider what factors, if any, give rise to diseconomies at the level of the firm. The main possible source of diseconomies at this level (although it may also operate to a lesser extent at the plant level) is diseconomies of management. It was argued above that the opportunity for management to specialise is an important source of firm-specific economies of scale. However, the firm's activities have to be coordinated and the increasing difficulty this presents in a large multiplant firm may mean that, above a certain level of output, management costs per unit of output stop falling and start to rise. This will happen if more managers and more hierarchical tiers of management are needed, especially if the lengthened chains of command mean that decisions are carried out less effectively and managers are less strongly motivated.

Measuring economies of scale

To provide estimates of economies of scale it is in principle necessary to obtain information on how production costs change as output increases *ceteris paribus*. There are three main methods available for measuring economies of scale: the survivor test, statistical cost analysis and engineering estimates. In the *survivor test*, plants or firms are grouped into classes in terms, say, of output, and the share of industry output in each size class is computed at the beginning and end of a period. Those size classes which increase their share of industry output are assumed to have lower unit costs. This type of test can obviously at best indicate the shape of the long-run average cost curve; it cannot say anything about the level of costs. The typical results are that firms over a wide range of size appear to operate at minimum cost and that the minimum optimal size of firm is small.

All sorts of problems, however, beset this particular technique. Sometimes the firms that do best in terms of increasing their share of industry output are those in the smallest and largest size categories, thus implying that the cost curve is bell shaped. Survival patterns are not always stable over time, and this implies that cost functions vary a lot more than may sensibly be expected. The basic idea behind the survivor principle is that competition weeds out the inefficient. For a correct test of this idea, firms need to be in a single market with no major imperfections. In fact, however, the industries that are used in the survivor tests will display various imperfections (e.g. product differentiation, collusive behaviour), which will play a part in explaining changes in market share. Following on from the last point, firms may increase their share of output not because they have lower costs but because of increased market power. If the objectives of firms are different, this will also play a part in explaining changes in market share. The long-run cost curve is drawn on the assumption of a given state of technology. The results of the survivor test, however, may reflect differences between firms in their innovative performance over a particular period of time.

These and other problems are sufficient to demonstrate that the survivor test will not normally give a good estimate of the shape of the long-run cost curve. This is because it shows not just the influence of costs on market share but rather the influence of all the factors that determine a firm's performance over a period of time.

The *statistical* approach to estimating economies of scale looks at the average production costs of plants or firms of different sizes. A fairly large number of observations is needed to give significance to the results, and this will tend to bias the results in the direction of finding relatively small minimum optimal sizes. The general pattern of the results is indeed that minimum optimal size tends to be small. Apart from this statistical point, however, there are other problems with statistical cost analysis.

Firms and plants classified to the same industry often produce a different mix of products. They may also pay different prices for their inputs. These differences should be allowed for, but in practice this will be difficult, if not impossible.

Another batch of problems surrounds the valuation of fixed assets. Even if firms have an identical stock of capital, they may use different accounting procedures, and this means that over the accounting period measured capital costs will vary between firms. This may be due to different depreciation methods or differences in the lifetime of capital assets that is assumed for depreciation purposes. In fact, of course, firms will have different capital structures, and this will cause further problems. Indeed, the long-run average cost curve is drawn on the assumption that the firm is using the most efficient available technology. But in practice the capital equipment of firms will represent a collection of capital of different vintages, and this profile of the capital stock will vary from one firm to another. Lastly, statistical cost analysis will in fact reflect short-run costs rather than long-run costs.

The third approach to measuring scale economies, the *engineering* approach, is in principle the most promising. This method obtains data directly from management and technical experts on the optimum size of plant with the use of best-practice techniques. This method has the disadvantage, as with all research using questionnaires, that great care must be taken not to obtain misleading information and also that it is an extremely time-consuming process, so that only a smallish sample of industries can be covered. The main advantage of the engineering method is that it should be possible to relate costs to output while holding constant all the other factors which affect costs (such as the price and quality of inputs) more effectively than with either of the other two methods.

This was the approach taken in a leading UK study by Pratten and Silberston, who estimated economies of scale in 25 manufacturing industries in the 1960s (Pratten 1971) and Silberston (1972). The sample was selected to cover different types of technology, but was biased towards capital-intensive industries. Their results showed that the importance of economies of scale varied considerably between industries. At one extreme, the sample included three industries (aircraft, diesel engines and certain types of machine tools) for which the estimated minimum efficient scale exceeded the whole UK market. At the other end of the scale – the footwear and engineering castings industries – it was calculated that plants could achieve all the available technical economies of scale at an output level corresponding to only 0.2 per cent of the UK market.

These findings indicate that economies of scale are an important determination of concentration in the following senses. First, the higher is MES in relation to market size, the higher concentration tends to be. Secondly, increased concentration (e.g. in beer, cement, turbo-generators and domestic appliances) was often due to technological change which made it possible to gain economies of scale by rationalising production. The implications for policy of these findings are that, in many industries, economies of scale are significant enough to create a conflict between maintaining competition and having plants big enough to be efficient. In 21 out of 30 cases, minimum efficient size for a product or group of products was estimated to be at least 20 per cent of the UK market, so that the UK could support a maximum of five plants of optimal size.

However, the findings of this study also suggest that the link between economies of scale and market structure is not a completely rigid one. For one thing, industries such as motor vehicle assembly, oil, beer, cement, and steel were found to have plants of sub-optimal size, so that not all available scale economies were being reaped. This may be explained by Pratten and Silberston's findings that the slope of the *LRAC* curve below MES is surprisingly flat, so that plants of less than optimal size suffer only a small cost disadvantage. For the assembly of a car in the 1300 cc range, they estimated that a plant of half the minimum efficient scale would have unit costs only 6 per cent higher than those for an optimal-sized plant. Secondly, as we have already emphasised, information on costs alone cannot fully explain concentration levels, for which it is necessary also to consider the demand side of the market. Therefore, in cases where the true size of the market is smaller (regional) or larger (international) than the UK, then the policy implications of concentration calculations based on the UK market need to be looked at again.

Although, as seen above, technological change which changes minimum efficient size will lead to changes in concentration levels over time, economies of scale are more significant in explaining cross-sectional variations in concentration level. Therefore we now summarise the extent to which plant and firm concentration can be explained by economies of scale before moving on to look at changes over time.

First, other studies agree with Pratten and Silberston that there is a positive relationship between MES and concentration levels. Second, the importance of technical factors in determining plant size is suggested by the fact that the ranking of industries by the average size of plant and by plant concentration ratios is similar across countries.

Since economies of scale are essentially a technical phenomenon, it might be expected that they would be more important in explaining plant than firm concentration. In fact, the ranking of industries by firm concentration ratios is similar across countries, which shows that technological factors are also important here. However, firm concentration ratios tend to be higher than those applying to plants, i.e. the proportion of output accounted for by the largest five, say, firms is much greater than that accounted for by the same number of plants. This suggests that high concentration is associated with multiplant operation, which is difficult to justify by reference to technical economies of scale. Multiplant operation is particularly important in industries with high firm concentration ratios, and is more marked in the USA than in Europe. It must be remembered, however, that no loss in efficiency is involved if the firm is operating under conditions of constant costs.

Lastly, it must be stressed that, while there is a general tendency for economies of scale to be associated with high levels of concentration, concentration does not depend on technical factors alone, so that the same technological conditions may be associated with high concentration in a relatively small closed economy, or with much lower concentration in an economy with a big domestic market or one in which international trade is important. Also, the relationship between economies of scale and concentration is an equilibrium relationship, which cannot be expected to hold in every industry all the time.

Changes in concentration

Let us now turn to examine the causes of changes over time in industrial concentration levels. Following on from the last argument, *changes in technology* are one such cause, although technology would not be expected to change much over a short period of time. Where technological change increases the optimal size of plants it will tend to increase concentration, but on the other hand technological developments such as the rapid advance in electronics and computer science may benefit small firms more than big firms, thereby enabling small firms to compete more effectively with big ones and reducing concentration levels. Empirical work in this area suffers from the previously mentioned problems of measuring economies of scale; the only alternative to detailed study of a small number of industries is to use a proxy measure for minimum efficient scale such as median plant size, i.e. the plant size which is exceeded by half the plants in the industry.

An alternative approach to changes in concentration is to regard these as the outcome of a random or *stochastic process*. According to the simplest version of this hypothesis, concentration levels emerge as the result of a random process whereby firms face a certain probability distribution of growth rates which is independent of the firm's initial size (the so-called 'law of proportionate effect'). Over a period of time, some firms will by this random process be subject to high growth rates several periods in succession while others will experience continual low growth rates. Since firms are subject to the same distribution of growth rates, i.e. of proportionate growth, the large firms will experience more absolute growth than smaller firms and inequality in firm size will tend to increase over time. The distribution of firm size becomes positively skewed and, over time, will approach the lognormal distribution. It is the empirical observation that many industries do have a lognormal distribution of firm size (basically a few large firms and a much bigger number of small ones), which gives the stochastic approach to explaining changes in concentration much of its appeal.

This approach, therefore, suggests that increasing concentration can come about as the result of a purely random process. The policy implication follows that a laissez-faire policy of no intervention in the competitive process will not preserve competitive market structures. In practice, however, even if the prevalence of lognormal distributions of firm size indicates that there are stochastic forces at work, such random processes operate alongside more systematic influences on concentration. To take the example of economies of scale; if larger firms have cost advantages over smaller ones then this will operate at the same time as the stochastic process and the movement towards increased concentration will take place faster than if firms of all sizes had the same costs. In this case, therefore, the distribution of growth rates is *not* independent of firm size; instead, large firms have a better chance of growing fast. This is inconsistent with the simplest kind of stochastic process outlined above, but does not indicate that no random forces are at work. Instead, other systematic effects may be seen as either accelerating or decelerating the stochastic process and it is to these remaining systematic influences on the level of concentration that we now turn.

Horizontal *mergers* between firms in the same industry speed up the concentration process by replacing two firms with one larger one, i.e. the number of firms falls and the average size of firms simultaneously increases. The importance of mergers compared with other causes of increased concentration varies from period to period, but certainly during 'merger booms' mergers are the single most important reason for increased concentration.

Assessing the contribution which mergers have made towards increased market concentration is not straightforward, since it involves comparing the observed size distribution of firms with a hypothetical distribution which would have resulted if the mergers had not taken place. A detailed survey of UK work in this area can be found in Curry and George (1983).

We can illustrate the problem by using a simple example (Table 5.8). In 1968 and in 1978 firm A has 40 per cent of total industry sales; in 1978 firm A acquires firm B, a smaller firm in the same industry, and by 1988 the merged firm has 55 per cent of industry sales. How much of the increase in concentration is due to the merger? The most usual method of answering this question is to assume that in the absence of merger the relative size of acquiring and acquired firms would remain the same, or equivalently that the acquired firm would have grown at the same rate as the industry as a whole. On this assumption, without the merger firm A would have had sales of 800 in 1988 and firm B's sales would have been 400. In this case, acquisition of B by A would have raised A's market share to 60 per cent, so we can say that A's share rose from 40 per cent to 60 per cent as a result of the acquisition and fell by 5 per cent owing to having an internal growth rate slower than the industry average. Here the hypothetical size distribution has been calculated for the end of the period, but an alternative within the same approach (and which in this particular example would give the

Table 5.8 Market shares before and after merger

| Year | Value of sales | | |
	Firm A	Firm B	Whole industry
1968	200	100	500
1978	400	200	1,000
1988	1,100		2,000

same result) would be to assess the contribution of mergers by constructing the hypothetical size distribution at the beginning of the period under study on the assumption that all the mergers took place in this year.

Obviously the assumption that in the absence of merger the acquired firm would have grown at the industry's average rate is open to criticism; for instance if the merger leads to managerial problems then the merged firm is likely to grow slower than the non-merged ones would have done. In this case the above method for assessing the contribution of the merger to increased concentration will overestimate the effect of the merger and underestimate that of internal growth. However, to make this kind of judgement demands case study analysis and inevitably restricts sample size. Therefore large-scale analyses, such as that of Hannah and Kay (1977), use the method outlined above.

Hannah and Kay studied the contribution of mergers to increased concentration in UK manufacturing industry during the interwar and postwar merger booms of 1919–30 and 1957–69. Therefore, for the latter period, they constructed a hypothetical population of firms to show what the size distribution of firms would have looked like in 1957 if all mergers of 1957–69 had taken place in 1957. Comparing this hypothetical 1957 distribution with the actual distribution for 1957 shows the contribution of mergers, while comparing the hypothetical 1957 with the actual 1969 distribution shows the effect of internal growth. Hannah and Kay found that similar results were obtained using the alternative method of calculating the hypothetical distribution at the beginning of the period.

For manufacturing as a whole, using several different measures of concentration Hannah and Kay's results suggested that about 70–80 per cent of the increase in concentration between 1919 and 1930 was due to mergers; for 1957–69, mergers accounted for 116 per cent of the increase in concentration. This means that if no mergers had occurred the effect of internal growth would have been to reduce concentration. This latter finding for the postwar period is explained by the fact that, although stochastic forces with growth rates unrelated to firm size were operating as explained above to increase concentration, these were outweighed by the tendency of growth rates to be negatively related to firm size so that small firms grew faster than large ones.

Other researchers, including Hart, Utton and Walshe (1973), Prais (1976), and Hart and Clarke (1980), have produced considerably lower figures for the contribution of mergers to increased concentration in the postwar period, and this shows that such a calculation is not a straightforward matter. The main reasons for differing results, apart from the assumptions used in producing a hypothetical 'no merger' size distribution of firms already discussed, are the choice of concentration measure and the sample of firms covered. Hannah and Kay went beyond companies quoted on the London stock exchange to include the acquisition by listed companies of unlisted companies and it has been argued that their methods led to upward bias in the estimate of mergers' contribution to increased concentration. The 1978 Green Paper on monopolies and mergers policy (Cmnd 7198) concluded that mergers probably accounted for about half the increase in concentration which took place in the late 1950s and 1960s. It must also be remembered that the relative contributions of mergers and differential internal growth rates to concentration vary from period to period.

A second factor which works systematically to speed up stochastic processes leading towards increased concentration is the effect of *advertising*. Particularly in consumer goods industries, the advantages which large firms have over smaller ones in advertising can both increase concentration and help large firms to maintain a dominant position. First, firms which do a lot of advertising may be able to bargain for lower rates from the advertising media, and therefore benefit from lower advertising costs. Second, advertising achieves its effect by repetition and the amount of money necessary is more likely to be available to large firms. This argument applies particularly strongly to television advertising; only a limited amount of advertising is available at peak viewing times and large firms' demand makes this time too expensive for smaller firms. Third, but related to the last point, the cumulative effect of repeated advertising will often be to establish a brand name, which may become synonymous with the product itself. In this way advertising can help to establish an entrenched position.

Empirical work on the effect of advertising on concentration is hampered by data problems; however, several studies (e.g. Blair 1972) have suggested that high levels of advertising expenditure do lead to increased concentration. The relationship between market structure and advertising intensity is complex and runs in both causal directions; this is discussed in more detail in Chapter 11.

The overall effect which *government policy* has on concentration is not clear *a priori*, since some kinds of policy have the effect of increasing, and others of decreasing, concentration. Disentangling the effects of policy is complicated because, apart from those areas of government policy expressly designed to affect concentration in one or other direction, all kinds of industrial policies may have effects on concentration as a largely unplanned by-product.

Let us start with policies aimed at concentration. The most important of these is competition policy, designed to encourage competition and therefore to limit increases in concentration. The most important plank of competition policy in this respect of course is merger policy, the effectiveness of which is discussed in more detail in Chapter 16. It is worth noting two points here however. The first is that, in the absence of merger policy, an unintended effect of other kinds of competition policy, notably of restrictive practices policy, may be to encourage firms to merge as an alternative, legal method of restricting competition. The second point is that British governments have usually displayed an ambivalent attitude towards mergers, wishing to have simultaneously the benefits of competition and those from having large enough firms to compete with large foreign companies. Therefore, despite the existence of a merger control mechanism, many mergers have been condoned. During the late 1960s this schizophrenic attitude towards mergers found institutional form in the coexistence of the Monopolies and Mergers Commission and the Industrial Reorganisation Commission which was set up to guide and encourage mergers for the sake of increased industrial efficiency.

What other strands of government policy have a, possibly unintended, effect on concentration? Several types of policy may be argued to lead to increased concentration. One such is any kind of planning or industrial strategy; the consultation process between the government and the firms in an industry will inevitably involve the big firms more than the smaller ones, and any policies agreed on will usually favour the larger firms. A second policy which may increase concentration is that towards patents; patents are granted to encourage firms to engage in research and development (see Chapter 9), but the ownership of patents may enable firms to obtain or consolidate an entrenched position. Lastly, the government is of course a major buyer of goods and services; it will usually find it easier to buy from big firms and therefore helps those to grow at the expense of their smaller rivals.

The net effect on concentration of all types of government policy taken together then is not at all clear; in industries where mergers have been prevented, concentration would have been higher without any government intervention, while in others government action has actually increased concentration.

We now turn to those factors which can be said systematically to lead to falling concentration. The first is having a high initial level of concentration. For several reasons there is a negative relationship between the initial level of concentration and the change in this level. One is statistical: the concentration ratio can vary only between zero and 100 per cent so a competitive industry with an initial concentration level of only 10 per cent can experience no more than a 10 per cent fall in concentration, while a more concentrated industry which starts with a ratio of 50 per cent can experience a bigger fall in concentration. Also, while it is true that some industries experience high concentration levels over a long period of time, it may also be true that certain kinds of behaviour characteristic of dominant firms will work to the advantage of the smaller firms and therefore towards a fall in concentration. This possibility is considered in the next chapter.

Lastly, we expect a negative relationship between *market growth* and changes in concentration: fast market growth encourages new entry and competitive behaviour and means bigger opportunities for small firms to expand, while slow-growing industries are more likely to become monopolised. The statistical evidence on this point, however, is not clear cut; some studies have found a significant negative relationship but others have not.

5.3 OTHER DIMENSIONS OF MARKET STRUCTURE

In this section we move on to consider briefly dimensions of market structure other than seller concentration. Concentration has received far more attention than these other dimensions, mainly because it is relatively easy to measure concentration and include it in empirical work. This should not be taken to mean that other dimensions are unimportant; two markets with identical size distributions of firms which differed in other structural characteristics would be expected to exhibit very different kinds of behaviour and performance.

Barriers to entry

One of the most important aspects of market structure, which has lately received a lot of attention from economists, is the presence and significance of *barriers to entry*. Because of its significance, potential competition will be dealt with separately in Chapter 10. Here we should just note that the effects of high barriers to entry into a market may interact with those of a high level of concentration. For one thing, the same fundamental cause, e.g. the technological factor of significant economies of scale, may both lead to an industry being highly concentrated and create high barriers to entry into the market. Where there are important economies of scale, a firm which tried to enter the market on a small scale could not compete and therefore the incumbent firms are free from the threat of new entry. This shows that, second, it is the combination of high concentration and high barriers to entry which creates the opportunity for existing firms to take full advantage of their market power to raise prices and earn high profits without inducing new entrants into the industry. Where there is freedom of entry, the firms in even a very concentrated oligopolistic market will be constrained to behave competitively. This is the idea behind the theory of contestable markets, which will also be covered in Chapter 10.

The point made in the last paragraph, that different dimensions of market structure interact with one another, has wide application, as will be evident from the remaining sections of this chapter.

Vertical integration

Vertical integration exists when a firm in a particular market also owns either an earlier stage of the production process (backward integration) or a later stage (forward integration). The reasons for vertical integration have already been covered in Chapter 3; here we are concerned with how vertical integration acts as an aspect of market structure. The point is that integration may confer market power on a firm over and above the level that the firm's sales in the market under consideration would suggest. If the integration has been brought about by efficiency considerations, then the integrated firm will have a competitive advantage over non-integrated firms, which will enable it either to undercut its rivals or to earn higher profits while charging the same prices. This advantage will be increased if the integrated firm is larger than its rivals, to the extent that bigger size confers an advantage in activities such as raising capital.

The most important way in which vertical integration confers market power is through its association with entry barriers. If one of the existing firms in a market owns a major input supplier, or a significant number of outlets, then it may become more difficult for new firms to enter this market. The integrated firm may refuse to supply the new entrant with the necessary input at all, or may agree to do so only on disadvantageous terms. In this case the only way a firm could successfully enter the market would be to enter as an integrated firm, having acquired its own source of input. This means that new entrants will need more capital, and therefore entry becomes less likely.

Diversification

Diversification is an aspect of market structure in a similar sense to vertical integration; a diversified firm has activities outside the market under consideration which will affect its behaviour and hence the nature of competition in this market.

Diversification has complex effects, not all of which operate in the same direction. A diversified firm will tend to be larger than a non- diversified one in the same market, and its size may give it some advantages of economies of scale, either real or pecuniary. Also, a diversified firm may be able to compete more fiercely in one of its markets than a specialist firm can, since any losses caused by price-cutting can be financed by profits earned in other markets. Diversification also has an effect on entry conditions. The knowledge that a diversified firm can behave like this may deter new entrants, and hence reduce potential as well as existing competition. On the other hand, diversification is a frequent and successful way for firms to enter a new market, and the presence of diversified firms already in a given market may encourage other firms to diversify into it.

Product differentiation

The degree of product differentiation present in a market is an element of the market's structure primarily because product differentiation is an important source of barriers to entry. Product differentiation creates consumer attachment to existing products and therefore makes it more difficult for new firms to enter the market. This applies whether the differentiation is based on objective differences between competing products or there is little innate difference but heavy advertising has created images associated with different brands and helped to create brand loyalty. In such a market, which will usually be a consumer good market, any new entrant has to be prepared to devote resources to building up a brand image from scratch.

Growth and elasticity of demand

Demand conditions may be seen as part of the structure of a market in the sense that they are largely beyond the firms' control, but do affect the firms' freedom of action.

We have already seen that the growth of market demand is expected to have an (inverse) effect on concentration. Market growth also influences entry conditions; entry is much more attractive into growing markets than into those which are stagnant or declining.

The elasticity of demand is a major determinant of the profit-maximising mark-up of price over cost; firms in a market where demand is inelastic will raise price further above costs than those operating with more elastic demand. Elasticity of demand is notoriously difficult to measure, which means that this theoretically important aspect of market structure is often ignored in empirical work.

Buyer concentration

In order to understand the nature of competition in a particular market, it is necessary to look at the number and size of customers, i.e. at buyer concentration as well as seller concentration. The same set of firms would be expected to charge different prices and earn different profits if they sell to many small customers than if they confront a few large customers.

Large buyers will be able to make contracts with sellers on terms which are more favourable to the buyer than a smaller buyer would be able to secure. Some of any price reduction may reflect real economies of scale if, for instance, the supplier can deliver large amounts at lower average cost, but the buyer may also be able to secure pecuniary economies for itself by virtue of its bargaining position. The simultaneous existence of buyer with seller concentration is known as *countervailing power*; the outcome of negotiations between a seller and a buyer where both have market power is indeterminate and depends on the relative bargaining strengths of the two parties (see analysis in Chapter 3). This in turn depends on factors such as: the state of demand, the aggressiveness of both parties in negotiations, and the number and size of firms on each side. In the extreme case, a single buyer (monopsonist) or seller (monopolist) is in the best position to drive a hard bargain since no alternative customer or supplier is available.

Foreign competition

Competition from imports has become an increasingly important aspect of market structure as trade liberalisation has led to an expansion in foreign trade in many industrial products, and this is a trend which is expected to continue in the future. In markets where there are substantial imports, domestic concentration indices calculated as some function of the shares of domestic firms in domestic sales will be a misleading guide to the existence of market power. One response to this situation is to calculate concentration ratios adjusted for international trade. In this case, instead of the usual (say) five-firm ratio defined as:

$$C_5 = \frac{\overset{5}{\Sigma}Q_i}{\overset{n}{\Sigma}Q_i} \times 100,$$

both the top and bottom of this expression will be changed to refer to sales of the product in the UK market, giving a foreign trade adjusted concentration ratio, A_5:

$$A_5 = \frac{\overset{5}{\Sigma}Q - \overset{5}{\Sigma}X}{\overset{n}{\Sigma}Q - \overset{n}{\Sigma}X + \overset{n}{\Sigma}M} \times 100,$$

where

$$\sum_{i=1}^{5} X_1$$

represents exports of the five largest firms,

$$\sum_{i=1}^{n} X_i \text{ and } \sum_{i=1}^{n} M_i$$

represent total exports and imports of the industry.

However, usually data on the exports of the five largest firms in the market will not be available, so that it is necessary to assume that these five firms account for the same proportion of exports as they do of production. In this case the foreign trade adjusted concentration ratio becomes:

$$A_5 = \frac{\overset{5}{\Sigma}Q_5}{\overset{n}{\Sigma}Q + (\overset{n}{\Sigma}M . \overset{n}{\Sigma}Q)/(\overset{n}{\Sigma}Q - \overset{n}{\Sigma}X)} \times 100.$$

If unadjusted and adjusted concentration ratios are calculated for the period 1979–84, then while the average unadjusted ratio for 195 industries fell from 51.4 per cent in 1979 to 49.1 per cent in 1984 (a fall of 2.3 percentage points), the ratio adjusted for foreign trade was both considerably lower and exhibited a faster fall. In 1979 the adjusted ratio was 39.3 per cent, and by 1984 this had fallen to 33.8 per cent, an absolute fall of 5.5 percentage points. These results indicate that British industries appear less concentrated once the effect of foreign trade is taken into account, and also that foreign trade had an increasingly important effect over this period. The number of (narrowly defined) industries with an adjusted concentration ratio above any threshold level will therefore be smaller than the number with unadjusted concentration ratios above the same level, and will consist mainly of those concentrated industries where foreign trade is relatively unimportant.

Competition from imports can therefore mean that an industry dominated by a small number of large domestic firms will function much more competitively than inspection of the unadjusted concentration ratio would suggest. The effects of foreign trade are of course more complex than can be covered by simply recalculating the concentration ratio as above; for instance, the effect of competition from abroad may be to shake up patterns of behaviour and induce more competitive conduct on the part of domestic firms. In general, then, competition from imports can work like any other kind of new entry, and its effects can be expected to grow in the next few years as Europe moves towards the establishment of a single market within the EC.

5.4 CONCLUDING COMMENTS

This chapter has reviewed the main elements of market structure, and has argued that market structure is a more complex concept than is sometimes recognised. This complexity includes the following: first, structure is multidimensional; secondly, structure is not exogenous, and the factors which influence it include the conduct of the firms in the market; and, thirdly, the links between the structure of a market, the behaviour of the firms in that market and the resulting performance are of varying strength and may operate in both directions.

Sometimes market structure is treated as though it boils down to seller concentration, and seller concentration is assumed to be measurable by concentration ratios. It is then assumed that an increase in the concentration ratio means an increase in market power and can be assumed to lead to less competitive behaviour, resulting in an increase in prices and profits. It should be apparent that, while this argument may hold true in a general way *ceteris paribus*, the *ceteris paribus* qualification here includes a great many reasons for caution. The effects of the same change in the concentration ratio in two markets can be totally different if the other structural features of the markets are different (for instance the significance of barriers to entry, or of foreign competition) or according to whether the firms have a history of cooperation in agreements or of competition among themselves. This obviously has implications for the conduct of empirical work on the relationship between market structure, conduct and performance, and these will be taken up in Chapter 11.

Chapter 6

Dominant firms

6.1 INTRODUCTION

In economic theory monopoly is a term used to describe a market in which there is only one seller of a good or service. This is obviously a case of dominance. The concept of dominance also extends to all those cases where one firm has a large share of the market. However, it is not possible to define precisely how large this share has to be. Dominance clearly exists when the leading firm has 80 per cent of the market, but what if it has 50 per cent? Much then depends on the size of the next largest firm. If the nearest rival has, say, 10 per cent of the market, most would agree that a measure of dominance exists, but if there are only two other firms with shares of 30 per cent and 20 per cent the position is less clear.

Dominance is thus viewed as a structural concept, and though it is not precisely defined it is a concept nevertheless which is recognised as important both in the theoretical literature and in policy matters.

Geroski and Jacquemin (1984) have, however, suggested an alternative approach. They argue that dominance should be defined in terms of the ability to exploit a strategic advantage at the expense of rivals, and that a high market share is one of the likely consequences of strategic behaviour. The suggestion is not very helpful. The authors themselves admit that strategic advantages are extremely difficult to measure even *ex post*, so that one is driven to infer the existence of a strategic advantage by one of its most likely consequences – the emergence and persistence of high market shares. So for policy purposes the starting point must be structural. Furthermore, many firms with relatively little market power will be able to make use of some strategic advantages over existing rivals and potential entrants. Nor is it the case that strategic behaviour explains all positions of high market share. It seems best, then, to stick with the traditional view and define dominance in structural terms.

The division of material between this and the next chapter is somewhat arbitrary. For instance, price discrimination and predatory behaviour are not confined to dominant firms; any firm with market power may engage in these practices. But there is an important distinction of degree if not of kind. Although perfectly collusive oligopoly will give the same results as simple monopoly, examples of perfect collusion are rarely if ever found. On average, therefore, we can expect dominant firms to be more successful in exploiting a market than an oligopolistic group accounting for the same market share. A dominant firm can always achieve at least as much as a group of firms acting collusively, and can work out its optimal strategy without having to resort to collusive arrangements. Such arrangements are not only liable to work imperfectly but also involve resource costs which the dominant firm escapes. If there are adverse effects associated with price discrimination, and if unwelcome predatory behaviour exists, the consequences are most likely to be important in cases of dominance. There is some justification, therefore, in considering such practices in this chapter.

The origins of dominance

There can be no doubt that dominance is an important feature of industrial structure. If we ask why this is so we have to look at the various forces governing the growth of firms, which have already been analysed in an earlier chapter. However, two factors stand out in explaining the emergence of dominant firm positions – mergers and innovation. The most spectacular examples of dominant positions created by merger are found in the first US merger wave around the turn of the century. Major consolidations in 1901 gave US Steel 65 per cent of domestic steel-making capacity. In the same year the consolidation of over 100 firms gave American Can a 90 per cent share of the US market. In a study of the impact of mergers during this period, Markham (1955: 180) concluded that: 'The conversion of approximately 71 important oligopolistic or near-competitive industries into near monopolies by merger between 1890 and 1904 left an imprint on the structure of the American economy that 50 years have not yet erased.' In some cases it is still not erased after nearly a century.

Mergers have also played a major role in the UK, and again the impact in many cases has been long-lasting. Large consolidations in cement and cigarettes in the first decade of this century gave the leading firms 59 per cent and 71 per cent market share, respectively; 80 years later they were 58 per cent and 66 per cent. In 1926, during the second merger wave of the 1920s, ICI was formed by the merger of the four largest firms in the chemical industry and has had a long history of dominance in branches of chemicals such as alkalis, dyes and dyestuffs.

Innovation has also played an important role both in establishing initial positions of dominance and in explaining its persistence. Examples that come immediately to mind include Eastman Kodak, Gillette, Alcoa, IBM, Xerox and Pilkington. Table 6.1 gives some examples of firms in the US and in the UK which have managed to retain positions of dominance over very long periods.

The plan for the remainder of this chapter is as follows. Section 6.2 examines the pricing strategies which may be adopted by dominant firms, and this is followed in section 6.3 by an analysis of non-price strategic behaviour. Section 6.4 reviews the difficulties of finding workable guidelines for the control of dominant firm conduct. Lastly, section 6.5 looks at the important question of the persistence of dominant positions.

Table 6.1 Some examples of persistent dominance

Company	Year	Market share %	Year	Market share %
United States:				
Eastman Kodak	1910	90	1975	80
Western Electric	1910	100	1975	98
American Can	1910	60	1975	35
Gillette	1948	70	1975	70
United Shoe Mach.	1948	85	1975	50
Du Pont (cellophane)	1948	90	1975	60
United Kingdom:				
Assoc. Portland Cement	1900	59	1978	58
Imperial Tobacco	1903	71	1976	66
Pilkington				
(flat glass)	1955	95	1980	77
British Plasterboard	1957	72	1978	100
British Oxygen	1953	98	1978	75

Sources: Shepherd (1975); reports of the UK Monopolies and Mergers Commission

6.2 DOMINANT FIRM PRICING

Much of the early theorising depicted a dominant firm as one that reacted pass-ively to a competitive fringe of much smaller rivals.

The suicidal dominant firm

Assuming a homogeneous product, the competitive fringe takes the price set by the dominant firm as given, and members of the fringe maximise short- run profits by extending output to the point where price equals marginal cost. The dominant firm sets its own profit-maximising price on the assumption that it has complete information on market demand, on the supply function of its small rivals and, of course, on its own costs. In Figure 6.1(a), market demand is DD', and the supply curve of the competitive fringe is SS'. If, as is assumed, the domi-nant firm is content to allow the fringe firms to produce their profit-maximising output at the price that it sets, the supply curve (SS') has to be subtracted from the market demand curve (DD') in order to derive the demand curve facing the dominant firm, which is MLD'. The dominant firm's marginal revenue curve is MR, and its marginal cost curve is MC. It maximises its own profits, therefore, by selling Q_d at price OP. At this price, quantity $PT (= Q_d - Q_c)$ will be supplied by the competitive fringe.

Assuming the supply curve of the competitive fringe to be positively sloped, the higher the price set by the dominant firm the greater the output of the competitive fringe until at OM it supplies the whole market. At price OM market demand is *MN*, which in Figure 6.1(a) is larger than *PT* by a factor of two to three, and it may seem unrealistic to assume that the competitive fringe is able to increase short-run output to this extent. One factor that determines the relative size of quantities *MN* and *PT* is the elasticity of the market demand curve at prices above O*P*. The more elastic it is, the larger the fall in demand as price is increased, and thus the smaller the demand that the competitive fringe will have to meet at price O*M*. Given the market demand curve, the relative size of *MN* and *PT* depends on the shape of the supply curve *SS'*. In Figure 6.1(a) it has been drawn with a rather gentle slope, reflecting a gradual increase in the marginal costs of the competitive fringe as short-run output is increased. An alternative possibility is shown in Figure 6.1(b), where the supply curve is perfectly elastic up to output *PT* and then becomes vertical. In this case the output of the competitive fringe will be exactly the same at prices O*P* and O*M*.

The theory of dominant firm pricing suggests that a position of dominance will be eroded, because if the price set by the dominant firm is high enough to allow members of the fringe to earn positive economic profit they will have an incentive to expand capacity. In addition, new entrants will be attracted into the fringe. As a result the supply curve of the competitive fringe shifts to the right and the dominant firm's demand curve shifts to the left. The dominant firm suffers a fall in market share and its position of dominance will eventually disappear. All this because the dominant firm stubbornly pursues a policy of short-run profit-maximising behaviour even though this erodes market share because of the incentive given to rivals to increase their capacity.

Pricing to deter entry

The dominant firm may well, however, choose not to behave suicidally, but choose instead to adopt policies that deter entry. In the extreme it may try to deter all entry. Assume that the dominant firm has the whole market so that the demand curve *DD'* in Figure 6.2 is also the firm's demand curve. Assume also

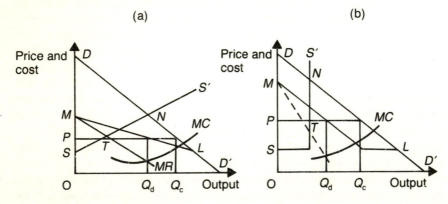

Figure 6.1 Dominant firm pricing

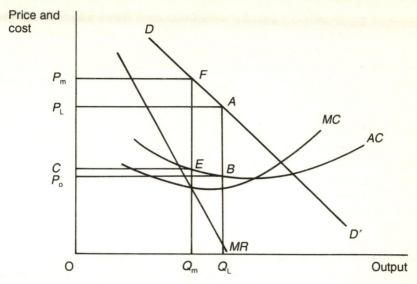

Figure 6.2 Dominant firm pricing to deter entry

that the dominant firm has a cost advantage over small rivals and that the latter can only operate with costs, including normal profits, of OP_L. By charging a price slightly below P_L and supplying an output slightly larger than Q_L there will be no inducement to new entry. The dominant firm will, year after year, be able to make a profit of P_LABP_o. This compares with higher short-run profits of P_mFEC, but the latter will of course be eroded as new entry occurs.

Will it pay the incumbent to pursue this entry-deterring policy? The answer depends on a number of factors: the cost advantage enjoyed and thus the extent to which the entry-deterring price can be elevated above costs; the discount rate applied to future earnings; and the speed at which entry would occur and profits would be eroded. A large cost advantage, a low rate of discount, and the expectation of a flood of entrants, should any departure from limit-pricing occur, will all encourage a long view to be taken.

Managing changes in market share

So far we have looked at two extreme cases. In the first, the dominant firm reacted passively to a competitive fringe, pursuing short-run profit maximisation regardless of the consequence this had for market share. In the second, the firm prices so as to deter all entry or any expansion by an existing competitive fringe. However it may be optimal, in terms of maximising the present value of the profits stream, to adopt other policies: of allowing some entry, or indeed of driving existing firms out of the market. This idea follows from the expectation that the speed of entry is likely to vary with the price set by the dominant firm or, more precisely, with the price–cost margin anticipated by entrants. A higher price–cost margin provides a greater stimulus to entry than a lower one and also makes it easier for the entrant to obtain the capital necessary to finance the entry.

A dynamic limit-pricing model developed by Gaskins (1971) incorporates this relationship between pricing and entry in the following equation:

$$\frac{dX}{dt} = k \, [P(t) - P_o].$$

$P(t)$ is the dominant firm's price at time t; and P_o is the unit cost of entrants. X_t is the output supplied by the competitive fringe at time t, so dX/dt is the rate at which this output expands. Lastly, the coefficient, k, gives the speed at which fringe output responds to the gap between $P(t)$ and P_o. By manipulating $P(t)$ the dominant firm is therefore able to control the rate of entry. Using optimal control theory, Gaskins finds the time path of prices that maximises the discounted present value of profits and at the same time the rate of entry which is optimal from the dominant firm's point of view. As in the earlier case of complete entry deterrence, the optimal price path depends on the dominant firm's cost advantage, the discount rate applied to future profits, and the speed at which fringe output responds to the profit stimulus.

It is possible of course that the dominant firm's cost advantage is so great that, even with short-run profit-maximising prices, no entry is induced. This is a case, to use Bain's (1956) terminology, of *blockaded entry*. In all other cases the dominant firm will hold prices below the short-run profit-maximising level.

If the dominant firm has no cost advantage, it will set prices somewhere between the short-run profit-maximising price and the limit price. The output of the competitive fringe will expand and asymptotically approaches total industry output. The dominant firm therefore eventually disappears into the fringe.

Where the dominant firm has a substantial cost advantage over members of the competitive fringe, there will be some optimal market share which will be reached asymptotically. The size of that market share is larger the greater the cost advantage, the lower the discount rate and the higher the value of the response coefficient k.

The Gaskins model assumes that entry occurs in infinitesimally small quantities. There is also a deterministic relationship between speed of entry and the gap between price and cost, which is known with certainty to the dominant firm. Fringe firms are also assumed to be price-takers and do not take account of the possible consequences of their behaviour on the conduct of the dominant firm; i.e. strategic interactions between the dominant firm and its smaller rivals are ignored.

Predatory pricing

The normal picture of price predation is that of a dominant firm cutting prices to a level that achieves one of the above objectives, and then raising prices again to a level high enough to recover the losses sustained during the period of predation.

Predatory behaviour may or may not involve cutting prices below the dominant firm's own costs, however defined, depending on the size of the cost advantage it has, if any, over smaller competitors.

The whole concept of predatory price-cutting behaviour was attacked by McGee (1958) as irrational. He argued that the cost to the predator would be far greater than that inflicted on small competitors in the fringe, because of the much larger output over which lower prices would apply. Therefore, the level of post-predation profits would have to be substantially higher to make the action worth-while. However, the dominant firm could have no guarantee that this would be the outcome. The victim of predation might indeed respond by immediately shutting down capacity and restarting as soon as a higher price is restored. And even if one firm is driven from the market there is no guarantee that another will not take its place. McGee also argued that, if the intention is to eliminate a rival, it might well be less costly to achieve this by acquisition. His general conclusion therefore was that predatory pricing was a high-risk strategy, likely to be unprof-itable and in all probability a rare occurrence. It is possible to criticise McGee's analysis on a number of points. At the theoretical level Gaskins demonstrated that by cutting prices below its own unit costs the dominant firm would in certain circumstances be behaving so as to maximise the discounted present value of profits. The circumstances are when the dominant firm has a large cost advan-tage over rivals; its discount rate is low; the competitive fringe is relatively large; and members of the fringe exit quickly in response to price cuts.

The extent of price predation is also dependent on what exactly is defined as predatory pricing. If it is only those cases where prices are cut below the domi-nant firm's own short-run marginal costs in order to deter entry, or to drive out a smaller rival, the practice may well be rare. It will be found more frequently if it includes, as surely it should do, a number of other cases including the following. A dominant firm may cut prices in order to place a small rival in financial diffi-culty and so reduce its value in a takeover bid. Another case is the use of price-cutting not to eliminate smaller competitors but to discipline them, possibly for their own price cuts. The worthwhileness of such disciplinary action will be greater the larger the share of output supplied by the competitive fringe. Preda-tory pricing should also include price cuts which are intended to forestall entry or to prevent the expansion of smaller competitors even when those price cuts still allow the dominant firm to earn an economic profit. If cost advantages allow effective predatory behaviour to occur without the need for the dominant firm to undercut its own unit costs, predation is more likely to occur. If the members of the competitive fringe have accurate information on their cost disadvantage they are also less likely to provoke the dominant firm into predatory actions.

Predation will also be more attractive when the market is segmented. If the segmentation is geographical, a small rival in a local market can be disciplined by price cuts in that market without disturbing prices elsewhere. Predation thus becomes less costly and more likely. Market segmentation and price discrimi-nation are considered more fully below.

Lastly, it is difficult to see how predatory pricing can be effective under conditions of certainty, when all firms are equally well informed and when there are no important intertemporal linkages on either the demand or supply side of the market. On the other hand, when these circumstances are not found, i.e. when there is uncertainty, asymmetric information and substantial intertemporal linkages, the scope for successful predation expands.

Take, for instance, the 'deep pocket' scenario in which a financially powerful dominant firm drives a financially weaker competitor into bankruptcy by predatory pricing, and then raises price to a level high enough to recover its losses. It would be realistic to assume that the dominant firm will be able to finance its predation internally. But why is the weaker firm unable to borrow from the capital market to finance its defence? If there was perfect information it would be able to do so, the dominant firm would recognise this and conclude that predatory price-cutting would not succeed. However, in the absence of perfect information, lenders have to rely on some imperfect indicator of a firm's creditworthiness. The firm's ability to borrow in one period may, for instance, depend on profits in the preceding period. The dominant firm will then have an opportunity for disciplining rivals – by reducing the small firm's profits in one period, it will make it more difficult for that firm to secure credit in the next period, with all the adverse consequences that that entails.

Another way in which predatory pricing, or the threat of it, might be effective is by creating a reputation for aggressive response to rivals. For strategic pricing to be effective, the dominant firm must develop a reputation that serves as a warning to small rivals or potential entrants. However, a reputation for toughness is unlikely to be established by threats alone. The time will surely come when the dominant firm will have to turn threat into action in order to maintain credibility. Will it pay to do so even if it would be more profitable in the short run to accommodate the expansion of an existing rival or the entry of a new firm? The dominant firm might well think so, especially if it fears that accommodating one firm would be the prelude to the expansion and/or entry of others. In this case, a clear demonstration by the dominant firm of what it is prepared to do may be sufficient to deter other small rivals.

Yet another way in which strategic pricing might influence the state of competition is by exploiting a situation in which information is asymmetric, i.e. the small competitor or potential entrant is less well informed than the incumbent dominant firm about the latter's costs or about the state of demand. The incumbent might then use pricing strategy in an attempt to mislead its smaller rivals – e.g. cutting prices in order to signal that the incumbent's costs are lower than they actually are, or that demand is less buoyant than it actually is.

Price discrimination

Any firm with market power may find it possible and profitable to practise price discrimination. This form of pricing behaviour is therefore not confined to dominant firms. Nevertheless it is convenient to examine the practice at this point. One justification for doing so is that in so far as price discrimination has deleterious welfare effects these are most likely to be found in dominant firm situations. We have already drawn attention to the objections that have been raised to the view that dominant firms frequently resort to predatory pricing. One of these objections was that predatory pricing costs the firm a great deal in lost profits – the loss being greater the larger the output affected by the price cut. However, if the dominant firm can discriminate between groups of customers, predatory behaviour can be targeted more finely and so the short-run losses are reduced.

Price discrimination is found where different units of a commodity are sold at different percentage mark-ups over marginal cost. In other words, relative prices do not reflect relative marginal costs. Thus price discrimination exists where different prices are charged for goods or services whose costs are the same, or where price differences are greater than the corresponding cost differences. It is also present where uniform prices are charged even though costs differ.

For price discrimination to be both possible and profitable the following conditions must hold. First, the firm must be able to divide its customers into groups with different reservation prices or with different elasticities of demand. Second, it must not be possible for buyers in the cheaper market to profitably resell in the more expensive market. If such arbitrage is possible, price discrimination will be undermined. Third, the costs incurred in segmenting the market must not exceed the additional profits that price discrimination yields net of these costs.

Three main categories of price discrimination are normally distinguished: first degree, second degree and third degree. In the case of first-degree price discrimination, each unit of product or service is sold at its full reservation price. In this case the firm's demand curve is also its marginal revenue curve and the monopolist finds it profitable to produce at the competitive level of output. In so doing, however, the monopolist appropriates the whole of consumer surplus. This extreme case of perfect price discrimination is clearly of theoretical interest only and not found in practice.

Second-degree price discrimination is a cruder version of the first-degree case. Rather than each individual unit of a good being sold at its reservation price, demand is divided into several blocks and each block is sold at its reservation price. Monopoly output is extended to the point where the reservation price of the marginal block equals marginal cost. The appropriation of consumers surplus in this case is not complete, but profits will be considerably higher than those realised under non-discriminatory pricing.

In the case of third-degree price discrimination, the firm divides customers into two or more markets each with its own demand curve.

Figure 6.3 illustrates the case where customers are divided into two groups with demand curves D_1 and D_2. The horizontal summation of the marginal revenue curves MR_1 and MR_2 gives the MR curve in diagram (c), and this curve, together with the firm's marginal cost curve (MC), determines the most profit-

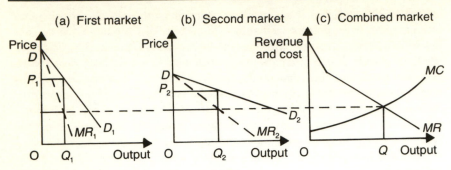

Figure 6.3 Third-degree price discrimination

able output (OQ). This output is divided between the two markets in such a way that the marginal revenue from additional sales in each market is equalised. The prices charged are OP_1 in the market with the less elastic demand curve and OP_2 in the other market. Price is highest in the market with the most inelastic demand curve.

Price discrimination is a very common form of behaviour in business. For instance, large buyers are often granted price discounts that exceed the cost savings associated with bulk supply. A firm may sell a particular commodity or service at a uniform price regardless of transport costs, thus absorbing freight charges and discriminating on a geographical basis. Firms often engage in price discrimination by selling different varieties of a product (e.g. cars, breakfast cereals) at price differentials far greater than the difference in cost of producing the varieties.

Another interesting case is intertemporal price discrimination – a practice whereby firms add a higher margin to costs for units sold in the early part of a product's life than in later periods (see Cyert and George 1969). In Figure 6.4, PP' represents the trend in price and CC' the trend in unit costs for a new product. The decline in CC' may be taken to represent the fruits of learning economies which the firm enjoys as cumulative production increases. The firm's strategy is to add a high mark-up on costs in the early period of the product's life when competition is absent. The firm may use the high profits to finance non-price activities such as advertising and R&D which will help it keep its lead over rivals, and make entry more difficult. It will also be part of the firm's strategy to allow the mark-up over costs to decline over time. This, together with non-price strategies such as advertising, will serve to expand the market. It will also help deter competition and to meet competition should it occur. The pricing strategy will be particularly effective if there is a marked downward trend in costs resulting from learning economies which are not available to potential entrants.

The price path may well follow a step-like pattern rather than the smooth downward adjustment depicted in Figure 6.4. Either way, the basic strategy is the same. It has been argued, however, that this strategy will be ineffective because

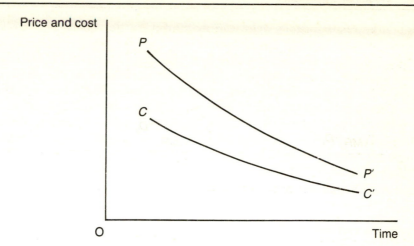

Figure 6.4 Intertemporal price discrimination

customers will postpone their purchases until price has fallen. The problem with this suggestion is that customers do not know with certainty how quickly competition will appear and how effective it will be in reducing price. In any case, with intermediate goods it may not be possible to shut down production in order to postpone purchases, and with consumer goods there always seem to be customers who are eager to be among the first to buy a new product. Certainly experience shows that markets do not seize up because everyone decides to postpone purchases in order to benefit from lower prices at some future date.

We have already drawn attention to the fact that price discrimination can be practised only by firms with some degree of market power. The static analysis of price discrimination tends to associate it with firms with considerable market power, and this is why the practice is usually condemned. Looked at in a dynamic context, however, the picture is not quite so simple. In the case of intertemporal price discrimination, for instance, the sequence of events may turn out to be similar to that under highly competitive conditions, with high profits in the short run followed by low profits in the long run. More generally, there is an important distinction to be drawn between systematic and unsystematic price discrimination, the former being more likely to be associated with entrenched monopoly positions. Unsystematic price discrimination may well add flexibility to prices by encouraging experimentation. A firm may be more prepared to reduce price if the lower price can, in the first instance, be limited to part of the market. It can then use its experience in one segment of the market to decide whether a general price cut would be profitable. In this way, and especially if price adjustments can be kept secret, oligopolistic price discipline may be undermined.

In contrast, systematic price discrimination by dominant firms is more likely to be anti-competitive in its effects. It may, for instance, reinforce a monopoly position by creating strong links with major distributive outlets, thus raising entry barriers to potential competition. It may also take the form of accepting lower profits where competition is strongest, and indeed may go so far as pricing below marginal cost in an attempt to bankrupt competitors. A good example of systematic price discrimination carried out by a dominant firm is that of British Gas. A Monopolies and Mergers Commission investigation found British Gas to be guilty of several actions which were against the public interest, including 'extensive discrimination' in the pricing of gas to large users. It imposed higher charges on those customers less well placed to use alternative fuels and was thus enabled selectively to undercut potential competing gas suppliers, which in turn acted to inhibit the development of competition and to deter new entrants.

Concluding comment on strategic pricing

A general criticism which has been made of the theory of strategic pricing behaviour is that it lacks credibility. This is because it does not involve the firm making an irreversible commitment. For instance, if a dominant firm threatens to cut price should entry occur, it may well find that it is in its own interests not to carry out the threat if entry actually does occur. Furthermore, the potential entrant will realise this. However, the force of this criticism is greatest when there is certainty and full information. Predatory pricing is more plausible under conditions of uncertainty and asymmetric information. It is also more plausible when conducted against small rivals or small-scale entry than against large rivals and large-scale entry, assuming, that is, that smaller firms are more easily intimidated and less likely to be as well informed as large competitors. Lastly, as we have seen in the section on intertemporal price discrimination, price and non-price strategic behaviour are interrelated. Although strategic pricing may be more plausible than has sometimes been argued, this does not of course deny that non-price strategies may be more effective. It is to these strategies that we now turn.

6.3 NON-PRICE STRATEGIC BEHAVIOUR

Dominant firms may obtain strategic advantages from a wide range of non-price behaviour. These strategies often involve the firm in making investments which, unlike price cuts, are not easily reversible. By making such commitments, the threats which are based on them are more credible and likely, therefore, to be more effective. Amongst the strategies available are various forms of vertical restraints, investment in over-capacity, brand proliferation, blanket patenting, and heavy advertising. Vertical restraints have already been discussed in Chapter 3 and will be examined further in a policy context in Chapter 15. Some of the other non-price strategies are considered more fully in Chapters 8–10. Here we examine one or two out of the many available strategies to illustrate the sort of advantage that dominant firms may possess. We will also draw attention to some limitations of these strategies and argue that, as in the case of pricing behaviour, it is often uncommonly difficult to distinguish innocent efficiency-enhancing behaviour from deliberate anti-competitive behaviour.

One possible form that non-price strategic behaviour may take, and one which has received a lot of attention in the literature, is where the dominant firm makes larger investments in capacity than it otherwise would (see Spence 1977). When the incumbent monopolist has this spare capacity, a potential entrant can expect it to react more vigorously in response to entry. Equally, existing small firms can expect a more vigorous response should they step out of line. This strategy will not work if the firm is operating under conditions of increasing costs; it may have some deterrent effect with constant costs, but is most important when costs are falling owing to economies of scale. In the latter case, a higher output, which is the incumbent's response to competition, can be produced at lower unit cost and, if scale economies are very important, at lower marginal cost.

A problem with this strategy is that maintaining excess capacity may, just like price predation, entail a long period during which profits are sacrificed. Indeed, the period of sacrifice may well be considerably longer than with predatory pricing, especially if industry demand is stagnant or declining. The risks associated with the strategy are also greater. Whereas a price cut can quickly be reversed, the whole purpose of excess capacity is to display to competitors, actual or potential, that an irreversible commitment has been made. The incumbent monopolist has to calculate how much excess capacity is needed to have the desired effect. That in turn will depend on future industry demand, which is not known with certainty. The success of the strategy is likely to be particularly sensitive to the rate of technological change. If products or processes are undergoing rapid change, the firm that over-invests may well find itself with a millstone hanging around its neck. It is easiest to see this strategy working where products and processes change little over time and where industry demand can be forecast with a high degree of certainty.

A further difficulty with this form of dominant firm conduct is that it may be difficult to distinguish between excess capacity maintained for anti-competitive purposes and excess capacity which results from investment decisions designed to minimise costs. We have already drawn attention to the point that the strategy is most effective as a fighting weapon when there are important economies of scale and costs are falling. But it is precisely under these conditions that the cheapest way of producing a given output is to build a plant which is then operated at excess capacity. Thus in Figure 6.5 output q_1 could be produced by building the plant depicted by short-run average cost $SRAC_1$ and operating that plant at full capacity. But this is not the cheapest way of producing q_1 when there are economies of scale. The cheapest way is to build the larger plant $SRAC_2$ and then operate that plant at less than full capacity.

In a dynamic setting, when demand is expanding, the same problem exists. Owing to indivisibilities and economies of scale in the construction of buildings, plant and machinery, firms will, on efficiency grounds alone, build capacity ahead of demand. Given the uncertainty attaching to forecasts of future demand

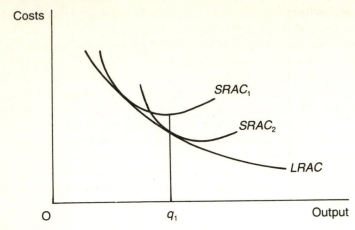

Figure 6.5 Excess capacity and entry deterrence

it will be extremely difficult to distinguish between this efficiency-based explanation for excess capacity and the anti-competitive 'positioning moves' of incumbent monopolists.

Another strategy which a dominant firm may use to disadvantage rivals is the
introduction of new products. One way of illustrating this is by using Lancaster's
theory of consumer demand (Lancaster 1966). In Figure 6.6, α and β represent
two characteristics of a product. Ray A shows the proportions in which these
characteristics are combined in product A, which, initially, is the only product on
the market and which is produced by the dominant firm and by smaller producers. All consumers of A are assumed to have the same indifference map and to
spend a given sum of money on the product. The highest indifference curve
attainable then depends on the price of A. Assume that the price is such as to
allow consumers to attain point a on I_1.

The dominant firm now introduces a new product B, which combines the
characteristics α and β in different proportions (more α, less β), and prices the
product so as to allow consumers to attain point b on I_2. All consumers will
switch to the new product, causing the small producers of A to leave the market.
If there are barriers to re-entry, the dominant firm will have increased its market
power.

The analysis can be extended to allow for differences in tastes. In Figure 6.7,
two groups of consumers are shown with indifference maps I_1, I_2 and I', I''.
Indifference curves I_1, I_2 belong to the customers of the dominant firms, I', I''
belong to customers of small rivals. Initially both the dominant firm and its small
rivals produce a single commodity A with characteristics α and β combined in
the proportions shown by ray OA. Both groups of consumers are at point a, on
indifference curve I_2 and I' respectively.

The dominant firm now introduces a new product targeted at customers of the

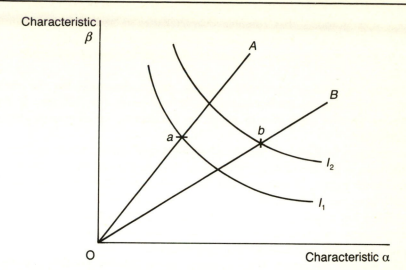

Figure 6.6 Product differentiation to deter entry

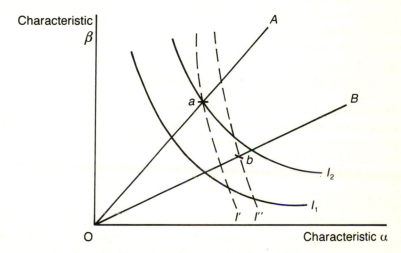

Figure 6.7 Product differentiation to deter entry where tastes differ

small rivals. Product B is introduced and priced so that consumers are able to attain point *b*. This induces the customers of the small firms to switch because by doing so they are able to attain a higher level of utility. The dominant firm's original customers, however, stay with product A.

When product differentiation is important and tastes differ, this analysis also suggests a strategy which the dominant firm may use to pre-empt entry. If economies of scale are unimportant, there will be opportunities for firms to enter the market with products that combine characteristics α and β in proportions different from those in A or B. However the dominant firm may pre-empt such entry by *brand proliferation*, i.e. by packing the product space on either side of A and B.

Packing the product space (and, likewise, geographic space) has the effect, then, of restricting the market niches available to prospective entrants. It also facilitates selective price-cutting aimed at disciplining or eliminating fringe competition.

A strategy which may be associated with product differentiation and brand proliferation is the use of heavy advertising. Advertising can have a substantial effect on the pattern of customer purchases where it reinforces brand images. Brand images may be the result of a history of successful product innovation and/ or promotional successes, and where they exist the firm will want to protect or reinforce them. Advertising is a means of achieving this; it also has the effect of raising rivals' costs and making entry more difficult.

The previous paragraph draws attention to yet another possible non-price strategy available to incumbent monopolists – the use of R&D and the patenting of inventions to block out competitors. It is usually possible to invent around a single patent, but, by accumulating an extensive portfolio of patents in a given area of technology, a firm may be able to prolong its period of dominance over a long period, allowing competition to appear only on its own terms.

6.4 CONTROLLING DOMINANT FIRM CONDUCT

If dominant firms have available to them all these anti-competitive strategies, what possibilities are there for controlling dominant firm conduct in a way that enhances efficiency and welfare? Unfortunately general rules are difficult, if not impossible, to find. The following sections illustrate the difficulties.

Predatory pricing

The difficulty here has been to define precisely what constitutes predatory behaviour. One obvious approach is to apply some sort of cost-based test. A suggestion made by Areeda and Turner (1974/5) was that behaviour was predatory if prices were set below short-run marginal costs. Assuming that short-run average variable costs are a good approximation to short-run marginal costs, they proposed that dominant firms found to have cut prices below short-run average variable costs in response to entry should be found guilty of predation and in violation of US antitrust law. Critics of this suggestion have pointed to a number of problems. Not least of these problems is that of obtaining reliable information from accounting data on the level of costs. Such a rule, it has also been pointed out, might encourage dominant firms to lower marginal costs by over-investing in capacity. More importantly, perhaps, the rule would be ineffective where the incumbent monopolist has cost advantages over new entrants. These advantages might be due to scale or to learning economies. During the period when the new entrant is attempting to establish itself in the market, the dominant firm will be able, by cutting prices, to make the entrant's operations unprofitable without violating the Areeda–Turner test. If, as argued earlier, profitability in one period affects the new entrant's prospects of attracting funds in subsequent periods, then the incumbent will succeed in retarding the entrant's growth if not in causing it to exit the market.

An alternative test proposed by Williamson (1977) is to restrict the dominant firm's reactions after entry has occurred. In other words, a dominant firm is allowed to attempt to deter entry by setting price and output at the entry-deterring levels, but is not allowed to react to entry, should it occur, by cutting prices and expanding output. Thus a dominant firm would not be able to charge high prices, react aggressively to the threat of entry by predatory price cuts and then raise prices again after the threat has subsided. A firm that wishes to deter entry would have to adopt a limit-pricing policy as a long-term strategy. Of course, if the dominant firm is successful in its limit-pricing policy, dominance will persist and industry structure will be frozen. How important this is depends on what the alternative outcome would have been. In the absence of the Williamson rule would the dominant firm have succeeded anyway in excluding rivals but by more efficiency-damaging modes of conduct, or would new entry have occurred and succeeded in loosening up market structure and increasing competitiveness? One possible disadvantage of the Williamson proposal is that it could result in more entrenched dominant firm positions. More important, however, is the difficulty of applying it in a dynamic situation where demand and supply conditions are continually changing and where firms make errors of judgement. To limit the responses of dominant firms is as likely to deter efficiency-enhancing responses as it is to deter predatory ones.

Price–cost margins

It would seem fairly obvious (setting aside second-best problems and the administrative costs of price control) that, where price–cost margins are excessive, a reduction in the prices charged by a dominant firm will lead to an increase in welfare, at least in the short run. This approach is evident in a number of cases that have come before the UK Monopolies and Mergers Commission; high prices may also constitute an abuse of a dominant position under Article 86 of the Treaty of Rome. However, it is not obvious that high price–cost margins are necessarily detrimental in the long run. The problem is caused by the interrelationships that exist between profitability on the one hand and incentives to invest and innovate, and inducements to entry, on the other. One of the incentives to invest in R&D is of course the prospect of gaining a dominant position. If price–cost margins are regulated and profits reduced, this incentive may be seriously weakened. High profitability is also an inducement to new entry. Price regulation may discourage potential entrants and result in the freezing of industry structure.

This is not to say that price–cost margins can never be excessive, or that any regulation will have the serious repercussions that have just been suggested. What it does mean is that there are no simple rules to guide policy making.

Non-price strategic behaviour

Advertising expenditure will serve to illustrate the problem with regard to a number of non-price strategies which may have anti-competitive consequences. Advertising is often considered to be a barrier to new entry. Yet it may be not advertising *per se* but advertising in conjunction with other factors that the firm uses to establish a reputation that constitutes the barrier. In a world in which there are information costs and transactions costs it will pay a firm to commit resources in order to build up a clientele of satisfied customers. It will do so by establishing a reputation for reliability and value for money, and by emphasising long-term relationships with customers rather than short-term opportunistic behaviour. These efforts at developing the firm's goodwill create entry barriers. In his analysis of advertising expenditure as a barrier to entry, Demsetz (1982: 50) argues that: 'it is the combination of information costs, the creation of a reputable history, and the commitment of industry-specific investment, not advertising *per se* that constitutes the barrier.' In a similar vein, Okun (1981: 178) argues that 'the customer market view ... accepts the attachment between buyer and seller as an inherently desirable institutional arrangement that economises on the expenses of shopping, trying out products, and otherwise engaging in transactions ... society pays the cost of monopoly elements and collects the benefits of genuine economies of transactions.'

Once again the important message is not that advertising and other promotional expenditures can never be anti-competitive or socially wasteful; it is that these activities also form part of business strategies for building long-term and efficiency-enhancing relationships with customers, and it is not easy to devise rules that will separate one from the other.

So far, then, economists have not been very successful in devising simple and workable rules for controlling dominant firm conduct which have unambiguously beneficial effects on efficiency and welfare. It has to be asked whether simple rules, however imperfect, can be justified. The answer depends on how prevalent is dominant firm abuse and how many cases have to be adjudicated. In the USA, where a large number of price predation cases are brought to the courts by private plaintiffs, there is a strong argument in favour of a simple Areeda–Turner type test. In the UK and EC, on the other hand, monopoly investigations are relatively rare, which is not to say of course that monopoly abuse is uncommon. In these circumstances a full-blown investigation of dominant firms, including the sources of dominance and an attempt to unearth the intent that underlies strategic conduct, can be justified.

6.5 HOW PERSISTENT IS DOMINANCE?

If positions of dominance decayed rapidly, dominant firm behaviour would not be of great concern. What expectations should we have about the persistence of dominance, and what does the evidence show?

Early thinking on this matter suggested the inevitability of decline. Much of this thinking, however, was based on models in which the dominant firm responded passively to the expansion of smaller competitors; adopting a myopic pricing policy which doomed it to decline. More recent theorising has emphasised the operating and strategic advantages which dominant firms have over existing and potential competitors and which might allow dominance to persist over long periods. One factor which is relevant in determining the outcome is the size of any advantage which the dominant firm has. If it is small, attempts at defending a position of dominance are liable to be costly and, quite likely, ineffective. The dominant firm may well therefore choose to make good profits while it can and accept the inevitability of decline. A large advantage, on the other hand, means not only that it is more worthwhile to defend a position of dominance but also that there are more profits out of which to finance that defence.

In a world of constant tastes and technology, the strategic advantages available to an incumbent might allow a dominant position to be sustained more or less indefinitely. These conditions may be approximated in mature industries where production and marketing methods are well established and where a firm which has achieved a dominant position has invested heavily in cementing customer attachments. In such circumstances it will be difficult for a newcomer to make a substantial impact. But, in a dynamic world in which tastes and technologies are constantly changing, management has to be continually alert to new opportunities. It may respond to the challenge and succeed in maintaining technological and managerial leadership over long periods, though if the changes come sufficiently thick and fast even the most efficient management may be unable to avoid some erosion of market share. On the other hand, dominant firms may fail to respond quickly enough. A sustained period of dominance which has given an easy life and led to an uncritical acceptance of traditional ways of doing things will produce a management ill equipped to respond to change, whether it comes in the form of new products, new processes or new forms of organisation.

What about the evidence? Studies in both the USA and UK suggest that there is a tendency for dominant firms to decline, but that *on average* this decline is slow. For the USA, Shepherd's investigations for the period 1910–35 suggest an average decline in market share of just under 1 percentage point a year (Shepherd 1975). For the period 1948–75 Shepherd argues that dominance was more persistent, the average decline in his sample of dominant firms being less than half a percentage point a year.

Figures for the UK suggest a similar average experience of slow decline. Shaw and Simpson (1985) examined leading firms that had been subjected to a Monopolies and Mergers Commission inquiry between 1959 and 1973. Changes in market share were analysed over periods ranging from 6 to 14 years after the inquiry. The median decline in market share was 6 percentage points, i.e. around half a percentage point a year. This certainly overestimates the rate of decline of the firms in the sample because many enjoyed a long period of dominance before they were referred for investigation. Information also taken from MMC reports shows that for 12 dominant firms that did lose market share the average rate of decline over periods ranging from 22 to 44 years, was just over half a percentage point a year.

The average experience of dominant firms tells only a part of the story and not necessarily a very interesting part. A small average rate of decline may, for instance, result from all firms declining by an amount near to the average or from one or two spectacular declines masking a picture of general stability. Reality in fact shows quite a wide range of experience. Some firms have managed to retain dominant positions for several decades; others have suffered spectacular decline. In the USA, for example, Eastman Kodak, which had a 90 per cent market share in 1910, still had an 80 per cent share in 1975. Other successful firms include Western Electric, Gillette and IBM. Part, at least, of their success in maintaining market leadership has been technologically based. In the UK, Pilkington has dominated both the flat glass and safety glass markets over several decades. Here, too, technological leadership has been important, though the acquisition of competitors has also played a role. Other examples of long-term dominance in UK industry shown in Table 6.1 include the Imperial Group (cigarettes), BOC (industrial gases), APCM (cement) and BPB (plasterboard). BPB increased its share of the market from around 70 per cent in 1951 to 100 per cent in 1978, largely as a result of acquisitions.

At the other end of the scale there have been some notable failures. For instance, International Harvester's share of the US market slumped from 80 per cent in 1910 to 33 per cent in 1935. Perhaps the most famous case of decline in US industrial history is that of US Steel, which saw its share of steel ingot production fall from 65 per cent in 1901 when it was formed, to 42 per cent in 1925 and 24 per cent in 1967.

There are several examples of UK firms that have lost positions of dominance. Often a dominant position that had been held for a long period was eroded because the firm was unable to adapt to entirely new market conditions. In beverage cans, for instance, the market share held by Metal Box fell from 94 per cent in 1968 to 31 per cent in 1982, a decline which to a large extent was due to the termination of agreements that had kept American competitors out of the UK market. In tyres, Dunlop's position with over 50 per cent of the market was held from the 1920s up to 1950. But by 1980 its market share had fallen to 20 per cent and later it moved out of tyre production completely, selling out to the Italian company, Pirelli. One reason for its decline was slowness in matching competitors in the production of radial tyres and failure to increase efficiency in a much more competitive market. In bicycles, the long-established market leader, Raleigh, saw its market share fall from 67 per cent in 1972 to 40 per cent in 1980 entirely as a result of a big increase in imports. Overseas producers were quick to supply new discount outlets whom Raleigh refused to supply.

Though the evidence is by no means complete, the distinct impression that one gets in comparing the USA and UK is that dominant positions in the UK have been much less secure. Part of the reason for this has been the greater exposure of the UK to competition from overseas. However, a number of MMC inquiries (e.g. those into cellulosic fibres, 1968, matches, 1952, and white salt, 1986) have shown that competition from imports is not always as effective as it may seem, because the dominant firm may be able to control the volume of imports by entering into agreements with foreign suppliers. Probably a more important explanation for the greater fragility of UK dominant firms has been management failure.

Another question which has been asked about the decline in dominance is whether there is any evidence to suggest that it is in any sense 'managed' by the dominant firm. This question follows from the work, reported earlier in this chapter, of economists such as Gaskins who have developed models which show that, under certain circumstances, it will be optimal for incumbent monopolists to adopt policies that allow a controlled expansion of the competitive fringe. There is very little evidence to support this managed-decline hypothesis. The experience of US Steel has been used as an illustration of a Gaskins-type model at work, but that experience is capable of more than one interpretation.

As noted earlier, the Gaskins model assumes that entry occurs in minute quantities, that a deterministic relationship exists between entry and the price–cost margin, and that this relationship is known to the dominant firm. It is difficult to imagine that these conditions apply even approximately in the real world. Successful entry often occurs because the dominant firm has become inefficient and fails to respond quickly enough to changes in technology, tastes, methods of distribution or management techniques. In addition, the competitive threat often comes from another large firm. Under these conditions it is unlikely that the dominant firm will be in control and able to manage its decline; mismanaged decline would be a more apt description.

If some form of control is possible, it is more likely to come from ownership of key inputs or sales outlets, which allow the dominant firm to employ various vertical strategies, than from pricing policy.

It is also worth noting that a long-term downward trend in market share may be punctuated by shorter periods during which dominance is strengthened, as a result either of change of management or, where competition policy allows it, of acquisitions. Just as acquisitions may be responsible for creating dominance in the first place, so they may strengthen existing dominant positions. This has certainly been the case for several UK companies such as Pilkington (glass), Courtaulds (cellulosic fibres) and BPB (plasterboard). Acquisitions and mergers, however, certainly do not guarantee success – the British motor industry provides a spectacular example of merger failure. In 1968, the merger of BMC and Leyland gave the new company, British Leyland, a near 50 per cent share of the UK market. However, BL staggered from one crisis to another and its market share fell steadily. Large government subsidies were needed to prevent a complete collapse. In 1988, the company, now known as the Rover Group and with just 15 per cent of the UK market, became part of British Aerospace and heavily dependent for survival on the Japanese company, Honda.

Although, as in the case of Dunlop and BL, decline may lead to complete collapse of the company, this is by no means always the case. In fact it is quite common to find that, although dominant firms may suffer a significant decline, they still retain the position of the largest firm in the industry. This must clearly have something to do with management changes and efforts to improve efficiency as the firm attempts to halt the decline. It may also be due in part to the type of market that evolves. Dominance is typically replaced by a tight oligopolistic structure. If we assume that the firms that succeed at the dominant firm's expense are small in number, are the most efficient of the dominant firm's competitors, and are accommodated by the dominant firm once they have become important players in the market, it may then become difficult for other firms to compete and the industry settles down to a tightly knit oligopolistic group with the previously dominant firm still playing a leading role.

The history of dominant firms shows that in many cases dominance tends to persist or to be eroded at a very slow pace. The explanation for this persistence, where it is found, is a combination of efficiency advantages, strategic manoeuvrings that disadvantage smaller competitors and potential entrants, and outright restrictive practices. The evidence is not sufficiently complete to allow general statements to be made about the relative importance of these factors, but numerous case studies and investigations by the competitive authorities suggest that efficiency advantages provide only a part of the explanation.

Chapter 7

Oligopoly pricing

7.1 INTRODUCTION

Chapter 5 looked at different aspects of market structure, and its importance. This showed that market structure is an important determinant of conduct and performance, but that it is necessary to realise both that structure does not rigidly determine performance, and also that structure is not exogenous but can be affected by firms' behaviour. Chapter 6 examined the market structure which is closest to the textbook case of simple monopoly – i.e. dominance. In this chapter we move on to consider industries which can be described as oligopolistic and focus attention on pricing behaviour in these industries. An oligopolistic industry contains a small number of firms, which means that the effect of any action taken by one of the firms will depend on how its rivals react. For instance, a price cut by one firm will result in a larger increase in sales if the other firms in the industry maintain their existing price than if they all follow its example.

It is this interdependence which is the defining characteristic of oligopoly and which makes the analysis of oligopolistic industries so much more difficult than that of either more concentrated (monopoly) or less concentrated (competitive) industries. Yet it is very important to be able to understand the behaviour of firms in oligopolistic industries because so many markets in advanced economies consist of a relatively small number of firms who are intensely aware of their rivals' reactions to any competitive move.

Monopolies or dominant firms are able to decide on their pricing and other policies without worrying about the reactions of any other, smaller, firms in the market. In oligopolistic markets, firms have a certain amount of scope for independent action, but are constrained by their rival firms to an extent which depends on, among other things, the number and size of the oligopolists and the similarity of their products. This chapter considers only price-setting behaviour, and only as influenced by competition among existing competitors. Other important aspects of oligopolistic behaviour include: product differentiation (Chapter 8), and research and development (Chapter 9). Potential competition and entry deterrence are covered in Chapter 10.

This chapter summarises a range of different approaches to analysing price-setting under oligopoly, and it will be seen that this is a dense and rich area of industrial economics. The plan of the chapter is as follows: section 7.2 introduces the game theory approach to oligopoly; sections 7.3 and 7.4 examine non-cooperative and collusive oligopoly models respectively; section 7.5 looks at average cost pricing as a way of achieving price coordination; and, lastly, section 7.6 briefly surveys the different types of empirical evidence on oligopoly pricing. Because the central issue is how to handle interdependence and firms' reaction to interdependence, the meaning of interdependence is spelt out in more detail in the next section.

Oligopolistic interdependence

Let us assume that all the firms in our industry are aiming to maximise their profits, that they produce a homogeneous product and that the market demand curve is given by $Q = \alpha - \beta P$; where Q is market output and P is market price. The problem for a single oligopolistic firm is that, unlike either a monopolist or a competitive firm, it does not face a given demand curve. Rather, the amount it can sell at any price depends on the behaviour of the other firms in the market. Therefore an oligopolist cannot reach a unique solution to the question of how much output it should produce and what price it should charge; it has to make a decision under uncertainty concerning the reactions of its rivals.

To illustrate this, consider the case of an oligopolist choosing output Q_i to maximise profits (π):

$$\pi_i = PQ_i - c_iQ_i - F_i,$$

where F_i represent fixed costs and c_i are constant marginal costs. For maximum profits, then:

$$\frac{d\pi_i}{dQ_i} = \left[\frac{dP.Q_i}{dQ_i} + P\right] - c_i = 0.$$

It is the first term on the right-hand side of this expression which shows the presence of interdependence: the effect which a change in firm i's output has on market price depends on whether the other firms react by changing their own outputs. We meet here the important concept of *conjectural variation*, which is the (proportional) alteration in firm j's output which firm i expects following a change in its own output, i.e. conjectural variation $= dq_j/dq_i$.

where $dq_j = dQ_j/Q_j$, etc.

Therefore, a conjectural variation of zero means that firm i believes that the other firms in the market will not change their output if firm i changes its own. We can rewrite the above expression, multiplying both top and bottom of $dp.Q_i/dQ_i$ by dQ to give:

$$\frac{d\pi_i}{dQ_i} = \left[\frac{dP.dQ.Q_i}{dQ.dQ_i} + P\right] - c_i = 0.$$

With zero conjectural variation, $dQ/dQ_i = 1$, i.e. the only change in market output is due to firm i. We can now proceed to derive the profit-maximising mark-up of price over cost:

$$\left[\frac{dP.Q_i}{dQ} + P\right] - c_i = 0.$$

$$P - c_i = -\frac{dP.Q_i}{dQ}$$

$$\frac{P - c_i}{P} = -\frac{dP.Q_i}{dQ.P}$$

$$\frac{P - c_i}{P} = -\frac{dP.Q.Q_i}{dQ.P.Q}$$

$$\frac{P - c_i}{P} = -\frac{1}{e} \times S_i,$$

where e is the market elasticity of demand and S_i is the market share of firm i.

The assumption of zero conjectural variation provides a useful benchmark in oligopoly analysis, and underlies the important Cournot model discussed in section 7.3 below. More generally, however, interdependence means that firms do react to changes in each others' outputs, so that conjectural variations are non-zero. If an increase, say, in firm i's output causes other firms also to expand output, then conjectural variation is positive and the dQ/dQ_i term in the expression above will be greater than 1. Therefore both profit-maximising output and the mark-up will be affected.

Suppose we have the general definition of conjectural variation:

$$\frac{dQ_j}{Q_j} = \alpha\frac{dQ_i}{Q_i} \text{ where } \alpha > 0$$

then

$$\frac{dQ}{dQ_i} = 1 + \alpha\frac{(Q - 1)}{Q_i},$$

which can be substituted into the condition for profit maximisation:

$$\frac{dP.dQ.Q_i}{dQ.dQ_i} + P - c_i = 0.$$

$$\frac{P - c_i}{} = -\frac{dP.dQ.Q_i}{dQ.dQ_i}$$

$$\frac{P - c_i}{P} = -\frac{dP.Q_i}{dQ.P}[1 + \alpha \frac{(Q - 1)}{Q_i}]$$

$$\frac{P - c_i}{P} = \frac{S_i}{e}(1 - \alpha) + \frac{\alpha}{e} .$$

This demonstrates, therefore, that the profit-maximising mark-up of price over cost depends on conjectural variation α, as well as the structural variables, market share and market elasticity of demand.

The obvious next question is, what determines the value of α? How do firms form an expectation of how their rivals will react to any change in their own output? We shall see during this chapter that this is not a simple question. One factor which influences the value of α is the number and relative size of the oligopolistic firms: the fewer firms and the more equal they are in size, the more likely it is that each firm will react to a move by one of the others. But firms also learn from experience and the past history of competition in an oligopolistic market will be relevant. The idea that other firms won't react ($\alpha = 0$) may characterise an inexperienced firm which hasn't got used to interdependence, but over time oligopolists will revise their conjectural variations on the basis of experience.

The logical limit to learning to live with interdependence is to recognise it explicitly, so that the interdependent firms collude to set a price which will maximise joint profits. If the firms agree to share the market in this way, then $\alpha = 1$, i.e. to preserve the agreed market shares, all firms change their output by the same percentage. In this case the above expression for the profit-maximising mark-up reduces to $1/e$, which is the same as for a single monopolist. Oligopolistic interdependence creates conflicting pressures on the firms concerned both to get together, i.e. to collude, and to try and get more profit for themselves alone by expanding output or cutting price. The operation of these conflicting pressures can be illustrated powerfully using some elementary concepts of game theory, as demonstrated in the next section.

7.2 THE GAME THEORY APPROACH TO OLIGOPOLISTIC BEHAVIOUR

Because the central feature of an oligopolistic market is the interdependence between firms, many important features of oligopolies can be illustrated using the techniques of game theory, which is a method of analysis applicable whenever the outcome for one party (player) depends on the choices made by another party. In this context each party has to develop a *strategy*. That is, firm i has to choose the course of action which will be best for it given firm i's expectations about how the other firms will behave.

A type of game which is useful in looking at oligopoly is the general type called the *prisoners' dilemma*, from the following story. Suppose the police hold two suspects for a crime in separate cells with no possibility of communication. The police wish to secure a conviction, and are willing to pardon one prisoner if he turns state's evidence, confesses to the crime and informs against the other prisoner. If both confess they both get a reduced sentence; if neither confesses they will both be prosecuted on a lesser charge. Each prisoner then has to decide independently whether or not to confess. The feature of this story which resembles the oligopolists' situation is that, although there is a conflict of interest between the two parties (each prisoner can gain from confessing if the other does not), there is also some common interest in that they can both gain by cooperating and agreeing not to confess.

In the context of oligopoly we can think of two firms, A and B, choosing between a low- and a high-output strategy. Each firm individually does best, i.e. makes more profit, by choosing a high level of output *as long as the other firm produces a low output*. If both firms choose a high output, however, industry output will also be high, price will be low and so will profits. If both firms choose low output the converse applies.

The profits accruing to firms A and B in every combination of chosen strategies are given in Figure 7.1. In each box the first figure (at the bottom) gives A's profits and the second figure gives B's profits. Now, what will each firm decide to do? Let us think about firm A's choice: if it thinks that firm B is going to produce a high output, then it will do better by also producing a high output level (with profit of 1) than if it went for low output (zero profit). If firm A thinks that firm B is going to choose low output, then again it will do better to produce a high output (profit of 3) than a low one (profit of 2). Therefore, it is better for A to choose a high output whatever it thinks B is going to do, and high output is said to be the *dominant* strategy. Exactly the same argument will apply to firm B's decision, and therefore the non-cooperative solution to this game is that both firms choose to produce high output and make profits of 1.

Without cooperation, then, both firms independently choose to produce high output, and this choice is an equilibrium in the sense that each firm, given that the other firm has chosen a high level of output, will not wish to change its own decision. Producing high output is the best each firm can do, given the other's

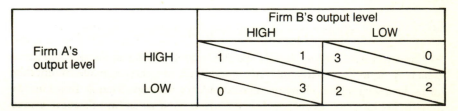

Figure 7.1 The 'prisoners' dilemma' game

choice of strategy. This concept of equilibrium is known as *Nash equilibrium* and will be encountered elsewhere in this chapter. However, although high output by both firms is an equilibrium position, it is obvious from Figure 7.1 that the firms could do better than this if they adopted a different approach to the problem of interdependence and agreed to cooperate. In this case both firms would agree to produce a low output level, giving each of them a profit level of 2, and total profit would be higher than with any other combination of strategies.

Later on in this chapter (section 7.4) we look at collusive models of oligopoly and the circumstances in which a collusive outcome can successfully be reached and sustained. Figure 7.1, however, demonstrates the essence of the problem. Despite the fact that the cooperative solution has the desirable effect of maximising joint profits, which gives the oligopolists an incentive to collude, it is also true that each firm could increase its own profits by cheating. If firm A reneges on the collusive solution by raising its output level, then as long as firm B sticks to the agreement to produce low output, the cheating firm A will make a profit of 3 and firm B will make no profit. Alongside the incentive to collude, then, such a structure of profits under different combinations of strategies simultaneously creates an incentive to cheat.

It should be clear by now that the simple structure laid out above can be used to illuminate various aspects of oligopolistic interdependence. These are not confined to the choice of price or output; on the contrary, any situation in which the outcome to one party depends on the behaviour of the other party may be analysed by game theory. In such a situation the firm's choice of behaviour is described as *strategic*, and we shall see in other chapters that oligopolistic behaviour with respect to entry prevention, advertising, product differentiation and research and development has been examined using the approach of game theory.

In reality, oligopolists coexist for what may be a very long time, and can therefore not be regarded as playing a 'one-off' game in which they make a single choice of strategy. Rather, they play a repeated game in which all the parties choose a strategy and can choose a different one next time round, depending on what everyone else chose last time. Lastly in this section, it is worth mentioning that the game theory approach has led to a large number of empirical studies in which the players choose price under different conditions relating to number of firms and completeness of information. Some of the results of this work are referred to in section 7.6 below.

7.3 NON-COOPERATIVE MODELS OF OLIGOPOLY PRICING

In this section we look at certain specific models of oligopolistic behaviour in which the firms do not collude. These models differ in how they characterise the firms' handling of the interdependence which is central to their situation. We start by looking at models in which the firms produce identical products, and then move on to models including heterogeneous products.

Models with homogeneous products

In this section we shall examine a group of oligopoly models which make restrictive assumptions in order to be able to concentrate on the central issue of how interdependent firms decide their price and output levels. Therefore, we shall assume initially that the industry consists of two firms only, which make an identical product, that there is a linear market demand curve ($P = \alpha - \beta Q$), that the firms face zero marginal costs, and that they seek to maximise profits.

Cournot model

The distinctive feature of the Cournot model of oligopoly is the way the firms handle their interdependence. Cournot (1838) assumed that each firm chooses its own output level on the assumption that the other firm will maintain its existing level of output. This corresponds, as will be obvious from section 7.1 above, to a zero conjectural variation. It amounts to an asymmetric recognition of interdependence: firm A recognises that it is interdependent with B when it chooses a level of output which depends on what B is doing, but its assumption that B will maintain this output level denies that B's choice is equally dependent on A's output level.

On the assumption of zero conjectural variation it is possible to derive each firm's *reaction curve*, as follows. Firm A seeks to maximise profits by choosing the level of output at which marginal cost (assumed zero) equals marginal revenue. However, the marginal revenue curve facing firm A, like its demand curve, depends on B's output level (which A is assuming won't change). The higher B's output, the less of the market demand is left for A to meet, and the lower its profit-maximising level of output will be. This can be shown in Figure 7.2.

If firm B is expected to produce Q_{B1}, the demand curve facing A is D_{A1} with associated marginal revenue curve MR_{A1}. In this case the profit-maximising level of output for A is Q_{A1}, where $MR_{A1} = MC = 0$. Supposing, however, firm B was expected to produce the higher level of output Q_{B2}. In this case firm A would be able to sell less at any price, would face the lower demand curve D_{A2} and marginal revenue curve MR_{A2}, and would choose the lower level of output Q_{A2}. Therefore, the more output firm B is expected to produce, the lower is firm A's profit-maximising output level. If we plot firm A's chosen output level against the output of firm B which determined this level, then we have firm A's reaction curve R_A, i.e. this curve tells us, for any level of Q_B, how much A will want to produce. Firm B's reaction curve, R_B, can be derived in exactly the same way. Figure 7.3 shows both reaction curves.

Given each firm's decision to set its output on the assumption that the other firm won't change its output, how much output will each firm end up producing? Suppose firm B is initially producing output Q_{B1}. Given this information, then firm A will, from its reaction curve R_A, choose to produce Q_{A1}. However, this

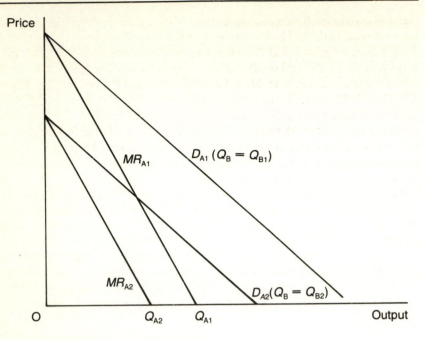

Figure 7.2 Derivation of reaction curves

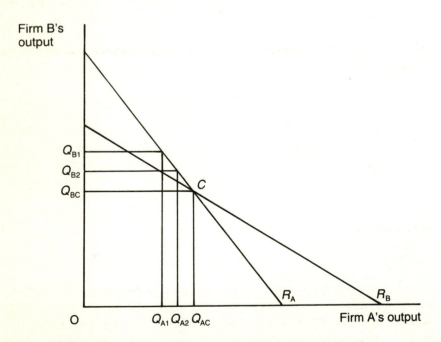

Figure 7.3 Reaction curves and Cournot equilibrium

fact will cause firm B to reduce its output, from Q_{B1} to the level Q_{B2}. Firm A in turn will react to this fall in B's output by expanding its output to Q_{A2}, and so on. This interactive process will continue, with firm B cutting its output and firm A expanding by smaller and smaller amounts, until we reach the point C where the two reaction curves intersect. Here A produces Q_{AC} and B produces Q_{BC}. The fact that C is on A's reaction curve means that, given that B is producing Q_{BC}, A's profit-maximising output level is Q_{AC}, i.e. here for the first time A will not want to change its output level. Exactly the same argument applies to firm B: each firm is doing as well as it can, given what the other firm is doing. The point C is therefore an equilibrium in exactly the sense of a Nash equilibrium explained above, and Cournot equilibrium is a special case of Nash equilibrium.

On the assumptions already made, we can work out the equilibrium output levels algebraically as well as showing them on a diagram. We have already seen that the condition for profit-maximisation gives, with zero conjectural variations:

$$\frac{dP.Q_i}{dQ} + P - c_i = 0.$$

On the Cournot assumption of zero marginal cost, and given that $dP/dQ = -\beta$, this becomes:

$$-\beta Q_A + P = 0$$

$$Q_A = \frac{P}{\beta}$$

and exactly the same expression can be derived for Q_B. Therefore, adding the two together we get:

$$Q_A + Q_B = Q = \frac{2P}{\beta} = \frac{2\alpha - 2\beta Q}{\beta}$$

$$\beta Q = 2\alpha - 2\beta Q$$

$$3\beta Q = 2\alpha$$

$$Q = \frac{2\alpha}{3\beta}$$

and therefore

$$P = \frac{\alpha}{3}$$

Since we have assumed that the two oligopolists are identical, each will produce exactly half of the market output. So $Q_A = Q_B = \alpha/3\beta$. If the same market demand curve were met by a single monopolist, profit-maximising output would be $\alpha/2\beta$, while if this were a competitive market, output would be α/β. Therefore the market output in the Cournot model is between the competitive and monopolistic output levels (two-thirds of the former, compared with half in the monopoly case) and market price will similarly be above the competitive price but not as high as monopoly price. If we relax the assumption that there are only two firms in the market, then output increases and price falls as the number of oligopolists increases. With n firms, market output is $n\alpha/(n+1)\beta$ and price is $\alpha/(n+1)$.

Let us now return to examine the nature of the Cournot solution and the assumptions on which it is based. First, the solution in Figure 7.3 above is stable, meaning that any move away from point C will set in force reactions by firms A and B which will move back towards point C. This is true as long as R_A is steeper than R_B. If the slopes are the other way round, than the firms' reaction to each other's output level will move away from C not towards it. Secondly, the solution depends on the assumption made by each firm that its own output decision will not cause the other one to adjust its output. The firms maintain this assumption in the face of contrary evidence: only at C in Figure 7.3 above is the expectation that the other firm won't change its output fulfilled. Why in general should firms go on acting on the basis of a belief which has been shown to be false? It seems more likely that firms will learn from experience that they do affect each other's output levels, and that, having recognised interdependence, they may be able to find a solution which will offer more profit than the Cournot solution. One such solution would be for the two firms to cooperate and agree to produce no more than the joint profit-maximising output; cooperative models of oligopoly behaviour are discussed in section 7.4 below.

Stackelberg model

Alternatively, if either firm recognises the nature of the interdependence, then a different non-cooperative solution from the Cournot equilibrium may be reached, as first suggested by von Stackelberg (1934). In Stackelberg's model, firms can choose whether to behave as followers or leaders. A follower behaves as in the Cournot model and will therefore choose a profit-maximising output level given its expectation about the other firm's output. A leader, however, goes a step further towards recognising the nature of the interdependence between the two firms. Suppose firm A is the leader. Firm A then realises that firm B's choice of output depends on how much it expects firm A to produce, i.e. A recognises that B is operating along a reaction function. The problem for firm A then becomes that of choosing the point on B's reaction function where its own profit is maximised. This can most easily be illustrated by combining B's reaction function with A's iso-profit curves.

An *iso-profit curve* for firm A shows all those combinations of Q_A and Q_B which give the same profit for firm A, and two of these curves are shown in Figure 7.4. The shape of these curves depends on the market demand curve and the firms' cost functions. Suppose firm B is expected to produce Q_{B0}. Then the profit-maximising level of output for A can be read off A's reaction function as

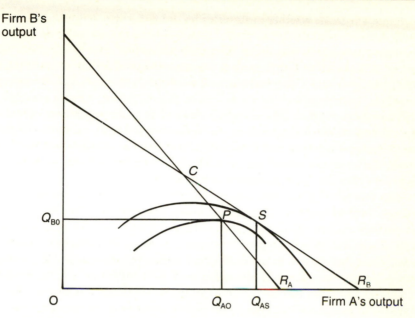

Figure 7.4 Reaction curves and Stackelberg equilibrium

Q_{A0}, at point P. If firm A were to produce either more or less than Q_{A0}, while B's output remained at Q_{B0}, A's profits would fall. The shape of the iso-profit curves shows that, moving in either direction from P, if firm A is to maintain the same level of profit as at P, then firm B must produce a lower level of output, because only then will an increase in the demand facing firm A compensate for the loss in profits incurred by moving away from Q_{A0}. Also, the lower the curve (i.e. the nearer to the Q_A axis) the higher is the level of profit earned by firm A. For a given level of Q_A, the lower is Q_B the higher will be the demand curve facing firm A, and therefore the higher its price and profit.

The Stackelberg leader's problem, then, is to find the highest level of profit consistent with R_B. The highest level of profit means the lowest attainable iso-profit curve on the diagram, and this is reached at the point where the reaction function is tangential to an iso-profit curve, at the point S.

Figure 7.4. shows that, if firm A acts as a leader and firm B as a follower, then A ends up making more profit than at the Cournot solution (point C), and firm B does worse than at C. Firm A also has a higher output level than firm B; at the point S in Figure 7.4 the leader produces an output equal to the monopoly profit-maximising level ($a/2\beta$) and the follower produces half as much. Their combined output is therefore three-quarters of the competitive output (compared with two-thirds in the Cournot model) and it follows that the market price will be lower and nearer to the competitive price with the Stackelberg than with the Cournot non-cooperative solution.

Firms will decide whether to act as leader or follower by comparing the profits to be made in each case. In the above case there is a profit incentive for the firms to behave as leader. If firm A can choose its output first, then it will gain a *first-mover advantage* over firm B, both in the sense that it makes more profit than B and in the sense that it does better than it would at C. However, if, following this argument, both firms wish to act as leaders and move first, then no equilibrium will initially be reached since each firm chooses its profit-maximising output on the assumption that the other firm will 'follow', i.e. take up the indicated point on its reaction function, and if the other firm has also decided to behave as a leader this expectation will not be fulfilled. If both firms decide to behave as followers, then the Cournot solution will be reached.

The existence of the Stackelberg equilibrium as a stable solution to an oligopoly model which is different from the Cournot solution, therefore, depends on one firm choosing to be the leader and one the follower. This raises the question of why this should happen. This can't be answered within the simplifying assumption that the two firms are identical, because if one firm would gain from being leader then so would the other and no equilibrium will be reached. However, if firm A is quicker than B to grasp the advantage of acting as a leader, then B will recognise that, once A has moved to its profit-maximising point on R_B, B's own profits will be better if it decides to act as follower than if it also tried to be a leader, since in this case their joint output will be high, profits will be low and they will be pushed towards the competitive solution.

An advantage which will enable one firm to act as leader might be conferred by superior size. However the Stackelberg model leads to a different result from price leadership models in which an industry consists of one big (dominant) firm and a competitive fringe of smaller firms (see Chapter 6). Another situation in which one firm has an advantage which will enable it to act as leader is where a market contains a single incumbent firm who is faced with the strategic choice of whether to allow another firm to enter the market, or to prevent entry. (See Chapter 10.)

Models incorporating heterogeneous products

In this section we look at a group of models which recognise an important aspect of oligopoly ignored by the models already discussed. This is that the interdependent firms may be producing differentiated products. If products are heterogeneous, the nature of the relationship between the firms will be changed. For one thing, if firms are producing related but slightly different goods, then they have more chance of separating their own demand curve from that of their competitors. There will be more scope for prices to vary. Also, charging a price above rivals' prices will not necessarily mean losing all sales, since some customers may value a specific version of the product enough to pay more for it. Secondly, the existence of heterogeneous products makes possible non-price competition, which is a strong feature of oligopolistic markets. The firms can compete by trying to introduce new and improved products and by advertising designed to capture more of the market for a specific brand. However these non-price mechanisms are dealt with in other chapters; here we wish to explore the consequences of heterogeneous products for pricing behaviour.

It is necessary first to recognise the difficulties of dealing with firms producing differentiated products; the main problem is to define the market, in other words to recognise a group of firms whose products are sufficiently similar for the firms to treat each other as rivals, so that the firms are interdependent in the true oligopolistic sense. This problem is discussed in more detail in Chapter 8.

Chamberlin's model

Chamberlin's 'small group' model contains a small number of firms (assumed for simplicity to equal two in the following analysis), so that each one's actions have a significant effect on the others, and differentiated products, so that each firm has some possibility of separating its own market (Chamberlin 1933). In this case we can distinguish two different demand curves facing each firm (see Figure 7.5). The less elastic, DD', curve, shows how demand would respond to changes in price if all firms charged the same price. The flatter curve, dd', shows how the quantity sold by firm A would vary if it changed its own price and none of the others followed suit.

Chamberlin assumed that the firms will recognise their interdependence, or

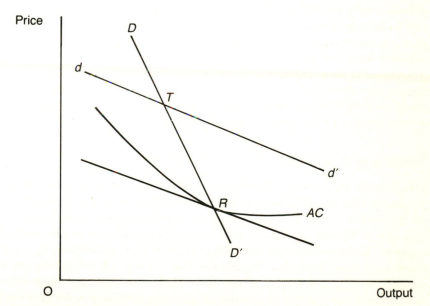

Figure 7.5 Chamberlin's model of oligopoly

that, even if they start with the Cournot assumption of zero conjectural variation, they will learn from experience that their own output decisions do affect the other firms. Suppose firm A initially chooses its profit-maximising output on the assumption that firm B has no output. In this case firm A will choose the monopolistic output (half of market demand), and firm B will respond, on Cournot assumptions, by in turn choosing an output which is equal to half the remaining half of the market. However, at this stage firm A recognises this sequence as proof of interdependence, and realises that the solution which will maximise industry profits is to share the monopoly output (equally, on the assumption of identical costs). Firm A therefore now chooses an output level equal to that of firm B, and they establish a profit-maximising outcome without collusion. Suppose this point is shown by T in the diagram above.

Although the point T corresponds to maximum *total* profits, each firm could increase its own profits by lowering price and increasing sales, provided that the other firm didn't follow the price change. This possibility is shown by the curve dd', which intersects DD' at the existing price. Therefore the joint profit-maximising solution in this model is subject to the same instability problem from the incentive to 'cheat' as when the solution is reached by an explicitly collusive process. Since both firms are subject to the same incentive, there will be a tendency for price to fall from its initial level, and so dd' will slide down DD'. The bottom of this slide is reached at the point R, where no supernormal profits are made; any further price reduction would lead the firms to make losses.

Chamberlin's model suggests that, with few sellers and differentiated products, it is impossible to say for certain where price will be established, but it will be somewhere within the limits set by joint profit maximisation and zero profits. Because of the differentiated products, the lower limit is set at a higher price and lower output than with homogeneous products; in the latter case dd' would be horizontal and price could fall to the lowest point of the cost curve, AC. Therefore the more differentiated are the products, the steeper dd', and the smaller the range of possible prices. In addition, the smaller the number of firms, the more likely it is that the joint profit-maximising point will be sustained, for reasons explained more fully in section 7.4 below.

Kinked-demand curve model

Like Chamberlin's model, the kinked demand curve examines a group of firms producing differentiated products, but, instead of explaining how an equilibrium price or output is reached, it predicts that an equilibrium price, however reached, will tend to be more stable than profit-maximising behaviour would normally suggest. This model assumes that firms recognise their interdependence in the following specific sense: each firm assumes that any price cut will be followed by its rivals, but that if it were to increase its price the other firms would not follow suit. On this assumption the demand curve facing each firm is discontinuous, with a kink at the current price. Since the firm expects its rivals to match price cuts but not increases, its demand curve is more elastic above than below the current price, as shown in Figure 7.6.

Since the demand curve for each firm has a kink in it, showing that it is essentially made up of two different demand curves embodying different conjectural variations, the corresponding marginal revenue curve is also discontinuous and in fact has a gap in it vertically below the current price. For all prices above current price OP the relevant marginal revenue curve is AC, marginal to the more elastic demand curve AB; while for prices below OP the demand curve is the less elastic segment BD and the appropriate marginal revenue curve is therefore FG.

It is the existence of the vertical gap CF which provides an explanation for price stability in oligopolistic markets. Consider first Figure 7.6(a). Suppose the marginal cost curve of the firm is initially MC_1; then it would be possible for marginal costs to increase by a considerable amount without affecting either profit-maximising price or output as long as the MC curve continues to pass through the discontinuity in the MR curve. Also, shifts in demand may not affect price, although in this case output will change, as long as the MC curve goes through the vertical gap in the MR curve (Figure 7.6(b)). So, the kinked demand curve model, unlike conventional profit-maximising models, predicts that price will be stable when faced with some degree of change in cost and demand conditions. The bigger the discontinuity in the MR curve, the more cost or demand can change without affecting price. Therefore, a bigger difference between the elasticities of the two segments, due for instance to less highly differentiated products, increases price stability.

The kinked demand curve model was developed, at least partly, as an interpretation of what businessmen said about how prices were set and why they were reluctant to change prices (see section 7.6 below). However, this model has been subject to many criticisms from both theoretical and empirical standpoints. One

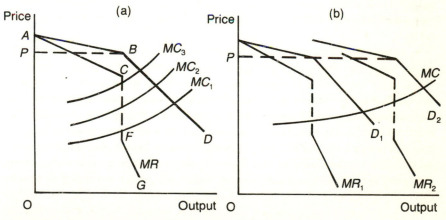

Figure 7.6 The kinked demand curve model of oligopoly

major criticism is that, while the model attempts to explain the stability of price, it provides no explanation at all of how that price is reached in the first place.

The second main theoretical criticism is that, while the assumptions about rivals' reactions which underlie the model may be justified for a group of firms who have little information about each other's reactions, over a period of time it would be in the interests of all the firms in the market to find some way of eliminating the kink. Suppose costs in the industry have risen to the extent where the *MC* curve no longer passes through the discontinuity in the *MR* curve. The firm would now like to raise its price but will be deterred by its belief about rivals' reaction. If one firm feels that it has to respond to the increase in costs by raising price, then the other firms will quickly follow, and the kink in the demand curve disappears.

Over time, as firms in a market acquire experience of each other's reactions to cost and demand changes, they are likely to develop ways of handling their interdependence which have the same effect of getting rid of the kink without relying on one firm to stick its neck out and raise its price first in order to test reactions. The logical conclusion to this argument is that some form of collusion will develop between the firms in the industry. This need not necessarily be a formal price-setting cartel; looser forms of agreement such as agreeing to exchange information or price leadership can achieve exactly the same effect of ensuring that price changes in either direction will be followed. We return to the issue of cartels and other forms of restrictive practice in more detail in the next section.

Empirical criticisms of the kinked demand curve model have cast doubt on its central prediction that prices will tend to be stable in oligopolistic markets. First, there is no evidence that rivals are less likely to follow price increases than price cuts. Second, prices have been found to be no more stable in oligopolistic than in monopolistic markets. Third, among oligopolistic markets the pattern of price changes does not fit with that predicted by the kinked demand curve model. For instance, prices are more stable when collusion operates. Also, greater price rigidity is associated with more differentiated products, contrary to the prediction made above that more heterogeneity makes for a smaller gap in the *MR* curve.

In conclusion, then, the specific version of interdependence assumed by the kinked demand curve model does not provide a successful general model of oligopoly. It seems unlikely that firms would continue to act on the assumption that rivals will not follow a price rise when it is in their interest to develop a way of eliminating the kink in the demand curve. While evidence does suggest that firms will not always change price immediately in response to small changes in cost and demand, the finding that prices are no more rigid in oligopolistic than in monopolistic markets suggests that the reason for such rigidity may lie elsewhere. One possible explanation is average cost pricing, to which we return in section 7.5.

Customer attachments

Another explanation of price rigidity has been put forward by Okun in his theory of customer attachments. Okun (1981) explains the existence of a kinked demand curve, and the associated price rigidity, as being a feature of what he calls customer markets. A customer market, as opposed to an auction market, is one in which sellers set prices and consumers search among alternative sellers. This search imposes shopping costs on the consumer, and by equating the marginal cost and benefit of search the consumer sets a reservation price. When the consumer finds a supplier offering the product at or below his reservation price he will buy it from that supplier.

The existence of search costs creates an incentive for both supplier and consumer to economise on such costs by forming a long-term relationship or customer attachment, so that consumers keep on going back to the same supplier. The price previously paid for the product, say P_0, is important here. If the repeat shopper can purchase the product at no higher than P_0, she will stay with the same supplier. If the price has gone up, she may decide to search else-where, so the demand curve for repeat shoppers is elastic above P_0. However, if the price has fallen, repeat shoppers will not necessarily buy more since they have already shown their willingness to pay P_0, and therefore the demand curve below P_0 is inelastic for repeat shoppers. However, there are also shoppers new to the market whose demand curve is random and therefore elastic throughout.

Therefore, and as shown in Figure 7.7, the firm faces two separate demand curves, one from new and one from repeat shoppers, and it is the addition of

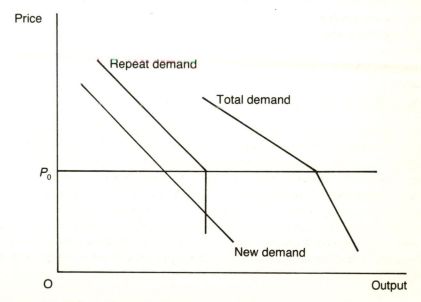

Figure 7.7 Kinked demand and customer attachments

these two curves which gives the kinked total demand curve, with demand being more elastic above than below P_0.

Okun's theory therefore explains the kinked demand curve as arising from customer attachments rather than from a specific view of the nature of oligopolistic interdependence which makes a firm reluctant to raise prices because it does not expect other firms to follow suit. Rather, the reluctance to raise prices results from not wishing to lose repeat shoppers, and this is not unique to oligopolists. Okun's theory is therefore more general in that it explains the existence of price rigidity in any type of market structure where shopping costs are important so that established customers are valued.

7.4 PRICE-FIXING CARTELS AND JOINT PROFIT MAXIMISATION

The previous sections have shown that in an oligopolistic market the interdependence between firms creates simultaneous incentives for the firms to compete and to cooperate. In this section we examine the outcome if the firms adopt the latter approach. One way of dealing with the problem of each firm's profits being dependent on the actions of the other firms in the industry is to internalise this interdependence. In this case, instead of each firm trying to take an independent decision on price and output, the firms act together and reach a joint decision on total output. As we shall see, the advantage of such cooperation is that the firms can increase their profits compared with a non-cooperative solution. Joint profits are maximised. However, such a solution is not easily reached, and we consider below the factors which make collusion relatively likely or unlikely to succeed. It follows from the discussion of game theory in section 7.2 that, although collusion may succeed in maximising the total profits of all the firms in a market, each individual firm may stand to increase its own profit by undercutting the agreed price and increasing its own sales. This incentive to cheat makes all collusive agreement inherently unstable.

The incentive to cooperate

The incentive for firms to cooperate can be illustrated using the diagram of Figure 7.4, and adding in the iso-profit curves of firm B. The result is shown in Figure 7.8. At the non-cooperative solutions reached in either the Cournot or Stackelberg models the iso-profit curves of firms A and B will intersect, at points C and S respectively. This indicates an inefficient solution, in the sense that at least one firm could benefit, without either losing out, by agreeing to cooperate.

What is meant by cooperation here is that it is possible for the firms to agree to reduce their output levels and thereby for at least one firm to earn more profit than without cooperating. For instance, starting at point C in this diagram, firm A could maintain its profit level while firm B increases its profits, by moving to point F; at this point firm B is earning the highest profit level for B consistent with A being as well off as at C. At F the iso-profit lines of the two firms are tang-

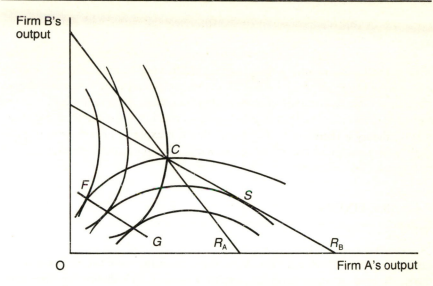

Figure 7.8 Reaction curves and cooperative oligopoly

ential, and this indicates a pair of output levels which is Pareto-efficient, i.e. it is not possible to increase the profits of one firm without reducing those of the other. Similarly, and starting again at C, firm B is made no worse off while firm A gains profit by a move from C to G, where again the iso-profit lines are tangential. The whole set of points of tangency between iso-profit curves constitutes a contract curve of efficient output pairs reachable by cooperation. However, only the segment FG of the contract curve corresponds to gains from trade, i.e. within this range neither firm is made worse off compared with the non-cooperative solution C, and anywhere between F and G both firms are actually better off and therefore gain from cooperation.

Although all the points on the contract curve represent efficient outcomes, given the costs of the two firms there is only one pair of output levels, i.e. one point on the contract curve, at which joint profits are maximised. Joint profit maximisation is demonstrated below. If all the firms in an industry agree to collude perfectly, i.e. to combine in a cartel, and to produce between them the level of output which will maximise joint profits, then the choice of profit-maximising output and price is exactly the same as that which faces a single firm monopolist, and the same solution will be reached. That is, the cartel will choose the level of output at which their combined marginal cost equals market marginal revenue. For profit maximisation to be achieved, this level of output must be allocated between the individual firms in the cartel so as to equalise marginal cost across firms (this is equivalent to a multiplant monopolist's decision about how to allocate output between different plants).

This process is illustrated in Figure 7.9, which for simplicity considers a cartel

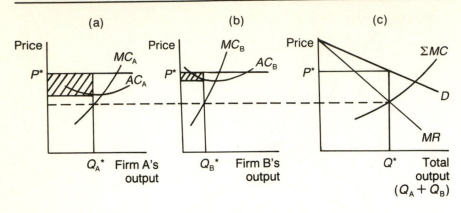

Figure 7.9 The joint profit-maximising allocation of output for a cartel

made up of only two firms. Firm A is a low-cost firm, while firm B has a higher marginal cost at every level of output. Figure 7.9(c) shows the combined marginal cost of the two firms, obtained by summing the individual marginal cost curves horizontally. Total profit-maximising output is determined in Figure 7.9(c) as Q^*, where total marginal cost equals marginal revenue. The market demand curve shows that output Q^* can be sold for P^* per unit. This level of output is divided between firms A and B to equalise their marginal cost: this means that the lower-cost firm A produces more than the higher-cost firm B. The pair of output levels Q_A^* and Q_B^* ($Q_A^* + Q_B^* = Q^*$) represents the joint profit-maximising output levels of the firms who make up the cartel.

The total level of output is lower, and therefore the price is higher, than that reached in the Cournot model. *A fortiori*, output is reduced below the competitive level. The collusive solution therefore leads to a deadweight loss equal to that imposed by a single monopolist. The high price charged by the cartel enables the inefficient firm B, which would be eliminated under competitive conditions, to earn profits and stay in business despite its high costs. This forms the basis of the argument for having a policy against cartels, such as the restrictive practices policy discussed in detail in Chapter 15.

Let us now return to the more general model used previously. It is possible to show that, if the possibility of making *side-payments* exists, then it will always be in the interests of both firms to agree on the joint profit-maximising solution. The argument is illustrated in Figure 7.10. Following from the argument above, the pair of output levels Q_A^* and Q_B^* is necessary for the earning of maximum joint profit. This maximum level of profit is written π^*; any other pair of output levels will produce a lower total profit. The levels of profit earned by each individual firm are also shown on the diagram; because firm B has higher costs it produces a lower output than A, and makes a much lower profit: π_A^* compared with π_B^*. These profit levels correspond to the shaded areas in Figure 7.9(a) and 7.9(b) respectively.

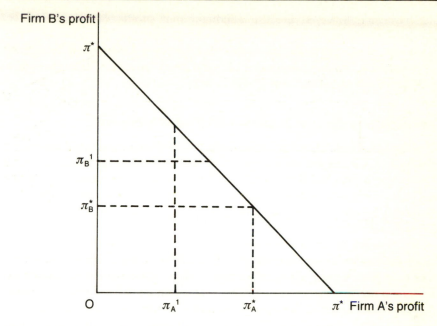

Figure 7.10 Joint profit maximisation and side-payments

Suppose that, in the non-collusive case, firm B has been producing a higher level of output than $Q_B{}^*$ and also earning more profit ($\pi_B{}^1$). Why then should firm B agree to cooperate with firm A? By moving to the joint profit-maximising pair of output levels, total profit can be increased to π^*, and, provided the firms stick to these output levels, this profit can be redistributed between the firms by means of side-payments. Because collusion increases total profits, it will always be possible to ensure by this means that neither firm loses by agreeing to collude. In the case above, although moving to the joint profit-maximising output levels initially means that firm A earns more and firm B earns less profit, firm A can restore firm B's profit to the pre-collusion level (by making a side-payment equal to $\pi_B{}^1 - \pi_B{}^*$) and will still be making more profit itself than it was before collusion.

Therefore, if side-payments are made it will always be possible to guarantee that collusion can make one firm better off without making the other one worse off. This is because, even if the unique point of joint profit maximisation is not on the segment *FG* of the contract curve in Figure 7.8, redistribution by side-payments can move the firms along the contract curve into this segment. If side-payments are not possible, the incentive to collude is reduced but still exists. Without collusion, in general, firm A will not be earning the highest possible profit consistent with a given level of firm B's profit (that is, the firms are not on the contract curve in Figure 7.8) and therefore at least one firm can be made better off by a movement onto the contract curve. The incentive is less than with side-payments, however, because although joint profits can in general be increased, the unique point of joint profit maximisation may not be reached. The institution of side-payments guarantees that this point *can* be reached; without side-payments, this will not be so if one firm would be worse off at the output level consistent with joint profit maximisation.

The incentive to cheat and the stability of collusive agreements

The discussion in the last section has made it clear that a cooperative agreement can succeed in increasing the total profits of the firms in an oligopolistic industry. However, if a particular firm realises that by increasing its own output above the level necessary for joint profit maximisation it can earn more profit, then it has an incentive to cheat on the collusive agreement, and the existence of this incentive will make the agreement unstable.

We therefore discuss in this section the conditions which will make it easier or more difficult for a cartel agreement to be established and to persist. In general terms a cartel is more likely to be successful when the firms involved are similar, so that no one firm has more to gain from cheating, and also when it is easy for the other firms in the cartel to detect and punish any instances of cheating.

Number and size distribution of firms

The first factor influencing the feasibility of joint profit maximisation is the number and relative sizes of the firms concerned. The fewer firms are involved, the easier it is to maintain a pricing agreement, for two reasons. First, the fewer firms the more obvious it is that they are interdependent, so that the alternative to joining together in a cartel is not being able to ignore the other firms but some type of competitive interaction which could leave all the firms worse off. Secondly, the collecting of information on firms' pricing and output policies which is needed to operate a cartel is obviously easier when fewer firms are involved.

However, it is not just the absolute number of firms involved but also their relative size which affects the stability of a cartel. The more similar in size are the firms involved, the more stable is the cartel, because this again makes it more likely that the firms will recognise their interdependence. If one of the firms involved is much larger than the others, it may well be able to ignore the reactions of the other firms, in the short run at least.

Heterogeneity of product

It is easier for a group of firms to agree on a common price and a set of outputs when they are making a homogeneous product. The more similar their products, the more interdependent the firms are and the more likely it is that they will be similarly affected by demand and cost changes. However, this is an instance where the existence of a price cartel may generate changes which threaten its stability. Where firms are forbidden by the terms of the cartel agreement to compete on price they will turn to non-price forms of competition such as advertising and product differentiation.

The more differentiated products become, the harder it is to negotiate a price agreement, since the amount of information required becomes larger and there is more scope for argument about the appropriate set of prices. Also, the more different firms' products are, the more likely it is that they will experience different changes in demand, say, which will put the set of outputs agreed by the cartel under strain. The economics of product differentiation are considered in more detail in the next chapter.

Another factor influencing the operation of cartels which can conveniently be mentioned under the heading of product heterogeneity is the rate of technical change. It is easier to set up and sustain a collusive agreement in an industry where there is not much technical progress, because rapid technical change will mean that product specification alters so that agreements have to be negotiated more often, and also the firms in the cartel will probably be differently affected by the technical change so that they do not all want to agree to the same changes.

Entry conditions

On the other hand, under some circumstances product differentiation can positively assist the operation of a cartel agreement by creating barriers to entry. In the absence of technical economies of scale, heavy advertising may be able to create brand loyalty so that entry is discouraged, and the existing firms in an industry are able to collude and earn high profits.

Demand conditions

The ideal demand conditions for oligopolistic collusion are found where the demand is stable and not 'lumpy'. Industries where demand is growing fast tend to encourage competitive rather than collusive behaviour by firms; rapidly expanding demand gives firms the necessary encouragement to hold on to their market share by competing on price. Also, where demand fluctuates, collusion becomes more difficult since it is difficult for the firms to agree on the output changes necessary to maintain profit maximisation in the face of changes in demand.

Therefore, collusion is more likely to be encountered in markets where demand is static or declining. However, a downturn in demand increases both the pressure on the cartel to stick together, and that on an individual firm to break ranks. When demand declines, the profits of all the firms in a cartel will tend to fall, and this will put pressure on their agreement; an individual firm may wish to break the cartel and cut its price in order to restore profits. However, if price discipline does break down then all the firms concerned may end up making losses, and price agreement may be difficult to re-establish even if demand improves. Therefore in practice a short period of price war may be followed by renewed collusion involving those firms who have survived the competition.

Lastly, it is difficult to organise a successful collusive agreement in an industry, such as shipbuilding, where demand comes in large lumps, i.e. in which a single order is large in relation to annual sales, because it is often impossible to share out demand among firms in such a way that they can all make a profit.

Cost conditions

The cost conditions which favour joint profit maximisation are found where firms have similar costs and their fixed costs form a small proportion of total costs. It is obvious from Figure 7.9 that the more different are the cost curves of all the firms which are party to the agreement, the more dispersion there will be in the profit-maximising output levels of the firms. Therefore where costs vary widely the higher-cost firms will be allocated small output levels with consequently low profits and, in the absence of side-payments, these firms may quickly become discontented and seek to renegotiate the agreement so as to give them more profits.

The problem with a high level of fixed costs, such as is found in the electrical engineering industry, is that in order to keep costs down each firm must operate near full capacity, and therefore each firm in the industry has an incentive to undercut the others by cutting price. In such industries there is a big gap between average total and average variable cost, and this increases the scope for short-run price wars. The problems of maintaining an agreed price under such conditions are obvious, especially if this is also an industry in which demand is lumpy.

Possibility for secret price-cutting

As we have already seen, it will usually be possible for a single firm to increase its profits by cheating on a collusive agreement, provided that the other firms maintain the agreed price. They are more likely to do this if they don't realise that one firm is cutting its price, and therefore 'secret' price cuts are often associated with cartels. This type of behaviour is more likely to be observed when it is difficult for the other firms to detect cheating, and/or difficult to punish cheats effectively.

Generally speaking, it is relatively easy to detect price cuts when there are few firms in the agreement and also a small number of customers, who usually go on buying from the same suppliers. Under these circumstances a switch of a customer to a different supplier may well suggest that the customer has been offered a lower price. Where a firm is detected reducing its price, the sanctions available to the other firms in the agreement are affected by the legal environment (see below). If the other firms react by matching the price cut, then all the firms concerned may face losses. This suggests that the type of firm most likely to cheat is a large firm with financial reserves which is more able than its partners to withstand a period of loss-making.

The legal environment

Most advanced economies have laws which restrict the ability of firms to enter into agreements to charge the same price, as well as other kinds of agreement. The mere existence of such a law is not, of course, enough to stop firms entering into agreements since they will weigh up the gain in profit from collusion against the penalties of being caught operating an illegal agreement. However, the legal framework will influence the type of agreements conducted, and also the sanctions which can be invoked against a cheat. For instance, a firm which cuts its price below an illegally agreed common price level can obviously not be brought to law by the other firms party to the agreement.

In general, as will be discussed in Chapter 15 which deals with restrictive practices policy in much more detail, policy has found it easier to deal with certain kinds of restrictive agreements than with others. Formal price-setting and market-sharing agreements are easier to detect and outlaw than are a whole range of behaviours such as concerted action and parallel pricing. The problem here is that a similar effect, i.e. all firms charging the same price, is achieved without the firms concerned operating anything which can be prosecuted as an illegal agreement, not even a verbal or tacit agreement. In an oligopolistic market, firms' pricing decisions are bound to be interdependent, and different industries will find different ways of managing this interdependence. In the next section we move on from fully fledged oligopolistic collusion to consider alternative means by which a group of firms may learn to manage uncertainty and interdependence.

7.5 AVERAGE COST PRICING AND THE DETERMINATION OF THE MARK-UP

As we have already seen, firms in oligopolistic markets have to make their pricing decisions under considerable uncertainty, which makes the goal of profit maximisation elusive. One way in which firms can proceed in the face of uncertainty is to adopt 'rules of thumb'. A rule of thumb is a relatively simple way of setting prices which does not demand full knowledge concerning demand and cost curves. A well-known rule of thumb, which has received some support from the empirical studies of oligopoly pricing discussed in the next section, is average cost pricing.

The basic idea of average cost pricing is that, rather than setting price by reference to *marginal* cost or revenue, price is equal to average cost plus a profit margin. However, average cost varies with output and therefore this rule raises the question 'set price equal to a margin plus average cost at what output level?' The level of output to be produced over the period in question will probably vary, and is in any case not known with certainty, and therefore unit costs have to be estimated on the basis of a standard volume associated with a given level of capacity utilisation. In Figure 7.11 the standard volume is OQ, average total cost (ATC) at this level of output is QR, the mark-up (whose determination is discussed below) is RS and therefore the price charged is QS (= OP).

What are the implications of this pricing rule? First, if the rule is rigidly adhered to then the price OP will not vary over the business cycle. However, the actual costs of production will change: the average cost curves in Figure 7.11 show that, at least initially, average costs fall as output increases because fixed costs are spread over a larger number of units of output. Therefore, in general, average costs fall in a boom and, if the standard price is maintained, profit margins will increase. Therefore profit margins vary pro-cyclically more than would be observed with short-run profit-maximising pricing behaviour, under which prices would be cut in slumps and raised in booms.

What advantages would firms get from average cost pricing to offset the loss of short-term profits (assuming this to be a feasible alternative)? Holding price constant when demand increases may discourage potential entrants and therefore contribute to profits in the longer term; the firm increases its sales and therefore achieves growth and enhances its long-run competitive position.

However, holding price constant when demand falls may mean making a loss. Competitive behaviour would mean reducing price so as to increase quantity sold. However, in an oligopolistic market following full-cost pricing rules the reaction may be quite different. If output is expected to be below the standard volume for some time, so that costs will be above the unit cost used when the original price was set, an attempt may be made to raise prices in order to main-

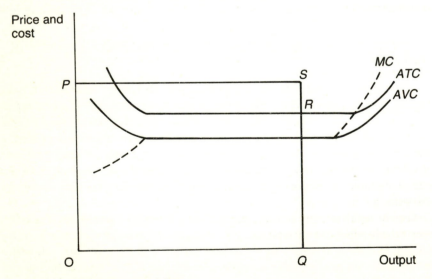

Figure 7.11 Average cost pricing

tain profit margins. Examples of oligopolistic industries where prices have increased during a recession, contrary to the predictions of neoclassical theory, have been found by Blair (1972) in the USA and by the Monopolies and Mergers Commission. For instance, the MMC (1976) found that the London Brick Company, with a market share of 40 per cent, had not used its market power to raise prices at times of high demand, but had been able to raise its prices during a recession to recover profitability.

Second, average cost pricing rules imply that prices will respond to changes in costs rather than changes in demand; any increase in costs of production will lead to an increase in the cost of producing the standard output and therefore, given the mark-up, to a rise in the price.

Third, the ability to raise prices in a recession depends on the ability of the firms concerned to coordinate their behaviour, and this raises the issue of how effectively average cost pricing works as a method of coordination. Many of the points made in the previous section apply here. For instance, it is easier to use average cost pricing as a way of colluding where few firms are involved and when they have similar demand and cost curves.

The presence of collusion strengthens the point made above that prices are likely to be stable through short-run, e.g. cyclical, changes in demand, and to be more responsive to changes in cost. This is because it is difficult for a group of firms to renegotiate an agreed price in the face of demand changes which are less likely to affect all firms in the same way than are cost changes.

Therefore, the use of average cost pricing may enable firms to coordinate their prices. This is more likely to be successful where all the firms concerned have similar costs and when the group has agreed to change price only in response to clear-cut changes in cost which affect all the firms concerned. Short-run changes in demand will be dealt with by changing the level of inventories or the length of order books rather than by price changes. However, average cost pricing does not determine the actual price charged, since this must depend on the mark-up applied to the standard cost. The 'rule of thumb' itself gives no account of how the mark-up is determined.

Determination of the mark-up

As suggested above, the average cost pricing rule is consistent with a number of different approaches to the theory of the firm. This is because different theories give different explanations of the mark-up included in the standard price. In this section we look at profit-maximising and target rate of return explanations of the mark-up; a third theory is that the mark-up is mainly determined by the need to prevent or regulate entry into the industry: this theory is covered in Chapter 10 under the heading of limit-pricing.

Individual profit maximisation

We have already seen that average cost pricing is inconsistent with short-run profit maximisation, but may be compatible with long-run profit maximisation for the group of firms as a whole. The profit-maximising mark-up of price over average cost, expressed as a ratio to price, depends only on the elasticity of demand (ε).

The relationship between marginal revenue and price (or average revenue) can be written:

$$\frac{MR}{AR} = 1 - \frac{1}{\varepsilon} \ .$$

For profit maximisation $MR = MC$ and if we assume constant costs, so that $MC = AC$, then we can replace MR in the above expression by AC to give

$$AC = P \left(1 - \frac{1}{\varepsilon}\right)$$

$$AC = P - \frac{P}{\varepsilon}$$

$$P - AC = \frac{P}{\varepsilon}$$

$$\frac{P - AC}{P} = \frac{1}{\varepsilon} \ .$$

Therefore, the application of the average cost pricing rule with a profit-maximising mark-up means that AC is the average cost of producing the standard volume of output. Given this value, the actual price charged and the mark-up over costs depend on the elasticity of demand. The less elastic the demand curve a firm faces, the higher its price for a given cost level. Similarly, for a given firm, the lowest mark-up will be charged on the product with the most elastic demand. Table 7.1 shows profit-maximising prices and mark-ups for different values of the elasticity of demand, assuming that average costs in each case equal 50.

It might be argued that following this pricing rule would be unlikely to lead to a group of oligopolistic firms all charging the same price even if they had the same costs. This is because the formula depends on the firm's elasticity of demand and this is notoriously difficult for oligopolists to estimate. The elasticity of demand facing an oligopolist does not depend in any simple way on the elasticity of market demand, but also depends on the assumed reaction of rivals to a price change. Therefore, if all the firms in a group are observed to charge the same price when following a profit-maximising mark-up, this can be taken as evidence of collusion. In its strongest form, as already explained, oligopolistic collusion removes the uncertainty from the elasticity of demand since the firms act together to maximise joint profits given the market demand curve.

Table 7.1 Price–cost margins and the elasticity of demand

Elasticity ε	Marginal and average cost $MC = AC$	Price = $MC(\varepsilon/\varepsilon-1)$	Mark-up over costs %	Mark-up as % of price $\dfrac{P-AC}{P} = \dfrac{1}{\varepsilon}$
2	50	100.0	100	50
4	50	66.5	33	25
5	50	62.5	25	20
10	50	55.5	11	10

However, if cost differences between firms are small, and there is not much disagreement about elasticities of demand, then a group of firms may be able to reach a stable structure of prices based on profit-maximising mark-ups without collusion. Under some circumstances a set of margins arrived at on the basis of this kind of profit-maximising process may be adhered to for such a long period of time that their origins are forgotten and the mark-up is regarded as 'conventional' rather than profit-maximising.

Initially the idea of a conventional mark-up on costs which firms are reluctant to depart from seems very far from profit-maximising behaviour. However, this is less obviously true in the context of a group of oligopolists trying to find a way of coordinating price so as to look after long-run profits. If price stability is seen as being in the firms' joint interests, then each individual firm will be reluctant to abandon a tried and tested formula without knowing in advance that the other firms feel the same, and, as we have seen, agreeing on a change in the mark-up can be a hazardous and complicated business.

A target rate of return

An alternative theory of the determination of the mark-up is that this is chosen so as to achieve a target rate of return on capital. This rule is compatible with a theory of the firm which has growth, rather than profits, as the firm's objective.

One growth-maximising model of the firm is that put forward by Marris, which has already been looked at in Chapter 2. What are the implications of this model for choosing a mark-up over costs? In this model, balanced growth means that the rate of growth of product demand, g_d, must be matched by the rate of growth of the firm's capacity, g_c. Charging a higher price by increasing the mark-up over cost can be expected to slow down the rate of growth of demand, but conversely makes it easier to raise finance and hence to finance increased capacity (see Figure 7.12).

This diagram shows that the optimum mark-up over cost is OM. A profit margin lower than this means that the growth of demand will exceed the growth of capacity so that order books will be lengthened, customers may decide to go

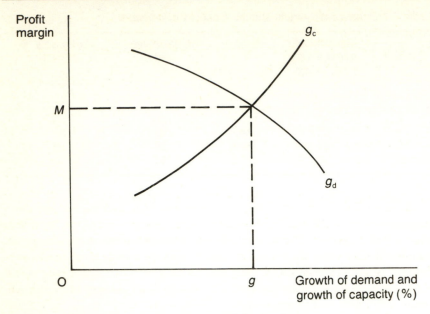

Figure 7.12 A target rate of return theory of the mark-up

elsewhere rather than wait for delivery and also new entry into the industry will be encouraged. On the other hand, if a profit margin above OM is charged, then the firm will suffer from excess capacity because capacity expands faster than demand. In either of these cases, then, the firm will fail in its objective of maximising growth, in that a faster rate of growth could be achieved by equating the growth of demand and the growth of capacity at mark-up OM.

If target rate of return pricing is likely to be adopted by firms whose main concern is growth rather than profits, then this argues that it is associated with firms who have sufficient market power to adopt their own objective independent of the other firms in the market. One example is General Motors of America, who set their price by adding to average cost at standard volume a margin sufficient to yield a 15 per cent post-tax return on capital employed. Smaller firms in the same market will have little choice but to follow the dominant firm's example.

In order to complete this section on the determination of the mark-up used in average cost pricing it is necessary to make a couple of qualifications, which argue that the determination of the mark-up is not necessarily a simple matter of following a formula. First, in the context of the target rate of return model just discussed, the choice of mark-up may be influenced by other forms of competition apart from pricing. If, say, the rate of growth of demand can be positively influenced by non-price competition such as advertising, then a profit margin higher than that indicated in Figure 7.12 will be able to be charged without reducing the rate of growth. One form of non-price competition, product differentiation, which is very significant in oligopolistic industries, is dealt with in more detail in the next chapter.

Secondly, the buyers' side of the market can have an important influence on the size of the market. Buyers can use their countervailing power to bargain mark-ups downwards, especially if buyers are better organised than sellers. Therefore, it is important to recognise that the determination of mark-ups is a complex issue which will vary from market to market according to circumstances.

7.6 EMPIRICAL EVIDENCE ON OLIGOPOLY PRICING

As we have seen at the end of the previous section, the determination of prices in oligopolistic markets is a complex issue and this conclusion is supported by the findings of empirical work in this area. As in other areas of industrial economics, different types of empirical work have been carried out to investigate how oligopolists set their prices. In this section we do not consider large-scale econometric studies of the determination of price–cost margins across markets; these are covered in Chapter 11. Other types of evidence include: surveys designed to find out from businessmen how they determine prices; experimental evidence on strategic behaviour when faced with a pay-off matrix of the general kind introduced in section 7.2 above; and case studies of pricing in individual industries.

One very well-known survey is that conducted by Hall and Hitch (1939). They interviewed 38 businessmen and found that average cost pricing with a 'normal' mark-up was the most common pricing procedure. The same finding has emerged from many more recent studies conducted in the USA and other European countries as well as the UK. To understand the implications of these findings it is therefore important to know more about the determination of the mark-up and the circumstances under which this will change. This has already been discussed in the previous section; empirical work lends some support to the suggestion made there that the use of a conventional mark-up can be interpreted as a way of setting a price which does not require a great deal of information, and which is consistent with moving towards profit maximisation in the long run. Therefore the use of average cost prices does not necessarily mean that prices are insensitive to changes in demand.

While surveys of this type have tended to support the prevalence of average cost pricing, they have also found that a minority of firms use different price-setting methods. These include price discrimination and dominant firm pricing. The more competitive are market conditions, as would be expected, the less discretion firms have about what price to charge and the more important demand becomes relative to cost. The interpretation of surveys of business behaviour, however, remains controversial. There is scope for disagreement between those who regard their results as inconsistent with the predictions of neoclassical economic theory and those who, on the other hand, think that the surveys show businessmen basically aiming to maximise profits but with imperfect information and without the economists' concepts of marginal cost and revenue.

The second type of empirical evidence to be considered is that collected from the playing of hypothetical oligopoly games under controlled conditions. In these experiments players are asked to choose price, say, given a matrix of profit outcomes. Explicit cooperation between players is impossible and therefore these experiments test how likely it is that some sort of tacit oligopolistic collusion will be arrived at, depending on the circumstances of the game. Broadly speaking, the results of this kind of work are consistent with the predictions of oligopoly theory in the following respects. The larger the number of players ('firms') involved, the lower are prices and profits, indicating that tacit collusion is more difficult. Second, the more information the players are given about the relationship between other players' price choices and their own profits, the higher are prices and profits, suggesting that a cooperative outcome can be approached more easily. Third, the less alike are the 'firms' in terms of product, cost and demand conditions, the longer it takes for price stability to be reached. The advantage of this type of empirical evidence is that attention can be concentrated on the effect of one specific factor on the outcome of the oligopolistic game. However, such experiments are too simple and artificial to be a perfect guide to the behaviour of firms in real markets.

The third type of empirical evidence we wish to look at briefly does come from such real markets. It is in the nature of case studies of pricing in individual markets that their results are hard to summarise; several such studies have been referred to in the preceding sections of this chapter. In the UK, the USA and the EC, interesting studies of pricing behaviour have emerged during the course of both restrictive agreement and monopoly investigations. Interdependent firms in oligopolistic markets are likely to recognise their interdependence and to want to find a way of setting output which takes this into account. Possible ways range from out-and-out collusion, illegal in most countries, to concerted practices which achieve parallel pricing without any actual agreement. These forms of behaviour are on the borderline between restrictive practices and monopoly policy, and have proved difficult for all competition policy systems to deal with – this point is taken up in Chapter 16. The reports of the Monopolies and Mergers Commission in the UK provide evidence of the range of competitive strategies adopted by oligopolists under different conditions. It is this range which makes the discussion of oligopoly pricing so much more complex than that of either competitive or monopoly pricing. In the case of oligopoly, furthermore, the choice of competitive strategy includes not just price but also such non-price variables as advertising and product differentiation, which form the subject of the next chapter.

Chapter 8

Product differentiation

8.1 INTRODUCTION

In this chapter we turn from oligopolistic pricing to an aspect of non-price competition which can be very important in oligopolistic markets. In contrast to the perfectly competitive model in which a large number of sellers all produce exactly the same product, in an oligopoly the firms typically produce differentiated or heterogeneous products and are thus able to compete by varying the characteristics of their products as well as, or indeed instead of, changing their prices.

Product differentiation refers to a situation in which two or more products are perceived by consumers to be close, but not perfect, substitutes. This is a very broad definition, and two types of product differentiation are usually distinguished and analysed separately. Horizontal differentiation (product range) occurs when a market contains a range of similarly priced products. An increase in the range of products means that consumers will, on average, be able to find a product which meets their preferences more exactly. With vertical (or quality) differentiation the products differ in respect of quality *and there is agreement on the ranking of the products*; buyers differ, however, in their willingness to pay for more quality. The scope for horizontal product differentiation, in particular, is greater in consumer than in producer goods industries and the definition of product differentiation shows the importance of consumers' perceptions to this phenomenon. Product differentiation can have a subjective dimension in that packaging or presentational variations can cause consumers to overestimate the difference between brands.

In fact, the concept of product differentiation is a subtle one and a full understanding of what is meant by product differentiation shows how ubiquitous the practice is. 'New' theories of consumer behaviour have analysed consumption as a form of productive process in which the household combines commodities in order to produce a desired mix of characteristics (Lancaster 1966) or combines bought commodities with time inputs in order to produce a desired mix of activities (Becker 1965). Because differentiated products may be seen as combining the same characteristics in different proportions, Lancaster's model has been widely used to analyse product differentiation, as we shall see in section 8.2 below. However, Becker's model also suggests some less obvious forms of product differentiation, because the purchased good represents only one differentiation in the other inputs such as time or amount of service offered. Thus, for instance, corner shops usually charge higher prices than supermarkets for the same products, but the local shops can be reached more quickly and cheaply and are often open longer hours.

Both horizontal and vertical product differentiation are widespread, and both raise the serious problem for industrial economics of how to define the market or the industry for differentiated products. In principle the market contains a group of products which are not identical but are closer substitutes for one another than for products outside the group. In practice this is a difficult definition to implement since it relies on the estimation of cross-elasticities of demand. A threshold value of cross-elasticity must first be determined; then products with cross-elasticities above this value are close enough substitutes to be included in the group. The selection of such a cut-off point may well be arbitrary to some extent.

However, the definition of the market is an important issue for many purposes in industrial economics. For instance, it is important for the measurement of concentration and the implementation of competition policy. In addition, the behaviour of the producers of differentiated products may well be affected by their perception of how many firms and products inhabit their market. Substitutability between differentiated products makes their producers' demand curves interdependent in the usual oligopolistic sense that each firm's own demand curve is affected by the output and pricing decisions of the other firms in the group. Therefore, when oligopolists producing differentiated products choose how many varieties, or how many different qualities, of a product to make, this is a strategic decision in that the outcome of one firm's decision on product range is affected by the product ranges made available by all the other firms. In fact, product differentiation is another aspect of oligopolistic behaviour which has been analysed by the techniques of game theory introduced in the last chapter.

Therefore, in a market characterised by product differentiation the firms have more decisions to make; they have to choose the number and quality of products to produce, and how much to spend on selling costs, as well as determine prices. Product differentiation is an important aspect of firms' behaviour in oligopolistic markets and their choices about product differentiation can act as an effective barrier to the entry of new firms into a market and thereby protect the profits of incumbent firms; this effect of product differentiation is discussed in Chapter 10. In section 8.2 we look at the theoretical analysis of markets in which products are differentiated, both horizontally and vertically. Because of the prevalence of product differentiation, all members of advanced societies are affected by it. In section 8.3 we consider the costs and benefits of product differentiation and, lastly, in section 8.4 go on to ask whether it is possible to identify an optimal level of product differentiation.

8.2 THEORETICAL ANALYSIS OF MARKETS CONTAINING DIFFERENTIATED PRODUCTS

Horizontal differentiation

Chamberlin's model of monopolistic competition

The first work to address itself to the problem of equilibrium of firms in a market characterised by product differentiation and selling costs was that of E.H. Chamberlin (1933). Chamberlin's model of a small group of oligopolists producing differentiated products who recognise their interdependence and experience simultaneous incentives to collude and to undercut the rest of the group has already been discussed in Chapter 7. Here we look at Chamberlin's 'large group' model, in which the group of firms constitutes a market in the sense that their products are close substitutes for one another and for no products outside the group.

Each firm has to decide exactly what version of the product to make (it is assumed that each firm produces only one version) and also how much to spend on selling costs as well as what price to charge. Because the firms' products are heterogeneous, each firm has some control over the price of its product, and therefore faces a downward-sloping demand curve. An increase in selling costs (e.g. more advertising) both shifts the demand curve to the right and makes it less elastic. Advertising has the effect of strengthening consumer preferences by increasing the perceived difference between products, so that any price rise has a smaller effect on sales. Average costs are also increased by any decision to incur more selling costs, hence selling costs underlie both the demand and cost curves shown in Figure 8.1. Chamberlin assumed that there were no significant barriers to the entry of new firms: under this assumption no firm will be able to earn excess profits in the long run. Price competition between the firms in the group will ensure that each firm reaches equilibrium at the level of output Q^*, where the firm's demand curve is tangential to its long-run average cost curve (LRAC).

Since equilibrium is reached at the point of tangency between the average cost curve and a downward-sloping demand curve, the firm will always be producing a sub-optimal level of output, costs are above their minimum level and price is above marginal cost. How serious this deviation from optimum output will be depends on the slopes of the average cost and demand curves, and is therefore related to the elasticity of demand. The more elastic the demand curve, the closer the tangential level of output will be to the minimum point of the *LRAC* curve. Chamberlin himself argued that this tangential equilibrium point represented the ideal trade-off between economies of scale and product variety: the excess of cost over minimum cost measures the cost of that variety, and consumers are willing to pay this cost because the slope of the demand curve represents the strength of consumers' preferences for that particular product. The question of whether Chamberlin's model of monopolistic competition really represents the optimal level of product differentiation is discussed in section 8.4 below.

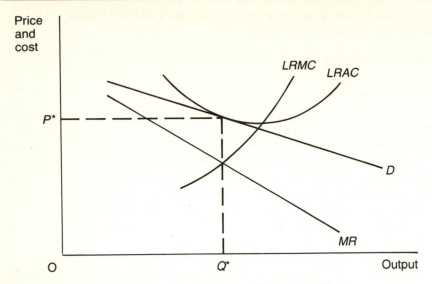

Figure 8.1 Long-run equilibrium under monopolistic competition

As a model of competition between producers of similar but differentiated products Chamberlin's theory is disappointing and has been subject to numerous criticisms. Chamberlin recognises the importance of product differentiation and selling costs, but in order to reach determinate solutions for the firm and for the group these features are then assumed away. For instance, the demand curve facing the group can be derived only on the assumption that each firm faces an identical demand curve because consumers' preferences are evenly distributed among the differentiated products. Costs are also assumed to be the same for all firms. However, if consumers' preferences are evenly distributed and there is no difference between the costs (including selling costs) of the products then it is hard to see any sense in which the firms' products can be differentiated from one another.

Product differentiation and characteristics

The difficulties of dealing adequately with differentiated products in the traditional framework of consumer theory have been mitigated by recent work which takes the *characteristics* of goods and not the goods themselves to be the object of consumer preferences. Goods can then be seen as bundles of characteristics, and differentiated products may be treated as goods which combine the same characteristics in different proportions. Chamberlin himself analysed monopolistic competition using characteristics of the differentiated products. He employed a spatial analogy for consumer behaviour: consumers have to pay the price of a product but also have to meet the cost of 'travel' from their preferred combination of characteristics to the nearest combination available in the market.

A more recent and generally applicable model is Lancaster's theory of demand, mentioned briefly in section 8.1. We discuss the application of Lancaster's model to the analysis of product differentiation with the aid of a simple example. In order to present the analysis diagrammatically we are restricted to goods with only two characteristics and also to a narrow definition of 'industry' and 'market'. This is purely for expositional convenience, and the implications of the analysis for a more realistic case are also discussed below.

In Figure 8.2, goods A, B and C are three varieties of chilli con carne which combine the two characteristics (chilli and carne) in different proportions. Good A contains the most chilli, and good C the most carne, per unit. Points a, b and c show the amount of each good which can be bought for equal expenditure on each; therefore the location of these points depends on the prices of each good. The consumer's indifference curves are defined over the characteristics, and in Figure 8.2 the consumer maximises her/his utility at point b on indifference curve I_3.

This framework may be used to provide answers to the problems, raised in section 8.1, which the phenomenon of product differentiation creates for economic analysis. First, an industry may be defined to include all the products which share the same characteristics – in terms of Figure 8.2 this means all the goods which can be located in chilli–carne space. Second, the nature of the interdependence between producers of differentiated products can be examined and the conditions necessary for Chamberlin's 'large group' solution, in which each firm faces an independent demand curve, can be established. Archibald and Rosenbluth (1975) have contributed to this analysis the concept of the 'neighbour' as

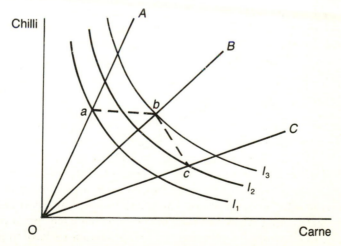

Figure 8.2 The 'characteristics' approach to product differentiation

the next-door good in characteristics space. In Figure 8.2, A and B are neighbours, B and C are neighbours but A and C are not. They have shown that interdependence between firms depends on two things: the number of characteristics in the market and the number of firms in the industry.

In our example there are only two characteristics. In this case each good can have no more than two neighbours and, no matter how many firms there are in the industry, their demand curves will be interdependent. It is not possible for the producer of good A, B or C to define a demand curve like that of Figure 8.1 on the assumption that the producers of rival differentiated products will not react to price changes. Instead, a change in the price of one of these goods will affect demand for the others. This interdependence will be weaker the more strongly the products are differentiated (i.e. the further apart are the rays in the diagram) and also depends on consumers' preferences across the characteristics. The more easily one characteristic can be substituted for the other, the flatter the indifference curves and the closer the interdependence between the firms' demand curves.

In Figure 8.3, the consumer is initially at equilibrium at point b on indifference curve I_3. Suppose that the price of good A begins to fall. This represents a fall in the relative price of the characteristic in which A is relatively rich, i.e. of chilli. The point a, which represents the amount of A that can be bought for a given expenditure, then moves outwards along the A ray. This consumer does not respond to the price fall in A immediately: she continues to maximise utility by purchasing B until point a reaches a', where the consumer is indifferent between buying A and buying B. If goods A and B can be mixed, then utility will be maximised by purchasing some of both goods and combining them to reach point d

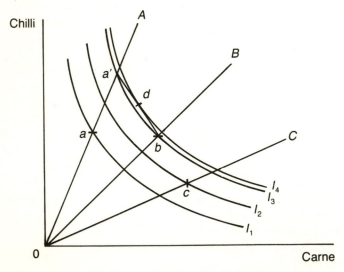

Figure 8.3 The effect of a price cut when the product is differentiated

on the higher indifference curve I_4. In our example the two varieties of chilli con carne could indeed be mixed to reach a preferred combination, but this is not often the case.

In the more generally realistic case, then, in which goods cannot be combined, if the price of A continues to fall the consumer will switch her expenditure completely from good B to good A. This analysis shows, therefore, that a fall in the price of one differentiated product will reduce the demand for its near neighbour. The rival firms will be forced to respond. If they respond by cutting their own prices, then market shares may be restored but lower profits will be earned all round.

To obtain Chamberlin's 'large group' result (in which each firm faces an independent demand curve), each good must have so many near neighbours that a price change has a negligible effect on the sales of each one. We have shown that this cannot be the case when the market contains only two characteristics: Archibald and Rosenbluth have demonstrated that for demand curves to be independent the market must include at least four characteristics, and also that increasing the number of firms weakens interdependence.

Lastly, Lancaster's theory provides insights into the firm's decisions about changing product variety and about selling costs which cannot be obtained from conventional theory. As well as changing the price of its product, a firm can change the nature of its product (thereby moving the ray in characteristics space) or introduce a new differentiated product (thereby adding a new ray). This is more likely to be profitable if a gap in the market can be spotted – an area of characteristics space already crowded with products is less attractive to a new product.

In Figure 8.4, two goods, A and B, are available and at current prices the consumer, for a given expenditure, can buy anything on the line *ab*. If the goods can be combined, the consumer's utility-maximising point is P, where goods A and B are combined to give the preferred mix of characteristics. In this case, market research would reveal an unmet consumer demand for a good with the combination of characteristics obtained at P, and a firm would find it profitable to produce a new good, N, with the desired combination of characteristics, as long as N could be sold cheaply enough. In order for the consumer to switch from her mix of A and B to good N, the price of N must be low enough so that expenditure on N puts the consumer at a point to the north-east of P, so that she can reach a higher indifference curve than I_1.

Lancaster's analysis can also explain why the producer of a differentiated product may decide to undertake advertising or to incur other selling costs. One reason is to inform consumers about the particular mix of characteristics offered by his own products, and another reason is to strengthen consumer preferences for this mix, i.e. to establish brand loyalty. The extent of brand loyalty may be assessed by seeing how quickly price increases lead to expenditure being shifted to other products.

So, Lancaster's 'characteristics' approach to demand theory has been used

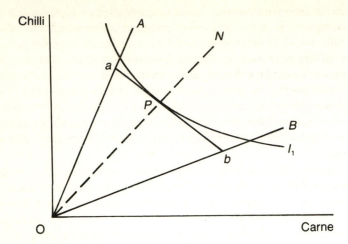

Figure 8.4 The introduction of a new product

to illuminate several aspects of markets containing differentiated products, and also as the basis for empirical work in this area, which will be mentioned later. So far, however, we have considered only markets in which products are differentiated horizontally and producers carve out a market niche for themselves in which they sell to those consumers whose tastes most closely match their mix of characteristics.

Vertical product differentiation

Vertical product differentiation exists when differentiated products are of different quality and can be unambiguously ranked in order of quality. In this case the lower-quality products will sell only if priced lower than the better versions. Vertical product differentiation could be analysed using Lancaster's model if the statement that good A is 'better quality' than good B can be interpreted as meaning that a unit of good A contains more characteristics than a unit of good B. However, the feature of markets containing vertical product differentiation which has received recent attention is the relationship between product differentiation and market structure.

Shaked and Sutton (1987) argue that the interaction between consumer preferences and the technology of product improvement is important in determining market structure. In particular, they draw attention to the possibility of 'natural oligopolies' in which a certain level of concentration is inevitable. In these markets a growth in the size of the market does not enable more firms to survive, so there is no tendency for concentration to fall as the market grows.

Improving product quality is bound to increase the costs of production, but the extra costs may be mainly fixed costs (e.g. if quality is improved by more

R&D effort to improve computer speed) or mainly variable costs (if higher-quality furniture can be made only out of more expensive wood, say). A natural oligopoly falls into the former group, so that variable costs increase only slowly as product quality improves. As long as consumer tastes are such that at least some consumers would be willing to pay more than the increase in variable costs in order to buy the higher-quality product, competition between the firms will take the form of spending increasing amounts on fixed costs in the pursuit of higher product quality. An increase in the size of the market leads not to the entry of more firms and a fall in concentration, but to higher levels of fixed costs and 'better' products.

In this case, then, there is an association between high levels of fixed costs and of concentration, but this is not a causal relationship. Rather, both the fixed costs and the concentration are explained by the firms' vertical product differentiation behaviour. The fixed costs are endogenous to the model, and structure and conduct are simultaneously determined by the fundamental forces of technology and consumer preferences.

Where products are heterogeneous, the competitiveness of firms cannot be judged by looking at price alone; what matters is value for money, i.e. the bundle of characteristics which the consumer gets compared with that obtainable from spending the same amount on the competing but different products of other firms. Cowling and Cubbin (1971) and Cowling and Rayner (1970) have looked at the UK markets for cars and tractors, respectively, using prices adjusted to take account of quality differences between competing products: quality-adjusted prices were found to be significant determinants of market shares, and the elasticity of demand calculated with respect to quality-adjusted price was higher than the simple price elasticity of demand. However, Curry and Rhys (1979) have pointed out that there are problems associated with the 'hedonic' technique of estimating price-quality relationships, so that results from studies using this method should be interpreted with caution.

8.3 THE COSTS AND BENEFITS OF PRODUCT DIFFERENTIATION

Product differentiation as an element of market structure

Product differentiation in its various forms affects us all: we are affected directly as consumers, and more indirectly by product differentiation as an element of market structure which helps to determine the way firms compete and how industry performs. Lastly, because of the sheer scale of product differentiation activities in industrial societies, they have a number of external effects, by-products of their main aim of selling more goods.

First, product differentiation is big business. The Advertising Association's estimates suggest that expenditure on advertising amounted to 1.5 per cent of GDP in the USA in 1985. The figure is lower than this in most other countries; in the same year, UK expenditure on advertising amounted to 1.3 per cent of GDP, but the highest ratio was in Australia (1.8 per cent). The amounts of money spent on advertising in advanced countries are enormous: around £4 billion in the UK in 1985. There is scope for argument about the extent to which advertising expenditure should be regarded as a waste of resources. At one extreme it has been argued that all advertising and promotional expenditures form a part of the overall social or resource costs of monopoly (Posner 1975), and empirical analysis of these welfare costs (see Chapter 12) has shown that they are highest in those industries characterised by heavy advertising, and also highest in the USA where expenditure on advertising is greatest.

The most obvious benefit of product differentiation for consumers is that it widens their range of choice. Consumers are offered a variety of different versions of a product and their choice between these versions is informed or guided by advertising which establishes the brand name in the public's mind. Can it be said that this widening of choice is unambiguously a gain for the consumer? It seems more likely that the introduction of a certain number of new varieties does increase consumer welfare, but that beyond this point further differentiation brings little benefit. Moreover, product differentiation may impose a resource cost in that sales per brand will be lower, so production runs will be shorter and economies of scale will be lost. We return to this point in section 8.4, which discusses the optimal level of product differentiation. In particular, brand proliferation may be expected to offer less benefit to consumers the smaller the objective difference between brands. In this case, differentiation is mainly subjective and is achieved by advertising and promotion to establish the brand name and create a consumer preference for the advertised brand which enables it to be sold at a higher price than a virtually identical unadvertised brand, such as supermarkets' 'own-label' versions of nationally advertised products.

Where a number of differentiated products exist, there is scope for advertising to inform as well as to persuade: advertisements may be seen as instructing consumers about the difference between the varieties of a good which are available or, in terms of Lancaster's theory of consumer demand, informing consumers about the exact mix of characteristics which each brand has to offer (the slope of the ray in characteristics space). It is certainly possible for product differentiation and its associated advertising to increase consumers' welfare by increasing the amount of information they have about the more complex types of differentiated products such as consumer durables. The technical nature of these products makes it difficult for consumers to assess different varieties adequately and, because consumer durables are, by their nature, purchased relatively infrequently, it is both difficult to learn from experience and costly to make a misguided purchase. However, many of the most heavily advertised consumer products are not technically sophisticated goods but things like food products, soft or alcoholic drinks, cosmetics, detergents and toilet products. Furthermore, advertisements for complex consumer durables like cars or washing machines often contain little objective information and rely instead on persuasive techniques.

Product differentiation means that consumers are able to associate products directly with their manufacturers, either by advertising or by the use of trademarks. This direct association can work to the advantage of both producer and consumer: the firm is thereby enabled to build up brand loyalty and goodwill among its customers, and consumers benefit from the responsibility imposed on the firm to maintain the quality of its products in order to protect its reputation. The customer comes to regard the manufacturer's brand name or trademark as a characteristic of the good in its own right which conveys information and provides an indication of quality. If the firm's products fail to come up to the required standard, its reputation and sales will be badly affected.

Related to this last point is the effect that product differentiation has had on the development of distribution systems. As already suggested, advertising forms a direct link between the manufacturer and the consumer which acts as a force leading towards increased concentration. The power of manufacturers is increased relative to that of the middlemen: wholesalers and retailers. Where consumers are informed at first hand about manufacturers' products, wholesalers lose much of their power to decide what goods to sell. Manufacturers have responded to this change in the balance of power by cutting out wholesalers and either selling direct to retailers or vertically integrating forwards to acquire distributive outlets.

However, more recent developments in distribution have led to a strengthening of the competitive position of retailers relative to manufacturers. The success in the UK of the big supermarket chains, and also of the voluntary chains such as Spar, has been based partly on their lines of own-brand products which undercut manufacturers' advertised brands and are sold with very little advertising. Retailers' advertisements are typically informative rather than persuasive, concentrating, for instance, on 'this week's special offers'. Consumers benefit from having the choice between the cheaper own-brand and the more expensive advertised versions of the same product.

One of the most important disadvantages of product differentiation is that, in conjunction with heavy advertising, it can act as a barrier to entry, making it more difficult for new firms to enter a market, and therefore enabling the existing firms in the market to raise prices and earn supernormal profits without having to worry about the threat of new entry. One way in which this result may come about is via the effect heavy advertising expenditure has on raising the capital required for entry to take place. Increased capital requirements will raise entry barriers as long as there are capital market imperfections. Another way in which entry may be made more difficult is through brand proliferation. This is clear from Lancaster's model, which has been discussed earlier. It is further illustrated by the following hypothetical example. Assume first of all that there are two existing firms. Each firm produces one brand of good; 50 per cent of consumers are attached to the existing firms by ties of goodwill, and the other 50 per cent are unattached. In this case a firm thinking of entering the market with a third brand may expect to pick up one-third of the unattached consumers (i.e. about

17 per cent of the market). Suppose, however, that each existing firm produces five brands of more or less equal popularity. In this case a new brand could expect to pick up about one- eleventh of the unattached customers or about 4–5 per cent of the whole market – a much less attractive proposition.

The reason why an existing firm decides to pre-empt an opportunity in product space is that the opportunity is more valuable to the established firm than to an entrant (Schmalensee 1978). This is because a new entrant might threaten price stability and reduce profits over the whole range of products produced by the incumbent. The latter calculates therefore that, by packing the product space, its profits will be higher than they would be if new entry occurred. For the strategy to work, however, there has to be some barrier to entry, and this may be in the form of heavy advertising outlays.

One market fitting the description above, where barriers to entry are caused by high advertising levels and a multiplicity of brands, is the market for detergents, discussed in the Monopolies and Mergers Commission *Household Detergents* report (1966). The MMC found that the expenditure on advertising and promotion (amounting to 17 and 18.5 per cent of retail price by Unilever and Procter & Gamble respectively) kept new entrants out of the market, weakened competitive restraints on price and profits and 'created a situation in which even the less successful of the two principal competitors can earn extremely comfortable profits while those of the more successful are outstandingly high'. The relationship between market structure, advertising and industrial performance is discussed more fully in Chapter 11.

However, product differentiation and the associated high levels of advertising expenditure do not necessarily have an adverse effect on market performance. Under certain circumstances, if advertising increases sales the consumer can benefit from lower costs of production and, therefore, lower prices. This will only happen, however, if there are technical economies of scale over the relevant output range and also if the effect of advertising is to concentrate demand on fewer firms. Otherwise the increase in demand and fall in costs for the advertised brands will be offset by lower demand and higher costs for competing brands. In industries where technical economies of scale are unimportant, advertising will actually raise costs above minimum production cost. This is the basis for the type of competition already discussed which takes place between advertised and 'own-brand' products. By not advertising at all, the manufacturers and retailers of the own-brand lines are enabled to sell at a lower price than the branded line of, for example, cornflakes (Monopolies and Mergers Commission, 1973). It is possible to argue, of course, that the sales of the own-brand products depend on the demand for the branded products and are thus parasitic on the brand advertising: what would happen to the demand for all varieties of cornflakes if Kellogg's stopped advertising?

Because advertising can increase the sales of advertised products, it has also been claimed that product differentiation increases the incentive for firms to innovate. If the market is informed by advertisements that a new product exists, sales will build up more quickly than they would without advertising and thus the benefits from innovation will accrue more quickly and certainly. Also, product differentiation, by building up brand loyalty, helps the innovating firm to protect its market from imitators. There certainly is a relationship between product differentiation and research and development, but many of the product innovations introduced in heavily differentiated, advertising-intensive industries are of very limited benefit to the consumer – the new products differ little from the older versions.

Product differentiation as a form of business behaviour

So far we have considered product differentiation as an element of market structure, but it is also a form of business behaviour and an important kind of non-price competition. What can we say about the costs and benefits associated with competition by product differentiation? Such competition may take place by advertising, by changing the nature or quality of the product, or by making it less or more widely available. The price competition associated with homogeneous products is replaced by a more complex form of competition in which firms have to decide how many varieties of a product to make, and then compete by a combination of price and selling costs. From the point of view of the firm, the decision about how many brands to produce must depend on the number of goods already on the market and how well these satisfy consumers' preferences (as discussed in the next section), as well as on the costs of producing another variety of the product. If the current range of differentiated products is too narrow, there will be gaps in the market which can be plugged either by the entrance of new firms or by the introduction of new brands by existing firms. However, if a firm is making too many similar products, each brand will simply take sales from the others with no overall effect on the firm's revenue.

In a stable, mature oligopolistic market, competition which takes the form of heavy advertising between a few large rival firms is unlikely to benefit the consumer. Advertising replaces price competition and leads to higher costs and prices all round. To a considerable extent the effects of each firm's advertising are mutually cancelling. A considerable reduction in or even abandonment of advertising would leave market shares substantially unaffected and would increase consumer welfare by reducing prices. An example of a market which fits this description is that for detergents investigated by the Monopolies and Mergers Commission (Monopolies and Mergers Commission, 1966). The duopolists in this market competed almost entirely by advertising and promotional expenditures rather than by price. This had the effect of creating barriers to entry, and the Monopolies and Mergers Commission found no evidence of benefits to consumers from the firms' behaviour.

However, advertising can actually increase competition under other circumstances, particularly when it serves to widen consumer choice by making it possible for products to penetrate new markets. Competition is interpreted here in a dynamic rather than a static sense. It may not be profitable for firms to sell their products in new markets without product differentiation and advertising to create demand for the product; in this case it is price competition rather than product competition which works to the advantage of the established firms.

An example of a market where advertising and promotion were considered essential to make new entry profitable is the market for spirits in the EC. Most of the member countries of the EC have their own national drink and, despite progress towards the single market, continue to protect the market against imported spirits by discriminatory taxation. The UK's national drink is Scotch whisky, which has about 50 per cent of the UK market but less than 10 per cent of the market in most other EC countries. The scope for whisky to increase its market share outside the UK on the basis of price is very limited. This is not only because of fiscal problems: the tax alone levied on a bottle of whisky in France exceeds the price of a bottle of rum. In this case increasing the market penetration of whisky depended crucially, in the view of the companies concerned, on advertising and other promotion to keep the product in the consumers' minds (George and Joll 1978). This, however, is strictly a short-term argument in favour of advertising, which recognises that the cost of winning a market is greater than the cost of maintaining it.

Competition by changing product design is most important for relatively complex products like consumer durables, and the classic example of an industry which competes through introducing new models is the motor industry. The experience of the UK motor industry underlines the importance of having successful new models if a motor manufacturer is to remain competitive. The introduction of even relatively minor styling changes is both a lengthy and an extremely expensive business. Therefore competition by new models tends to favour larger over smaller manufacturers, and to increase the likelihood of a vicious circle in which ageing model designs mean a fall in profits, so that insufficient money is generated to finance investment in new models. As far as the consumer is concerned, frequent style changes mean that if the consumer wants to remain up to date he will have to trade in his car long before it is actually worn out; this has the effect of stimulating the secondhand market in cars.

Some of the new models introduced by motor manufacturers do embody genuine improvements in design, safety or performance; others represent purely cosmetic changes. The effect of the latter may be to change consumers' preferences if the 'new look' becomes a desirable characteristic in its own right: people with older but perfectly serviceable cars feel dissatisfied. However, in some cases the kind of accelerated obsolescence to which the introduction of new models leads can have more serious effects on consumers' welfare. Manufacturers sometimes introduce new models of consumer durables, such as electric cookers, every couple of years and it becomes increasingly difficult or even impossible to get spare parts for an older model even if the rest of it is still working perfectly well. For a product like a cooker, where there is relatively little technical advance and not much scope for style changes, the manufacturer cannot hope to sell many new models unless the old ones become prematurely obsolescent.

The external effects of product differentiation

Lastly, let us consider the external effects of product differentiation mentioned at the beginning of this section. The reason why firms differentiate their products is to appeal to more consumers and increase sales; however, product differentiation is so ubiquitous in advanced economies that its effects go far beyond this and impinge on virtually every member of society, whether or not they have any interest in the product in question. For one thing, the existence of independent broadcasting and television networks and of large numbers of newspapers, magazines and periodicals is completely dependent on advertising revenue. This dependence undoubtedly curtails the freedom of the press to some extent, from the fear of offending large advertisers.

Second, advertising is so inescapable in our society that it can to some extent be assessed as an activity in its own right, independent of the products it is trying to sell. Advertisements can be a source of pleasure if they are beautiful or amusing, but can also give offence, for instance by using degrading images of women or by being located on an otherwise beautiful stretch of road. It is possible to imagine a system by which those who enjoy advertisements could choose to consume them while other people did not have to. At the moment however, it is all but impossible for people who would rather not be subjected to advertising messages to opt out.

Third, product differentiation, in the form both of consumer advertising and of frequent changes in product design, may be assigned considerable responsibility for the increasing materialism of modern societies. To be constantly bombarded by the praises of the latest model of car, video recorder, and so on, must help to make consumers dissatisfied with their current possessions and envious of any friends or neighbours who have more up-to-date versions.

Having established that product differentiation does have both costs and benefits, we go on in the next section to ask whether it is possible to identify an optimal level of product differentiation.

8.4 THE OPTIMAL LEVEL OF PRODUCT DIFFERENTIATION

The previous section suggested that in assessing the desirability of product differentiation the gain in welfare from increased variety must be weighed against the increased costs of production. The result of this trade-off will identify an optimal level of product differentiation. This optimal level will vary for different kinds of product: in an area like footwear in which economies of scale are insignificant and variety is important, the optimal level of product differentiation will be high, while for a product like electrical fittings where the reverse is true a much smaller range of products will be desirable. The trade-off presents a serious dilemma for policy only when economies of scale and the consumer's demand for variety are both important, as in the case of motor cars.

The ideal level of product differentiation is easier to define than to identify in operational terms. The ideal combination of products is that which maximises the sum of consumers' and producers' surplus, but the information required to find out which of the enormous number of possible combinations of products brings about the largest surplus is not available. Nor can we be confident that the existing variety of products represents the optimum, because there is no market mechanism which allows consumers to express a preference for products currently unavailable.

We can, however, say something about the conditions under which a given change in the level of product differentiation (e.g. the introduction of a new product) will bring about a gain or a reduction in welfare, and about what kinds of market structure are likely to lead to the most product differentiation. These questions can be approached using a number of different theoretical frameworks, just as product differentiation itself can be analysed in a number of different ways (see section 8.2). Following the approach used in that section, we here use Lancaster's characteristic approach to demand theory to examine the optimal level of product differentiation (Lancaster 1975).

The consumer's indifference curves are defined over characteristics, as before, and we now add the product differentiation curve (PDC) shown in Figure 8.5. The PDC shows all the different combinations of characteristics 1 and 2 which can be produced with a given level of resources. This enables us to identify, for a

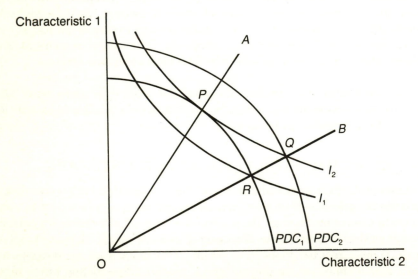

Figure 8.5 The optimal level of product differentiation

given consumer, the optimal combination of characteristics and therefore the optimal variety of the product. This is the variety which, for a given resource availability, enables the consumer to reach the highest indifference curve. In Figure 8.5 it is good A which is the optimum product variety because, with the level of resources available along PDC_1, any other good would make the consumer worse off. Suppose, however, that only good B was available. Then, in order to make the consumer as well off as at point P (i.e. to put the consumer on indifference curve I_2), more resources will be needed. Because the consumer is not offered her preferred combination of characteristics, a given level of utility cannot be reached for the minimum amount of resources. In fact, to make the consumer as well off as she is at P by consuming good B requires that she have a quantity OQ of B, which demands the level of resources embodied in PDC_2, which is greater than that along PDC_1.

The proportional increase in the amount of resources needed to make the consumer as well off by consuming B as she would be at P, consuming the preferred good A, is measured by OQ/OR, which Lancaster called the compensating ratio. This ratio measures the resource or welfare cost of a sub-optimal product variety, i.e. the amount needed to compensate the consumer for the non-availability of the preferred good. The size of this cost depends on three things: the slope of the indifference curves (which reflects the degree of substitutability between the characteristics from the consumer's point of view); the distance between the preferred and available goods in characteristics space (which indicates the objective difference between the two goods), and the slope of the PDC curve (which measures the opportunity cost of each characteristic). The welfare cost incurred by having only a non-optimal product variety available will be higher when the consumer has pronounced preferences between the two characteristics, when the available good is substantially different from the preferred good, and when the resource cost of each characteristic is sharply increasing.

The implications of this analysis for the optimal level of product differentiation depend on the technology of the production function – on whether it exhibits increasing, decreasing or constant returns to scale. If there are constant or decreasing returns to scale, no cost penalty is incurred by producing a large number of varieties, and, in terms of Figure 8.5, each consumer's particular preferred combination can be produced. If the goods can be mixed, then fewer goods need to be produced since consumers can combine varieties themselves to achieve their ideal combination of characteristics. However, this condition does not apply to most complex differentiated produces (e.g. consumer durables).

Without increasing returns, then, it will be socially optimal for each consumer's preferred goods to be produced. This is not the case when the production function exhibits increasing returns. If production exhibits great enough economies of scale, indeed, it may be optimal for only one product to be made. In this case, owing to increasing returns, the available resources permit the single product to be produced in such large quantities that all consumers can be paid their compensating ratios and be made as well off as they would be with a smaller amount of their preferred version of the good. For the more general case, with some but not overwhelming economies of scale, Lancaster showed that it is possible to derive conditions for the optimum level of product differentiation and that the optimum number of goods falls as economies of scale become more important. However, it is difficult to relate the optimum number of goods to any easily observable variables.

What can we say about the type of market structure most likely to bring about the optimum level of product differentiation? As mentioned in section 8.2, Chamberlin claimed that monopolistic competition achieves the ideal in this respect. Goods are produced at above minimum cost, i.e. there are unexhausted economies of scale, but the consumer is willing to pay the higher cost in order to have the choice between different varieties. This argument, however, ignores the fact that consumers are not offered the choice between greater variety and a narrower choice at less cost. Lancaster suggested that the freedom of entry characteristic of a monopolistically competitive market will result in the production of more than the socially optimal number of goods, and therefore be associated with too much product differentiation. This is because a new entrant does not take into account the effect which an extra product has on the profits of existing firms. If the profit earned on a new product is partly at the expense of existing products, it will exceed the net addition to the profits of the industry as a whole.

Whether a monopolist is likely to produce too few or too many varieties of a product is difficult to determine. On the one hand variety tends to be under-provided because, unless the monopolist can practise perfect price discrimination, the profit contribution of a new product falls short of its contribution to consumer plus producer surplus. This tendency will be accentuated if a new variety causes customers to switch from existing brands and if economies of scale mean that costs increase as more brands are produced. On the other hand, and as we stated earlier, a monopolist has a powerful incentive to pack the product space in order to pre-empt entry.

Scherer (1979) attempted an empirical application of the theory of optimal product differentiation to the US ready-to-eat breakfast cereal industry. Like household detergents, this industry is characterised by high concentration, heavy advertising and the production of many brands by the leading firms. The industry has been the subject of antitrust investigation in both the USA and the UK. Scherer found evidence of extensive 'cannibalisation', that is, that the introduction of new brands had reduced the sales of existing cereals rather than increased the total market. This supports the view that different brands of cereal are close substitutes for one another, so that there is little increase in consumer welfare from the introduction of new brands. However, by leading to an overall rise in prices, the brand proliferation caused a transfer from consumer to producer surplus, i.e. it increased profits. The relatively high profit margins earned on cereal products stimulate product differentiation beyond the level that would exist in a more competitive industry.

To test the hypothesis that brand proliferation had been carried beyond the socially optimal in the breakfast cereal industry, Scherer compared the increase in net consumers' surplus with the high launching costs of introducing a new brand of cereal, estimated at $4.4 million per product in 1959–64. This sum covered the costs of R&D, market research, test marketing and advertising expenditure over the first 14 months of the product's life. Scherer found that, of 51 new brands introduced between 1958 and 1970, only 22 added more to surplus than they cost to launch. Thus, 29 new brands were not socially desirable, and to these must be added a further 25 brands withdrawn after test marketing. Thus there is considerable evidence that, for this industry at least, product differentiation has been carried beyond the optimal level.

Chapter 9

Invention and innovation

9.1 INTRODUCTION

The previous chapter examined product differentiation both as a determinant of market structure and as an instrument of business behaviour. We are also concerned with the level of expenditure and effort committed by firms to the development and introduction of new products and also new methods of production.

The subject matter of this chapter is often referred to for simplicity as technological change. However, it is important to recognise at the outset that the process of technological change is a complex one. Schumpeter (1947) distinguished between three main stages: invention, innovation and diffusion. Invention is the production of new knowledge in the form of a new product or method of production. Innovation covers the whole range of activities that are needed to translate a new idea into commercial practice for the first time. They include the further, possibly extensive, development and refinement of an idea before the stage of commercial application can be reached. It may involve extensive laboratory and clinical testing, as in the case of pharmaceuticals, or the building of prototypes, as in the case of vehicle or aircraft development. In many cases the development of a new idea may depend on other scientific advances. The development of new aero engines, for instance, has depended on the parallel development of new materials. The innovation stage also includes identifying the market for a new product, investing in the capital goods needed for production and distribution, and raising the funds for that investment. The third of Schumpeter's stages – diffusion – is the stage when a product or process innovation is spread through the market, either through the efforts of the innovator or as a result of imitation by other firms.

It is also quite common to distinguish between the following categories of R&D activity: basic research, strategic research, applied research and development. *Basic* research is aimed at the discovery of new knowledge for its own sake with no thought for immediate application. *Strategic* research has foreseeable application though this may not be clearly defined. *Applied* research is aimed at obtaining knowledge for specific industrial application. *Development* refers to the application of *existing* knowledge to the production of new products or processes. These categories do not represent watertight compartments but the distinctions made can be useful. In particular, the distinction drawn between basic and other forms of research activity will be of importance when we come to discuss the adequacy of markets in funding R&D activity.

We now turn to the main issues in the economics of technological change. The next section examines the relationship between firm size and R&D activity. This is followed in section 9.3 by an analysis of the interrelationship between R&D and market structure. Section 9.4 examines the wider issue of whether the free play of market forces would tend to allocate too few resources to R&D activity. Lastly, section 9.5 considers the diffusion of new technology and the economics of the patent system.

9.2 R&D AND FIRM SIZE

How far should we expect R&D activity to be associated with firm size? A number of arguments have been advanced to suggest that the large firm has certain crucial advantages.

Galbraith (1963) argued that the high costs involved in modern-day research are such that only large firms have the necessary resources to carry out the work. In addition, large firms are better placed to handle the high risks associated with R&D work. The small firm may have to concentrate its efforts on developing a single innovative idea, the success or failure of which may make or break the firm. The large firm, on the other hand, is able to support several projects simultaneously and failure in one area will be more than made good by successes elsewhere. Large firms have a further advantage where there are substantial economies of scale in R&D work. For instance, they are better able to afford the specialist staff and expensive equipment which may be needed. The marketing power of large firms may also be important in inducing a high level of R&D expenditure. Established links with distributor outlets, heavy advertising and other sales promotion expenditures will allow large firms to penetrate new markets more quickly with new products and thus increase the return on R&D investment. In the case of process innovations that reduce production costs, the large firm's advantage is that the lower unit costs apply to a larger output, so that total savings are greater than they will be for a small firm.

The broad evidence on formally organised R&D strongly suggests that R&D is dominated by large firms. In 10 out of 11 industrial countries analysed by the OECD (1969) the 100 largest R&D programmes accounted for more than two-thirds of total industrial R&D expenditure. However, the concentration of R&D by firm size (as measured by employment) was lower, indicating that not all large firms have large R&D programmes and that some medium-sized firms do. For the UK, in 1978, firms with over 5,000 employees accounted for 58 per cent of total manufacturing employment but for 89 per cent of R&D employment. A similar picture applies to the USA where in 1972 firms with over 5,000 employees accounted for 53 per cent of manufacturing employment but 89 per cent of R&D expenditure. The evidence on formally organised R&D may be summed up by saying that almost all large firms engage in some R&D but only a small fraction of small firms do so, and that the great bulk of recorded R&D expenditure is undertaken by large firms.

Yet the evidence given so far needs to be qualified in some important respects. First, the statistics show that, although many small firms do not have formal R&D programmes, nevertheless they do undertake some work in this area. To the extent that the data are incomplete, it is the contribution of firms in the smaller size classes which is most likely to be underestimated, so that the concentration of R&D in large firms is overstated. Second, there is a great variation in the size of firm in the large size category, and it is of some importance to know whether the R&D performance of the very largest firms in industry is superior to that of those which are relatively much smaller but still quite large in absolute terms. For if R&D performance does improve up to the size of the very largest firms this would have important implications for optimal industrial structure.

The evidence (mainly US) shows that in most industries the absolute level of expenditure is correlated with size. This of course is what one would expect. The picture is less clear, however, with regard to the *intensity* of R&D effort – that is, R&D expenditure as a percentage of output, or R&D employment as a proportion of total employment. In many industries where the intensity of R&D effort has been found to be positively correlated with size the correlations are weak. In other industries the correlations are negative. In a study of 21 industry groups, Comanor (1967) found that in 7 cases R&D employment increased less than proportionately to total employment, and in no case was there a statistically significant positive association between R&D employment and firm size. Nelson, Peck and Kalachek (1967: 67) summarised their findings in this area as follows:

> While in most (but not all) industries the R&D to sales ratio rises as one moves from the group of firms with less than 1,000 employees to the group in the 1,000–5,000 range, there is no clear tendency for these ratios to be larger for the giants in the above 5,000 range than for the firms in the 1,000–5,000 range.

A third comment which may be made about the statistical evidence is that figures of R&D intensity are of course a measure of the *input* of R&D and should be used with caution. A high figure is not necessarily a good thing and may indeed reflect inefficiency in the organisation of research and development programmes. In a study of the iron and steel, petroleum refining and chemical industries in the USA for instance, Mansfield (1968) found that the number of significant inventions per dollar of expenditure was lower in the very large firms than in the large and medium-sized ones. For the UK, Pavitt et al. (1987) examined the relationship between firm size and innovative activity using information on more than 4,000 significant innovations commercialised in the UK between 1945 and 1983. They found that the distribution of significant innovations by firm size was very different from that of R&D expenditures. Firms with fewer than 1,000 employees accounted for only 3.3 per cent of total R&D expenditure in 1975, but for 34.9 per cent of the identified significant innovations between 1970 and 1979.

In addition to the qualifications which have already been made, other considerations have to be taken into account in order to form a balanced picture of the relative importance of large and small firms. In particular, R&D is not one activity but a series of activities varying in costliness and in the risks involved. Thus the argument that only large firms can afford the costs of R&D needs to be qualified because the different stages of the R&D process vary greatly in costliness. The contribution of small firms, and indeed of individuals, to invention is likely to be much greater than their contribution to the commercial application of new ideas, where the costs involved are so much higher.

Similarly, the argument that only large firms can afford the risks involved in R&D is too simple a view. A firm need not start on full-scale development until the main technical uncertainties have been eliminated in the early inexpensive stages of the R&D process, where there is plenty of scope for small businesses. Furthermore, large firms may be at a disadvantage in the early stages of R&D. One factor which may work in this direction is the danger that with the emphasis on team work and an efficient, easily managed research department, not enough freedom will be given to the individual to develop novel ideas. Individual initiative may be swamped by excessive organisation. Another factor working in the same direction may be a tendency, particularly in management-controlled firms, for there to be a bias against the really innovative ideas which carry the greatest risks. It has been suggested by Nelson *et al.* (1967: 54) that, apart from a small number of areas, the bulk of R&D carried out by large firms is relatively safe and achieves modest advances.

> Outside defence and space related R&D, however, and possibly some segments of the civil electronics and chemical industries, the bulk of corporate R&D is modest design improvement work not reaching very far – the type of work that results in yearly changes in automobile design, gradual improvements in refrigerators and vacuum cleaners, and steady improvements in the automaticity, speed and capacity of machine tools, rather than radically new products and processes.

There can be little doubt, however, about the importance of individuals and small firms in inventive activity, especially as a source of major inventions. Jewkes, Sawers and Stillerman (1969), for example, in tracing the origins of 61 major inventions which occurred in the main between 1930 and 1950, found that only 12 could be clearly attributed to large firms; 38 were due to the work of individuals and small firms, and 11 were unclassifiable. In a later review of new evidence the authors concluded that there did not seem to be a need for substantial modification of their earlier views relating to the importance of individuals and small firms. Similar case-study research in the USA has also shown the importance of the small unit in inventive activity, as has analysis of patent statistics.

In areas where there are important economies of scale in R&D, the large firm will certainly have the advantage of being able to afford specialised equipment and a team of specialists. In addition, where size is associated with market power the firm will be able to take a long view. In other words, R&D will not be hindered by the prior consideration of short-term survival. Small firms can overcome these disadvantages to some extent by hiring the services of outside consultants, but this will not always be as effective as having one's own team.

It would also seem, as mentioned earlier, that large firms have an important advantage in commercial application because they can ensure quicker market penetration of new products and processes. It is in the development and commercial application of proven ideas rather than as a source of invention that large firms are most likely to have the advantage over their smaller competitors. Freeman (1974) found that 80 per cent of 1,100 innovations introduced into 50 UK industries between 1945 and 1970 were made by firms with more than 1,000 employees. But how large a firm needs to be in order to be a successful innovator varies from one industry to another. In mechanical engineering, for instance, there are many opportunities for small-scale, low-cost innovations, and here the small and medium-sized firms can hold their own. In heavy chemicals, on the other hand, the advantage is overwhelmingly with the large firm. The study by Pavitt *et al.* already referred to confirms the variation between sectors in the size distribution of innovating firms. Firms with fewer than 1,000 employees were particularly important in machinery, instruments and R&D laboratories, in which they accounted for 45 per cent of all significant innovations made between 1945 and 1983, while in mining, food, chemicals, electrical products and defence, firms with more than 10,000 employees were responsible for more than 75 per cent of innovations. In the majority of industries it is probably true to say that a range of R&D work exists in terms of both cost and the degree of risk involved. Under these conditions, an important contribution to R&D can be made by individuals and small firms as well as by larger corporations.

Even where large firms do have important advantages in the commercial application of new knowledge, the possibility exists that the introduction and diffusion of this knowledge may be delayed by the vested interest which the firms have in traditional products and processes. Such delay is most likely where an industry is dominated by one firm. We shall deal with this problem in greater depth in the next section.

The final point to be emphasised here is that successful R&D effort is a management technique that must be considered as an integral part of the total activity of the firm. This brings out two matters of some importance.

First, the task of the successful research manager is not simply to solve technical and scientific problems but, in particular, to solve those that are relevant to the production and marketing objectives of the firm. This involves a clear view of what these objectives should be, the time period involved, and the finance that is likely to be available for R&D work. There has to be effective communication, therefore, between the various departments of the firm, particularly between R&D, production and marketing. It was mentioned earlier that freedom from the need to worry about short-term survival is an advantage in the prosecution of R&D work. This is true, but does not mean that R&D effort should be isolated from the basic marketing objectives of the firm. The problem of deciding on the most appropriate level of research expenditure and choosing the projects which are most likely to have usable results is, of course, an extremely difficult one. The outcome of R&D work is by its very nature highly uncertain, and it is hardly surprising that firms of much the same size in the same industry reach different conclusions about how much money it is worth spending in this field.

A second important part of the management function is to keep open lines of communication to sources of technical knowledge outside the firm, and to be aware of their relevance to the firm's own position. These external sources include developments in other industries and countries, research associations, and technical and scientific journals. One way of keeping abreast with the latest technical advances is by using or producing under licence the processes or products developed by other companies at home or abroad. The availability of outside information also means that even where smallness is a disadvantage it is still possible for small firms to be technically progressive. So long as the management of small firms keep in touch with the various outside sources of technical information, and of course have the ability to understand the relevance of such knowledge to the firm's position, they will be able to take advantage of the results of research.

9.3 R&D AND MARKET STRUCTURE

Theoretical arguments

From the viewpoint of industrial policy, a crucial question is what kind of market structure is most conducive to R&D and thus to the promotion of technological change.

Arrow (1962) argued that a purely competitive industry would provide greater incentives for cost-reducing innovations than would a simple monopoly. The argument, for the case of a large cost reduction, is illustrated in Figure 9.1(a). Industry demand is DD' and the pre-innovation cost curve, assuming constant cost conditions, is at level C. For the competitive case, price equals cost, and output is where the cost curve intersects the industry demand curve. For the monopolist with identical demand and cost conditions price $= P_m$ and output $= Q_m$, and monopoly profits are earned equal to $(P_m - C)Q_m$.

Consider now the returns to an innovation that lowers unit costs at all levels of output to C_n. In the competitive case Arrow assumes that the innovation is the work of an independent inventor who charges all firms a uniform royalty for each unit of output sold. In order to maximise his returns the royalty will be fixed at r.

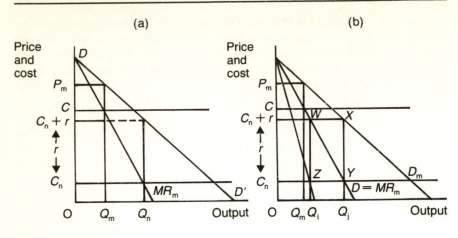

(a)   **(b)**

Figure 9.1 The returns to cost-reducing innovation

The unit cost facing each firm will thus be $C_n + r$. Competition between firms ensures that they will all adopt the innovation; price falls to $C_n + r$ and competitive output is Q_n. Total proceeds from the royalty equal rQ_n. By charging a per unit royalty of r the inventor has restricted output to the profit-maximising level and has appropriated all the monopoly profit for himself. Given the cost of innovation, K, the incentive to innovate is thus given by $rQ_n - K$.

Compare this with the monopoly case. Here Arrow assumes that it is the monopolist who does the innovative work. In the pre-innovation state the monopolist earns economic profit of $(P_m - C)Q_m$. Following the innovation and the reduction in costs to C_n, profit-maximising behaviour by the monopolist will again result in output Q_n and a price equal to $C_n + r$, giving a return (before deducting the cost of the innovation) of rQ_n. However, unlike the competitive case, the monopolist was earning economic profits in the pre-innovation stage, equal to $(P_m - C)Q_m$, and these have to be deducted. Assuming the cost of introducing the innovation to be the same as in the competitive case, the strength of the incentive to invent is thus given by $rQ_n - K - (P_m - C)Q_m$, which is less than the incentive to invest under competitive conditions.

This analysis of the relative incentives to invest under pure competition and simple monopoly was questioned by Demsetz (1969), who argued that Arrow's results depended on monopoly output being less (only half as much with a linear demand curve) than competitive output. If both industry structures are assumed to have the same initial levels of output, the result, Demsetz argued, is reversed. This is shown in Figure 9.1(b). In order to equalise industry size at the pre-innovation stage, the industry demand curve for the competitive case shown in Figure 9.1(b) is the same as the monopolist's marginal revenue curve MR_m in Figure 9.1(a). In this case the pre-innovation level of output will be equal to Q_m for both monopolist and competitive industry, and the monopolist again earns profits of $(P_m - C)Q_m$. The maximum amount which the inventor can extract in royalties in the competitive case is then rQ_i. The monopolist's profit-maximising output after the innovation will be Q_j, where $C_n = MR_m$, and profits earned will be given by rQ_j. Thus in Figure 9.1(b) the monopolist produces a larger output than the competitive industry. Also, ignoring the costs of innovation, the monopolist has a greater incentive to innovate as long as the excess of monopoly profits over competitive profits, shown by area $WXYZ$ in the diagram, is greater than the monopoly profit lost after the innovation $(P_m - C)Q_m$. With linear demand curves this condition will always be met.

Though it may be of some theoretical interest, the above analysis has little practical value. One problem with Arrow's approach is the assumed absence of competition in the innovative process, thus implying that the inventor knows with certainty that his invention will not be imitated, i.e. there is no problem of appropriability. Arrow's results also depend on immediate diffusion of an innovation. On the other hand, Demsetz's argument that comparisons should be made on the basis of the same pre-innovation industry size makes little sense *if* monopoly output does in practice tend to fall below the competitive level. If it does then this should be taken as one of the relevant factors determining incentives to invest in R&D. Indeed it is not even clear that any adjustment is needed to the analysis in order to meet Demsetz's point. This is because the *post*-innovation output in the first part of our analysis (Figure 9.1(a)) is the same for both the monopoly and competitive cases, and, given complete information, it is post-innovation output that is surely relevant in determining incentives. The real problems with Arrow's analysis lie elsewhere – e.g. in the assumption that, in the competitive case, the innovation comes from an independent inventor, and that there are no problems of appropriating the benefits. The question of whether conditions in purely competitive industries are conducive to R&D is therefore conveniently by-passed.

A major problem with theoretical attempts to compare extreme cases is that assumptions are often made which strain credulity. Take another model which has been used to compare monopoly and pure competition, shown in Figure 9.2. In this case a process innovation results in a downward shift in the marginal cost curve from MC_1 to MC_2. Cost conditions are identical for the monopolist and the purely competitive industry, and pre-innovation output for both is OQ. As a result of the innovation the monopolist expands output to OQ_m where $MR_m = MC_2$, but the competitive firm expands output further – to OQ_c, where $MR_c = MC_2$. Given the cost of the innovation, the return to the competitive firm exceeds that of the monopolist by area ABC. This result is due to the fact that, following a cost reduction, output is expanded more by the competitive firm than by the monopolist. However, the result here that competition is more favourable to innovation than monopoly rests on the assumption that a single firm in a competitive industry is the same size as a firm with monopoly power. In fact if, following an innovation, all firms in a competitive industry were to expand output, price would fall and the analysis of Figure 9.2 breaks down.

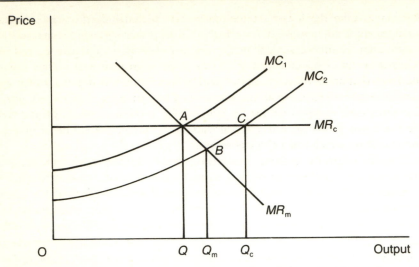

Figure 9.2 The returns to cost-reducing innovation where output is smaller under monopoly than under competition

The ideas discussed so far, then, are of very limited usefulness. What we need is a better understanding of both the ability to undertake R&D and the incentives to do so, for different kinds of industry structure. We start with the view, associated with Schumpeter (1947), that monopoly power is necessary for a high level of R&D activity. There are two separate reasons why firms with a substantial degree of monopoly power may engage in more R&D activity than firms in competitive markets. The first concerns the incentive to innovate. A firm with a high market share can expect to appropriate a large share of the financial gains from any innovation. More generally, incentives exist in the form of either creating or strengthening positions of market power. In highly competitive markets on the other hand, where an innovation is rapidly imitated by a large number of competitors, the innovating firm may not expect to secure a sufficient share of the gains to make the innovation appear worthwhile. Indeed, in the extreme case of pure competition, where new ideas are copied immediately, there can be no incentive at all to invest in R&D. Thus large numbers of equally matched firms and easy entry conditions may both have adverse effects on the incentive to innovate.

The second argument relates to the ability to innovate. Firms with market power will have larger profits out of which to finance R&D work. Also, such firms have a greater degree of certainty about their future prospects, which makes them better able to bear the risks associated with R&D and also to equip themselves adequately for R&D effort. The protection they enjoy from competition, for instance, makes it easier for them to engage staff on projects which may take several years to come to fruition. A firm with market power is thus in a better position to take the long-term view necessary for such R&D work because management is not completely absorbed in the short-run struggle for survival.

The main counter-argument to the case for monopoly concerns the relative incentives to innovate experienced by firms with a great deal of market power and firms that are exposed to a great deal of competition. A dominant firm will certainly expect to appropriate the gains from innovation, but in another sense it has *less* reason to innovate than a firm with a modest share of the market, because it has less to gain in terms of increased market share. Furthermore, a dominant firm which is not threatened by entry may be slow to innovate because of its vested interest in existing products or processes. Innovation brings an end to the monopoly profits from outmoded products or processes and the protected monopolist will thus tend to delay the introduction of the innovation.

However, though a dominant firm has relatively little to gain from innovation, it has a lot to lose if another firm – in the form of either an existing small competitor or a new entrant – should threaten to undermine its position through innovation. Therefore, although a dominant firm might not be expected to take the lead in innovation, it can be expected to react vigorously to the innovative activity of a smaller competitor by either rapid imitation or acquisition.

Another advantage of having several competitors is that competition in innovation should have the advantage of improving the quality as well as the quantity of innovation. Different approaches to the problem will be tried, and it will be the market which determines which product or process is successful.

The discussion so far suggests that oligopolistic market structures, which combine elements of competitiveness and market power, are likely to provide the best framework for a high level of R&D. The case for oligopoly may be summarised as follows. First, although firms in an oligopolistic industry may collude on price it is more difficult for them to collude on R&D. Unlike a price cut, successful R&D is not easy to follow. Each firm will therefore hope that a successful innovation will at least give it a temporary advantage over its competitors. Second, competition between firms has the advantage that there are several centres of initiative, so that different approaches to design or solving a technical problem will be adopted. Third, each oligopolist will have a sufficiently large share of the market to allow it to appropriate a large enough share of the benefits of any innovation which may be imitated by competitors. Fourth, oligopolistic price discipline means that economic profits are earned. This provides the financial resources to fund R&D. In addition, price discipline allows the firm to take the long view which is often necessary for successful innovative activity.

Although a useful guide, the case for oligopoly has limited practical value because the range of oligopolistic industries is so wide. Starting from a position near to that of simple monopoly, an increase in the number of firms could, up to a point, be expected to have beneficial effects. It would increase the competitive stimulus to R&D without damaging the ability to undertake it. There would also be the benefit of having more centres of initiative. Beyond some point, however, an increase in numbers will be counterproductive. Price discipline will collapse, thus damaging the ability to fund R&D work. In addition, incentives will be blunted because of the appropriation problem. Much the same problem applies to entry conditions. Up to a point the threat of entry will act as a stimulus to the R&D efforts of incumbent oligopolists, but if entry barriers are too low the effect may be to reduce the level of R&D.

It must also be borne in mind that R&D is affected by factors other than market structure. These include the size and growth of markets. For a given size distribution of firms, the larger the market the greater the expected returns from successful innovation. Similarly, a rapidly expanding industry will promise higher returns to R&D than a declining one. The last point is related to the enormous differences that exist between industries in *opportunities* for technical advance. These opportunities are much higher, for instance, in science-based industries such as electronics, pharmaceuticals, chemicals and electrical engineering, than in the clothing and footwear, and food, drink and tobacco industries.

One complicating factor in assessing the determinants of R&D effort is the correlation that exists between the potentially important explanatory variables. For instance, the opportunity to innovate may be a determinant of market structure. Thus, in some industries high R&D activity may result in high concentration as a result of patent protection. High concentration may also result in so far as research-intensive industries tend to be those where economies of scale are relatively important and where product differentiation is marked. Another possibility is that the variance of growth rates is higher in those industries where technological opportunities are greatest and that this leads to high concentration as a result of the law of proportionate effect (see Chapter 5). Whatever the true relationship between market concentration and the opportunity to innovate, it is important to try and distinguish between these two influences on R&D. It is time to turn to the empirical evidence.

Empirical evidence

Empirical work on market structure and innovation is of two kinds: industry case studies and cross-sectional analysis.

Industry studies

Industry studies are by their very nature difficult to summarise. They do suggest, however, that no simple relationship exists between market structure and technical progressiveness, and that other factors (e.g. opportunities to innovate, entrepreneurial attitudes) have an important part to play.

While many industries with highly competitive market structures engage in little or no R&D, some (e.g. certain electronic products) have good R&D records. Conversely, while some industries characterised by dominant firms or tight oligopolies have been resistant to technical change, there are examples of dominant firms which have led the way in R&D. The UK glass manufacturer

Pilkington is one example. Another is the German chemical giant I.G. Farben, which between the wars had the largest R&D programme of any chemical firm in the world, and alone accounted for 17 per cent of the international plastics patents issued up to 1945.

There is also plenty of case-study evidence to show that dominant firms are often rapid imitators of innovations introduced by smaller rivals, thus supporting one of our theoretical predictions. Thus, for instance, Wilkinson Sword introduced the stainless steel razor blade but was quickly and aggressively followed by Gillette. IBM in computers and AT&T in microwave radio relay systems also fit into this category. Dominant firms not only have the ability to respond rapidly to an innovation, they also have the marketing clout which facilitates a more rapid diffusion of their own products.

In the hope of finding more general results we have to turn to cross-sectional analysis, which covers a range of industries.

Cross-section regression analysis

We begin by looking at a basic problem encountered in this field of research; that of measuring R&D performance. What we would like to have is a measure of the value of the results of R&D activity that recognises that not all innovations are equally valuable, either to the firm that does the innovating or to consumers. However, in practice, data limitations rule out such a measure, and the choice is between an imperfect output measure and, even less satisfactory, various measures of firms' input into R&D – such as the ratio of R&D expenditure to sales, or the ratio of scientists and engineers to total employment.

The most readily available and frequently used measure of the output of R&D activity is the number of patented inventions issued to a given firm or market. This is an unsatisfactory measure of innovative output for a number of reasons: patented inventions may never reach the innovation stage, they vary widely in their economic importance, and different industries display different tendencies to take out patents.

Despite these problems, counting patents obviously gives an index more closely related to what we want to measure than does measuring the inputs into the innovative process, since the mere expenditure of huge sums on R&D is no guarantee of finding a profitable innovation. However, one study by Mueller (1966) found that in fact there was a high correlation between R&D inputs and number of patents issued, so that, although this is obviously not true for every single project, in general, increasing expenditure on R&D does lead to greater output.

It is not easy to assess either from data on R&D inputs or from figures on patents how much benefit consumers derive from R&D activities. While some R&D programmes lead directly to the introduction of completely new products or new technologies, many result in only minor improvements in product design.

With these introductory comments on the problems of measuring R&D activity we turn to the evidence.

In the mid 1980s approximately 70 per cent of all privately funded R&D expenditure in the UK occurred in three sectors: electronic engineering (34.1 per cent), chemicals (18.3 per cent) and aerospace (16.9 per cent). Some further information which reflects the opportunity to innovate is shown in Table 9.1, which also gives data on five-firm employment concentration ratios.

There is not enough information in Table 9.1 to draw any firm conclusions about the relationship between the intensity of R&D expenditure and the level of industry concentration. The general impression one gets is that differences between industries in the opportunity to innovate are far greater than differences in concentration and that the former is likely to be far more important than the latter in explaining R&D expenditure. In view of the preceding discussion about the complexity of the relationships involved, it is not surprising that very few empirical studies have simply regressed a measure of innovation on one of concentration. The differences between industries in opportunity for innovation mean that it is necessary to allow for these differences before a valid assessment of the role of industry structure can be made.

A great deal of empirical work has been done in this area based almost entirely on US data. Studies by A. Phillips (1966), Scherer (1967), Comanor (1967), Rosenberg (1976), Wilson (1977) and Shrieves (1978), are among those surveyed by Kamien and Schwartz (1982). The following tentative conclusions emerge from this work.

A positive correlation is generally found between R&D intensity and concentration, but the strength of this correlation is considerably reduced when technological opportunity is taken into account. In Scherer's study the correlation

Table 9.1 Intensity of R&D expenditure and five-firm employment concentration ratios, selected industries, UK, 1978

Industry	R&D expenditure as % of sales	Weighted average concentration ratio
Aerospace	18.5	77
Electronic computers	16.1	70
Electronic components	12.1	59
Pharmaceutical products	10.4	40
Misc. electrical goods	2.5	32
Motor vehicles	1.4	64
Insulated wires	1.2	82
Domestic (elect.) appliances	1.0	57
Pottery, china, glass	1.0	52
All manufacturing	1.6	43

Sources: *Industrial Research and Development Expenditure and Employment, 1978,* Business Monitor MO 14, London: HMSO, 1980; *Report of the Census of Production 1978: Summary Tables*, Business Monitor PA 1002, London: HMSO, 1981

coefficient falls from 0.46 to 0.20. This indicates that R&D intensity is more strongly affected by differences in opportunity to innovate than by differences in concentration. Nevertheless, a positive relationship between R&D effort and the level of concentration remains after adjusting for technological opportunities, that is, technologically progressive industries tend to be more concentrated than others. Does this provide support for Schumpeter's hypothesis and suggest that high concentration encourages innovation? The evidence seems to give only qualified support to Schumpeter's hypothesis.

One important point to note is that the strength of the positive correlation between R&D intensity and concentration varies for different industry groups and is greatest for those groups with the lowest opportunities for innovation. For instance, the industry sample in Comanor's study is divided into two categories according to whether the opportunity for product differentiation is high or low, this division being justified on the grounds that, where product differentiation is an important dimension of competition, product innovation opportunities are liable to be abundant. Comanor found that R&D intensity was higher in industries where product differentiation is important (investment goods and consumer durables), but that the positive correlation between R&D and concentration was much weaker in these industries than in those where product differentiation opportunities were low (material inputs and consumer non-durables). Similar conclusions are arrived at in the study by Shrieves. He found a strong positive correlation between R&D intensity and concentration for consumer goods and material inputs, but no significant correlation for durable goods industries where both R&D intensity and concentration tended to be above average. Increased concentration levels thus have less effect on R&D effort in the high-opportunity industries, which tend to be more concentrated anyway.

Another point to note is that, within the group of industries characterised by low to moderate technological opportunities, the relationship between concentration and innovation is non-linear. Almost no R&D effort takes place in the least concentrated industries in these groups; maximum effort appears to take place in industries with a four-firm concentration ratio of around 50–55 per cent, and a further increase in concentration brings about very little increase in innovation. Thus, the empirical evidence suggests that, for industries with limited opportunities for technological advance, a rather loose oligopolistic market structure is the one most likely to induce innovation.

The empirical work done in this area also illustrates the importance of other structural features in affecting innovation. We have previously argued that the ease or difficulty of new entry into an industry will have an important effect on existing firms' attitude to R&D. Where entry is very easy, the gains from innovation will be rapidly eroded by new firms entering the market and imitating the product; where barriers to entry are very high, firms will be so protected from competition that they will feel little incentive to innovate. Comanor (1967) found that industries with moderate barriers to new entry have the highest proportion of expenditure on R&D personnel. There is also a lot of evidence from case studies which testifies to the large contribution made by new entrants, especially in pioneering completely new products and processes.

Turning now to the influence that market size has on R&D, Schmookler (1966) showed from both time-series and cross-sectional analysis that the number of inventions of capital goods is positively related to the output of capital goods; the higher the current sales of capital goods, the greater the expected return from the invention of an improved type of capital good. This shows that invention, like other economic activities, responds to expected returns and is encouraged by large markets. Freeman (1962) showed that there is also a strong positive correlation between research expenditure by industry and the rate of growth of output in that industry. The relationship here is likely to be two-way: not only does the prospect of a rapidly growing market provide an increased incentive to spend money on research, but the results of such research will themselves contribute to growth.

Empirical work does, then, give some support to the theoretical predictions of the previous section. Moderate levels of concentration appear to have a beneficial impact on R&D, especially when opportunities for advance are modest. They are also likely to have a positive role to play when rapid imitation of new ideas is difficult to prevent. There is little evidence however to support very high levels of concentration. The same sort of conclusions apply to entry barriers. New entry has played a crucial role in innovation, especially in the introduction of completely new processes and products. High entry barriers are almost certainly inimical to progress. At the same time, and especially where opportunities for advance are modest and innovations can be quickly imitated, moderate entry barriers may have some benefit. Lastly, large market size and rapid demand expansion play a positive role, though both are related to the opportunity to innovate.

9.4 THE ALLOCATION OF RESOURCES TO R&D

Having reviewed the evidence concerning links between market structure and R&D, we now turn to the more general topic of the overall level of R&D activity, and in particular to the question of whether the allocation of resources to R&D is likely to be optimal in a market economy. We shall see that there are reasons for supposing that too few resources will be allocated to R&D activity, so that some action by governments will be called for. First we look at some evidence on R&D spending.

Table 9.2 provides information on R&D spending for the UK and its major competitors for 1985. The first column of figures suggests that, measured by R&D expenditure as a percentage of GDP, UK performance is somewhat, but not greatly, inferior to that of some of its major industrial competitors. The second column of figures shows the proportion of total R&D spending which is government funded. Here there are considerable differences between countries, but again there would seem to be no particular cause for concern, the UK figure

Table 9.2 R&D expenditure in selected countries, 1985

	R&D expenditure as % of GDP	Proportion of total R&D funded by government
UK	2.3	43.1
Japan	2.6	19.1
Sweden	2.8	34.0
West Germany	2.7	36.7
Italy	1.1	51.7
France	2.3	52.9
USA	2.8	50.3
OECD average	2.4	41.1

Source: Stoneman and Vickers (1988)

being very near the average for all OECD countries. However, the figures in Table 9.2 conceal some important details, in particular the breakdown of government-funded R&D into defence-related and civilian application. This breakdown is shown in Table 9.3. It shows that, with the exception of the USA, UK government-funded R&D expenditure is more strongly orientated towards defence applications than that of its competitors.

Several authors have strongly criticised the high defence component of government funded R&D, arguing that it distorts the pattern of technological activity in the industrial sector and that it necessarily reduces the productivity performance of the supply side of the economy. This is because the 'spin-off' potential of military technology has, arguably, only limited civilian application, and therefore a significant opportunity cost, in terms of foregone technical progress, is attached to this form of R&D activity. If this is the case, then the R&D performance of the UK, as detailed in the first column of Table 9.1, becomes much less impressive, since the UK government's role in R&D expenditure is rather higher than the OECD average.

Concern over the level of R&D activity in the UK is heightened when consideration is given to long-term trends. In 1963, UK expenditure on R&D as a percentage of GDP was 2.2 per cent, compared with an average of 1.8 per cent for OECD countries. In Japan the figure was 1.4 per cent, in West Germany 1.5 per cent, and in Sweden 1.2 per cent. Therefore, as a proportion of GDP, R&D expenditure in the UK has not increased; indeed it may have declined slightly. However, and again with the exception of the USA, other major industrialised countries have significantly increased their R&D effort, and this increased level of activity has come mainly in civilian rather than defence-related applications. The upshot is that studies of privately funded R&D show the UK lagging well behind some of its closest competitors such as West Germany over quite a wide range of industries.

Table 9.3 The defence component of government-funded R&D, 1985

	Total government expenditure £m	Defence-related R&D £m	Defence as % of total
UK	4,589	2,259	49.2
Sweden	764	199	26.0
West Germany	4,920	596	12.1
Italy	2,695	229	8.5
France	5,421	1,775	32.7
USA	30,479	21,159	69.4

Source: Stoneman and Vickers (1988)

Government versus markets

A question that arises naturally from the preceding discussion of the level of R&D effort is why the government is regarded as so important to technological activity in market-orientated economies. If we were confident that the free operation of market forces would guarantee a socially optimal allocation of resources to R&D then the role of the state would be of little importance. Unfortunately this is not the case. There are strong reasons for believing that owing to market failure the amount of resources allocated to R&D will be sub-optimal. Three main arguments have been advanced to suggest that too few resources will be allocated to R&D activity so that some action by governments is called for. These are arguments associated with the cost and risk of R&D, the public good nature of R&D activity, and the distinction between basic and applied research.

The costs and risks of R&D

The first argument concerns the costs and risks associated with investment in R&D. We have already said that for an individual firm the returns to R&D expenditure cannot be predicted with any confidence; large amounts may be spent on research without making any worthwhile discoveries. The element of risk inherent in R&D activity means that firms that are risk averse will undertake too little R&D from the resource allocation point of view. This is because, even if the expected value of gains from a given research programme equals its expected cost, if the firm is risk averse the expected gain in utility from the project's success will be less than the loss in utility from paying for it, and so the firm will not undertake the project. The more risky the research, the more serious the underinvestment.

One way in which expenditure decisions under uncertainty can be made optimal is by arranging insurance, under which payment of an insurance premium guarantees compensation for any losses incurred. However, the risks associated with R&D projects are not of a kind that are insurable in this way, because of unpredictability and *moral hazard*. Moral hazard is a general problem of insurance markets and arises because the fact of being insured changes the insured party's behaviour and thus affects the insurance company's costs in a way that the company cannot control. In the case under discussion, if a company were fully insured against the possibility of an R&D project being unsuccessful, its financial incentive to be efficient in innovation would be removed, and the firm would tend to commit resources to wasteful and extravagant research projects. This happens because, with insurance, the marginal private cost to the company of using resources in R&D falls below the marginal social cost. This is one example of a more general problem associated with the allocation of resources to risky activities, namely, that arrangements to improve efficiency with regard to risk-bearing may cause efficiency losses elsewhere in the economy.

A good example of this problem is where the government bears the risk of failure through the specification and funding of 'cost-plus' research contracts. Important examples are to be found in the defence-related industries. The use of cost-plus contracts, by which the government pays the full costs of production plus a flat-rate fee or percentage mark-up, passes risk-bearing on to the taxpayer. The problem of course is that it eliminates incentives to minimise costs. Indeed, in the case of a percentage mark-up on actual costs, there is an incentive to incur wasteful expenditures.

Public good characteristics of R&D

The second reason for supposing that in a free market too few resources will be allocated to R&D expenditure is that the product of such expenditure (i.e. information) has the two characteristics of public goods: indivisibility and inappropriability. Information is indivisible because its use by one person or firm doesn't prevent its being used at the same time by others. Thus, the opportunity cost of using information is zero, and in order to achieve a social optimum it should be made freely available at zero price. But to encourage firms to invest in the production of information it is necessary to guarantee an inventing firm exclusive rights in the information that it produces, for a limited period at least. However, because information is inappropriable as well as indivisible, it is difficult to make such a guarantee. This is because it is, if not impossible, at least extremely costly to exclude interested parties from the benefits of the information. This applies particularly to product inventions; as soon as a new product is available on the market, other firms will be able to copy it and thus appropriate some of the benefits of R&D paid for by the inventing firm. Where the invention is a new manufacturing process rather than a new product, it is easier for the firm that did the research to keep new knowledge to itself, but firms in the same industry may have the know-how to work out how the new process functions.

Once a new invention has been developed, therefore, it is virtually impossible for the inventor to secure all the economic gains from his invention; the costs of excluding other interested parties from the benefits may be too high. Moreover, from an optimal resource allocation point of view they ought not to be excluded, as the knowledge should be made freely available. This clearly poses a policy dilemma since treating knowledge as a public good and making it generally available would completely destroy the individual firm's incentive to invest in R&D.

It might be expected that the market would evolve institutional arrangements for dealing with the problems that have so far been discussed. One such arrangement is the use of joint ventures.

Joint ventures

A mechanism for financing R&D which overcomes some of the cost, risk and appropriability problems is the formation of joint ventures. A cooperative approach to R&D has the benefits of spreading risks, limiting wasteful duplication, and speeding up the diffusion of new knowledge, while at the same time ensuring that the fruits of success are appropriated by the cooperating firms. The strength of the case for joint ventures will clearly vary according to circumstances. The more complex and risky an R&D programme is, the more likely that a joint venture will be superior to non-cooperative action. Joint ventures are also likely to be superior to non-cooperative action when R&D spillovers are high.

On the debit side, however, it must be remembered that collaboration results in additional costs – of negotiation, supervision and coordination, as well as problems that may arise out of differences in 'management style'. In addition, joint ventures reduce the number of independent centres of initiative, and may depress both the overall level of R&D effort and also the diversity of approach to a particular problem. The importance of this danger depends on the scale and complexity of the R&D programme. It may be that both the scale and complexity of the programme are such that there is simply no alternative, as in the case of European collaboration in designing and constructing civilian aircraft. Another relevant factor is the market share of the firms participating in a joint venture. It may be possible to have several joint ventures in an industry so that the benefits can be reaped while at the same time preserving the advantages of having several independent R&D centres.

Another problem with joint ventures is that the full exploitation of the R&D results may require cooperation at the level of production and even distribution. If firms are prevented from such joint exploitation, and if it is anticipated that the benefits of cooperative R&D will be quickly dissipated through intense product-market competition, some valuable joint ventures will be discouraged. As d'Asprement and Jacquemin (1988) argue, joint cooperation in *both* R&D and production may bring R&D activity closer to the social optimum. Of course the danger is that the more cooperation extends downstream the greater the danger that joint ventures will weaken competition and, indeed, may be used to underpin collusive behaviour. Ordover and Willig (1985), for instance, conclude that the intensity of downstream competition in the post-innovation stage is an important determinant of the social desirability of a joint venture.

The case for joint ventures thus depends on several factors: the risks and complexity of R&D investments, the level of R&D spillovers, the extent to which cooperation needs to extend downstream, and the market share of the participants. George and Jacquemin (1990) explain how these considerations are dealt with in the European Commission's approach to the handling of cooperative R&D.

Basic versus applied research

Joint ventures are unlikely to be an adequate response to the problems posed by basic research. While applied research has a reasonably immediate commercial application to one particular technology, product or industry, basic research is concerned with the advance of scientific knowledge generally and may come up with findings of interest to a number of different industries or to none. Basic research is of fundamental importance, because its discoveries will later serve as the inputs for further applied-research projects with commercial outputs. Therefore, in order to encourage R&D expenditure as a whole it is essential to invest sufficient funds in basic research. But the two problems already discussed, of uncertainty and the public good nature of information, both apply *a fortiori* to basic research. Indeed the problems in this area of research are particularly acute. The pay-off from the point of view of an individual investing firm is more uncertain the further the research project is towards the basic end of the spectrum. And the possibly wide implications of basic scientific discoveries increase the desirability of making the results freely available. Nelson (1959) suggested that, as far as the problem of uncertainty is concerned, large diversified firms may play a positive role. These firms he argued will be more willing to undertake research which is not tied to commercial possibilities in any one market. This is because any inventions thrown up as a result of basic research are more likely to be applicable somewhere in the firm's product range. Firms which are already diversified may also be ready to extend their range of interests in order to exploit an innovation. The wide range of markets in which they operate will also allow the spreading of risk; in effect the firm operates a self-insurance system whereby unsuccessful projects are offset against successful ones.

There are of course disadvantages as well as advantages associated with the role of the large firm in R&D which have been considered earlier in this chapter. As to the evidence, there is little as yet which gives firm support to the view that large diversified firms contribute disproportionately to basic research.

Any tendency, therefore, for too few resources to be allocated to R&D in a market economy is likely to apply most strongly to basic research, and it is here that the case for government action is strongest.

We have now reviewed the arguments for supposing that the market mechanism, left to itself, will allocate too few resources to R&D. Governments may adopt a number of policies to correct this tendency. They include the direct allocation of funds to R&D especially for basic research; the encouragement of R&D joint ventures; and the use of the patent system. The patent system is considered in the next section.

9.5 DIFFUSION OF NEW TECHNOLOGY AND THE PATENT SYSTEM

The speed of diffusion

The creation of new knowledge is clearly an important determinant of economic welfare, but so too is the rate at which new knowledge is diffused.

The pioneering work in this area is that of Mansfield (1968), who examined the diffusion of 12 techniques in four industries in the USA; brewing, bituminous coal, iron and steel, and railroads. He measured the speed of diffusion as the number of years it took for a new technique to be adopted by a given proportion of firms. Not unexpectedly his results showed a wide variation in the experience of different industries. For the 12 techniques in Mansfield's study the average time taken for half the firms to adopt a new technique was 7.8 years. The range, however, was from 0.9 to 15 years.

What are the factors most likely to influence the speed of diffusion? The profitability of the new technique is obviously an important consideration. In empirical studies in this field profitability is often measured by the estimated length of the payback period, i.e. the number of years taken for investment in the new technology to pay for itself. The shorter the payback period, the more attractive the investment will be, given the risks associated with it.

Another important determinant will be the size and complexity of the investment required to adopt a new technology. The finance needed to purchase new machinery; the labour training that is necessary to ensure that the workforce is sufficiently well acquainted with the new technology; the investment needed in servicing new machines, and in adapting the technology to local conditions etc., will vary substantially from one innovation to another. Teece (1977) found that technology transfer is expensive even when it is a transfer from one subsidiary of a multinational company to another. For 26 case studies the median transfer cost (calculated as a percentage of 'total project cost') was 17 per cent, with a lower to upper decile range of 6 per cent to 42 per cent. Technology transfer between independent companies will typically be more costly since it may have to be done with less than full cooperation from the innovator. Mansfield *et al.* (1981) examined 48 product innovations in the chemical, pharmaceutical, machinery and electronics industries of the USA. On average, they calculated imitation costs to be around 65 per cent of innovation costs. Again, there was considerable variation around the average.

Empirical studies such as those by Mansfield (1968), Romeo (1977) and Davies (1979) confirm the expectation that speed of diffusion is positively related to profitability and negatively related to the investment costs of installing new technology.

But what part does market structure play in the diffusion process? On the one hand it might be expected that competitive market structures would speed up the rate of diffusion. This expectation is given some support in Romeo's study of the diffusion of the numerically controlled machine tool in ten industries in the USA over the period 1951–70. He found that diffusion tended to be faster the larger the number of firms, though the association was not a very strong one. He also found a strong negative association between the rate of diffusion and a measure of the inequality of firm size.

On the other hand, a good *a priori* case can be made out for expecting the rate of diffusion to be faster in industries where there are few firms and where those firms are well matched in terms of size. One argument is that information can be transmitted more easily when there are few firms. And if firms are also similar in size they are more likely to share the same expectations and objectives (Davies 1979). In addition, a technology which is appropriate for large firms may be unsuitable for small ones. For instance, mining machinery designed for use in large pits with thick mineral seams may be quite inappropriate for pits operating on a small scale. Here then is another reason why equality of firm size may be conducive to the rapid spread of a new technique. Another possibility is that industries where firms are relatively few and well matched might be more conducive to the emergence of information-sharing agreements, a point we return to below. A study of 22 process innovations in 13 UK industries by Davies (1979) produces results which support these arguments, and finds that the rate of diffusion tends to be faster the smaller the number of firms and the smaller the differences in firm size.

R&D agreements

It was mentioned above that one advantage of a market with relatively few firms of similar size is that it might facilitate the emergence of arrangements, overt or tacit, for the exchange of R&D information. Baumol (1990) has argued that market forces will impel the interchange of technical information between firms.

His simple model, of what he tentatively calls a 'technology-sharing cartel', assumes that there is a group of identical firms; each firm spends the same amount on R&D for cost-reducing innovations, and each has the same expected return on its R&D expenditure. If all but one of the firms agree to exchange the results of R&D the odd one out will be faced with a growing loss in competitiveness. The reason for this is that, though each member of the information-sharing group will not get as *much* benefit out of the R&D efforts of other firms (because there are costs involved in adopting the innovations of others) as it will out of its own innovations, there is still *some* positive benefit to be gained. The firm which holds out from exchanging information can thus expect its costs to fall more slowly. More generally, so long as a sufficient number of firms agree to exchange information, they can expect their costs to fall more quickly than those of firms which choose to act independently. Furthermore, the cost advantage will grow cumulatively over time, and this serves to discourage cheating. For, while cheating may pay off in the short run, the firm that is cheating will eventually be caught out and expelled from the group, and will therefore be barred from enjoying the long-term benefits of more rapidly falling costs.

The *ex ante* incentive to agree to exchange information will be weakened in the case of a firm that believes its own R&D effort will produce a more valuable stream of new ideas than those of its rivals because, for instance, its R&D effort is much larger. Even in the case of equally matched firms which share the same expectations as to the value of R&D output, one firm is liable to produce an innovation of exceptional value. The temptation to renege on an information-sharing agreement will then be strong.

An obvious way to overcome these problems is to have an *ex post* sharing agreement on a bilateral basis. In this case the exchange is of innovations already made and which, over a period of time at least, will be of more or less equivalent value to the participating firms. One important advantage of an *ex post* sharing arrangement is that it gives each firm an incentive to produce worthwhile innovations because unless it puts something into the R&D pot it gets nothing out.

In principle this arrangement should also allow exchange agreements to be entered into by firms of very unequal size because the information which a firm has to hand over is limited in value to what it receives. However, this possibility may be limited in practice by several considerations. For instance, a firm with a large R&D effort may have a constant flow of new ideas whereas a small firm may produce innovations only intermittently. In these circumstances it may be difficult to achieve a workable and continuing agreement. One large firm is also more likely to be concerned about another of similar size gaining a competitive advantage through successful innovation. Successful innovation by a much smaller firm on the other hand is of less immediate concern and can be dealt with in a variety of ways including acquisition. This leads to the possibility that information-sharing agreements between large firms in a tightly knit oligopolistic industry might have the *adverse* effect of squeezing out the competitive fringe and perhaps reducing the flow of really radical ideas.

The patent system

The patent system is an attempt to resolve the dilemma outlined earlier: namely, that to encourage firms to invest in R&D the firms need some kind of property rights in the information that comes out of the R&D, but that, on the other hand, since information is indivisible, it should be made available to all potential users. The patent system attempts to resolve the dilemma in the following way. An inventor, the firm or other owner of information, can register his sole rights in the information by taking out a patent on it. This gives the inventor legal protection against the appropriation of the benefits from his information by other interested parties for a certain period of time. But to obtain a patent the inventor has to disclose full details of the process or product concerned. This ensures that, when the patent expires, the information becomes freely available. While the patent is in operation, other firms have no legal right of access to the information unless the patent-holder abuses his monopoly position, but the patent-holder may license other firms to use it if they pay either a flat sum or a royalty payment which depends on the amount of the product made under licence. The central question to be asked about the operation of a patent system is whether it achieves the right trade-off in reconciling conflicting interests.

An individual or firm can apply for a patent for any invention that is susceptible of application in industry or agriculture, that is new, and that involves an inventive step and does not form part of the existing state of the art. But the patent system is essentially an administrative device and cannot deal flexibly with the intricate economics of research and innovation; both the economic importance of patented inventions and the degree of monopoly power conferred on the patentee vary enormously from case to case.

The number of patent applications made every year is huge, and their validity is checked only when the application is opposed, say by a rival firm. This means that many patents are granted that are in fact invalid (i.e. contain nothing new). The vast majority of patents are never actually used, having been applied for to establish priority of invention 'in case'. The propensity to patent varies across industries, and this means that, while many patents apply to inventions of little or no economic value, conversely some significant inventions are never patented. This suggests that the number of patents granted is not necessarily a good measure of technical progressiveness.

How much benefit does the individual firm undertaking R&D derive from the operation of the patent system? The patent system does give innovating firms a temporary monopoly over their new product or process, and some kind of exclusive right is necessary to encourage investment in R&D in a market economy. However, the amount of encouragement provided by the patent system varies considerably. In some industries, e.g. chemicals and pharmaceuticals, holding a patent is an effective way of preventing imitation by rival companies that haven't themselves done R&D, but in others, e.g. electronics, rivals can easily get round the patent and produce a substitute product without infringing the patent protection. In fact, applying for a patent can make imitation easier, since the know-how behind the invention must be disclosed and can then be adapted by other firms. This is one reason why the propensity to patent inventions varies across industries.

Thus, the amount of incentive to R&D generated by the patent system varies according to the competitive situation in the market concerned, and the empirical work in this area quoted below shows that in only a small minority of firms is R&D activity crucially dependent on patent protection. Given that the patent system encourages some but not all firms to do more R&D, what is the effect of the system on the wider public interest? There are two important issues: the effect of the system on the production and diffusion of new knowledge, and the effect on market power.

Patents and the production and diffusion of knowledge

Does the patent system encourage the production and rapid dissemination of new knowledge? Several general points can be made in answer to this question.

First, the patent system encourages not R&D as such but patentable inventions. This may involve misallocation of R&D resources, since patented inventions are not always those of most economic importance. In addition, considerable research effort may be devoted to 'inventing round' existing patents, thus resulting in social waste.

Second, it can be argued that the patent system increases the risk inherent in R&D activity by turning such activity into a race. Firms that expend money on research will face a heavy loss not only if they make no discoveries but also if they do come up with a new product or process only to find that it has already been patented by someone else, perhaps only a few days earlier. In a patent race, a 'near miss' is just as bad as 'missing by a mile', so firms may adopt risky research strategies, cut corners, etc., in order to win the race. This danger probably applies more to product than to process innovation and is of particular concern in areas such as pharmaceuticals.

Third, the patent system now operates to protect a firm during the process of innovation rather than at the invention stage, by enabling a firm to recoup the costs of R&D by granting a monopoly for the period in which the new product or process is introduced. However, it can be argued that competition and not monopoly in innovation would encourage the dissemination of new knowledge most rapidly.

Fourth, we can ask in what kinds of market, where the incentive to innovate is otherwise lacking, will the patent system prove effective in increasing R&D? Earlier in this chapter we have seen that there is least incentive to innovate in perfectly competitive markets, owing to the ease of imitation and consequent impossibility of appropriating the benefits of innovations, and also in monopolistic markets with high barriers to entry where the existing firms have little to gain from innovating. The patent system will do nothing to help in the latter case and will merely provide another barrier to entry. In the perfectly competitive case, it is true that patents will make it possible (to some extent at least) for innovating firms to keep the advantages of their innovation to themselves, but it must be asked how important this consideration is in practice.

In the real world there exist imperfections in markets that afford some protection to an innovating firm even without patent protection. In imperfectly competitive oligopolistic markets, competition in product innovation may be the most important form of competition, and the need to remain competitive by producing differentiated products will ensure that plenty of R&D activity takes place without patents. Indeed, in most product markets it is difficult to argue that the gains from innovation to the innovating firm would be completely wiped out by imitation. For this to happen, imitation by rival firms must be both rapid and widespread. In practice, as we have seen, there will inevitably be time lags involved in imitation. Since the innovating firm will always have a headstart, it will have a period during which it can, through price and non-price strategies, develop a market position.

Empirical work on whether the patent system effectively increases R&D has been carried out in the UK by Taylor and Silberston (1973). They questioned 44 firms in research-intensive industries about the extent to which their R&D activity depended on patent protection. Only 6 out of the 33 firms that answered this question said that 20 per cent or more of their R&D expenditure depended on patents. Most of the firms regarded innovation as an essential part of their competitive strategy. Similar conclusions were reached by Scherer *et al.* (1959) in a US survey of 91 large corporations; only 7 firms said that patent protection was the most important factor influencing their R&D decisions.

Thus, the evidence that the patent system does increase R&D expenditure is not very strong. It is not particularly effective in providing an incentive to innovate where such incentive is naturally lacking, or in increasing the allocation of resources towards the kind of research (i.e. basic research) that is particularly underprovided by a market system.

Patents and market power

The second important public-interest question regarding the operation of the patent system is concerned with the market power that the system creates and whether this is abused. In the most extreme case of abuse, a firm can use its patent monopoly over a product or process to prevent its being introduced at all; more generally, it can restrict output and keep prices high. Other firms can break the patent-holder's monopoly by applying for a licence to use the process or make the product concerned. Normally, the patent-holder can choose whether or on what terms to grant a licence, but in the UK, for instance, after a patent has operated for three years the Comptroller General of patents can grant a compulsory licence of right if the patent-holder is shown to have abused its monopoly position by restricting output.

Do these licensing arrangements offer sufficient protection against the abuse of market power? Probably not, since patent-holders can use their control over licences to maintain this power. The expansion of capacity can be controlled through the grant of licences, very high royalty payments can be exacted, or the licence can be granted only on certain conditions; for example, about market-sharing, so that the licensee can use the product or process only in markets where the patent-holder doesn't operate. In addition, a group of firms in research-intensive industries may operate a patent-pooling and licensing arrangement by which all the firms agree to license one another but no outside firms. Indeed, Silberston and Taylor found that in the pharmaceutical industry the most important advantage claimed for the patent system was that it gave the firms something to put into such a patent-pooling system so as to gain access to the other firms' patented drugs. This evidence gives some support to Baumol's views on the diffusion of new knowledge which were reported in section 9.4.

In some cases, then, patent protection is a significant structural feature of the market and adds to the market power of existing firms by creating another barrier to entry. It is therefore relevant to ask whether possible abuse of the market power afforded by patents is satisfactorily controlled by competition policy. In the UK, patents have been afforded a relatively privileged position by competition policy, since they are supposed to have the beneficial effect of increasing R&D to set against the disadvantage of increasing market power. Patent-pooling and licensing agreements have been registrable and referable to the Restrictive Practices Court only since the Fair Trading Act 1973. The Monopolies and Mergers Commission cannot investigate patents *per se*; it can look at patent abuses discovered during an investigation, but these can be corrected only by the Comptroller General of patents. In the EC it is also recognised that patent licensing agreements may have beneficial effects, but such agreements are covered by Article 85 and will be allowed by the EC Commission only if they contain no restrictive provisions other than those essential for the purposes of the agreement.

The precise balance of the advantages and disadvantages of a patent system will depend on the legal terms and administrative details, which vary from country to country. It is true to say that various inquiries into the patent system have concluded that it does on balance yield positive net benefits and should therefore be retained. Some kind of legal protection of property rights in information is necessary to counteract the private market's tendency to underinvest in R&D.

However, the above discussion suggests that patent systems as currently operated tend to favour the private interests of the patent-holder rather than the public interest. Most of the suggestions for reforming the system, from economists at least, have involved a reduction in the degree of protection afforded a patent-holder for the sake of both reducing market power and encouraging the rapid dissemination of new knowledge. Such reforms could be effected in a number of ways.

First, the number of years for which a patent is valid could be reduced. In most countries the period is 15 to 20 years, and in fact the tendency has been for this to increase in recent years; in the UK, for instance, the term for a patent was increased from 16 to 20 years by the Patents Act 1977. In the UK a patent-holder can apply for extension of the patent where he has not received an economic return on his investment, but there is no provision for a patent to be withdrawn earlier when an economic return has been made.

Second, patents could be subjected to an annual renewal fee and cancelled in the event of non-payment. This happens in West Germany, where as a result only 5 per cent of patents remain in force for the full term of 18 years and the average life of a patent is only 8 years.

Third, a two-tier patent system could be created that recognises that not all patented inventions are equally important. Full patents would be awarded for basic inventions and only shorter-term patents for minor inventions and improvements.

Fourth, and most radically, the conditions for granting licences could be tightened up, even to the extent of making licensing compulsory. This clause need not take effect immediately but after a short period, say three years, of absolute patent rights. Just as the empirical evidence has shown that in most cases patent protection is not a major reason for R&D effort, so Taylor and Silberston for the UK and Scherer *et al.* for the USA found little evidence that compulsory licensing would be a disincentive to research activity, except in the pharmaceutical industry.

Chapter 10

Potential competition and entry deterrence

10.1 INTRODUCTION

It is a clear prediction of the simple structure-conduct-performance explanation of industrial organisation that the smaller the number of firms operating within a market the more likely it is that they will restrict competition within it. The restriction of competition may take the form of collusive pricing or market-sharing agreements, and may also extend to restricting entry into the market by new firms, for, without some form of barrier to new competition, market power is a short-run phenomenon only. Thus a barrier to entry can be part of the competitive strategy of firms already producing in a market (the incumbents). However, an entry barrier is not an unambiguous concept. It is possible in theory to distinguish between 'natural' or 'innocent' barriers, which occur independently of the conduct of the incumbent firms, and 'strategic' barriers which are the result of the conscious actions of incumbents. In practice however, the distinction between natural and strategic barriers is not so easily made, as we shall see below.

In his pioneering work in this area Bain (1956) defined entry barriers as factors that allow established firms in an industry to earn supernormal profits without attracting new entry. Stigler (1968) offered an alternative definition. He defined entry barriers as costs that have to be borne by an entrant that are not borne by established firms. Demsetz (1982) took an entirely different approach, identifying entry barriers with various types of government intervention in the market, and arguing that only these imperfections could persist in the long run. Further consideration is given to this view in section 10.2. In section 10.3 we examine the way in which firms may set prices in order to deter entry, and this is followed in section 10.4 by a review of non-price strategies of entry deterrence. Lastly, section 10.5 examines the theory of contestable markets in which entry is perfectly free and exit is completely costless.

10.2 BARRIERS TO ENTRY

Bain (1956) identified four main 'natural' sources of entry barriers: absolute cost advantages of incumbents at any level of output, economies of scale, product differentiation advantages of incumbents, and total capital requirements to set up a firm of minimum optimal size.

With *absolute cost advantages* the incumbent's cost function lies everywhere below that of the potential entrant. This may occur because the incumbent has access to superior and/or cheaper inputs, or it may be due to advantages which the incumbent enjoys as a result of past R&D effort. This brings us immediately to the problem of distinguishing in practice between innocent and strategic entry-deterring conduct. There are many ways in which a firm can maintain a cost advantage over potential entrants and so protect an established position. Many of these are in the interest of consumers and the economy generally. They include cost-reducing innovations, and securing the supply of inputs by means of long-term contracts. An established firm may also gain an advantage over later arrivals simply as a result of learning economies. Although these activities may be used quite innocently by any firm with an interest in long-term competitiveness, they also merge into less innocent strategic behaviour designed to eliminate entry that would be beneficial to consumers and society. Thus a firm may take out a large number of patents as a means of obstructing entry, or it may increase entry barriers by tying up a high proportion of the supplies of some essential input. Similarly, it will be difficult to distinguish between innocent capacity extensions which are part of the normal process of expansion, and capacity extensions designed to pre-empt increases in demand.

A second source of entry barrier under the Bain definition is the existence of *scale economies* which are significant in relation to total market size. An example is shown in Figure 10.1. For a given market demand of q_n it is clear that scale economies are a more effective barrier to entry with cost conditions given by the long-run average cost curve $LRAC_2$ rather than $LRAC_1$. This is because the minimum efficient size (MES) in the former is at output level q_2 compared with q_1

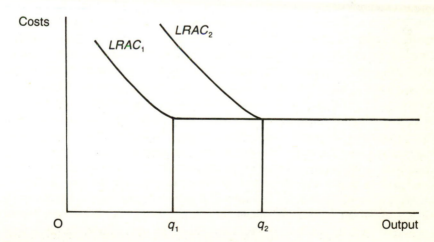

Figure 10.1 Economies of scale as an entry barrier

and so this market can efficiently support only q_n/q_2 firms rather than q_n/q_1, where $q_n/q_2 < q_n/q_1$. Here again there is the possibility that the entry barrier may, in part at least, be due to strategic behaviour on the part of an established firm. This can occur if the incumbent is able to raise MES and thereby increase the *capital requirements* of a potential entrant (another of Bain's entry barriers). Since all costs are averaged in $LRAC_1$ and $LRAC_2$, any cost which is subject to greater than average unit cost reductions will tend to increase MES. The clearest example is that of advertising and sales promotion expenditures, which are typically subject to discounts for bulk orders and which often imply high levels of expenditure before significant effects on sales are realised. If we redefine $LRAC_1$ and $LRAC_2$ in Figure 10.1 to represent the cost conditions of an industry with and without advertising expenditures, then the effect of such a strategy on entry possibilities is clear. The market will support fewer firms (unless the demand curve shifts by a greater proportion than MES) and the capital requirements for entry at scale q_2 rather than q_1 are considerably increased.

The argument that total capital requirements constitute an entry barrier has been criticised because it appears to depend on the assumption of capital market imperfections, i.e. that incumbents have access to investment funds on more favourable terms than an entrant. Equally of course, if capital markets *are* imperfect, total capital requirements may be an obstacle to entry. The willingness of the market to finance entry, especially on a large scale may, for instance, be affected by the posturing of an established firm (see Chapter 6). If the latter signals its intention to react vigorously to new entry and is able to finance this out of internal funds, it will depress the entrant's expected profits. Consequently the entrant, unless it is itself a large firm established in another market, may not be able to get sufficient backing in the capital markets.

A barrier to entry may also exist in the form of *product differentiation.* In so far as an established firm is simply catering for the varied tastes of consumers, product differentiation can be thought of as a natural entry barrier. The firm will also wish to create for itself a reputation for producing good value for money across a range of products. The more successful it is, the stronger customer attachments will be and the more difficult it will be for successful entry to occur. Advertising will form part of the firm's attempt to build a reputation. All of this, up to a point at least, will benefit consumers and society generally. Once again, however, the dividing line between welfare-enhancing activities and strategic behaviour designed to deter entry is not easy to identify. Brand proliferation may be excessive (see Chapter 8) and designed to pack the product space so as to forestall entry. It may be backed by heavy advertising aimed more at raising entry costs than at imparting information to consumers. Intuitively we would expect the impact of product differentiation upon entry to be greater the more important are scale economies, since the entrant will require a higher price to cover costs if he is constrained by the incumbent to produce along the downward-sloping portion of the long-run average cost curve. Since product differentiation is typically accompanied by large advertising expenditures, which themselves exhibit scale economy characteristics, this makes it more likely that it will be an effective entry barrier, especially in the case of some consumer goods industries.

As noted earlier, Stigler defined entry barriers as costs which potential entrants have to pay but which are not paid by established firms. There could be several reasons why such a situation might occur, implying the existence of several different types of entry barrier. For example, the incumbent may have access to higher-quality inputs (e.g. skilled labour) which are in short supply. Or it may have more favourable access to long-term capital either through larger amounts of internally generated funds or because of lower risk-adjusted interest rates in an imperfect capital market. Similarly, in markets where important learning economies are available, which in turn are a function of cumulative production, entrants will operate at a cost disadvantage. It is clear that under such a definition the list of potential barriers to entry is considerable. However, unlike Bain, the Stigler definition does not include economies of scale as an impediment to entry because they are available to both the incumbent and the entrant. Provided the entrant has sufficient capacity installed to produce at the minimum efficient size (MES), its production costs will be the same as those of the established producer. If the entrant cannot produce at MES, perhaps because of a shortage of inputs or a lack of funding, then these are the relevant barriers to entry rather than the existence of economies of scale.

Demsetz (1982) argues that effective barriers to entry can persist in the long run only if they are erected and supported by the State. Restrictions upon entry into a market, or the numbers allowed to operate there, are the most obvious examples. Similarly, government restrictions which raise the costs of firms considering entry will also constitute an entry barrier under this definition. Hence tariffs imposed on the import of foreign foods will inhibit the ability of foreign producers to compete effectively in domestic markets. Pollution and safety requirements imposed on the production of certain goods and services will raise costs above the level that would occur under the free workings of the market and so constitute an entry barrier. The obvious example here is the stringent pollution standards imposed by Japan upon imported cars which has impeded the ability of foreign producers to compete effectively in Japanese markets. That such restrictions impede entry is incontrovertible. What is unclear is the claim that the free operation of markets can be relied on to prevent the emergence and persistence of monopoly power in the long run. The Demsetz position is that, in the absence of government-imposed restraints, it is not possible for firms that earn supernormal returns to impede the entry that is attracted by such high returns. However, the fact that some industries *are* persistently characterised by higher than average rates of return suggests that it is unrealistic to assume that the market invariably bids away the emergence of monopoly rents. There are private markets unprotected by government-imposed entry restrictions in which firms do earn *economic* profits in the long run.

10.3 PRICING TO DETER ENTRY

As well as identifying the sources of entry barriers Bain also categorised barriers in terms of their height. He did so by reference to the extent to which firms found it possible and profitable to elevate price over cost. There are four categories:

1   *Easy entry* is the situation in which existing firms have little or no cost or other advantage over potential entrants. It is not possible in these circumstances for price to be held above minimum average costs for any length of time.
2   *Ineffectively impeded entry* occurs when established firms have an advantage over potential entrants and can therefore earn persistent abnormal profits by exercising price restraint. However, the entry barrier is not sufficiently high to make this strategy superior to short-run profit maximisation.
3   *Effectively impeded entry* occurs when established firms have an advantage over potential entrants and judge that an entry-preventing price policy will secure higher profits than short-run profit maximisation.
4   *Blockaded entry* occurs when entry is not induced even when price is set at the level which maximises short-run profits.

It is case (3) that is most interesting from the viewpoint of limit-pricing theory.

A point that is crucial to the theory is that the profits anticipated by a potential entrant depend upon the assumed reaction of existing firms after entry has occurred. This is because an entrant will be concerned with the relationship between his unit costs and the post-entry price and, given the elasticity of market demand, the post-entry price will depend on total output after entry has occurred. The greater the post-entry output, the lower the price. Given the output that an entrant plans to produce, total industry output will depend upon the reaction of the existing producers. Will they react to entry by reducing their output so as to 'accommodate' the new entrant, or will they fight to maintain their output or indeed to increase it? The assumption made by Bain and Sylos-Labini (1962), the two pioneers of limit-pricing theory, was that existing firms are expected to maintain their output at the pre-entry level, so that a new entrant can expect its output to be a net addition to total supply. Another fundamental assumption of limit-pricing models concerns the degree of information which exists in the market – the entrant knows with certainty that the incumbent will maintain output. Given the Bain–Sylos postulate, and the assumption of perfect information, the entrant can determine what effect its entry would have on total industry output, and the incumbent can work out the price necessary to deter entry. With these two assumptions we proceed to examine limit-price theory, first, when existing firms have an absolute cost advantage over potential entrants and, second, when they have an economies-of-scale advantage.

Absolute cost advantages

Consider the case where established firms have a cost advantage over potential entrants, owing, say, to a superior technology that is protected by patents. In Figure 10.2, DD' is the market demand curve, and AC_1 and AC_2 are the average total cost curves of existing firms and potential entrants respectively, the vertical distance between the two measuring the absolute cost advantage of the incumbents. The entry-preventing price, or limit price, is OP_L. To maintain the limit price, the output of existing producers has to be OQ_L. This is because, if a potential entrant assumes that existing producers will maintain the same output after entry occurs, the demand curve facing the potential entrant is that section of the market demand curve (DD') to the right of the quantity produced by existing firms (i.e. segment BD'). If price is kept at OP_L, the potential entrant's demand curve lies underneath his average cost curve throughout its length, so that there is no way of making a profitable entry into the market.

In the case of absolute cost advantages, therefore, if potential entrants assume that existing firms will maintain the pre-entry output level, the mark-up that existing firms add to costs can be as great as their cost advantage over potential entrants.

Economies-of-scale advantages

We now assume that cost conditions are identical for established firms and potential entrants, so that we have an economies-of-scale barrier to entry only. As in the previous analysis, potential entrants expect established firms to maintain pre-entry output. Given the elasticity of the market demand curve, the effect of entry on price will depend on the scale at which entry occurs. We examine first the case of entry at minimum efficient scale.

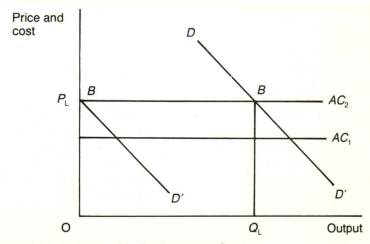

Figure 10.2 Limit-pricing with absolute cost advantage

The extent to which price can be held above minimum average cost depends on the minimum efficient size of firm in relation to the size of the market and on the elasticity of the market demand curve. The greater the minimum efficient size of firm, the higher the price–cost margin can be set, because with a given demand curve the greater will be the difference between the pre- and post-entry prices. And, given economies of scale, the more inelastic the demand curve the greater the extent to which price can be elevated above average cost for a given scale of entry.

Consider Figure 10.3. Assume first that the long-run cost curve for both established firms and a new entrant is given by $LRAC_1$ and that the market demand curve is DD. The minimum efficient size of firm (MES) is at output Q_M. Knowing that the entrant expects his output to be a net addition to pre-entry industry output, the incumbent will produce a limit output of Q_L, which is slightly larger than the difference between competitive output Q_C and MES (Q_M). This output will be sold at the limit price of P_L. The firm that is contemplating entry will know that adding Q_M to the pre-entry output Q_L will produce a total output slightly greater than the competitive level Q_C, and price will fall below the minimum level, P_C, necessary to cover costs. Entry will thus be forestalled.

Figure 10.4 shows that the limit price P_L depends on the importance of economies of scale. With cost conditions $LRAC_1$ and market demand DD, the limit output and limit price are Q_L and P_L respectively, as in Figure 10.3. However, if scale economies become more important, as shown by $LRAC_2$, limit output is reduced to Q'_L and limit price is elevated to P'_L. This is unsurprising since, if scale economies are more important, a new entrant must produce a larger output in order to avoid a cost penalty. Hence the incumbent is able to charge a higher price without inducing entry. An alternative way of interpreting Figure 10.4 is as a comparison of two industries with differing degrees of scale economies: the

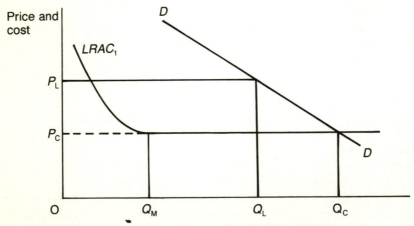

Figure 10.3 Limit-pricing with economies-of-scale advantage

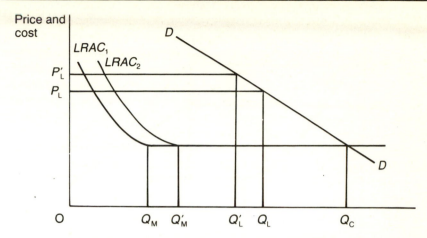

Figure 10.4 The effect of size of the economy-of-scale advantage on limit price

industry with the greater scale economies in relation to market demand will have the higher price–cost margin.

The effect of demand elasticity on the limit price is shown in Figure 10.5. With demand curve DD, limit price is P'_L, but if the established firms are able to take measures that reduce the elasticity of demand so that market demand changes to $D'D'$ then the limit price increases to P''_L. Again we could interpret this result as a comparison between markets: the market with the lower demand elasticity having, *ceteris paribus*, the higher limit price.

So far the analysis has proceeded on the assumption that entry occurs only at minimum efficient size. However, entry may occur at less than MES, though this means that the new entrant would suffer a cost penalty. Entry at a size below MES may be contemplated because a potential entrant is unable to raise sufficient capital for entry at the most efficient scale.

The effect of sub-optimal entry on the limit price may be to raise it above or lower it below the level that would prevail with entry at MES. Consider Figure 10.6 where Q_L and P_L are the limit output and limit price respectively when entry takes place at MES. What is the effect of entry at half MES, i.e. at $\frac{1}{2}Q_M$? Assume that the cost curve is $LRAC_1$ so that the entrant would suffer a cost disadvantage of AB. The entrant's unit costs are thus given by AC'. In order to deter entry the incumbent has to produce a pre-entry output, Q'_L, such that if the entrant's output, $\frac{1}{2}Q_M$, were added to it, price would fall below the entrant's average costs. Total output would then equal Q_S, so the entry-preventing output Q'_L is given by $(Q_S - \frac{1}{2}Q_M)$. The entry-preventing price is therefore P'_L, which is lower than P_L, which would have been the limit price with entry at optimal size. However, if the cost curve is $LRAC_2$, exhibiting larger scale economies and thus a bigger cost penalty, FB, for sub-optimal sized entry, the limit price would be above P_L. (The reader is invited to complete the diagram for this case.)

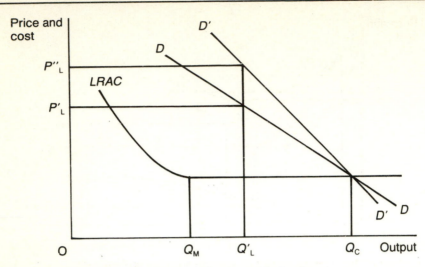

Figure 10.5 The effect of elasticity of demand on limit price

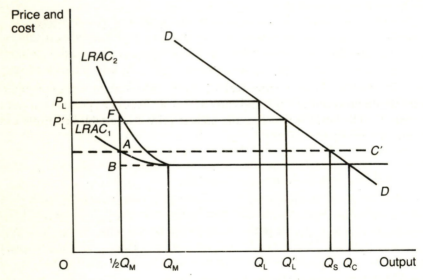

Figure 10.6 The effect of sub-optimal size entry on limit price

More generally, entry at a sub-optimal size results in a cost penalty the importance of which depends on the size of scale economies. Sub-optimal entry also means a smaller 'price effect' compared with entry at MES, i.e. the smaller the addition to industry output caused by entry, the smaller the depressing effect on industry price. These two influences are shown in Figure 10.7. The long-run average cost curve, $LRAC$, shows the size of the cost disadvantage incurred by

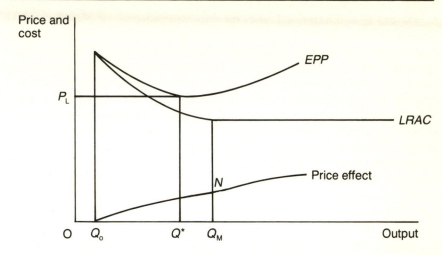

Figure 10.7 The combined effect of demand and cost on limit price

entry at a size less than Q_M. The price effect curve shows the extent to which price will fall at different scales of entry. Thus, with entry at size Q_o there is a considerable cost disadvantage but no noticeable effect on price. At Q_M there is no cost penalty but a price effect of $Q_M N$. Adding the price effect curve to *LRAC* gives the entry-preventing price curve, *EPP*, which shows the combined cost and price disadvantage for alternative scales of entry. The scale of entry that minimises the disadvantage is OQ^*, and entry at that size would be profitable if price exceeds P_L. The latter is therefore the highest price that established firms can charge without attracting entry.

Critique of limit-pricing theory

Limit-pricing policy is consistent with the main elements of full-cost pricing which were outlined in Chapter 7. The analysis of full-cost pricing suggests that firms tend to change prices only in response to industry-wide cost changes. This makes sense if firms wish to deter entrants, since cost changes will tend to affect established and potential entrants more or less equally. Once a limit price has been established, therefore, existing firms may play safe and adjust this price only in response to cost changes that are likely to affect all firms to much the same extent.

Another interesting feature of limit-pricing is that it is quite consistent with a firm operating on the inelastic segment of its demand curve. A standard conclusion of the theory of monopoly is that a profit-maximising monopolist will always be operating along the elastic segment of his demand curve. This is not necessarily the case for a firm that practises limit-pricing and therefore produces a larger output than a short-run profit-maximising monopolist.

The theory of limit-pricing raises the important question of what determines whether a firm will choose a limit-pricing strategy or pursue short-run profit maximisation? The answer in a nutshell is that it depends on a comparison of the discounted streams of profits expected from the two pricing strategies, which in turn will depend on a number of factors. First, it will depend on the rate at which future profits are discounted. The lower the rate of discount, the more likely it is that a limit-pricing policy will be pursued. Second, it will depend on the degree of competition that is expected after entry. If established firms anticipate that new entry would mean a sharp intensification of competition, they are more likely to pursue limit-pricing policies than if their expectation is that new entrants would cooperate in joint profit-maximising behaviour. Third, it will depend on the speed at which potential entrants are likely to respond to an entry-inducing price, and on the scale of entry. The faster the response and the larger the market share that new entrants are expected to enjoy, the more likely it is that limit-pricing will be adopted. The scale of entry is, of course, a function not simply of the number of entrants but also of the size of individual entrants. It has been suggested that an optimum strategy for established firms to pursue would be to allow entry on a limited scale. This would be a viable strategy if there were only one or two potential entrants who would not account for a large share of the market. It would also be possible with a large number of potential entrants if there are big cost differences between them. In many instances, however, a controlled entry policy will be difficult, if not impossible, to achieve.

The difficulty of forming a judgement on these matters may lead us to ask whether limit-pricing is at all practicable, and there are in fact several difficulties with the theory.

First, there is the problem that established firms must have accurate information on demand and cost conditions in order to discover the limit price. In practice, firms will not have this information and will have to proceed by a process of trial and error. Here, then, is another example of the importance of learning. But what firms learn by trial and error will not necessarily achieve the desired result in this case. If firms make an error and set prices too high, entry will occur, and they will have to accept the consequences. On the other hand, prices may be set below the limit price. In this case entry will not be induced, but the established firms will have no way of finding out that their prices are too low and will therefore forego profits needlessly.

Second, for a limit price to be maintained, industry sales have to be kept at a certain level. In Figure 10.3, for example, limit price P_L can be maintained only if total sales equal Q_L. This in turn means that there must be some agreement on market shares, so that the outputs of individual firms add up to the level of market sales necessary to sustain the limit price. In a world of change, total output even of a well-behaved group of firms will often turn out too high or too low in relation to demand at the established price. This is where changes in the level of inventories and in the length of order books will be important in keeping price at the entry-preventing level. Even with this flexibility, however, it may be difficult to achieve the desired level of total output if, for instance, there are large cost differences between the existing firms. Unless established firms can agree on a market-sharing policy, the limit price will not endure.

Third, there are problems concerning the assumption that potential entrants make about the post-entry behaviour of established firms, namely, that they will maintain their pre-entry output. As emphasised earlier, it is this assumption that forms the rationale of limit-pricing behaviour. On this assumption, established firms can set a price–cost margin that is equal, say, to the absolute cost advantage that they have over potential entrants without attracting newcomers to the market. But why should potential entrants make this assumption? They could just as realistically assume that, once entry has in fact occurred, the best policy open to established firms will be to accept them as members of the oligopolistic group. This will be particularly likely if the new entrants are large firms diversifying from other industries, so that all-out price warfare could be just as damaging to established firms as to new entrants. Once the expectations of potential entrants have been changed in this way, entry may occur even if established firms set their price–cost margins at a level that is less than their cost advantage over potential entrants. This suggests an alternative strategy for established firms. Why not set prices at the short-run profit-maximising level and try to prevent entry by threatening that, if entry occurs, prices will be cut to a level that will make it impossible for entrants to cover their costs, including an acceptable return on capital? If this happens, cost advantages will not set an upper limit to the price–cost margins of established firms. This strategy of threatening entrants with predatory behaviour may be more successful if potential entrants are small and have no base in any other industry. It may have some effect, however, even on potential entry by large diversified firms. It is frequently the case that these firms consider entry into an industry as one of a number of alternative investments. If established firms in an industry can issue credible threats, even a large firm may be persuaded that its investment is likely to be better made elsewhere.

These doubts about the expected reaction of established firms suggest that, if entry does in fact occur, almost anything may happen. Prices may be driven down below the average costs of entrants if established firms react aggressively. On the other hand, prices may be maintained at the pre-entry level by collusive behaviour, or indeed even increased. New entrants with higher unit costs, owing, for instance, to heavier advertising expenditure, may want a higher price, and established firms may be prepared to follow. Indeed, a price increase may be to the common advantage of the larger group of firms now comprising the industry as long as there are no further potential entrants on the horizon.

Fourth, limit-pricing becomes a less plausible entry-deterring policy when demand is expanding rapidly or when there are important technological advances. For one thing, changes in demand and in cost conditions make it more difficult for established firms to calculate the limit price, so that mistakes are more likely. More important, however, demand expansion and technological change may increase the attraction of an industry for a potential entrant to such an extent that the pricing behaviour of established firms becomes relatively unimportant. Rapid demand expansion is an important magnet for a firm that is seeking to grow by diversification and makes it more likely that entrants will expect to be accommodated by established firms rather than to face a price war. Where technological change is important, a new entrant may have a superior product or process. In this case, of course, limit-pricing breaks down completely. The development by potential entrants of a new product or process may very often determine the timing of entry into an industry.

Lastly, it should be noted that an implicit assumption of the simple limit-pricing model is that at any given time the incumbent is concerned only in totally impeding entry into the market. A less extreme, dynamic version of the model recognises that the incumbent basically faces a trade-off between short-run and long-run profitability. That is, the incumbent can set a price in excess of the limit price and earn high levels of profitability in the short run, but knows that this behaviour will encourage entry so that it will suffer a reduction in market share in the long run. The profit-maximising firm will choose the strategy which yields the profit stream with the greatest discounted present value. This will be influenced by the incumbent's discount rate (its opportunity cost of capital) and by the speed with which the entrant can set up and compete in the market. In turn such influences will vary with the type of entrant, the technological structure of the industry and the degree to which restrictions, other than those induced by the behaviour of the incumbent, impede the speed of entry. The crucial point is that the established firm may choose to regulate the *rate* of entry into its market rather than blockade entry altogether. Such a strategy naturally implies that the incumbent possesses considerable information concerning the number of potential entrants and the scale at which they would choose to enter the market. The analysis is exactly the same as that reviewed in Chapter 6.

Concluding comment on limit-pricing

To be effective, business conduct aimed at raising entry barriers must be *credible*. It must also be profitable – i.e. expected profits net of the costs incurred in pursuing entry-deterring policies must be higher than if no entry-deterring costs are incurred and entry is allowed to take place. As we have seen, credibility is a major problem with limit-pricing policies. The incumbents' threat to maintain output after entry has occurred is not credible because it would be in their own interests to accommodate the entrant.

The best hope that established firms have of influencing entrants through pricing behaviour is either by establishing a *reputation* for aggressive behaviour, or by making use of information asymmetries. Thus an established firm may threaten and sometimes engage in predatory pricing to create a reputation for aggressiveness and an expectation that it is prepared to act irrationally in order to repel an entrant (see Chapter 6). Where a potential entrant is unaware of the costs of established firms, the incumbents may set price–cost margins below the short-run profit-maximising level in order to signal to an entrant that costs are lower than they actually are and to convince the entrant that it has little chance of matching the efficiency of incumbents.

Even with strategic signalling and asymmetric information, however, there must be doubts about the effectiveness of limit-pricing. It depends heavily on the ability of incumbents to influence the expectations of entrants without doing anything to change the underlying cost and demand conditions. The credibility of limit-pricing is again seen to be the problem and this arises because established firms have not made any irreversible commitments to changing cost and demand conditions so as to make entry less attractive.

10.4 ENTRY DETERRENCE – NON-PRICE STRATEGIES

Non-price entry deterrence strategies involve making an *irreversible commitment*. That is, an incumbent commits itself to expenditure on some line of action which strengthens its ability to repel an entrant. And the potential entrant knows that this commitment has been made. Consequently these non-price strategies are credible. Possible non-price strategies include additional expenditures on capacity, product differentiation, and R&D.

An established firm inevitably incurs a cost in making a commitment and the firm has to decide whether the cost is worthwhile. Suppose there is one incumbent, and let monopoly profit $= \pi_m$. Assume that if entry is to be deterred an expenditure of α has to be incurred on, say, capacity extensions. If the expenditure is not incurred, entry will occur and the incumbent's monopoly profits will fall to $(\pi_m - \pi_e)$ where π_e is the entrant's share of total profit. If the expenditure is incurred, the incumbent gets $\pi_m - \alpha$. The incumbent will decide to incur the expenditure if $\pi_m - \alpha > \pi_m - \pi_c$. We now go on to consider some of the main non-price strategies.

Investment in capacity

Strategic moves influencing cost and demand conditions require irreversible commitment. That is, the incumbent adopts a policy which necessarily commits it to a line of action should entry take place. Hence, if the incumbent builds capacity ahead of demand, a clear signal is sent to the potential entrant concerning the future behaviour of the incumbent should entry occur. This is because, once capacity is built, a high proportion of the costs may be non-recoverable. The costs are 'sunk', i.e. the resale or scrap value of the capacity is low or zero. An incumbent that builds such capacity has irrevocably committed itself to a line of action – using the capacity to cover overheads – should entry take place.

It is clear therefore that sunk costs play an important role in entry deterrence for both the incumbent and the entrant. To the incumbent, sunk costs commit it to a course of action. To the entrant, their presence as part of the costs of operating in the market will act as a disincentive to entry. Entrants will be averse to entering markets that involve them bearing sizeable sunk costs since they are an impediment to leaving the market as well as to entering it. Barriers to exit may therefore act as a barrier to entry.

Spence (1977) related capacity investment to limit-pricing. He noted that an incumbent's irreversible pre-entry investment in capacity could make limit-pricing a credible threat since such investment will lower the incumbent's post-entry marginal cost of production. In this situation the incumbent has more of an incentive to maintain high levels of production after the entrant has appeared in the market (see also Dixit 1979). A related model is that advanced by Schmal-ensee (1981) where the incumbent over-invests before entry. As in the static limit-pricing model, pre-entry output tends to exceed the short-run profit-maxi-mising level and hence profits are lower.

As in the case of limit-pricing, however, the use of capacity extensions to deter entry runs into difficulties when there are two or more incumbents. Unless econ-omies of scale are very important, over-investment may result in a large fall in pre-entry profit. The strategy of over-investment might then be adopted only if all incumbents agree to share the cost, for if one firm adopted the policy without the others it would weaken its competitive position. On the other hand, if all firms do agree to over-invest they will increase the dangers of a damaging price war should there be a decline in industry demand.

Empirical work has not given much support to the view that firms maintain spare capacity in order to deter entry. Caves and Ghemawat (1986) examined the relationship between capital commitment and performance as measured by profi-tability. Analysing a cross-sectional sample of high-concentration producer goods industries they found a negative relationship between profitability and capital commitment. This result, however, does not necessarily support the theory of entry deterrence. An alternative interpretation is that high capital intensity is part of the competitive strategy of incumbents towards each other rather than an entry-deterring strategy.

Product proliferation and advertising

An alternative entry-deterring strategy is for the incumbent to fill the market with a sufficient number of closely related products or brands so that it is difficult for an entrant to find a niche in the market. The opportunity to adopt such a strategy is provided by the economies of scale and of scope that exist between the produc-tion and marketing of related products. Moreover, such opportunities will be reinforced by the increasing returns and brand externalities available from adver-tising expenditures.

Increasing returns to advertising occur for a variety of reasons. Often there are discounts attached to the size of advertising contracts so that the average cost of successive units of advertising falls. Similarly 'threshold effects' have been identified where a minimum amount of advertising expenditure has to be incurred before demand is affected. And advertising possesses investment and externality characteristics. Repeated advertising establishes brand names and increases consumer awareness (the investment characteristic) as well as influencing the demand for a range of firm products (spillovers or externalities). Such expenditures are likely to induce or strengthen entry barriers, though it is possible to classify them as either strategic or innocent. Either way the presence of considerable product proliferation combined with large levels of advertising expenditure makes it more difficult for the entrant to find 'space' in the incumbent's market and will raise the capital requirements for profitable entry. Schmalensee (1983) considers the use of advertising as a strategic weapon, and Cubbin and Domberger (1988) suggest that established firms may intensify advertising campaigns in response to entry.

Pre-emptive patenting

The previous chapter discussed the rationale for, and some of the effects of, the patent system. Gilbert and Newberry (1982) suggest that patents may be used by incumbents to maintain or strengthen their market dominance. Their results resemble those derived from other strategies such as product proliferation and capacity expansion in that pre-emptive action lowers the expected returns of potential entrants. They show that the incumbent has an incentive to preserve its position by patenting new technologies before potential competitors, and that this might lead to 'sleeping patents', a case where patents are neither used nor licensed to others. Basically the incumbent will pre-empt if the cost is less than the profits gained by discouraging entry. However, the existence of patent rights is neither necessary nor sufficient for pre-emption. What is important is that there are significant 'first mover' advantages. This occurs where the return to acting first is large compared with the returns accruing to later investors. In this particular case, of course, the patent goes only to the firm acting first, and, although in practice the effective patent protection may be quite small, it is being first in the acquisition of technical knowledge that provides the returns from increased investment in research and development.

It is clear that pre-emptive patenting has several undesirable features. The incumbent can maintain market dominance through pre-emption. It can expend resources on the search for new technologies and then refrain from introducing them and/or deny other producers the opportunity to use them. Either way social welfare is reduced. Interestingly, however, prohibiting pre-emptive patenting might not necessarily induce an increase in economic welfare, because were pre-emption to be prohibited then the incumbent might resort to other entry-deterring strategies, some of which might involve even greater social costs. For instance, capacity expansion may be introduced or increased and its welfare effects may well be greater than those associated with pre-emptive patenting.

A major problem with pre-emptive patenting, as with other non-price entry-deterring strategies, lies in being able to identify it. In practice it would be extremely difficult to distinguish between the introduction and development of product lines which are the outcome of considerations such as the anticipation of demand changes, and a product line policy designed to deter potential competition. This in turn makes the effective monitoring of such practices problematical since the regulators would require access to considerable amounts of technical and market information before an accurate verdict could be arrived at.

10.5 THE THEORY OF CONTESTABLE MARKETS

So far in this chapter we have been concerned with the ways in which incumbent firms can impede the entry of competitors into their established areas of operation. In recent years great emphasis has been laid upon the importance of potential competition and the welfare implications of market structures characterised by costless entry and exit. The theory of perfectly contestable markets (Baumol, Panzar and Willig 1982) is concerned with markets where there is 'ultra-free' entry, i.e. barriers of the kind discussed by Stigler and Bain do not exist. Exit, too, is costless. Firms can recoup any investment made in entering the market and so are not deterred by the costs attached to withdrawing. If such conditions hold then it is possible to seize a temporary profit opportunity existing in the market and then withdraw. A contestable market is therefore said to be susceptible to 'hit and run' entry.

If a market is truly contestable then it follows that in equilibrium it will possess several desirable features from an economic welfare point of view. First, price must equal average cost since, if it is less (greater) than average cost, firms would exit (enter) the market. Secondly, industry output is being produced efficiently at minimum cost, otherwise a firm will enter in order to reap the economic profits available by producing efficiently. Thirdly, price is at least equal to marginal cost. If this were not the case, an entrant operating at a slightly smaller scale would enter and make profits. Fourthly, when there are two or more firms in the market, price cannot exceed marginal cost. Hence it follows that, in a contestable market, price must *equal* MC in equilibrium. Also, there is no cross-subsidisation between products or there would be a profit opportunity for potential entry. So if a market is contestable then, *in equilibrium*, the number of firms and the distribution of output between firms is such as to guarantee that output is produced at minimum cost.

Notice the key difference between a contestable market and one categorised as perfectly competitive. Both types of market guarantee efficiency of production and the absence of market power. However, whereas the perfectly competitive structure implies the presence of a large number of similar-sized producers, a contestable market can be highly concentrated and yet still possess the desirable features of efficiency and competitiveness. It is the threat of potential competition caused by the ease of entry into and exit from the market that guarantees that the market possesses such attractive characteristics.

Clearly the concept has particularly strong implications in the area of industrial policy. It will be recalled that the traditional structure–conduct–performance paradigm implies that only by changing market structure will behaviour and performance within the market be affected. A high level of concentration is a potential source of abuse of market power and losses of efficiency and welfare. The theory of contestable markets suggests that if markets are contestable *or can be made contestable* then the threat of potential competition will be sufficient to ensure that intervention is unnecessary since discretionary power is removed. The market may be made contestable through the removal of entry barriers and the opening up and liberalisation of markets. Hence the focus of industrial policy is shifted from intervention and regulation of conduct in the market to loosening up the competitive environment within which incumbents operate.

Critique of contestability

Clearly, from a welfare point of view contestable markets are highly desirable. Since the theory has such profound policy implications it is important that its assumptions and conclusions are subjected to close scrutiny. Contestability guarantees economic efficiency because entry and exit are costless. What underlies this result? A crucial assumption is that the market is not characterised by sunk costs, i.e. all costs other than normal wear and tear are recoverable on exit. A market can be contestable when there are fixed costs but the presence of sunk costs precludes the hit and run entrant. However, empirical evidence suggests that most markets contain some degree of sunk costs. Another important assumption is that it is possible for the entrant to build capacity and start production before the incumbent can make any response. Again, this would seem to be a most unlikely state of affairs. Hence a major criticism of contestability theory is that its practical relevance is limited if such markets do not exist or cannot be brought into existence.

To the reader raised on the assumptions of perfect competition, market clearing, perfect information, etc., this may seem a little harsh. After all, economics abounds with models which bear only a passing resemblance to the real world but simplify the market setting sufficiently to provide useful and fruitful analysis. Why should contestability be any different? Sunk costs are a feature of many markets but to different extents. Some activities (railway operation, power transmission, telecommunications networks) involve considerable investment in equipment which has no secondhand market and which is non-recoverable. Others, however, may involve considerable fixed costs, only a relatively small amount of which is sunk (e.g. large areas of manufacturing and heavy engineering). In these markets, then, do not the conclusions of contestability still hold? Unfortunately the answer is 'no'. Contestable market theory is non-robust; its conclusions are materially altered by only small changes in the underlying assumptions (see Schwartz and Reynolds 1983, Dasgupta and Stiglitz 1980).

Two assumptions are of critical importance: first that sunk costs are zero; second that the time taken for an entrant to set up in production is less than the time it takes for an incumbent to react to entry. The significance of these assumptions will now be examined in more detail (see Vickers and Yarrow, 1985). Suppose there is a single incumbent (firm A) in a market and one potential entrant (firm B) is considering producing in this market. Let T_A be the length of time it would take for firm A to respond to firm B's entry into the market, and let T_B be the length of time it takes for the entrant to set up in production. (Note that this information is known to both incumbent and entrant with certainty). Hence if $T_A > T_B$ then the entrant can enter before the incumbent can react. Now define the difference between these times, T, as

$$T = T_A - T_B \quad \text{if } T_A > T_B \text{ and}$$
$$T = 0 \text{ otherwise}$$

Hence, T takes a positive value if the entrant can produce before the incumbent can react, and a zero value if it cannot. An element of sunk costs, S, has to be borne in order to enter the market. Lastly, let the incumbent charge price P in the current period. The question is, will firm B effect entry?

We can answer this question with the help of Figure 10.8. Market demand is given by DD' which, with constant costs of production CC', gives a breakeven level of output Q_C. If B does enter and undercuts A by charging a price of say P' then it will earn a profit of $\pi(P') = (P' - C)D(P')$ given by the area $P'EFC$. Let such a profit flow continue for n periods by which time price will have been driven down to C as competition between entrant and incumbent proceeds. Clearly it is worth-

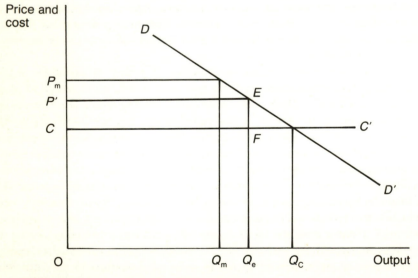

Figure 10.8 The theory of contestable markets

while for firm B to enter the market if the present value of the profit flow $\pi^*(P')$, discounted at the entrant's opportunity cost of capital, exceeds the discounted sunk costs, S^*; i.e. $\pi^*(P') > S^*$. If sunk costs are zero and the entrant can set up before the incumbent can respond ($T > 0$) then entry will occur at *any* price greater than C, i.e. the market is contestable. But if the incumbent can react at least as quickly as the entrant can set up ($T = 0$) and reduce price to C, then *any* minimal level of sunk costs would be sufficient to deter entry. Indeed in such a case the incumbent could charge the monopoly price P_m and still not attract entry into the market.

A final possibility is that the entrant can set up in production before the incumbent can react ($T > 0$) but sunk costs are present ($S > 0$). The condition for entry in this case is that the discounted profit flow $\pi^*(P')$ exceeds the ratio of discounted sunk costs to the time it takes for A to respond to B's entry; i.e. $\pi^*(P') > S^*/T$. Given the importance of sunk costs in many markets and the likelihood that even if $T > 0$ its value will be very small, it seems unlikely that entry would be considered.

Contestable market theory has also been criticised (Shepherd 1984) for the assumption that entrants suffer no cost disadvantage in terms of production techniques, perceived product quality, access to distribution networks, etc. In practice, incumbents will often have substantial advantages in these and other respects. Certain assumptions, such as equal access to finance, may apply well enough to entry associated with the diversification of a large firm's activities, but then large firms are unlikely to spoil each other's markets by hit and run tactics. And even if contestable markets were to be approximated in some real world cases it is doubtful whether they could be taken as an ideal once consideration is given to those factors that determine the incentive to innovate (see Chapter 9).

The theory of contestable markets has been much criticised for the strong assumptions on which it is based. But the real weakness of the theory lies not in the simplifying assumptions as such but in the fact that it is not robust, i.e. a small change in the assumptions completely upsets the results.

10.6 CONCLUDING COMMENTS

From the discussion contained in this chapter it is clear that there are many ways in which entry by potential competitors may be effectively prevented. Entry may be precluded either because of the market behaviour of an incumbent firm or despite its actions. Entry barriers may therefore be classified as strategic or innocent. An elementary form of strategic entry deterrence is limit-pricing. It is elementary because it rests on the assumption that the incumbent makes a threat which is not credible; i.e. the threat to maintain production levels after entry has occurred. Limit-pricing strategy is made more credible in the presence of uncertainty and asymmetric information. Incumbents may then engage in strategic signalling in an attempt to influence the potential entrant's expectations. Other more realistic methods of strategic entry deterrence involve attempts to influence entrants' expectations through instruments such as capacity extensions and strategic advertising expenditures, brand proliferation and pre-emptive patenting. These are more realistic, in the sense of being more effective, since they imply a degree of irreversible commitment on the part of established firms.

In each of the above cases the aim of the incumbent is to limit the influence and the extent of potential competition. The theory of contestable markets highlights the role of potential competition at its most extreme. If entry and exit are costless, implying the absence of sunk costs, then production is efficient even if the industry is highly concentrated. This theory therefore totally contradicts the conclusions of the structure–conduct–performance model of industrial organisation. However, contestability theory appears largely bankrupt in terms of practical applicability. The presence of only small levels of sunk costs and/or relatively short reaction times on the part of the incumbent significantly reduces the influence of potential competition on industry performance.

Chapter 11

Market structure, conduct and profitability

11.1 INTRODUCTION

In this chapter we examine the links between market structure, conduct and profitability. One possibility that has received much attention from economists is that high profits are the result of high market concentration. This may be because high concentration facilitates collusion, enabling the firms to achieve profits near to the joint profit-maximising outcome. In addition, firms in highly concentrated markets may be able to protect their positions by various forms of strategic behaviour, including, for instance, product differentiation and heavy advertising expenditure. An alternative explanation of a positive relationship between market structure and profitability is that this comes about not because of market power but because of the greater efficiency of large firms. Firms that are more efficient, perhaps because of superior innovative performance, will expand their market share at the expense of the less efficient. A positive correlation between high concentration and high profitability may thus simply reflect these efficiency differences.

In section 11.2 we examine the complex links between market structure and profitability, looking first at theoretical issues and then at the empirical evidence. Section 11.3 examines more directly the role of advertising and looks at the interrelationships between market structure, advertising intensity and profit performance.

11.2 MARKET STRUCTURE AND PROFITABILITY

Causal links between market structure and profitability

The link between market structure and profitability comes from firms' pricing behaviour. In perfectly competitive markets each firm faces a perfectly elastic demand curve. They have no discretion at all about what price they can charge; freedom of entry into, and exit from, the industry ensures that each firm earns no more than normal profits, and price will be set equal to marginal cost. In all other types of market structure, however, a firm faces a downward-sloping demand curve and thus has the possibility of earning supernormal profits.

In general, the profit-maximising relationship between a firm's price and marginal cost will depend on the elasticity of demand for the firm's product. For the case of simple monopoly, where one firm produces the whole of the output in the relevant market, the optimal excess of price over marginal cost depends solely on the market elasticity of demand. The price–cost margin, $p - mc/p$ is in fact the Lerner index of market power and is equal to the inverse of market elasticity of demand, $1/e$.

For the Lerner index to be an accurate measure of market power it is necessary to assume that: (i) there is one seller of the product; (ii) the seller has market power over only one product; (iii) increases in the price of this product do not result in price changes for other products; and (iv) there are no intertemporal cost or demand linkages. Whenever these assumptions are violated, use of the elasticity of market demand could lead to a substantial overestimate or underestimate of market power. The various possibilities are outlined in Ordover (1990).

Suppose, for instance, that the relevant product is produced by a dominant firm, with say 80 per cent of the market, and a fringe of small firms. If price is raised much above marginal cost, and assuming the fringe firms do not suffer a major cost disadvantage, the result might be a substantial increase in the market share of the fringe. In other words, if the elasticity of supply of the fringe, at prices near to marginal cost, is high, the dominant firm's ability to raise price will be severely restricted. In these circumstances market elasticity of demand will overestimate the market power of the dominant firm. The Lerner index of market power becomes equal to $1/(e^m + s^f \eta^f)$ where e^m is market elasticity of demand, s^f is the market share of the fringe and η^f is the elasticity of supply of the fringe. In an oligopolistic industry with a competitive fringe, the market power of any one of the oligopolists depends not only on the market elasticity of demand and the elasticity of supply of the fringe but also on the firm's market share, market power being greater, *ceteris paribus*, the greater the firm's market share.

Just as the market power of a dominant firm or a group of oligopolists is affected by the supply responses of a competitive fringe, it will also be affected by conditions of entry. If substantial new entry occurs when price is raised much above marginal cost, and this new entry results in higher output, the elasticity of market demand will again overestimate the market power of the incumbent monopolist or oligopolists.

There are also circumstances when market elasticity of demand will underestimate market power. If a dominant firm increases the price of product x, this will tend to increase the demand for products which are substitutes for x, so that the prices of these products may also increase. If so, the monopolist will be able to increase the price of x by more than would otherwise be the case. Where 'learning economies' are important there is an incentive to push output beyond the point where short-run marginal revenue (*MR*) equals short-run marginal costs (*MC*), because a higher level of output in the short run has a beneficial effect on long-run costs. If the dominant firm is operating under increasing cost conditions, in the short run this policy of expanding short-run output beyond the point where $MR = MC$ will mean that market elasticity of demand would underestimate market power.

It should be clear from the foregoing discussion that it is not easy to derive a measure of market power based on estimates of suitably adjusted market demand elasticities. Consequently, it is common to use market share as a proxy for market power. But this measure too raises problems relating to the proper definition of the relevant geographical and product markets. Too narrow a definition will overestimate the extent of market power, and vice versa. These problems have already been addressed in Chapter 5.

So far in this discussion the influence of concentration on profitability has not appeared explicitly. In so far as concentration determines profitability the causal link works through the effects of concentration on anticipated rivals' reaction. The more highly concentrated the market, the more each firm will anticipate that the others will respond to a price cut by increasing their own output, and therefore the less elastic will be the demand curve facing each firm, and the higher will be the optimal excess of price over marginal cost, and profitability. Alternatively, the more highly concentrated the market, the greater the likelihood of effective collusion and of a joint profit-maximising outcome.

Thus, on theoretical grounds we would expect to observe a positive relationship between concentration and profitability, given profit-maximising behaviour by the firms concerned. This expectation, however, needs to be qualified in several important respects.

The prediction is based on the assumption of profit-maximising behaviour. To the extent that firms in more highly concentrated markets are less concerned with profit maximisation, the relationship will be obscured. This may be either because large firms are concerned to maximise something other than profits or because they fail to minimise costs because of X-inefficiency.

The relationship need not necessarily be a linear one, nor need it be continuous. The possibility of a discontinuous relationship is indicated by the fact that the positive link between concentration and profitability is related to the interdependence of firms in concentrated markets, particularly to the possibility of collusive behaviour or to the way in which firms' behaviour may be influenced by the expectation of a reaction from competitors. The possibility of effective collusion and expectations concerning the reaction of competitors may well show a marked change at certain thresholds of concentration.

The theoretical relationship between concentration and profitability is a long-run equilibrium relationship. Firms are likely to be out of equilibrium to a greater or lesser extent at any point in time. Indeed, in the short run, firms in perfectly competitive industries may earn very high profits. This points to the fact that we are interested in the long-run relationship between concentration and profitability and so should look at the empirical evidence over a fairly long period, which draws our attention to two other important factors. If we examine the profits of firms over, say, a ten-year period, allowance will need to be made for differences in the rates of growth of the firms. Also, the ability of firms in concentrated markets to earn excess profits in the long run depends on the existence of barriers to entry. Where entry is possible, short-run profit maximisation may not be in the firm's long-run interests, and the relationship observed between concentration and profitability will be affected. An attempt should therefore be made to measure the height of entry barriers so as to estimate their effect on profitability.

More generally, the profit performance of firms is affected by many factors apart from concentration – factors such as barriers to entry, the rate of growth of markets, the level of imports, the degree of vertical integration, business goals, the amount of risk involved and the ability of management. Simple regressions are therefore not an adequate way of testing for the effect of concentration on profitability, since the effect of omitted relevant variables biases the results. However, estimating the effect of concentration on profitability by a multiple regression analysis including several explanatory variables raises new problems for the interpretation of the results, particularly because some of the independent variables are likely to be correlated. This is the econometric problem of multi-collinearity. For instance, the variables used to explain profit performance may include capital intensity and scale economies as well as the level of concentration. But these three explanatory variables are likely to be correlated, so that it will be difficult to determine what independent effect each is having on profitability.

Some of the 'independent variables' included in the equation used to determine profitability may not be exogenous but determined, together with profitability, by underlying supply and demand conditions. Furthermore, an explanatory variable such as the level of concentration or advertising intensity may not only affect profitability but also be affected by it. Thus a high level of concentration may allow prices to be elevated well above costs, but high profits in turn may allow firms to follow strategies that maintain or increase the level of concentration. High profits, however, may be not the result of monopoly pricing but a reflection of the superior efficiency of large firms, a superiority based on economies of scale or on more dynamic factors such as success in developing and marketing new products. Efficiency may also explain why concentration is high. It is possible, therefore, that a positive correlation between concentration and profitability reflects the greater efficiency of large firms.

This raises a related question of whether it is concentration or the market share of leading firms that matters most in explaining profitability. Disentangling the effects is difficult because concentration and market share are likely to be correlated. Nevertheless it is important to know which of the two variables is the more important explanator.

To get around the related problems of simultaneity and causality, researchers have to use more sophisticated estimation techniques using simultaneous equations, in which, for example, profitability, advertising intensity and concentration are simultaneously determined by exogenous variables. The empirical attempts at disentangling the various interactions are reported on later.

Data problems

Having looked at the problems in specifying and interpreting the theoretical links between market structure and profitability we now turn to look at the further difficulties of finding available data to represent the theoretically appropriate concepts. We start by looking at profitability. This can be measured in a number of ways. Since monopoly power implies the ability to elevate price above marginal cost, a natural way to proceed is to use the Lerner index of market power (suitably adjusted as explained earlier), which is the ratio of price minus marginal cost to price. One difficulty with this measure is that estimates of marginal cost are not generally available. Measures of this kind usually have to make do with average cost data, which will give the same result as marginal cost data only under constant cost conditions.

More problematic is the fact that, apart from the case of simple monopoly, the use of the price–cost margin may give a misleading measure of market power. As we have already seen, the profit-maximising price–cost margin for an oligopolistic firm depends not only on concentration (which affects it through rivals' expected reactions) but also on market elasticity of demand and the firm's market share. The observed effect of concentration on the price–cost margin will be concealed, or at least weakened, if elasticity of demand is higher in highly concentrated industries than in industries with low concentration. Therefore, in industry studies the elasticity of demand should be included as an explanatory variable; otherwise the study should be confined to industries with similar elasticities. Many of the empirical studies that have been carried out do not meet this test.

Profitability can also be measured as a rate of return on some measure of capital. Several alternatives are available, such as the pre- or post-tax return on stockholders' equity, and the pre- or post-tax return on total assets employed. Rate of return measures also give rise to a number of difficulties. Profitability comparisons might be distorted because of variations across firms in the accounting practices adopted for dealing with such matters as the valuation of stocks, depreciation of physical assets and the writing off of research and development expenditure. Variations in accounting practices may not be systematically correlated with industry structure, in which case estimated structure–profitability relationships will not be biased one way or another. However such biases may result. During a takeover, for instance, any monopoly profits that are expected from the enlarged company may be capitalised, especially if the acquiring firm incorporates the assets of the acquired firm at market value. This will have the effect of depressing the rate of return. If highly concentrated industries experience a high level of takeover activity in the period preceding an empirical investigation, the result, other things being equal, will be an underestimation of the strength of the concentration–profit relationship.

Another systematic bias will arise if concentration and capital intensity are correlated. We might expect such a correlation to exist because capital intensity tends to be associated with economies of scale, which may create barriers to entry. If so, concentrated industries will have a higher ratio of capital assets to sales than less concentrated industries and profitability expressed as a rate of return on capital will be depressed. This will weaken the concentration–profitability relationship, unless differences in capital intensity are allowed for.

A further major problem with the use of rate of return data is that these are generally available only at a much higher level of aggregation than the level at which structural data are collected. Rate of return data may be available only at the company level, whereas structural data are collected at the plant level. For diversified, multiplant firms, this means that costs which are common to each plant, such as general R&D, head office management, and joint purchasing and distribution costs, have to be allocated between plants, and this inevitably involves a degree of arbitrariness. For vertically integrated firms, an even bigger problem may arise in the form of a divergence between internal transfer prices and arm's length prices. Vertically integrated oil companies, for instance, can depress the reported profits of their refining operations by setting the internal transfer price of crude oil at a level higher than the one which would prevail with arm's length transactions.

We turn now to the variables that may be expected to affect profitability. The most obvious is industry concentration. The problems of measuring concentration were dealt with in Chapter 5. The choice of concentration variables for studies of the concentration–profitability relationship is important if different measures rank industries differently. In practice, the choice of concentration variable is affected largely by the availability of data, and most studies have used the concentration ratio. Unsound results are, however, far more likely to result from an inappropriate definition of the market than from the use of the 'wrong' measure of concentration. If the geographic and/or product market is defined too narrowly, the concentration measure will be too high and structural monopoly will be overestimated, and vice versa. Great care clearly has to be taken in defining markets appropriately if misleading results are to be avoided.

Excessive profits are of concern only if they persist, for even competitively structured industries can earn supernormal profits in short-run equilibrium. Supernormal profits can persist, however, only if there is some entry barrier to new competition. It is important therefore to include some measure of entry barriers in statistical analysis. One way of doing this is to form subjective estimates, based on detailed study of the particular circumstances of each industry under investigation, of whether barriers are high, moderate or low. This was the method adopted in Bain's (1956) pioneering study. One problem with this approach is that, armed with the knowledge that profits are high in a particular industry, the investigator may 'find' entry barriers where none exist. An alternative approach is to use some objectively measurable proxy for entry barriers. For instance, product differentiation barriers are commonly measured by the ratio of advertising expenditure to sales revenue, and technical economies-of-scale barriers are often proxied by the ratio of median plant sales to industry sales.

Other supply-side factors that may influence profit performance are foreign trade and capital intensity. Foreign trade may be taken into account by adjusting the concentration ratio so that it measures the domestic sales of the n largest firms as a proportion of total domestic production less exports plus imports. It may also be argued that a given volume of imports is likely to have a more pro-competitive effect than the same volume of sales from an additional domestic producer. One possible reason is that importers are less likely to enter into collusive agreements; another is that foreign producers may be practising price discrimination and selling more cheaply in foreign markets. Foreign competition may thus have the effect of increasing the demand elasticities facing domestic producers and reduce their ability to earn supernormal profits. On the other hand, it is well known, in Europe at least, that international cartels are not uncommon, and foreign suppliers may use high domestic prices as an umbrella under which to make high profits on foreign sales. In any event, several studies include the share of imports in domestic sales as an additional explanatory variable. The case for including a capital intensity variable has already been mentioned in the earlier discussion of the use of rate of return variables to measure profitability. Without it, biased estimates of the concentration–profitability relationship may be obtained because profitability in high-concentration industries tends to be depressed. Another reason for including this variable is that the temptation to cut prices during a recession may be particularly great in those industries where fixed costs form a high proportion of total costs.

Several demand-side factors are also used in estimating structure–profitability relationships. One of these is the rate of growth of market demand. The hypothesis here is that fast-growing industries are, *ceteris paribus*, likely to be more profitable than slow-growing ones because capacity is more likely to have failed to keep pace with demand, thus resulting in capacity shortages. Another variable that is potentially important, for reasons already discussed, is elasticity of demand. There are also several demand-side differences between producer and consumer goods industries, such as better-informed customers and lower advertising intensities in the former compared with the latter. Empirical studies therefore often distinguish between these two groups of industry by, for instance, using dummy variables or by restricting the sample to consumer or producer goods industries only.

This account of the variables used in concentration–profitability studies is by no means exhaustive, but it does serve to underline the large number of variables which, potentially at least, affect the concentration–profitability relationship. Empirical work in this area is made more hazardous by two other considerations. First, some variables such as elasticity of demand are often, in practice, unobservable. The omission of potentially important, but unobservable variables from regression equations may produce biased results. Even when a measure for a particular variable is available, it may well be a very imperfect one; this is particularly the case for estimates of the height of entry barriers. Second, even where reasonably reliable estimates are available there is still the problem that these estimates may not be available at the same level of aggregation.

Empirical evidence

An enormous number of empirical studies of the relationship between market structure and profitability have been carried out for the USA and a growing number in the UK. This section does not attempt to survey the results of all these studies. Rather, a sample of studies is taken in order to convey to the reader the sorts of results that have been achieved and the questions that remain unanswered.

US evidence

The pioneering work in this area was carried out by Bain (1951 and 1956). In his 1956 study Bain attempted to measure the effects of concentration and entry barriers on the profit performance of a sample of 20 manufacturing industries. The industry sample was divided into three entry barrier categories – 'very high', 'substantial' and 'moderate or low' – and into two seller concentration categories – 'high' and 'medium or low', with an eight-firm concentration ratio of 70 per cent as the dividing line. The measure of profitability used was the average after-tax profit rates on stockholders' equity for the leading firms in each industry for 1936–40 and 1947–51.

Bain found that profit rates were substantially higher in the high-concentration industries. In addition it was found that highly concentrated industries with very high entry barriers had higher profits than other highly concentrated industries with lower entry barriers.

The Bain studies suggest that the relationship between concentration and profit performance is a discontinuous one, with concentration having to reach a certain threshold before a noticeable effect on profitability is found.

Mann (1966) also found a discontinuous relationship between concentration and profitability. This study examined concentration, barriers to entry, and rates of return of leading companies in 30 industries over the period 1950–60, and looked at the question of whether concentration and barriers to entry influence rates of return independently. A distinct cleavage was found between the average profit rate of the 21 industries with an eight-firm concentration ratio above 70 per cent and that of those with lower concentration. The 30 industries were also divided into three groups with very high, substantial and moderate-to-low barriers to entry and the average profit rates in the three groups were found to be 16.4, 11.3 and 9.9 per cent respectively. These results show a distinct difference between the group with very high barriers to entry and the other groups, and a smaller difference between the substantial and moderate-to-low barrier groups. All 8 industries in the very high barriers group, 8 of the 9 in the substantial barriers group and 5 of the 13 in the moderate-to-low barriers group had a concentration ratio above 70 per cent, so this study provides some rough and ready evidence that barriers to entry and concentration do affect profitability separately.

Mann's analysis was extended by George (1968) to take account of the effect of growth on profitability. The industries that grew at more than 10 per cent per annum between 1950 and 1960 were found to have a higher profit rate than the slower-growing industries with the same height of barriers to entry or level of concentration. Within each growth class, profitability increased with concentration and with barriers to entry, but concentration seemed to have most effect on profitability within the group of industries with very high barriers to entry. For the other groups it is more doubtful whether concentration exerted an independent influence.

The broad conclusion to be drawn from these studies is that concentration has most effect on profits where it is combined with high barriers to entry, which give the firms concerned the freedom to set prices above marginal costs and to earn excess profits for a long period of time. In some cases the barriers may arise from technical economies of scale, in which case there is a trade-off between reduced costs of production and monopolistic misallocation of resources, but the barriers to entry may also arise from such artificial causes as control of sales outlets or heavy advertising expenditure. It is interesting to note that a study by Comanor and Wilson (1967: 437) came to a similar conclusion about the relative importance of barriers to entry and concentration. Their conclusion was that much of the differential in profits 'is accounted for by the entry barriers created by advertising expenditure and by the resulting achievement of market power'. Furthermore, 'the role of concentration appears closely linked to that of technical entry barriers and there is little remaining influence which is evident' (1967: 435).

One further problem of interpretation in these studies arises because of a possible interrelationship between growth and barriers to entry. Several studies have reported a positive correlation between growth and profitability (see Chapter 4), and this should be borne in mind when assessing whether or not high profits are acceptable. The assessment is complicated by the fact that growth and barriers to entry may be related. A high growth rate may be due to barriers to entry, in so far as they allow a firm to earn the high profits out of which capacity extensions are financed. In addition, the capacity extensions may themselves have an entry-deterring effect, because, if existing firms are able to maintain a measure of spare capacity, potential competitors may be dissuaded from entering the market because of their concern that entry would result in a big increase in output and price reductions by existing firms.

The first large-scale studies using industry price–cost margins as the dependent variable were those undertaken by Collins and Preston (1968, 1969). In both studies the authors found that, in general, concentration had a significant and positive impact on price–cost margins, and that this relationship survived when additional explanatory variables were added. The following equation reproduces one of their results for the complete sample of 417 four-digit industries covered in their 1969 study using 1963 data:

$$PCM = 19.54 + .096\ CR - .029\ GD + .092\ K/S \quad R^2 = 0.19$$

where PCM is the price–cost margin; CR is the concentration ratio; GD is an index of geographical dispersion to control for industries selling in regional or local markets, and K/S, the ratio of capital to sales, is a measure of capital intensity. The concentration ratio and capital intensity variables were both significant at the 1 per cent level, whereas the GD variable was significant at the lower, 5 per cent, level. However, the overall level of explanation, as indicated by the R^2 statistic, was low, only 19 per cent of the variation in the price–cost margin being explained.

In the equation shown above, concentration has a small but significant effect on price–cost margins; an increase of 10 percentage points in the concentration ratio being associated with a 1 percentage point increase in the price–cost margin. This result, however, is an average for all 417 industries, and the strength of the concentration–profitability relationship was found to vary substantially between industry groups. Two other interesting findings emerge from the 1969 study. One is that the relationship between concentration and price–cost margins tended to be strongest for those industries in which concentration increased between 1958 and 1963. The other is that the concentration/price–cost margin relationship was stronger for consumer goods industries than for producer goods, indicating, possibly, that buyers of producer goods are better informed and have greater bargaining power than the buyers of consumer products.

The Collins and Preston studies have been followed by several others which, while adopting the same basic approach, have added more explanatory variables. One of the most comprehensive is that of Weiss (1974), which used 1963 data for 399 Census industries. The following is one of the regression equations estimated by Weiss, with standard errors shown in parentheses:

$$PCM = 16.3 + .05\ CR - .03\ GD + .12\ K/S + 1.3\ A/S - 1.9\ CO/TE$$
$$(.02)\quad (.01)\quad (.02)\quad (0.2)\quad (4.2)$$
$$+ .02\ I/S + .26\ G + .0008\ C.CR + .10\ MID - .03\ PLANT\ K \quad R^2 = 0.43$$
$$(.14)\quad (.09)\quad (.0003)\quad (.13)\quad (.02)$$

In addition to the variables included in the earlier equation from the Collins and Preston study, Weiss includes the following: the ratio of advertising to sales (A/S); the ratio of central office employment to total employment (CO/TE); the ratio of inventories to sales (I/S); past output growth (G); the product of the concentration ratio and the percentage of industry sales going to consumer goods markets ($C.CR$); the ratio of median plant sales to total industry sales (MID); and the capital required by a median plant ($PLANT\ K$).

The equation shows that concentration has a positive and significant effect on price–cost margins in general, and a further effect on consumer goods industries as shown by the coefficient on $C.CR$. Price–cost margins are also positively and significantly correlated with capital intensity, advertising intensity and growth. A significant and negative correlation is found between price–cost margins and GD, which measures the degree of geographic dispersion. Other correlations (including the two entry barrier variables, MID and $PLANT\,K$) were not significant at the 5 per cent level. However, it should be noted that these are very crude measures of entry barriers and also that entry barrier effects may also be picked up in the variables measuring capital and advertising intensity.

Another hypothesis concerning the relationship between profitability and market structure which has been examined in the USA is that profit rates will be not only higher but also more varied in more concentrated markets. In competitive industries, the forces of competition – and in particular freedom of entry into, and exit from, industries – will serve to equalise the rates of return across industries, and also the rates of profit earned by firms within an industry. In concentrated industries, the existence of barriers to entry will mean not only that firms in some markets will be able persistently to earn higher profits than those in markets with lower entry barriers, but also that within an industry some firms may be able to earn consistently higher profits than others. The relationship between market structure and dispersion in rates of return has been examined by McEnally (1976) using data for 16 US industries for the years 1960–65. The influence of market structure was measured by dividing the industries into two groups with 'very high' and 'other' barriers to entry, respectively, and McEnally found that the standard deviation of industry returns (a weighted average of rates of return of firms in the industry) was significantly higher for the industries with very high barriers to entry than for the others. He also found that the average intra-industry dispersion of returns was significantly larger for the very high barriers industries, so that the hypothesis that profit rates will vary more both within and between monopolistic industries is supported by his findings.

US studies based on 1950s and 1960s data show a reasonably robust correlation between profitability and industry structure. Industry concentration appears to have a marked effect, especially when it rises above a critical threshold – variously estimated as a four-firm concentration ratio somewhere between 40 and 60 per cent. Entry barriers too seem to be important in many studies.

However, as indicated earlier a problem with single-equation estimates is that some of the explanatory variables may be not truly exogenous but determined simultaneously with the dependent variable, profitability. This problem has been addressed with the use of simultaneous equation estimation techniques. The results suggest a weaker role for concentration than that shown in single equation models. Strickland and Weiss (1976), using data on 407 Census industries in 1963, estimated a three-equation model in which price–cost margins, advertising intensity and concentration are treated as endogenous variables. The effect of allowing for the endogeneity of the concentration and advertising intensity variables was that their impact on price–cost margins ceased to be statistically significant. However, it is possible, as they suggest, that the result for concentration may be due to problems of collinearity with a scale economy barrier to entry variable. A similar study by Martin (1979) also found concentration to have a positive but insignificant effect on price–cost margins.

An even stronger attack on the market power hypothesis that high concentration is the cause of high profitability came from Demsetz (1973a). He argued that a positive correlation between concentration and profitability reflected the superior efficiency of large firms. Concentration is high because of the superior efficiency of large firms, which also explains high profit levels. The average level of profits in highly concentrated industries will in fact tend to be high both because of the high profits of leading firms and because of the high weight accorded to these profits in calculating industry averages.

How can these competing hypotheses be tested? According to the market power hypothesis, Demsetz argued, all firms in high-concentration industries should benefit from the power to elevate prices above costs. The profitability of small firms should thus be higher in more concentrated industries. If, however, high concentration and high profits result from superior efficiency, profitability differences between large and small firms should be greater in high-concentration industries than in low-concentration ones. Using a sample of 95 three-digit industries for 1963, Demsetz found that these predictions are confirmed. Unfortunately his results are marred by faulty market definitions – three-digit Census industries are far too broadly defined and liable to understate the effect of structural variables. In addition Demsetz used absolute size differences between firms rather than relative size differences, which would have been more appropriate.

Another attempt to discriminate between the market power and efficiency hypotheses using industry-wide, whole company, data is that of Carter (1978), who used four-digit industry data for 1963, 1967 and 1972. He fitted an equation to the data using, as the dependent variable, first the average price–cost margin of the top four firms in each industry, then the average margin for the firms ranked 5–8. He found that the concentration variable had a significant and positive effect on the price–cost margins of the top four firms, but not on the firms ranked 5–8, thus supporting the efficiency hypothesis. Once again, however, this result cannot be taken as conclusive. One crucial problem is that it says nothing about the determinants of concentration.

More reliable tests of the market power and efficiency hypotheses require not only more sophisticated estimation techniques but better data – in particular data on market share and individual firm performance, disaggregated to product class or line of business. Data of this kind became available in the USA under the Profit Impact of Market Strategy (PIMS) programme of the Strategic Planning Institute. Using these data, Gale and Branch (1982) found that, while both the four-firm concentration ratio and market share are correlated with firms' rate of return, the correlation is far stronger for the market share variable. Furthermore, when both are included in a multiple regression equation only market share shows a positive and significant association with profitability. These results are taken to support the efficiency explanation of high profitability and to cast doubt on the market power hypothesis.

However, this conclusion would be too hasty. There are of course the usual comments one has to make about the data base which may influence the results. The firms in the PIMS samples are not fully representative of all businesses, with leading firms in particular being over-represented. Of more significance, however, is the fact that it is not possible to distinguish industries where economies of scale are important from those where they are not. Product differentiation effects, which can be differently interpreted, also exist. If all the firms in each industry produced a homogeneous product thus forcing firms to charge uniform prices, and if it could be established that high market share and scale economies were closely correlated, then a positive correlation between profitability and market share would be strong evidence in support of the efficiency hypothesis. However, product differentiation is widespread, and large firms may be able to exploit product differentiation opportunities more effectively than small ones and thus charge higher prices. And, in the absence of conclusive evidence that market share is no higher than it need be on efficiency grounds, market power may still have a role to play in explaining high profits. Indeed it is perfectly possible that what the PIMS results reflect is not the relative efficiency of leading firms but their market power. As Shepherd (1989) argues, and as pointed out in Chapter 6, a dominant firm can pursue any anti-competitive conduct *at least as* effectively as a group of colluding oligopolists with the same aggregate share of the market. With the present state of knowledge, however, the safest conclusion is that the positive correlation between market share and profitability reflects a combination of efficiency and market power advantages.

UK evidence

There is even less agreement among UK than US studies about whether concentration has a significant effect on profitability. Hart and Morgan (1977), using 1968 data on 113 industries, did a simple regression and found a significant positive relationship between the logarithm of profitability (measured by the share of profits in value added) and that of concentration (five-firm employment concentration ratio), but variations in concentration 'explained' only 10 per cent of the variation in profitability across industries.

However, as already discussed, such simple regressions are likely to be misleading, and Hart and Morgan went on to add other independent variables, which increased the explanatory power of the relationship to about 46 per cent. They found that some theoretically relevant variables were insignificant: the rate of growth of sales, the ratio of imports to domestic sales, and the median size of enterprise by employment. This last variable was included as a measurement of barriers to entry, and it remained insignificant even when the concentration variable was omitted. However, it seems likely that sources of barriers to entry other than absolute firm size were captured by the two most significant variables included in their calculations: the ratio of capital expenditure to labour, and the ratio of advertising to sales. In fact, when the capital–labour ratio was included, the effect of the concentration ratio became statistically insignificant.

However, the interpretation of the positive and significant coefficients on the capital–labour and advertising–sales ratios is affected by data problems. A spurious correlation between each variable and the dependent variable (gross profits as a share of value added) is introduced because gross profits include both provision for depreciation and advertising expenditure. A UK study by Holterman (1973), which also found that the advertising–sales ratio had a significant effect on gross profitability, corrected for this data problem by subtracting advertising expenditure from gross profits. The advertising–sales ratio had an insignificant effect on the resulting net profits dependent variable.

Table 11.1 summarises the results of six of the early UK studies on the relationship between concentration and profitability. In only a minority (two out of six) of these studies did concentration have a significant effect, and the equations did not in general achieve a high level of explanatory power. These studies also illustrate vividly the data problems involved in this type of work. For example, the use of the advertising–sales ratio is unsatisfactory to the extent that the present performance of firms is also affected by the absolute level of advertising expenditure both currently and in the past. The use of such proxy variables as the average size of the largest plants that account for half of industry employment, to measure the effect of economies-of-scale barriers to entry, has met with mixed success, and there is also a difficulty of interpretation because of the close relationship between such proxies and the concentration measures. Again, the use of proxies for the international trade variable may or may not be significant, but the measures used have often been very rough and ready, so that it is difficult to know how much importance to attach to the results.

It is clear that it is not easy to conduct a satisfactory multiple regression analysis of the effect of concentration on profitability. The addition of more explanatory variables often raises severe data problems and also problems of multicollinearity, but if relevant variables are omitted the results will be misleading. One theoretically relevant variable usually omitted from empirical studies, because it is so difficult to measure, is the elasticity of demand. Assuming that elasticities of demand remain reasonably constant over the relevant time period, the mis-specification caused by leaving elasticity out of the equation can be reduced by specifying the relationship between profitability and concentration in terms of *changes* rather than levels. If other explanatory variables have remained constant, they too can be omitted without biasing the results.

Two such studies of the relationship between changes in profitability and changes in concentration have been carried out for the UK with conflicting results. The first study was that of Cowling and Waterson (1976), for a sample of 93 industries. They regressed the proportional change in gross price–cost margins between 1963 and 1968 on the proportional change in concentration

Table 11.1 Summary of results of UK empirical studies on the relationship between concentration and profitability

Study	Level of industrial classification	No. of firms in concentration ratio	Industries	Profit measure	Time period Concentration	Time period Profits	R^2	Coefficient on concentration ratio	Rate of growth of demand	Advertising	Capital intensity	Other barriers to entry	Foreign companies
(1) Shepherd (1972)	3-digit	5	91	Price–cost margin	Average of 1958 and 1963	Average of 1958 and 1963	0.114	0.062	Yes	No	Yes*	No	No
(2) Phillips (1972)	3-digit	3	71	Gross profits–gross output	1951	1951	0.260[a]	0.001*	Yes	Yes*	No	Yes*[b]	No
(3) Holterman (1973)	3-digit	5	113	Gross profits–gross output	1963	1963	0.454[a]	−0.026	Yes*	Yes*	Yes*	Yes*	No
(4) Khalilzadeh-Shirazi (1974)	3-digit	5	60	Gross price–cost margin	1963	1963	0.544[a]	0.009	Yes	Yes*	Yes*	Yes*	Yes*
(5) Hart and Morgan (1977)	3-digit	5	113	Gross profits–value added	1968	1968	0.432	0.21	Yes	Yes*	Yes*	Yes	Yes
(6) Hitiris (1978)	3-digit	5	80	Gross price–cost margin	1963 and 1968	1963 and 1968	0.444	0.099*	Yes*	No	Yes*	No	Yes*

(Header: Variables included to measure effects of: Rate of growth of demand, Advertising, Capital intensity, Other barriers to entry, Foreign companies)

* Coefficient significant at 5% level.
[a] $\bar{R}^2$
[b] Wrong sign.

(between 1958 and 1963), measured by the Herfindahl index, with the following result (t-value in parenthesis):

$$\Delta \left[\frac{\pi}{R}\right] = 0.0220 + .2501 \ \Delta H \quad R^2 = 0.067$$
$$(2.572)$$

Changes in concentration were found to have a significant effect on price–cost margins, although the level of explanatory power of this relationship was low. Cowling and Waterson found that the inclusion of other explanatory variables that would be expected to be related to changes in price–cost margins (e.g. changes in union density, changes in sales, changes in the percentage of the workforce unemployed) added little to explanatory power. However, they also split the sample into durable and non-durable goods industries, on the argument that durable industries will show more marked cyclical behaviour, and found that changes in concentration had a significant effect on price–cost margins for durable goods but not for non-durables. This result is consistent with the view that there is more scope in durable goods industries to achieve price flexibility by changing the quality of the goods.

Hart and Morgan (1977) repeated Cowling and Waterson's test with a smaller sample of 76 industries, having eliminated those which couldn't be compared between 1958 and 1968 and using a different and unbiased estimate of the Herfindahl index of concentration. Their results conflicted with Cowling and Waterson's in that they found changes in concentration to have no significant impact on changes in profitability, as shown by the following relationship (standard error in parentheses):

$$\Delta \left[\frac{\pi}{R}\right] = 0.03 + .05 \ \Delta H \quad R^2 = 0.02$$
$$(0.04)$$

More recent studies also show rather mixed and inconclusive results. Lyons (1981), using 1968 data, found that concentration had a positive effect on price–cost margins which was significant at about the 5 per cent level. This study was particularly concerned to measure the impact of foreign trade variables. It found that margins tended to be lower the higher the level of import penetration. Margins were also found to be positively related to the proportion of domestic production which was exported. The degree of intra-industry trade is another foreign trade variable which was found to exert a positive and significant effect on price–cost margins. This variable was used as an indicator of product heterogeneity, the argument being that the higher the degree of heterogeneity the more protected domestic producers will be from import competition.

Geroski (1981), again using 1968 data, found that the relationship between concentration and price–cost margins was not continuous, but that there were critical threshold levels for concentration. Concentration, measured by the five-firm concentration ratio, was found to have a small positive effect on profits as it increased to a level of around 35 per cent; very little effect between 35 and 75 per cent; a sharp negative effect as it increased from 75 to 85 per cent and a sharp positive effect above 85 per cent. This complex relationship is hard to explain and runs counter to much of the US evidence.

Clarke (1984) found little evidence of a positive link between concentration and profitability for the period 1970–76. Both advertising intensity and capital intensity had a positive and significant effect on price–cost margins, but the five-firm concentration ratio had a negative impact. The effect of concentration on trends in margins, though positive, was not found to be significant. The most noticeable effect concentration had was in explaining the variability of profit margins, the variation in margins tending to be higher the more highly concentrated the industry. Clarke suggests that this result is consistent with *greater* competition in concentrated industries. However, an alternative explanation offered by McEnally (1976), who found the same relationship between concentration and the variability of profits, is that this might be due to high entry barriers in concentrated industries which weaken the tendency for competitive forces to equalise rates of return.

In the UK, the market power versus efficiency hypothesis has been tested by Clarke, Davies and Waterson (1984), using data for 104 industries over the period 1971–77. As we have seen, one way of trying to discriminate between these competing hypotheses is to compare the price–cost margins of large and small firms in high- and low-concentration industries. This comparison offered no support for the efficiency hypothesis; indeed if anything there was a slight tendency, on average, for the five largest firms to have lower margins than the rest. The authors also examined the relationship between individual firms' price–cost margins and market share in each industry. A large estimated impact of market share on profitability would support the efficiency hypothesis; a low value of the regression coefficient would favour market power as the most likely explanation. Only 29 industries showed a positive relationship between market share and price–cost margins, and the range of results across these industries suggested that efficiency and price-raising effects are important in different markets. The degree of market power, as estimated by the strength of the relationship between market share and price–cost margins, was also found to be strongly correlated with concentration, giving further support to the market power hypothesis.

Individual industry studies

Substantial problems are clearly encountered in the use of econometric analysis to determine the effect that industry structure has on profit performance and to disentangle complex causal relationships. A major part of the difficulty lies in the poor quality of the data which are available for cross-section analysis. An advantage of detailed studies of individual industries is that the quality of the data can be improved. This means not only better data on industry structure and performance variables, but also an economically more meaningful definition of markets than is available for econometric studies.

In the UK, the reports of the Monopolies and Mergers Commission (MMC) provide a rich source of information. Most of the MMC's inquiries have concerned highly concentrated markets, and indeed several of them have approximated monopolies. The inquiries cover a wide range of issues including costs, prices, profitability, advertising and other promotional expenditure, discriminatory behaviour and other forms of anti-competitive behaviour which are not covered by restrictive practices legislation.

Up to January 1989 the MMC had produced 98 monopoly reports. In about 14 cases profits and/or prices have been judged to be excessive. These cases, together with others where the dominant firm had at least 50 per cent of the market or where a near duopoly situation existed, are shown in Table 11.2. The MMC has always looked at the rate of return on capital employed measured on a historic cost basis and these are the figures which are shown in the table. However, it should be noted that the reports span periods with widely varying rates of inflation. Periods of rapid inflation increase the difference between rates of return measured on a historic cost and on a replacement cost basis and for this reason little attention should be paid to differences in the profitability figures in different reports. The more interesting and useful comparison is that between the profitability of the leading firms in the reference markets and that of a broader sector of the economy such as the average for all industrial companies. The figures used for this purpose in Table 11.2 are the Bank of England series of returns on capital for large companies in the industrial sector.

The cases of British Oxygen (1956) and Fisons (1959) show that, in the early years of the MMC's life, profitability did not have to be all that much higher than average to be considered excessive. In the British Oxygen case it was the near-complete monopoly and the limited financial risk facing the company that led to the conclusion that profitability was unjustifiably high. The risk factor was also important in the report on *Colour Film* (1966). The MMC drew attention to the fact that Eastman Kodak 'has suffered no serious setback throughout its history' and recommended that prices should be cut. In *Household Detergents* (1966) it was the excessive advertising and sales promotion of the two leading companies to the detriment of prices that was the crucial factor leading to the conclusion of 'unduly high profits'. The profitability of the companies in the *Chlordiazepoxide and Diazepam* (1973) and *Contraceptive Sheaths* (1975) references was so high that a conclusion of excessive profits could hardly be avoided, however efficient the companies, particularly in view of the near-monopoly positions held by Hoffman La Roche and the London Rubber Co. in their respective markets.

However, the MMC has cleared several cases where the profitability of a dominant firm may appear to have been excessive. In three of these cases (*Clutch Mechanisms*, 1968, *Breakfast Cereals*, 1973 and *Primary Batteries*, 1974) profits had been excessive but were not so at the time of the inquiry. Consequently the recommendation was one of surveillance. In *Cigarette Filter Rods* (1969), efficiency, high risk and ease of entry were important factors justifying a high return on capital. Efficiency was also an important factor in explaining why the

MMC was satisfied with the high profits of Pedigree Pet Foods in the supply of *Cat and Dog Foods* (1977).

In more recent cases there has been a noticeable tendency to avoid administrative controls if at all possible and to rely instead on new entry or measures designed to loosen up the market. In *Tampons* (1986), for instance, though it was recognised that profits were higher than they would have been if the dominant firm had less market power, it was concluded that in the absence of any entry barriers 'the currently rewarding profit levels should act as a magnet to attract new entry'. In *Postal Franking Machines* (1986), although the MMC estimated a rate of return of 72 per cent over a six-year period on the supply of reference products, it did not recommend measures to control prices or margins but proposed instead to reduce or remove factors restricting competition. In *White Salt* (1986), however, it was concluded that the absence of effective competition was unlikely to be rectified by the threat of imports or of new entry and so direct price controls were recommended as the only workable solution.

It should be noted (see Table 11.2) that there have been several monopoly cases where high concentration has been associated with only moderate or low profitability. Having said this, however, one interesting tendency does emerge, and that is for high profits to be associated with dominance. Utton (1986) examined data from a sample of 50 MMC reports. He defined dominance as a leading firm having a market share of about 50 per cent or more, and at least twice the share of its nearest rival, and concentrated oligopoly as two leading firms having a combined market share of at least 50 per cent. He found that the profits of the market leaders relative to the industry average were notably higher for cases of dominance than for those of concentrated oligopoly. Of course, this still leaves unanswered the question of whether the high profits of dominant firms are the result of price-raising power or efficiency. The MMC reports suggest a mixed answer.

Concluding comments on structure–profitability relationships

We have examined a small proportion of the vast quantity of empirical work on the relationship between market structure and profitability. So far this work has yielded very few generally agreed results. The relationship between economic performance and market structure is too complex to be captured satisfactorily by single-equation regression models, and more complicated simultaneous equation models have as yet added little to the sum total of knowledge in this area.

It is not clear that there is a positive relationship between concentration and profitability, *ceteris paribus* (i.e. independent of such other factors as barriers to entry, elasticity of demand and rate of growth of demand). Including these additional variables introduces multicollinearity problems; leaving them out introduces equally serious problems of mis-specification. Nor is it clear whether a correlation between seller concentration and profitability can be considered a general sign of a serious monopolistic misallocation of resources. In the absence

Table 11.2 Market share and profitability in monopoly references

(1)		(2)	(3)	(4)
Monopoly reference	Year of report	Market share of leading firm %	Profitability of leading firm[a] %	Column (3) ÷ average profitability for all large industrial companies[a]
Electronic valves & tubes	1956	Mullard 51	40 (1954)	2.0
Industrial & medical gases[b]	1956	British Oxygen 98	23 (1952–54)	1.3
Chemical fertilisers[b]	1959	Fisons 40–50	24 (1954–57)	1.4
Cigarettes & tobacco machinery	1961	Molins 57	36 (1951–58)	2.0
Cigarettes & tobacco	1961	Imperial Tobacco 63	13 (1951–59)	0.7
Elect. equip. for vehicles[b]	1963	Champion 71	57 (1954–60)	3.4
Wallpaper	1964	Wallpaper Man. 79	16 (1960–62)	1.1
Colour film[b]	1966	Kodak 70	50 (1961–64)	3.7
Household detergents[b]	1966	Unilever 44	29 (1960–65)	2.0
		Procter & Gamble 46	53 (1960–65)	3.8
Infant milk foods	1967	Glaxo } 80+	10 (1962–66)	0.8
		Cow & Gate }	16 (1962–66)	1.2
Clutch mechanisms	1968	AP 63	31 (1962–67)	2.4

Product	Year	Company				Return
Flat glass	1968	Pilkington	91	20	(1960–65)	1.4
Cellulosic fibres	1968	Courtaulds	89	17	(1964–67)	1.3
Cigarette filter rods	1969	Cigarette Comp.	100	45	(1963–67)	3.3
Metal containers	1970	Metal Box	77	19	(1963–68)	1.4
Breakfast cereals	1973	Kellogg	60	70	(1962–66)	5.2
Chlordiazepoxide & diazepam[b]	1973	Hoffman La Roche	99	70	(1970)	6.0
Plasterboard	1974	British Gypsum	100	16	(1967–71)	1.3
Batteries	1974	Mallory	70	34	(1967–72)	2.6
Contraceptive sheaths[b]	1975	London Rubber	90	100	(1969–73)	7.7
Photocopiers	1976	Rank Xerox	93	36	(1971–75)	2.3
Copying materials	1977	Ozalid	52	34	(1972–75)	2.1
Cat & dog foods	1977	Pedigree Pet	50	47	(1972–75)	2.9
Tampons[b]	1980	Tampax	66	62	(1974–79)	3.6
Roofing tiles[b]	1981	Redland	48	43	(1976–80)	2.6
		Marley	40	23	(1976–80)	1.3
Contraceptive sheaths[b]	1982	London Rubber	90+	25	(1978–82)	1.7
Tampons	1986	Tambrands	60	66	(1979–84)	4.4
Postal franking machines[b]	1986	Pitney Bowes	60	72	(1979–84)	4.8
White salt[b]	1986	ICI	45	36	(1979–84)	2.4
		British Salt	50	43	(1979–84)	2.9
Steel wire fencing	1987	Twil Ltd	65	20	(1980–85)	1.3
Gas[b]	1988	British Gas	100	18	(1984–88)	–

[a] Return on average capital employed (historic cost basis) before tax and interest for the period indicated in column (3).
[b] High profits and/or high prices criticised.
Sources: MMC reports, and *Bank of England Quarterly Bulletin*

of very high entry barriers, at least, the high profits may be a temporary phenomenon signalling to new entrants. In other cases, the high level of concentration may be the result rather than the cause of high profit rates if the superior performance of the leading firms in the industry has enabled them to increase their market shares. This might be the case, for instance, where firms owe their high market share to leadership in research and development. We therefore reach a largely agnostic conclusion concerning the possibility, in the current state of knowledge, of formulating general policy rules on the basis of empirical evidence on the relationship between market structure and profitability. Perhaps the one conclusion that comes through more clearly than any other is the link between profitability and market share, and in particular between profitability and positions of dominance. Although positions of dominance may be due to efficiency, there is sufficient evidence to suggest that more rigorous competition policy standards should be applied to these positions than to other types of market structure.

11.3 STRUCTURE, ADVERTISING AND PROFITABILITY

The second structure–conduct–performance relationship that we propose to look at is that between market structure, advertising intensity and profitability, which raises a number of interesting questions. Is there a positive association between concentration and advertising intensity, so that firms in more highly concentrated markets spend more on advertising? And do firms that spend more on advertising achieve higher profitability? As we shall see, the hypothesised links between these variables are not completely straightforward, nor is the attempt to test the relationship empirically.

Causal links between market structure and advertising

Let us first consider the relationship between market structure and advertising intensity, and note at once that, if there is a positive relationship between these two variables, the direction of causality may run either way. On the one hand, as originally suggested by Kaldor (1950), advertising can work to increase concentration if there are economies of scale in advertising, because then advertising will tend to increase the range of output over which average costs (including selling costs) fall and to increase the minimum efficient size of the firm. Advertising expenditure thus works to increase barriers to entry and concentration. Scale effects in advertising may exist because large firms are able to obtain discounts from the media so that the advertising cost per message is lower. It may also be the case that a certain threshold of advertising expenditure has to be reached before it becomes effective. Above this threshold, increased repetition of an advertising message may, over a certain range, have a more than proportionate effect on sales revenue.

In addition to any scale effects, advertising may also impede entry by increasing capital requirements. Assuming capital market imperfections, new entrants (unless they are existing large firms) may find it more difficult to raise the necessary capital for entry into industries where advertising is heavy because of the high risks involved in advertising expenditure.

The most obvious barrier to entry associated with advertising, however, is product differentiation. Product markets in which product differentiation is important lend themselves to advertising. In turn, advertising may be used to further strengthen product differentiation, thus lowering price elasticities of demand and making it more difficult for successful entry to occur. There has been a considerable debate as to whether advertising does in fact create an entry barrier. Demsetz (1982) has argued that it is the successful attempts of established firms to create a reputation for quality and reliability that create an entry barrier, not advertising as such. The more successful established firms are in developing customer attachments, the more difficult it will be for newcomers to break into the market.

The Demsetz argument still leaves open the possibility that customer loyalty and advertising interact, and that advertising is therefore not entirely innocent of the charge of creating entry barriers. The important problem then is to distinguish between the advertising that is beneficial – because it is associated with a firm's reputation and long-term commitment to customers – from the advertising that is anti-competitive. In other words, given that some level of advertising can always be justified because it increases long-run efficiency, at what level does it become excessive?

Another way in which advertising may increase concentration has been suggested by Mann (1974). Advertising activity, he argued, contains a large element of chance, and when advertising expenditure is an important dimension of competition it increases the volatility of market shares. In Chapter 5 it was pointed out that, according to the law of proportionate effect, chance factors alone can explain why concentration tends to increase over time. Furthermore, the rate at which it increases depends on the variance of growth rates facing each firm. By increasing this variance, advertising has the effect of increasing concentration. Furthermore, as concentration increased to the level where interdependence is recognised, price competition weakens and non-price competition, including advertising, becomes the dominant form of competition. Thus there is a cumulative effect, with advertising expenditure resulting in higher concentration, and the latter in turn causing firms to put less emphasis on price and more on non- price competition. We proceed then to examine in more detail the way in which concentration may affect advertising.

The link from concentration to advertising is likely to be a complicated one because of the large number of factors determining advertising expenditure. Theoretical arguments about advertising expenditure take place at the level of the individual firm and suggest that the amount that an optimising (profit-maximising) firm spends on advertising will depend on the increase in sales revenue anticipated from advertising. This in turn depends on the responsiveness of sales to changes in advertising expenditure (i.e. on the advertising elasticity) and on the price elasticity of demand.

Dorfman and Steiner (1954) showed that for a profit-maximising firm the ratio of advertising expenditure to sales should equal the ratio of advertising elasticity of demand to price elasticity of demand. Following Schmalensee (1972), who further developed the Dorfman–Steiner model, assume that the firm is able to purchase advertising messages at a constant cost T per message. Total messages, A, enters the demand function facing the firm:

$$Q = Q(A, P)$$

where Q is output and P is price. More advertising is assumed to increase demand, and a higher price to reduce it. Therefore $\partial Q/\partial A > 0$ and $\partial Q/\partial P > 0$.

Non-advertising costs are a function of output, $C[Q]$, and the firm's profit function is:

$$\pi = PQ(A, P) - C[Q(A, P)] - AT.$$

Differentiating with respect to A and setting this equal to zero gives the profit-maximising condition for advertising messages for any given price:

$$\frac{\partial \pi}{\partial A} = \left[P - \frac{\partial C}{\partial Q}\right]\frac{\partial Q}{\partial A} - T = 0$$

and multiplying by A/PQ gives:

$$\frac{AT}{PQ} = \left[\frac{P - (\partial C/\partial Q)}{P}\right]\frac{A}{Q}\cdot\frac{\partial Q}{\partial A}.$$

The expression in brackets is the price–cost margin as a proportion of price, and the remaining term on the right-hand side, $-A/Q.\partial Q/\partial A$, is the advertising elasticity of demand.

If price is fixed so as to maximise profits the price–cost margin is equal to the inverse of the elasticity of demand, $1/\eta$, and if we let the advertising elasticity of demand be a, we have:

$$\frac{AT}{PQ} = \frac{a}{\pi}$$

Thus the ratio of advertising expenditure to sales revenue will be higher, the greater the advertising elasticity of demand relative to the price elasticity of demand.

Nature of the product

The relative size of these elasticities will vary substantially across products. One important distinction to be made is that between consumer and producer goods. There are a number of reasons for supposing that advertising elasticity of demand will be higher for the former. The justification most commonly used is that buyers of producer goods can generally be expected to be better informed and thus less susceptible to persuasive advertising. Differences in customer requirements are also important. Advertisements for consumer goods compete for the expenditure of a consumer who can choose from a bewildering variety of goods. In a big proportion of cases the choice actually made, e.g. of chocolate bar, tin of cocoa, toilet cleaner, will have an insignificant effect on the consumer's welfare. 'Mistakes' can easily be rectified. The buyer of producer goods, however, is in the market for a very limited range of products. Accurate product specification and reliable delivery dates are often crucial. Mistakes can be costly to both buyer and seller. Promotional activities are thus more likely to take the form of direct contact between buyer and seller in order to determine such things as delivery dates and product specification. Because of this distinction, many studies of advertising have focused attention on the consumer goods sector of the economy.

Within the consumer goods sector, however, the scope for advertising expenditure varies substantially from one product to another. One relevant factor is the degree of heterogeneity, or the number of 'characteristics' embodied in a good. Thus there is more scope for advertising toiletries and motor cars than there is for advertising paper clips or nuts and bolts. Porter (1974) distinguishes between 'convenience' goods and 'shopping' goods. The former have low unit value and are purchased frequently with a minimum of search costs; e.g. breakfast cereals and confectionery. Shopping goods, on the other hand, have a high unit value and are purchased infrequently after, possibly, considerable search; e.g. motor cars and furniture. Convenience goods are more susceptible to advertising because relatively little time and effort goes into their purchase. For shopping goods, however, customers are more likely to be influenced by product specification and direct contact with sales outlets. As in the case of producer goods, when the cost of making mistakes is high the customer is less likely to be influenced by advertising messages. We would expect, therefore, to find advertising intensity to be higher for convenience goods, and this is confirmed by Porter's study.

Several other product market characteristics may affect the level of advertising expenditure. High advertising may be associated with products characterised by frequent design changes, e.g. motor cars and cameras, or with products with a high fashion content, e.g. perfumes and certain types of clothing.

Market structure

Given product characteristics, it can be expected that the intensity of advertising expenditure will be affected by market structure. A firm's advertising may increase sales either by shifting the industry demand curve outwards or by diverting sales from other firms in the industry. Under perfectly competitive conditions the individual firm has no incentive to advertise. Demand is perfectly elastic and each firm can sell any quantity at the market price, the only constraint being its productive capacity. Although no individual firm has any incentive to advertise, the industry as a whole may do so because the market demand curve is negatively shaped. Thus, in the market for milk there is no incentive for an individual farm to advertise, but all farmers, through their milk marketing board, may try to persuade consumers to 'drinka pinta milk a day'. More generally, an industry, although not perfectly competitive, may have a large number of sellers. In these cases an individual firm can expect to gain little from an expansion of market demand if it starts to advertise because it will be too small for its advertisements to have much impact on the whole market. Additional sales, if they are forthcoming, are more likely to be at the expense of its nearest competitors. At the other end of the structure scale, when conditions approximate those of simple monopoly, the dominant firm may benefit from an increase in the total market, but there will be very little scope for attracting sales from competitors. This argument suggests that the greatest incentive to advertise, from the combined effect of generated and diverted sales, is for firms in moderately concentrated oligopolistic industries. In these industries an individual firm can expect to receive a worthwhile share of generated sales and also has the possibility of gaining substantially at the expense of competitors.

The Dorfman–Steiner result reported earlier does not take oligopolistic interdependence explicitly into account. When interdependence is taken into account, a firm's demand function depends not only on its own price and advertising policies but also on those of its competitors, and its choice of policy will depend on how it expects rivals to react. Thus, if a firm increases advertising expenditure, it will have some expectation of how this will affect the advertising expenditures of its rivals and what effect that reaction will in turn have on its own sales.

We have already discussed the reason why the price elasticity of demand facing a firm will be affected by market structure; the argument is that, in more highly concentrated markets, interdependence will be stronger, and any individual firm will thus expect a price cut to evoke a larger output response from rivals. Price elasticity of demand thus falls as the number of rivals is reduced, and the price–cost margin increases. This result implies that, as concentration increases, there will be a general tendency for advertising intensity to increase because advertising elasticity increases relative to price elasticity.

However there is a counteracting tendency at work. As concentration increases, firms will tend to give more weight to interdependence. Each firm will recognise that the positive effect an increase in advertising has on sales may be more or less offset by the negative impact of an increase in advertising by rivals. The possibility that advertising expenditure might be mutually offsetting becomes stronger as concentration increases to some critical level.

The argument so far suggests that advertising intensity will increase with concentration until the latter reaches moderate to high levels, and will then decline. *A priori* reasoning, however, does not tell us what the critical level is likely to be. At what level of concentration will interdependence be strong enough to induce firms to eschew price competition and at what level will it have a dampening effect on advertising expenditure?

There are reasons to believe that competition through advertising may persist after price competition has been severely attenuated. First, it is more difficult to follow a rival's successful advertising campaign than it is to follow a price cut. Though much advertising expenditure may be mutually offsetting, there is always the possibility that one brilliant idea will have a major impact which rivals will find difficult to follow. Second, advertising may play an important role as an entry barrier, especially when technical scale-economy entry barriers are low. In these cases, even though advertising expenditures are largely mutually offsetting, and are recognised by rivals to be so, intensive advertising policies may nevertheless be pursued in highly concentrated industries because of their entry-deterring effects.

Economic analysis suggests therefore that advertising intensity is likely to be positively correlated with market concentration up to some critical level. It is less easy to predict what that level is. Some arguments suggest that advertising intensity may peak at relatively modest levels of concentration, others suggest that a positive correlation may be found up to very high levels. To proceed further we must turn to the evidence.

Empirical evidence

Both the hypotheses outlined above concerning the relationship between market structure and advertising intensity have been subjected to empirical testing.

Let us look first at the evidence concerning the 'Kaldor hypothesis' that advertising increases concentration. Reference has already been made in Chapter 5 to the work of Blair (1972) for the USA, which concluded that the effects of advertising were largely responsible for increased concentration in the adver-tising-intensive industries studied. This finding is repeated in Mueller and Rogers (1980), whose results suggest that advertising accounted for the whole of the increases in concentration in consumer goods industries over the period 1947–72. In the UK this hypothesis has been tested by Cowling et al. (1975). They regressed minimum efficient firm size on minimum efficient plant size, adver-tising and R&D expenditures per firm for a sample of 15 industries, and they found that advertising had a significant positive effect on minimum efficient firm size. This work, then, supports the argument that advertising expenditure exhi-bits increasing returns to scale and tends to raise the minimum efficient size of firm. However, in view of data limitations and the large number of other variables affecting minimum efficient firm size, these results cannot be taken as conclusive. Another major problem is that much of the association between advertising and concentration may be due to the reverse causal relationship, with heavy advertising being the result of high concentration. It is very likely that both causal relationships are at work and that they may have a mutually reinforcing effect.

The hypothesis of an inverted U-shaped relationship between advertising and concentration has been tested by many empirical studies. One British study along these lines is that of Sutton (1974), using 1963 data for 25 minimum list heading industries selling mainly consumer goods. Sutton initially divided his industries into 'high', 'medium' and 'low' concentration groups according to whether the five-firm concentration ratio was above 80 per cent, between 48 and 80 per cent or below 48 per cent, and he examined the advertising–sales ratios for each group. His findings provide support for the inverted U-shaped hypothesis. Most of the unconcentrated industries had low advertising–sales ratios, most of the medium-concentrated group had a high advertising–sales ratio, and most of the highly-concentrated industries fell into the medium advertising category.

Sutton then ran regressions of advertising intensity on concentration ratio in both linear and quadratic forms. He found that the explanatory power of the quadratic form was significantly higher ($R^{-2} = 0.34$ as against 0.01) and also that both concentration and its square had significant coefficients in the quadratic form, while concentration had an insignificant effect on advertising intensity in the linear regression. The two estimated equations were as follows:

$$A = 0.99 + .013\,C \qquad\qquad\qquad R^2 = 0.01$$
$$(1.29)\,(1.13)$$

$$A = -3.15 + .19\,C - .0015\,C^2 \qquad\qquad \bar{R}^2 = 0.34$$
$$(2.36)\ (3.71)\quad (3.51)$$

where A is the advertising to sales ratio and C is the five-firm concentration ratio, with t ratios in parentheses. From the quadratic equation it is estimated that advertising intensity increases as concentration rises, reaching a peak when the five-firm concentration ratio is 64 per cent.

Sutton's work has been criticised for using industries that were too broadly defined and for omitting potentially important explanatory variables which were liable to vary significantly across these industries.

Cowling *et al*. (1975), for instance, argued that Sutton's relationship between advertising intensity and concentration is mis-specified, since it excludes all the other important determinants of advertising intensity, and it cannot be assumed that these did not vary between the 25 industries concerned. Their own empirical work covered 26 narrowly defined non-durable goods markets, mainly food items, for which it was thought that the effect of excluded variables would be more nearly constant. They also included explanatory variables other than concentration: namely, the total number of brands in each market, the ratio of new to existing brands, sales growth, and a dummy variable for products 'close to sensitive psychological drives'. Their equations achieved higher explanatory power when the dependent variable used was 'goodwill' (a six-year weighted average of advertising–sales ratios) than when it was the current level of advertising intensity. Using the Herfindahl index to measure concentration, they found an inverted U-shaped quadratic relationship, with advertising intensity rising from around 4 per cent in a competitive market to over 15 per cent under duopoly. Thus advertising intensity was estimated to peak at a much higher level of concentration than was the case in Sutton's study. Indeed, when concentration was measured by the three-firm concentration ratio, a monotonic relationship between advertising intensity and concentration was found to exist.

More recently Buxton, Davies and Lyons (1984) have found evidence to support a quadratic relationship between advertising intensity and concentration. Their industry sample consisted of 51 UK industries in 1968 at the minimum list heading level of disaggregation. One of the equations which they fitted to the data gave the following result:

$$A = -1.90 + 7.66\ P + .12\ \pi/S + .18\ (SC/S)C - .0014\ (Sc/S)C^2 \quad \bar{R}^2 = 0.75$$
$$(-2.35)\quad(6.31)\quad(3.01)\quad\quad(5.21)\quad\quad\quad(-3.53)$$

where A is advertising intensity, P is a dummy variable for 'personal goods', π/S is the rate of return on sales, Sc/S is the proportion of industry sales made to consumers, C is the five-firm concentration ratio, and t-values are in parentheses. A crucial factor in this study was the Sc/S variable. When no allowance was made for this variable, the authors found no evidence of a statistically significant relationship between advertising intensity and concentration, thus confirming the importance of consumer goods industries in the study of advertising. Advertising intensity was estimated to peak at a five-firm concentration ratio of 64 per cent – the same level as in Sutton's study. Buxton *et al.* also estimated a two-equation model to take account of the possibility of a two-way causal relationship between advertising intensity and concentration, but the results were similar to those of the single-equation model with advertising intensity as the dependent variable.

Several US studies have also given support to a quadratic relationship between advertising intensity and concentration. This result is found, for example, in Strickland and Weiss (1976), with advertising intensity in consumer goods industries peaking at a four-firm concentration ratio of 46 per cent.

Overall, therefore, there is support for the hypothesis of an inverted U-shaped relationship between advertising intensity and concentration. Several studies suggest that peak advertising intensity may occur at moderate levels of concentration, but this estimate may be biased downwards because industries are defined too broadly. Studies using more narrowly defined industries tend to show advertising intensity peaking at higher levels of concentration.

Advertising and profitability

Having considered the relationship between market structure and advertising, we now turn to that between advertising and profitability. As outlined earlier in this chapter, one argument is that advertising expenditure creates barriers to entry and thus enables firms to increase their price–cost margins and achieve higher profitability. One influential early study that looked specifically at the effects of advertising was that of Comanor and Wilson (1967), who regressed profit rates for 41 consumer goods industries on different combinations of several explanatory variables. The following equation reproduces one of their results:

$$\pi = 0.039 + .343\ A/S + .0105\ K(\text{logs}) + .015\ G(\text{logs}) + .0043\ Cd$$
$$\quad\ \ (2.3) \qquad (2.8) \qquad\qquad (1.4) \qquad\qquad (0.3)$$

$$+ .0278\ Rd \qquad R^2 = 0.40$$
$$(1.5)$$

where π is profitability, A/S is advertising intensity; K is the capital required to set up a single efficient plant; G is the growth of demand; Cd is a concentration dummy variable; Rd is a regional industry dummy variable, and t statistics are shown in parentheses. In this equation, only advertising intensity and capital requirements are significant at the 5 per cent level or higher. One of the main conclusions from the Comanor–Wilson study is that advertising intensity has a significant effect on the profit rate. Industries with high advertising outlays earned, on average, a rate of profit 4 per cent above that of other industries; this represents a profit differential of 50 per cent. On the other hand, concentration was not found to exert a significant independent effect on profits, and so Comanor and Wilson concluded that a successful policy to control market power should be directed at factors that facilitate product differentiation, and hence encourage advertising, rather than at influencing the size distribution of firms.

Other US studies, e.g. Weiss (1974), have also found a significant correlation between profitability and advertising intensity.

These studies have been subject to a good deal of criticism. One criticism is that results in this area depend heavily on the inclusion or exclusion of particular industries in the sample being investigated. A related problem is that product markets may be inappropriately defined. Second, and following from our earlier discussion of causality, there is a simultaneity problem. High advertising intensity may be both a cause and an effect of high profitability, so that simultaneous equation models are needed to establish whether there is a causal relationship leading from advertising intensity to profitability. Third, there is a potential problem in the way advertising expenditure is treated for accounting purposes. Because advertising expenditure is treated as a current expense rather than as an investment, accounting profit will tend to deviate from true profit when advertising has long-lived effects on demand. Because intangible advertising capital is not included in the denominator of the rate of return, this will mean that accounting profit overstates the true rate of return. However, since accounting profits are calculated after deducting advertising expenditure the numerator of the rate of return is also affected. If current advertising expenditures exceed (fall short of) current depreciation charges on intangible advertising capital, the effect will be that the accounting rate of return will understate (overstate) the true rate of return. It has been argued that the general effect is for accounting profitability to overstate true profitability and that the overstatement is greater the higher the advertising/sales ratio and the longer the period over which advertising depreciates. If there is a tendency for an overstatement of accounting rates of return to be positively correlated with advertising intensity, this could clearly wipe out the Comanor–Wilson result reported above.

To get round some of these problems, Cowling *et al*. (1975) conducted a test of the relationship between profitability and advertising using data for 88 individual firms from one industry, namely, the food industry. Both profit rates and advertising expenditure were measured over a five-year period, to allow for the 'goodwill' effects of advertising. The other independent variables included were firm size, concentration and two alternative measures of advertising at the market level. The results suggest that advertising creates barriers to entry and therefore increases the market power of the firms in the industry.

In response to criticism concerning the direction of causation, Comanor and Wilson (1974) used the same data base employed in their 1967 study to test a two-equation model in which both profit rates and advertising/sales ratios are treated as endogenous variables. They found that a two-way causal relationship between advertising intensity and profitability exists but that this tends to strengthen the impact of advertising intensity on profitability. However, other simultaneous equation studies (e.g. Strickland and Weiss 1976) produced results which offer only heavily qualified support for the role of advertising in increasing profitability.

Comanor and Wilson (1974) also responded to the criticism that advertising should be treated as an investment because of its long-lasting effects. In fact they produced estimates which suggest that advertising effects decay rapidly and that, in many industries, treating advertising as a current expense does little to violate underlying economic realities. Their tests therefore showed that treating advertising as an investment left the positive impact of advertising intensity of profitability intact.

Following from the above it is hardly surprising that the studies which have challenged the Comanor–Wilson results have used low depreciation rates for advertising expenditure. This is true, for instance, of Bloch (1974) and Ayarian (1975) who, not surprisingly, found no evidence of a statistically significant impact of advertising intensity on profitability.

Individual industry studies

One of the difficulties with a cross-section analysis is that it is all too easy, because of data limitations, to omit potentially relevant and important variables from the analysis. These include the extent to which consumers are informed about the offers made by firms, and the role played by retailers. Case studies, however, can pick up these more subtle influences. For instance, Benham (1972) found that prices of eyeglasses in the USA were higher in states which restricted advertising than in those where restrictions were few or non-existent. In this case advertising had a pro-competitive effect by improving customer information and increasing the elasticity of demand of individual retail outlets. Advertising is likely to be particularly effective in this context when it is associated with the expansion of new, low-cost forms of retailing. Advertising may then serve as a means of speeding up the transfer of sales to low-cost outlets and also of accelerating the diffusion of new selling methods. It is worth noting, however, that these beneficial effects of advertising, when advertising is largely informative rather than persuasive, may be confined to industries which are relatively fragmented and subject to rapid change.

For highly-concentrated manufacturing industry, advertising expenditure in the UK has come under scrutiny in a number of the investigations of the Monopolies and Mergers Commission. The classic case is that of *Household Detergents* (1966) in which the role of advertising was singled out for special analysis. The industry was found to be extremely highly concentrated; Procter & Gamble and Unilever exerted a virtual duopoly, with 46 per cent and 44 per cent of sales, respectively. Profit rates on the sales of detergents were much higher than the average for manufacturing industry – about twice as high for Unilever and nearly four times as high for Procter & Gamble. The MMC found that the aspect of the firms' behaviour that operated against the public interest was the extremely high level of advertising expenditure. Price competition had been largely replaced by competition in advertising at a level that deterred new entrants, protected the existing market structure and permitted the earning of excess profits.

The analysis of the detergents market is interesting in a number of respects. First, a very high level of advertising expenditure is maintained in a highly-concentrated market. It has been suggested that duopolists may recognise that much of their advertising is merely cancelling out the other firm's, so that recognition of interdependence may lead to a reduction in advertising expenditure. However, Unilever and Procter & Gamble clearly prefer to compete by advertising rather than in any other way. Second, a possible reason for this maintenance of advertising in a duopolistic industry is that the advertising is an essential determinant of the industry's structure. Economies of scale in advertising, but not in production, serve to raise the minimum efficient scale of production of detergents and thereby create barriers to entry.

The MMC recommended that Procter & Gamble and Unilever should be made to reduce both retail prices and selling costs, so that advertising expenditure and profitability would both fall. Without any accompanying structural change (e.g. selling off factories by Procter & Gamble and Unilever) or the positive encouragement of new entrants, it is doubtful how much this would have achieved, at least without continuous monitoring from the government. In the event, the government didn't take up the MMC's recommendations, and instead Procter & Gamble and Unilever agreed to introduce a new range of cheaper and less heavily advertised detergents. Thus, the MMC's analysis of high levels of advertising as the main problem in the detergents industry failed to lead to the adoption of any remedies that would really deal with this problem. The levels of advertising expenditure that the MMC considered excessive in the

Household Detergents report were 17 per cent of retail price for Unilever (11 per cent on advertising and 6 per cent on promotions) and 18 per cent for Procter & Gamble (10 per cent on advertising and 8.5 per cent on promotions).

This is the only MMC case in which the level of advertising expenditure has specifically been found to operate against the public interest. In *Breakfast Cereals* (1973) Kellogg's ratio of advertising and promotion to sales averaged 14 per cent between 1960 and 1965, but this was not found to be excessive, although the MMC recognised that, by acting as a barrier to entry, this heavy advertising increased the amount of discretion that Kellogg had in setting its prices.

Thus, although the MMC has reported on a number of markets in which advertising is important (other cases include *Chlordiazepoxide and Diazepam, Contraceptive Sheaths, Cat and Dog Foods* and *Ice Cream*), *Household Detergents* remains the only case in which the level of advertising has been singled out for adverse comment.

11.4 CONCLUDING COMMENTS

The preceding discussion of the links between market structure, advertising and market performance shows that few general statements can be made with a high degree of confidence at either the theoretical or the empirical level. There is evidence of a positive correlation between concentration and advertising intensity over a certain range of concentration, but this correlation is consistent with causation running in either direction. It seems that advertising is one factor leading to increased concentration, especially in consumer goods industries, but when concentration has reached a level where mutual interdependence is recognised this will tend to increase advertising intensity. There is also evidence, disputed by some, that advertising interacting with product differentiation, increases entry barriers and, thereby, profitability. In all cases, however, the significance of these relationships is likely to vary between markets.

Chapter 12

Welfare losses and resource misallocation

12.1 INTRODUCTION

This chapter is concerned with the magnitude of the welfare losses resulting from the existence of monopoly power. Traditional welfare economics tells us that perfect competition is one way of achieving an efficient allocation of resources, but the preceding chapters have shown us how far away a modern industrialised economy is from even approximating to the perfectly competitive paradigm. Instead of a large number of firms in each market, each taking price as given and earning only normal profits, we have found many markets dominated by a small number of large firms with some degree of market power. The existence of market power means both that firms have some measure of control over the price that they set and also that firms will compete by methods unheard of in a perfectly competitive model: by product differentiation, by advertising, by innovation, for instance.

Clearly, the real world is far from perfectly competitive, but in order to decide what, if anything, should be done about this we need some measure of the seriousness of the problem. How bad is the misallocation of resources arising from market power? The view that there is some misallocation, which needs correcting, underlies all the various forms of intervention in industry, particularly competition policy, which are the subject of the next three chapters.

In the next section we look at the traditional analysis of welfare losses from monopoly, which is the static analysis of resource misallocation. Section 12.3 examines the problems associated with this approach. In subsequent sections we broaden the concept of monopoly losses. Thus in section 12.4 we look at Leibenstein's suggestion that monopoly will give rise to technical costs as well as allocative costs, while the possibility that monopoly may bring about cost savings, so that a welfare trade-off is involved, is considered in section 12.5. Section 12.6 considers the argument that the process of competing for a monopoly absorbs resources which should be counted as part of the welfare loss of monopoly.

12.2 THE DEADWEIGHT LOSS FROM MONOPOLY

It is beyond the scope of this book to show exactly how and why the institution of perfect competition in all markets will lead to an optimal allocation of resources, in the Paretian sense that no reallocation is possible that will make one consumer better off without at the same time making someone else worse off. The general condition for a Pareto optimum that the marginal rate of substitution between any two goods (i.e. the ratio between their marginal utilities) should equal the marginal rate of transformation between them (i.e. the ratio of their marginal costs) is met by using the price mechanism, so that price comes to equal marginal cost for all commodities.

Under monopoly, on the other hand, this equation between price and marginal cost ceases to hold, and price is raised above marginal cost in the monopolised sector. Thus, the conditions for an efficient allocation of resources are violated, but how can we measure the consequent loss of welfare?

Consider Figure 12.1, which shows demand and cost conditions in an industry under the simplifying assumption of constant costs; that is, average cost (AC) equals marginal cost (MC). If the industry were perfectly competitive, output would expand to the point at which price equals marginal cost; that is, output OQ_c would be sold at price OP_c. If the same industry, with no change in demand or costs, were to be monopolised, there would be a fall in output to OQ_m, at which output marginal cost and marginal revenue (MR) are equated, and this output would be sold at price OP_m, in excess of marginal cost.

One consequence of the monopolisation of this industry is that consumers are worse off; they suffer a reduction in consumer surplus (i.e. the excess of how

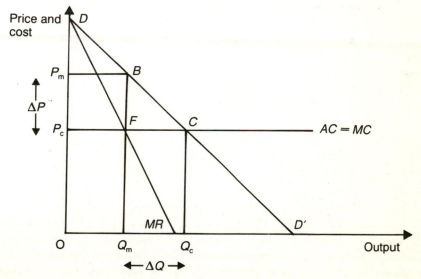

Figure 12.1 Monopoly welfare loss with identical demand and cost conditions

much they would be prepared to pay for a certain quantity of the good over how much they have to pay) from triangle DP_cC to triangle DP_mB. But not all of this reduction in consumer surplus represents a loss in welfare, since some of it is transferred to the producer in the shape of producer surplus. Producer surplus is any excess of receipts over the amount needed to induce the producer to produce this commodity, as measured by the marginal cost curve. At price OP_c and output OQ_c there is no producer surplus, whereas after monopolisation, at price OP_m and output OQ_m, the monopolist earns a surplus (monopoly profits) of P_mBFP_c. Therefore, only the remaining triangle BCF represents a net loss in welfare, and this is the area referred to as the deadweight loss.

The size of this deadweight loss in welfare is given by

$$\tfrac{1}{2}(Q_c - Q_m)(P_m - P_c) = \tfrac{1}{2}\Delta Q \Delta P$$

where Q_c and P_c are respectively the quantity and price under perfect competition, Q_m and P_m the quantity and price under monopoly, and ΔQ and ΔP the quantity and price changes between perfect competition and monopoly. This can be expressed in terms of the elasticity of demand, ε, at (P_m, Q_m) as follows:

$$\text{Welfare loss} = \tfrac{1}{2}\Delta Q \Delta P$$

$$\varepsilon = \frac{\Delta Q}{Q_m} \cdot \frac{P_m}{\Delta P}$$

$$\Delta Q = \varepsilon Q_m \cdot \frac{\Delta P}{P_m}$$

$$\therefore \text{Welfare loss} = \tfrac{1}{2}\varepsilon Q_m \cdot \frac{\Delta P}{P_m} \Delta P$$

$$= \tfrac{1}{2}\varepsilon Q_m P_m \cdot \frac{\Delta P}{P_m} \cdot \frac{\Delta P}{P_m}$$

$$= \tfrac{1}{2}\varepsilon P_m Q_m \left[\frac{\Delta P}{P_m}\right]^2$$

where $\Delta P/P_m$ is the proportionate excess of price under monopoly over price under competition, and $P_m Q_m$ is the monopolist's revenue.

This formula has been used to work out the magnitude of the welfare losses resulting from monopoly either in money terms or as a percentage of gross national product (GNP) by dividing the above expression by the money value of the economy's total output. However, the application of this formula involves estimating, first, the elasticity of demand and, second, $\Delta P/P_m$ (i.e. the price mark-up resulting from monopolisation). There has been considerable disagreement about how these elements should be calculated and consequent disagreement about how quantitatively significant the losses from monopoly are.

The first estimate of the welfare loss from monopoly was that of Harberger (1954), who calculated that the cost of monopoly distortions in the manufacturing sector of the economy was very low – only about 0.1 per cent of GNP. This has been criticised as an underestimate on a number of grounds. Harberger assumed that the elasticity of demand was equal to 1, which is inconsistent with profit maximisation at the industry level (profit maximisation entails being on a section of the industry demand curve where elasticity is greater than 1). ΔP was estimated by looking at the deviation of industry profit rates from the average for all manufacturing. But the average profit rate in manufacturing is higher than that which would prevail under competition, and this measure therefore leads to an underestimate of ΔP; Harberger found a price differential of only 4 per cent. Monopoly welfare losses were calculated for the manufacturing sector, which accounted for only a quarter of GNP, and no allowance was made for the costs of monopolies outside the manufacturing sector. The manufacturing industries were broadly defined, and so the study failed to capture the full effect of the high monopoly returns in more narrowly defined lines of activity. A further downward bias was imparted by assuming that all firms sell to final consumers. However, when there are vertical links, as when one firm supplies inputs to another, and assuming similar price–cost margins at all stages in the production chain, monopoly distortion at one stage in the vertical chain increases the distortion at the next stage. Lastly, part of the monopoly effect is likely to be found in the form of inflated costs rather than high profit margins – a point that is taken up in more detail in section 12.3.

Subsequent studies have used different methods to estimate elasticities and the price differential ΔP. Some of these, e.g. Schwartzman (1960), Scherer (1970) and Worcester (1973), have confirmed Harberger's finding of a low cost attributable to monopoly. However, Kamerschen (1966), using elasticities of demand consistent with monopoly pricing behaviour at the industry level, found welfare losses as high as 6 per cent of GNP. More recently, Cowling and Mueller (1978) emphasised that, for a firm with market power, the profit-maximising increase of price over competitive price, $(P_m - MC)/P_m$, will be given by the reciprocal of the elasticity of demand facing the firm (see Chapter 7). Thus a mark-up of 25 per cent implies an elasticity of demand equal to 4. In other words, the sort of monopoly mark- up that one would expect to find implies, for profit-maximising firms, a much higher elasticity than that assumed in the Harberger study.

The expression $(P_m - MC)/P_m = 1/\varepsilon$ will be recognised as the Lerner index of monopoly power which was discussed in Chapter 11. It simplifies the expression for welfare loss as follows:

$$\text{Welfare loss} = \tfrac{1}{2}\varepsilon P_m Q_m \cdot \left[\frac{\Delta P}{P_m} \right]^2$$

becomes: Welfare loss $= \frac{1}{2}\varepsilon P_m Q_m \cdot \dfrac{\Delta P}{P_m} \cdot \dfrac{1}{\varepsilon}$

$$= \frac{1}{2} P_m Q_m \cdot \dfrac{\Delta P}{P_m}$$

$$= \frac{1}{2} Q_m \Delta P$$

which is equal to half of the monopoly profits of the firm. Using data on the profits of large firms in the UK and USA, Cowling and Mueller went on to derive high estimates of welfare losses – about 4 per cent in the USA and 10 per cent in the UK of the total output of the manufacturing sector.

However, there are reasons to question the method of imputing price elasticities from price–cost margins. First, where there is more than one seller, oligopolistic collusion is likely to fall short of achieving joint profit maximisation, for reasons that have been detailed in Chapter 7. Second, even with singlefirm dominance or perfectly coordinated oligopolistic behaviour, price may be set below the short-run profit-maximising level. This may be explained by the longrun effects of pricing policy on new entry. Indeed entry-deterring pricing models are consistent with prices being set in the range of inelastic demand (see Chapter 10). The same can be said of non-profit-maximising behaviour.

The general method of calculating the costs of monopoly power which has been described above does, however, have the advantage that it indicates whereabouts in the economy most of the welfare losses come from. It shows that the welfare loss is a function both of the size of the mark-up and the size of the monopolist's market. If the mark-up is high but the market is small, the welfare loss will be small. Even if the total loss is fairly small it may nevertheless be significant in a number of industries which are both large and highly monopolised. Siegfried and Tiemann (1974) found that 67 per cent of total loss in the USA was concentrated in only five sectors: plastic materials and synthetics, drugs, petroleum-refining and extraction, office and computing machinery, and motor vehicles. In fact, 44 per cent (or nearly one half) of the total welfare loss was accounted for by motor vehicles alone. Those studies which have used data at the individual firm level (e.g. those of Worcester, and Cowling and Mueller) can go further than this and point out which firms contribute most to the overall welfare loss. Such studies have an obvious use for antitrust policy in indicating where limited policy resources could do most good.

12.3 PROBLEMS IN ESTIMATING MONOPOLY WELFARE LOSSES

Apart from the arguments already mentioned about how elasticity of demand and the price differential resulting from monopoly should be measured to calculate welfare losses, the whole method pioneered by Harberger has been subject to criticism at a more profound level, indicating that the whole idea may be misconceived.

Partial equilibrium vs. general equilibrium

The first such criticism that we deal with is that of Bergson (1973), who suggested that the welfare costs of monopoly should be measured using a general equilibrium model rather than the partial equilibrium approach used by Harberger. Bergson argued that the derivation of total costs of monopoly by summing the deadweight welfare-loss triangles in different sectors is justified only if the income elasticity of demand for each monopolised product is zero and if the cross-elasticities of demand between monopolised products are also zero. Where such cross-elasticities are not equal to zero, Harberger's method may be completely misleading. Suppose that we have two products that are close substitutes for one another, but for no other good, and that one of them is produced under monopolistic conditions, so that its price exceeds marginal cost. Now, according to Harberger's calculations total welfare loss would rise if the second product were also to be monopolised, but in fact, according to second-best optimising considerations, the allocation of resources in this sector would actually improve if the two goods showed the same excess of price above marginal cost.

The theoretical force of Bergson's argument that a general equilibrium approach should be used to calculate welfare losses from monopoly is undeniable, but it is very difficult to put his argument into empirical practice, owing to the difficulty of allowing for the necessary interrelationships between sectors. Bergson himself presented hypothetical rather than empirical results, based on the use of a constant elasticity of substitution indifference map, which assumes that the elasticity of substitution is the same between each pair of goods in the economy. Bergson got relatively high estimates of the cost of monopoly – up to 8 per cent of national income, depending on the value of the price–cost ratio assumed in the monopolistic industries. But Bergson's own article shows that, in order to derive an estimate of the welfare costs of monopoly using a general equilibrium framework, assumptions will have to be made that are just as restrictive as the assumption that cross-elasticities of demand between monopolised products are equal to zero, which is implicitly made in the partial equilibrium approach.

Consumer surplus and welfare changes

A second argument against Harberger's method of calculating the deadweight loss from monopoly is that it relies on measuring the loss of consumer surplus resulting from an increase in price and reduction in output, but the use of consumer surplus to measure changes in welfare is itself problematic. The main problem here is whether or not the marginal utility of money can be treated as constant for all the individuals affected and at all income levels. If not, changes in consumer surplus are not strictly proportional to changes in welfare and should be multiplied by the marginal utility of money in order to obtain correct measures of welfare or utility.

The same problem concerning the constancy of the marginal utility of money affects the treatment of the transfer of surplus that takes place in Figure 12.1. Of the total reduction in consumer surplus, one part is the deadweight loss, and the remaining part is transferred to the producer in the shape of monopoly profit. Should this transfer be treated as having no effect on welfare? This is a distributional question. If the monopolisation results in a redistribution away from consumers to a richer monopolist, we may well regard this as an additional source of welfare loss. If the monopolist is richer, he will have a lower marginal utility of money than the consumers (i.e. gain of £1 gives him a smaller increase in utility than the loss in utility from consumers losing £1). In this case, multiplying the transferred surplus (area P_mBFP_c in Figure 12.1) by the marginal utility of income of consumer and producer respectively would reveal that in fact the consumers lose more utility than the producer gains, so that the redistribution causes a loss in welfare which should be added to the deadweight welfare loss.

Monopoly behaviour

A third set of problems relates to the behaviour of the monopolist. The analysis so far assumes a single-product monopolist charging a single price for a product which has no close substitutes. Furthermore, the range and quality of products is the same as that which would exist under perfectly competitive conditions. To the extent that these assumptions are violated in practice, the above formulae can underestimate or overestimate the welfare costs of monopoly.

For instance, a monopolist can adopt more complex pricing techniques such as multi-part tariffs, price discrimination and a whole range of discount schemes. In the case of perfect price discrimination, monopoly output equals competitive output and there is no deadweight loss, although there are of course distributional implications (see Chapter 6). This rather unlikely case does serve to emphasise the point, however, that output is a function of the pricing policy adopted by the monopolist, and complex pricing policies may result in an output closer to the competitive level and thus in lower welfare losses. On the other hand of course, it is also possible (see Chapters 6 and 16) that the pricing tactics adopted by the monopolist serve to increase market power by excluding entrants or inducing discipline amongst small competitors.

The issue of product numbers and product quality is perhaps even more problematic. The calculation of monopoly welfare losses is based on the existing range of products in the economy. One familiar proposition is that monopoly may lead to excessive product proliferation and wasteful advertising (see Chapter 8). This hypothesis and the suggestions made for capturing this element of welfare loss are examined further in section 12.4. There is another aspect of product range, however, which has not generally figured in the analysis of welfare losses. It most certainly cannot be included in the statistical analysis. This is the possibility that powerful monopolies may have succeeded in suppressing or eliminating competition from rival industries. It has been argued, for instance, that the monopoly behaviour of the powerful automobile and tyre manufacturers contributed to the decline of public transport in parts of the USA. To the extent that monopoly behaviour has resulted in the suppression or elimination of substitute products, there is an important social loss which is not captured by conventional estimating methods.

Turning to product quality, it has been argued that conventional methods of measurement will overestimate monopoly welfare losses. The reasoning is that the monopolist may offer a better-quality product and there will be circumstances where some market power will be needed to protect that quality. These circumstances are where quality depends on the level of service supplied by retailers and where the appropriate level of service is only ensured by vertical restraints (see Chapters 3 and 15).

Natural monopolies

In some cases, including the natural monopolies, marginal cost pricing would be loss making, and the usual comparison between monopoly and competition then makes little sense. The implication for the size of the welfare loss associated with this category of monopolies is, however, unclear. On the one hand, since marginal cost pricing is not sustainable, it is an inappropriate base from which to measure price distortions. To that extent the formulae given earlier overestimate the welfare loss. Ideally, of course, government regulation of these industries should eliminate most if not all of the welfare loss. However, as will be seen in the next chapter, regulation may itself have adverse effects, including adverse effects on allocative efficiency.

The duration of welfare losses

The welfare loss of monopoly power would be of little concern if it was short-lived. In the extreme case of perfectly contestable markets (see Chapter 10), there can be no deadweight welfare loss because incumbents have to charge competitive prices and can earn only a competitive return. The other extreme would be the case of a monopolist which can protect its position indefinitely. Clearly the rate at which monopoly positions decay (see Chapter 6) is of crucial importance.

Schmalensee (1982) has shown, assuming a market for a homogeneous product, that the effect of the rate of decay of monopoly power on the deadweight welfare loss is as follows:

$$\text{Welfare loss} = (1/r) \, [r(DW_S) + \gamma(DW_L)] \, (r + \gamma)^{-1}$$

where:

r = rate of discount used to capitalise future welfare losses

DW_S and DW_L = short- and long-run deadweight welfare losses, respectively

γ = the annual fractional reduction in the gap between DW_S and DW_L; i.e. the rate of decay of market power.

For the case of perfect contestability, $\gamma = \infty$ and $DW_L = 0$, so welfare loss is zero. Where, on the other hand, market power is preserved indefinitely, $\gamma = 0$ and $DW_S = DW_L$. Consequently welfare loss equals the present discounted value of the short-run welfare loss, i.e. $1/r(DW)$.

Empirical evidence finds no support for either extreme. Market power does tend to decay, but the rate of decay varies substantially and in some cases may be at a snail's pace.

So far we have concentrated on the possible allocative losses associated with monopoly power. In the next two sections we broaden the concept of welfare losses of monopoly and look at arguments that suggest that the static allocative loss from monopoly is only one element, and not necessarily the most important element, of the total costs involved.

12.4 X-INEFFICIENCY

Measurement of the welfare costs of monopoly by the triangular deadweight loss area BCF of Figure 12.1 rests on the assumption that the costs of the industry will be the same under monopoly as under perfect competition. In fact, there is no reason why this should be so, and plausible arguments can be put forward to suggest either that costs will be higher under monopoly or that they will be lower.

Costs will be lower if the monopolisation of an industry enables the monopolist to achieve economies of scale by expanding output and moving along a downward-sloping long-run average-cost curve. The idea that this will at least sometimes be the case lies behind the cost–benefit case-by-case approach to competition policy adopted by the UK in particular, in which the disadvantages of market power are traded off against any benefits of lower-cost production in order to decide whether a particular merger or monopoly operates against the public interest. This welfare trade-off has already been examined in Chapter 4; we return to it later in this section.

Here, we are concerned initially with the opposite argument, namely, that costs of production may be higher under conditions of monopoly than under perfect competition. This argument is associated with the name of Leibenstein (1966), who suggested that the allocative inefficiency of monopoly already discussed is likely to be unimportant compared with the internal inefficiency possible under imperfect competition; he coined the phrase 'X-inefficiency' to describe this technical inefficiency of monopoly.

Why should monopolies be technically inefficient and face higher costs of production than competitive firms? A firm with market power will be able to earn excess profits as long as it is protected from competition by barriers to entry and is thus under little pressure to behave efficiently and minimise costs. In this case the firm may use its resources inefficiently and not produce the maximum possible output from given resources, and therefore its cost curves will rise above the minimum cost of producing a given level of output.

If monopolies are technically as well as allocatively inefficient, this should be taken into account in measuring the welfare cost of monopoly, and the argument of Figure 12.1 should be amended. In Figure 12.2, as in Figure 12.1, we consider an industry that is initially perfectly competitive, producing output OQ_c sold at price OP_c, and then becomes monopolised. Output falls to OQ_m, sold at OP_m, and there is a consequent reduction in consumer surplus from area DP_cC to area DP_mB.

The total loss in consumer surplus is thus P_mBCP_c, of which BFC is the deadweight loss due to resource misallocation, and AC_mEFP_c is the technical cost of the monopoly owing to the fact that the cost of producing output OQ_m is higher under monopoly than under competition conditions. The remaining loss of consumer surplus, P_mBEAC_m, is offset by an equal increase in producer surplus.

This argument, then, suggests that a measure of the total social cost of monopoly must include the technical cost due to the relatively inefficient use of factors of production under monopoly, as well as the allocative cost due to the reduction of output below the competitive level, so that previous studies have led to a serious underestimate of the total cost of monopoly. Comanor and Leibenstein (1969) argued that the technical cost may well be the largest component of the total welfare loss. They argued that the degree of allocative inefficiency will be underestimated if monopolistic price–cost margins are used to measure $\Delta P/P_m$ (i.e. the price differential between monopoly and perfect competition) on the assumption that price would equal cost under competitive conditions. If in fact costs would be lower under perfect competition, the true price differential would be greater by the extent of this cost differential. The size of the cost differential between monopoly and perfect competition then becomes

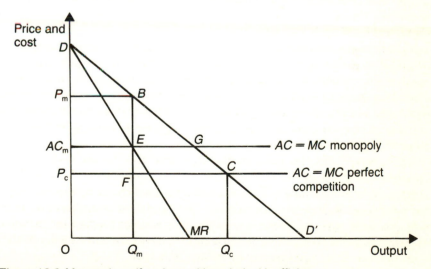

Figure 12.2 Monopoly welfare loss with technical inefficiency

a vital element in calculating the total cost of monopoly, which increases more than proportionately with the cost differential. Using the hypothetical examples of price elasticity of demand equal to 2, a cost differential of 18 per cent and a price–cost margin of 6 per cent in the monopolised sector, Comanor and Leibenstein calculated that the welfare loss as traditionally measured (i.e. area BGE of Figure 12.2) is 0.18 per cent of net national product (NNP), but the full allocative loss (area BCF) amounts to nearly 3 per cent, to which should be added the pure X-inefficiency loss (area AC_mEFP_c) of 9 per cent of NNP, thus arriving at a total cost of monopoly of 12 per cent of NNP.

The argument of this section so far can be summarised as saying that, if costs of production are higher under monopoly than under perfect competition, the welfare costs of monopoly are far larger than has previously been suggested. This is clearly an important point and one that can be argued at both the theoretical and the empirical levels.

At the empirical level there is little systematic evidence on the importance of X-inefficiency and the extent to which this elevates costs above the competitive level. However, there are plenty of examples which suggest that it is important. In the UK, for example, the steel industry was transformed when it moved from a highly protected market, characteristic of the 1950s and 1960s, to the more competitive environment of the 1970s and 1980s. In the early 1970s, steel production in the UK was renowned for its overmanning and general inefficiency. By the end of the 1980s the British Steel Corporation had become one of the most efficient bulk steel producers in the European Communities. The same can be said of US steel production, which also made significant improvements in efficiency and profitability following exposure to increased competition from abroad.

But can X-inefficiency be considered as representing a pure waste of resources? This was certainly the view of Comanor and Leibenstein. The output OQ_m in Figure 12.2 is produced using more than the minimum necessary amount of inputs, and hence output could be increased without any reallocation of resources to this sector. This kind of waste is more likely to occur under monopolistic conditions, because an X-inefficient monopolist will not be eliminated from the market as an X-inefficient competitive firm would be. All that happens is that the producer surplus (i.e. monopoly profit) is reduced by the amount of the X-inefficiency cost. This suggests a relationship between X-inefficiency and non-profit-maximising behaviour on the part of the firm, which in turn calls into question the idea that X-inefficiency represents a complete loss of welfare.

Suppose that costs are above the minimum level not simply because resources are being used inefficiently but because the firm's decision-makers are maximising something that does not require cost minimisation (i.e. not profits, sales, or growth) and may indeed specifically require that costs are not minimised. Such a theory has been put forward by Williamson (1963), who proposed that managers maximise their own utility and that they derive utility from employing a large staff, because this not only tends to increase their own salary (in a hier-archical pay structure) but also gives them security, status and prestige. In this case the firm will employ more people than a profit-maximising firm would and will produce any level of output at a higher cost, but it is no longer the case that lowering costs to the competitive level would represent a pure gain in welfare, since the managers at least would be made worse off by such a move.

This is not the only case in which the X-inefficiency area of Figure 12.2 in fact represents a benefit to someone, so that the argument for eliminating it is less clear. Other examples include the case in which costs are raised because some of the monopoly profit is transferred to the firm's workers, who get higher wages than they otherwise would. Alternatively, the owner-manager of a firm may be prepared to sacrifice some profits in order to enjoy more leisure, and thus his costs may not be minimised. Just as it may be argued that some element of monopoly power is necessary for a firm to protect product quality, so it may also be argued that one benefit of monopoly power is an enhancement in the quality of life of those employed by the monopolist.

The concept of X-inefficiency may also have some significance in relation to allocative efficiency. The theoretical argument for supposing that X-inefficiency will be associated with monopoly rather than with competition is that, under monopolistic conditions, the firm will be subject to less market pressure to be efficient in production and minimise costs. This means that managers have more discretion to pursue goals other than profit maximisation: for example, maxi-misation of discretionary expenditures, sales or growth. The implications of these managerial models for the theory of the firm are discussed in Chapter 2, where it has been pointed out that sales- or growth-maximising firms will choose to produce a higher level of output than a profit-maximising firm. Therefore, if monopolistic firms are, say, sales maximisers, their output will not fall by as much as is suggested in Figures 12.1 and 12.2, and the allocative loss due to monopoly has been overestimated.

12.5 COST SAVINGS AND WELFARE TRADE-OFFS

It is possible to argue, in contradiction to Leibenstein's theory, that costs of production will actually be lower for a monopolist than they would be under competitive conditions. There are two possible reasons. First, although industry output falls on monopolisation, the monopolist will be producing a level of output higher than that previously produced by each individual competitive firm. Thus, to the extent that there are economies of scale, the monopolist will be able to produce at lower cost, and instead of technical inefficiency there will be cost savings and efficiency gains due to monopolisation. This is the case of the market power–efficiency trade-off applied to mergers in Chapter 4.

Second, there is the argument concerning the relative innovative efficiency of monopoly and competition. If monopoly is dynamically superior to competition, this can lead to costs being lower under monopoly. The arguments and evidence on this issue have been reviewed in Chapter 9, where it has been shown that some element of monopoly power is necessary to induce firms to undertake research and development (R&D) but that monopolists or dominant firms have little incentive to innovate on their own account, although they will follow innovations of other firms extremely rapidly. Thus there is no conclusive argument that monopolists will be more dynamically efficient than competitive firms. The relative lack of incentive to innovate experienced by monopolists is related to their lack of incentive to produce a wide variety of brands or products. In Chapter 8 it has been suggested that monopoly may lead to a sub-optimal level of product differentiation, and to the extent that this is true the normal methods of calculating welfare loss will lead to an underestimate, since there is no way of calculating loss due to the non-availability of products that consumers would have welcomed.

In the absence of completely convincing theoretical or empirical arguments that costs of production will be higher under monopoly than under perfect competition, it seems best simply to say that, unless costs are actually the same, there will be considerations of technical efficiency to be taken into account when assessing the desirability of a certain market structure, as well as considerations of allocative efficiency. If costs are higher under monopoly, these technical factors will add to the allocative loss; if costs are lower, technical efficiency will reduce the allocative loss and may indeed result in a net gain in welfare under monopoly. If costs are sufficiently lower for the monopoly, then output will increase, and there will be an unambiguous gain in welfare.

It is possible to derive separate expressions for the allocative loss resulting from monopoly and for the technical effect and hence to derive conditions for the technical gain to outweigh the allocative loss, so that monopoly represents a gain in welfare. For convenience of exposition we use Figure 12.3, in which costs of monopoly production are lower than costs of competitive production. (This is similar to Figure 4.2, in which the same general argument is applied to the particular problem of assessing mergers.)

In Figure 12.3 the monopolisation of the industry results in a fall in consumer surplus from area DCP_c to area DBP_m. Of this, triangle BCE represents the deadweight loss, and the remaining area P_mBEP_c is transferred to the monopolist as producer surplus (i.e. profits). However, in this case costs of production are *lower* under monopoly, and this results in cost savings to the amount of area P_cEFAC_m, which must be weighed against the deadweight loss (BCE).

As above, the area of deadweight loss is given by

$$\tfrac{1}{2}(Q_c - Q_m)(P_m - P_c) = \tfrac{1}{2}\varepsilon P_m Q_m \left[\frac{\Delta P}{P_m}\right]^2$$

where $\Delta P/P_m$ is the proportionate excess of price under monopoly over price under competition. The value of cost savings is given by $Q_m \Delta C$, where ΔC is the cost differential between monopoly and competition. The expression for the total welfare loss attributable to monopoly is therefore

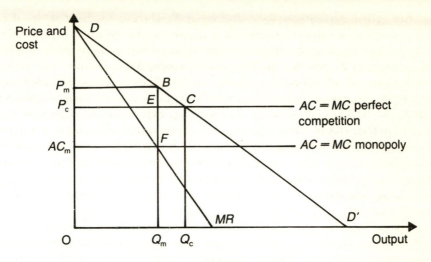

Figure 12.3 Welfare changes with economies of scale

$$\text{Total welfare loss} = \tfrac{1}{2}\varepsilon P_m Q_m \left[\frac{\Delta P}{P_m}\right]^2 - Q_m \Delta C.$$

For monopoly to result in an overall gain in welfare, this expression must be negative; that is,

$$Q_m \Delta C > \tfrac{1}{2}\varepsilon P_m Q_m \left[\frac{\Delta P}{P_m}\right]^2$$

$$\frac{\Delta C}{P_m} > \tfrac{1}{2}\varepsilon \left[\frac{\Delta P}{P_m}\right]^2$$

This expression shows that, the greater the price elasticity of demand (ε), the larger the percentage cost saving from monopoly ($\Delta C / P_m$) needed to offset the welfare losses of a given price increase resulting from the monopoly. Suppose that prices rise by 15 per cent. If the elasticity of demand is high (e.g. 6), costs must fall by more than 6.75 per cent for welfare to be improved. If the elasticity of demand is only 2, however, the monopolisation would result in a net gain in welfare if costs fell by as much as 2.25 per cent. These hypothetical calculations show, moreover, that, even with a high elasticity of demand, only moderate cost savings are required to offset relatively large increases in price.

12.6 THE SOCIAL COSTS OF MONOPOLISATION

In this section we consider another argument for supposing that the conventional welfare loss calculations discussed in section 12.2 result in a serious underestimate of the costs of monopoly. This argument is due to Posner (1975), who suggested that the existence of an opportunity to earn monopoly profits will attract resources into competing for these profits and that the opportunity cost of these resources should be counted as a cost of monopoly.

The effect of this kind of competitive activity is to transform the whole of monopoly profits into social costs, since firms will incur costs in order to obtain a monopoly position until the costs incurred equal the expected return from the position (i.e. the profits). Thus there are no intra-marginal monopolies that have an excess of profits over costs. There are a variety of different ways in which resources may be consumed in the competition for a monopoly: forming a cartel, registering a patent, lobbying for the imposition of tariffs or import quotas, bribing government officials, and various forms of non-price strategic behaviour. The last includes wasteful advertising and sales promotion expenditure – i.e. expenditure by competing oligopolists which is mutually offsetting. Firms may also maintain excess capacity as a weapon in non-price rivalry with existing competitors and as a deterrent to new entry.

Thus, Posner's argument suggests that the whole value of monopolists' profits represents a social cost of monopoly, so that the total social cost of monopoly should be measured as shown in Figure 12.4. This diagram assumes, for the sake of simplicity, that costs of production are the same under monopoly and perfect competition. The deadweight welfare loss is given by triangle BCF, but the area P_mBFP_c represents social costs rather than monopoly profits. This assumes, first, that the supply of all inputs to the monopolisation process is perfectly elastic and, second, that the costs incurred in obtaining the monopoly have no social benefits.

In this case total social cost (TSC) is given by

$$TSC = BCF + P_m BFP_c$$

$$= \tfrac{1}{2}\Delta P\Delta Q + \Delta P Q_m$$

$$= \tfrac{1}{2}\Delta P\Delta Q + \Delta P(Q_c - \Delta Q).$$

This expression can be used to show the relative size of the deadweight and social cost components:

$$\frac{\text{Deadweight loss}}{\text{Social costs}} = \frac{\tfrac{1}{2}\,\Delta P\Delta Q}{\Delta P(Q_c - \Delta Q)}$$

$$= \frac{\Delta Q}{2(Q_c - \Delta Q)}.$$

If μ denotes the elasticity of demand at (P_c, Q_c),

$$\mu = \frac{\Delta Q}{\Delta P} \cdot \frac{P_c}{Q_c}$$

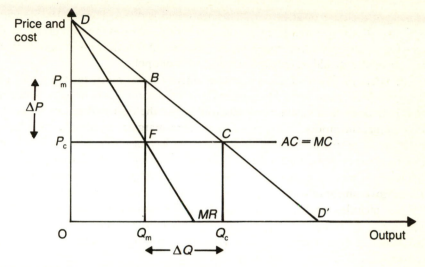

Figure 12.4 The social costs of monopoly

$$Q_c = \frac{1}{\mu} \cdot \Delta Q \cdot \frac{P_c}{\Delta P}$$

$$\therefore \frac{\text{Deadweight loss}}{\text{Social costs}} = \frac{\Delta Q}{2 \left[\dfrac{1}{\mu} \cdot \Delta Q \cdot \dfrac{P_c}{\Delta P} - \Delta Q \right]}$$

$$= \frac{\dfrac{\Delta P}{P_c}}{2 \left[\dfrac{1}{\mu} - \dfrac{\Delta P}{P_c} \right]}.$$

This shows that the deadweight loss is smaller in relation to total social cost the lower is the elasticity of demand at price P_c and the smaller is $\Delta P / P_c$ (i.e. the proportionate price increase over the competitive level).

The total social cost of monopoly, as before, is given by

$$TSC = \tfrac{1}{2}\Delta P \Delta Q + \Delta P Q_m$$

$$= \tfrac{1}{2}\Delta P \Delta Q + \Delta P (Q_c - \Delta Q)$$

$$= \Delta P \left[\frac{\Delta Q}{2} + Q_c - \Delta Q \right]$$

$$= \Delta P \left[Q_c - \frac{\Delta Q}{2} \right]$$

$$= \frac{\Delta P}{P_c} \left[P_c Q_c - P_c \cdot \frac{\Delta Q}{2} \right].$$

But $P_c Q_c$ equals total revenue at competitive price (R_c). Therefore,

$$TSC = \frac{\Delta P}{P_c} R_c - \frac{\Delta P}{P_c} \cdot P_c \cdot \frac{\Delta Q}{2}$$

$$= \frac{\Delta P}{P_c} R_c - \frac{\Delta P \Delta Q}{2}$$

$$= \frac{\Delta P}{P_c} R_c - \tfrac{1}{2}\mu P_c Q_c \left[\frac{\Delta P}{P_c} \right]^2$$

$$= \frac{\Delta P}{P_c} R_c - \tfrac{1}{2}\mu R_c \left[\frac{\Delta P}{P_c} \right]^2$$

$$= R_c \left[\frac{\Delta P}{P_c} - \tfrac{1}{2}\mu \left[\frac{\Delta P}{P_c} \right]^2 \right]$$

and this shows that, as would be expected, the total social cost of a monopoly increases as the size of the industry's competitive revenue increases, as the price differential under monopoly increases, and as the elasticity of demand increases.

Posner's own empirical estimate of the total social cost of monopoly was confined to the single example of air travel. Assuming an elasticity of demand of 2.5 at the monopoly price and a 66 per cent price increase above the competitive level, he calculated the total social cost to be 20 per cent of monopoly revenue. This result draws attention to another point made by Posner, namely, that previous studies of the welfare costs of monopoly have concentrated on the private manufacturing sector, but in fact a good many of the monopoly positions in the economy are established and protected by government regulation. Government controls of one kind or another operate in all kinds of markets, from the market for doctors' services to that for broadcasting or providing rail transport. The controls are initially established for good reasons (e.g. to protect the consumer, to guarantee the safety of the product), but they also have the effect of limiting entry. Controls and regulations may therefore keep prices above the competitive level and thus have social costs just as much as private monopolies. In fact, Posner's own calculations suggest that the social costs arising from government regulation of industry may be greater than those in the manufacturing sector.

Cowling and Mueller (1978) presented a set of alternative estimates of the social cost of monopoly power using different definitions and assumptions. Their highest estimate includes both advertising expenditures and after-tax profits as elements of social cost, as suggested by Posner's argument. On this definition estimated welfare losses amounted to 13 per cent of the gross corporate product of the 734 US firms included in the analysis. Of the 40 firms with the largest losses, 6 were subject to government regulation (airlines and telephone companies), and their advertising expenditure accounted for most of the welfare loss.

Cowling and Mueller applied the same methodology to a sample of UK firms and found that the welfare loss due to the top 103 firms amounted to 7 per cent of their product. The main reason why this figure is lower than that for the USA is the lower level of advertising expenditure in the UK. Cowling and Mueller's estimates of the social costs of monopoly power are among the highest quoted in this chapter, but they themselves mentioned the attempt by J. Phillips (1966) to estimate the economic surplus of the USA, in which he calculated that over 50 per cent of GNP was on types of expenditure that depended on the existence of monopoly capitalism.

Let us look more closely at this argument that competition for monopoly profits will transfer the whole of that profit into social cost. This argument rests on a profound belief in the market mechanism's ability and willingness to respond to incentives in the shape of excess profits. Any such surplus anywhere in the economy will attract resources into the surplus-earning sector, until the total value of the surplus has been consumed in costs.

The idea that monopoly profits form part of the social costs of monopoly is sufficiently novel to raise all sorts of questions in the reader's mind. Here, we deal first with the problem about whether monopoly profits are a satisfactory measure of the resources consumed in the competition for monopoly power, and then we return to the more basic question of whether such competition should really be described as social cost.

Posner's argument is that resources will be attracted into competing for monopoly profits until the cost of the resources equals the expected gain from attaining the monopoly position, so that the cost of the resources can be fairly accurately measured by total monopoly profits. What about a monopolist who is protected from competition by barriers to entry? In this case the resources will be used in trying to break down or get around the barriers: for example, by lobbying for a change in the law or by merging to form a larger company. Posner argued that there are no intra-marginal monopolies for which profits exceed the costs incurred in competing for profits.

There are a number of reasons for suggesting that monopoly profits will underestimate the resource cost of monopolies. First, some of the expenditures incurred by firms in competing for monopoly positions (e.g. hiring lawyers, wining and dining politicians) will inflate the firm's costs, and this rise in costs is part of the resource cost of monopoly. Inevitably, some of this expenditure and raised costs will be incurred by firms that are unsuccessful in the competition and thus may escape detection. The decision about how many resources to invest in competing for a monopoly position must be taken under conditions of uncertainty, so each firm will be willing to incur costs equal to its *expected* gain from the monopoly, which is given by monopoly profit multiplied by the probability of obtaining the monopoly.

Second, the total value of monopoly profits also understates the social cost of monopoly by omitting the value of resources used up by competition policy and regulatory agencies in controlling monopolies. A low level of profit in a certain industry may indicate not a low level of social cost, but that some public agency has expended a lot of resources in monitoring the firm's performance.

There are, on the other hand, arguments that suggest that monopoly profits overestimate the resources used in competing for monopoly positions. First, Posner's idea was to treat obtaining a monopoly as a competitive activity into which there was free entry – so that in equilibrium monopoly profits are reduced to zero. This situation, however, is unlikely to be reached, and for the usual reasons. Dominant firms are likely to find that they are in a favourable position to retain their dominance without squandering all their profits. The favourable conditions include absolute cost and product differentiation advantages which give dominant firms operating advantages over actual and potential rivals. In addition, by colluding, firms may be able to secure a joint monopoly position with a much lower total expenditure of resources than if each firm competed separately.

Second, and more importantly, Posner assumed that the costs incurred in competing for a monopoly position have no socially valuable effects at all. This is an extreme assumption and will inevitably lead to an overestimate of the social costs of monopoly. Firms may compete for a monopoly in various ways, including advertising, product differentiation, maintaining spare capacity and innovation. Although any of these activities can be wasteful if carried to excess, it is difficult to deny that there is also benefit, often appreciable, to the customer. Thus consumers benefit from the information content of advertising expenditure; customers benefit if suppliers have spare capacity which ensures uninterrupted supply even when there is an upsurge in demand; and even though firms may be larger and have more market power than is needed to induce a high level of R&D activity, some degree of monopoly power is needed for optimal performance.

This brings us on to the fundamental criticism of Posner's argument. This is that he treats all resources used in competing for monopoly profits as social costs, while in fact competition for profit lies at the heart of a dynamic efficient market system. If resources were not attracted into profitable areas, we should have a totally static economy with no innovation in new products or processes. The prospect of gaining market power and monopoly profit is a strong incentive to invest in R&D; an incentive which is absent in perfectly competitive markets. In addition, as noted in Chapter 10, the ability and willingness to invest may also be positively related to existing market power. This being so, dominance may, in some cases at least, persist because of superior technological performances. Monopoly profits provide an incentive to which the market economy responds, and to describe the competition for monopoly power as incurring social costs is equivalent to abusing, if not killing, the goose that lays the golden eggs.

In the context of gauging the welfare costs of monopoly, consideration of technological advance draws attention to at least two points of importance. First, in analysing monopoly it is important to ask *how* a position of dominance was achieved – to what extent can it be explained by superior technology rather than predatory behaviour or takeovers. Second, comparisons of monopoly with a competitive 'ideal' are to some extent misguided, because perfect competition provides no incentives to invest in research and development.

12.7 CONCLUDING COMMENTS

The purpose of this chapter has been to discuss the nature and quantitative significance of the welfare losses associated with monopoly power. The first estimates made of the welfare costs of the allocative effects of monopoly indicated that these are very low, so that there is not much to be gained from policies designed to correct the effects of monopolies. Subsequent work in this area has led to Harberger's original estimates being very considerably increased, both by changing the method of calculation and by extending the concept of welfare loss beyond the allocative loss originally measured. Some of these decisions, while they make monopoly losses appear much more substantial and policy intervention therefore more urgent, go too far in totting up the costs of monopoly. This applies particularly to the idea that monopoly profits measure the costs to society of resources used in competing for monopoly positions. Such competition is essential for the dynamic efficiency of the economy and cannot be said to represent purely social costs.

The difficulties of estimating the welfare losses of monopoly are enormous. Even in relatively simple models there are both theoretical and practical problems. In reality there are a large number of factors at work, often pulling in opposite directions. As a result it is not possible to do more than hazard a guess at the importance of these losses.

Few would put the losses higher than 3 or 4 per cent of GNP. The reason for this rather modest estimate is that large tracts of the economy are workably competitive, though, with respect to the UK economy, this statement can be made with greater confidence in the 1990s than it could have been in the 1950s and 1960s. This is partly because of legislation against restrictive agreements but, most important, because industry generally has become much more exposed to international competition. In addition to these changes in the market environ- ment, allowance must also be made for the fact that firms may be deterred from fully exploiting short-run monopoly positions because of the threat of entry, or product substitutions, or loss of customer goodwill.

This is not to deny, however, that monopoly welfare losses may be important.

If they do amount to 3–4 per cent of GNP, this in itself is a significant sum. But more importantly, from the perspective of policy, the welfare losses tend, as indicated earlier, to be accounted for by a small number of industries. This of course is helpful from the point of view of policy, which can (or should) be focused on those areas of the economy where intervention is most likely to have a positive impact.

Chapter 13

Natural monopoly

13.1 INTRODUCTION

The previous chapter dealt with the costs that the incidence of private monopoly may impose upon society owing to the lower levels of output and higher prices than would prevail under a competitive environment. Clearly the outcome of such an approach is that, at the static level at least, monopoly may be undesirable from the viewpoint of economic efficiency. However, there are instances where efficiency dictates that demand is met by a single producer. This is the case of *natural monopoly*. In such a situation the costs of supply exhibit characteristics such that single-firm production is always more efficient than multi-firm production. In the single-product case such a situation is caused by substantial (and often unexploited) economies of scale induced by a high fixed cost component. In a multiproduct industry it is largely caused by a combination of economies of scale and scope. In such circumstances there is clearly a public policy problem. This is because, although efficiency requires single-firm production, this may occur at the expense of allocative efficiency. The monopolist is in a powerful position to charge prices that more than cover costs of production. The natural monopoly problem therefore is one of ensuring that industry output is produced at minimum cost (private and social) and sold at prices that reflect these costs. The postwar approach in the UK until the 1980s was the exclusive public owner-ship of such activities. Apparent dissatisfaction with this solution has led to the recent programme of privatisation accompanied by regulation. In this chapter we first consider the conditions which give rise to the natural monopoly problem and the welfare issues raised. We also look at the practical policy issues raised and the 'solutions' adopted: public ownership (section 13.4), privatisation (section 13.5) and regulation (section 13.6). A major conclusion is that ownership (whether public or private) by itself is not an adequate solution to the natural monopoly problem. Just as public ownership may be criticised on internal efficiency grounds, the system of privatisation and regulation so far adopted appears vulnerable to the charge of permitting potential allocative as well as internal inefficiencies. Moreover, both approaches imply a high level of outside involve-ment in decision-making. This in turn raises questions concerning the adequacy of either approach as a solution to the natural monopoly problem and once again highlights the importance of introducing competitive pressures into the industries concerned. The feasibility of introducing competition is the subject matter of the next chapter.

13.2 SINGLE-PRODUCT NATURAL MONOPOLY

In early writings on the monopoly problem, discussion revolved around the *single-product* firm with falling average costs throughout the relevant ranges of output, so that one producer can always supply the market more cheaply than two or more. This is shown in Figure 13.1. In such a situation there will be a monopoly equilibrium where the single firm equates MC and MR, earning per unit profits of AB. Entry at small scale will not occur despite the attraction of high prices because of the high costs of production. Figure 13.1 depicts three cases. First the private monopoly outcome with price P_m and output Q_m; secondly the constrained breakeven outcome with price P_n and output Q_n; and thirdly the marginal cost pricing outcome with price P_c and output Q_c. In the last case, because of decreasing costs, marginal costs are below average costs so that marginal cost pricing results in losses. This case will be referred to again later.

A natural monopoly exists if the cost function of an industry is such that no combination of two or more firms can produce a given level of output cheaper than a single firm (see Baumol *et al.* 1982). When these conditions exist, the cost function is said to be *subadditive*. In other words, an industry is a natural monopoly if $C(Q) < \Sigma C(Q_i)$, i.e. no combination of firms can produce the chosen level of output Q (where $\Sigma Q_i = Q$) cheaper than the single firm. If the

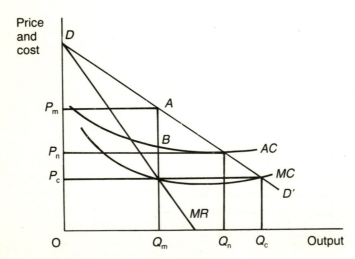

Figure 13.1 A single-product natural monopoly

cost function is subadditive at *all* levels of output, as in Figure 13.1, then the cost function is *globally* subadditive and changes in demand conditions will not alter the condition of natural monopoly. An important consequence of the concept of subadditivity is that costs can be rising under a natural monopoly. It is also possible for an industry to be a natural monopoly at one level of production but not at another (local subadditivity). To see this, consider Figure 13.2.

With the state of demand given by D' the industry is clearly a natural monopoly; splitting production will not lower costs – and entry is not feasible. At demand level D'' the industry is still a natural monopoly since although we could now have two firms, one producing at the minimum efficient size of Q_m and the other producing the residual market demand of $Q_m Q_r$, the combined costs of doing so would be the weighted average of $C_m + C_f$. This exceeds the cost of single-firm production C_s. Hence the case of increasing average costs of production is not sufficient to remove natural monopoly status. However consider the situation with demand curve D''' giving a market size $2Q_m$. Single-firm cost of production is C^* which is greater than the weighted combined costs of production of two firms of size Q_m, i.e. $C^* > 2C_m$. Hence shifts in demand can transform an industry from a natural monopoly to a multi-firm industry. In this case the cost function is locally but not globally subadditive.

In the example depicted in Figure 13.2 it was the doubling of market demand, with cost conditions held constant, which served to transform the industry from a natural monopoly into a duopoly. A change in technology, inducing a change in cost conditions, can have the same effect. In Figure 13.3 the combination of demand conditions DD' and average cost function AC_1 gives rise to a natural monopoly because C_s is less than the weighted average of $C_m + C_f$. However, if

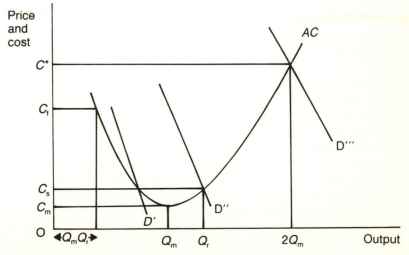

Figure 13.2 Demand conditions and natural monopoly

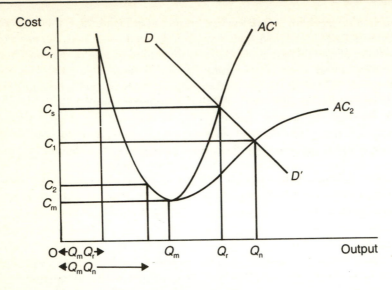

Figure 13.3 Technology and natural monopoly

average cost conditions change to AC_2, the industry ceases to be a natural monopoly because the lowest multi-firm cost, the weighted average of $C_m + C_2$ is less than C_1. In this case, then, it is the change in cost, with demand held constant, that has changed the status of the industry. Without detailed knowledge of demand and cost conditions, the most we can say in the single-product case is that if there remain unexploited economies of scale then the industry is a natural monopoly.

Two other important points emerge from the analysis. The first is that the interaction of cost and demand conditions determines not only whether an industry is a natural monopoly but also whether marginal cost pricing is feasible without a subsidy being required. For instance, under decreasing cost conditions (Figure 13.1) marginal cost pricing would result in losses to the natural monopolist since at all positive levels of output $MC < AC$. However, when demand is being met under conditions of increasing average costs marginal cost pricing would yield profits since marginal costs exceed average cost at levels of production in excess of the minimum efficient size.

The second point is that, although from an economic welfare viewpoint it is desirable that only one firm produce in a natural monopoly industry, it is possible under certain market conditions for the monopolist to be vulnerable to 'hit and run' entry. This is clearly shown in Figure 13.2. If the natural monopolist facing demand D'' sets prices to break even, i.e. charges C_s, then it is possible for a firm to enter and agree to supply part of the market at less than price C_s and make profits. If this occurs it destroys the optimal market structure, resulting in price and output instability in future periods. If the natural monopolist operates in such market conditions then its position is not *sustainable* and can be removed by destructive competition.

It is clear therefore that the existence of natural monopolies raises important questions for public policy in terms of their regulation (how do we prevent them abusing their monopoly positions?) and their vulnerability (how do we prevent destabilisation of the market via harmful competition?). We return to these themes later.

13.3 MULTIPRODUCT NATURAL MONOPOLY

The above discussion showed that in the single-product case the question of whether or not an industry is a natural monopoly is rather a difficult one to answer. Demand and/or cost changes can change the status of the industry. The only clear case is where there remain unexploited scale economies of the type depicted in Figure 13.1.

Not surprisingly the situation is even less clear in the more realistic multi-product case. We use the term 'more realistic' because most firms produce more than one product. This includes those activities that produce seemingly homogeneous outputs such as electricity generation, railway services, gas distribution, telephone services, etc. This is because they are subject to variable time-of-day demands which should be treated as different products with different costs of production.

Since we are now dealing with more than one output (for ease of illustration assume two, say peak and off-peak electricity), an analysis of how total costs of production vary in response to changes in demand makes it necessary to combine the two outputs. This is done through the construction of a bundle of (two) outputs, Q^*, in fixed proportion to each other (e.g. $Q^* = q_1 + 2q_2$). We can then examine the relationship between costs and the fixed bundle as successive units are added to or subtracted from it. This gives rise to the concept of *ray average cost* (RAC). Hence the RAC of producing q_1, q_2 would be:

$$RAC(Q^*) = \frac{C(tQ^*)}{t}$$

where t is the number of units of the bundle Q^*. Hence if we increase the number of units by t per cent and cost increases by less than t per cent then we have declining ray average costs, implying *multiproduct economies of scale* of:

$$S = \frac{C(Q)}{\Sigma q_i MC_i} \qquad i = 1, 2$$

where q_i refers to each output and MC_i is the independent marginal cost of producing each. Naturally if we have declining RAC then this implies that the sum of marginal costs weighted by each output is less than total cost, hence $S > 1$ and we have multiproduct scale economies.

Two other multiproduct cost concepts are important here. The first is *average incremental cost* (AIC_i), i.e. the average cost of producing *only* good i. This is given by:

$$AIC_i = \frac{C(q_i,q_j) - (0,q_j)}{q_i}$$

where AIC_i is total (joint) cost minus the stand-alone cost of producing only qj, divided by the output of good i. This provides us with a measure of *product-specific returns to scale*:

$$S_i = \frac{AIC_i}{MC_i}$$

i.e. the presence of individual product scale economies is indicated as an excess of average incremental cost over the marginal cost of production of output i.

The other important multiproduct cost concept is that of *economies of scope*, which occur when joint production of a set of outputs is cheaper than their separate production, that is

$$C(q_1,q_2) < C(q_1,0) + C(0,q_2).$$

How do such economies occur? Basically, because some factors of production are 'public' inputs; i.e. their acquisition for use in the production of one output does not preclude their use elsewhere and at zero cost. A clear example is that of peak-load pricing (see Demsetz 1973b and Panzar 1976). Here it is the time-of-demand characteristic which determines the nature of the product. No additional inputs are required for the production of peak compared with off-peak production. It must therefore be cheaper to produce peak and off-peak outputs jointly rather than separately. It should also be noted that, apart from the presence of externalities, the conditions that promote economies of scope are similar to those that promote economies of scale. The specialised use of labour and productive capacity may result in efficiency gains in the production of related products as well as in the larger production of a single homogeneous good. Often this occurs because of indivisibilities or 'lumpiness' in the plant and usually takes the form of shared overheads, as for instance when a producer uses the same vehicles to distribute a range of products to its wholesale or retail outlets.

Many of the industries in the UK that are believed to possess scope-economy characteristics have been the large public sector corporations of electricity generation, gas distribution, railway services and telecommunications. Indeed, such a belief was part of the rationale for their retention as single corporations. Since these activities appeared to possess both scale and scope economies it was felt until recently that the consumer was best served (on grounds of economic efficiency) through these services being produced by state-owned natural monopolies to preclude monopoly abuse. However, recent years have seen a marked change in the attitude of policy makers towards the natural monopolies. This is characterised by the recent programmes of privatisation and, to a lesser extent, liberalisation. We return to these important issues later in this chapter.

Returning to the issue of cost subadditivity for the multiproduct firm, it is important to realise that the simultaneous existence of economies of scale and scope does not *necessarily* imply that the firm must engage in multi-output production in order to minimise costs. For example, it may be that joint production yields scope economies but only at the expense of losing scale economies from, for instance, shorter production runs. At the margin therefore there may be a trade-off between the two cost characteristics. Naturally, for joint production to be always preferable, the efficiencey gains from economies of scope must at least outweigh the loss of potential economies of scale for each output.

Baumol, Panzar and Willig (1982) have shown that decreasing average incremental costs of each product plus economies of scope are *sufficient* to guarantee subadditivity. Intuitively this makes sense, since falling AIC_i implies subadditivity for each individual product, and economies of scope imply that it is cheaper to produce the output set jointly. The problem with this result is that, when assessing whether or not an industry is characterised by a subadditive cost function, a rather important piece of information is usually missing. The ability to calculate AIC for a given product line implies knowledge of the 'stand-alone' costs of production, but this information is rarely available. What empirical work has been done in this area has focused on the evaluation of economies of scale and of scope over a limited range of production, i.e. at observed levels of production rather than at all feasible ones. The empirical estimation of multiproduct cost functions (see Baumol and Braunstein 1977) makes a useful contribution to the debate on optimal industry structure but is necessarily of limited usefulness. This is because the estimated cost functions are applicable only to cost structures associated with observed output levels. We have seen earlier how changes in demand and cost conditions can transform the optimal structure of an industry. Therefore, without global cost information we cannot be sure that such changes are not possible. Inevitably, the difficulties of assessing which industries or which product lines are subadditive make the formulation of public policy toward the natural monopolies rather difficult. However, this does not mean that it should not be attempted. What is striking about recent privatisation programmes in the UK and elsewhere is that they are being conducted in almost total absence of *any* cost information. This problem is considered in greater detail in a later section.

If it is accepted that certain activities are natural monopolies, then economic efficiency demands that production be undertaken by a single producer. This then raises the question of how to prevent the natural monopolist abusing its dominant position either by over-pricing or by failing to minimise costs. Several alternative approaches have been suggested, including exclusive public ownership, regulated private ownership and the introduction of competition. The first two approaches are considered in the remainder of this chapter. The possibilities of introducing competition are dealt with in the chapter that follows.

13.4   PUBLIC OWNERSHIP

The most important form of public ownership in Britain has been the public corporation, which has been the legal form adopted for all the major utilities. There have been two major problem areas with this form of ownership. The first has been the relationship between the board of the corporation and the responsible government minister; the second has been the setting of objectives and the putting in place of incentives and monitoring systems.

In theory, accountability and control are straightforward. Public corporations have statutory duties which are laid down by Act of Parliament. The relevant minister, who is answerable to Parliament, appoints the members of the management board. The division of responsibility between the minister and the board is that the former lays down general directions, leaving the latter to get on with the day-to-day tasks of managing the business. One of the major difficulties in the postwar history of the nationalised industries is that the original intention of having an 'arm's-length' relationship between the minister and the board quickly disappeared. Ministerial interventions in decision-making have been common. They include interventions to keep wages and prices down as part of government anti-inflationary policy; at other times to push prices up so as to reduce the public sector borrowing requirement; and to influence decisions on plant location or plant closures because of government concern over regional unemployment.

Turning to objectives, the statutory duties of the public corporations, as laid down by Act of Parliament, were expressed in very broad terms and thus were of little use as a guide to management. More specific objectives were contained in a series of White Papers in 1961, 1967 and 1978. In 1961 the emphasis was on setting financial targets, typically in the form of a return on capital employed. However nothing was said about pricing policy. The corporations could therefore meet their financial targets by raising prices as well as by cutting costs. There was also no guidance on how prices should relate to costs, so that there was no impediment to cross-subsidisation as a means of supporting non-commercial activities. The 1961 White Paper was also silent on methods of investment appraisal.

These weaknesses were addressed in the 1967 White Paper. The emphasis now switched to optimal pricing and investment policy, and the financial targets given to each corporation were, as far as possible, to be consistent with the pricing and investment objectives. Prices were to be set equal to long-run marginal cost, though, if capacity happened to be way out of line with demand, prices could be adjusted to reflect short-run marginal cost. A test discount rate was introduced for investment decisions, and non-commercial activities were to be identified so that the government could decide whether or not to subsidise them.

Marginal cost pricing

A pricing criterion based on setting prices equal to marginal cost is appealing on grounds of allocative efficiency, but it gives rise to several theoretical and practical problems. As a means of achieving allocative efficiency, the marginal cost pricing rule for an industry is generally correct only if prices equal marginal costs in other industries. This is an application of the general theory of second-best. As an illustration take the simple case of a toll bridge for which there is an alternative route in the form of a road that is congested at peak hours. Figure 13.4(a) shows peak demand, DD, for the toll bridge and the constant marginal costs, MC, of using the bridge (it is assumed that there is no congestion on the bridge). Figure 13.4(b) shows the demand curve $D'D'$ for using the congested route at peak hours and the marginal social costs (MSC), in the form of traffic congestion, of using the route. For the bridge alone, the optimal price is P, but when congestion on the alternative route is taken into account, optimality requires that the toll be set below P so that traffic is diverted away from the congested road; i.e. by setting a price below P the demand curve for the congested road shifts from $D'D'$ to $D''D''$. The optimum toll P^* is the one that equates the marginal welfare loss on the bridge with the marginal welfare gain on the congested road.

Another problem with marginal cost pricing, as we have already seen, is that, under conditions of increasing returns to scale, losses are incurred and these have to be financed by government subsidy. This raises the problem of managerial incentives. If managers know that losses are inevitable and will be met out of taxation, they may fail to minimise costs. The allocative benefits of marginal cost pricing can be preserved by adopting more complex pricing policies such as multi-part tariffs and other forms of price discrimination. With a two-part tariff, for instance, there can be a charge per unit based on marginal cost and a fixed charge to cover overheads. A more complex system of price discrimination can also enable industry output to approximate the optimal level. However, these pricing structures are not appropriate to all industries. They also do not, of course, overcome the practical problems with any form of marginal cost pricing

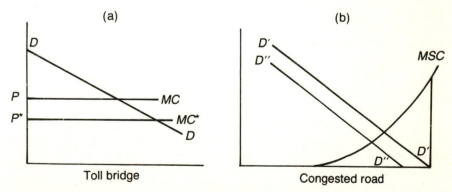

Figure 13.4 The effect of an externality on optimum prices

which are the identification, calculation and monitoring of marginal cost, especially in the presence of sunk costs and multiproduct supply. There is also the problem of specifying the time horizon over which marginal costs are to be calculated in order to produce tariff schedules. Furthermore, whatever time period is chosen, demand and cost conditions cannot be known with certainty so that a whole spectrum of out-turns is possible. This allows the managers of public enterprises to introduce elements of discretion into pricing schedules which accord with their own ideas of how the industries should be run. Similar problems exist in relation to investment appraisal. Rates of return calculations, like prices, are subject to demand and cost uncertainties, so that once again it is possible for a large amount of managerial discretion to be present in investment decisions and in the reporting of outcomes.

It is clear from the above that an important problem with marginal cost pricing is providing strong enough managerial incentives to minimise costs. The benefit that marginal cost pricing might have in terms of more efficient resource allocations could easily be outweighed by an inefficient use of resources. As Sir D.H. Robertson (1957: 168) put it as far back as 1957: 'A right distribution of productive resources between employments is a "good thing" economically, but not the only good thing even economically.'

Financial targets

In the 1978 White Paper the focus of attention shifted once again to financial targets, and marginal cost pricing was given less prominence. Each industry was also required to produce performance indicators such as productivity and unit cost indices, so that a check could be kept on internal efficiency. The same concern for devising directives that could be easily monitored led to the test discount rate for individual investment projects being replaced by a rate of return target for investment expenditures as a whole. The emphasis, therefore, was very much on the setting of objectives that were more amenable to effective monitoring. The judgement had been made that, in practice, there was more to be gained from greater internal efficiency, brought about by tighter financial control and more effective monitoring, than would be lost through departures from optimal price and investment policy.

A policy that gives financial targets pride of place is, of course, not without its problems. Where, as is often the case, the corporation has market power, the target may be met by monopoly pricing rather than by increased efficiency. The corporation may also impede or distort competition by engaging in price discrimination or cross-subsidisation. (See, for instance, the Monopolies and Mergers Commission reports on the London Electricity Board 1983, British Airports Authority 1985, and British Gas, 1988.) The government may relate financial targets to macroeconomic objectives such as a reduction in the public sector borrowing requirement. One example of this is the price increases imposed upon the electricity supply industry throughout the 1980s, which consistently exceeded the rate of inflation and which were not justified on grounds of cost or investment needs. The external financing limits (EFLs), introduced by the government in 1979 as a further financial constraint on the public corporations, resulted in the rejection of many worthwhile investment projects.

Rejection of investment projects on the grounds of poor profit performance in the past is also misconceived. For instance, in its report on coal the Monopolies and Mergers Commission (1983) argued that financial performance must improve before any major new investment should take place. The argument is wrong. Investment decisions should be based on expected returns. So long as an investment yields the required return, it is worth having, irrespective of past performance.

In Figure 13.5 the world price of coal is given by P, and the marginal cost curve is initially MC. In a free market, demand of q_c would be met by domestic production of q_d and imports of $q_c - q_d$. If imports are kept out and the whole of demand q_c is met domestically, there is a welfare loss of ade. Assume investment in new capacity q_1 takes place which yields the required rate of return and has average and marginal cost of OM. The new marginal cost curve is now MC'. If the new capacity replaces old so that output is kept constant, the welfare gain is $q_1 (P - M)$ plus $abcd$ which is the cost saving from closing the old pits. Even if the new investment results in a net addition of q_1 to output, there is still a welfare gain of $q_1 (P - M)$ so long as the extra output can be sold at the world price, P.

The UK experience of public ownership certainly demonstrates that there have been important obstacles in the way of attaining allocative and internal efficiency. Arguably (see, for instance, Vickers and Yarrow 1988) many of these obstacles could be removed without a change of ownership. Efficiency could be

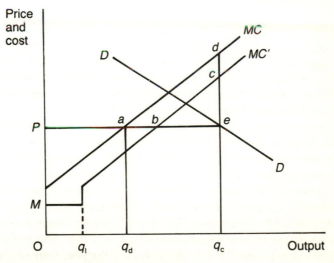

Figure 13.5 Optimal investment decisions

increased, for instance, by using independent bodies to scrutinise the perform-ance of public sector bodies, including their price and investment decisions. Several efficiency audits of public corporations have in fact been carried out by the Monopolies and Mergers Commission and there is no doubt that some measure of success has been achieved. In addition, efficiency-enhancing effects would very likely occur if managerial rewards were more closely related to performance. More important perhaps would be the salutary effect of exposing public corporations to competition wherever that is feasible. It would also be beneficial to have a more arm's length relationship between the government and the boards of public corporations, for there can be little doubt that some of the problems facing these corporations have been government imposed. These include the use of the corporations to achieve macroeconomic objectives, the external financing limits and restrictions on diversification. To give one example of the latter: while under public ownership British Gas successfully diversified into oil and gas exploration but was forced by the government to divest itself of this activity. In the run-up to privatisation one of the advantages which the minister claimed for the change of ownership was the freedom that the new corporation would have to diversify into new areas, including oil exploration!

It is one thing, however, to argue that the government should adopt a 'hands off' approach; whether this can be achieved in reality is another matter. So long as major activities are under direct government control it is hard to imagine that ministers will not make use of this for short-term economic policy objectives or indeed (especially!) for political gain. The fact of the matter is that successive administrations failed to establish and operate an effective arm's length regu-latory mechanism with a consistent set of objectives. The difficulty in practice of achieving a durable arm's length relationship between the government and public sector corporations is one of the more compelling arguments for privatisation.

The performance of nationalised industries

The question remains to be asked, however, as to how badly the nationalised industries have actually performed. Several different approaches have been used in an attempt to answer this question; none is entirely satisfactory. Some inter-national productivity comparisons, e.g. Aylen (1980) and Pryke (1981), have indicated that UK nationalised industries perform less well than privately owned counterparts overseas. However, international comparisons show UK industry generally to perform relatively badly. The important question is whether the relatively poor performance is even worse for publicly owned firms. The specific contribution of the form of ownership *per se* to relative performance is not at all clear. Some studies, e.g. Collins and Wharton (1984), have looked for clues in the public sector investigations of the Monopolies and Mergers Commission. In each of the 27 public sector investigations carried out by the MMC between 1979 and 1989 the MMC found something to criticise, and often the criticism was of a serious kind relating to failures in allocative or managerial efficiency. In particu-

lar, attention has been drawn on several occasions to inadequacies in management information flows; failure to relate prices to costs; insufficiently challenging
performance targets; and the absence of effective monitoring mechanisms.
However, in the majority of cases the MMC has also found much to commend,
and in only three cases did it judge a problem to be sufficiently serious to merit an
adverse public interest finding. Moreover, MMC investigations of private sector
monopolies have also on many occasions been highly critical. The results of the
MMC's efficiency audits of public sector bodies do not therefore form a safe
basis from which to draw conclusions about relative performance.

We are on somewhat safer ground when dealing with productivity comparisons with privately owned domestic industries. These studies have proceeded on
the basis of comparing *changes* in productivity, which are not necessarily a good
measure of relative *levels* of efficiency. Consequently the results have to be
viewed with caution. The figures in Table 13.1 show the findings of two such
studies. Both suggest that the nationalised industries have, on the whole,
performed well relative to the average performance of the manufacturing sector.
The striking improvement in the performance of Coal, the Post Office, British
Rail and British Steel shows what can be achieved under public ownership.

It is on the basis of financial performance indicators that the public corporations come out badly. For instance, for all public corporations over the ten-year
period 1970–79 gross trading surpluses, net of subsidies, averaged 4.3 per cent of
the net capital stock at replacement value. By comparison, for all industrial and
commercial companies gross trading profit as a percentage of net capital stock at
replacement cost averaged 17.1 per cent. This profitability comparison cannot
however be taken as evidence of a high level of internal inefficiency within public
corporations. Part of the difference may be due to monopoly price distortions in
the private sector and government price controls in the public sector. In some
cases, e.g. rail transport, financial results may be depressed because public sector

Table 13.1 Productivity changes (output per head)

	1960–75 % change		1968–78 % per annum	1978–85 % per annum
British Airways	150	British Airways	6.4	6.6
British Gas	242	British Gas	8.5	3.8
Electricity	127	Electricity	5.3	3.9
Coal	25	Coal	−0.7	4.4
Postal services	−6	Post Office	−1.3	2.3
Telecommunications	169	British Telecom	8.2	5.8
		British Steel	−0.2	12.6
		British Rail	0.8	3.9
All manufacturing	51	All manufacturing	2.7	3.0

Source: NEDO (1976)   *Source*: Molyneux and Thompson (1987)

pricing policy is being used to correct for external diseconomies in the private sector. More generally, the use of profit as an indicator of efficiency is valid only if the price of a good or service reflects society's valuation of it relative to other commodities, and if the costs of inputs reflect the social value of those inputs. When these conditions do not hold, owing for instance to monopoly or externalities, financial measures may be a poor indicator of relative performance. It is impossible to estimate the extent to which these factors explain the disparity in the financial performance of the public and private sectors in the 1970s, but it is improbable that all of it could be explained away. However, what *is* clear is the emphasis that came to be placed on financial performance by successive governments after 1979. This was particularly noticeable during the dispute over pit closures in the early 1980s when financial performance clearly dominated wider economic and social appraisal. (See, for instance, George *et al.* 1989.) The overriding aim of government during the 1980s was that 'every tub should stand on its own (financial) bottom'; subsidy became a dirty word and wider economic efficiency arguments stood little chance when confronted with the virtues of financial rectitude. For whatever reason, the poor financial performance of public corporations proved a major handicap to those seeking to defend public ownership.

13.5 PRIVATISATION

An alternative to instituting reform of the nationalised industries is to return their activities to the private sector. This policy has been pursued by a number of countries in recent years, but nowhere so enthusiastically as in the UK, where several major industries, including telecommunications, gas, airports, water and electricity supply, have been privatised.

It is important to note that privatisation simply transfers a monopoly from the public to the private sector. All the resource allocation problems of monopoly thus remain. If there is a case for privatisation *per se* it must rest on a link between *internal* efficiency and the form of ownership and control. This involves *inter alia* the relationship between shareholder and manager or, in the case of nationalised industries, between government and managers. These belong to a more general set of problems known as *principal-agent* or *agency* relationships. A principal-agent relationship exists where one party (the agent) agrees to act in the interests of another party (the principal). Thus managers are appointed by shareholders to run companies on their behalf. Likewise the government appoints managers to run nationalised undertakings in accordance with policies laid down by Parliament. Two conditions are necessary for agency relationships to pose interesting problems. First, the agent's objectives must differ from those of the principal. Second, the principal must have access to less information than is available to the agent, e.g. on cost, market conditions and the agent's behaviour. There is, in other words, a problem of asymmetric information and thus a need for monitoring the agent's behaviour and performance.

Agency-type relationships exist between managers and other employees as well as between owner and manager. At the latter level, which is the one that interests us here, these relationships pose no problems in firms where there is no divorce between ownership and control, e.g. the single proprietor who also manages the firm. A problem does exist, however, in large firms where, typically, there is a degree of separation between owner and manager and where organisational complexity, together with imperfections in product and capital markets, allow managers to pursue objectives other than the maximisation of shareholders' wealth. On the face of it the agency problem would appear to be more acute under public ownership. In large part this is due to the fact that there are more layers of responsibility and thus more opportunity for directives to be distorted, messages misunderstood and grievances left unresolved. The management board is given directives by a government minister who is answerable to Parliament, which in turn represents the owners, who are the taxpaying public. In addition, the civil servants, who advise the minister and the rest of the Cabinet, may not support him on key issues. There are more principal-agent relationships therefore than one would find in a typical large private company. The objectives of the various parties involved are also liable to display more variety, so the potential for conflict is greater. For instance, in transport, social as well as economic objectives are likely to be important to the 'owners'. Indeed, governments have often set nationalised industries social as well as economic objectives, but the trade-off between the two has never been entirely clear. This reflects the fact that, given the different weights attached to these objectives by members of the public, the trade-off *is* not clear. This in turn allows politicians wide discretion and ample opportunity to manipulate the weights accorded to economic and social objectives in decision-making for maximum political advantage. The setting of several, possibly conflicting, goals also increases the scope for managers to exercise discretion.

Arguments for privatisation

It would seem therefore that there is an *a priori* case in favour of privatisation on the grounds that it imposes more binding constraints on management and is thus likely to increase efficiency. More specifically the following arguments in favour of privatisation have been advanced. They are put rather strongly in order to make clear the main points at issue.

1 The profit motive provides *incentives* to employees generally but to management in particular, which are largely absent in state-owned corporations. Generally, rewards are more closely linked to performance.
2 Privately owned firms have a clearly defined objective – the maximisation of profits – which is easy to monitor. This aids the coordination of effort within the firm. State-owned firms, however, have to pursue a mixture of economic and social goals, which results in inefficiency in day-to-day operations and ambiguities in pricing and investment decisions.

3 Private companies are more responsive to market conditions and will more readily take advantage of new opportunities such as diversification into new growth areas. This is aided by the fact that privately owned firms have greater freedom in raising capital.

4 Private companies are not plagued by government intervention when making decisions on prices, wages, investment, location, etc., whereas such intervention is common in the public sector.

5 Private companies are more accountable to their owners, who are better able to monitor performance and organise a revolt against inefficient management.

6 Efficiency is encouraged in privately owned companies not only by the profit motive and clearly defined objectives but also by the threat and occurrence of takeover.

Points (1)–(4) could in principle be tackled with or without change of ownership. Greater incentives could be introduced into publicly owned corporations as an inducement to greater efficiency. Where social objectives are important these could be identified and the efficiency with which socially desirable activities are supplied could be monitored; otherwise the corporation could be instructed to behave commercially. Public corporations could be given greater freedom to raise capital and to diversify, and with sufficient will the government could adopt an arm's length approach to day-to-day operations. In addition, it should not be supposed that the advantages claimed for private ownership are always realised, especially when considering large firms, which is the appropriate comparison to make. Managerial incentives may be severely attenuated in large firms; there may be an asymmetry in managerial rewards – failure being punished more harshly than success is rewarded – which tends towards excessive caution in decision-making; and, because of the vested interests of different groups within the firm, clearly defined overall objectives may be just as elusive in large private companies as in public corporations. Of particular concern is the charge that the private sector has failed to generate adequate funds for investment on a long-term basis. Spokesmen for the financial sector tend to argue that there is no evidence of any shortage of funds for profitable investment projects. However, this defence has to be heavily discounted if the financial markets themselves take a short view in investment appraisal.

On point (5) there are several reasons to doubt the effectiveness of shareholder monitoring. Take, for instance, the case where shares are highly dispersed amongst individuals. An individual will typically find it difficult and costly to get detailed information on company performance. If he feels sufficiently discontented it will not be easy to organise a revolt and any attempt to do so may be thwarted by management's use of the proxy vote. Further, the incentive to upstage management is severely attenuated by the free-rider problem. If a small number of shareholders succeed in removing management and improving performance, the consequent rewards will be enjoyed by the whole body of shareholders, and the 'activists' will gain only a small proportion of the benefits. The position should be better where institutional shareholders are important. Again, however, there is the problem of obtaining access to the detailed information needed to judge performance. The institutions are liable to make judgements on the basis of readily available indicators such as earnings per share which say nothing directly about efficiency. Institutions also typically hold a small percentage of shares in a single company, so the free-rider problem is still present. Lastly, the alternative to getting involved is getting out. In the UK the choice which institutions have between active supervision and passive portfolio adjustment has generally been exercised in favour of the latter.

This brings us to the argument that privatisation will result in efficiency gains because private sector firms are exposed to the discipline of the takeover bid. It would seem reasonable to suppose that the threat of takeover would have a beneficial effect on efficiency. One way of modelling this effect is to adapt an approach applied by Leibenstein (1979) to product market competition. In the context of product market competition this approach has already been examined in Chapter 2. The analysis is repeated here for convenience. In the context of the takeover bid the essence of the argument is that the threat of takeover is directly related to managerial or internal efficiency, as measured by long-run average costs, and that the latter is a function of managerial effort. We assume that it is long-run costs that are important, i.e. that the threat of takeover will be high if outsiders see large unexploited opportunities for increasing efficiency, including long-term programmes of modernisation, rationalisation, R&D effort, labour force training, and so on. The emphasis on long-run efficiency and the effort required to achieve long-run improvements as opposed to short-run cost cutting, which may imply *less* effort, is crucial.

In Figure 13.6 curve A shows that, as effort increases, average cost falls. The

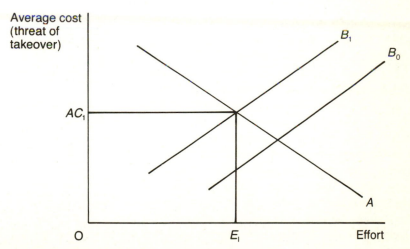

Figure 13.6 X-efficiency and the threat of takeover

degree of effort is in turn a function of cost, because if costs increase as a result of inefficiency the firm will be more exposed to takeover. The higher costs are, the more pressure there is to increase effort in order to avoid takeover. This relationship is shown in curve B_1. The optimum amount of effort is E_1 with average costs AC_1. There is a family of B curves, each representing a different level of the perceived takeover threat. The more protected the firm, the lower the pressure to minimise costs and thus the less effort there will be at any given level of average cost, and vice versa. If the takeover threat increases, the relevant B curve will be positioned to the right of B_1, e.g. at B_0; managerial effort will be higher and costs lower.

This result depends on the assumption that takeovers are motivated only by long-run cost and profit considerations and that the potential for cost improvements is known equally well to both incumbent managers and raiders. However, there are several grounds for doubting the reasonableness of this assumption. Where cost conditions are not well known by outsiders there may be a large random element in takeover activity. Takeovers may also be motivated by considerations such as empire building, which are not closely related to costs. When costs are important, the emphasis may be on opportunities for short-run gains rather than on longer-term efficiency considerations. In these circumstances the effect of a more hostile environment, in the form of increased probability of takeover, might be the opposite to that suggested above. The incumbent management might judge the extra effort needed to improve long-run competitiveness to have no noticeable effect on the chance of being taken over and may decide to reduce effort. Indeed, in certain circumstances a reduction in effort will be clearly indicated. For instance, a firm's costs may be temporarily high, and profits and share prices temporarily depressed, because it is in the middle of a modernisation or rationalisation programme, and predators may see this as an opportunity for launching a takeover bid. Some examples of this possible outcome, taken from investigations of the Monopolies and Mergers Commission, are given in George (1989). Where the threat of takeover is high, one possible effect, therefore, is that firms eschew longer-term investments and concentrate on the less arduous cost-cutting exercises needed to boost short-run profits, even though this may have adverse consequences on long-run competitiveness.

There are other reasons why too much emphasis should not be placed on the efficiency-enhancing effects of takeovers, especially in the case of the large utilities. First, although it seems that even very large companies are not immune from the threat of takeover, there is still a general tendency for the incidence of takeover to be negatively related to size. Certainly the size of the major utilities gives them a substantial measure of protection, and their strategic importance suggests that they are unlikely to be exposed to the full rigours of capital market competition. Second, studies of the effects of mergers such as Singh (1971), Meeks (1977) and Kumar (1984) do not yield very reassuring conclusions. One specific aspect which is particularly relevant in the present context, and which ties up with the earlier analysis, is the suggestion that a high level of takeover activity may lead to short-termism in managerial decision-making. To the extent that this tendency exists it is serious because by the very nature of their activities the utilities need to take a long view.

The performance of privatised firms

In assessing the case for privatisation it is also relevant to consider the evidence. The majority of firms that have been privatised were, prior to privatisation, operating in 'competitive' markets. Three of these are often described as 'clear success stories' – Cable and Wireless, The National Freight Corporation and Associated British Ports (Yarrow 1989). Even for these three, however, the evidence to support the view that privatisation *per se* has had a major impact is not clear cut, and there are several other cases where post-privatisation performance has not improved (George 1990).

It should also be noted that many successful companies now operating in the private sector (e.g. Enterprise Oil, Britoil and Amersham International) would not have existed but for initiatives taken in the public sector. There are many examples of large private companies which have failed to adjust to changing market conditions – the UK manufacturing sector can hardly be held up as a shining example of efficiency. Some of the bankrupt companies (e.g. British Leyland and later the much-diminished Rover Group, Ferranti, and Rolls-Royce) were rescued with public funds. There are many examples (Cable and Wireless, BP, British Telecom, British Airways, British Gas, the British Airports Authority and British Steel) of companies that were operating successfully in the public sector before they were privatised. An examination of efficiency and productivity gains shows that the performance of corporations such as British Telecom, the BAA and British Gas has not changed dramatically since privatisation. A comparison of productivity gains over the period 1979–88 shows British Steel (under public ownership up to 1988) to be the star performer, with annual productivity gains of 10 per cent, and privatised British Telecom and British Gas to be outperformed by publicly owned British Rail.

The evidence then is by no means clearly in favour of privatisation. Of course, the fact that privatisation has been on the agenda may well have played an important part in changing management attitudes and thus in improving on pre-privatisation performance. All in all, however, it is difficult to avoid the conclusion that privatisation is not necessary for improving efficiency.

It may not be sufficient either, for there is another important consideration. Some of the companies that have been privatised (e.g. Amersham International and BP) were operating in a competitive environment when they were in public ownership, a factor which was clearly important in explaining their efficiency. However, effective competition is not always present and in such cases privatisation means simply the substitution of a private monopoly for a public one. In these cases (e.g. British Telecom, British Gas, BAA) the competitive stimulus is weak or missing, and efficiency gains are therefore less certain. At the same time there is a danger that the privatised firm will exploit its monopoly position and will shed uneconomic services that have social value. There are two possible solutions. One is to make the industry more competitive by restructuring and reducing barriers to new competitors. This option is dealt with in the following chapter. The other is to introduce some form of regulatory control.

13.6 REGULATION

The arguments for state intervention to regulate the behaviour of privatised corporations largely revolve around specific features of these industries that induce market failure. Hence, it is argued, the free workings of the market would lead to a sub-optimal allocation of resources. The most obvious source of market failure, discussed in this chapter, is that of natural monopoly. The major corporations that have been privatised are public utilities and as such their outputs involve the establishment of transmission and distribution networks which necessarily imply natural monopoly characteristics since their replication by competitors would preclude economic efficiency. And since the asset structure of such industries tends to be specific and durable, they are also characterised by significant sunk costs. This makes it unlikely that an entry-liberalising competitive solution such as contestable markets is feasible. There is therefore considerable danger of abuse of monopoly power.

A second argument for the regulation of these industries revolves around the relationships that exist with other producers in related activities. For instance, electricity generation and distribution imply a complementary demand for electric appliances by households. Similarly, the outputs of the public corporations are often the intermediate inputs for other production activities. Gas, electricity, telecommunications, water, etc. are used in most production activities to a varying degree. Hence an expansion of output confers inappropriable external benefits on complementary producers. Because the benefits are inappropriable there is insufficient incentive for a private producer to expand production. So, it is argued, investment will be socially sub-optimal, output too low and prices too high, in the absence of regulation.

Other arguments for regulation rest on considerations of economic *equity*. The first is to do with the differing costs of supplying consumers in different locations. For instance, the cost of supplying postal, energy, transport and telecommunications services to rural areas tends to exceed that in densely populated urban areas. On straightforward marginal cost pricing criteria, consumers would face prices that reflect the true costs of supply, so that prices would be higher in rural than in urban areas. Furthermore, demand and cost conditions might be such that no service can be supplied economically. On grounds of equity, however, it might be argued not only that these basic services should be *available* to all consumers but also where necessary they should be subsidised so that they are available at 'reasonable prices'. Regulation would be required to achieve this objective.

In this example the equity problem is associated with the principle of charging according to true cost. In other cases, however, equity problems may arise as a result of departures from this principle. The monopoly supplier may take advantage of market segmentation to charge what the market will bear. Price–cost margins will then be higher for the customers with the most inelastic demand, and this may also offend one's sense of justice. Discriminatory pricing will often be an option available to the monopolist and again regulation will be needed to control it.

Price controls and efficiency

A central feature of regulation is some form of price control, and a central objective is the maximisation of allocative and internal efficiency. In setting allowable prices, the regulator will want to ensure not only that the firm will be able to recover its costs over the regulatory period, but that it will also earn a 'fair rate of return'.

The concept of a fair rate of return has been a cornerstone of the US approach to regulation. This approach suffers a major weakness, which is that the guarantee of a fair return weakens incentives to reduce costs. It would be better to relate the allowable rate of return to operating efficiency, since this would give shareholders an incentive to pressurise managers to maximise efficiency. Better still perhaps would be to combine performance-related allowable returns with performance-related executive compensation. More complicated schemes of this kind, however, require the availability of reliable indicators of operating efficiency, and the more detailed the information that is required, the greater the burden on the regulator. In addition, we have here an example of asymmetric information. Managers will always be better informed than the regulator and they may exploit this by passing on misleading information.

The UK has attempted to avoid the disadvantages of the fair rate of return approach to regulation by adopting the use of price formulae. As we shall see, however, the basic problem of how to ensure allocative and internal efficiency remains.

Since allocative efficiency depends upon relative prices and costs, there is a good case for indexing allowable prices to the prices of a suitable basket of other goods and services. In addition, it may be possible to foresee that real costs in the regulated firm should fall as a result of unusually rich opportunities for technological advance or above-average growth in demand, in which case these forecasts can be incorporated into the pricing formula. Thus in the case of British Telecom (BT) an $RPI - X$ formula was adopted so that in any one year BT could not increase the average price of its regulated services by more than the increase in the retail price index *minus* a figure initially set at 3 percentage points. The formula can be further elaborated by linking it to changes in the cost of one or more inputs. If these costs are largely under the firm's control, the pricing formula would then incorporate the disadvantage of cost-plus pricing, i.e. a weakening of incentives to minimise costs. However, if the cost components of the pricing formula are largely outside the firm's control and are competitively determined, there is little cause for concern. In the case of British Gas, the pricing formula is $RPI - X + Y$, the Y element allowing the company to pass on changes in gas purchasing costs.

With either of the above formulae there is a danger that, over time, prices and costs will diverge and so result in allocative inefficiency. From the point of view of allocative efficiency, therefore, the shorter the interval between price reviews the better. Likewise, the shorter the interval the less important becomes the precise formula used for determining allowable prices. On the other hand, a short 'regulatory lag' means that the firm gets little benefit from efficiency improvements and incentives to reduce costs may be seriously weakened. The choice of time interval between price reviews is thus a compromise in which the desirable goals of allocative and internal efficiency have to be weighed in the balance.

As already intimated, the allowable increase in prices in a multi-product firm generally relates to a basket of goods/services rather than to individual goods/services. This can be defended on grounds of administrative simplicity and also as a way of minimising the problem of allocating sunk and joint costs. However, just as a fair rate of return regulation fails to discriminate between different parts of a firm's activities, so too does price control by reference to a basket of goods or services. Problems include that of determining which goods and services should be included in the regulatory basket, and the extent to which the relative prices of regulated goods/services are to be permitted to vary. Ideally, the prices that are regulated should be those where the danger of monopoly abuse is high. However, abuse is a matter of degree and the regulatory authority may not choose an appropriate dividing line. If there is no control over relative prices within the regulated basket, the firm has an incentive to loosen the regulatory constraint by increasing the output of low-priced goods/services and reducing the output of high-priced goods/services, thus changing the weights of the price index.

What evidence is there that any of these problems have surfaced in the UK? Looking first at internal efficiency, the evidence for BT is not entirely reassuring. Molyneux and Thompson (1987) and Bishop and Kay (1988) conclude that BT's productivity performance has not changed materially post-privatisation. The latter study estimates that total factor productivity increased at an average annual rate of 2 per cent between 1979 and 1983 and at 2.5 per cent between 1983 and 1988. Allowing for the faster growth in demand for BT services over the latter period, implying scale economy benefits rather than shifts in cost functions, the authors conclude that there is no evidence of a significant improvement in productivity performance. This conclusion has to be seen against the productivity gains that BT could have been expected to achieve. It is not possible to put precise figures on this, but there is sufficient evidence to suggest that BT's performance has been disappointing. For instance, immediately before privatisation a major network modernisation programme was planned. Foreman-Peck (1989) suggests that, using North American experience as a benchmark, a 50 per cent productivity gain was feasible. Similarly, Beasley and Laidlaw (1989) argue that in local network operations BT has, on the basis of international comparisons, some 75,000 more employees than would be needed with best-practice techniques. That the Office of Telecommunications (OFTEL) underestimated attainable productivity gains is indicated by the fact that in 1989 the X component in the pricing formula was increased from 3 per cent to 4.5 per cent and in 1991 this was raised to 6 per cent. Here it should be noted that, if X is periodically revised in the light of the corporation's *own* cost performance, tariffs are tied to costs and the incentive to increase efficiency is weakened – one of the problems of rate of return regulation.

Although there is little sign of a positive impact on the total volume of telephone services or on overall efficiency, the composition of output has changed. Foreman-Peck, using an econometric model designed to simulate the dynamic impact of liberalisation and the change of ownership, estimated that business connections were 26 per cent higher and residential connections 12.5 per cent lower than would otherwise have been expected. This reflects not only a reorientation of the business towards more profitable segments, but also a response to the presence of Mercury, which has concentrated mainly on the business section of the market.

Evidence on tariffs suggests that BT is making substantial relative price changes within the basket of regulated services. In July 1990 the company announced a new price structure, effective from September 1990. Though there were a number of changes to the structure of call charges (e.g. cheap rate calls would become more costly relative to peak rate calls), the major change was a substantial increase in line rental and connection charges relative to call charges. Overall, the average household bill would increase by 9 per cent, but there would be little change for large businesses. BT argues that the readjustments were necessary to bring charges more closely into line with costs, but in the absence of detailed cost information this is impossible to verify. What is clear is that an increased loading of costs on to line rental will increase competitive pressure on Mercury, since trunk calls, where the two companies are in competition, are included in the regulatory basket.

The evidence does not, however, suggest that BT and Mercury are aggressive price competitors. It is more consistent with a model of non-collusive oligopoly in which the smaller firm is content to live under the monopoly price umbrella of the dominant firm, setting prices somewhat lower but not so low as to trigger a price war. This has been particularly noticeable in the (unregulated) international calls market. Since Mercury's entry into the market, international call charges have increased substantially at the same time as costs have fallen dramatically. In March 1990 it was disclosed that BT was a member of an international cartel and that gross profit margins on international calls averaged 60 per cent.

The performance of British Gas since privatisation has also been less than satisfactory. In June 1990 the regulatory body, the Office of Gas Supply (OFGAS), announced a review of the formula governing the prices set for tariff customers (i.e. those consuming up to 25,000 therms annually). As a result of this review the Corporation will, as from April 1992, be faced with a much stiffer pricing formula. The X in the $RPI - X + Y$ formula will be increased from 2 to 5 percentage points, and there will also be constraints on the extent to which the corporation can pass on gas purchasing costs.

Evidence of allocative inefficiency also exists in the supply of gas, especially for contract business (i.e. supplies to users with annual gas consumption in excess of 25,000 therms), which is not regulated. In 1988, just two years after privatisation, British Gas's (BG) contract business was referred to the MMC following complaints about abuse of monopoly power. The MMC criticised BG, amongst other things, for extensive discrimination in the pricing and supply of gas, and for failing to provide adequate information on the costs of common carriage. The MMC was of the view that BG's behaviour served to deter new entrants and to inhibit the development of competition.

As with the case of telecommunications, so experience with gas suggests that the monopoly will make use of whatever discretion is available in the price control formula, and will often do so anti-competitively. Experience also shows that in attempting to tackle this problem the regulator is drawn into ever more detailed scrutiny and control of pricing behaviour.

Price controls and quality of service

Even if price regulation is successful in reducing costs there is a danger that this may be at the expense of service quality. The incentive to improve quality is weakened because, though such improvement will benefit the firm in so far as it increases sales, the firm is unable to appropriate any of the benefit to the main body of consumers who purchased the good/service before the quality improvement was made. In the absence of competition, failure to maintain or improve quality will not threaten the firm's position.

In principle, the problem of service quality can be met head on by linking allowable prices to indicators of service quality. In practice, there may be great difficulty in the choice of suitable indicators and in determining their weights in the pricing formula. Furthermore, it involves yet more detailed intervention by the regulator. An alternative approach is to introduce some form of contractual liability whereby customers receive compensation if service levels fall below predetermined levels. A scheme of this sort was introduced by BT in 1988 following an upsurge in customer complaints. Even so, BT's procedures for handling complaints remain one of OFTEL's biggest continuing concerns. Contractual obligations to meet service standards are also to be introduced for gas. Following the review mentioned earlier, British Gas will have to publish regular figures on its overall quality of service and will have a legal commitment to provide a comprehensive package of services.

Price controls and investment

A major concern in the analysis of regulatory problems has been the adverse incentives which regulatory control might imply for investment decisions. In analysing the effects of rate of return regulation, Averch and Johnson (1962) showed that the result might be an adverse choice of technique, with too much capital being employed relative to other factors. The incentive to employ too much capital exists because this enlarges the rate-base, so that for a given allowable *rate* of return the firm achieves a higher *level* of profit.

This tendency exists when the allowable rate of return, r, exceeds the current cost of capital, c. This is because setting $r > c$ is equivalent to a subsidy on capital. The firm therefore perceives the cost of capital to be less than the market cost. In Figure 13.7, I is the relevant isoquant which shows the combinations of labour and capital capable of producing a given output. P_1 is an isocost line whose slope gives the ratio of the market price of labour to that of capital. The optimal combination of inputs is thus A. However, if the firm perceives the cost of capital to be lower than the market rate, it will decide its factor input combination on the basis of an isocost line such as P_3, which shows capital to be cheaper relative to labour. The firm will then select the input combination at point B. In terms of market prices, point B is inefficient, and this is shown by drawing isocost line P_2 parallel to P_1 so that it too reflects market prices. Clearly the output given by isoquant I is being produced at higher cost at B than at A. The degree of distortion in factor proportions depends on the elasticity of factor substitution. It will also depend on the elasticity of demand for the final product, a high elasticity making it difficult for the higher costs associated with non-optimal production techniques to be passed on to customers in the form of higher prices.

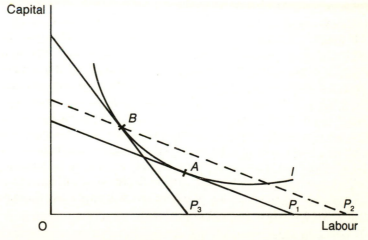

Figure 13.7 Rate of return regulation and the choice of technique

Research in the USA, however, has produced little evidence of the 'rate-base padding' effect. There are several possible reasons for this. The incentive to extend the rate-base uneconomically depends on the allowable return on capital being in excess of the market rate for new funds. There is no difficulty in showing this in theory, but in practice, given capital market imperfections, the relationship between the two rates may be less than clear cut. In addition, the technical possibilities of substituting capital for labour may be very limited – and in the extreme case of zero elasticity of substitution there will be no factor proportion distortion. Another important consideration is that, although an allowable rate of return may be an objective, what the regulator actually sets is prices. The rate of return enters as an input into the determination of maximum prices, but it may not be the only input into the price formula. As suggested earlier, the regulator may also take into account performance indicators designed to measure operating efficiency, and this may have the effect of depressing prices. The firm also has to allow for the effects of *regulatory lag* – the time interval between price reviews. The longer the lag, the longer the time period over which the firm has to absorb cost increases before it has a chance to pass them on in the form of higher prices, and the less inclined it will be to engage in wasteful capital expenditure. Caution will be reinforced if it is thought that the regulator, aware of the possibility of rate-base padding, will scrutinise investment decisions and perhaps disallow some items of capital expenditure. Where sunk costs are important, the dangers of over-investment are particularly acute since, once the investment has been made, the firm's bargaining power at rate-setting time will be considerably weakened. This consideration is particularly important given the specificity and durability of public utility assets and the very long pay-off periods that are involved. In sum, investment decisions have to be made on the basis of the firm's expectations of future allowable prices and of what the regulator will accept as a reasonable rate-base. These and other uncertainties are likely to act as a powerful offset to any forces tending in the opposite direction.

Too short a period has elapsed for any reliable analysis to be made of the effects of the UK privatisation programme on investment. An examination of BT's post-privatisation investment does not, at first glance, suggest any reason to suspect underinvestment, since real capital expenditure has grown steadily since 1984. However, this may indicate that price control generally has been too slack and that BT has been allowed to earn an excessive rate of return. One area where BT is closely regulated is in value added services such as the provision of cable TV, where it has been barred from entry. It is interesting to note that in 1990 BT announced that it was shelving a £200 million investment programme to provide local optical cables because the profitability of the investment depend upon the telephone network being allowed to carry TV services. Doubts about permission to enter profitable markets have the same effect on investment as doubts about the extent to which future allowable price increases will cover full cost – the tendency will be to underinvest. The BT example parallels the 'investment strike' of the Bell operating companies in the USA, who are delaying the modernisation of their networks whilst they are barred from several service areas, including cable TV.

13.7 CONCLUDING COMMENTS

One of the arguments in favour of privatisation was to get the government off the backs of management. However, it is clear that when it is a large monopoly that is privatised, so that a regulatory agency is required, management can by no means be free from outside interference. The regulator has to be involved not only in setting general tariff levels but also in more detailed matters such as relative prices, investment policy and quality of service. In addition to these problems, there is a whole range of others connected with the regulation of new entry, which are discussed in the next chapter.

The difficulties of regulation suggest that, wherever possible, we should look for ways of introducing competition. Where effective competition can be introduced, the need for a regulator disappears. But, as the next chapter will show, the ideal is rarely available. Even so it is usually possible to introduce an element of competition. This is likely to be resisted by the incumbent monopolist, who will argue that new entry will result in some loss of benefit from economies of scale and of scope. Management and unions will agree about this since the unions usually manage to appropriate some of the benefits of the monopoly in the form of higher wages.

However, it is important to determine as far as possible the extent to which a natural monopoly situation truly exists. Some parts of a firm's activities may constitute a natural monopoly but not others. Even when there is a natural monopoly, the quantitative importance of the cost benefits may be modest. In these cases the potential economies may be worth sacrificing in return for the advantage of having more than one firm and, of course, the advantage of the competitive stimulus.

Chapter 14

Introducing competition

14.1 INTRODUCTION

The previous chapter discussed two alternative approaches to the natural monopoly problem, namely, public ownership, and private ownership accompanied by regulation. Both approaches belong to a wider class of problems involving principal–agent relationships. In the case of public ownership, a major difficulty is the specification and enforcement of a set of incentives and constraints which ensure internal efficiency. In the regulated private ownership case, even if internal efficiency is less of a problem there is a major difficulty in specifying and enforcing a set of regulatory constraints which ensure allocative efficiency. These difficulties highlight the natural monopoly problem of ensuring internal and allocative efficiency in a single-producer market. For these reasons an alternative approach involving the introduction of competition into natural monopoly situations has been proposed and it is with this that the present chapter is concerned.

At first glance a policy of introducing competition into a natural monopoly market seems by definition to be undesirable. After all, a natural monopoly implies that the socially optimal industry structure is one in which a single producer supplies the market. Therefore the introduction of competition necessarily introduces inefficiency through the wasteful duplication of production facilities, possibly involving the destruction of that structure. This problem is particularly important in those industries where the natural monopoly is non-sustainable and 'hit and run' entry is feasible. However, it has been argued that several of the industries traditionally regarded as natural monopolies have cost functions that are only subadditive between certain activities and that, outside these areas, the industry has the potential to become more competitive. An appropriate policy approach, therefore, might be to facilitate the liberalisation of, and entry into, those areas where natural monopoly does not prevail. Allied to this is the suggestion that, even if an industry is a natural monopoly, it may on balance be desirable to sacrifice some potential economies of scale in order to have two firms in competition, rather than suffer the consequences of an inadequately regulated single-producer market. Although liberalisation of entry conditions does not necessarily mean that entry will actually occur, the threat of entry might be sufficient to change the behaviour of the incumbent monopolist. If entry does occur there is, of course, the benefit of competition. In addition, with two or more competitors the regulating authority has a sounder basis on which to make assessments of efficiency.

There are several ways in which competition might be introduced. One approach, discussed in section 14.2, is to restructure the industry by splitting up an incumbent monopolist, a policy solution that may be facilitated by the effect which technical progress sometimes has of removing natural monopoly status. Another approach, discussed in section 14.3, is deregulation and liberalisation of markets so as to attract new competitors. Both restructuring and deregulation are aimed at increasing competition *in* the market. Where this is not possible, an alternative is the introduction of a system of franchising and competitive tendering – that is, competition *for* the market, which is the subject of section 14.4. First, however, we examine the proposition that, under certain conditions, even an unregulated private monopoly will be socially optimal – this of course is the case of perfectly contestable markets.

14.2 CONTESTABILITY AND THE NATURAL MONOPOLY PROBLEM

In the single-product natural monopoly case of Figure 13.1 we depicted three alternative outcomes. These were the breakeven price and output of p_n, q_n; the competitive, marginal cost outcome of p_c, q_c and the private monopoly outcome of p_m, q_m. Price is highest and output and consumer surplus lowest in the last case. The problems of natural monopoly revolve largely around the situations depicted in Figures 13.1 and 13.2. If the industry cost function is subadditive and there remain unexploited economies of scale, then the maximisation of economic welfare via marginal cost pricing will cause the natural monopolist to make losses. Furthermore, as Figure 13.2 shows, constrained breakeven pricing could also be problematic if demand and costs conditions are such that the natural monopoly is unsustainable.

Non-sustainability is of course not a problem if potential entrants are prevented from supplying a portion of the market at a lower price by state-erected restrictions, as was the case under the nationalised industry approach. However, it clearly could be a problem for the regulated natural monopolies whose markets are opened up to competition.

Nevertheless it has been argued that for some natural monopolies outside regulation is unnecessary provided that entry into and out of the market is cost-less – the contestable market case. It has been shown that, under certain conditions (see Baumol, Panzar and Willig 1982), a private unregulated natural monopoly can simultaneously exhibit the characteristics of socially optimal (or Ramsey) pricing, efficient production and sustainability. These conditions are that if the natural monopolist, characterised by cost subadditivity, operates in a perfectly contestable market then the above highly desirable outcomes *necessarily* occur. How does this work? If *MC* pricing is not feasible because of the losses it implies, then the second-best solution for maximising social welfare requires a pricing rule which minimises the deviation of price from *MC*. Ramsey prices arise from the maximisation of net surplus defined as the difference between the total utility derivable from the outputs of the multiproduct natural monopolist and their costs of production, i.e.

$$\text{Max } U(y_1 \ldots y_n) - C(y_1 \ldots y_n)$$

subject to the breakeven constraint

$$\sum_i p_i y_i = C(y_1 \ldots y_n).$$

The solution to such a problem (see Baumol 1977) implies that the percentage deviation of prices from marginal costs for each product should be inversely proportional (denoted by a factor *k*) to the product's own demand elasticity, i.e.

$$\frac{p_i - MC_i}{p_i} = \frac{k}{\varepsilon_i} \ .$$

The rationale for such a pricing rule is as follows. If prices must deviate from marginal costs, then it is preferable that the deviations cause the minimum possible distortion of demand. It follows, therefore, that the largest deviations should fall on those outputs with the lowest demand elasticities. The more inelastic the demand for an output of the natural monopolist, the less a given percentage change in price from marginal cost will distort its use from the Pareto-optimal level. Therefore the prices of outputs with inelastic demands should deviate from marginal costs by a relatively large percentage, and smaller deviations should apply to products with more elastic demand.

Hence if we have a multiproduct natural monopolist characterised by cost subadditivity and operating in a contestable market – *thereby guaranteeing that the firm produces efficiently and breaks even* – then second-best Ramsey prices result and external regulation is unnecessary. And Baumol *et al.* (1982) have shown that under this 'weak invisible hand theorem' such a set of Ramsey prices will guarantee that the market is sustainable. Note that such a result holds only under the conditions of the observed industry cost function. Were an alternative means of supply feasible, exhibiting different cost characteristics and hence implying a different set of optimal prices, then Ramsey prices based on the incumbent monopolist's costs may not be sustainable.

The implications for public policy are clearly considerable. Provided that entry and exit are completely free (*or can be made so*) then outside regulation of the private natural monopoly is unnecessary, since socially optimal pricing is guaranteed and the market is not vulnerable to destructive competition. The crucial question is whether the natural monopolies are, or can be, transformed into contestable markets? The discussion in Chapter 10 showed how stringent the conditions for the existence of contestability were and how the influence of positive sunk costs and relatively short reaction times on the part of the incumbent caused severe problems for its competition-inducing conclusions. In addition, it has been argued (see Weitzman 1983) that scale economies arise not merely from the presence of fixed costs but also through sunk costs. If this is the case then subadditivity precludes the possibility of contestability. Either way, as in the more general case of non-natural monopoly, the main contribution of contestability theory has been to emphasise the benefits of potential competition and of the dismantling of entry barriers. Such results have undoubtedly been influential in several areas of deregulation enacted recently in the United States. Little or no work has been attempted in the UK to assess which activities are natural monopolies and whether any such markets approximate contestability (though see Starkie 1986). However, the inevitable conclusion to be drawn is that the introduction of competition into natural monopoly industries is dependent upon the nature of cost conditions prevailing there. In the next section we discuss this in more detail.

The role of costs

Although certain industries are traditionally regarded as natural monopolies, it has been suggested that a useful alternative, or complementary policy, to regulation, would be the introduction of competition and the intensification of competitive pressures. This is based partly on the idea that only specific areas of operation contain natural monopoly elements and that other areas do not. Hence it might be contended that in telecommunications, for example, whereas local networks are naturally monopolistic, long-distance networks are not. In addition, since it is the network aspect of these activities that provides the major element of cost subadditivity, it follows that if access to networks were liberalised then the natural monopoly element would be significantly reduced.

Given the discussion of entry deterrence in Chapter 10 and in the previous section, it is clear there is a close relationship between the nature of cost conditions within and between market segments in an industry, and the extent to which those segments could be successfully opened up to competition. For example, the presence of sunk costs makes it difficult to feel confident that the free play of market forces will, in the long run, ensure the emergence of the socially optimal industry structure. We have already noted that such costs often accompany economies of scale and that often it is the latter that explain natural monopoly. In fact many of the industries traditionally regarded as natural monopolies derive their status from the networking aspect of their operations. Gas, water, telecommunications and electricity all use grid-type distribution systems whose average costs decline rapidly with intensity of usage. More importantly, such networks also exhibit sunk cost characteristics, since expenditures in the networks are 'committed' and largely irrecoverable. Hence, it is argued, natural monopolies cannot be opened up to competition, or be made contestable, because of scale economy and sunk cost considerations.

In several cases, however, the sunk element of total costs is confined to specific areas of operations, in particular the networking areas. Thus one approach to introducing competition into these industries might be to retain public ownership of networks and open up the possibilities for multi-firm usage of the system. In the case of rail operations, for example, this might involve public ownership of tracks, platforms, embankments and cuttings. Rail vehicles, locomotives, wagons, carriages, etc. have secondhand value and are in some cases mobile between markets, which, in theory at least, raises the possibility of competing rolling stock using shared track. This is analogous to competing express coach services (deregulated in 1980) using the state-owned public motorway system, or competing airlines hiring access to airspace, terminals and runways. Similarly, private rail companies might hire track and platform space. In each case the sunk cost element is removed as a factor influencing the entry decision of the potential competitor.

Alternatively, if the industry is privatised the regulatory authority can try to ensure that entrants have access to the incumbent's distribution network at reasonable cost. The incumbent, however, has a clear incentive to prevent competition or to minimise its effectiveness by fixing interconnection costs for entrants as high as possible. In these circumstances the terms under which access is offered are of crucial importance. This *access to network* problem has been faced, for instance, by Mercury and the regulatory body, OFTEL, in the telecommunications industry. In 1985 Mercury applied to OFTEL for a ruling after it had failed to agree on terms for interconnection with BT. BT in turn challenged OFTEL's power to make a ruling by taking the matter to the courts. After a ruling against BT, OFTEL established interconnection arrangements but only after a lengthy delay which postponed the emergence of more effective competition.

Another way of introducing competition would be by dismembering the incumbent. Once again this approach calls into question exactly which service areas have truly natural monopoly status. It will be recalled that a necessary condition for natural monopoly in a multiproduct market is the existence of economies of scope as well as economies of scale. Hence in a multiproduct natural monopoly it is cheaper for a single firm to produce two or more goods than it would be for two or more firms to engage in specialised production. Such 'joint' production arises because some factors of production are 'public' inputs. They are acquired for use in the production of one output and are available costlessly for the production of another. Perhaps the clearest example is that of peak-load pricing (see Demsetz 1973b and Panzar 1976). So an economy of scope is basically an unavoidable externality arising from multiproduct production. Apart from the presence of these externalities, the conditions which promote economies of scope are the same as those which promote economies of scale. The specialised use of labour and productive capacity may result in efficiency gains in the production of related products as well as in the increased production of a single homogeneous good. Hicks (1952) has shown that this often occurs owing to indivisibilities in the plant and usually takes the form of shared overheads. Hence the adoption of a policy of divestiture might be based on the argument that scope economies do not exist (in which case there is no natural monopoly) or that their loss would be more than outweighed by the efficiency gains from the intensification of competitive pressures.

A major example of this approach is the case of the US telecommunications industry. In 1982 the dominant supplier of network telephone services in the US, AT&T, agreed to divest itself of its local operating companies. This followed an eight-year legal battle after the Federal Trade Commission (FTC) had brought charges of anti-competitive conduct. The decision meant that AT&T's local and long-distance operations were to be separated and its 22 local operating companies would be reconstituted into seven regional holding companies – the so-called 'Baby Bells'. In its evidence to the FTC, AT&T had repeatedly claimed that voice telephony was a natural monopoly and hence that divestiture would lead to inefficiency. However, empirical evidence suggested the absence of economies of scope between local and long-distance operations (see Evans 1983 and Evans and Heckman 1984). In fact it implied that it would be more efficient to separate such services rather than retain integrated production. Since its full divestiture in 1984 AT&T has reduced its manpower requirements and embarked on a network modernisation programme in order to meet competition from its direct rivals MCI and GTE Sprint (Bailey 1986). Although AT&T has remained the market leader and its rivals have struggled, it appears that divestiture had some success, since tariffs to consumers in certain areas have fallen. Interestingly, it appears that the Baby Bells will in the future be allowed access to the long-distance market outside the area of their local operations, so that they will be in direct competition with the original parent company. In this case, therefore, it appears that the restructuring of the vertically integrated dominant incumbent has had the effect of strengthening competitive pressures.

An interesting question naturally follows: would restructuring along these lines be feasible in the UK? The Telecommunications Act 1981 and the Oil and Gas (Enterprise) Act 1982 heralded the introduction of more competitive markets. In some areas of telecommunications, such as the retailing of customer apparatus and certain value-added network services, a substantial increase in competition has occurred, with noticeable benefits to consumers. In BT's core network operations, however, the government has deliberately restricted competition. Mercury Communications was licensed as a new network operator in 1982, its aim being to take a small percentage of the lucrative business market. The privatisation of BT in 1984 was seen by some commentators as an ideal opportunity for creating a more competitive industry structure along the lines of the AT&T divestiture in the USA. However, the government announced that no new licences for network operation would be issued before 1990. Thus the market structure was left with a dominant supplier facing limited competition from the much smaller Mercury Communications Co. and a local network company operated by Hull City Council.

In the case of gas, the Gas Act 1986, which privatised the British Gas Corporation, gave the privatised company a monopoly in the supply of tariff (mainly domestic) customers but, in line with the 1982 legislation, allowed new entrants into the contract business (generally large industrial and commercial users). Any new entrant would, of course, have to use British Gas (BG) pipeline systems and would have to negotiate terms, including matters relating to safety of supply. In the event, deregulation failed to induce any new entry.

BG also has very substantial vertical market power. It has been a monopoly purchaser of gas from UK fields, a monopoly which, a recent MMC report recommended, should be ended (see below). Another MMC report in 1980, on the supply of domestic gas appliances, was highly critical of the Corporation's conduct as a dominant buyer, and concluded that its retailing monopoly was against the public interest. The MMC offered two possible solutions. Either the Corporation should withdraw from the retailing of gas appliances, or a number of restrictive practices should be abandoned, which would have the effect of reducing its power as a retailer. In July 1981 the Minister of State for Consumer Affairs announced that the Corporation would be required to cease selling domestic appliances and dispose of its showrooms over a five-year period. However, in October 1981 the Secretary of State for Energy announced that the sale of gas showrooms would be delayed until complex safety legislation had been debated in Parliament, but that the government remained fully committed to breaking up the monopoly as soon as possible. The management of the British Gas Corporation argued vigorously against enforced division, and four years later the government announced its intention to privatise the corporation intact!

The government also set its face against restructuring in the case of the British Airports Authority (BAA). BAA owns and operates seven airports in Britain – Heathrow, Gatwick and Stansted near London, and Prestwick, Glasgow, Edinburgh and Aberdeen in Scotland. Competition between airports is bound to be blunted by the inevitable government involvement in this sector. In view of the sensitive environmental issues, and other externalities, it would be naive to imagine that airports could be allowed to engage in unfettered competition. Even so, a beneficial increase in competitive pressure by, for instance, privatising the three London airports as separate companies, could have been achieved without jeopardising the government's legitimate concern with wider issues. The possible benefits, which are examined in detail by Starkie and Thompson (1985), include more competition for off-peak business, thus making better use of capacity, and more information to the regulatory authority, which would be beneficial in the setting of regulatory standards. However, the government argued that any benefit from a more competitively structured industry would be very limited and would be more than offset by efficiency losses. Doubtless, the government was also concerned with the proceeds of the asset sale. In addition, and as in the case of British Gas, the management of BAA campaigned vigorously against enforced division of the company.

Thus, in the case of telecommunications, gas and airports, the government, at the time of privatisation, decided against restructuring. As a result, a heavy burden was placed on the regulatory agencies to curb monopoly abuse, a matter already referred to in the previous chapter. Yet for telecommunications, gas and airports it would appear that a more competitive industry structure could have been achieved. In view of the MMC's highly critical 1980 report on the sale of gas appliances, more effective measures would have been justified at that end of the market. The area gas boards could also have been privatised as separate companies – a policy which has been adopted in the case of the electricity supply industry. The same can be said of BT and the privatisation of local networks as separate companies, and also of the division of BAA into two or more separate entities. In all three cases, reducing the size of the company would have reduced the scope for anti-competitive behaviour. Decision making would have been spread more widely and the existence of a number of separate companies would have allowed performance comparisons to be made which would have facilitated the setting of standards for regulatory purposes.

To what extent, however, if at all, would this restructuring be achieved at the expense of economies of scale or of scope? Relatively little is known about the nature of cost conditions within the newly privatised utilities. A long-held presumption is that they exhibit natural monopoly features and that they should be kept intact, whether in public or private ownership. Some recent work in this area has yielded interesting results. For telecommunications, Hunt and Lynk (1990a, b) have estimated logarithmic, multiproduct cost functions, using time-series data for the period 1950/1 to 1980/1. The aim of their study was to examine the case for the divestiture of British Telecom along the lines advocated by Beesley and Littlechild (1986) and Vickers and Yarrow (1988). The former suggested the separation of domestic (local and trunk) from international voice telephony services as a means of introducing an element of competition. The latter advocated the separation of local from long-distance (trunk and international) services along the lines of the AT&T divestiture in the USA. Hunt and Lynk found cost complementarities, and thus economies of scope, between internal and external services, but not between local and long distance. The implication of their results is that the divestiture of local services would not result in efficiency losses. This finding is perhaps not surprising. After all, the USA, Japan and Denmark operate local and regional services, and the Hull Telephone Co. also operates a profitable local telephone service.

The preceding discussion has emphasised the importance of cost conditions in determining the extent to which the introduction of competition into natural monopoly situations is likely to produce the desired outcomes of effectively constraining the market behaviour of the dominant producer and increasing efficiency. In several situations the presence of sunk costs is likely to deter entry into such markets and so a policy designed to encourage entry would need to remove this influence. One approach would be for the sunk cost elements to be owned and maintained under public ownership with private producers hiring these facilities for a specified charge. Another would be the divestiture of the natural monopolist in those areas where economies of scope were unimportant or where the intensification of competition would more than compensate for their loss.

The role of technical change: the case of telecommunications

In Chapter 13 we saw that, in a multiproduct market, economies of scale and scope are necessary conditions for natural monopoly, *for a given level of output*. We also showed how changes in demand and cost can change the status of an industry, and that *global* information on cost and demand conditions is necessary before an industry can unequivocably be regarded as naturally monopolistic. Cost conditions faced by the firm are influenced by several factors, including movements in input prices and also the technology with which the firm operates.

The influence of technical progress in general is to move the cost function downward. In reality, however, it is likely that costs are reduced over some output levels more than they are over others. These cost changes may have strong implications for optimal industry structure. For example, an innovation which accelerates the rate at which scale economies are exhausted would (in a single-product industry) imply an increase in the number of firms the industry could support for a given level of demand without sacrificing efficiency. Evidence suggests that in certain segments of the market this is precisely the situation occurring within telecommunications. The replacement of coaxial and copper wire with large-capacity optical fibre by BT and Mercury in their trunk lines has greatly reduced operating costs. Similarly, the digitalisation of switching and signalling, which increases the ability of networks to carry different types of traffic, is removing the distinctions between voice telephony and other services. Within telecommunications, the service area that appears to exhibit the most rigid natural monopoly characteristics is local network services. The choice by Mercury to compete in the main in the long-distance market reflects the view that wasteful duplication of capacity might occur should it move into certain local markets. However, Mercury is building local capacity and introducing competition in local switched services in some British cities.

One area where there is considerable potential for local competition is through the participation of cable television companies. These companies could compete in local services because they would be able to share costs that are common to television and telephone systems, thereby making competition economically feasible. This is a fascinating example of technical change inducing scope economies which remove the natural monopoly status of an activity originally conferred by substantial scale economies. At present, however, cable TV companies can provide voice telephony only if they do it via an agreement with BT or Mercury.

A further obstacle to the emergence of local competition has been the perceived low profitability of local call business relative to long-distance business. One remedy would be to increase the standing charge, which pays for the provision of the exchange line from the consumer to the local exchange, but this might induce unwelcome externalities in the form of falling network participation, which would reduce the value of the service to everyone. However, technical change is again facilitating local competition by reducing the overall costs of the network and making it possible for the standing charge to rise in relative terms without an absolute increase, thereby reducing call charges within the overall basket of services. Within telecommunications, then, the effect of technical change is increasingly to reduce the incidence of cost subadditivity in the service area most often regarded as a natural monopoly. Hence there appears to be considerable scope for introducing competition into the industry, which will further reinforce the regulatory process.

The potential for introducing more competition into the telecommunications industry was recognised in a government White Paper published in March 1991. Following widespread criticism of the post-privatisation performance of BT in the areas of service quality and productivity, the government announced its intention of ending the licensed duopoly, and of introducing competition, particularly in the local and long-distance markets. Local network competition is envisaged through the entry of cable television companies, who will be permitted to carry telephone services as well as television services. Several operators, including British Rail, which already has its own dedicated fibre-optic network in place, are expected to enter the long-distance market. Though these proposals are undoubtedly radical, it is unlikely that effective competition will emerge before the mid-1990s at the earliest. This is why some commentators have argued for a restructuring of BT as a complementary policy to the liberalisation of entry conditions (see Hunt and Lynk 1991).

Tariff structures

Another problem facing the regulator in trying to promote competition is the pricing policy of the incumbent, which may be used as a weapon to deter entry. Pricing problems are particularly difficult in industries where there are strong peaks in demand and where a high proportion of the assets are in the form of fixed and sunk costs. It has already been noted in this chapter that, for optimality, fixed costs should be allocated to customers in inverse proportion to their demand elasticities, so giving a set of 'Ramsey prices'. These demand elasticities will be determined by the availability of alternative suppliers and of substitute products or services. This causes a major problem because it is exactly the basis on which systematic, and anti-competitive, price discrimination may take place. And, where fixed and sunk costs are high, there is great scope for discriminatory pricing behaviour. The pricing policy of British Gas, which was condemned in the 1988 report of the Monopolies and Mergers Commission (see Chapter 13), is a classic example.

The choice of tariff structure is particularly relevant where, as in the UK, regulation constrains overall price movements but leaves the incumbent free to adjust the structure of prices within the overall constraint.

14.3 DEREGULATION

In some industries, regulation has had little or nothing to do with natural monopoly. It has existed for other reasons – for instance, to protect cartel arrangements, to protect safety standards, or to meet social needs. The less important the natural monopoly element, the easier it will be to introduce competition. Deregulation will increase competition between existing firms, and it will also expose incumbents to new entry, though where safety is important new entry will be limited to those firms that can meet the required standards.

Take the case of stage-fare bus services in the UK. Up until 1986 local bus undertakings, often owned by the municipality, had a virtual monopoly. They operated a network of services which could be divided into three parts: (i) profitable services; (ii) unprofitable services subsidised by (i); and (iii) other unprofitable services financed by the local authority. The larger the 'breakeven network' made up of the first two categories, the less support was needed from public funds. The cross-subsidisation of services within the breakeven network was thus regarded by many local authorities as an important part of local transport policy; indeed cross-subsidisation was often a condition of revenue support. The means of achieving cross-subsidisation was the charging of common fares regardless of variation in cost.

Although the natural monopoly element in local bus services is small compared, say, with gas or electricity distribution, there are nevertheless some interesting similarities. In particular the emphasis is on maintaining a *network* of services, including a high proportion of unprofitable but socially desirable ones. In addition, it was argued that in large conurbations the system facilitated the coordination of public transport, resulting in external benefits that would not otherwise be achieved. The common fare policy was easy to administer and was widely regarded as equitable. The arguments for the system were thus based not so much on natural monopoly arguments but on the need to defend as large a network of coordinated services as possible on grounds of social need and beneficial external effects.

However, the old system was open to a number of criticisms. First, the resources used in providing local bus services were misallocated because of the common fare policy and thus fares failed to reflect the relative cost of providing individual services. Second, the fairness of the system was open to challenge, especially in the cities where some of the most profitable services were to and from areas with a high proportion of low-income households. In these cases the common fare policy meant that low-income households were subsidising those on higher incomes. Third, the combination of cross-subsidisation and revenue support in the form of a general subsidy for a whole network gave the bus undertaking little incentive to minimise costs on individual routes. Fourth, the protection given to the monopoly supplier meant that there was little incentive to relate services more closely to passenger needs, to introduce more economical mini and midibuses, and generally to exercise the managerial authority needed to increase efficiency. Fifth, the problems facing management were exacerbated by the political element in decision-making.

In principle there is no reason why desirable changes such as increased use of passenger surveys, more flexible use of manpower, and more rapid introduction of smaller buses could not have come about under the old regime. Recommendations to this effect were made in the MMC's report on *Stage Carriage Services* (1982). However, deregulation might, at the very least, have given an impetus to much-needed reforms.

The purpose of deregulation was, of course, to expose incumbent monopolists to competitive pressures. But how was this competition likely to manifest itself? Would it be widespread and permanent or localised and sporadic? Entry into commercial services was expected to occur on the most profitable routes, i.e. there would be a substantial amount of 'cream skimming'. It was also expected that the incumbent would respond aggressively to any attempt at entry. Overall profitability in providing bus services is, at best, modest, and loss of the more profitable services would have serious consequences. The incumbent could therefore be expected to react to entry by matching lower fares and increasing service frequency, very often with the use of smaller, more economical, vehicles. A sharp response could be expected, even to very small-scale entry on profitable routes, because other potential entrants might be deterred if a reputation for toughness could be established.

Thus competition could be expected to lead to a closer matching of fares to costs and thus to greater allocative efficiency *within* the sector. (There are limits to what can be achieved in practice because of the administrative costs of having a multiplicity of fares, and because high- and low-cost routes frequently overlap.) There would also be greater incentives to increase efficiency. On the other hand, there could well be some unwelcome effects. The increased competition would be most likely to occur where services were already frequent, and this might lead to unnecessary duplication as well as increased congestion in town centres. Indeed, if substantial excess capacity emerged, the position would not be sustainable in the longer term. Another possible adverse effect would be a decline in the size of the network. If the incumbent monopolist loses revenue on the most profitable routes then, for a given level of revenue support paid by local authorities, fares on other services would have to be increased and some services would have to be abandoned altogether.

Deregulation of bus services in the UK followed the 1985 Transport Act. The available evidence on the effects of the deregulation is patchy but does give some support to the predictions made earlier. Deregulation does seem to have given an impetus to the introduction of new methods of operation. There are also examples of attempts at 'cream skimming'. The success of entry, however, has depended very much on the efficiency and financial power of the incumbent. Where the incumbent is in a strong position, the challenge of new entry has been successfully met and most entry attempts have been short-lived. Fare structures have sometimes come to reflect costs more closely but not invariably so. Where there was not a strong incumbent, deregulation has sometimes resulted in the breakdown of a dependable network of services (George and Lynk 1990).

While there has to be flexibility to meet changing market requirements, there also has to be a long-term commitment from bus operators who are prepared, in Demsetz's words, to invest in permanence rather than in fly-by-night operations (Demsetz 1982). One of the less fortunate aspects of the 1985 Act is that by encouraging cream skimming and hit and run entry it failed to recognise sufficiently clearly the importance of the network. While competition is important in minimising costs, the most appropriate form of competition will vary according to the circumstances of individual markets. Under the 1985 Act there is virtually unregulated entry. Operators have to meet minimum safety and other criteria, but many well-established firms would argue that these are not rigorously enough enforced. A more regulated and less disruptive form of entry would exist if, for those bus operators under municipal control, greater use was made of the tendering system. For privately owned bus operators it would be more appropriate if management inefficiency was punished by takeover rather than by piecemeal sniping at parts of the business.

Business failures and takeovers on a sufficient scale might of course produce a more disciplined market, and the benefits of increased competition might then be short-lived. This is what has happened following the deregulation of passenger air services in the USA. Once again we find that a good and sustainable balance between the benefits of competition and the benefits of efficient supply is not easy to find.

So far we have looked at ways in which the problem of regulating monopolists might be eased by introducing competition *in* the market. Monopolies might be exposed to competition in a number of ways. The natural monopoly element might be removed by state ownership of sunk cost elements or by ensuring that entrants have access to the distribution network of the incumbent monopolist. Alternatively, in those cases where economies of scale and of scope are small, or where they would be outweighed by the efficiency-enhancing benefits of a more competitive market structure, the industry could be restructured by breaking up the incumbent monopolist. This policy will be facilitated where technical change reduces the importance of economies of scale and of scope. Lastly, competition can be introduced by deregulating an industry.

14.4 FRANCHISING

Where restructuring and deregulation are not appropriate, an alternative is to introduce competition by allocating monopoly rights of supply – i.e. competition *for* the market, in which firms bid for franchises entitling them to be the sole producer of a given product or service in a particular segment of the market. The practice is widespread. It is used in oil exploration, coach and bus services, radio and television broadcasting, cleaning and catering services in public buildings, to mention just a few examples. It is a practice used by private as well as public bodies. The British Airports Authority (BAA), for instance, has concessionaires operating shops, restaurants and other services in its airports around the country.

Franchising would appear to be an eminently suitable approach to natural monopoly. In a natural monopoly, production is most efficient with only one firm. In a franchising system, firms compete for the right of being the sole supplier. The potential at least would seem to exist for an ideal solution to the natural monopoly problem. Competition for the franchise should eliminate the adverse monopoly elements in single-firm markets without impairing the efficiency benefits of monopoly supply. Furthermore, there would appear to be no need for regulation. Once the franchise has been awarded, the franchisee would have freedom to operate the business. In reality, however, the ideal is unlikely to be achieved.

Contract specification

Firms will bid for a franchise on the basis of their expectations about the future stream of profits from the business. One method of awarding a franchise is to award it to the firm that offers the largest sum of money for the business. In this case a proportion of the monopoly profits will accrue to the franchisor, that proportion being greater the more competition there is at the bidding stage. Not surprisingly, this is the system adopted by the BAA, the allocation of concessionaires at the BAA-owned airports being based on the proportion of sales revenue that a bidder undertakes to pay the BAA. While obviously benefiting the franchisor, this method of awarding a franchise suffers the disadvantage of monopoly pricing and consequent loss of consumers' surplus.

The alternative is to award a franchise to the firm that offers to supply the products or services at the lowest prices. This proposal, first made by Chadwick (1859) and developed by Demsetz (1968), is known as the Chadwick–Demsetz proposal. It avoids the problem of monopoly pricing and has the apparent merit of simplicity.

Franchising, however, does present a number of difficulties. The first concerns the bidding process itself. Ideally this should be between a large number of independent firms all with access to the same information. In reality some firms will be better placed than others. This will be so even when the franchise is being offered for the first time, because some firms will have experience of the general line of business – for instance, large catering organisations bidding for the catering franchise at London Airport. Another problem is the possibility of collusion between bidders. This is most likely when the bidders are few in number and compete for franchises on a regular basis so that there is a danger of market-sharing arrangements. Where there is already an incumbent, a further problem is that the incumbent is liable to have access to more information than is available to potential entrants. In particular, the incumbent is likely to have better information on cost conditions within the business and have a better 'feel' for the franchisor's priorities and objectives. This is particularly important once factors other than price enter the contract and complex decisions involving, for instance, price–quality objectives have to be made.

This brings us to the next difficulty. Franchising is complicated by multiproduct operation and by having to consider non-price dimensions such as product quality or quality of service. In these circumstances the Chadwick–Demsetz proposal of awarding a franchise on the basis of the lowest price ceases to have precise meaning. The magnitude of the problem will of course vary from one business to another, depending on the range of performance criteria that enter the contract, and the problems involved in evaluating the quality of service. For example, it would be easier to specify a contract embodying price and quality of service components for window-cleaning than for a shop or restaurant. In the former it is a relatively simple matter of price and frequency of cleaning; in the latter, product specification and range, opening hours, staffing levels and so on have to be detailed, as well as the prices to be charged. Again, it would be easier to specify a contract for a school bus service than for broadcasting, since quality in the latter embraces subjective and non-quantifiable elements.

Length of contract and contract enforcement

An important problem with franchising is to determine the length of the contract. To some extent the problem will be resolved by the nature of the product or service in question. A franchise for the sale of ice cream can be of considerably shorter duration than one for the supply of cable television; the reason being, of course, that the latter involves a considerably larger resource commitment than the former.

However, even when considering a given franchise there is considerable scope for argument about the optimal length of the contract. This is because there are both advantages and disadvantages in lengthening a contract. The resources commited to a franchise may involve substantial sunk costs, including the sunk cost of making the bid itself. A longer contract is therefore likely to attract a large number of bidders, since investments can be written off over a longer period. Similar considerations suggest that a long contract period acts as an inducement to the incumbent to invest in the business. If, on the other hand, the contract period is short, and the incumbent fears that his franchise will not be renewed, the likelihood is that investment will be deterred. This presents a problem. On the one hand, short-term contracts have the advantage, that they can be made more *complete*; on the other hand, they may deter investment.

A contract is complete when it contains a full description of what is to happen to price, and all other dimensions of performance that are stipulated, under every conceivable set of circumstances over the life of the contract. Clearly, the shorter the contract period the less likely that there will be substantial shifts in demand or cost conditions, or that the incidence of technical progress will substantially alter the operating environment. The shorter the term, therefore, the easier it is to specify a contract that contains an agreed set of price and non-price variables which can be satisfied throughout the period. The longer the period, the more uncertainty attaches to future demand, cost and technological conditions, and the more difficult it becomes to specify a contract. One response might be to specify prices, product range, etc. that would apply regardless of any change in circumstances over the contract period. However, an *unconditional* contract of this kind is liable to break down. A collapse in demand following a change in fashion, for instance, would ruin a business that was not able to respond by adjusting prices and the range of products sold. The alternative is to have an incomplete contract that allows prices, etc. to be adjusted in response to changes in underlying conditions. But this implies the need for periodic renegotiation of contracts and thus for continual regulation of the business by the franchisor.

Lastly, what about the interaction between contract length and investment? With perfect capital markets and no sunk costs there would be no problem. The incumbent would, in the event of his franchise not being renewed, be able to recover the full value of his investment net of depreciation. The difficulty arises, therefore, because of problems of asset valuation where capital markets are imperfect, especially for sunk investments where secondhand markets do not exist and a valuation is not possible. A further consideration is that the franchisee's overall commitment to a business is liable to be weak unless there is a reasonably long contract, and this may have adverse effects not only on investment but also on other aspects of business performance such as quality of service.

One way of resolving some of these difficulties is to have an 'operating' franchise rather than an 'ownership' franchise. With an ownership franchise, the franchisee owns the assets used in supplying the good or service. With an operating franchise, however, the franchisee rents the assets from the franchisor. Where sunk costs are important, the operating franchise has the advantage of widening the range of potential bidders. But it is not without its disadvantages. The assets may not embody best-practice techniques as perceived by the franchisee. The franchisee may also have less control over the way in which assets are used. Operating franchises, in other words, are liable to involve more regulation by the franchisor.

Concluding comment on franchising

There are several potential advantages in operating a franchising system where conditions of natural monopoly are found. In theory it is able to combine the benefits of competition with those of operating efficiency. In the operating franchise the problem of sunk costs can be avoided. Efficiency constraints can be placed on the incumbent franchisee through the threat of non-renewal of contract, and the periodic bidding process provides the franchisor with an important element of 'yardstick information'. However, there are also problems – of ensuring competitive auctions; of specifying contracts under conditions of multiproduct supply, when non-price factors are important, and when there is considerable uncertainty over future demand and cost conditions; and of choosing the length of contract which strikes the right balance between the threat of non-renewal and the offer of adequate incentives so that the franchisee feels that he has a sufficient stake in the business. The right balance will vary from one industry to another. In some cases the investment required in the business may be small and continuity of relationship between consumer and producer unimportant. In other cases the reverse will be the case. Lastly, franchising often has to be accompanied by regulation. Even in relatively simple activities such as cleaning services, where contracts are short and the task easily defined, intervention by the franchisor to deal with unforeseen circumstances and to see that the job is properly done is not uncommon. Regulation is all the more likely as the contract period is lengthened and the contract itself becomes more complex.

14.5 CONCLUDING COMMENTS

Both public ownership and regulation fall short of being ideal ways of dealing with monopoly. As a result it is generally accepted that, wherever possible, ways should be found of introducing competition. This chapter has discussed a number of ways in which this may be accomplished. It has also become clear that a policy of introducing competition serves to complement rather than to replace the other policy options. Where there are strong natural monopoly elements, competition alone is not likely to be sufficient. A particular difficulty of introducing competition into certain industries is the necessity of allowing entrants reasonable access to an incumbent monopolist's network. It is in the incumbent's interests to inflate connection charges and thereby restrict the emergence of effective competition. Regulation is needed to guard against this conduct. Alternatively, entry-deterring obstacles can be reduced by retaining important sunk cost elements in public ownership and allowing competition in other parts of the business. Where it is judged that economies of scale and of scope have been greatly exaggerated, or that any loss of economies would be outweighed by the efficiency-enhancing effects of a more competitive market structure, it may be possible to have a measure of industry restructuring with the incumbent broken up into smaller units. The extent to which this is possible depends very much on technology and on the cost conditions prevailing in the industry.

In some industries the main obstacle to competition may have been legal rather than technical. Regulation, for instance, may have supported cartel or other arrangements that stifled competition between potentially close competitors. In these cases competition can easily be introduced simply by changing the rules of the game. However, the removal of that regulation may lead to a level of competition which is not sustainable in the long term. Bankruptcies and/or mergers may be needed to bring capacity more in line with demand, but this process may go too far and result in an overly concentrated industry. Here deregulation may need to be accompanied by merger policy to secure better results.

Where it is not possible to have competition *in* the market, an alternative is to have competition *for* the market – i.e. a system of franchising. Franchising appears to combine the benefits of competition with the cost efficiencies of single-firm operation, without the need for regulation. In practice, however, there are often substantial difficulties in conducting competitive auctions and in specifying and enforcing contracts. These problems are particularly important when it is desirable to have a long-term relationship between customer and supplier. Once again it is not possible to rely exclusively on competition : regulation and competition have to be present, one complementing the other, in order to get the best results.

Chapter 15

Maintaining competition: restrictive practices policy

15.1 INTRODUCTION

The previous chapter examined the possibilities of introducing competition into markets where, because of technical or institutional constraints, effective competition has been either completely absent or stifled. The other main area of competition policy is that of maintaining competition in markets where the main problems are the restrictive practices of a number of firms acting together and the anti-competitive behaviour of firms that hold dominant positions in their markets. In this chapter we first give a brief overview of competition policy in the USA, UK and European Communities, before going on to examine restrictive practices policy in more detail. Section 15.2 describes the different types of restrictive practices. Section 15.3 examines policy towards horizontal collusive behaviour in the UK, EC and USA, and this is followed in section 15.4 by a review of policy approaches to vertical arrangements between firms.

A brief overview of legislation

US legislation

The USA is the home of antitrust policy in the historical as well as the philosophical sense. Policy started with the passing of the Sherman Act 1890. Section 1 of this Act made contracts, combinations or conspiracies in restraint of trade or commerce among the several states illegal. Section 2 declared that 'every person who shall monopolize or attempt to monopolize ... any part of the trade or commerce among the several States, or with foreign nations, shall be deemed guilty of a misdemeanour'.

In 1914 two additional laws were enacted. The Clayton Act declared illegal certain specific practices – price discrimination, exclusive-dealing arrangements and tying contracts, the acquisition of shares in competing companies and interlocking directorates – which were not covered in the 1890 legislation. (Policy towards vertical arrangements was later to be extensively modified.) Its most important provision was to prohibit certain mergers where the effect would be substantially to lessen competition or to tend to create a monopoly. This merger control was strengthened by the Celler–Kefauver Anti-Merger Act of 1950 which included the acquisition of assets as well as shares within the scope of the legislation. Also in 1914, the Federal Trade Commission Act was enacted which established the Federal Trade Commission and gave it powers to outlaw 'unfair methods of competition'.

So by 1914 the main lines of US policy had been established. Policy actions are enforced by two separate agencies, which have largely similar functions. The Antitrust division of the US Department of Justice prosecutes alleged violators of the law before a federal district court, whose decisions in important civil actions may be appealed against, on matters of law, by either party to the Supreme Court. The Federal Trade Commission (FTC) investigates and prosecutes civil complaints internally. With majority approval of its five-member staff, complaints are brought before one of the Commission's administrative law judges, who can recommend that the Commission issue an order against firms found to be guilty of breaking the law. Appeals against decisions can be made to a US Court of Appeal and from there to the Supreme Court. FTC procedures are therefore more cumbersome than those of the Justice Department. In both cases policy outcomes depend on decisions made by the two agencies as to which cases to prosecute, and on judicial decisions.

An important feature of US policy is the role played by private litigants. Private prosecutions may be brought under both the Sherman and Clayton Acts, and appeals may be made to higher courts. The vast majority of all antitrust cases are brought by private litigants who, if they win, are rewarded with triple damages.

UK legislation

Policy in the UK dates effectively from 1948 with the passing of the Monopolies and Restrictive Practices Act, which set up a Monopolies and Restrictive Practices Commission with powers to investigate monopolies and cartels. The work of the Commission turned out to be that of inquiry rather than control. By 1956 it was clear that a tougher approach was needed. The 1956 Restrictive Trade Practices Act took restrictive practices policy away from the Commission and established separate machinery to deal with them – the Registrar of Restrictive Practices and the Restrictive Practices Court. The Act established compulsory registration of restrictive agreements, and such agreements were presumed to be against the public interest. The legality of individual agreements was to be established by the Court, with the Act laying down the conditions under which an agreement could be upheld. The Act made collective resale price maintenance illegal *per se*.

Competition policy was further strengthened in the 1960s with the enactment of three pieces of legislation. The Resale Prices Act 1964 introduced a general prohibition of individual resale price maintenance (rpm) but with the possibility of exemption. The Monopolies and Mergers Act 1965 brought mergers within the scope of Monopolies Commission investigations, while the Restrictive Trade

Practices Act 1968 brought information agreements within the scope of restrictive trade practices legislation.

Competition policy currently falls under four main Acts, and is enforced by four main competition authorities.

The *Fair Trading Act 1973* replaced the Acts of 1948 and 1965. The most important institutional change was the creation of a new office – that of Director General of Fair Trading. The Director General was empowered to make monopoly references, subject to the approval of the Secretary of State. The functions of the Registrar of Restrictive Trading Agreements were transferred to the Director General, so that the surveillance of monopolies, mergers and restrictive practices were brought together for the first time. The Monopolies Commission was reconstituted and renamed the Monopolies and Mergers Commission (MMC). The Act changed the definition of the public interest, introducing for the first time explicit mention of the desirability of competition. The *Restrictive Trade Practices Act 1976* consolidated previous enactments relating to restrictive trade practices. The *Resale Prices Act 1976* consolidated Part II of the 1956 Act which prohibited collective rpm and the 1964 Act which introduced the general prohibition, subject to exemptions, of individual rpm. The *Competition Act 1980*, which was a new piece of legislation, enabled the Director General of Fair Trading to investigate the anti-competitive practices of single firms and to make 'competition references' to the MMC. Previously the anti-competitive behaviour of single firms could be examined only as part of a full-scale monopoly reference. The 1980 Act also empowered the Secretary of State to refer public sector bodies to the MMC.

The four main competition authorities are the Office of Fair Trading (OFT), the MMC, the Restrictive Practices Court, and the Secretary of State for Trade and Industry. The OFT monitors restrictive trade practices, monopolies and mergers. Its Director General (DG) takes restrictive trade practices to the Court unless otherwise directed by the Secretary of State. The DG also makes monopoly references and competition references to the MMC, subject to the approval of the Secretary of State. Only the latter has the power to make merger references and public sector references under section II of the 1980 Act. The MMC investigates the monopolies, mergers, anti-competitive practices and public sector bodies that are referred to it. If it decides that a merger, for instance, may be expected not to operate against the public interest, there is no power to stop it; similarly if there is no adverse public interest finding with respect to the conduct of a monopolist. In these instances the MMC effectively has the power of decision. In the event, however, of an adverse public interest finding, the MMC can only make recommendations, the power to decide on remedies resting with the Secretary of State. The latter has considerable powers at his disposal including, for instance, the power to stop a merger or to prevent monopolies from pursuing a particular course of conduct. But he is not bound by the MMC's recommendations. He decides at his own discretion whether to accept the conclusions and recommendations of the Commission.

EC legislation

The European Community's competition policy is laid down in Articles 85 and 86 of the Treaty of Rome (1957).

Article 85(1) states that 'agreements between undertakings, decisions by associations of undertakings and concerted practices which may affect trade between Member States and which have as their object the prevention, restriction or distortion of competition within the Common Market shall be prohibited as incompatible with the Common Market'. There is, however, provision for exemptions, including block exemptions as, for instance, in the case of franchising agreements.

Article 86 states that 'any abuse by one or more undertakings of a dominant position within the Common Market or in a substantial part of it shall be prohibited as incompatible with the Common Market in so far as it may affect trade between Member States'.

These basic principles have been translated into an effective policy by various implementing Regulations, notably no. 17, which came into force in 1962. This Regulation gives exclusive power to the Commission to enforce policy. For this purpose one of the European Commissioners is given responsibility for the implementation of competition policy and he is assisted by a Directorate-General for Competition, DG IV.

There is no article in the Treaty of Rome that deals specifically with mergers, though both Articles 85 and 86 have been used, with mixed success, to deal with merger cases. In 1973 the Commission put forward a draft merger-control proposal to the Council of Ministers, but this never succeeded in becoming law. However, in December 1989 the Council accepted a merger regulation which would give the Commission powers for dealing with mergers above a prescribed minimum size in terms of turnover, and which have a 'Community dimension'.

The EC has adopted an administrative approach to competition policy in which the Commission has extensive powers to investigate suspected breaches of the law, to require the ending of anti-competitive practices and to impose penalties on offending parties. With the powers of both prosecution and judge there has to be provision for appeal against the Commission's decisions. This power of review lies with the European Court of Justice.

15.2 RESTRICTIVE PRACTICES

In most industrialised economies, policy towards restrictive practices is the oldest and most highly developed form of competition policy and is more hostile than policy towards single large firms. Firms can combine in a huge variety of different forms of restrictive behaviour. What these have in common is that, by engaging in such behaviour, the firms concerned manage to some extent to reduce the pressure of competition and the level of uncertainty about how other firms react. This uncertainty, which is healthy for competition and the consumer, is uncomfortable for the firms concerned, and it has long been observed that firms will try to get together to temper the bracing winds of competition.

The general case against restrictive practices rests on the theoretical argument in favour of competition and against monopoly, which has been discussed fully in Chapter 12. This is that any restriction of pure competition will tend to raise prices and/or restrict output, *ceteris paribus*. The fact, mentioned above, that competition policy tends to be more severe on restrictive agreements between firms than on non-competitive conduct by large firms acting on their own can be largely explained by the fact that one of the most important *ceteris paribus* conditions in this argument – namely, that cost conditions should remain unchanged between the perfectly competitive monopolistic industries – is more likely to hold for agreements between independent firms that promise no gain in efficiency from possible economies of scale to offset against the loss in efficiency due to increased market power. Indeed, as argued in Chapter 7, restrictive agreements are likely to raise the level of costs in the industry by protecting the inefficient firms that would be eliminated under competitive conditions. However, as we shall see, policy against restrictive practices has usually stopped short of total prohibition, and this indicates that at least some restrictive practices promise beneficial effects which may be thought to outweigh their disadvantages.

For convenience, restrictive practices may be divided into the following four main categories: horizontal agreements, vertical agreements, concerted practices and industrial property rights. These categories are discussed separately below, but it should be recognised that in practice many of the agreements that firms enter into are hybrids that combine elements from more than one category.

Horizontal agreements are those between firms in the same industry. This is the most familiar category of restrictive practice and includes price-fixing cartels, market-sharing agreements, sales syndicates, coordination of investment plans, research agreements, and standardisation and specialisation agreements. Restrictive practices policy usually assumes initially that the first three types of agreement are illegal, since they restrict competition without any other beneficial effects, although in particular cases such benefits may be claimed.

The last three types are more problematic for policy. Coordination of investment plans is often one aim of indicative planning, since without such coordination the fear of creating excess capacity may keep investment at a sub-optimal level, particularly in industries that are not growing and in which investment has to be made in large indivisible units. This is an example where competition and industrial policies may conflict. Similarly, allowing firms to combine to finance and undertake research may be an effective way of encouraging research and innovation (see Chapter 9), but it may also have undesirable effects in reducing competition between the firms involved. Lastly, if firms agree between themselves to specialise in different products, then, although competition is clearly reduced, such an agreement may enable each firm to produce on a more efficient scale than before.

Concerted practices are observed when firms collude to behave in a non-competitive way without any explicit agreement between them. This form of restrictive practice is on the boundary of policy, since it is clearly more difficult to prove that collusion has taken place without an actual agreement, and also such parallel behaviour is likely to become more common where more traditional forms of restrictive practice are illegal. Concerted practices are facilitated by information agreements between firms, by which firms inform each other of current prices, projected increases, and so on. It is then possible for firms to align their prices without actually agreeing to do so.

Industrial property rights are agreements concerning patents, copyrights, trademarks, and so on. These form a separate category, in that such agreements are legal forms designed to achieve a compromise between encouraging firms to engage in research and development (R&D) by allowing them a monopoly on any innovations and a general encouragement of competition. The considerations governing this compromise have been discussed in Chapter 9.

Vertical agreements are made between firms in successive stages of production or distribution. These include exclusive-dealing agreements, by which a single firm or group of firms agrees to buy only from, or sell only to, another firm or group of firms, and also resale price maintenance (rpm), by which the producer of a good controls the price at which it is sold to the final customer and makes sure that all retailers charge the same price.

This section has described various types of restrictive practice and also explained both why a policy towards restrictive practices is needed and why such a policy is unlikely to be simple. Despite a general preference for competition over collusion, which is itself felt with varying degrees of fervour in different societies, there are certain policy aims (e.g. the encouragement of a high level of investment in R&D) where allowing firms to get together may seem likely to work better than forbidding them to do so. Many restrictive agreements do offer some sort of advantage, not just to the firms concerned but also to consumers in the form of improved production or distribution, which must be weighed up against the reduction in competition due to the agreement. The trade-off between competitive pressures and efficiency benefits is especially important in the case of vertical price and non-price relationships. Contractual vertical relationships are considered in a separate section. First we turn to horizontal agreements.

15.3 HORIZONTAL COLLUSIVE BEHAVIOUR – POLICY IN THE USA, THE UK AND THE EC

Policy attitudes towards restrictive practices may be compared at a number of different levels. First, we can look at the broad philosophy behind policy and the strength of its commitment to competition. Second, we can look at the details of legislation to see how this philosophy comes through in terms of prohibiting restrictive agreements. Third, we can look at how forcibly the legislation has actually been applied in practice.

Broad policy approaches

The range of possible broad policy attitudes towards restrictive practices ranges from such a strong commitment to competition that all forms of restrictive behaviour are outlawed, on the one hand, to a system that has no laws against restrictive practices, on the other. On this scale the USA is nearest to the first end, with laws that make certain forms of restrictive agreement illegal *per se*, and the EC and the UK occupy an intermediate position at which a wide variety of restrictive agreements are prohibited but not *per se*; that is, there is provision for agreements to be exempt from prohibition. However, it is noteworthy that at least one constituent country of the EC, namely Italy, occupies a position close to the other end of the policy scale and operates no effective internal policy against restrictive practices.

The severity of US antitrust policy can be explained by historical and political factors as much as by economic arguments.

> Unrestrained interaction of competitive forces will usually result in the best allocation of our economic resources, the lowest prices, the highest quality and the greatest material progress, while at the same time providing an environment conducive to the preservation of our democratic, political and social institutions. (UK Green Paper 1978: 136–7)

For the EC, however, a competitive system is chosen for primarily economic reasons, as it is seen as the best means of achieving the fundamental aims of the EC, namely, economic integration and increased prosperity. The Treaty of Rome, which established the EC, contains a specific commitment to the 'institution of a system ensuring that competition in the Common Market is not distorted'. No such unequivocal statement can be found in UK legislation on competition policy, but although in principle the EC is more committed to competition than the UK, the practical policy differences are less significant than may be supposed.

Legislation against horizontal agreements

Let us now turn to examine legislation against restrictive practices in the USA, the UK and the EC. Legislation in all three cases reflects a compromise between the benefits of competition and those of restriction, and it is the different terms of compromise reached that we shall be examining. To some extent these can be explained by the different purposes of competition policy in the three systems: one national, one federal and one international. Thus, US federal antitrust policy is concerned with trade between, not within, states, EC competition policy covers only trade between member states, while UK policy deals with restrictions that affect the national economy.

US policy

Restrictive practices legislation in the USA started in 1890 with the Sherman Act, Section 1 of which made contracts, combinations or conspiracies in restraint of trade or commerce among the several states illegal. The scope of this Act is virtually all-embracing, and any exemptions have themselves to be legislated. The meaning of 'restraint of trade' has been decided by judicial interpretation over 100 years of antitrust cases. Neale (1966: 12) summed it up as 'business behaviour which in pursuit of profit prevents some form of competition from operating in the market', but he stressed that the existence of a restraint of trade has to be decided separately for each case that comes up. There are several categories of agreement, however, that are exempted from legal prohibition: these include restrictive practices by labour; agreements concerning public utilities and agriculture; export agreements; intra-state activity; and certain professional and financial services.

The American attitude towards the most flagrant forms of horizontal collusion, such as price-fixing and market-sharing, has been that these practices have no redeeming features. There is no need therefore for detailed inquiry into why they are pursued or the degree of injury they cause. They are illegal *per se*. Since there are no offsetting benefits, there is no need to apply the *rule of reason* under which a plaintiff would have to demonstrate not only anti-competitive effects but also that these effects outweighed any efficiency benefits that might be claimed by the parties to the restriction. However, although this view has dominated policy in this area, there has been some softening in more recent years and on at least one occasion an efficiency defence has been both allowed and upheld by the Supreme Court. The Court adjudicated that the collective action of copyright owners of musical compositions in preventing unauthorised use of their compositions resulted in substantial cost savings compared with the alternative of having thousands of individual transactions. It concluded that this collective action 'should be subjected to a more discriminating examination under the rule of reason'.

The rule of reason is applied to all practices which may facilitate collusive outcomes in the absence of explicit agreements. They include exchange of information agreements and certain pricing arrangements such as the use of 'basing-points'. The rule of reason is applied to these cases because they may have efficiency benefits as well as possibly facilitating collusive outcomes.

UK policy

The UK government began to take action against restrictive practices more than 60 years after the Sherman Act was passed in the USA. The Restrictive Trade Practices Act 1956 was followed by further legislation in 1968 and 1973 and these enactments were consolidated in the Restrictive Trade Practices Act 1976. The Act provides for registration with the Director General of Fair Trading of agreements between two or more persons in the production or supply of goods in which the parties concerned accept restrictions in respect of such matters as the prices to be charged, the terms on which goods are supplied and the markets to be supplied. The definition of an agreement is widely drawn, encompassing agreements which are expressed or implied as well as those that are written. Similar provisions are made in respect of designated services, and the Act also provides for the registration of information agreements.

The Director General is obliged to refer every registered agreement to the Restrictive Practices Court unless discharged from doing so by the Secretary of State. Registrability depends on whether an agreement contains restrictions of a *form* specified in the legislation, and not on whether it has the *effect* of reducing competition. UK legislation is thus described as 'form-based' rather than 'effects-based'. Registrability also depends on whether an agreement falls under an exempted category. The list of exemptions is long, including a wide range of professional, transport and financial services and labour market agreements.

Registered agreements are presumed to be against the public interest and the burden of proof is on the parties to an agreement to demonstrate benefit. To do so they have to convince the Court that each restriction in an agreement has beneficial effects in one or more of eight categories (the so-called 'gateways'). In addition, the benefits must outweigh any detriment caused by the restrictions – this requirement is known as the 'tailpiece'. The gateways allow a restriction on competition to be defended because it: protects the public against injury; confers benefits on the public; is needed to counteract the restrictions or market power of other parties; has beneficial effects on employment or exports; is needed to maintain another restriction upheld by the Court; or because it has no material effect on competition.

The gateways have been much criticised, in particular for being too widely drawn. However, out of several hundred agreements referred to the Court since 1956, only a handful have been upheld, the majority of these in the early years of policy enforcement.

EC policy

Restrictive practices policy in the EC has adopted a broadly similar attitude to that of the UK in that restrictive agreements are in general prohibited, with specific grounds for exemption. EC policy is laid down in Article 85 of the Treaty of Rome, which says that 'agreements between undertakings, decisions by associations of undertakings and concerted practices which may affect trade between Member States and which have as their object the prevention, restriction or distortion of competition within the Common Market shall be prohibited as incompatible with the Common Market'. Article 85(3) specifies the following conditions for exemption from prohibition. An agreement, decision or concerted practice may be allowed if it contributes to improving the production or distribution of goods, or to promoting technical or economic progress, while allowing consumers a fair share of the resulting benefits, as long as the restriction is necessary for attainment of the objective and the firms concerned are not thereby enabled to eliminate competition in respect of a substantial part of the products in question.

The policy laid down in Article 85 has been translated into practice by means of a number of implementing regulations of the EC Commission, notably Regulation 17, passed in 1962. This states that agreements and concerted practices as defined in Article 85 are prohibited. Registration is not compulsory, but firms that wish to continue operating an agreement legally can apply either for exemption under the terms of Article 85(3) or for 'negative clearance' – a declaration by the Commission that the agreement is not prohibited by Article 85. This may be granted on a number of grounds (e.g. that the agreement does not affect trade between member states). There are two remaining sets of circumstances in which restrictive agreements may be permitted: when they don't have a 'noticeable effect' on the market, and when they come under a 'block exemption'. The first criterion consists of a test of significance similar to tests operated in both the UK and the USA. Since 1970 it has been established that an agreement between firms is not prohibited by Article 85 if its effect on competition and trade between member states is insignificant, insignificance being defined in terms of the combined market share of participating firms or in terms of aggregate turnover. Second, the Council of Ministers can empower the Commission to issue block exemptions, by which whole categories of agreements are exempted from prohibition. Block exemptions have for instance been issued to cover agreements relating to specialisation, R&D, and patent licensing.

From the outset the Commission has dealt firmly with agreements involving price-fixing, quantity restrictions, or market-sharing. The position here is virtually one of *per se* prohibition. This being so it can be expected that more subtle collusive arrangements would emerge – such as parallel pricing, information agreements and the use of industrial property rights – to restrain competition. All these practices are embraced by Article 85, and in some cases have been condemned – for instance, parallel pricing by manufacturers of dyestuffs in 1967, and an information agreement amongst the three major European producers of fatty acids in 1987. In a number of cases involving property rights the Commission and the Court have established that these rights cannot be used to restrain competition.

While the Commission has taken a consistently hard line in relation to classic anti-competitive violations such as price-fixing and market-sharing agreements, it recognises that unfettered competition may not always produce the best results. Free market forces may work too slowly to bring about a desired result, or they may involve unacceptably high social costs. There is thus a role, within carefully defined limits, for cooperative agreements between firms. In a number of cases the Commission has looked sympathetically at agreements aimed at reducing capacity in industries with a structural over-capacity problem, and has also viewed favourably cooperative agreements aimed at fostering research and the strengthening of key industries of the future.

An important strand running through the Commission's thinking is the conviction that special attention should be given to small and medium-sized firms (SMEs). These firms 'are an essential and major component of a healthy, competitive environment'. They are also often at a disadvantage compared with large firms in their ability to raise funds, to benefit from economies of scale and to get access to specialised services. In markets characterised by dominance, they may also be the victims of predatory behaviour. The administration of policy attempts to correct these imbalances. For instance, the competitive restrictions of small firms are exempt from Article 85(1) on grounds of insignificance, and the block exemptions on specialisation agreements apply only when certain combined market shares and turnover thresholds (currently 20 per cent and 500 million ECU) are not exceeded.

A comparison of the legislation

Having outlined the main provisions of restrictive practices policy, we can now proceed to compare the attitudes towards competition and restriction revealed by these provisions. With regard to a wide range of the most seriously restrictive forms of behaviour (e.g. price-fixing and market-sharing) the comparison may appear relatively straightforward. The US approach towards such agreements has in almost all cases been to prohibit them; they are *per se* illegal and no amount of evidence concerning the alleged beneficial effects of such restrictions will cause this rule to be relaxed. Even in this area of policy, however, an efficiency defence has been allowed and upheld, but this is the exception that proves the rule. The US position is still that competition is (almost!) always and necessarily to be preferred to restriction. Neither UK nor EC legislation takes such a hard line as this, since both allow the effects of a restrictive agreement to be assessed in order to determine its legality.

On the basis of the legislation, the UK may appear to take a softer line than the EC. This is because the conditions for exemption from prohibition of restrictive agreements are more stringent in the EC than in the UK. First, the beneficial effects that can be claimed in support of an agreement are narrower. In the EC, only improving production or distribution and contributing to technical or economic progress may be used as arguments for maintaining an agreement, while the list of gateways in UK policy goes beyond such microeconomic efficiency considerations to include the goals of macroeconomic policy. Thus, a restrictive agreement can be upheld under UK law if it contributes to exports or to employment in areas of high unemployment and can be exempted from registration if it combats price rises. Second, UK legislation is more ambiguous about whether competition is the best means of achieving the ends of economic policy, both micro and macro. One of the gateways says that an agreement may be upheld where removal would deny the public other benefits or advantages arising from the restriction or arrangements or operations resulting from it. This is the clause that has allowed through most of the agreements upheld by the Restrictive Practices Court since 1956, and its wording suggests no initial presumption in favour of competition and against restriction. Third, the conditions for exemption under EC law contain a 'cut-off' clause; that is, no agreement shall be allowed, however beneficial its effects, if the firms concerned are enabled to eliminate competition in respect of a substantial part of the products in question. This suggests that competition must be maintained and that the benefits from preserving competition necessarily outweigh those of restriction. In the UK, the benefits claimed for a restriction must be shown to outweigh any disadvantages if the restriction is to be upheld by the Court. However, there is no 'cut-off' clause as in the EC.

This discussion of the provisions of policy towards horizontal collusive behaviour suggests that it is the USA that has been most and the UK that has been least committed to competition, and this accords with the broader philosophical attitudes to competition of the three systems which were outlined earlier. However, this conclusion as it stands may be too simple, because the difference between policy as *actually* enforced may be less important than the wording of the legislative provisions suggests.

The enforcement of policy

Let us then go on to compare policy towards horizontal agreements practices in the USA, the UK and the EC at the third level distinguished above, namely, the level of enforcement. The effectiveness of policy depends not only on the mere existence of legislation outlawing restrictive practices but also on how successfully this legislation is implemented. This means that there must be mechanisms for the detection of restrictive behaviour, procedures for examining agreements to determine whether they are legal, and appropriate penalties to end agreements found to be illegal.

The normal case with restrictive practices policy is that there is no shortage of agreements to be investigated. In all three systems under discussion, the antitrust authorities can initiate investigations into any sector or market when the presence of restrictions is suspected or when complaints have been received from members of the public adversely affected by restrictions. Also, in both the UK and the EC the only way for an agreement to be operated legally is for it to be registered and upheld, and unregistered agreements are declared automatically null and void. This does not mean that all agreements will be registered, so that there is no problem of detection, but it does mean that in general the problem for the restrictive practices policy authority is to choose which of a large number of cases in front of it is the most important to deal with.

This raises the point that to some extent, as with other forms of policy, the effectiveness of restrictive practices policy depends on the volume of resources devoted to it. Other important factors are how easy the provisions of policy are to interpret and the efficiency of the procedures for examining agreements. In the EC, restrictive practices policy is enforced through an administrative procedure by the Commission and the Directorate-General for Competition; in the UK the procedure is judicial, with the Restrictive Practices Court; and US policy is enforced jointly by the Antitrust Division of the Department of Justice and by the Federal Trade Commission, which is an executive agency.

What are the advantages and disadvantages of a judicial against an administrative procedure for examining restrictive practices? One advantage of a judicial system is that it is relatively open. The arguments on both sides can be heard by all those concerned and assessed by an impartial judge, while there have been complaints against the EC restrictive practices procedure that it can be bureaucratic and arbitrary, since the Commission acts as prosecutor, judge and jury. However, it may also be argued that the desirability or otherwise of a given restrictive agreement, which is essentially an economic question, should not be decided by a judicial procedure and by persons whose training and expertise is legal rather than economic. This argument is stronger where the law against restrictive practices is less clear cut and requires more in the way of interpretation. Thus, it can be claimed that, while a judicial procedure may be able to enforce satisfactorily US antitrust policy, which declares many forms of restrictive agreement illegal *per se*, this is not so for British policy, which requires much more weighing up of economic arguments in order to decide whether an agreement should be upheld or not. The British case-by-case approach, coupled with a wide range of possible grounds for exemption, has also been criticised on the grounds that it leads to inconsistent results. The US, UK and EC systems have in common, however, the feature that they are resource intensive; investigation into a single case may take months or years and use a vast quantity of man-hours from both the investigating authority and the companies under investigation.

Where the existence of an illegal restrictive agreement has been established, what can the competition policy authorities do to stop the agreement from working? In the UK, if the Restrictive Practices Court finds that an agreement is against the public interest, it can issue an order that forbids the companies concerned to operate either that agreement in its original form or another agreement to like effect. However, a serious weakness in UK policy has been the absence of penalties for those caught operating illegal restrictions. In the EC, the Commission can terminate an agreement found to be prohibited under Article 85 by issuing a formal decision that legally enforces abandonment of the agreement and can impose substantial fines on the firms involved. In the USA, the Federal Trade Commission issues a 'cease and desist' order – an injunction to the companies concerned to abandon those practices which have been found to be against the law. The penalties imposed by the courts in US antitrust cases depend on whether the case is a civil or a criminal one. Criminal penalties include the payment of fines and the imprisonment of offending businessmen, although in practice this latter sanction is rarely used. In civil proceedings (i.e. those cases not involving blatant *per se* offences) the court issues a decree that regulates the future conduct of the parties concerned in some detail. As indicated earlier, however, the vast majority of cases in the USA are brought to court by private parties. This provision for private litigation clearly improves the detection rate, and with triple damages being awarded when the plaintiff is successful there is also a considerable deterrent effect.

Lastly and most importantly we have to consider how successful policy has been in discouraging the most damaging forms of collusive behaviour.

One way of approaching this question is to look at the number of agreements discovered, upheld and struck down. By this criterion all three systems come out well. In the UK for instance, where in terms of legislative toughness results might be expected to be least impressive, out of over 900 agreements referred to the Court over the period 1956–87 only 11 were upheld. Such figures, however, tell only part of the story. On the one hand an unknown number of agreements will be abandoned in the light of decisions made by the competition authorities, and to that extent figures of agreements registered and struck down underestimate the effects of policy. On the other hand, the extent of evasion is also unknown. But we do know that it exists. In 1988, for instance, the European Commission reported that 15 major petrochemical producers had operated a market-sharing and price-fixing cartel. This, and other recent examples, underline the persistence with which firms will resort to quite explicit agreements even in the knowledge that if caught they may face a heavy fine.

But what happens when an agreement is abandoned? Will the firms concerned actually begin to behave competitively? This is particularly a problem in (the vast majority of) cases that are dealt with informally, since there is then no legal obligation on the firms concerned not to enter into another agreement and no provision for monitoring the subsequent behaviour of the firms.

Little research has been done into the effects of the abandonment of restrictive practices. An early enquiry into the effects of the disappearance of agreements (Heath 1960) found that in two-thirds of the cases manufacturers reported no change in prices or in the intensity of competition. A much later enquiry (O'Brien et al. 1979) also found that there was no significant difference between the profitability and other performance aspects of a group of firms that had been affected by the abandonment of restrictive agreements and those of a group that had not been affected by restrictive practices legislation. Although there are several methodological problems with these studies, the results are not entirely surprising. In general, the firms affected will usually be reluctant to embrace price competition wholeheartedly and will adopt any one of a number of devices to avoid this. Competitive behaviour will be most likely when the industry contains a large number of firms, including new entrants, and when the economic climate is buoyant. In other circumstances firms may attempt to restrict the degree of competition by entering into a new and legal form of agreement, or by recognising a price-leader or by some other form of oligopoly behaviour.

Many firms, previously party to an illegal agreement, will seek to replace this with a less restrictive form of agreement that will offer some of the same advantages of reduced uncertainty. The most common form of agreement entered into in these cases is an information agreement, by which the firms in an industry exchange information on prices, costs, investment plans, and so on through a central agency, but no agreements are made between the firms themselves on these matters. The prevalence of information agreements, where more restrictive agreements have been abandoned, has forced both the USA and the UK to evolve a policy towards such agreements. The Restrictive Trade Practices Act 1968 made information agreements registrable in the UK, which means that details of the agreement are available to all concerned, but as yet no cases involving information agreements have been heard by the Restrictive Practices Court. US antitrust policy has evolved guidelines to decide whether an information agreement is restrictive or not. In order to be allowed to continue, the information exchanged under an information agreement must be available to all buyers and sellers, must not identify individual companies, must cover only past sales, must not circulate average prices, and must not contain any controls or penalties on sellers. In the EC, information agreements have been included in the general prohibition of Article 85 from the outset of policy, and in several cases such agreements have been disallowed.

The evidence shows that firms are often very persistent in pursuing anticompetitive conduct, and that when one form of restriction is made illegal new forms will be invented that may achieve the same result. In oligopolistic industries, where the problem is most serious and durable, a collusive outcome may be achieved simply by recognition of mutual interdependence. This brings us to the last and most vexing problem of all – what constitutes a restrictive agreement?

In the USA, parallel pricing – which is one possible outcome of oligopolistic interdependence – does not violate the Sherman Act, even though the *result* may be exactly the same as in an explicit price agreement. Policy in fact focuses not on the result but on the *process* by which prices are set. The key issue therefore is the existence of evidence of an agreement, which means inevitably that explicit agreements are more easily detectable than tacit ones. This approach clearly means that important anti-competitive behaviour may go untouched while rather trivial cases will be caught. As a result Posner (1976) has argued that policy should focus on results and that all collusion, explicit or tacit, should be treated even-handedly. Although admirable in theory, the problem with such an approach is of course one of enforceability. To be effective it would be tantamount to instructing oligopolists not to recognise their interdependence.

A similar problem, but in even more acute form, has afflicted the UK approach. UK policy is based on the form of an agreement rather than on its effects. All agreements of a certain form are registrable even if their effects on competition are trivial. On the other hand, as in the USA, tacit collusion with substantial anti-competitive effects may escape. In addition, in the UK even explicit agreements may be immune if they are carefully worded.

This, and other weaknesses, have been recognised, and in 1988 the government announced its intention to switch to an effects-based policy, which would introduce a general prohibition of all agreements and concerted practices which have the 'effect of preventing, or restricting or distorting competition'. In order to *deter* anti-competitive conduct, especially tacit agreements which are difficult to detect, the new administration authority, which is to implement the new policy, will have substantial powers, including the power to impose fines. As an added deterrent, provision for private actions along USA lines is also proposed.

These changes will bring UK policy closely into line with that of the EC, where the approach from the outset has been to prohibit agreements, tacit as well as explicit, which have the object of preventing, restricting or distorting competition, but with clearly defined conditions for exemption.

In a number of respects, then, policies towards horizontal collusive agreements have shown some convergence. Although the legislative provisions show the USA as adopting the toughest stance with its *per se* approach, this has also been the outcome recently in both the UK and EC as far as the textbook examples of cartel behaviour are concerned. The EC, however, has adopted a more positive approach to certain kinds of restriction such as rationalisation and restructuring schemes which are deemed to be beneficial.

The most difficult problem confronting policy, even when it is effects-based, is that of promoting competition in oligopolistic industries. The problem stems from the structure of the industry, which forces the firms concerned to take account of one another's pricing behaviour. In such a situation, how can policy detect and distinguish illegal collusion, and what remedy should be applied? This has proved a very intractable problem for competition policy authorities everywhere, and it is on the borderline between policies towards restrictive practices and policies towards large dominant firms. If parallel pricing behaviour can occur in oligopolistic industries without any illegal meeting or agreement between the firms concerned, is it possible to infer that any illegal activity has taken place on the basis of circumstantial evidence? Policy in the USA, the UK and the EC has not reached a definite answer to this question, although evidence of coordinated price changes, for instance, may indicate collusion. However, even where the existence of collusion is proved and condemned, there remains the problem of what to do about it. Remedies available to restrictive practices policy authorities consist mainly of regulating future behaviour, which in the case of oligopolistic collusion consists of telling oligopolists that they shouldn't behave like oligopolists. This seems unlikely to be successful in the long term in the absence of more drastic structural policies.

15.4 VERTICAL ARRANGEMENTS

Many anti-competitive practices may be related to vertical arrangements between firms. They include both price and non-price vertical restraints, examples of the latter being distribution agreements and exclusive dealing.

Legislation against vertical agreements

The one thing that the USA, UK and EC have in common is the illegality of *collective* resale price maintenance (rpm) – the practice whereby a group of manufacturers combine to set the same resale price. In the USA, collective rpm is illegal under the Sherman Act; in the UK it was prohibited by the Restrictive Trade Practices Act 1956; and in the EC it comes under the general prohibition of Article 85. In other respects, however, there are major differences in policy.

US policy

The vacillations of US policy are most evident in relation to individual rpm. In 1911 the Supreme Court had declared rpm to be a *per se* violation of the Sherman Act. Then, however, a long period of legislative action under the banner of 'fair trading' established the legality of rpm, culminating in the Federal Fair Trade Act 1952. Under this Act not only were manufacturers and retailers permitted to sign rpm agreements, but retailers who had not signed an agreement could be forced to charge the same price. This policy stance survived into the 1970s. It had arisen because of an overriding concern for business interests during the interwar years. However, during the period of postwar prosperity the mood changed. But it was not until 1975 that the fair trade legislation was repealed and the original *per se* prohibition reinstated. However, the *per se* ruling was again to come under attack.

It came about as a result of developments relating to non-price vertical restraints. The first cases to be heard by the Supreme Court were in the 1960s, and in the *Schwinn* case (1967) the Court ruled that, so long as 'all indicia of ownership' had been transferred, territorial and customer restrictions were *per se* violations. A decade later this position had been overturned. In the *Sylvania* case (1977), which involved the distribution of television sets, it was accepted that vertical restraints may increase efficiency and promote inter-brand rivalry, and thus be in the interest of consumers as well as producers. Producers should thus be free to determine their distribution arrangements.

The effect of this judgment was to focus attention again on the *per se* ruling on price restraints. Since price and non-price restraints may lead to the same economic effects, the inconsistency in policy was plain to see. In 1982 the Department of Justice unsuccessfully argued that the *per se* treatment of rpm should be removed. However, although the Supreme Court retained the *per se* rule, the scope of the prohibition or rpm was narrowed, and over the decade of the 1980s the challenge to vertical restraints virtually ceased.

UK policy

Vertical relationships are dealt with under all four of the main competition acts. Individual rpm is caught by the 1976 Resale Prices Act; vertical relationships can be investigated as part of a full-scale monopoly investigation under the 1973 Fair Trading Act; some, such as franchising agreements and exclusive dealerships, fall under the 1976 Restrictive Trade Practices Act; and, in so far as they might involve anti-competitive practices, vertical relationships can also be investigated under the 1980 Competition Act.

UK policy has been more severe towards rpm than to any other aspect of business conduct. The 1964 Resale Prices Act, which declared a general prohibition of individual rpm, provided for exemption in cases where its abandonment would harm consumer welfare by: reducing the quality or variety of goods or the number of retail outlets; increasing retail prices; allowing goods to be sold under conditions dangerous to health; or reducing necessary services provided with or after the sale of the goods. However, the narrowness of these gateways has made it difficult to defend the practice, and in only two cases – pharmaceutical products and books – has there been a successful defence.

There is nothing to prevent suppliers from fixing maximum resale prices or from recommending resale prices. There is a danger that the latter practice might have the same result as rpm. This possibility was recognised in the MMC's report on *Recommended Resale Prices* (1969), but no clear evidence was found that the practice was harmful.

Non-price vertical arrangements are dealt with on the merits of each individual case. It is recognised that these arrangements may be efficiency enhancing but they may also be anti-competitive.

EC policy

Vertical arrangements between firms have from the outset been a central part of EC policy. Individual rpm agreements are allowed, so long as retailers remain free to buy from any supplier. This means that national rpm systems can be broken down by parallel imports from other EC countries. This ensures that rpm will not restrict or distort trade between member states.

The Commission has always recognised the legitimate interests that producers have in choosing their methods of distribution. At the same time, it has been mindful of the possible anti-competitive effects of certain vertical arrangements, especially market segmentation. The policy that has evolved is one that permits vertical relationships so long as certain basic conditions relating to the maintenance of effective competition are preserved. In particular, great emphasis is placed on sweeping away any barriers to parallel imports.

Vertical price restraints

As already noted, there is a marked difference in attitude in the USA and UK towards rpm. For over 50 years, rpm in the USA had legislative approval, and after a short period of hostility during the 1970s the official attitude became favourable once again. In the UK on the other hand rpm has been condemned. What accounts for the difference?

One possible reason is to be found in the underlying aims of US antitrust policy. An important motive has been the essentially political one of preventing concentrations of economic power. In those sectors of the economy where the free play of competitive forces would lead to the elimination of many small firms, this motive will lead to serious conflict with the economic aim of encouraging free competition. Retailing is one such sector and the 'fair trade' lobby was politically successful over a long period in its advocacy of rpm as a means of protecting the small shop against 'unfair' competition from large retailers.

More recently, however, the defence of rpm has its roots in the new developments in industrial organisation theory. Generally, it is argued, vertical arrangements do not add to entry barriers nor do they facilitate collusion. It can be shown, for instance, that under certain circumstances the maximum monopoly profits available to a fully integrated firm can be appropriated by a firm which is a monopolist at just one stage of the production–distribution chain. Monopoly power then is a horizontal problem, and so long as there is *inter-brand* competition there is no cause for concern.

If there is no monopoly element in vertical arrangements, there must be other motives, and these are found in the form of increased efficiency and lower transactions costs. These benefits could be attained through vertical integration (see Chapter 3). Alternatively, a manufacturer may seek to attain them by choosing a particular method of distribution and imposing restrictions on his distributors. This can be seen as another application of the principal–agent relationship, with distributors acting as the agents of the manufacturer. But whether firms choose to integrate activities internally or seek to impose restraints on their agents, the new theorising argues that there is no cause to interfere, for in both cases the outcome benefits both producers and consumers.

Since rpm restricts competition between distributors it has the effect, in general, of increasing prices. On this there is no dispute. Why then do manufacturers pursue a policy which *ceteris paribus* reduces output and profits? The answer is that by protecting retail margins the retailer can offer better service, which stimulates demand. This service may come in the form of more expert advice, better after-sales service, more advertising, and an increase in the number of retail outlets. In addition, the retailers who practice rpm are signalling quality to the customer. The rpm 'label' is an assurance of quality which maintains the reputation of the manufacturer.

An important feature of this analysis is the argument that the manufacturer cannot achieve the same results by forgoing rpm and widening retail margins by reducing his own price to retailers. This is because, even if some retailers used the improved terms on which they acquired the goods to improve service, others would not but would attempt instead to gain sales by cutting prices. In other words, they would be free-riding on the backs of their rivals. The price-cutting retailers would be gaining sales of products whose reputation for quality was being financed by others. Some might even use the product as a 'loss leader', a practice that would injure both the quality retailer and the reputation of the manufacturer.

By widening retail margins, therefore, retailers can offer more services; this stimulates demand so there is an outward shift in the demand curve. Thus, as well as increasing prices, rpm also increases output. The fact that consumers buy more at a higher price means that they must be better off. Consumers as well as producers have gained. This, in essence, is the argument in favour of rpm and one which has been accepted as the conventional wisdom by antitrust officials in the USA.

However, this position has been developed from theories whose assumptions may make them an unreliable guide to likely competitive outcomes. For instance, as Comanor (1985) has shown, the argument that increased output automatically benefits consumers rests on the assumption that consumers have identical preferences for various price/service combinations offered by retailers. Where differences exist, which they surely do, consumers in general do not necessarily benefit.

It is also not at all clear that rpm results in increased output. It may be used to facilitate collusion amongst either manufacturers or distributors, in which case the whole argument in favour of rpm collapses.

Also worth noting is the fact that the ways in which rpm is supposed to expand sales – quality signalling, more outlets and improved services – are all included as a possible defence of rpm in UK legislation. Yet in the UK manufacturers and distributors have been singularly unsuccessful in using these gateways to defend the practice. Let us then turn to the case against rpm which underpins UK policy. The basic point is that rpm restricts competition by imposing a uniform price on a commodity and that typically it raises distributors' margins above the competitive level. From this basic proposition a number of consequences follow.

First, whereas the preferences of consumers vary in terms of the desired price–service combination, the practice of rpm does not give them a choice. Thus, the consumer is not able to choose between a shop that sells a commodity at a relatively high price but also offers a lot of service, and one that sells at a lower price but offers very little service.

Second, rpm means that the price charged by different distributive outlets is the same, regardless of differences in their location, their efficiency and the amount of service actually supplied with the sale of goods. The more efficient firms are unable to attract more customers by offering lower prices, so that the growth of the efficient at the expense of the less efficient is retarded. This does not mean that the more efficient firms will be unable to increase their share of the market. Their greater efficiency will enable them to attract more customers by offering a better service and/or to earn higher profits with which to finance a faster growth rate. However, rpm does remove price competition, which is a powerful force affecting market shares. This is why, of course, the pressure to retain rpm has often been exerted by retailers rather than manufacturers.

Third, rpm is an obstacle to the development of new forms of distribution based on lower prices and less service. Again, this is not to say that it is *impossible* for new methods of distribution to develop. Thus, in the UK new retail firms based on self-service developed rapidly in the grocery field even under rpm, although it should be added that rpm in the UK was never as firmly established in this field as in the case of other consumer goods. Pressure on rpm can also come about by the diversification of large retail firms, as occurred in the case of the sale of cigarettes and alcoholic drink in supermarket stores. The development by large retailers of their own-branded goods also exerts pressure in the same direction.

Fourth, because rpm prevents price competition, it tends to increase competition in service to levels in excess of what is demanded by consumers, in the sense that, if given the choice, a substantial proportion of consumers would prefer to have lower prices and less service in the form, for instance, of elaborate packaging and attention from sales staff.

One particular aspect of competition in service that has received much attention is the argument that rpm results in a larger number of shops than would exist under a more competitive situation, and thus creates excess capacity. Even where rpm does not exist, the theory of monopolistic competition leads us to expect some degree of excess capacity because of the structure of the distributive trades. That is, where there are many close competitors each with a downward-sloping demand curve, and where entry conditions are easy, the forces of competition will *tend* to push the demand curve to a point of tangency with the downward-sloping portion of the average cost curve. This suggests that the same total output could be produced at a lower real cost by a smaller number of larger firms. It is difficult, however, to draw any firm implications from this analysis about the welfare of consumers, especially in the retail trades, because much of the excess capacity that is generated is associated with the existence of peak demand. How much differentiation do consumers demand, and how much are they prepared to pay for it in terms of the lost opportunities of a more standardised, lower-cost system? Accepting the fact that consumers demand *some* differentiation, is the amount of excess capacity actually generated by the competitive process too large? Chamberlin (1933) regarded the 'tangency solution' in the case of large numbers of competing sellers as a 'sort of ideal', arguing that the elasticities of the individual demand curves form a 'rough index of buyers' preferences for the 'product' of one seller over that of another'. This argument, however, is not tenable, because consumers are not in fact given a choice of having *either* more standardisation and lower prices *or* more differentiation and higher prices. They are offered one or the other, but not both.

With the existence of rpm, however, there is a much stronger presumption that too much surplus capacity will be generated. The maintenance of margins at a level higher than that which would prevail under freely competitive conditions protects the inefficient firms and promotes the entry of new ones. Small retail firms may also be encouraged by extensive delivery services, credit facilities, and so on, supplied by wholesalers and manufacturers. Competition in service therefore is not restricted to distributive outlets but may extend back to the manufacturers.

This brings us to the last point about the effects of rpm, namely, the way in which it is related to manufacturers' competition. The importance of rpm in this connection is that it strengthens manufacturers' price agreements. Price competition among retailers obviously endangers manufacturers' price agreements, especially if this competition changes market shares. The interrelationship between retailer and manufacturer competition and the importance of rpm in bolstering restrictive agreements among manufacturers are commented on in several reports of the Monopolies and Mergers Commission and its predecessors, including those on dental goods and cigarettes. In the report on dental goods (1950) the Commission said that 'manufacturers themselves claim that part of the value of resale price maintenance to them lies in the fact that if dealers compete in price the result very soon is a request for increased discounts (that is, for a reduction in the manufacturer's price)'. In the cigarettes, tobacco, and cigarette and tobacco machinery report (1961) the Commission argued that the 'manufacturers, who with few exceptions do not at present compete with one another in price for products of the same class, might be more willing to vary their own selling prices if there were no longer any standard retail prices'.

The argument against rpm is thus that it restricts consumer choice, supports inefficient forms of retailing, and also possibly facilitates collusion amongst manufacturers.

The virtual elimination of rpm in the UK, together with the growing dominance of the big retail chains, has shifted the area of concern. In the 1950s and 1960s it was about obstacles to the emergence of more efficient forms of retailing; now it is about the bargaining power of the retail chains. In its report, *Discounts to Retailers* (1981), the MMC concluded that more often than not discriminatory discounts were a reflection of effective competition between suppliers and buyers rather than a sign of monopolistic behaviour, and that thus competition had benefited consumers. However, the report warned that concentration in the retail trade might go too far.

Non-price vertical restraints

Non-price vertical restraints include exclusive dealing, tied sales, selective distribution and franchising. Following the *Sylvania* judgment in 1977, the US position is that these restraints hardly ever have anti-competitive effects.

Take exclusive dealing for instance. The dealer benefits from having to face less competition, so that a higher margin on sales can be maintained. The manufacturer benefits from having his product sold by enthusiastic dealers who, with the higher margin, have an incentive to carry larger stocks and offer an improved service. The arguments are the same as those used to justify rpm. Critics argue that exclusive dealing forecloses part of the market to competitors. One response to this criticism (again in common with the arguments that support rpm) is that exclusive dealing only achieves what could otherwise have been achieved by full integration. No additional element of market power is thus involved. Furthermore, even if competitors are foreclosed from one stage in the distributive chain, the effect is limited to that stage. A rival would still be able to compete by entering two adjoining stages simultaneously. Thus exclusive dealing arrangements that tied retailers to existing manufacturers would not impede new entry by a manufacturing firm with its own retail outlets.

These arguments form the basis of the US acceptance of vertical restraints. Note that they assume that there are no capital market imperfections which make entry more difficult for vertically integrated firms. In addition, the conclusions are based on a theory which assumes single-product firms in manufacturing and distribution. When the reality of multiproduct firms is taken into account, the conclusion that vertical restraints have no anti-competitive effects has to be modified. The problem arises when there are substantial economies of scope or of scale in the distribution of goods. If there are, vertical arrangements may foreclose competitors from access to low-cost distributive outlets. They are then forced to use more costly alternatives, which puts them at a competitive disadvantage. The existence of economies of scope in distribution also calls into question the assumption that vertical integration is always a viable alternative strategy for the manufacturer who is engaged in exclusive dealing arrangements.

The UK and EC have adopted a more selective approach. In the UK, the view is that, although exclusive dealing tends to reduce *intra-brand* competition, this may not be of much concern if *inter-brand* competition remains vigorous. The likely outcome will depend on circumstances. Beneficial effects are most likely where the product market is unconcentrated, and product differentiation is weak, so that strong inter-brand competition can exist. It is most likely to be harmful when the market at the manufacturing stage is highly concentrated and dominant suppliers can use exclusive dealing arrangements to blunt competition amongst themselves and to foreclose a large proportion of the market from competitors (see the MMC reports on *Frozen Foodstuffs*, 1976, and *Ice Cream and Water Ices*, 1979). Similar considerations apply to closely related vertical restraints such as tied sales.

Exclusive dealing agreements pose a problem to the EC Commission because the assignment by manufacturers of exclusive sales territories may partition the European market at the distribution level. The first important test case in this area was *Grundig–Consten* in 1964. Grundig, a German manufacturer, had given Consten, a French manufacturer, exclusive selling rights for its products in France, and also prohibited its non-French dealers from exporting to France. As a result, price levels in France, across a range of products, were between 20 and 50 per cent higher than in West Germany. The Commission's decision (upheld by the European Court) was that the agreement infringed Article 85. The key factor in this case, which became the cornerstone of policy towards exclusive dealing agreements, was Grundig's prohibition of parallel imports, thus giving its appointed dealers complete protection from intra-brand competition. The Commission has been prepared to grant temporary territorial protection to firms which have a small market share if that protection helps them to establish a market. But this defence is not available to large firms, as was evident in the

Distillers case. As in the UK, therefore, EC policy has regard to market structure in assessing the likely effects of vertical restraints.

Another example of vertical restraints is given by the case of selective distribution. In a wide range of products – e.g. motor vehicles, photographic products, many household appliances – it is common for suppliers to restrict their outlets to dealers who have suitable premises and who are able to offer a minimum standard of service. In the USA, the policy approach to these arrangements would be the same as that outlined above in relation to exclusive dealing. No anti-competitive effects can normally be expected. The UK and EC approach is more cautious. The European Commission has always recognised the legitimate interests that firms have in protecting their reputation in this way. However, it also recognises the danger of abuse, especially by dominant firms. In 1977 the European Court decided that the requirements which a supplier makes of his resellers must be laid down uniformly and must not be applied in a discriminatory fashion. Furthermore, selective distribution systems must not be used as a vehicle for restricting or distorting competition. In the *AEG–Telefunken* case the company was found guilty of violating these conditions. It had used its distribution system to protect existing dealers by excluding competitors who were able to meet the minimum standards laid down by the supplier.

In the UK, the MMC investigation of *Bicycles* (1981) also draws attention to the importance of the relationship between the effects of vertical restraints and the market power of the firm involved. In this case the company, Raleigh, argued that its distribution policy was in its commercial interests because, amongst other things, it maintained Raleigh's brand image, which had been built up hand in hand with the goodwill of its dealers. To protect its reputation it had a policy of not supplying discount stores. The MMC could not accept that a company's right to determine how its goods should be distributed was an entirely unfettered right regardless of circumstances. It argued that: 'The case for some restriction of the right is particularly strong where a manufacturer is a dominant supplier and his goods are differentiated ... from other manufacturers' goods of the same kind.' Having emphasised the importance of market power in determining the acceptability of the vertical restraints involved, the MMC unfortunately went on to overestimate the market power which Raleigh actually had, and concluded that the company was guilty of anti-competitive behaviour. In fact Raleigh's refusal to supply was more a cause of its decline than a manifestation of monopoly power. However, the interest in the case rests on the emphasis that is placed, when investigating vertical restraints, on the market power of the firm exercising those restraints, an approach which is very much in line with EC policy.

Concluding comments: price vs non-price vertical restraints

From what has already been said it would appear that, by and large, price and non-price vertical restraints may have similar effects.

However, it has been argued that, if anything, non-price restraints are likely to impose greater costs on consumers. The reasoning is as follows. With rpm, non-price competition among distributors continues and, in equilibrium, the wider margins enjoyed by distributors will go entirely to support additional services such as more quality signalling and a larger number of outlets. Non-price constraints such as exclusive dealing and territorial protection, on the other hand, restrain both price and non-price competition. There is less certainty, therefore, that the higher distributors' margins will be entirely used up in supporting extra service to consumers. So, for a given volume of service, distributors' margins and consumer prices will have to be higher with non-price than with price restraints. This argument challenges the wisdom of policies which place greater emphasis on preventing price than non-price restraints.

There are, however, some counter-arguments to consider. First, are *all* the extra services generated by rpm welfare enhancing? Probably not. More importantly, the dynamics of the interrelationships between manufacturer and retailer need to be examined. It is an oversimplification to believe that the manufacturer sets the resale price and competition amongst retailers then uses up the margin to provide extra services without further repercussions. Where in particular the additional service comes in the form of more retail outlets, there may emerge a growing problem of excess capacity and higher retailing costs, with the result that retailers put pressure on manufacturers to increase prices even further. With territorial protection this is less likely. Price restraints may also be more dangerous, not only because they might lead to more coercion by retailers, but also because they facilitate collective action by manufacturers more effectively than do non-price restraints.

Chapter 16

Maintaining competition: monopoly and merger policy

16.1 INTRODUCTION

In this chapter we examine competition policy towards single firms that are enabled by their size or dominant market position to behave in an uncompetitive way. The reasons for having such a policy have been discussed in earlier chapters, in which we have seen how the possession of market power enables large firms to behave in an uncompetitive manner with possible adverse effects on industrial performance. How can large firms most successfully be controlled to prevent them from exploiting their market power at the expense of competitors and consumers?

Competition policy towards single firms tends to be more ambivalent than policy attitudes towards groups of firms acting together, as discussed in the last chapter, because large firms may offer real efficiency gains through economies of scale, which are not available when several firms combine to act uncompetitively. Thus, in the case of competition policy towards large firms there is a trade-off between increased market power and efficiency from economies of scale, and this conflict is very important to understanding the operation of monopoly and merger policy.

The aim of monopoly and merger policy is to modify aspects of the performance of the firms in a certain industry or market, but there are a number of different methods by which this aim may be approached. In terms of the structure–conduct–performance paradigm, it is true to say that policies towards market power may take the form of intervention at any of the three stages. Policy may be aimed directly at performance (e.g. by regulating the rate of return that firms earn on assets), at aspects of firms' behaviour (e.g. their pricing or advertising) or at the control of market structure, to attempt to maintain competitive market structures.

Alternative approaches to monopoly and merger policy

The two most important approaches to the control of market power are the cost–benefit and structural approaches. The cost–benefit approach involves a case-by-case study of large firms to assess whether in each individual case the benefits of large size (e.g. possible economies of scale, increased foreign competitiveness) outweigh or are outweighed by the costs (i.e. increased market power). Thus, the attitude that underlies this approach to policy is basically neutral; no general stand is taken, and the merits of competition versus market power are assessed in each case. The structural approach is more radical and holds that competition and competitive market structures should be defended, because the benefits from competition will outweigh any potential benefits from increased firm size. Thus, the structural approach to the control of market power implies that large firms should be controlled by preserving or creating a competitive market environment, which would prevent the firms from acting in undesirable anti-competitive ways, and the structural approach to mergers is to prohibit any mergers that would create or consolidate an undesirably concentrated market structure. In other words, the philosophy behind the structural approach to policy – which accepts the importance of the causal links between structure, conduct and performance, with a definite preference for competitive structures – is that, if we look after market structure, market conduct and performance will look after themselves.

The policy implications of the cost–benefit approach are less simple, but it should not be thought that structural remedies are precluded. Both monopolies and mergers must be assessed in order to decide whether the activities of the large firm, or the merger of two firms, would be 'in the public interest', to use the British expression. If the finding goes against the firm(s) involved, the appropriate remedy may be structural (e.g. to forbid a merger). Alternatively it may involve the control of certain aspects of the firms' conduct. For instance, a large firm may be instructed to lower its prices or reduce its advertising expenditure, or a merger may be allowed to go ahead on certain conditions about the behaviour of the newly created firm. Acceptance of the cost–benefit approach implies, as well as a neutral pragmatic approach to the virtues of competition, that it makes sense to regulate market conduct without changing the underlying market structure, because the causal links between structure, conduct and performance are seen as less than deterministic.

The above point also illuminates the relationship between monopoly and merger policy. A structural approach to policy must necessarily include a policy for merger control as well as a policy towards existing large firms, since to maintain competitive market structures it must be possible to prevent mergers and also to break up existing firms. The cost–benefit approach, on the other hand, does not object to large firms and the existence of market power as such, but it does object to anti-competitive manifestations of such power. Thus, a merger policy is not strictly necessary, since a firm created by merger can be assessed by cost–benefit analysis and controlled in the same way as an existing large firm.

Indeed there is one school of thought – the neo-Austrian or 'Competitive Process' school – which adopts the view that monopoly and merger policy, and particularly the latter, is largely misconceived. Some of the main arguments in this approach are as follows: (i) the prospect of monopoly profit is a powerful incentive to entrepreneurial activity; (ii) the authorities should adopt a light-handed approach to monopolies, otherwise they may discourage innovation; (iii) so long as there are no artificial barriers to entry, monopolies will survive only if they can maintain a competitive advantage; (iv) mergers are an important part of the competitive process and to prevent them would protect inefficient firms; (v) firms will strive in a variety of ways such as advertising and sales promotion to build up or maintain a reputation, and expenditure on these activities is often wrongly condemned. The general conclusion to be drawn from this school of thought is one that reinforces the point made earlier in connection with the cost–benefit analysis approach – that merger policy is not necessary. It is not necessary because in the vast majority of cases mergers are beneficial. In the exceptional cases where they result in monopoly abuse, this can be dealt with by policy for the control of monopolies.

Before going on to look at policies towards monopolies and mergers in the UK, the USA and the EC, what can be said in general about the pros and cons of the cost–benefit and structural approaches to policy? The theoretical argument underlying the cost–benefit approach has been explained in Chapter 12. If large firms can produce at lower costs than smaller ones owing to economies of scale, there will be a welfare trade-off between market power and efficiency. Each case must therefore be examined separately to see whether the cost savings from increased size outweigh the welfare losses due to increased market power. The arguments against the cost–benefit in favour of the structural approach, apart from the underlying greater commitment to competition, are essentially empirical and practical. The empirical argument concerns the importance in practice of economies of scale as a justification for increased size of firms and has already been discussed in Chapter 4. The practical argument in favour of a structural policy approach is that the cost–benefit approach is unduly costly in terms of the resources used to investigate each separate case and that a structural approach not only uses less resources and is easier to administer but also makes it clearer to firms when intervention by the antitrust authorities can be expected.

The remainder of this chapter looks in some detail at policies towards monopolies (in section 16.2) and mergers (in section 16.3) in the UK, the USA and EC.

16.2 MONOPOLY POLICY IN THE USA, THE UK AND THE EC

In this section we compare the approaches taken by the UK, the USA and EC to the control of dominant firms. As with restrictive practices policy, discussed in the last chapter, it is the USA that has by far the longest history of anti-monopoly policy and also the toughest policy. US monopoly (and merger) policy is based firmly on the structural approach, while UK policy is equally clearly cost–benefit based. EC policy towards large firms is less fully developed and less easy to classify, but it inclines more towards the cost–benefit approach.

The legislation

US legislation

US monopoly policy, like restrictive practices policy, started with the Sherman Act of 1890, Section 2 of which declared : 'Every person who shall monopolize, or attempt to monopolize, or combine or conspire with any person or persons to monopolize any part of the trade or commerce among the several States, or with foreign nations, shall be deemed guilty of a misdemeanour.' The significance of this Act depends on what is meant by 'monopolizing' – a concept peculiar to American law. The use of the active verb 'to monopolize' implies that it is actions taken with the deliberate intention of establishing a monopoly that are illegal, not monopolies as such, and that a monopoly attained by superior products or skill in the competitive process will not necessarily be illegal. For instance, in February 1980 the US Supreme Court ruled that the Eastman Kodak company had been acting within its rights when it introduced the Instamatic camera and cartridge film in 1972. One of Kodak's competitors, Berkey Photo, alleged that the company had abused its monopoly position when it introduced the Instamatic without prior warning. Berkey Photo as a camera manufacturer relied on Kodak film but did not have a camera that would take the new cartridges, because Kodak had not informed it of the change. Berkey Photo was awarded damages of $87 million by a lower court, but this decision was reversed in an appeals court. The appeals court decision, upheld by the Supreme Court, said that the antitrust laws will allow a 'monopolization' if it comes about through innovation, cost-saving or product improvement rather than through anti-competitive practices. This still leaves the important question of what is meant by a monopoly in American law. This involves both the always difficult problem of defining the relevant market and that of specifying the monopoly share of that market, which is not statutorily defined as in British law but has been held by the courts to vary according to the structural and other features of the market concerned. The wording of Section 2 of the Sherman Act implies that it can be used to attack oligopolistic firms if these can be shown to be combining or conspiring 'to monopolize'. We return later to look at the efficacy of monopoly policy in dealing with the problems posed by oligopolistic industries.

As well as the act of 'monopolization', US monopoly policy controls various forms of abuse of monopoly power. Under US law certain types of anti-competitive conduct (e.g. acquisitions, vertical integration, tying agreements, price discrimination) may be dealt with under the Sherman Act as 'attempts to monopolize', but they have also been the subject of subsequent legislation addressed more directly to these problems. The Clayton Act of 1914 declared illegal the following four specified types of anti-competitive behaviour when their effect was substantially to lessen competition or to tend to create a monopoly: price discrimination, exclusive-dealing and tying contracts, acquisition of shares in competing companies, and interlocking directorates. The provisions of this Act relating to mergers were amended by the Celler–Kefauver Anti-merger Act of 1950, which is discussed in the section on merger policy. The Clayton Act's provisions against price discrimination were interpreted very loosely and were tightened up by the Robinson–Patman Act of 1936, which was intended to reduce the competitive advantage that large buyers were able to gain over small buyers through the operation of quantity discounts.

US monopoly policy therefore can be seen to operate a wide battery of provisions. The Sherman Act (and antimerger laws to be discussed later) offers ways of controlling market structure, and the Clayton and Robinson–Patman Acts offer means of controlling the behaviour of existing large firms.

UK legislation

Monopoly policy in the UK started with the passing of the Monopoly and Restrictive Practices (Inquiry and Control) Act 1948. This Act, which created the Monopolies and Restrictive Practices Commission, defined a monopoly as existing where one-third of the UK supply of any good was supplied, processed or exported by a single firm, or by two or more persons who 'conduct their respective affairs so as to prevent or restrict competition in connection with the production or supply of goods of the description in question'. References to the Commission might be for the purpose of establishing whether a legal monopoly existed and, if so, what practices it had led to. More generally, the Commission would be asked to report on whether the monopoly operated against the public interest.

In defining the public interest the 1948 Act instructed the Commission to take into account, among other things: the need to achieve efficient production and distribution, a more efficient organisation of industry and trade, the fullest use and best distribution of men, materials and industrial capacity, and the development of technical improvements. There was no suggestion that the best way of achieving these goals would be through maintaining competitive markets, and indeed there was no mention of the word 'competition' in defining the public interest.

The Monopolies and Mergers Commission, as it is now known, can also be given 'general references' in which it is asked to report on the effect on the public interest of certain practices that appear to be uncompetitive. Up to 1990 there have been seven such references: *Collective Discrimination, Recommended Resale Prices, Refusal to Supply, Professional Services, Parallel Pricing, Discounts to Retailers* and *Full-Line Forcing and Tie-in Sales*.

The pragmatic and neutral approach of UK monopoly legislation has remained unchanged since the 1948 Act. However, there have been some important developments. For instance, the Monopolies and Mergers Act 1965 enabled the then Monopolies Commission, after a reference had been made, to inquire into the supply of monopolised services as well as monopolised goods, and also to undertake general inquiries into practices likely to restrict competition that were not registrable under the Restrictive Trade Practices Act 1956 (the Act under which the Commission was reconstituted and renamed the Monopolies Commission).

In 1973 the Acts of 1948 and 1965 were repealed and replaced by the Fair Trading Act. The most important institutional change was the creation of a new office: that of Director General of Fair Trading. The Director General was given the duty of collecting information about market structure and business conduct and of generally keeping under review commercial activities in the UK. The Director General was empowered to make monopoly references in the private sector, subject, however, to the approval of the relevant Secretary of State, who was given the power of veto.

Under the 1973 Act the Monopolies Commission was reconstituted and renamed the Monopolies and Mergers Commission (MMC). The definition of a 'monopoly situation' was changed from a market share of one-third to a share of one-quarter. The Act made it possible for a local monopoly to be referred; it also made it possible for ministers to refer a nationalised industry or part of a nationalised industry for investigation. The 1973 Act changed the definition of the public interest, including for the first time explicit mention of the desirability of competition. Clause 84 of the Act stated that the MMC 'shall have regard to the desirability of maintaining and promoting effective competition between persons supplying goods and services in the United Kingdom'. However, the MMC was still instructed to take into account 'all matters which appear to them in the particular circumstances to be relevant', and specific mention was made of the desirability 'of maintaining and promoting the balanced distribution of industry and employment in the United Kingdom'. In practice, therefore, it is unlikely that this change in the definition of the public interest did much, if anything, to alter the conduct of monopoly policy in the UK.

The latest development in monopoly legislation in the UK is the Competition Act 1980. The aim of this Act is to strengthen the attack on anti-competitive practices, and its main elements are as follows. The Director General of Fair Trading is able (subject to veto by the relevant Secretary of State) to carry out preliminary investigations on an anti-competitive practice, defined as a course of conduct that has, is likely to have or is intended to have the effect of restricting, preventing or distorting competition. The Director General has to publish his findings. If he has identified important anti-competitive practices, he may accept an undertaking from the firm concerned to stop or modify the practices in question, or he may decide (again subject to the approval of the Secretary of State, who has the right of veto) to make a reference to the MMC. Such a reference is known as a 'competition reference'. If the MMC confirms the finding of an anti-competitive practice, it must go on to consider whether the practice operates against the public interest. A reference may also follow a preliminary investigation by the Director General into prices or charges in areas that appear to be of public concern. The MMC has six months to complete its report on a competition reference (with a possible extension to nine months). In the event of an adverse finding, the Secretary of State may order the prohibition of the practice or take steps to remedy its adverse effects.

The Secretary of State is also empowered to refer such public bodies as the nationalised industries. The MMC may be asked to inquire into matters of efficiency, cost, service to consumers and abuse of a monopoly position, but it is not allowed to comment on financial obligations or objectives (e.g. profitability targets, cash limits) laid down by the government. The time allowed to carry out these 'public sector references' is the same as for the 'competition references' in the private sector. The Secretary of State has the power to require a public sector body to produce a plan of action to remedy any adverse finding.

In spite of these developments, the basic approach towards monopoly has remained largely unchanged. Each reference is dealt with on its merits; there is no presupposition built into the legislation that monopoly is necessarily bad; and the onus is on the Commission to show that a monopoly operates against the public interest. The public interest guidelines are intended to guide the MMC as to what matters should be taken into account in reaching conclusions on the public interest, but these guidelines are very widely drawn, so that a great deal of discretion can be exercised in deciding how the public interest should be interpreted.

EC legislation

EC monopoly policy resembles UK policy in that it sets out to control market conduct and not market structure. EC policy is contained in Article 86 of the Treaty of Rome, which states that 'any abuse by one or more undertakings of a dominant position within the Common Market or in a substantial part of it shall be prohibited as incompatible with the Common Market in so far as it may affect trade between Member States'.

The terms of EC policy, then, are quite different from those of UK policy, which operates a statutory definition of a monopolist. EC policy is directed against firms that have 'a dominant position', and this means both that the relevant market must be established and that the meaning of dominance must be clarified. The difficulties of interpretation raised by Article 86 help to explain the slow start to monopoly policy in the EC. Article 86 was used for the first time in 1971. Although Article 86 does cover oligopolistic as well as monopolistic abuses of dominance, no case against an oligopoly has been heard under EC law.

The wording of Article 86 makes it very clear that it is the abuse of a dominant position that is condemned and not the existence of such a position, so that an uncompetitive market structure, with a dominant firm, will be permitted as long as the firm doesn't take advantage of its position to behave uncompetitively. Like UK policy and, to some extent, US policy, EC law admits the possible existence of a 'good' monopolist – a firm with market power that doesn't use this power to the detriment of its competitors, suppliers and consumers. In UK terms, the MMC can (and often does) find that, although monopoly conditions exist in a market, they do not operate against the public interest. However, the actual possibility of such a theoretically feasible finding has been problematic in the EC. In a 1965 memorandum the Commission asserted that dominance is 'primarily a matter of economic potency, or the ability to exert on the operation of the market an influence that is substantial.' With this approach, dominance is proved by the *existence* of abusive conduct. If there is no abusive conduct there is no dominance. There is no way of establishing therefore the existence of a 'good' monopolist. In more recent case law, however, the EC has, as we will see later, recognised the ambiguities in the legislation, and has edged towards a more structuralist approach.

This brief account of the provisions of monopoly policy in the USA, the UK and the EC makes it clear that the approaches to monopoly policy vary considerably in the emphasis attached to market structure, market conduct and performance at three different stages of policy: the determination of the existence of monopoly power, criteria for enforcing remedial measures, and the remedial measures applied – or, in other words, what constitutes a monopoly, when something should be done about it, and what should be done. Let us now look at each of these three stages in turn.

Definition of monopoly

In Britain and America it is a monopoly that must be shown to exist; in the EC it is a 'dominant position' that is the legal term for the relevant economic concept of a firm with market power. Proof of the legal existence of a monopoly is most straightforward in Britain, where a monopoly is defined by law in purely structural terms as a firm with 25 per cent of the market of the good or service that has been referred to the MMC. However, the reference market is not necessarily the economically relevant market, and a market share of 25 per cent doesn't automatically qualify a firm for investigation. In the USA, a monopoly is also defined in structural terms, but there is no legal definition of a monopoly share; this depends on interpretation and case law. The rule of thumb passed down from the Alcoa case of 1945 by Judge Hand says that '90 per cent is enough to constitute a monopoly; it is doubtful whether 60 or 64 per cent would be enough; and certainly 33 per cent is not'. In the EC, as we have already seen, early interpretations made the existence of dominance coincide with its abuse. This unsatisfactory position was to some extent resolved by the Court's judgments in the *United Brands* (1978) and *Hoffman-La Roche* (1979) cases. From these cases it is clear that extremely large market shares, 80 per cent in the Hoffman-La Roche case, of themselves constitute evidence of dominance. Also, dominance can generally be said to exist once a market share of the order of 40–50 per cent is reached, but this does not automatically give control, so that other structural, conduct and performance indicators have to be taken into account. Of particular interest is the emphasis which the Court has attached to the gap between the market share of the leading firm and its nearest rival. For example, in *Michelin Nederland* (1981) the firm's dominant position was found to result first and foremost from the fact that it held 60 per cent of the Dutch market in replacement tyres with none of its main competitors accounting for more than 8 per cent. It seems that the European Court is of the view that dominant firm market structures pose a greater threat to competition than tight-knit oligopolies.

The main problem in determining the existence of monopoly power, which is common to all three systems, is that of defining the relevant market in both product and geographical terms. In order to exert market power, a firm must have a significant share of the market, but any firm's share can be varied enormously in percentage terms by adopting a broader or narrower definition of the product market (e.g. spirits, or alcoholic drink, or beverages) or of its geographical extent (e.g. Scotland, or Britain, or the EC). Which of these definitions is economically relevant will vary from case to case, but there is always scope for disagreement and because of this monopoly judgments may be overturned on appeal. For instance, it was the problem of defining the market that resulted in the European Commission losing its case against *Continental Can*, brought in 1971. The Court upheld the company's appeal on the grounds that the Commission had defined the product market too narrowly, thus underestimating competition from substitutes.

Criteria for taking action against monopolies

If we go on now to look at the criteria applied in the USA, the UK and the EC for the enforcement of remedial measures (i.e. what the firms must do in order for some action to be taken), we again find some differences. In the USA, policy has wavered at different times between using mainly structural and mainly conduct criteria. In certain cases antitrust policy has come close to saying that the existence or possession of a monopoly is itself illegal, regardless of how the position was acquired or how it is being used. The most famous case in which this line was taken was that of Alcoa, in which Judge Hand said that 'the [monopoly] power and its exercise must needs coalesce'. This implies that it makes no sense to talk about a monopolist not using its power, because in simply setting price such a firm has a freedom of choice not available to firms in a competitive environment. For the most part, however, in order to be attacked under Section 2 a firm not only must have market power but must also have pursued anti-competitive conduct. But what constitutes a monopoly share of the market?

Judge Hand's view that not even a 60–64 per cent share necessarily confers market power does not square easily with the view that market power is the power to have some control over prices. For this, much lower shares might be sufficient. However, whatever market share is needed, the US approach is based on demonstration of market power plus evidence of anti-competitive conduct. Most of the actions taken have been brought by private plaintiffs who, if successful, can recoup triple damages.

In the UK there is no problem of defining the market share which qualifies a firm for investigation of suspected monopoly abuse. This is laid down by statute and is currently 25 per cent. Though a legal requirement, this is not the only factor that enters into a decision to initiate a monopoly investigation. Typically, a reference to the MMC will be made after the Director General of Fair Trading has carried out a preliminary investigation, which may itself have been triggered by complaints from third parties.

There has never been a suggestion in the UK policy that a structural standard is sufficient. Intervention has been based on either conduct or performance criteria. In the report on *Man-Made Cellulosic Fibres* (1968), the MMC did not find that Courtaulds had earned excessive profits, but it did condemn the company for its anti-competitive conduct. On the other hand, in the *Primary Batteries* (1974) case the MMC did not find any conduct that was against the public interest, but it did find that Mallory, the dominant supplier of mercury batteries, was charging high prices for its photographic batteries and that this operated against the public interest in that the high prices gave rise to excessive profits.

Anti-competitive practices, however, are not necessarily condemned in the UK unless they affect the performance of the market in a way that operates against the public interest; for example, by making excess profits, holding back inno- vations or restricting supply. There are also certain types of conduct that the MMC is not allowed to investigate under present legislation. Section 54(5) of the Fair Trading Act 1973 says that the MMC cannot investigate agreements that are registrable under Part I of the Restrictive Trade Practices Act 1956. Much time can be wasted on a monopoly reference discovering what agreements exist and whether they are registrable under the 1956 Act. A registrable agreement may also be found to be the most crucial issue for the public interest, but even so the MMC is not allowed to pursue it. (For a good example of these difficulties, see the report on *Diazo Copying Materials*, 1977.)

In the EC it is non-competitive market conduct (i.e. the abuse of a dominant position) that is condemned by Article 86, if it affects trade between member states. A very wide interpretation of what counts as an abuse is possible – namely, that any form of behaviour that could not have occurred in a competitive market is abusive – but it has been gross forms of abuse that have been prose- cuted. One interesting question, which arises in EC anti-monopoly policy as in US antitrust policy, is whether the consolidation of a dominant position can count as an abuse. Can Article 86 be used to preserve competitive market struc- tures? In the controversial *Continental Can* case, the EC Commission attempted to prevent the takeover of Europemballage by Continental Can on the grounds that it would seriously reduce competition in the market. Although the European Court of Justice reversed the Commission's decision, it supported the Commis- sion's argument that Article 86 could be used to preserve competitive market structure: 'the strengthening of the position held by the enterprise can be an abuse and prohibited under Article 86 of the Treaty regardless of the method or means used to attain it', if the degree of dominance essentially affects competition. This dictum raises the possibility that Article 86 could even be used to prevent dominant firms from extending their dominance through internal growth. However, the Commission itself has not attempted to interpret Article 86 in this way, and there is no case of a firm simply being accused of dominance with no attempt to prove deliberate anti-competitive behaviour.

Policy remedies

US policy provides both structural and conduct remedies under the Sherman Act and conduct remedies under the Clayton Act. Where both are available, the choice between structural and conduct remedies is dictated primarily by practical considerations and may therefore be considered discriminatory. If two companies have committed equally serious offences of monopolisation but one consists of several plants and the other has only one plant, the former company is far more likely to be subjected to the more drastic remedy of dissolution.

The structural solution, 'trust-busting', was used most enthusiastically in the early years of antitrust policy before the First World War. The companies involved in the oil and tobacco trusts, the explosives trust and the early railway cases consisted of large numbers of plants, and physical dissolution was therefore practicable. More recently there has been the successful dissolution of the American Telephone and Telegraph Company. However, dissolution is not a popular remedy and has been used very sparingly. In many cases dissolution presents insuperable practical problems, so the courts have had recourse to conduct remedies and have prohibited specific monopolistic practices. For instance, the United Shoe Machinery Co. manufactured all its machines in a single plant and therefore could not be split up. Instead, the court issued an injunction ordering the company to remove restrictive conditions from the agreements to lease its machines and also to make the machines available for sale. Under the Clayton Act the Federal Trade Commission is empowered to issue 'cease and desist' orders, which have the force of law, to make firms abandon any practice that has been found to be an unlawful method of competition.

The power of the courts under the Sherman Act is not limited to banning specific practices. They can in effect legislate a detailed programme for the future conduct of the firms in any industry that has been found to violate the Sherman Act. For instance, in the *Paramount* case the major producers and distributors of films were found to have colluded in favour of major cinema circuits, and detailed rules were laid down by the courts to regulate and change the arrangements by which films were made available to cinemas.

In the UK, on completion of a monopoly investigation the MMC reports to the appropriate Secretary of State concerning what, if any, monopoly conditions have been found to operate against the public interest and what remedies it recommends to deal with these. The Commission's conclusions are advisory only; the Secretary of State is not obliged to accept them.

The Secretary of State has wide powers to compel a firm to take whatever action is necessary to remedy the adverse effects of its monopoly position. The future conduct of firms can be regulated, and they can also be obliged to sell assets or shares to change the structure of the market. In the UK, structural remedies have only rarely been recommended and their implementation has been even rarer. The most important example is the *Supply of Beer* (1989). In this case the MMC concluded that, in view of the powerful market position of the national brewers, basic structural changes were needed if the adverse effects stemming from their ownership of public houses was to be remedied. One of the main recommendations was that a brewer should be limited to owning no more than 2,000 public houses, the rest to be divested. This recommendation was subsequently amended by the Secretary of State with the effect that brewers have to release from a tie half the pubs they own in excess of 2,000. Still, an important measure of divestment was put into effect.

The remedies commonly applied to monopoly problems in the UK are conduct remedies, which control aspects of firms' behaviour. These remedies can be applied either formally or informally, but in practice informal agreements are much more common. The Director General of Fair Trading meets the companies concerned to secure voluntary undertakings that they will implement the recommendations of the Monopolies Commission. For instance, in the case of *Frozen Foodstuffs* (1976), Birds Eye agreed to reform its discount structure and to stop lending freezer cabinets to retailers on restrictive terms. The operation of such undertakings is regularly reviewed by the Director General of Fair Trading and, in cases where it is found that the undertakings are not being adhered to, the Commission can be asked to undertake a 'follow-up' reference. On the rare occasions when no voluntary agreement can be reached between the Office of Fair Trading and the firms concerned, Parliament can issue a statutory order that compels the recommendations of the Monopolies Commission to be carried out.

In the EC there is no provision for the dissolution of existing monopolies, although, as suggested above, in theory at least, Article 86 could be used to preserve the existing structure by preventing the extension of a dominant position. The EC Commission can prevent a dominant firm from continuing to abuse its position, either informally or by issuing a formal decision, which has the status of law.

An assessment of alternative approaches to monopoly policy

The previous section has shown that US, UK and EC monopoly policies place different emphasis on market structure, conduct and performance in the various stages of policy. We now look at the effectiveness of these three systems of policy to see which offers the most promising approach to monopoly problems. The fact that the problems persist in all three systems testifies to the difficulty of adequately controlling very large firms and to the need for an effective merger policy to prevent the emergence of dominant firms – a point to which we return later.

The last section has demonstrated that the most practical way of defining a monopoly is in structural terms, although this does not mean that the existence of a monopoly problem can be simply identified with any given market share, nor does it mean that any firm with such a market share is necessarily suspect. The function of a legal definition of a monopoly is to identify those markets or firms which could be the subject of investigation, not to say that all of them will be. In fact, the choice of markets or firms to be dealt with must always be the result of a complex investigation of the competitive conditions in a market, involving a lot more than just market shares. In practice, no monopoly policy has ever taken or could ever take the line that all monopolies, no matter how achieved or what their effects, are to be condemned, and thus it is necessary and sensible to define a monopoly first and then to go on to specify the circumstances under which a monopoly will be liable to government intervention. From this point of view the UK approach has much to commend it. It is also the approach which, since 1973, has been adopted by West Germany, where a legal presumption of dominance exists where one firm has a market share of one-third or more. The EC system is unsatisfactory in that it tends to confuse these two stages of policy.

Having defined a monopoly in structural terms, how should policy proceed to establish criteria for intervention? The UK uses both conduct and performance criteria, the EC uses a conduct criterion (i.e. the abuse of a dominant position), while the US offence of monopolisation has been variously interpreted in structural and conduct terms, although the emphasis now seems to be very much on conduct.

To take a structural approach at this stage would mean a failure to distinguish a monopoly that has been acquired by 'bad' methods (i.e. anti-competitive or predatory behaviour) from one attained by 'good' methods (i.e. successful clean competition), in order to condemn the former only. This is a problem associated with the structural approach, which is intended to maintain competition by preventing one or a small number of firms from acquiring dominance. In some industries, free competition may itself lead to the emergence of one dominant firm, in which case the artificial preservation of a number of competing firms would entail government intervention into the competitive process. Nevertheless, it is the logical approach for those who believe that to maintain competition it is necessary to maintain competitive market structures. In one important respect, however, the dilemma is eased. In many industries, competition from overseas suppliers will mean that there is effective competition, even though domestic supply is highly concentrated.

For the cost–benefit type of monopoly policy, performance criteria for intervention seem to be the logical approach. Large firms and market power are not viewed as bad in themselves but are subject to intervention only when they have bad effects on the performance of the firm or market in question.

However, the task of undertaking anything like a complete assessment of market performance is a formidable one. There are several dimensions to performance (e.g. profitability, prices, selling costs, technical efficiency, innovativeness), and they will all have to be examined before it can be decided whether or not a monopoly operates against the public interest. For some aspects of performance, a conclusion may be reached without too much difficulty. For instance, in some cases advertising and other sales costs may be low, both in absolute terms and as a percentage of sales, so that it will be possible to arrive quickly at the conclusion that selling costs do not present a public interest issue. In other instances, however, problems of assessment are likely to be greater. Large firms are often defended on the grounds that they achieve important economies of scale. The measurement of these economies is highly technical and demands a great deal of information. The MMC in the UK has been accused of failing to deal with this crucial aspect of monopoly in a systematic fashion, in particular with failing to quantify the cost savings that are claimed to be associated with size.

Another aspect of performance that may well cause great difficulty is profitability. The evaluation of the profit performance of a firm invariably involves a reference to the concept of a 'normal' rate of profit, so much so that it can be said that such a concept is essential to the sensible implementation of monopoly policy. In static analysis, normal profits are thought of as the minimum level necessary in the long term to maintain capital in an industry. However, monopoly policy has to be conducted within a dynamic environment, in which firms and industries have different growth rates and profits are necessary to attract finance for expansion, either by means of retentions or by means of funds raised externally. It has been suggested, therefore, that a normal rate of profit should be defined by reference to the rate of growth of the firm, so that the higher the growth rate, the higher the normal or 'necessary' rate of profit.

Let us suppose that for a number of firms, say the 100 largest manufacturing companies, a distinct positive correlation between profitability and growth is observed over a given time period. Diagrammatically, we can, as in Figure 16.1,

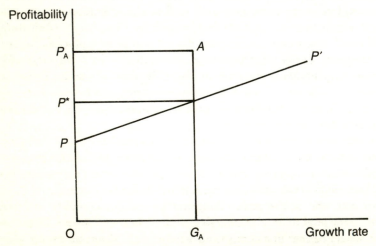

Figure 16.1 The profitability–growth relationship as a guide to policy

draw a line PP' that shows the *average* relationship between the two variables. The actual scatter of observations lies on either side of the line. The usefulness of this relationship as a starting point for the assessment of the profitability of a given firm depends on its stability. The greater the stability of the average profitability–growth relationship over time, the greater the confidence with which we can look on this relationship as establishing a *desired* relationship between profitability and growth. On the other hand, if the height and/or slope of the PP' curve showed a great deal of instability, it would be of no great use as a policy guide.

Even assuming a reasonable measure of stability in the profit–growth relationship, there are still some major problems in assessing the profit performance of an individual firm. Take firm A in Figure 16.1, which is located well above line PP'. On the basis of the average relationship between profitability and growth, the profitability of A, P_A, appears excessive. For a rate of growth of OG_A the PP' curve suggests a 'normal' return of OP^*, but A's profitability is well above this. Further information is needed, however, in order to decide whether or not A's profits are excessive. A number of factors need to be distinguished and their relative importance assessed.

First, the high profitability may be due entirely or in part to abnormally high risks. In this case, although firm A has been successful over the period concerned, it operates in a field where the risks of failure are greater than the average for all manufacturing activity. Since this is an argument frequently but not always correctly made in defence of exceptionally high profitability, it is important that the strength of the argument be assessed. It will certainly be relevant to see if, for individual investment projects, there is evidence of substantial losses as well as substantial profits both for other firms in the same line of activity and for periods in the history of the firm under examination. Such an assessment was made in the MMC's report on the supply and processing of *Colour Film* (1966). The opinion of the majority of the commissioners who investigated this case was that 'photographic manufacturing is not a particularly high risk activity, and that, so far as colour film is concerned, a monopoly position founded upon Kodak's reputation with the public is not likely to be suddenly eroded. So far as we are aware the Eastman Kodak organisation has suffered no serious setback throughout its history'.

Second, high profitability may be due to monopoly power. The firm may maintain a high profit margin by such practices as restricting output, creating barriers to new competition by exercising a restrictive control over sources of supply or distributive outlets, and heavy promotional outlays. Examples of such practices are revealed in the reports of the MMC. Thus, in the case of *Man-Made Cellulosic Fibres* (1968), the Commission found that the behaviour of Courtaulds exemplified 'one of the classic disadvantages of monopoly, the limitation of supply to the level most advantageous for the producer, which is below the level which would be met in a competitive situation'. In the same case it was found that Courtaulds' vertical integration forward into the textile industry was done for the purpose of preserving its monopoly position, by increasing the entry barriers to new competitors, limiting the entry of imports and reducing the seriousness of competition from other fibre producers. An example of a case in which heavy promotional expenditure led to high profitability is *Household Detergents* (1966). The firms' price policies and policies on advertising and promotion had operated against the public interest by restricting entry, inflating advertising and sales promotion to the detriment of direct price competition, and raising prices.

Third, high profitability may be the result of exceptionally able management, not only in terms of the day-to-day task of the efficient organisation of production and distribution, but also in 'getting in first' with new developments or in being prompt in adopting successful innovations made elsewhere. The management factor also draws attention to the importance of managerial attitudes, in particular the extent to which management is willing to exploit a favourable market situation. Recognition of the wide variation in internal efficiency and in managerial attitudes also leads to the conclusion that monopoly power is not necessarily reflected in high profits. The potentialities for high profits may be forgone in favour of a quiet life.

The performance approach to the second stage of policy, namely, that of establishing criteria for taking action, is therefore full of difficulties. Performance cannot be assessed without looking at the causes of performance, and this will involve considerations of market structure and business conduct. High profits, for instance, need to be seen against the background of such factors as the structure of the industry, the existence of substitutes, restrictive agreements between firms, and the growth and innovative record of the firm being investigated, before any conclusion can be reached.

This brings us to the part played by conduct in the second stage of policy. It would seem that it must play an important part because it is hard to imagine how certain aspects of performance can be properly assessed without regard to the conduct of firms. The emphasis placed on conduct in US, UK and EC policy would seem not to be misplaced. In particular, predatory conduct and conduct designed to raise rivals' costs would be condemned in all three systems. The problem is to distinguish between conduct that is predatory and that which deliberately sets out to raise rivals' costs from conduct that is innocent. Several aspects of conduct may be both welfare enhancing and anti-competitive in their effects. Firms may use advertising and other marketing expenditure to develop a good reputation and create customer attachments which benefit both the firm and its customers. The effect, even if this is not an overt objective, may also be to strengthen positions of dominance. Price discrimination may also be pro- or anti-competitive. In short, because of the strategic nature of conduct, it is necessary to determine intent before drawing policy conclusions. By the same token, rules designed to modify business conduct will often have ambiguous effects on efficiency and welfare.

Lastly, what can be said about the effectiveness of different types of remedy?

Both conduct and performance remedies involve government interference with the running of companies and are costly in terms of monitoring costs. For instance, in the UK, Kodak was not released from an undertaking concerning profit levels until 18 years after the MMC report on *Colour Film*. Studies of the effect of MMC investigations have suggested that they often come too late and have only a small impact. A further difficulty is that an attack on one form of conduct may lead to other forms having much the same result. This is particularly problematic in the case of oligopolistic industries which are discussed in more detail below.

The problems associated with conduct and performance remedies raises the question of whether large firms can be controlled satisfactorily without changing the underlying market structure. A structural remedy is available in both the USA and UK, but it has been used with great hesitancy in the former and hardly at all in the latter.

Policy towards oligopoly

As explained above, the legislation on monopolies in the USA, the UK and the EC covers oligopolies in all three cases, but policy has been even less successful in dealing with oligopolistic industries than in dealing with monopolistic ones. This can be largely ascribed to the problem raised at the end of the previous section, namely, that of finding an effective solution. How can a group of oligopolists be stopped from behaving as oligopolists? The root of the problem is clearly structural. In an oligopolistic market the firms are aware of their interdependence and are likely to evolve an appropriate form of behaviour, ranging from actual collusion to concerted practices to price leadership, and so on. Dealing with oligopolistic behaviour under restrictive practices legislation, which has been attempted, is not likely to provide a permanent solution, since it will not change the structure of the industry concerned; the most likely effect is that firms will substitute a new form of concerted behaviour for that which has been outlawed. Moreover, these important oligopoly problems must remain on the frontiers of restrictive practices policy, since there is often nothing between the firms concerned that can possibly be described as an agreement, and so concerted behaviour will have to be inferred from circumstantial evidence related to pricing behaviour, and so on. The difficulties of extending restrictive practices legislation to cover oligopolistic collusion have been discussed in Chapter 15. The point being made here is that oligopoly problems arise from a particular form of market structure and are consequently better dealt with under a policy that allows for the possibility of changing that structure.

In practice, in the USA some oligopoly cases have been heard under Section 1 of the Sherman Act (i.e. illegal conspiracy) and some under Section 2 (i.e. the 'monopolization' clause), but neither approach has been very successful. In particular, US policy has never got a sufficiently firm hold on oligopoly to be able to use the drastic remedy of dissolution, and, in the absence of effective remedies, the many tight oligopolies in the USA are immune from prosecution.

British monopoly policy extends to cover oligopoly via the 'complex monopoly' provisions of the Fair Trading Act 1973, which says that a market may be liable to investigation by the MMC when two or more companies together have a market share of 25 per cent and act in a way that prevents, restricts or distorts competition. The investigation of an oligopoly depends on finding that a complex monopoly exists. As a result, assessment of the effect of the oligopoly on the public interest is limited in two ways. First, it is limited to an examination of those practices which form the basis of the complex monopoly, and, second, it is limited to the companies that engage in those practices. A member of an oligopolistic group that cannot be shown to engage in the said practices will escape investigation as long as its market share is less than 25 per cent. The fact-finding stage of a reference would be greatly simplified if, as in the case of a monopoly, a structural approach could be taken in defining an oligopoly. This in fact is the position in West Germany, where a legal presumption of market domination by a group of firms exists when three firms have a market share of at least 50 per cent or five firms have a market share of at least two-thirds. This approach makes it far easier for the authorities to prepare a full examination of competitive effects.

In the EC, oligopolistic markets exhibiting parallel-pricing behaviour have been investigated under Article 85, but no oligopoly has been held to come under Article 86, which prohibits the abuse of a dominant position by more than one firm.

The difficulties of applying competition policy to oligopolists remain among the most urgent and intractable problems facing competition policy, because of the prevalence of oligopolistic market structures. Not all oligopolists exhibit uncompetitive behaviour, but when they do behave uncompetitively it has proved particularly difficult for policy to come up with an effective way of enforcing competition.

The difficulty of finding effective and practicable remedies for abuse of a dominant position is a fundamental problem of monopoly policy, while the handling of oligopolistic industries is even more problematic. This emphasises yet again the importance of having a structural policy to prevent the emergence of intractably dominant firms, and it is to the question of merger policy that we now turn.

16.3 MERGER POLICY IN THE USA, THE UK AND THE EC

The preceding sections of this chapter have demonstrated the importance to a successful competition policy of maintaining competitive market structures, and also the difficulty of adequately controlling firms that have acquired a position of dominance. Therefore, an extremely important part of competition policy is a policy for the control of mergers that can prevent the formation of such dominant firms. Acceptance of the need for a merger policy is acknowledgement that market structure matters, and we now turn to examine the systems of merger control in the USA, UK and EC.

The legislation

US legislation

The first antimerger provision was contained in the Clayton Act of 1914, which controlled the acquisition of shares in another company. This was amended by the Celler–Kefauver Anti-Merger Act of 1950, which also prohibited the acquisition of physical assets where the effect would be substantially to lessen competition or to create a monopoly. After this Act, policy against mergers tightened up and was codified in a set of guidelines issued in 1968. These guidelines were designed to make clear which mergers were thought substantially to lessen competition and would therefore be challenged by the Justice Department.

The 1968 guidelines represented something of a high water mark in USA merger policy. The emphasis was firmly on the preservation and promotion of competitive market structures which 'generally produce economic predictions that are fully adequate for the purpose of a statute that requires only a showing that the effect of a merger "may be substantially to lessen competition or to tend to create a monopoly"'. It was made clear that an efficiency defence would be accepted as a justification for a merger only in exceptional circumstances and the onus of proof was on firms to show that a merger would not substantially lessen competition. Horizontal, vertical and conglomerate mergers were covered. For horizontal mergers, for instance, the guidelines were a combination of industry concentration ratios and the market shares of the acquiring and acquired firm; the more highly concentrated the market, the smaller firms had to be if they were not to be challenged. For instance, in a market where the four-firm concentration ratio was 75 per cent or more, a merger would be challenged if both acquiring and acquired firms had market shares of at least 4 per cent, or if the acquiring firm had 15 per cent and the acquired firm 1 per cent or more of the market.

In 1982 and 1984, however, revised merger guidelines were issued by the Department of Justice. There is some dispute whether the new guidelines merely represent a more careful formulation of long-established principles or whether they represent a fundamental change in official attitudes as a result of theoretical developments and the growing exposure of domestic industry to foreign competition.

The revised guidelines continue to emphasise the importance of market structure, and acknowledge that mergers, by creating more tightly knit oligopolistic structures, increase the risk of collusion and monopoly outcomes. The change comes in the definition of markets, the market share tests to be applied, and the weight to be given to other considerations.

The 1982 guidelines define the appropriate market as a 'group of products ... for which a hypothetical monopolist could profitably impose a small but significant and non-transitory increase in price', the hypothetical price increase normally to be applied being 5 per cent. The ability of the hypothetical monopolist to raise prices depends on the degree of substitutability amongst products in both consumption and production. In contrast with the 1968 guidelines, where the emphasis was on actual competitors, the 1982 guidelines gives prominence to potential competition. In defining the market, an assessment has to be made of the likely response to a price rise not only of consumers but also of firms outside the market. In so far as this widens the market definition it has the effect of lowering the concentration index. The index used is the Herfindal index (HI) of market concentration – defined as the sum of the squares of market shares for all firms in the market, the shares being expressed as percentages. Thus for five equally sized firms the index would be 2000. Markets with an HI between 1000 and 1800 are regarded as moderately concentrated and mergers here will be challenged if they lead to an increase in the index of 100 points or more. In highly concentrated markets, with an HI greater than 1800, mergers are likely to be challenged if the index is increased by only 25 points. In practice, the HI gives results very similar to those yielded by the old market share/concentration ratio thresholds.

The 1982 guidelines were still cautious about expanding market boundaries outside the USA. The efficiency defence was also still considered to be limited to exceptional cases. The 1984 guidelines, however, give full weight to international competition in the sense that if foreign firms import into the relevant market they will be included in the market along with domestic firms. The efficiency defence is also extended to all cases where it can be established by clear and convincing evidence. Indeed, the aim of merger policy 'is to take into account all relevant factors'.

In certain respects the revised guidelines are an improvement. The generally ad hoc approach to defining markets has been replaced by a more careful appraisal that recognises the importance of potential competition. The HI also has theoretical advantages over the n-firm concentration ratio, though, in practice, the two measures are highly correlated.

Critics, however, object to equal weight being given to actual and potential competitors. It is much more difficult to assess the strength of potential than of actual competition, and estimates of how much entry is likely to result from a price increase above existing levels are bound to be highly speculative. Furthermore, existing prices may already reflect substantial monopoly power. If so, it is more instructive to ask why new entry hasn't occurred than to speculate about the future – i.e. actual competition should be given most weight.

Whatever the differences in detail, the most noticeable change has been in the tone of the guidelines. In 1968 the emphasis was unambiguously on the importance of maintaining competitive market structure. In the revised guidelines the emphasis is that most mergers do not threaten competition, that many are in fact pro-competitive and enhance efficiency. Thus there is 'need for economic evidence of harm or potential harm to competition before a merger will be challenged'.

There has also been a marked change in the evaluation of non-horizontal mergers. Conglomerate mergers are virtually free of control. As to vertical mergers, evaluation used to be based on the foreclosure theory, e.g. forward integration by a supplier denies part of the downstream trade to competitors of the supplier. Thus, with the 1968 guidelines, if a supplying firm accounted for at least 10 per cent of market sales and a buying firm for at least 6 per cent of purchases, a merger between the two would be challenged unless there were no significant entry barriers.

New theorising, however, has argued that vertical integration does not necessarily increase market power. A single-firm monopolist can under certain circumstances achieve the same profit as a fully integrated one. The revised guidelines are in line with this thinking. A vertical merger, it says, will be challenged in the following circumstances: (a) where markets are already highly concentrated and where vertical merger forces potential competitors into more costly dual-stage entry; (b) where it facilitates collusion at the upstream stage; and (c) where it is a device to avoid government rate regulation.

UK legislation

Merger policy in the UK started with the passing of the Monopolies and Mergers Act 1965, which made mergers liable to investigation by the MMC on the basis already existing for monopoly references. A reference may be made where a merger creates or strengthens a monopoly (currently defined as 25 per cent of the relevant market) or where the value of the assets taken over exceeds a specified threshold. All types of merger are covered. They are initially considered by the Mergers Panel – an interdepartmental committee with representatives of all interested government departments – which advises the Director General of Fair Trading, who in turn advises the Secretary of State responsible for competition policy.

The MMC has to decide whether a merger operates or may be expected to operate against the public interest. The guidance which is given for evaluation is extremely wide. Although, since 1984, successive secretaries of state have said that references will be made primarily on competition grounds, once a reference is made the Fair Trading Act 1973 stipulates that the MMC 'shall take into account all matters which appear to them in the particular circumstances to be relevant.'

The onus of proof is on the MMC to demonstrate that a merger may be expected to operate against the public interest, and in so doing it must be able to demonstrate specific adverse effects. If there is an adverse public interest finding, the Secretary of State has discretionary powers to prevent the merger. Without an adverse public interest finding there is no power to stop a merger.

A review of policy in 1988 did nothing to change the fundamental approach. The two most important legislative changes that were announced were (a) a voluntary pre-notification procedure, and (b) a mechanism whereby parties to a merger can give legally binding undertakings to meet competition objections as an alternative to a MMC reference.

EC legislation

The absence of a merger control provision was, for a long period, a major gap in EC competition policy. Case law established that both Article 85 (the *Phillip Morris* case, 1981) and Article 86 (the *Continental Can* case, 1971) could be applied to mergers. However, merger policy did not fall neatly into either article. In its 1987 Report on Competition Policy the Commission complained that 'it is very serious if it is not possible to respond adequately to mergers that so increase the concentration of markets that there is little room for competition', and again in the 1988 Report it emphasised that prior control of mergers 'is crucial to the preservation of competitive structures'.

The Commission finally succeeded in getting the Council of Ministers to adopt a merger Regulation in December 1989. The Regulation applies to mergers having a Community dimension as defined by a combination of criteria relating to total turnover and geographical distribution of turnover within the Community – aggregate worldwide turnover must exceed Ecu 5 billion, and aggregate EC turnover of each of at least two firms has to exceed Ecu 250 million. These figures are considerably higher than those originally proposed by the Commission, but had to be accepted largely on the insistence of the UK and West Germany who wanted to protect their own merger policies.

Of the mergers that are covered by the Regulation, only those which create or strengthen a dominant position, as a result of which effective competition would be significantly impeded in the Common Market or a substantial part of it, are prohibited. In making its appraisal the Commission will take into account a range of considerations, including various dimensions of market structure, potential competition, supply and demand trends, the interests of consumers, and the development of technical and economic progress, provided it is to the consumers' advantage and does not restrict competition.

Although considerations of efficiency enter into merger appraisal, there is no explicit efficiency defence. Here again the Commission was forced to depart from an earlier draft which did contain such a defence so that an anti-competitive merger might have been allowed if the competitive detriment was outweighed by the contribution it made to attaining other objectives such as promoting technical or economic progress. It was feared that the efficiency defence was too widely drawn and would give the Commission too much power in determining industrial strategy.

The wording in the adopted Regulation puts the emphasis firmly on preserving effective competition, and a merger which threatens competition cannot be permitted because of overriding efficiency gains. It is difficult to see therefore what useful role efficiency considerations can play in assessing mergers, because whenever there is a conflict with competition the latter must win. In practice, of course, given the ambiguities that will often surround the attempt to assess the impact of a merger on competition, efficiency criteria might well play a bigger role than the wording of the Regulation suggests. That, however, remains to be seen.

Lastly, on matters of procedure, it appears that the Commission intends to adopt a neutral approach to mergers. This is suggested in the preamble to the Regulation, which states that greater unification of the EC market will result in major and beneficial restructuring via merger. Also it appears that it will be for the Commission to show detriment rather than for the firms to demonstrate benefit.

Merger policy: an assessment

In the 1960s the USA was adopting a tough policy, particularly towards horizontal mergers. Between 1960 and 1973 the Department of Justice and the Federal Trade Commission had between them brought over 300 cases without losing a single important one. The onus of proof fell on firms to prove that a merger would not substantially lessen competition, and the record shows that this was not easily done. Efficiency arguments at that time carried little weight – efficiency gains could usually be achieved by internal growth. Of course, by 1960 many US markets were already highly concentrated, many as a result of earlier merger waves.

The 1980s, in contrast, was a decade of very weak enforcement of merger policy. The emphasis had swung towards the efficiency benefits of merger. And whereas the onus of proof had previously been placed squarely on firms, there was now need for evidence of harm before a merger would be challenged. A major factor in explaining this change was the upsurge in competition from abroad, which exposed the inefficiency of much of US industry.

The growing internationalisation of competition has had a general weakening effect on merger policy in all countries. It has widened markets and increased competition between large firms. Furthermore, when one country gains or threatens to gain ascendancy in an industry it is liable to trigger off defensive mergers in others. But is there a danger that the process will go too far and that mergers will continue to be nodded through on the grounds of efficiency gains needed to meet international competition, even when those grounds are distinctly shaky? The EC Commission certainly thinks so, which is why it fought over many years for a merger regulation. As argued elsewhere in this book, international competition and the widening of markets disturbs the accustomed balance between safety and competition. Mergers are a quick way of restoring that balance. But while some sort of balance has a beneficial effect on business ability and willingness to invest, that balance can also be tipped unduly towards safety – i.e. the monopolisation of markets through either dominance or collusion. It is or should be the task of merger policy to guard against this.

What then should be the main ingredients of an active merger policy?

First, there should be guidelines which identify those mergers that are likely to be challenged. They should give prominence to actual competition as indicated by the main dimensions of actual market structure. Longer-run influences of substitution and new entry have to be taken into account, but it is doubtful whether they should be accorded equal prominence. There should, in other words, be a move back towards the standards applied by the USA in the 1960s. UK merger policy has suffered from not having any guidelines, one consequence of which has been inconsistencies in making referrals to the MMC. The EC guidelines are the outcome of a political compromise. They are based on firm size rather than market concentration, which is clearly suspect on economic grounds. In addition, they will capture only the very largest mergers within the Community.

Second, within the relevant market the objective of merger policy should be that of maintaining competition. Wider economic and social issues such as the balance of payments and regional impacts, which are included in the UK definition of the public interest, are best dealt with by other policies. They should not form part of the assessment of mergers.

Third, that assessment should be based on such factors as trends in demand growth, the strength of competition from imports, economies of scale benefits and the rate of technological change. These factors will vary considerably from industry to industry. It will be easier to allow a merger to proceed, for instance, in an industry characterised by strong demand growth, international competition and a high rate of technological change than in one where the opposite characteristics apply.

Fourth, there is a strong case in favour of having an efficiency defence so long as there is an initial presumption in favour of competition. In the USA, the balance has probably shifted too far towards efficiency arguments. In the UK, merger references are made mainly on competition grounds, but here too the actual recommendations made by the MMC may give undue weight to efficiency arguments, as in the case of the merger between British Airways and British Caledonian (1987).

Fifth, the onus of proof in merger cases should be on the parties to a merger to demonstrate benefit. The purpose of merger policy is, after all, to maintain competition and it is only those mergers that pose the greatest threat to competition that are challenged. Where it is thought that competition might be endangered, it would seem both reasonable and logical to expect the parties to bear the burden of convincing the authorities either that this would not occur, or that any detriment to competition would be outweighed by efficiency benefits which could not be achieved in other ways. This stance is further supported by two other considerations: empirical work on the effects of mergers does not support a general presumption in favour of mergers (Chapter 4), and efficiency benefits in particular are more easily claimed than demonstrated – the detailed evidence needed to demonstrate benefit is available only to the parties to a merger, who should be expected to use it to prove their case. For the time being, however, these arguments have fallen on deaf ears. The USA has moved away from the policy of the 1960s when the burden of proof was placed squarely on the firm. In the UK it has always been for the MMC to demonstrate adverse effects, and this will also be the case with EC merger control.

It remains to say a few words about conglomerate mergers. The basic questions to be asked about conglomerate mergers are the same as those relating to horizontal and vertical ones. What are the prospects of realising gains in efficiency, and what are the dangers in terms of loss of competition? As far as efficiency is concerned, a conglomerate merger may result in gains from the more efficient management of existing assets. Further gains may be realised as a result of scale and scope advantages in finance, management, marketing and R&D. How important in quantitative terms these economies are likely to be clearly depends on how closely related the new activity is to the conglomerate's existing activities, in terms of either production or marketing. The more tenuous the links between a company's various interests, the less likely it is that any important economies exist.

There are several ways in which competition might be affected by conglomerate mergers, the outcome depending on such factors as the structure of the industry being entered, the feasibility of entry by internal expansion rather than by acquisition, the particular firm acquired and the behaviour of the conglomerate after entry. Conglomerate mergers may infuse badly needed managerial skills into an industry, which results in an all-round improvement in performance. Some of the dangers that might be associated with highly diversified firms have already been outlined in Chapter 4. Their financial strength, for instance, means that they always pose a threat to smaller specialised competitors.

In the USA there is in effect no obstacle to conglomerate mergers. In the UK and EC they do come under general merger regulations. It is right that they should. To subscribe to this view is not to say that conglomerate mergers are in general undesirable or that efficiency is maximised by a neat division of companies on the basis of existing industry boundaries. The past history of the sources of invention and innovation, for instance, does not justify such a view. This is part of a more general point, which is the danger of emphasising the present to the neglect of the future. Just as the theory of the firm is concerned with intertemporal problems, so must the government consider these in dealing with problems of industrial structure. Having said all that, however, conglomerate mergers should not be excluded from merger policy. This statement can be justified on political arguments concerning undue concentration of power. But there are economic reasons as well. When business conduct is viewed strategically, the anti-competitive opportunities available to large diversified firms become more credible. Of particular concern is the merger that takes a firm already with substantial market power in existing product lines into related lines of activity, acquiring, that is, companies which are its most likely potential competitors. This must be of concern even to those who give potential competition at least equal weight to actual competition. To them, allowing conglomerate mergers which enable dominant firms to acquire potential competitors would be tantamount to killing the goose that laid the (contestable) golden egg.

References

Archibald, G. and Rosenbluth, G. (1975), 'The "new" theory of consumer demand and monopolistic competition', *Quarterly Journal of Economics*, 89.

Areeda, P.E. and Turner, D.F. (1974/5), 'Predatory pricing and related practices under Section 2 of the Sherman Act', *Harvard Law Review*, 88.

Arrow, K.J. (1962), 'Economic welfare and the allocation of resources for invention', in National Bureau of Economic Research, *The Rate and Direction of Inventive Activity: Economic and Social Factors*, Princeton, NJ: Princeton University Press.

Averch, H. and Johnson, L. (1962), 'Behavior of the firm under regulatory constraint', *American Economic Review*, 52.

Ayarian, R. (1975), 'Advertising and rate of return', *Journal of Law and Economics*, 18.

Aylen, J. (1980), 'Britain's Steelyard Blues', *New Scientist*, June.

Bacon, R. and Eltis, W. (1976), *Britain's Economic Problem: Too Few Producers*, London: Macmillan.

Bailey, E.E. (1986), 'Price and productivity change following deregulation: the US experience', *The Economic Journal*, 96.

Bain, J.S. (1951), 'Relation of profit rate to industry concentration: American manufacturing 1936–40', *Quarterly Journal of Economics*, 65.

Bain, J.S. (1956), *Barriers to New Competition*, Cambridge, Mass: Harvard University Press.

Baumol, W.J. (1967), *Business Behavior, Value and Growth*, rev. edn, New York: Harcourt, Brace and World.

—— (1977), *Economic Theory and Operations Analysis*, 4th edn, Englewood Cliffs, N.J.: Prentice-Hall.

—— (1990), 'Technology-sharing cartels', paper presented to the European Association for Research in Industrial Economics, Lisbon, September.

Baumol, W.J. and Braunstein, I.M. (1977), 'Empirical study of scale economies and production complementarity: the case of journal publication', *Journal of Political Economy*, 85.

Baumol, W.J., Panzar, J. and Willig, R.D. (1982), *Contestable Markets and the Theory of Industry Structure*, New York: Harcourt, Brace, Jovanovich.

Beasley, M.E. and Laidlaw, B. (1989), *The Future of Telecommunications: an assessment of the role of competition in UK policy*, London: Institute of Economic Affairs, Research Monograph 42.

Becker, G. (1965), 'A theory of the allocation of time', *The Economic Journal*, 75.

Beesley, M.E. and Littlechild, S. (1986), 'Privatisation: principles, problems and priorities', in J.A. Kay, C. Mayer and D. Thompson (eds), *Privatisation and Regulation: the UK experience*, Oxford: Clarendon Press.

Benham, L. (1972), 'The effect of advertising on the price of eyeglasses', *Journal of Law and Economics*, 15.

Bergson, A. (1973), 'On monopoly welfare losses', *American Economic Review*, 63.

Berle, A. and Means, G. (1932), *The Modern Corporation and Private Property*, London: Macmillan.

Bishop, M. and Kay, J.A. (1988), 'Does privatisation work? Lessons from the UK', London Business School, mimeo.

Blair, J.M. (1972), *Economic Concentration*, New York: Harcourt, Brace, Jovanovich.

Bloch, H. (1974), 'Advertising and profitability: a reappraisal', *Journal of Political Economy*, 82.

Buxton, A.J., Davies, S.W. and Lyons, B.R. (1984), 'Concentration and advertising in consumer and producer markets', *Journal of Industrial Economics*, 32.

Carter, J.R. (1978), 'Collusion, efficiency and antitrust', *Journal of Law and Economics*, 21.

Caves, R.E. (1968), 'Market organisation, performance, public policy', in R.E. Caves and associates, *Britain's Economic Prospects*, London: Allen & Unwin.

Caves, R.E. and Ghemawat, P. (1986), 'Capital commitment and profitability: an empirical investigation', *Oxford Economic Papers*, 38.

Chadwick, E. (1859), 'Results of different principles of legislation and administration in Europe of competition for the field as compared with competition within the field of service', *Journal of the Royal Statistical Society*, 22.

Chamberlin, E.H. (1933), *The Theory of Monopolistic Competition*, Cambridge, Mass: Harvard University Press.

Clarke, R. (1984), 'Profit margins and market concentration in UK manufacturing industry; 1970–6', *Applied Economics*, 16.

Clarke, R. and Davies, S.W. (1983), 'Aggregate concentration, market concentration and diversification', *The Economic Journal*, 93.

Clarke, R., Davies, S.W. and Waterson, M. (1984), 'The profitability–concentration relation: market power or efficiency?', *Journal of Industrial Economics*, 32.

Coase, R.H. (1937), 'The nature of the firm', *Economica*, 32.

Collins, N. and Preston, L. (1968), *Concentration and Price–Cost Margins in Manufacturing*, Berkeley: University of California Press.

—— (1969), 'Price–cost margins and industry structure', *Review of Economics and Statistics*, 51.

Collins, B. and Wharton, B. (1984), 'Investigating public industries: how has the Monopolies and Mergers Commission performed?', *Public Money*, September.

Comanor, W.S. (1967), 'Market structure, product differentiation and industrial research', *Quarterly Journal of Economics*, 81.

—— (1985), 'Vertical price-fixing, vertical market restrictions and the new antitrust policy', *Harvard Law Review*, 98.

Comanor, W.S. and Leibenstein, H. (1969), 'Allocative efficiency, X-efficiency and the measurement of welfare losses', *Economica*, 36.

Comanor, W.S. and Wilson, T.A. (1967), 'Advertising, market structure and performance', *Review of Economics and Statistics*, 49.

—— (1974), *Advertising and Market Power*, Cambridge, Mass: Harvard University Press.

Cosh, A. *et al*. (1980), 'The causes and effects of takeovers in the United Kingdom', in D.C. Mueller (ed.), *Determinants and Effects of Mergers*, Cambridge, Mass: Oelgschlager, Gunn & Hain.

—— (1985), 'Conglomerate organisation and economic efficiency: a report to the Office of Fair Trading', University of Cambridge, mimeo.

Cournot, A.A. (1838), *Research into the Mathematical Principles of the Theory of Wealth*, translated by N.T. Bacon, Homewood, Ill: Irwin, 1963.

Cowling, K. and Cubbin, J. (1971), 'Price, quality and advertising competition', *Economica*, 38.

Cowling, K. and Mueller, D. (1978), 'The social costs of monopoly power', *The Economic Journal*, 88.

Cowling, K. and Rayner, A. (1970), 'Price, quality and market share', *Journal of Political Economy*, 78.

Cowling, K. and Waterson, M. (1976), 'Price–cost margins and industry structure', *Economica*, 43.

Cowling, K. *et al.* (1975), *Advertising and Economic Behaviour*, London: Macmillan.

—— (1980), *Mergers and Economic Performance*, Cambridge: Cambridge University Press.

Cubbin, J. (1981), 'Advertising and the theory of entry barriers', *Economica*, 48.

Cubbin, J. and Domberger, S. (1988), 'Advertising and post-entry oligopoly behaviour', *Journal of Industrial Economics*, 37.

Curry, B. and George, K.D. (1983), 'Industrial concentration: a survey', *Journal of Industrial Economics*, 31.

Curry, B. and Rhys, D.G. (1979), 'The price–quality relationship: some comments', *Bulletin of Economic Research*, 31.

Cyert, R.M. and George, K.D. (1969), 'Competition, growth and efficiency', *The Economic Journal*, 79.

Dasgupta, P. and Stiglitz, J. (1980), 'Industrial structure and the nature of innovative activity', *The Economic Journal*, 90.

d'Asprement, Q. and Jacquemin, A. (1988), 'Cooperative and non-cooperative R&D in duopoly with spillovers', *American Economic Review*, 78.

Davies, S.W. (1979), *The Diffusion of Process Innovations*, Cambridge: Cambridge University Press.

Demsetz, H. (1968), 'Why regulate utilities?', *Journal of Law and Economics*, 11.

—— (1969), 'Information and efficiency: another viewpoint', *Journal of Law and Economics*, 12.

—— (1973a), 'Industry structure, market rivalry and public policy', *Journal of Law and Economics*, 16.

—— (1973b), 'Joint supply and price discrimination', *Journal of Law and Economics*, 16.

—— (1982), 'Barriers to entry', *American Economic Review*, 72(1).

Dixit, A. (1979), 'A model of duopoly suggesting a theory of entry barriers', *Bell Journal of Economics*, 10.

Dorfman, R. and Steiner, P.O. (1954), 'Optimal advertising and optimal quality', *American Economic Review*, 44.

Downie, J. (1958), *The Competitive Process*, London: Duckworth.

Evans, D.S. (ed.) (1983), *Breaking up Bell: Essays on Industrial Organisation and Regulation*, New York: North Holland.

Evans, D.S. and Heckman, J.J. (1984), 'A test for subadditivity of the cost function – with an application to the Bell system', *American Economic Review*, 74.

Evely, R. and Little, I.M.D. (1960), *Concentration in British Industry*, Cambridge: Cambridge University Press.

Foreman-Peck, J.S. (1989), 'Ownership, competition and productivity growth: the impact of liberalisation and privatisation upon British Telecom', University of Hull, mimeo.

Freeman, C. (1962), 'Research and development: a comparison between British and American industry', *National Institute Economic Review*, no. 20.
—— (1974), *The Economics of Industrial Innovation*, Harmondsworth: Penguin.

Galbraith, J.K. (1963), *American Capitalism*, Harmondsworth: Penguin.
—— (1972), *The New Industrial State*, London: Andre Deutsch.
Gale, B.T. and Branch, B.S. (1982), 'Concentration versus market share: which determines performance and why does it matter?, *Antitrust Bulletin*, 27.
Gaskins, D.W. Jr (1971), 'Dynamic limit pricing: optimal pricing under threat of entry', *Journal of Economic Theory*, 3.
George, K.D. (1968), 'Concentration, barriers to entry and rates of return', *Review of Economic and Statistics*, 50.
—— (1989), 'Do we need a merger policy?' in J.A. Fairbairn and J.A. Kay (eds), *Mergers and Merger Policy*, Oxford: Oxford University Press.
—— (1990), 'Public ownership vs. privatisation' in Peter de Wolf (ed.), *Competition in Europe: Essays in Honour of Professor Henk W. de Jong*, Amsterdam: Kluwer Academic Publishers.
George, K.D. and Jacquemin, A. (1990), 'Competition policy in the European Community', in W.S. Comanor *et al.*, *Competition Policy in Europe and North America: Economic Issues and Institutions*, London: Harwood Academic Publishers.
George, K.D. and Joll, C. (1978), 'EEC competition policy', *Three Banks Review*, no. 17.
George, K.D. and Lynk, E.L. (1992), 'Privatisation', in F. Hahn (ed.), *The Market: Practice and Policy*, London: Macmillan.
George, K.D. and Shorey, J.C. (1985), 'Manual workers, good jobs, and structured internal labour markets', *British Journal of Industrial Relations*, November.
George, K.D. *et al.* (1989), 'Coal', in K.D. George and L. Mainwaring (eds), *The Welsh Economy*, Cardiff: University of Wales Press.
Geroski, P. (1981), 'Specification and testing the profit–concentration relationship: some experiments for the UK', *Economica*, 48.
Geroski, P. and Jacquemin, A. (1984), 'Dominant firms and their alleged decline', *International Journal of Industrial Organisation*, 2.
Gilbert, R.J. and Newberry, D.M.G. (1982), 'Pre-emptive patenting and the persistence of monopoly', *American Economic Review*, 72.

Hall, M. (1967), 'Sales revenue maximisation: an empirical examination', *Journal of Industrial Economics*, 75.
Hall, R.L. and Hitch, C.J. (1939), 'Price theory and business behaviour', *Oxford Economic Papers*, 2.
Hall, M. and Weiss, L.W. (1967), 'Firm size and profitability', *Review of Economics and Statistics*, 49.
Hannah, L. and Kay, J.A. (1977), *Concentration in Modern Industry*, Cambridge: Cambridge University Press.
Harberger, A. (1954), 'Monopoly and resource allocation', *American Economic Review*, 45.
Hart, P.E. (1962), 'The size and growth of firms', *Economica*, 9.
Hart, P.E. and Clarke, R. (1980), *Concentration in British Industry: 1935–75*, Cambridge: Cambridge University Press.
Hart, P.E. and Morgan, E. (1977), 'Market structure and economic performance in the United Kingdom', *Journal of Industrial Economics*, 25.
Hart, P.E., Utton, M.A. and Walshe, G. (1973), *Mergers and Concentration in British Industry*, Cambridge: Cambridge University Press.

Heath, J. (1960), 'Restrictive practices legislation: some economic consequences', *The Economic Journal*, 70.

Hicks, J.R. (1952), 'Annual survey of economic theory – monopoly', *Econometrica*, 1935, 1–20; reprinted in G.J. Stigler and K.E. Boulding (eds), *Readings in Price Theory*, Chicago: R.D. Irwin Inc.

Hitiris, T. (1978), 'Effective protection and economic performance in UK manufacturing industry, 1963 and 1968', *The Economic Journal*, 88.

Holterman, S. (1973), 'Market structure and economic performance in UK manufacturing industry', *Journal of Industrial Economics*, 22.

Hughes, A. (1989), 'The impact of merger: A survey of empirical evidence for the UK', in J.A. Fairburn and J.A. Kay (eds) *Mergers and Merger Policy*, Oxford: Oxford University Press.

Hughes, A. and Kumar, M.S. (1984), 'Recent trends in aggregate concentration in the UK economy', *Cambridge Journal of Economics*, 8.

Hunt, L.C. and Lynk, E.L. (1990a), 'Telecommunications industry structure in the UK: an empirical examination of the case for restructuring BT', University College of Swansea, mimeo.

——— (1990b), 'Divestiture of telecommunications in the UK: a time series analysis', *Oxford Bulletin of Economics and Statistics*, August.

——— (1991), 'Competition in UK telecommunications: restructure BT?', *Fiscal Studies*, 12.

Jacquemin, A. and de Jong, H. (1977), *European Industrial Organisation*, London: Macmillan.

Jewkes, J., Sawers, D. and Stillerman, R. (1969), *The Sources of Invention*, London: Macmillan.

Kaldor, N. (1950), 'Economic aspects of advertising', *Review of Economic Studies*, 18.

——— (1966), *Causes of the Slow Rate of Economic Growth of the United Kingdom*, Cambridge: Cambridge University Press.

Kamerschen, D. (1966), 'An estimation of the welfare losses from monopoly in the American Economy', *Western Economic Journal*, 4.

Kamien, M.I. and Schwartz, N.L. (1982), *Market Structure and Innovation*, Cambridge: Cambridge University Press.

Kelly, E. (1967), *The Profitability of Growth through Mergers*, Philadelphia: Pennsylvania State University Press.

Kendrick, J.W. (1961), *Productivity Trends in the United States*, Princeton, NJ: Princeton University Press.

Khalilzadeh-Shirazi, J. (1974), 'Market structure and price–cost margins in the UK manufacturing industries', *Review of Economics and Statistics*, 56.

Kitching, (1967), 'Why do mergers miscarry?', *Harvard Business Review*, 45.

Kumar, M.S. (1984), *Growth, Acquisitions and Investment*, Cambridge: Cambridge University Press.

Kuznets, S. (1977), *Economic Growth of Nations*, Cambridge, Mass: Harvard University Press.

Lancaster, K. (1966), 'A new approach to demand theory', *Journal of Political Economy*, 74.

Lancaster, K. (1975), 'Socially optimal product differentiation', *American Economic Review*, 65.

Leibenstein, H. (1966), 'Allocative efficiency vs X-efficiency', *American Economic Review*, 56.

—— (1979), 'A branch of economics is missing: micro-micro theory', *Journal of Economic Literature*, 17.

Llewellyn, W.G. and Huntsman, B. (1970), 'Managerial pay and corporate performance', *American Economic Review*, 60.

Lyons, B.R. (1981), 'Price–cost margins, market structure and international trade', in D. Currie, D. Peel and W. Peters (eds), *Microeconomic Analysis*, London: Croom Helm.

McEnally, R. (1976), 'Competition and dispersion in rates of return: a note', *Journal of Industrial Economics*, 25.

McGee, J.S. (1958), 'Predatory price cutting: the Standard Oil (NJ) case', *Journal of Law and Economics*, 1.

McGuire, J.W., Chiu, J.S.Y. and Elbing, A.O. (1962), 'Executive incomes, sales and profits', *American Economic Review*, 52.

Mann, M. (1966), 'Seller concentration, barriers to entry and rate of return in thirty industries, 1950–1960', *Review of Economics and Statistics*, 48.

—— (1974), 'Advertising, concentration and profitability: the state of knowledge and directions for public policy', in H.D. Goldsmith, H.M. Mann, and J.F. Weston (eds), *Industrial Concentration: The New Learning*, Boston: Little, Brown.

Mansfield, E. (1968), *Industrial Research and Technological Innovation: An Econometric Analysis*, New York: Norton.

Mansfield, E., Schwartz, M. and Wagner, S. (1981), 'Imitation costs and patents: an empirical study', *The Economic Journal*, 91.

Markham, J.W. (1955), 'Survey of the evidence and findings on mergers', in National Bureau of Economic Research conference report, *Business Concentration and Price Policy*, Princeton: Princeton University Press.

Marris, R. (1963), 'A model of the managerial enterprise', *Quarterly Journal of Economics*, 77.

Martin, S. (1979), 'Advertising, concentration and profitability: the simultaneity problem', *Bell Journal of Economics*, 10.

Marx, Karl (1887), *Capital*, translated by Ernest Untermann; Chicago: Kerr, 1912.

Meeks, G. (1977), *Disappointing Marriage: A Study of the Gains from Merger*, Cambridge: Cambridge University Press.

Meeks, G. and Whittington, G. (1975), 'Directors' pay, growth and profitability', *Journal of Industrial Economics*, 24.

Molyneux, R. and Thompson, D. (1987), 'Nationalised industry performance: still third rate?', *Fiscal Studies*, 8(1).

Mueller, D. (1966), 'Patents, research and development and the measurements of inventive activity', *Journal of Industrial Economics*, 14.

Mueller, W.F. and Rogers, R.T. (1980), 'The role of advertising in changing concentration of manufacturing industries', *Review of Economics and Statistics*, 62.

National Economic Development Office (1976), *A Study of UK Nationalised Industries*, London: HMSO.

Neale, A.D. (1966), *The Anti-Trust Laws of the United States of America*, Cambridge: Cambridge University Press.

Nelson, R.L. (1959), *Merger Movements in American Industry, 1895–1956*, Princeton, NJ: Princeton University Press.

Nelson. R.R., Peck, M.J. and Kalachek, E.D. (1967), *Technology, Economic Growth and Public Policy*, Washington DC: Brookings Institution.

Newbould, G.D. (1970), *Management and Merger Activity*, Liverpool: Guthstead.

Nyman, S. and Silberston, Z.A. (1978), 'The ownership and control of industry', *Oxford Economic Papers*, 30.

O'Brien, D.P. *et al.* (1979), *Competition Policy, Profitability and Growth*, London: Macmillan.

OECD (1969), *The Overall Level and Structure of R&D Efforts in Member Countries*, Paris: Organisation for Economic Co-operation and Development.

Okun, A.M. (1981), *Prices and Quantities: A Macroeconomic Analysis*, Oxford: Basil Blackwell.

Ordover, J.A. (1990), 'Economic foundations of competition policy', in W.S. Comanor *et al.*, *Competition Policy in Europe and North America: Economic Issues and Institutions*, London: Harwood Academic Publishers.

Ordover, J.A. and Willig, R.D. (1985), 'Antitrust for high technology industries: assessing research joint ventures and mergers', *Journal of Law and Economics*, 28.

Panzar, J.C. (1976), 'A Neoclassical approach to peak load pricing, *Bell Journal of Economics*, 7.

Pavitt, K., Robson, M. and Townsend, J. (1987), 'The size distribution of innovating firms in the UK: 1945–1983', *Journal of Industrial Economics*, 25.

Penrose, E.T. (1966), *The Theory of the Growth of the Firm*, Oxford: Basil Blackwell.

Phillips, A. (1966), 'Patents, potential competition and technical progress', *American Economic Review*, 56.

Phillips, J. (1966), Appendix to P. Baran and P. Sweezy, *Monopoly Capital*, New York: Monthly Review Press.

Phillips, S. (1972), 'An econometric study of price-fixing, market structure and performance in British industry in the early 1950s', in K. Cowling (ed.), *Market Structure and Corporate Behaviour*, London: Gray Mills.

Porter, M.E. (1974), 'Consumer behaviour, retailer power and market performance in consumer goods industries', *Review of Economics and Statistics*, 56.

Posner, R.A. (1975), 'The social costs of monopoly and regulation', *Journal of Political Economy*, vol. 83.

—— (1976), *Antitrust Law: An Economic Perspective*, Chicago: University of Chicago Press.

Prais, S.J. (1976), *The Evolution of Giant Firms in Britain*, Cambridge: Cambridge University Press.

—— (1989), 'Qualified manpower in engineering: Britain and other industrially advanced countries', *National Institute Economic Review*, February.

Pratten, C.F. (1971), *Economies of Scale in Manufacturing Industry*, Cambridge: Cambridge University Press.

Pryke, R. (1981), *The Nationalised Industries: Policies and Performance since 1968*, Oxford: Martin Robertson.

Reid, S.R. (1968), *Mergers, Managers and the Economy*, New York: McGraw-Hill.

Roberts, A. (1956), 'A general theory of executive compensation based on statistically tested propositions', *Quarterly Journal of Economics*, 70.

Robertson, D.H. (1957), *Lectures on Economic Principles*, vol. 1, London: Staples Press.

Robinson, E.A.G. (1958), *The Structure of Competitive Industry*, Cambridge: Cambridge University Press.

Romeo, A.A. (1977), 'Rate of imitation of a capital-embodied process innovation', *Economica*, 44.

Rosenberg, J.G. (1976), 'Research and market share: a reappraisal of the Schumpeter hypothesis', *Journal of Industrial Economics*, 25.

Rowthorn, R. (1986), 'De-industrialisation in Britain', in R. Martin and R. Rowthorn (eds), *The Geography of De-industrialisation*, London: Macmillan.

Salter, W.E.G. (1966), *Productivity and Technical Change*, 2nd edn, Cambridge: Cambridge University Press.

Samuels, J.M. (1965), 'Size and the growth of firms', *Review of Economic Studies*, 32.

Sargent Florence, P. (1961), *Ownership, control and success of Large Companies*, London: Sweet & Maxwell.

Scherer, F.M. (1965), 'Corporate inventive output, profits and growth', *Journal of Political Economy*, 73.

—— (1967), 'Market structure and the employment of scientists and engineers', *American Economic Review*, 57.

—— (1970), *Industrial Market Structure and Economic Performance*, Chicago: Rand McNally.

—— (1979), 'The welfare economics of product variety: an application to the ready-to-eat cereals industry', *Journal of Industrial Economics*, 28.

Scherer, F.M. *et al.* (1959), *Patents and the Corporation*, Boston, Mass: Galvin.

Schmalensee, R. (1972), *The Economics of Advertising*, Amsterdam: North Holland.

—— (1978), 'Entry deterrence in the ready-to-eat breakfast cereal industry', *Bell Journal of Economics*, 9.

—— (1981), 'Economies of scale and barriers to entry', *Journal of Political Economy*, 89.

—— (1982), 'Another look at market power', *Harvard Law Review*, 95.

—— (1983), 'Advertising and entry-deterrence: an explanatory model', *Journal of Political Economy*, 91.

Schmookler, J. (1966), *Invention and Economic Growth*, Cambridge, Mass: Harvard University Press.

Schumpeter, J. (1947), *Capitalism, Socialism and Democracy*, London: Allen & Unwin.

Schwartz, M. And Reynolds, R.J. (1983), 'Contestable markets: an uprising in the theory of industry structure: comment', *American Economic Review*, 73.

Schwartzman, D. (1960), 'The burden of monopoly', *Journal of Political Economy*, 68.

Scitovsky, T. (1943), 'A note on profit maximisation and its implications', *Review of Economic Studies*, 11.

Shaked, A. and Sutton, J. (1987), 'Product differentiation and industrial structure', *Journal of Industrial Economics*, 36.

Shaw, R. and Simpson, P. (1985), 'The Monopolies Commission and the process of competition', *Fiscal Studies*, 6.

Shepherd, W.G. (1972), 'Structure and behaviour in British industries, with US comparisons', *Journal of Industrial Economics*, 21.

—— (1975), *The Treatment of Market Power*, New York: Colombia University Press.

—— (1984), 'Contestability vs competition', *American Economic Review*, 74.

—— (1989), 'The process of effective competition', Department of Economics, University of Massachusetts, Working Paper.

Shorey, J.C. (1975), 'The size of the work unit and strike incidence', *Journal of Industrial Economics*, 23.

Shrieves, R.E. (1978), 'Market structure and innovation: a new perspective', *Journal of Industrial Economics*, 26.

Siegfried, J. and Tiemann, T. (1974), 'The welfare cost of monopoly: an inter-industry analysis', *Economic Inquiry*, 12.

Silberston, Z.A. (1972), 'Economies of scale in theory and practice', *The Economic Journal*, supplement.

Singh, A. (1971), *Take-overs*, Cambridge: Cambridge University Press.

—— (1977), 'UK industry and the world economy: a case of de-industrialisation?', *Cambridge Journal of Economics*, 1(2).

Singh, A. and Whittington, G. (1968), *Growth, Profitability and Valuation*, Cambridge: Cambridge University Press.

—— (1975), 'The size and growth of firms', *Review of Economic Studies*, 42.

Solow, R. (1971), 'Some implications of alternative criteria for the firm', in R. Marris and A. Wood (eds), *The Corporate Economy*, London: Macmillan.

Spence, M. (1977), 'Entry, capacity, investment and oligopolistic pricing', *Bell Journal of Economics*, 8.

Stackleberg, H. von (1934), *The Theory of the Market Economy*, translated by A.T. Peacock, London: William Hodge, 1952.

Starkie, D. (1986), 'British Railways: opportunities for a contestable market', in J. Kay, C. Meyer and D. Thompson (eds), *Privatisation and Regulation: the UK Experience*, Oxford: Clarendon Press.

Starkie, D. and Thompson D. (1985), 'Stanstead: A viable investment?', *Fiscal Studies*, 6.

Stigler, G.J. (1968), *The Organisation of Industry*, Homewood, Ill.: Irwin.

Stoneman, P. and Vickers, J. (1988), 'The economics of technology policy', *Oxford Review of Economic Policy*, 4.

Strickland, A.D. and Weiss, L.W. (1976), 'Advertising, concentration and price–cost margins', *Journal of Political Economy*, 84.

Sutton, C. (1974), 'Advertising, concentration and competition', *The Economic Journal*, 84.

Sylos-Labini, P. (1962), *Oligopoly and Technical Progress*, Cambridge, Mass: Harvard University Press.

Taylor, C.T. and Silberston, Z.A. (1973), *The Economic Impact of the Patent System*, Cambridge: Cambridge University Press.

Teece, D.J. (1977), 'Technology transfer by multinational firms: the resource cost of transferring technological know-how', *The Economic Journal*, 87.

Thirlwall, A.P. (1982), 'Deindustrialisation in the United Kingdom', *Lloyds Bank Review*, 144.

Utton, M.A. (1974), 'On measuring the effects of industrial mergers', *Scottish Journal of Political Economy*, 21.

—— (1979), *Diversification and Competition*, Cambridge: Cambridge University Press.

—— (1986), *Profits and the Stability of Monopoly*, Cambridge: Cambridge University Press.

Verdoorn, P.J. (1949), 'Fattori che regolano lo sviluppo della produttività del lavoro', *L'Industria*, 1.

Vickers, J. and Yarrow, G. (1985), *Privatisation and the Natural Monopolies*, London, Public Policy Centre.

Vickers, J. and Yarrow, G. (1988), *Privatisation: An Economic Analysis*, London, MIT Press.

Weiss, L.W. (1974), 'The concentration–profits relationship and antitrust' in H.D. Goldschmid *et al.*, *Industrial Concentration: The New Learning*, Boston: Little, Brown.

Weitzman, M. (1983), 'Contestable markets: an uprising in the theory of industry structure: comment', *American Economic Review*, 73.

Weston, J.F. (1961), *The Role of Mergers in the Growth of Large Firms*, Berkeley, California: University of California Press.

Whittington, G. (1972), 'Changes in the top 100 quoted companies in the United Kingdom, 1948 to 1968', *Journal of Industrial Economics*, 21.

Williamson, O.E. (1963), 'Managerial discretion and business behavior', *American Economic Review*, 53.

—— (1968), 'Economies as an antitrust defence: the welfare tradeoffs', *American Economic Review*, 58.

—— (1971), 'Managerial discretion, organisation form, and the multi-division hypothesis', in R. Marris and A. Wood (eds), *The Corporate Economy*, London: Macmillan.

—— (1977), 'Predatory pricing: a strategic and welfare analysis', *Yale Law Journal*, 87.

Wilson, R.W. (1977), 'The effects of technological environment and product rivalry on R&D effort and licensing of inventions', *Review of Economics and Statistics*, 59.

Worcester, D. (1973), 'New estimates of the welfare loss of monopoly: US 1956–69', *Southern Economic Journal*, 40.

Yarrow, G.K. (1989), 'Privatisation and economic performance in Britain', *Carnegie-Rochester Conference Series on Public Policy*, 31, North Holland.

OFFICIAL REPORTS

UK: Reports of the Monopolies and Mergers Commission

Report on the supply of dental goods	HC 18	1950
Report on the supply and export of matches and the supply of match-making machinery	HC 161	1952
Collective Discrimination: a report on exclusive dealing, collective boycotts, aggregated rebates and other discriminatory trade practices	Cmnd 9504	1955
Report on the supply of certain industrial and medical gases	HC 13	1956
Report on the supply of electronic valves and cathode ray tubes	HC 16	1956
Report on the supply of chemical fertilisers	HC 267	1959
Report on the supply of cigarettes and tobacco and of cigarette and tobacco machinery	HC 218	1961
Report on the supply of electrical equipment for mechanically propelled land vehicles	HC 21	1963
Report on the supply of wallpaper	HC 59	1964
Colour Film: a report on the supply and processing of colour film	HC 1	1966
Household Detergents: a report on the supply of household detergents	HC 105	1966
Infant Milk Foods: a report on the supply of infant milk foods	HC 319	1967
Flat Glass: a report on the supply of flat glass	HC 83	1968
Man-Made Cellulosic Fibres: a report on the supply of man-made cellulosic fibres	HC 130	1968
Clutch Mechanisms for Road Vehicles: a report on the supply of clutch mechanisms for road vehicles	HC 32	1968

Recommended Resale Prices: a report on the general effect on the public interest of the practice of recommending or otherwise suggesting prices to be charged on the resale of goods   HC 100   1969

Cigarette Filter Rods: a report on the supply and exports of cigarette filter rods   HC 335   1969

Refusal to Supply: a report on the general effect on the public interest of the practices of refusing to supply goods required for business purposes and of entering into certain exclusive supply agreements   Cmnd 4372   1970

Metal Containers: a report on the supply of metal containers   HC 6   1970

Professional Services: a report on the general effect on the public interest of certain restrictive practices so far as they prevail in relation to the supply of professional services   Cmnd 4463   1970

Breakfast Cereals: a report on the supply of ready cooked breakfast cereal foods   HC 2   1973

Chlordiazepoxide and Diazepam: a report on the supply of chlordiazepoxide and diazepam   HC 197   1973

Parallel Pricing: a report on the general effect on the public interest of the practice of parallel pricing   Cmnd 5330   1973

Plasterboard: a report on the supply of plasterboard   HC 94   1974

Primary Batteries: a report on the supply of primary batteries   HC 1   1974

Contraceptive Sheaths: a report on the supply of contraceptive sheaths in the United Kingdom   HC 135   1975

Building Bricks: a report on the supply of building bricks   HC 474   1976

Frozen Foodstuffs: a report on the supply in the United Kingdom of frozen foodstuffs for human consumption   HC 674   1976

Indirect Electrostatic Reprographic Equipment: a report on the supply of indirect electrostatic reprographic equipment   HC 47   1976

Diazo Copying Materials: a report on the supply in the United Kingdom of copying materials sensitised with one or more diazonium compounds   HC 165   1977

Cat and Dog Foods: a report on the supply in the United Kingdom of cat and dog foods   HC 447   1977

Ice Cream and Water Ices: a report on the supply in the United Kingdom of ice cream and water ices   Cmnd 7632   1979

Domestic Gas Appliances: a report on the supply of certain domestic gas appliances in the United Kingdom   HC 703   1980

Tampons: a report on the supply in the United Kingdom of tampons   Cmnd 8049   1980

Full-Line Forcing and Tie-In Sales: a report on the

practice of requiring any person to whom goods or services are supplied to acquire other goods or services as a condition of that supply	HC 212	1981
Discounts to Retailers: a report on the general effect on the public interest of the practice of charging some retailers lower prices than others or providing special benefits to some retailers where the difference cannot be attributed to savings in the supplier's costs	HC 311	1981
Concrete Roofing Tiles: a report on the supply in the United Kingdom of concrete roofing tiles	HC 12	1981
Bicycles: a report on the application by T.I. Raleigh Industries Ltd and T.I. Raleigh Ltd of certain criteria for determining whether to supply bicycles to retail outlets	HC 67	1981
Bristol Omnibus Company Limited, Cheltenham District Traction Company, City of Cardiff District Council, Trent Motor Traction Company Limited and West Midlands Passenger Transport Executive: a report on stage carriage services supplied by the undertakings	HC 442	1982
Contraceptive Sheaths: a report on the supply in the United Kingdom of contraceptive sheaths	Cmnd 8689	1982
London Electricity Board: a report on the direction and management by the London Electricity Board of its business of retailing domestic electrical goods, spare parts and ancillary goods	Cmnd 8812	1983
National Coal Board: a report on the efficiency and costs in the development, production and supply of coal by the NCB (2 volumes)	Cmnd 8920	1983
Guest Keen and Nettlefolds PLC and AE PLC: A report on the proposed merger	Cmnd 9199	1984
Hepworth Ceramic Holdings PLC and Streetley PLC: A report on the proposed merger	Cmnd 9164	1984
British Airports Authority: a report on the efficiency and and costs of, and the service provided by, the British Airports Authority in its commercial activities	Cmnd 9644	1985
Tampons: a report on the supply in the United Kingdom of tampons	Cmnd 9705	1986
Postal Franking Machines: a report on the supply, maintenance and repair of postal franking machines in the United Kingdom	Cmnd 9747	1986
White Salt: a report on the supply of white salt in the United Kingdom by producers of salt	Cmnd 9778	1986
Steel Wire Fencing: a report on the supply of steel wire fencing in the United Kingdom	Cmnd 79	1987

British Airways Plc and British Caledonian Group plc: a report on the proposed merger	Cmnd 247	1987
Gas: a report on the matter of the existence or possible existence of a monopoly situation in relation to the supply in Great Britain of gas through pipes to persons other than tariff customers	Cmnd 500	1988
The Supply of Beer: a report on the supply of beer for retail sale in the United Kingdom	Cmnd 651	1989

UK: Green Papers

A Review of Monopolies and Mergers Policy: A consultative document, Cmnd 7198, London: HMSO, 1978.
Review of Restrictive Trade Practices Policy, Cm 331, London: HMSO, 1988.
Mergers Policy, London: HMSO, 1988.

UK: White Papers

H M Treasury (1961), *Financial and Economic Obligations of the Nationalised Industries*, Cmnd 1337, London: HMSO.
H M Treasury (1967), *Nationalised Industries: A Review of Economic and Financial Objectives*, Cmnd 3437, London: HMSO.
H M Treasury (1978), *The Nationalised Industries*, Cmnd 7131, London: HMSO.
Competition and Choice: Telecommunications Policy for the 1990s, Cm 1461, London: HMSO, 1991.

US: Competition Cases

United States v Arnold Schwinn and Co., 388 US 365 (1967).
Continental TV v GTE Sylvania, 433 US 36 (1977).
Berkey Photo, Inc. v Eastman Kodak Company, 444 US 1093 (1980).
United States v Aluminum Company of America, 148 F.2d 416 (2d Cir. 1945).

US: merger guidelines

US Department of Justice, *Merger Guidelines*, issued May 30 1968.
US Department of Justice, *Merger Guidelines*, issued June 14 1982.
US Department of Justice, *Merger Guidelines*, issued June 14 1984.

European Communities Reports

Summaries of the decisions made in the various cases cited in this book may be found in the annual *Reports on Competition Policy*, published by the Commission of the European Communities.

Full details of the 1989 merger regulation may be found in: Council Regulation (EEC) No/89 on the control of concentrations between undertakings, Brussels, 21 December 1989.

Index

accounting for advertising expenditure, 310–11

acquisitions and mergers: and bankruptcy, 88; capital accumulation, 114–16; and competition, 91–2, 115, 428; and concentration of industry, 91–2, 107–9, 116, 120, 150–2; and control of firm, 60, 64; and corporate control 93–4; cycles of activity, 84–5; and diversification, 83, 97, 125–6; and economies of scale, 89–90, 110; effects of, 104–16; and efficiency, 107–14, 352, 424, 428; and excess capacity, 91; and fixed costs, 89; government policy, 151–2, 422–9; and growth of firm 61, 83–96, 104–16, 150–2; horizontal, 87, 91, 106, 115–16; and investment, 114–16; and management, 114; and market power, 91–2, 108, 160; motives of firms, 88–96; and plant size, 89; predatory, 86, 89, 93, 97, 105; and privatisation, 350, 351–2; and profitability, 60, 104–16; regulation, 151–2, 422–9; and resource allocation, 109; and shareholders, 93, 94, 105, 113–14; and size of firm, 60, 86, 88, 96, 104–16; and stock market, 105–7; welfare effects, 107–9, 428–9

advertising: accounting for expenditure, 310–11; and concentration of industry, 116, 120, 152, 302–3, 306–9; consumer goods, 304–5; detergents, 312–13, 420; economies of scale in, 145, 302; and elasticity of demand, 304–5; and entry to markets, 223, 225, 226, 262, 274–5, 289, 302–3, 309; expenditure on, 303–5; and growth rate of firm, 50, 53; and interdependence of

firms, 306; and market dominance, 174, 176, 203; and market structure, 302–9; MMC investigations, 224, 312–13, 420; oligopolistic industries, 53; producer goods, 304–5; and product differentiation, 215, 221–2, 223, 224, 225, 227, 303; and profitability, 294, 309–13; and size of firm, 307

agency relationships, 348–9

aggregate concentration, 116–22

aggressive behaviour, 166, 272

agriculture, 2–5

Areeda, P.E., 174, 175

assets: disposal, 85; management, 93; specificity, 63, 66; valuation measurement, 146

asymmetric of information, 34, 35, 74, 166, 272–3

average cost pricing, 205–11

average incremental cost (AIC), 340, 341

Bacon, R., 14–15

Bain, J.S., 164, 260, 264, 286, 288

balance of payments, 10–11, 13

bankruptcy, 88

bargaining: buyers, 211, 223; costs, 70, 72; within firms, 36; large firms, 73–5

barriers to entry, see entry

Baumol, W.J., 46–7, 52, 53, 257, 276, 336, 341, 363, 364

behavioural school approach to profit maximisastion, 39–40

behavioural theory of firms, 33, 57, 58–9

benefits of scale, 110, 406

bilaterial monopoly, 70–2, 74–5

Blair, J.M., 152, 207, 307

blockaded entry, 164, 264